The Naturalist's Guide to the Southern Rockies

Logan
Cundiff

The Naturalist's Guide to the Southern Rockies

Colorado, Southern Wyoming, and Northern New Mexico

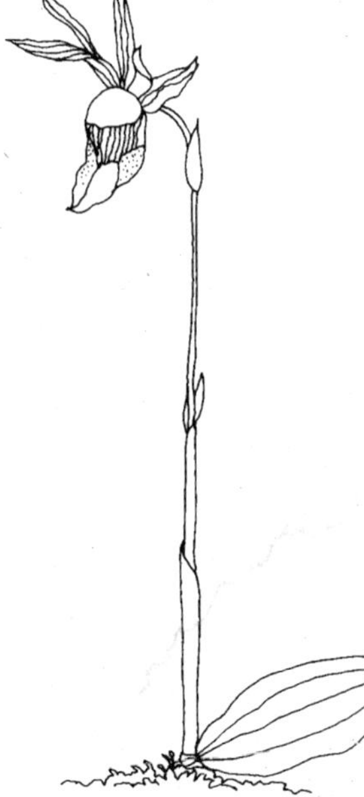

The Naturalist's Guide to the Southern Rockies

Colorado, Southern Wyoming, and Northern New Mexico

Audrey DeLella Benedict

Illustrations by
Barbara Bash

FULCRUM
GOLDEN, COLORADO

Originally published by the Sierra Club Books in 1991

Library of Congress Cataloging-in-Publication Data

Benedict, Audrey D.
The naturalist's guide to the southern Rockies : Colorado, southern Wyoming, and northern New Mexico / by Audrey DeLella Benedict ; illustrations by Barbara Bash.
p. cm.
Includes bibliographical references.
ISBN-13: 978-1-55591-535-3 (pbk.)
1. Natural history--Rocky Mountains. 2. Rocky Mountains--Description and travel. I. Benedict, Audrey D. Sierra Club naturalist's guide to the southern Rockies. II. Title.
QH104.5.R6B46 2008
508.78--dc22

2007051378

Printed in Canada by Friesens Corporation

0 9 8 7 6 5 4 3 2 1

Design by Ann W. Douden

Fulcrum Publishing
4690 Table Mountain Drive, Suite 100
Golden, Colorado 80403
800-992-2908 • 303-277-1623
www.fulcrumbooks.com

To my grandchildren—
Zoe, Noah, Jayne, Lauren, and Steven Benedict—
so that they may continue to know the joy
that comes from discovering the intricate details
of the natural world.

At Wheeler Geologic Area, near Creede, multiple layers of volcanic tuff and ash are sculpted by erosion into fanciful shapes.

Contents

Acknowledgments xv
Introduction 1

CHAPTER ONE
Mountains in the Clouds: The Southern Rocky Mountains 5

CHAPTER TWO
Landscape Evolution: A Geologic Introduction 53

CHAPTER THREE
Opening Scenes: Precambrian Landscapes 69

CHAPTER FOUR
The Paleozoic: Mountain Islands and Desert Seas 79

CHAPTER FIVE
The Mesozoic: Rising from the Sea 93

CHAPTER SIX
The Cenezoic: The Age of Mammals 110

CHAPTER SEVEN
Finishing Touches: The Quaternary 128

CHAPTER EIGHT
Climate and Weather in the Southern Rockies 148

CHAPTER NINE
The Winter Landscape 172

CHAPTER TEN
Landscape Patterns 189

CHAPTER ELEVEN
Land within the Rain Shadow: The Shortgrass Prairie 199
Ecological Distribution 200
Physical Environment 201
Community Characteristics 203
Plant Adaptation: Designs for Survival 207

Descriptions of Common Plants ... 211
Common Plants of the Shortgrass Prairie ... 213
Environment and Adaptation: Animals of the Shortgrass Prairie ... 216
Life Histories of Selected Animals ... 220
Common Animals of the Shortgrass Prairie ... 227

CHAPTER TWELVE

The Shrubland Tapestry: Semidesert, Sagebrush, and Mountain Shrublands ... 230
Plant Adaptation: Designs for Survival ... 231
Environment and Adaptation: Shrubland Animals ... 237

CHAPTER THIRTEEN

Living Dry: Semidesert Shrublands ... 240
Ecological Distribution ... 241
Community Characteristics ... 241
Descriptions of Common Plants ... 243
Common Plants of the Semidesert Shrublands ... 245
Environment and Adaption: Animals of the Semidesert Shrublands ... 247
Life Histories of Selected Animals ... 247
Common Animals of the Semidesert Shrublands ... 252

CHAPTER FOURTEEN

Heart of the Rain Shadow: Sagebrush Shrublands ... 254
Ecological Distribution ... 255
Community Characteristics ... 256
Descriptions of Common Plants ... 259
Common Plants of the Sagebrush Shrublands ... 262
Environment and Adaptation: Animals of the Sagebrush Shrublands ... 264
Life Histories of Selected Animals ... 267
Common Animals of the Sagebrush Shrublands ... 270

CHAPTER FIFTEEN

A Resilient Beauty: Mountain Shrublands and Gambel's Oak Woodlands ... 273
Ecological Distribution ... 274
Community Characteristics ... 275

Descriptions of Common Plants 276
Common Plants of the Mountain Shrublands and Gambel's Oak Woodlands 279
Environment and Adaptation: Animals of the Mountain Shrublands and Gambel's Oak Woodlands 281
Life Histories of Selected Animals 283
Common Animals of the Mountain Shrublands and Gambel's Oak Woodlands 288

CHAPTER SIXTEEN
Sun Forests: Piñon-Juniper Woodlands 291
Ecological Distribution 291
Physical Environment 293
Community Characteristics 293
Plant Adaptation: Designs for Survival 295
Descriptions of Common Plants 298
Common Plants of the Piñon-Juniper Woodlands 303
Environment and Adaptation: Animals of the Piñon-Juniper Woodlands 305
Life Histories of Selected Animals 311
Common Animals of the Piñon-Juniper Woodlands 316

CHAPTER SEVENTEEN
Music in the Pines: Ponderosa Pine Forests 319
Ecological Distribution 320
Physical Environment 322
Community Characteristics 322
Plant Adaptation: Designs for Survival 323
Descriptions of Common Plants 327
Common Plants of the Ponderosa Pine Forest 332
Environment and Adaptation: Animals of the Ponderosa Pine Forest 334
Life Histories of Selected Animals 341
Common Animals of the Ponderosa Pine Forest 345

CHAPTER EIGHTEEN
The Raven's Forest: Douglas-fir Forests 348
Ecological Distribution 350

Physical Environment 351
Community Characteristics 351
Plant Adaptation: Designs for Survival 352
Descriptions of Common Plants 353
Common Plants of the Douglas-fir Forest 356
Environment and Adaptation: Animals of the Douglas-fir Forest 358
Life Histories of Selected Animals 359
Common Animals of the Douglas-fir Forest 362

CHAPTER NINETEEN
Open Country: Mountain Grasslands and Meadows **364**
Ecological Distribution 365
Physical Environment 366
Community Characteristics 367
Plant Adaptation: Designs for Survival 371
Descriptions of Common Plants 375
Common Plants of the Mountain Grasslands and Meadows 379
Environment and Adaptation:
Animals of the Mountain Grasslands and Meadows 383
Life Histories of Selected Animals 388
Common Animals of the Mountain Grasslands and Meadows 394

CHAPTER TWENTY
Streambank and Shoreline: Mountain Wetlands **397**
Ecological Distribution 398
Physical Environment 400
Community Characteristics 400
Plant Adaptation: Designs for Survival 408
Descriptions of Common Plants 410
Common Plants of the Mountain Wetlands 416
Environment and Adaptation: Animals of the
Mountain Wetlands 419
Life Histories of Selected Animals 425
Common Animals of the Mountain Wetlands 434

CHAPTER TWENTY-ONE
Riffle, Pool, and Tarn: Aquatic Ecosystems **438**
Lotic Ecosystems: Mountain Streams and Rivers 439

Lotic Environments: Community Characteristics 441
Lentic Ecosystems: Marsh, Pond, and Lake 445
Community Characteristics 450
Common Plants of Aquatic Ecosystems 454
Life Histories of Selected Animals 455
Common Animals of Aquatic Ecosystems 458

CHAPTER TWENTY-TWO

Leaf Dance: Aspen Forests 461
Ecological Distribution 462
Physical Environment 463
Community Characteristics 464
Plant Adaptation: Designs for Survival 468
Descriptions of Common Plants 473
Common Plants of the Aspen Forests 479
Environment and Adaptation: Animals of the Aspen Forests 482
Life Histories of Selected Animals 487
Common Animals of the Aspen Forests 492

CHAPTER TWENTY-THREE

The Fire Forest: Lodgepole Pine 495
Ecological Distribution 497
Physical Environment 498
Community Characteristics 498
Plant Adaptation: Designs for Survival 500
Descriptions of Common Plants 502
Common Plants of the Lodgepole Pine Forest 506
Environment and Adaptation: Animals of the Lodgepole Pine Forest 508
Life Histories of Selected Animals 512
Common Animals of the Lodgepole Pine Forest 516

CHAPTER TWENTY-FOUR

The Wind Forest: Bristlecone Pine and Limber Pine 518
Ecological Distribution 518
Physical Environment 522
Community Characteristics 523
Plant Adaptation: Designs for Survival 524

Descriptions of Common Plants 525
Common Plants of the Bristlecone Pine and Limber Pine Forests 528
Environment and Adaptation: Animals of the Bristlecone Pine and Limber Pine Forests 529
Life Histories of Selected Animals 533
Common Animals of the Bristlecone Pine and Limber Pine Forests 535

CHAPTER TWENTY-FIVE

The Snow Forest: Engelmann Spruce and Subalpine Fir 537
Ecological Distribution 538
Physical Environment 540
Community Characteristics 542
Plant Adaptation: Designs for Survival 546
Descriptions of Common Plants 556
Common Plants of the Spruce-Fir Forest and the Forest-Tundra Ecotone 559
Environment and Adaptation: Animals of the Spruce-Fir Forest 562
Life Histories of Selected Animals 565
Common Animals of the Spruce-Fir Forest and the Forest-Tundra Ecotone 572

CHAPTER TWENTY-SIX

Islands in the Sky: Alpine Tundra 574
Ecological Distribution 575
Physical Environment 576
Community Characteristics 579
Plant Adaptation: Designs for Survival 594
Descriptions of Common Plants 601
Common Plants of the Alpine Tundra 604
Environment and Adaptation: Animals of the Alpine Tundra 609
Life Histories of Selected Animals 623
Common Animals of the Alpine Tundra 626

Selected References 629
Index 636

Acknowledgments

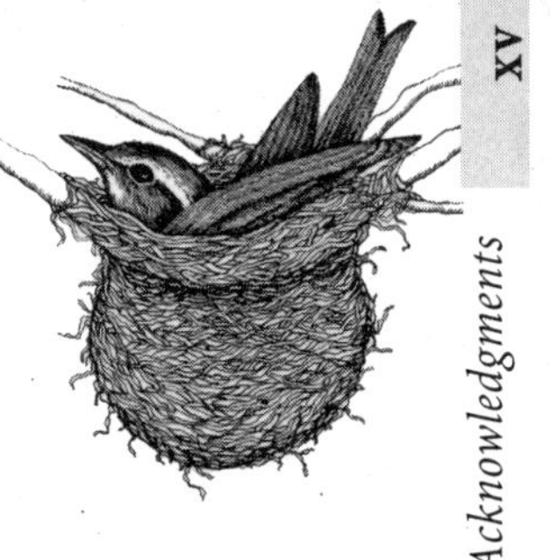

The often-quoted adage "It takes a village to raise a child" applies equally well to the challenge of writing a field guide to a region as geologically and biologically diverse as the Southern Rockies. A daunting project, indeed, without the scientific expertise, generous support, and encouragement of many people. I have relied on the research and descriptions published in the professional and popular literature by a talented group of geologists, climatologists, and biologists far too numerous for me to list individually but without whom a book like this would be impossible. In both the first edition of this field guide, published by Sierra Club Books in 1991, and in the current edition, several individuals were especially influential in shaping my thinking about the natural history of the Southern Rockies: Dr. David Armstrong, Dr. James Benedict, Dr. William Bradley, Constance Brown, Dr. Steve Cassells, Dr. Jameson Chase, Dr. Alex Cruz, Dr. Boyce Drummond, Michael Elliot, Dr. Emmett Evanoff, Susan Quimby Foster, Dr. Joyce Gellhorn, Paul Gilbert, Dr. Geoff Hammerson, Dr. Yan Linhart, Dr. Brian Linkhart, Dr. Martin Lockley, Willard Louden, Dr. Rich Madole, Dr. John Marr, Dr. Carron Meaney, Chris Pague, Dr. Robert Michael Pyle, Dr. Richard Reynolds, Bob Rozinski, Dr. Mike Scott, Wendy Shattil, Dr. Wayne Shepperd, Dr. Marc Snyder, Dr. Diana Tomback, Dr. William Weber, Dr. Tom Veblen, Dr. Ed Wick, Dr. Olwen Williams, and Ann Hammond Zwinger. I owe a tremendous debt of gratitude to Dr. James Benedict and Dr. David Armstrong for their critical review of the entire first edition manuscript. In addition, several individuals read one or more chapters for scientific content and clarity, including Dr. Peter Birkeland, Dr. William Bradley, Abigail Bridges, Liz Caile, Fran Enright, Dr. Emmett Evanoff, Dr. Freeman Hall, Mehry Khosravi, Dr. Art Mears, Dr. Brainerd Mears, Dr. William Rense, Judith Schaefer, and Deb Tewell. I extend my sincere thanks to Sam Scinta for his belief in the importance of this book, Derek Lawrence, and the entire staff at Fulcrum Publishing for their support and encouragement. Every page in this book reflects the consummate skill and deft hand of Faith Marcovecchio, my editor at Fulcrum, as well as the book design genius of Ann Douden. Over the years, the many wonderful books and friendship of Ann Hammond Zwinger have inspired me to write natural history from the heart and from the mind, without comprise. My most profound and heartfelt gratitude goes to my husband, Jim Benedict, for his loving support in all things. He has shown me throughout nearly forty-five years of his own multidisciplinary research in the Colorado Front Range that getting the science "right" and expressing the beauty of a place are never incompatible in teaching or in writing; they are the best legacy we can leave for future generations.

Introduction

A map of the Southern Rocky Mountains is musical with the names of ranges: Sangre de Cristo, La Garita, Never Summer, Medicine Bow, La Plata, Culebra, San Juan, Grenadier, and so many more. To those who have had the pleasure of exploring this most complex of North American mountain regions, these names bring to mind memories of summers gladdened, meadows rich with the colors of flowers, snowmelt cascades, and peaks lit with alpenglow. But the scenery does not stop at mountains. Deep canyons and broad, sweeping valleys cleave the ranges and create a landscape of extraordinary beauty and diversity.

Sangre de Cristo twilight.

To the geologist or biologist, the urge to unravel the histories of landscapes or the complex relationships governing natural communities is irresistible. Our exploration of the ecosystems of the Southern Rockies begins with a geographical introduction to its mountain ranges, plateaus, and basins.

To appreciate the scenic diversity that is the region's hallmark, one must walk through the geologic archives, from nearly 3 billion years ago to the tectonically restless present. The tumultuous geologic story of the Southern Rockies occupies several chapters of this book and is crucial to understanding the landforms and ecosystems we see today. The effects of climate and weather, the subject of Chapter 8, are clearly imprinted on the land and its people, setting the stage upon which all physical, chemical, and biological processes operate. Snow, the subject of Chapter 9, is a critical component of the mountain environment, influencing landscape processes, controlling the distribution and composition of plant communities, and shaping many of the adaptations that plants and animals must have for survival.

The second half of the book describes the major ecosystems, beginning with the shortgrass prairie and ending with the alpine tundra. Each is described in terms of its environmental setting, principal plant and animal species, and community characteristics. The emphasis throughout is on the adaptations of the organisms associated with these ecosystems—their form, physiology, and behavior—and the ways in which these adaptations are shaped by the environment in which the organisms live. To maintain the usefulness of this guide over such a broad region, ecosystem descriptions and species lists have been somewhat generalized. Readers primarily interested in identification should refer to the list of comprehensive field guides in the Bibliography. Plant and animal species lists, once again limited by space constraints, are provided to give an idea of the representative species associated with each ecosystem; the scientific names for plants and animals are restricted to the species lists. This is intended to improve readability of the text without sacrificing the greater precision of scientific names or the usefulness of the guide; in some cases, subspecies and varieties are indicated when essential in identifying a particular organism occurring in the Southern Rockies. Nomenclatural differences are also noted where appropriate.

Human-wrought changes threaten nearly every corner of the Southern Rockies: we trample, build roads, clear-cut, overgraze, bulldoze, drain, fill, flood, and poison with reckless abandon. Even in the once-remote, pristine watersheds of our highest mountains, the effects of acid rain are increasingly apparent. Nonnative plant species such as Canada thistle, cheatgrass, knapweed, tall whitetop, Russian-olive, tamarisk, and so many others continue to thrive and spread in response to human disturbance and land-use patterns. Sadly, we must be as wary of the impacts of recreation and all its accoutrements as we are of the effects of unregulated logging or mining. In the Colorado River system, for example, the fourteen surviving native fish species must now compete with more than forty nonnative species. The stocking of nonnative game fish such as the northern pike and the channel catfish has decimated populations of Colorado squawfish (northern pike minnow), a species that evolved more than 3 million years ago and was once the top predator in the Colorado River, reaching a length of six feet or more. Every habitat altered or destroyed, whether through unwitting overuse or careless disregard, makes every remaining habitat exponentially more important—and with it the crucial web of life strung through all its parts.

We are only beginning to understand the intricate relationships that characterize natural communities. The impact of global warming and the role that it will play as a force for environmental change is even more difficult to quantify. My intent with this book is to provide an introduction to the varied ecosystems of the Southern Rockies and to share some of the marvelous adaptations that bind organisms to their environments. In so doing, my ultimate wish is to underscore the fragility of such systems and the importance of stewardship.

Physiographic provinces of the Rocky Mountain region.

CHAPTER ONE

Mountains in the Clouds: The Southern Rocky Mountains

To the traveler journeying west across the Great Plains, the first sighting of the cloud-capped ramparts of the Rockies makes a lasting impression. Appearing on the western horizon like a line of storm clouds, the Rocky Mountains form the eastern front of an immense cordon of mountain ranges, the Western Cordillera, which extends from Alaska and northwestern Canada to the southern tip of South America. North of the border between Canada and the United States, the Canadian Rockies stretch for some 900 miles, from the Laird River in northern British Columbia to Helena, Montana. Within the United States, the ranges that make up the Rocky Mountains are divided physiographically into four provinces: the Northern, Central, and Southern Rocky Mountains, and the Wyoming Basin. The Wyoming Basin, separating the Central and Southern Rocky Mountains, is connected by narrow passages to the Great Plains Province to the east and the Colorado Plateau Province to the south.

A Geographic Orientation

The Southern Rocky Mountains lie mostly in Colorado, with extensions north into Wyoming and south into New Mexico. These mountain ranges and their intervening basins dominate the landscape from the northern edge of Wyoming's Laramie Mountains south to northern New Mexico, a distance roughly 500 miles in length and as much as 250 miles wide from east to west. The region covered by this book extends beyond the eastern mountain front to include the High Plains, Colorado Piedmont, and Raton

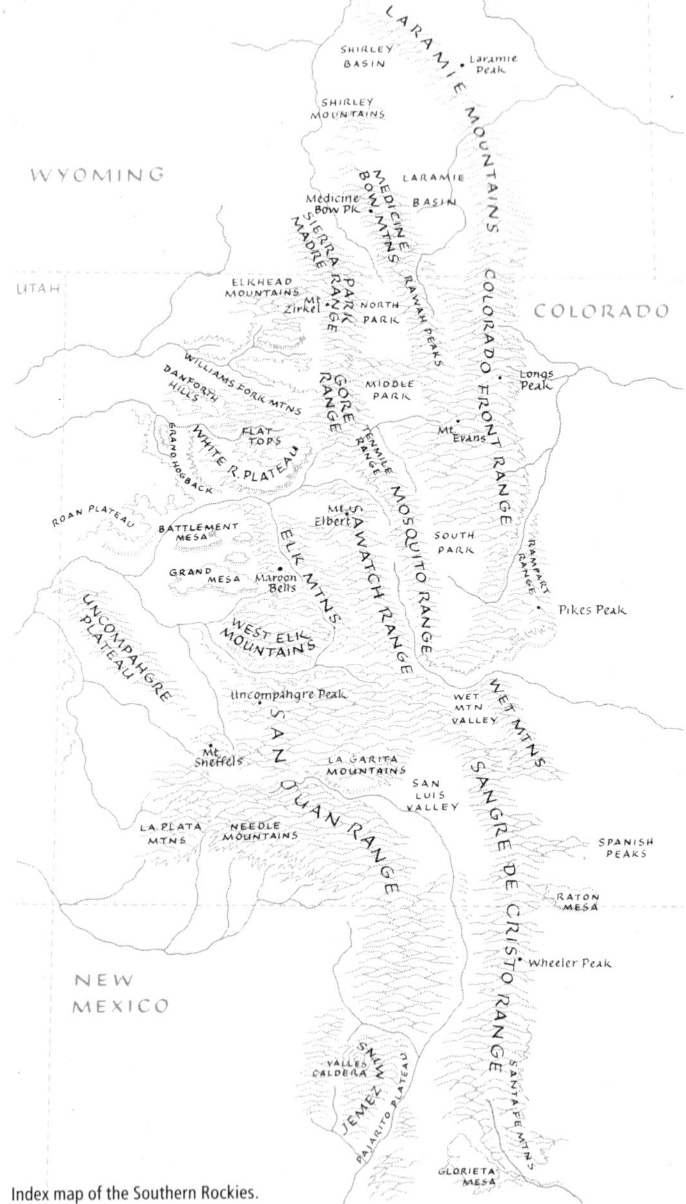

Index map of the Southern Rockies.

sections of the Great Plains Province, all lying within the rain shadow and ecological influence of the Southern Rockies. The western boundary borders the mesa and canyon country of the Colorado Plateau, along a line roughly drawn through the towns of Jemez Springs, New Mexico; Durango, Grand Junction, Rifle, and Craig, Colorado; and Saratoga, Wyoming. Biologists use the term *ecoregion* to refer to a large contiguous landscape that shares similar geological, physical, and biological characteristics. In areal extent, the Southern Rocky Mountain Ecoregion encompasses approximately 63,654 square miles, an area that approximates the size of Maine, New Hampshire, Vermont, Connecticut, Rhode Island, and Massachusetts combined.

With the exception of the San Juan Mountains in southwestern Colorado, the principal mountain ranges of the Southern Rockies fall into two north-south belts. The eastern ranges include the Laramie Mountains, the Colorado Front Range, the Wet Mountains, and the Sangre de Cristo Range. The principal ranges of the western belt are the Sierra Madre, Park, Gore, and Sawatch ranges, and the Elk, San Juan, and Jemez mountains. Separating the two mountain belts is a chain of large, intermontane basins: Laramie Basin, North Park, Middle Park, South Park, the Wet Mountain Valley, the San Luis Valley, and the Rio Grande Valley.

High Peaks

Alpine scenery—high country—distinguishes the Southern Rockies. During the opening of the American West, the spectacular scenery that now attracts millions of visitors each year proved to be a major barrier to transmountain travel. The most heavily used emigrant trails followed routes around the northern and southern ends of the Southern Rockies, never through their heart. Colorado contains the loftiest summits in the entire Rocky Mountain system, including all of the chain's fifty-four "Fourteeners" (peaks that exceed 14,000 feet). In fact, excluding Alaska, Colorado contains more high mountains than any other state; more than 1,000 Colorado summits rise above 10,000 feet, and 300 exceed 13,000 feet. Looking west from Denver, the difference in elevation between the peaks and the nearby lowlands is particularly striking; the square-topped silhouette of Longs Peak, the northernmost Fourteener, towers 9,000 feet above the adjacent plain. Both north and south of Colorado, the ranges of the Southern Rockies decline only slightly in elevation.

The Continental Divide

The backbone of the North American continent, the Continental, or "Great," Divide, runs from northwestern Canada along the crest of the Rocky

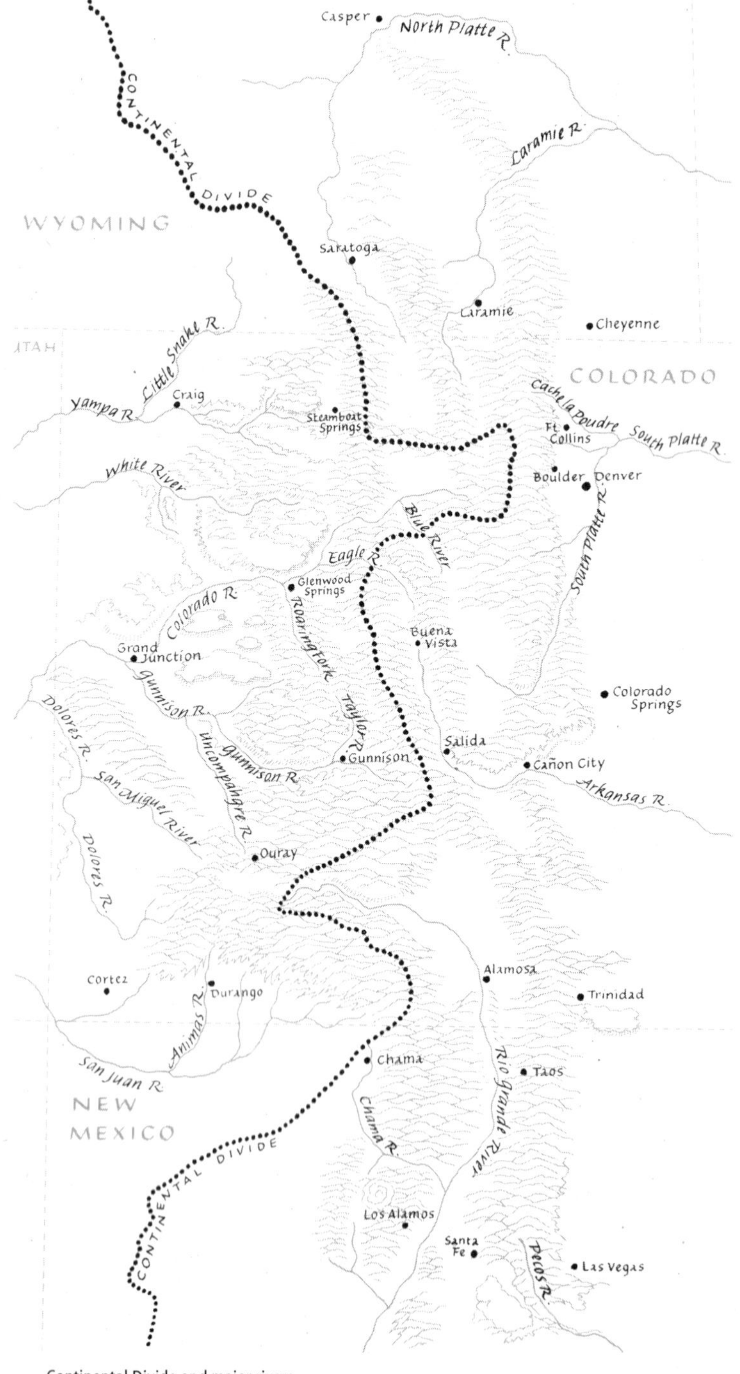

Continental Divide and major rivers.

Mountains to New Mexico. South of the Mexican border, the divide travels along the Sierra Madre Occidental into Central America and then along the towering Andes Mountains to the southern tip of South America. On most maps of the United States, the Continental Divide is represented by a series of dashes, a meandering line drawn from north to south along the chaotic and sometimes confounding geography of the Rockies. Streams and rivers originating in mountain watersheds along the eastern side of the Continental Divide in the United States flow into the Gulf of Mexico and the Atlantic Ocean, while those on the western side flow to the Gulf of California and the Pacific Ocean.

To most flatlanders, crossing the Continental Divide invokes visions of traversing a skyscraping, continuous ridge from which the bounty of mountain watersheds flows predictably toward one ocean or another according to the laws of gravity. The high drama associated with the divide's more mountainous ramblings becomes lost in cartographic ambiguity in places where it must thread its way between mountain ranges and across wide open spaces with little visible relief. In southern Wyoming's Great Divide Basin, the Continental Divide frays apart, like the strands in an old rope, encircling a couple of million acres with no visible means of surface drainage to either ocean. Recombining its separate strands as it angles south, the Continental Divide regains its legendary grandeur in the Southern Rockies, charting a sinuous course that traverses one range crest after another.

Not surprisingly, the Continental Divide attains its highest elevations in Colorado. Wandering along the crest of the Sierra Madre and Park ranges, the divide angles across the southern end of North Park and then east around the headwaters of the Colorado River in Rocky Mountain National Park. At the park's southern boundary, the highest peaks of the Indian Peaks Wilderness Area carry the divide south; Sawtooth Peak, a conspicuous landmark at the northern end of the wilderness area, marks the extreme eastern point reached by the Continental Divide in the United States. Near the southern end of the Colorado Front Range, the divide swings sharply west around the headwaters of the Arkansas River to ride the crest of the Sawatch Range. In a great looping switchback that roughly defines the headwaters of the Rio Grande, the divide then traverses the San Juan Mountains before angling south into the San Juan Basin, between the San Juan and Chama rivers.

The influence of the Continental Divide on regional climate—and politics—is undeniable. Along the East Slope of the Southern Rockies, rivers such as the Platte and the Arkansas roll down from the mountains and out across the plains. Along the West Slope, the Colorado River and its many tributaries wind their way down spectacular canyons to an eventual rendezvous with the Gulf of California. Precipitation varies considerably from one place to another along the entire length of the Rocky Mountains. In the Southern Rockies, average annual precipitation can range from as little as seven inches to as much as sixty inches, depending on topographic location and elevation. Though nearly two-thirds of the Southern Rocky Mountain watersheds drain eastward, more than 75 percent of the precipitation falls on the west side of the Continental Divide, 60 percent in the Colorado River Basin alone. This natural imbalance, paired with the concentration of most of the population and political power along the Front Range urban corridor, places the upper Colorado River and its tributaries squarely at the center of an ongoing legal and environmental controversy. Colorado grew by 1 million people in the last decade, with growth projections estimated for another 2 million residents by 2020. Faced with an ever-increasing population, the poorly understood environmental and socioeconomic impacts of global warming, and our failure to adopt long-term strategies for conservation, the future of our precious water resources—for people, plants, and animals—remains in jeopardy.

Eastern Ranges of the Southern Rockies

Laramie Mountains

Early exploration accounts referred to the Laramie Mountains as the Black Hills because of their dark profile when viewed from the east, near old Fort Laramie. These low, weather-beaten, and unglaciated mountains mark the western edge of the High Plains in southern Wyoming and provide a striking contrast to the rugged, ice-sculpted scenery of the Medicine Bow Mountains to the west. Rounded bedrock knobs and unusual rock formations characterize much of the range crest, particularly in the area of Vedauwoo Rocks and the Sherman Mountains. Laramie Peak, the highest peak in the range at 10,272 feet, was a famous landmark along the Oregon Trail, which passed just to the north of the mountains. Along their eastern front, the Laramie Mountains merge with the plains along a ramplike slope called the Gangplank. This unusual landform, located about sixteen miles west of Cheyenne and visible from U.S. I-80, marks the only place between Canada and Mexico where the thousands of feet of sediments that once buried the Rockies remain largely undisturbed, the only place where you can step from the High Plains surface directly onto the ancient Precambrian rocks that distinguish the crest of the range.

The rough-and-tumble country along the southern edge of the Laramie Mountains was the stage for one of the most famous swindles of the nineteenth century: the Great Diamond Hoax of 1872. The perpetrators of the hoax, two gold rush forty-niners from backwoods Kentucky, cousins Philip Arnold and John Slack, found that their heretofore-unrealized theatric skills more than made up for their failures as prospectors. As gold fever waned in California, the two men, in connivance with another Kentuckian, Asbury Harpending, hatched a plot to capitalize on the furor resulting from the discovery of diamonds in South Africa. Another dedicated son of the Confederacy, Harpending had no aversion to working both sides of the law. In fact, during the turbulent years of the Civil War, Confederate president Jefferson Davis had sent Harpending to California to hijack ships bearing Yankee gold before they could set sail out of San Francisco Bay. After the war, reinventing himself as a "respected" mining banker in San Francisco, the wealthy and well-connected Harpending was the perfect foil for Arnold and Slack.

With investors' imaginations stoked anew by Jim Bridger and Kit Carson's tales from the Rockies of "jewels littering the ground like stars fallen from the heavens," the conspirators found that gathering a gullible audience was amazingly easy. Choosing a little-visited maze of granite knobs and low ridges just south of the Colorado-Wyoming border, the men salted their bogus diamond field with more than fifty pounds of rough gemstones garnered from diamond dealers in London, a booty most likely paid for by Harpending. Embellishing their "discovery" with one dramatic flourish after another, the conspirators succeeded in embroiling a large group of unsuspecting investors, including William Ralston and several other prominent California financiers, British banking magnate Nathan Rothschild, two former Civil War generals, Colorado territorial governor William Gilpin, a U.S. senator, two presidential candidates, a well-respected California mining engineer, and the country's leading jeweler, C. L. Tiffany. Caught up in diamond fever, these men invested a total of about $2 million dollars. Hearing rumors of the diamond discovery in Colorado and the investment frenzy, Yale-educated geologist Clarence King and members of his Fortieth Parallel Survey crew traveled to the purported diamond field to investigate. Finding too many geologic inconsistencies and suspicious circumstances to support the claim's validity, the incorruptible King made haste to the San Francisco–based offices of the Bank of California to expose the scam. Unfortunately, King's revelations were largely too late to undo many of the financial repercussions and personal tragedies that resulted from the Great Diamond Hoax. The conspirators, in fact, escaped legal action altogether. Clarence King's role in the exposé, however, made him an international celebrity, a confidant of Theodore Roosevelt, and led to his tenure as the first director of the United States Geological Survey.

Ironically, in 1965, geologist M. E. McCallum noted the occurrence of a distinctive type of diamond-bearing rock (kimberlite) not far from the scene where the Great Diamond Hoax had played out nearly a century before. Outcrops of kimberlite are exceedingly rare, occurring only where volatile, diamondiferous magmas originating in the Earth's upper mantle surge upward along a system of volcanic conduits, or pipes. At current count, there are fewer than twenty active kimberlite mines in the world, the most important being those in South Africa, Australia, and northern Canada. McCallum's discovery triggered a Colorado-scale diamond rush, leading to the identification of several other kimberlite pipes in the region. In 1975, a geology graduate student discovered the first verified in situ diamond not far from McCallum's site. The kimberlites at Kelsey Lake were discovered in 1987, and full-scale mining began in 1996. Though small by world standards, the Kelsey Lake Diamond Mine in Colorado is the only commercial producer of diamonds in the United States. The biggest rough diamond unearthed at the mine weighed 28.3 carats. After cutting and polishing, this spectacular golden-hued diamond weighed 16.9 carats and sold for nearly $300,000, making it the largest faceted diamond ever produced in the United States. Current estimates by the mine's owners suggest that the remaining Kelsey Lake kimberlite may hold between 60,000 and 250,000 carats of diamonds.

Snowy Range, Medicine Bow Peak, Medicine Bow Mountains, Wyoming.

Medicine Bow Mountains

In the Medicine Bow Mountains, two groups of glaciated, snowcapped peaks rise above the otherwise flat, benchlike surface of the range: the Snowy Range in Wyoming and the Rawah Peaks in Colorado. The white, quartzitic peaks of the Snowy Range rise nearly 2,000 feet above the thickly forested Medicine Bow upland, appearing like sparkling whitecaps on a storm-tossed sea. Medicine Bow Peak (12,014 feet) marks the highest point in the range. A seasonal road over Snowy Range Pass (10,847 feet), long considered one of the most beautiful scenic byways in the Southern Rockies, provides easy access to Lake Marie and to the many prime fishing streams that characterize the rolling subalpine upland.

The origin of the name Medicine Bow is thought to reflect the spiritual significance of these mountains to Native Americans, especially the Cheyenne and Arapaho. One of the earliest explanations of the name comes from an account by the historian C. G. Coutant and dates from around 1889. He reported that various tribes of Plains Indians frequented spots along the base of these mountains where they could replenish the wood needed for making hunting bows: juniper (or cedar), mountain mahogany, and mountain-ash. The Arapaho are also known to have called the Medicine Bows the "Hammer

Mountains," referring to the hammerstones that they made from a special white quartzite found only there. The healing qualities and ceremonial importance of the region's hot springs, such as those near the present-day community of Saratoga, no doubt contributed to its reputation as a destination known for its good medicine. Ethnographic accounts suggest that these hot springs played an important role in rituals that conveyed special powers to the implements used in hunting or in traditional medicine.

The Medicine Bow Mountains were also a favorite haunt of trappers and mountain men as early as the 1830s, most attracted by the rich bounty of beaver pelts and other furs. French explorers gave the docile river that emerged from the mountain's flanks the name Riviere de Plat (flat river), because for most of its 122-mile length the North Platte bears little resemblance to the tumbling cascade near its source. Today, when adventuresome rafters and kayakers answer the siren call of the North Platte, they head to the river's upper reaches, where challenging Class III and IV rapids dance their way through 800-foot-deep, 12-mile-long North Gate Canyon. The resort town of Saratoga, located along the banks of the North Platte River, serves as the western gateway to the Medicine Bow Mountains and provides weary travelers with a Wyoming-style hot-spring experience to be savored.

Flanking the eastern edge of North Park and extending from Cameron Pass to the Wyoming border, the Rawah Peaks mark the southern extension of the Medicine Bow Mountains in Colorado. The 76,000-acre Rawah Peaks Wilderness Area was one of the first areas to enter the National Wilderness Preservation System. The East Sand Hills and North Sand Hills, east of Cowdrey, nestle against the western Rawah foothills and form a northern analog to the enormous dune system found at Great Sand Dunes National Park, on the western slope of the Sangre de Cristos. The Michigan and Canadian rivers, tributaries of the North Platte in North Park, drain the mountains along their western flank. The cottonwood-edged Laramie River, another tributary of the North Platte, meanders along the eastern flanks of the mountains out onto the plain.

Colorado Front Range

Looking west from Denver, the mountains appear to rise from the plains in two giant steps, from an average elevation of 5,600 feet to alpine summits above 14,000 feet. Beginning at the north fork of the Cache la Poudre River, near the Colorado-Wyoming border, the Colorado Front Range stretches south to the Arkansas River near Cañon City. Along much of its length, the Eastern Slope of the Front Range is edged by a conspicuous ridge of buff-colored sedimentary rocks known as the Dakota Hogback, the frayed, upturned edge of a vast sheet of sedimentary rock that spreads out for thousands of square miles beneath the surface of the eastern plains.

Several mountain ranges are collectively referred to as the Colorado Front Range. These include the Never Summer Mountains and the Mummy Range (both in Rocky Mountain National Park), the Indian Peaks (west of Boulder), and a lower, more timbered series of ranges south of the Indian Peaks that define the Williams Fork Mountains, Vasquez Mountains, Platte River Mountains, Tarryall Mountains, Kenosha Mountains, and Rampart Range. The Lost Creek Wilderness Area, located on the northeastern slopes of the Tarryall Mountains, preserves an unusual landscape animated by uniquely weathered granite formations.

The Colorado Front Range contains some of the most accessible alpine scenery to be found in the Southern Rockies. Rocky Mountain National Park preserves thousands of acres of mountain meadows, glacier-fed streams, deep U-shaped valleys, rolling alpine uplands, and glacially carved peaks. Trail Ridge Road in Rocky Mountain National Park traverses a fifty-mile skyscraping sampler of the Colorado Front Range between the resort communities of Estes Park and Grand Lake. As you travel the eleven-mile section of the road that lies above tree line, you parallel the Continental Divide, surrounded on all sides by a seemingly endless expanse of alpine tundra and snowcapped peaks. More than 300 miles of hiking trails provide access to remote areas of this popular national park.

The highest peaks in Rocky Mountain National Park, such as Longs Peak (14,255 feet) and Ypsilon (13,514 feet), challenge rock climbers from all over the world. Longs Peak was first officially climbed in 1868 by a small party that included the one-armed explorer and geologist John Wesley Powell. The infamous Diamond of Longs Peak, which ranks as the largest, highest, and steepest wall in the Southern Rockies, remains as alluring to rock climbers as Yosemite's El Capitan. Several early attempts to climb the Diamond failed, and the wall remained unconquered until 1960, when

Trail Ridge Road, Rocky Mountain National Park.

two California climbers made the first ascent. Enos Mills, the self-taught naturalist who led the fight to establish Rocky Mountain National Park in the early 1900s, was to Longs Peak what Thoreau was to Walden Pond; his books on regional natural history, written "in the evening shadow" of this legendary peak, remain classics in their field.

The North Fork of the Colorado River comes to life each spring in a snowy amphitheater beneath Thunder Mountain, in the northwestern corner of Rocky Mountain National Park. From there and from tributary streams along the western side of the national park and the Indian Peaks, the Colorado River gathers force and begins its 1,450-mile odyssey to the Gulf of California. At Shadow Mountain Reservoir, located between the towns of Grand Lake and Granby, the river encounters the first of man's many attempts to tame it; from here to its mouth it bears only an occasional resemblance to the snow-nourished tributary streams that cascade from its uppermost reaches.

South of Rocky Mountain National Park, the Indian Peaks and a long string of alpine summits extend south along the Continental Divide to reach their greatest elevation at Grays Peak (14,270 feet). The 70,000-acre Indian Peaks Wilderness Area sits astride the divide, providing a network of spectacular hiking trails that complement those in Rocky Mountain National Park. Mountains in the Indian Peaks area are named for the Indian tribes that frequented the Southern Rockies and the eastern prairies: Ogallala, Kiowa, Pawnee, Shoshoni, Arikaree, Arapaho, and others. Two influential Arapaho chiefs, Niwot and Neva, are commemorated in the naming of Niwot Ridge and Mount Neva; Niwot Ridge is the site of the University of Colorado's Mountain Research Station and is one of the most thoroughly studied alpine environments in the world.

South of the Indian Peaks, three Fourteeners dominate the Front Range skyline: Mount Evans and the twin peaks of Grays and Torreys. Mount Evans boasts the highest automobile road in the United States, providing seasonal road access to the 14,264-foot summit and a panoramic view of the Colorado Front Range from Longs Peak, fifty miles due north, to Pikes Peak, fifty-eight miles to the southeast. In 1863, Albert Bierstadt, one of the world's great landscape artists, was among the first white men to climb Mount Evans. Grays and Torreys peaks are named for two nineteenth-century American botanists, Asa Gray and John Torrey, whose extensive collections and classification of western plants paved the way for the modern botany manuals used in the Southern Rockies today.

South of Mount Evans, the benchlike crest of the Rampart Range is broken only by the pyramidal outline of one of North America's most famous mountains: Pikes Peak. In 1806, the U.S. Army dispatched Lieutenant Zebulon Pike and a small exploring party to trace the headwaters of the Arkansas and Red rivers. Crossing the High Plains on a crisp November day, Pike's expedition spotted a strange apparition, a "small blue cloud" on the distant horizon; the cloud, of course, would one day be called Pikes Peak. Major Stephen Long's expedition in 1820, sent to chart the boundaries of the Louisiana Purchase, made short work of Pike's claim that the mountain would never be climbed. The expedition's surgeon and botanist, Dr. Edwin James, scaled the peak in three days, making the first collections of the Colorado columbine, now Colorado's state flower, as well as a wide assortment of previously unknown alpine plants. In California, gold rush fever had largely subsided by 1849, leaving thousands of restless fortune seekers anxiously awaiting the "next California." In 1858, newspaper accounts of the discovery of gold nuggets in the gravels along Colorado's South Platte River, just west of the river's confluence with Cherry Creek, brought a fresh wave of prospectors and settlers west, straight into the heart of Pikes Peak country and up and down the Front Range. The slogan "Pikes Peak or Bust" was synonymous with events that heralded the opening of the American West. Countless mining claims were filed, roads built, towns established, and enormous quantities of gold sluiced from gravels along the channels of most of the major streams. With few passes lower than 11,000 feet, engineering bravado was necessary to breach the formidable crest of the Front Range. John Rollins pioneered the first wagon road across the Continental Divide west of Denver in 1873. The Rollins Pass Road (or Corona Pass Road, as it was also called) was soon joined by many others: Berthoud Pass, Loveland Pass, Argentine Pass, Guanella Pass, and Kenosha Pass, to name just a few.

Wet Mountains

The green, somewhat flat-crested range known as the Wet Mountains extends from the Arkansas River southeast to Badito Cone. No doubt the name Wet was coined by some weary prairie traveler in response to the respite these mountains offered after the long, dusty march across the Great Plains. The scenic expanse of the Wet Mountain Valley separates this narrow, forty-five-mile-long range from the rugged eastern ramparts of the Sangre de Cristo Range. Rounded granite knobs are typical of the higher portions of the Wet Mountains, with discontinuous patches of volcanic rock particularly prominent along the western margin. Elevations along the north-northwest-trending crest of the Wet Mountains vary from around 9,200 feet at Tanner Peak to more than 12,000 feet at Greenhorn Mountain. Aspen and Douglas-fir forests interspersed with streams and lush meadows are characteristic of the range's eastern flanks and provide a striking contrast to the arid grasslands and open stands of bristlecone pine that typify the western slope of the mountains.

Spanish explorers preceded the American and French frontiersmen by nearly a hundred years in their familiarity with the mountains that lay between their Santa Fe and Taos outposts and the Arkansas River country.

In 1779, while American colonists were fighting for independence from England, Juan Bautista de Anza, then governor of Spanish-controlled New Mexico, was pursuing the defiant, elusive Comanches through the verdant valleys of the Wet Mountains. De Anza named Greenhorn Mountain in grudging admiration for the Comanche chief Cuerno Verde (meaning "greenhorn"), who died in a fierce battle with the Spanish along its flanks.

Spanish Peaks

The twin cones of the Spanish Peaks rise abruptly out of the arid plains southwest of Walsenburg and the Cucharas River. Native Americans named the Spanish Peaks Huajatolla, meaning "breasts of the Earth." Isolated from the main Sangre de Cristo Range, the Spanish Peaks were long thought to be the much-eroded remnants of ancient volcanoes. We now know that the peaks were eroded from sedimentary rocks that had been intruded by molten rock rising from great depths along a series of fractures and cracks. Vertical walls of solid rock, called dikes, radiate from the flanks of the two peaks and run for miles up and down the foothills, bearing a striking resemblance to the man-made Great Wall of China. The dikes, in contrast to the easily eroded sedimentary rocks into which they were intruded, are resistant to erosion and remain as a dramatic record of the ancient fires that once burned deep beneath the Earth's surface. The Apishapa Pass and Cuchara Pass roads skirt the flanks of East and West Spanish peaks (13,626 feet and 12,683 feet, respectively), offering travelers an unparalleled look at the radiating network of dikes and the legendary landscapes of the Spanish Peaks.

Some tribes, such as the Utes, traditionally believed the Spanish Peaks to be the home of evil spirits and avoided them. Spanish explorers, disregarding Indian superstitions, were drawn to the peaks. Legend has it that one of the priests left behind by the Coronado Expedition in 1541 traveled north to Huajatolla after hearing tales of rich Indian gold mines there. As the story goes, the priest found the gold and, after loading his mules with as much as they could carry, started south for New Mexico—never to be heard from again.

The Highway of Legends Scenic Byway loops westward from either Walsenburg or Trinidad and crosses 9,994-foot Cuchara Pass, which marks the divide between the Cucharas and Purgatoire river valleys. The route provides a fascinating sampler of a region rich in human history and dramatic geology, and is a must for travelers interested in the history of the Santa Fe Trail.

Sangre de Cristo Range

The crest of the Sangre de Cristo Range stretches south, almost unbroken, for more than 200 miles, from the Arkansas River near Salida to Glorieta Pass southeast of Santa Fe. As late as 1827, an American map of the Santa Fe Trail showed no routes through this seemingly impenetrable range. In the autumn of 1540, however, Francisco Coronado and his men made their way east from Pecos Pueblo through present-day Glorieta Pass, becoming the first Europeans to cross the Continental Divide north of Mexico. The Spanish named this range Sangre de Cristo, meaning "the blood of Christ," inspired by the rich red glow of these mountains at sunset.

For 250 years, the fortunes of the Spanish waxed and waned in missions established along the foothills of the Sangre de Cristos. As Spanish dreams of empire faded, French and American traders, followed by U.S. Army explorers and surveyors, poured into the Sangre de Cristos in ever-increasing numbers. The Santa Fe Trail became a bustling trade route, and mountain men such as Ceran St. Vrain, Antoine Robidoux, and Kit Carson explored the Sangre de Cristo high country and trapped beaver along the streams that danced down its side canyons.

The winter of 1807 found Zebulon Pike and his men attempting to cross the Sangre de Cristos from the east, struggling through snowdrifts, bitterly cold, and near starvation. On January 28, 1807, the expedition finally reached Medano Pass. The view from the pass must have seemed like a strange mirage to the weary men, a virtual seascape of "sandy hills" trapped in a cul-de-sac at the foot of the mountains. Today, Pike's sandy hills are preserved within Great Sand Dunes National Park and Preserve and rank among the world's tallest inland dunes.

The northern portion of the Sangre de Cristos, extending from the Arkansas River south to La Veta Pass, is geographically and structurally considered to be part of the western belt of mountain ranges. Seven Fourteeners—Blanca Peak, Ellingwood Point, Little Bear Peak, Kit Carson Peak, Challenger Point, Crestone Peak, and Crestone Needle—grace the

Dunescape, Great Sand Dunes National Park.

northern crest of the range. South of Blanca Peak and La Veta Pass, the range is offset to the east by a fault, rejoining the ranges that form the eastern mountain belt. From La Veta Pass south to the Colorado–New Mexico border, the Sangres are known locally as the Culebra Range (*culebra* means "snake" in Spanish). Culebra Peak (14,047 feet), the southernmost Fourteener in the Southern Rockies, and Purgatory Peak (13,676 feet) mark the high points along this section of the range.

Between the Colorado–New Mexico border and Taos, the Sangre de Cristo Range folds into two north-south-trending groups of mountains, the Taos Mountains on the west and the Cimarron Range on the east, separated along their length by the Costilla and Moreno valleys. Wheeler Peak (13,160 feet), northeast of Taos, is the highest peak in New Mexico and is encompassed by the 6,000-acre Wheeler Peak Wilderness Area. The Cimarron Range is located on private land, and special permission from the current landowners (Philmont Scout Ranch and Vermejo Park) is required prior to entering this area.

From Taos south, the Sangre de Cristos form two north-south ridges: the Truchas Peaks and the Santa Fe Range on the west and the Mora and

Las Vegas ranges on the east. Near the Truchas Peaks, an east-west ridge connects the Santa Fe Range with the Las Vegas Range, enclosing the upper Pecos Valley. First climbed by the Wheeler survey party in 1874, South Truchas Peak, at 13,103 feet, is the second highest point in New Mexico. The Sky Line Trail, beginning near Aspen Basin and extending in a forty-eight-mile arc around the entire upper Pecos River drainage basin, offers an unparalleled sampling of the scenic 167,000-acre Pecos Wilderness Area.

Western Ranges of the Southern Rockies

Jemez Mountains

The Jemez Mountains mark the southern end of the western ranges of the Southern Rockies. The Spanish, awed by the sight of thousands of sandhill cranes flying over these mountains during spring migration, gave them the name Sierra de las Grullas, or "Mountains of the Cranes." These dark volcanic mountains rise ominously above a maze of lava-capped mesas, vermillion cliffs, and deep canyons just south of the Colorado–New Mexico border and the San Juan Mountains. The Chama River, one of the Rio Grande's major tributaries, winds its way south from the high San Juans bringing much-needed moisture and softening the rough edges of this austere volcanic landscape. Rising along the rim of an enormous volcanic depression, the fourteen-mile-wide Valles Caldera, the Jemez Mountains extend from Cerro Pedernal, west of Abiquiu, to Borrego Mesa, near Jemez Pueblo (or Walatowa). The highest summits in the range, Santa Clara Peak (11,561 feet) and Polvadera Peak (11,232 feet), tower above the caldera's rim.

Geologists often refer to New Mexico as the "Volcano State" because it contains one of the greatest concentrations of young, largely uneroded volcanoes on the continent. The "supervolcanoes" that created the Jemez Mountains are among the most famous of all, their origin coinciding with the cataclysmic intersection of two major zones of crustal weakness and volcanism: the western edge of the Rio Grande Rift, which runs north-south through southern Colorado and New Mexico, and the Jemez Lineament, a line of dormant young volcanoes that extends from east-central Arizona through northeastern New Mexico to westernmost Oklahoma. Other prominent volcanoes associated with the lineament rise both to the west and east of the Jemez Mountains and include Mount Taylor (11,301 feet), which looms above the desert plain west of Albuquerque and is one of four mountains considered sacred to the Navajo, and the near-perfect cone of Capulin Mountain (8,182 feet), which lies just to the east of the Sangre de Cristos and is accessible to the public as part of Capulin Volcano National Monument.

In the Jemez Mountains, two major volcanic eruptions are responsible for the mountains we see today, the first occurring more than 1.4 million years ago, and the second a little over 1 million years ago. Taken together, these eruptions are believed to have been 600 times more powerful than the 1980 eruption of Mount St. Helens. In all, more than 100 cubic miles of volcanic ash and other ejecta were erupted, covering a 1,500-square-mile area with as much as 1,000 feet of volcanic debris. Valles Caldera formed as a result of the explosive eruption and collapse of one of these supervolcanoes. This spectacular caldera, one of the largest in the world, was once part of the Jemez section of the historic Baca Ranch. In 2000, President Bill Clinton signed groundbreaking legislation that enabled the federal purchase of the 89,000-acre ranch and created Valles Caldera National Preserve. Stunning mountain grasslands sweep across the floor of the caldera, an area known locally as the Valle Grande, and a forest-topped, resurgent lava dome, Cerro La Jara, distinguishes the otherwise flat expanse of the caldera's floor. The remarkable volcanic features associated with the Jemez Mountains attract geology students and research professionals from all over the world.

The Jemez Mountain Trail National Scenic Byway penetrates the heart of this fascinating region, beginning near the village of San Ysidro and winding past Jemez Pueblo, home to more than 3,000 tribal members, before entering the spectacular Cañon de San Diego. Virgin Mesa towers above the junction of the Jemez and Guadalupe rivers, a landscape distinguished by high volcanic cliffs, cone-shaped tent rocks, and clouds of steam rising from the bubbling hot springs along the Jemez River at Soda Dam. Nearby Jemez State Monument protects the Puebloan ruins of Giusewa (Place of the Boiling Waters), one of the numerous villages built about 600 years ago in the canyons and on the mesa tops by the Jemez people. Hot springs, reminders of the region's turbulent volcanic past, are common throughout the Jemez Mountains. Many of the deep-seated geothermal resources that underlie the Jemez volcanic field have undergone extensive study

Puebloan ruins of Ginsewa, Jemez State Monument.

by government agencies and private energy corporations to determine their potential for electric power generation. Ancient Puebloan peoples frequented these springs, and Spanish explorers are known to have visited Jemez Sulphur Springs as early as 1542. Modern travelers along the Jemez Mountain Trail National Scenic Byway may enjoy a soothing dip at the historic Jemez Springs Bath House or at La Cueva. For hikers, spectacular Spence Hot Springs or McCauley Warm Springs provide the perfect setting for a backcountry soak.

Some of the Southwest's least-known archaeological treasures are to be found in the Jemez Mountains, hidden away on the pine-topped mesas above Jemez Springs. Here, the Jemez people lived, farmed, and hunted from about A.D. 1350 until their final subjugation by the Spanish in 1696. At the time the Spanish penetrated what is now northern New Mexico, the Jemez were among the most numerous and powerful of all the Puebloan tribes; one early Spanish estimate suggested that at least 30,000 people occupied the region at the time of European contact in 1541. By 1696, only a few hundred had survived the ravages of war, famine, and disease. In the most comprehensive survey of the Jemez Mountains, archaeologist Michael Elliot mapped at least forty large pueblo (village) ruins within an eight-mile radius of Jemez Springs; he classified nine of the largest of these ruins, all located on high mesas, as Great Pueblo Villages. A typical village site included one great kiva (a semisubterranean ceremonial chamber), multiple plazas (town squares), and multistoried room blocks. Tovakwa, the largest of the Jemez villages, had an estimated 1,800 rooms, more than twice the size of Pueblo Bonito in Chaco Canyon, New Mexico. The most interesting aspect of the Jemez lifeway was the network of small, isolated fieldhouses (a single-family, seasonal dwelling) associated with each pueblo. Archaeologists estimate that as many as 10,000 fieldhouses may have existed in the area. Fieldhouses have been found at elevations of up to 8,450 feet, the highest elevation known for corn agriculture in the American Southwest. Most were located at a distance from the pueblo but close to communal fields where corn and other crops were cultivated.

Pajarito Plateau

Massive eruptions of volcanic ash spewed from Valles Caldera around 1 million years ago to form the Pajarito Plateau, a gently sloping bench skirting the eastern flank of the Jemez Mountains. The striking canyons and mesas of the Pajarito, with their stacks of vertical colonnades and cone-shaped tent rocks, were carved from the volcanic tableland by the erosive forces of water and wind.

The Pajarito Plateau contains a wealth of archaeological ruins providing evidence of almost 500 years of Indian occupation. Bandelier National Monument, south of Los Alamos, occupies the southernmost section of the Pajarito Plateau and preserves the finest examples of these ruins. At Bandelier, early peoples used stone scrapers to enlarge the natural caves and depressions found in the ashflow tuff, creating chambers that were used for dwellings, storage, or ceremonial purposes. The most impressive and beautiful ruins are located within easy walking distance of the visitor center in Frijoles Canyon.

Nacimiento Mountains

The Nacimiento Mountains form a low, north-south ridge that parallels the Jemez Mountains for nearly thirty miles, from San Ysidro to beyond Cuba. Unlike the volcanic Jemez Mountains, the Nacimiento Mountains are cored with crystalline rock and flanked along their eastern side, near Jemez Springs, by spectacular red cliffs of sedimentary rock. The highest summits in the range include Pajarito Peak (9,040 feet), San Miguel Mountain (9,473 feet), and Nacimiento Peak (9,801 feet). Deposits of travertine and calcium carbonate are common around once-active hot springs along the southern portion of the range, most notably in the Arroyo Peñasco area and at Ojo del Espiritu Santo. The Nacimiento Mountains are mostly forested, with ponderosa pine and aspen typical of higher elevations and Gambel's oak and New Mexican locust common along valley walls at lower elevations.

San Juan Mountains

Rugged and colorful, the San Juan Mountains encompass more than 10,000 square miles, space enough to enclose the entire state of Vermont and a sliver of New Hampshire. Unrivaled as the largest single range in the U.S. Rockies, the San Juans include at least seven mountain groups: the Sneffels Range, the Grenadier Range, the Needles and West Needles, the La Plata Mountains, the Rico Mountains, and a northwestern offshoot called the San Miguel Mountains. A southeastern arm of the San Juans, the La Garita Mountains and the Cochetopa Hills, forms the hill country along the western boundary of the San Luis Valley. South of the Colorado border, the Tusas Mountains rise between Tres Piedras and Tierra Amarilla and include the prominent landmarks of Brazos Peak and the Brazos Cliffs along the Rio Brazos and the great volcanic dome of San Antonio Mountain (10,908 feet). The San Juan Mountains include three national forests: the Rio Grande, San Juan, and

Uncompahgre. These enormous expanses of federal forestlands encompass six spectacular wilderness areas: the Weminuche, South San Juan, Big Blue, La Garita, Mount Sneffels, and Lizard Head, together protecting more than 800,000 acres.

Engineer Pass, San Juan Mountains.

No other range in the United States contains as much land above 10,000 feet as the San Juans, with nearly a dozen peaks exceeding 14,000 feet. Uncompahgre Peak (14,309 feet) marks the highest point in the San Juans and is considered one of the most beautiful mountains in the entire Southern Rocky Mountain chain. The San Miguel Mountains, a skyscraping collection of peaks located just west of Lizard Head Pass, includes three Fourteeners (Mount Wilson, Wilson Peak, and El Diente) and one near-Fourteener (Lizard Head Peak); many climbers regard Mount Wilson (14,246 feet) as the most challenging of all the Fourteeners and tout Lizard Head Peak (13,113 feet) as the most difficult single peak to climb in the Southern Rockies.

The San Juan Mountains are split nearly in half by the Rio Grande, the third longest river in the United States. The Rio Grande arises deep within the heart of the San Juans, near Stoney Pass, and bears little resemblance in its headwater reaches to the muddy, powerful river that sweeps 1,885 miles to the Gulf of Mexico. The Conejos River and the Chama River, both originating in the San Juans, are among the Rio Grande's main tributaries. In addition to the Rio Grande, the Dolores, the San Juan, the San Miguel, the Chama, and eight other rivers have headwaters in the high San Juans; of these rivers, only the upper reaches of the Rio Grande and the Chama River are included in the Wild and Scenic Rivers System.

Much of the beauty of the San Juan Mountains can be attributed to their geologic history, a unique mixture of fire and ice. The western portion of the range is constructed of vividly colored layers of sedimentary rock. The central and eastern portions reflect millions of years of violent volcanic activity. Between 40 and 25 million years ago, incredible outpourings of lava and ash covered most of the central and eastern San Juans and extended north to merge with volcanic rocks in the West Elk Mountains. Ice caps and valley glaciers reworked the volcanic landscape, scouring the spectacular U-shaped valleys and multicolored peaks we enjoy today. Wheeler Geologic Area, near Creede, preserves some of the most interesting rock formations to be found in the Southern Rockies.

Once the homeland of the far-ranging Ute Indians, the San Juans were among the last regions in the Southern Rockies to be overrun by settlers and gold seekers. Discoveries of rich lodes of gold and silver in the early 1870s increased public pressure to displace the Utes. In 1873, the Brunot Treaty removed a large rectangular area of the San Juans from Ute control and paved the way for white settlement. As the trickle of prospectors and miners became a raging torrent, towns sprang up in the richest parts of the range: Silverton, Ouray, Telluride, Lake City, and Creede. The new prosperity attracted the interest of some of the West's most legendary outlaws. Butch Cassidy began his bank-robbing career in 1889 with a stickup of Telluride's silver-rich San Miguel County Bank. To combat the growing lawlessness and to tame their more colorful citizens, Silverton's town fathers imported the infamous Bat Masterson from Dodge City.

As the mining boom continued, the need for year-round access into the heart of the San Juans intensified. The Denver and Rio Grande Railroad, a slim ribbon of track climbing up from Durango along the Animas River, ended Silverton's isolation in 1882. A journey on the narrow-gauge Silverton-Durango train remains a popular way for travelers to sample the historic and scenic flavor of the San Juans. Several spectacular gravel roads—the Alpine Loop, Engineer Mountain, Cinnamon Pass, Ophir Pass, Imogene Pass, Black Bear Pass, and Stony Pass—penetrate the San Juan backcountry along historic routes; high-clearance four-wheel-drive vehicles are required for most backcountry routes. The Alpine Loop National Back Country Byway traverses the remote, rugged heart of the San Juan Mountains and passes hiking trail access to five Fourteeners. Avalanches still pose a serious threat to winter travel on even the paved, more civilized routes over Red Mountain and Wolf Creek passes; state-of-the-art avalanche sheds protect the highway in several areas along these routes.

Uncompahgre Plateau

A forested tableland, the Uncompahgre Plateau stretches northwest from the San Juan Range for nearly 100 miles. The name Uncompahgre, an adaptation of the Ute word for "red-water canyon," originated with the Spanish friars Dominguez and Escalante, whose expedition traveled through the region in 1776. Linked geologically to both the Colorado Plateau and the Southern Rockies, the Uncompahgre Plateau forms a scenic and ecological transition between the two geographical provinces. Precambrian crystalline rocks, similar to those that form the cores of other ranges in the Southern Rockies, lie at the heart of the Uncompahgre Plateau. Unlike most of those ranges, however, the Uncompahgre Plateau remains draped with a thick overlay of the same colorful sedimentary rocks that distinguish the slickrock country of the Colorado Plateau. Unaweep Canyon, one of the major scenic attractions of the Uncompahgre, exposes the plateau's Precambrian core. Geologists believe that this spectacular canyon was carved by a large river, either the ancestral Colorado or the west Gunnison River, and was then abandoned when the regional drainage pattern shifted dramatically as a result of mountain building. At the northeast edge of the plateau, high above the Grand Valley of the Colorado River, the geologic story of the Uncompahgre Plateau is spectacularly revealed at Colorado National Monument.

Grand Mesa and Battlement Mesa

Grand Mesa and Battlement Mesa rise abruptly from the flat, fertile sweep of irrigated green that defines the Grand Valley of the Colorado River. Both mesas are erosional remnants of a lava-capped plain that once spread across much of west-central Colorado. Grand Mesa, the larger of the two mesas and one of the world's largest flattop mountains, begins near the confluence of the Colorado and Gunnison rivers and extends eastward to the Elk Mountains, encompassing nearly 800 square miles; Battlement Mesa is situated about fifteen miles to the northeast of Grand Mesa.

The sixty-three-mile-long Grand Mesa Scenic and Historic Byway climbs gradually upward along the narrow canyon of Plateau Creek to traverse the lake-dotted, forested expanse of Grand Mesa. The Utes referred to Grand Mesa as "Thunder Mountain," an altogether fitting name for a mountain that routinely gives rise to some of the region's most ominous, anvil-topped storm clouds on hot summer afternoons. Climate and vegetation vary enormously from the bottom to the top of Grand Mesa, with four distinct vegetation zones visible within a remarkably short vertical distance. The summit of Grand Mesa, averaging about 10,000 feet in elevation, lies almost a mile above a valley floor dotted with desert shrublands. As you climb above the arid lowlands, oak brush and streamside forests of aspen are quickly replaced by spruce-fir forests, flower-filled subalpine meadows, and, along the mesa's windswept western edge, by an uncommonly verdant expanse of sagebrush shrubland. The rich pageant of color changes with the seasons, the greens and wildflower hues of spring and summer giving way to the gold and russet colors of autumn.

During glacial times, Grand Mesa was host to a succession of thick ice caps that covered most of the mesa top and, in places, cascaded down the flanks along old stream courses. Later, landslides created a broad bench of rotated lava blocks along the mesa's flanks and dammed numerous small lakes. In all, there are some 300 lakes on the bench and the glaciated upland of Grand Mesa. Many of these lakes have been developed as reservoirs to augment the water-intensive agriculture of the Grand Valley. Toward the western end of Grand Mesa, the Lands End Road, one of the most dramatic roads in the Southern Rockies, spirals downward over the lip of the mesa and offers spectacular views of the confluence of the Gunnison and the Colorado.

West Elk Mountains

The West Elk Mountains, like the San Juans, are somewhat detached from the western belt of ranges. Rising to the north and west of the San Juans, the West Elks are bounded along their southern and eastern flanks by the Gunnison River. Essentially circular in outline, the West Elks cover an area no more than thirty miles in diameter. Two spur ranges, the Anthracite Range and the Ruby Range, angle off from the main mass of the West Elks toward the historic and colorful resort town of Crested Butte. High and relatively inaccessible, the West Elks contain a number of peaks that exceed 12,000 feet; West Elk Peak (13,035 feet), located at the heart of the West Elk Wilderness Area, is the highest peak in the range.

The West Elk Mountains formed during the same interval of intense volcanic activity that produced the San Juans. Castlelike outcrops of a distinctive volcanic rock, the West Elk Breccia, edge the mountain front with colorful spires and form the palisades along the Gunnison River. The peaks and ridges in the southern half of the range, including West Elk Peak, are carved from layers of lava and consolidated ash that were once continuous with those of the San Juan region. Summits in the northern West Elks, on the other hand, are carved from the once deeply buried roots of enormous volcanoes. Lava flows originating in the West Elk Mountains wreaked havoc with the course of the ancestral Gunnison River. Once volcanic activity came to an end, about 18.5 million years ago, the river was able to cut its way through the layers of lava and ash, through the underlying sedimentary rocks, and into the ancient crystalline rocks beneath the West Elk Mountains, a process that took nearly 2 million years.

Black Canyon of the Gunnison National Park, the most visited spot in the West Elks, protects a fourteen-mile-long section of one of North America's most magnificent canyons. No other North American canyon combines the depth, narrowness, sheerness, and forbidding countenance of the Black Canyon. At Warner Point, on the park's south rim, the Gunnison River thunders some 2,722 feet below the visitor lookout. Chasm View marks the canyon's narrowest width, at 1,100 feet. The twin summits of Mount

Sopris and the Black Canyon of the Gunnison anchor either end of the West Elk Loop Scenic Byway. This route provides access to the White River and Gunnison national forests, Black Canyon of the Gunnison National Park, Curecanti National Recreation Area, and Crawford and Paonia state parks. During the summer months, the Kebler Pass and Crested Butte/Gothic portions of the West Elk Loop offer travelers lush, flower-filled meadows and aspen forests. With the coming of fall, from one end of this spectacular byway to another, visitors are treated to the most beautiful display of autumn foliage anywhere in the Southern Rockies.

Elk Mountains

The sunset-hued peaks of the Elk Mountains rank among the most beautiful in the entire Rocky Mountain chain. This northwest-trending range rises to the north of the West Elks and extends for nearly fifty miles, from just to the west of the Sawatch Range to the Huntsman Hills near Glenwood Springs. Unlike most mountain ranges in the Southern Rockies, a number of the highest peaks in the range are capped with enormous thicknesses of steeply slanting red sedimentary rocks. In the central portion of the mountains, richly colored peaks such as the Maroon Bells and Castle Peak contrast sharply with the gray crystalline summits of Capitol and Snowmass peaks. Of the six elegant Fourteeners that grace the crest of the Elk Mountains—Castle Peak, Pyramid Peak, North and South Maroon peaks, Capitol Peak, and Snowmass Mountain—only one has a walk-up route to the summit. Today, these peaks are included within the 181,000-acre Maroon Bells–Snowmass Wilderness Area.

Situated high on the western slope of the Continental Divide, the Elk Mountains are drained on the north by the Roaring Fork and Crystal rivers and on the south by the East and Taylor rivers, tributaries of the Gunnison. Stream valleys within the Elk Mountains are generally steep-sided and narrow, their walls dramatized by cliffs of red rock; waterfalls cascade from hanging valleys left behind by long-vanished glaciers. Passes between drainages are high and treacherous, and the primitive roads that cross the most dramatic of these—Schofield, Pearl, Conundrum, and Taylor—are legendary for their difficulty.

Following the Leadville silver boom in the late 1870s, prospectors swarmed across the Sawatch Range along Independence Pass, searching for similar lodes in the Elk Mountains. They were not disappointed. In 1879, silver was discovered along Castle Creek, near the historic town of Ashcroft, and on Aspen Mountain. During the early days of the boom, before a wagon road was built over Independence Pass, miners using Taylor Pass were forced to dismantle their wagons and lower them, piece by piece, along with their cargo, over drops of about forty feet. By 1890, Aspen, then known as Ute City, surpassed Ashcroft as a mining center, its population of nearly 10,000 served by two railroads, three newspapers, and a municipal electric lighting system. Elsewhere in the Elk Mountains, mining activity concentrated on extensive deposits of coal and marble, leading to the establishment of the towns of Redstone, Marble, Crystal, and Crested Butte. The town of Marble became nationally famous for its high-grade marble, known as the Yule Marble; one enormous, fifty-six-ton block of this frost-white marble was quarried for the Tomb of the Unknown Soldier.

Yule Marble quarry, Elk Mountains.

During World War II, the U.S. Army's 10th Mountain Division ski troops trained for mountain duty at Camp Hale, near the former boomtown of Aspen. Some of these men returned to Colorado after the war and were influential in the development of a downhill ski area at Aspen Mountain, which today ranks as one of the finest winter-sports centers in North America.

Sawatch Range

Sailing into the distance like a row of battleships, the Sawatch Range dominates the high country south and east of the Elk Mountains. Beginning at the Eagle River, near Wolcott, the range stretches south for almost 100 miles. Peak after peak line up to form a towering wall that ranks as the highest range in the U.S. Rocky Mountains. Fifteen Fourteeners mark the crest of the Sawatch Range, including the three highest peaks in the Southern Rockies: Mount Elbert (14,433 feet), Mount Massive (14,421 feet), and Mount Harvard (14,420 feet). Unlike the mountain ranges to the east and west, all traces of the sedimentary rocks that once draped the range crest have been stripped away by erosion.

Isolated within the heart of the northern Sawatch, Mount of the Holy Cross (14,005 feet) stands guard over the 123,000-acre Holy Cross Wilderness Area. The peak is named for the snowy, cross-shaped couloir on its northeast face. The first photograph of the peak, made in 1873 by Hayden survey photographer William Henry Jackson, brought the mountain and its photographer international fame. Inspired by Jackson's photograph, Thomas Moran, a noted English landscape artist, traveled to the Sawatch Range to paint the peak. Moran's painting of this famous peak, with its cross wreathed in clouds, ranks among the finest examples of nineteenth-century landscape painting.

The Collegiate Peaks (all Fourteeners)—Mounts Harvard, Yale, Columbia, Oxford, and Princeton—grace the central section of the Sawatch Range just south of Leadville. The three symmetrical summits of Mount Princeton, at the southern end of the Collegiates, are flanked to the southeast by a 2,000-foot escarpment known as the Chalk Cliffs. These striking white cliffs are formed of kaolinite, a soft, chalklike rock produced by hot springs percolating through the fault-riddled crystalline rocks at the core of Mount Princeton. Hot springs persist along the eastern mouth of the Chalk Creek Valley, and at Mount Princeton Hot Springs there is a public health spa and swimming pool. South of Mount Princeton, across Chalk Creek, several summits—Mounts Antero, Shavano, and Tabeguache—break above 14,000 feet before the Sawatch Range merges with the northernmost foothills of the Sangre de Cristos and the San Juans.

Bordering the Sawatch Range are some of the most scenic rivers in the Southern Rockies: the Arkansas on the east, the Eagle on the north, the Roaring Fork on the northwest, and the Taylor and Gunnison drainages on the west. In its first 125 miles, the Arkansas River tumbles 5,000 feet in a series of deep green pools and chutes, a spectacular beginning for the Mississippi's second-longest tributary. From its headwaters to Royal Gorge, the Arkansas ranks as one of the finest white-water rivers in the country; more than 75,000 people a year ride rafts and kayaks through rapids such as the Zoom Flume and the Staircase in Browns Canyon.

By the 1880s, mining camps had sprung up in almost every valley of the Sawatch; nearly every outcrop bears the mark of some hardrock miner's can't-miss claim. Roads built of bravado and greed soon traversed Monarch, Tincup, Cottonwood, Independence, and Marshall passes, connecting the Sawatch communities with mining centers west of the Continental Divide. During the winter, horse-drawn sleighs replaced the wagons and stagecoaches that rumbled along these tortuous routes. An army of men with shovels was required to keep the freight traffic moving. The windswept summit of Independence Pass must have presented an eerie spectacle to the winter traveler in 1880, a solid double line of traffic moving in opposite directions through twenty-foot-deep trenches excavated through the snowdrifts. During the summer, specially trained dogs raced ahead of the stagecoaches to warn uphill traffic to get out of the way. Independence Pass, at 12,095 feet, remains the nation's highest passenger-car crossing of the Continental Divide.

Mosquito and Tenmile Ranges

The Mosquito Range rises from a low gap in the mountains near Hoosier Pass and angles due south to Trout Creek Pass, paralleling the Sawatch Range and separating the windswept grasslands of South Park from the upper Arkansas Valley. At its southern end, near the dark summits of the Buffalo Peaks, the Mosquito Range loses elevation rapidly and merges with the low volcanic country of the Arkansas Hills. A cluster of Fourteeners—Lincoln, Democrat, and Bross—distinguishes its northern end.

With scarcely a break, the comparatively small Tenmile Range curves north from Hoosier Pass to Tenmile Canyon, near Frisco. Bordered on the east by the Blue River and on the west by Tenmile Creek, the Tenmile Range forms a lofty and somewhat linear ridge as it angles northward to the Gore Range. One Fourteener, Quandary Peak (14,265 feet), marks the southern end of the range; north from Quandary, several peaks—Pacific, Fletcher, and Crystal—approach 14,000 feet as the narrow crest winds toward Tenmile Peak at the northern end of the range.

Layers of sedimentary rock still drape much of the Mosquito Range, giving the upland surface a broad, rolling appearance. These sedimentary layers are best displayed west of Fairplay, where glacial erosion has created the spectacular bowl of Horseshoe Cirque. In contrast, the rugged peaks of the Tenmile Range and the cluster of high peaks gracing the northern end of the Mosquito Range are capped with crystalline rocks. Buffalo Peaks, the double-summited mountain southwest of Fairplay, is an erosional remnant of the many layers of volcanic rock that once spread over this portion of the range.

In 1859, gold-rich gravels were discovered near Fairplay and Breckenridge and at California Gulch, north of Leadville. The gentle incline of Kenosha Pass and the flat expanse of South Park proved to be a veritable speedway for prospectors heading to these new goldfields. From the summit cairns to the valleys below, nearly every inch of the Mosquito and Tenmile ranges has felt the impact of miners' picks. By 1873, however, the first placer boom was on the wane, leaving the valley bottoms littered with gravel piles. Prospect fever began once again when miners at Leadville discovered cerussite, a silver ore, along with the gold in their gravels. This second boom period produced nearly $100 million worth of silver and made Horace Tabor the bonanza king of Colorado.

The numerous roads in these ranges are a legacy of the frenzied mining activity of more than a century ago. During the winter of 1863–64, Methodist preacher John Dyer pioneered a route across Mosquito Pass in order to make regular mail deliveries between the communities of Fairplay and Leadville. Dyer made his trips across the pass alone and at night, when the hard-frozen snow allowed him to make good time on his homemade skis. Eventually, a road was built over the pass, and by the summer of 1879, more than 150 wagons and stagecoaches were traveling the route daily. Life insurance policies issued to miners during the boom period stipulated that no payoffs would be made if the insured met his end on Mosquito Pass. Once the railroads arrived in Fairplay and Leadville, however, the treacherous pass route fell into disuse.

Gore Range

The Gore Range rises steeply from the glaciated valley of Tenmile Canyon and angles northwest along the Blue River Valley. Except along its western flank, few traces remain of the sedimentary rocks that once draped the crest of the range. A line of serrated peaks distinguishes the southern end of the range, with several summits breaking above 13,000 feet: Eagles Nest, Mount Powell, Keller Mountain, and several more as yet unnamed. North of Eagles Nest Wilderness Area, at Gore Canyon, the Colorado River has carved a four-mile-long, 2,000-foot-deep gorge, exposing pastel-hued sedimentary rocks as well as the crystalline core of the range. North of Gore Canyon, the range loses elevation gradually as it winds north to Rabbit Ears Pass. Unlike so many other ranges in the Southern Rockies, the Gore Range offered very little to the prospector, and few roads penetrate its high country.

The Gore Range is named for the Irish baronet Lord George Gore. Colorful to a fault, Gore seems an unlikely candidate for immortality. Arriving at Fort Laramie in the summer of 1854, Gore was intent on trophy hunting his way up the North Platte. Jim Bridger, legendary mountain man and scout, signed on as hunting guide for the expedition, inflating his guiding fee to thirty dollars a day to compensate for Gore's nasty disposition. No luxury was spared; Gore's entourage included forty attendants, a hundred and twelve horses, twelve yokes of oxen, fourteen dogs, six wagons, and twenty-one carts full of wine and champagne. Lord Gore had few qualms about the wholesale slaughter of wildlife in the name of sport. During three summers spent hunting in the Rockies, Gore and his men are believed to have killed more than 2,000 bison, 1,600 elk and deer, and 100 bear.

White River Plateau and the Flat Tops

The White River Plateau towers above the valley of the Colorado River north of Glenwood Springs, at the eastern doorstep of canyon country. This steep-sided, forested uplift extends northwest for nearly fifty miles, its southwestern flank bordered by a sinuous ridge of steeply upturned sedimentary rock known as the Grand Hogback. The White River Plateau ranges in elevation from 6,000 feet along its southern margin to 12,354 feet at Flat Top Mountain, near the northern end, where the plateau is capped with thick, tablelike layers of volcanic rock: the Flat Tops escarpment. The most spectacular of these lava-capped flattop mountains are encompassed within the 235,000-acre Flat Tops Wilderness Area, the second largest wilderness area in Colorado. The northern edge of the White River Plateau is defined by the low Yampa–Williams Fork Mountains (not to be confused with the string of peaks paralleling the Blue River north of Dillon).

Glenwood Canyon, a fifteen-mile-long gorge carved by the Colorado River, reveals the White River Plateau's core and provides a dramatic look at the geologic events that built this broad uplift. Atop the plateau, in the Flat Tops, almost 660 feet of layered volcanic rocks representing at least three periods of volcanic activity are dramatically exposed at Trappers Peak (11,990 feet) and in the colossal Chinese Wall. Elsewhere on the White River Plateau, in striking contrast to the volcanic terrain, the upland surface is blanketed with multiple layers of light-colored sedimentary rocks. Deep Creek Canyon, slicing 2,300 feet into the White River Plateau, winds its way between Deep Lake and the Colorado River and exposes nearly 300 million years of sedimentary deposits. Just below the canyon's rim, an exposed layer of limestone forms near-vertical walls up to 250 feet tall. Because of its high solubility, the limestone provides an ideal environment for the formation of caves. The greatest concentration of caves in the Southern Rockies is found within this limestone layer; Groaning Cave, with an estimated twelve miles of passageways, is believed to be the largest.

The White River Plateau is the first "rock in the stream," the first impediment to moisture-laden storms flowing into the region out of the northwest. The high precipitation and gently rolling upland result in a parklike landscape: groves of aspen and coniferous forests interspersed with lush mountain meadows. The Flat Tops are dotted with small lakes, including Skinny Fish, Surprise, Big Fish, and Paradise. The beauty of Trappers Lake, situated at the headwaters of the White River, inspired Arthur Carhart, a young forest service engineer, and Aldo Leopold to promote the idea that certain federal lands could best serve the needs of the public if left in their wild state. The year was 1918. Though the idea of protecting wilderness was slow to gain support, Congress finally created the National Wilderness Preservation System in 1964, and the Flat Tops Wilderness Area became one of the first to join the system. The Flat Tops Trail Scenic Byway, beginning at either of the gateway towns of Meeker or Yampa, provides seasonal road access to a wonderful diversity of wilderness hiking, fishing, and camping opportunities.

Both of the major rivers of northwestern Colorado, the White River and the Yampa River, have their headwaters in the Flat Tops. On the western side of the Flat Tops, the White River gathers its waters from Trappers Lake and a network of small streams in adjacent valleys before flowing out through desert country to its confluence with the Green River near Ouray, Utah. The Yampa River headwaters arise within the shadow of Derby Peak, on the eastern edge of the Flat Tops; some maps and local residents still use the name Bear River for the uppermost headwaters west of the town of Yampa. The Utes gave the river the name Yampa because it flowed through a traditional harvesting area for an important root plant, *Perideridia gairdneri*, that they called *yampa*. Snowmelt streams and rivers originating in the Middle Fork Mountains and in the Gore and Park ranges join the Yampa River on its 170-mile journey across the broad, fertile sweep of the upper Yampa Valley and into the desert and canyon country of northwestern Colorado. By the time the Yampa reaches the eastern boundary of Dinosaur National Monument, its flow has been nearly doubled by additions from its western tributaries—the Elk, Elkhead, and Little Snake rivers—before joining the Green River at Echo Park, near the Colorado-Utah border.

Rabbit Ears Range

The jumble of ancient volcanoes and lava flows that forms the Rabbit Ears Range carries the Continental Divide eastward from the southern tip of the Park Range to the Never Summer Mountains. North of the Rabbit Ears

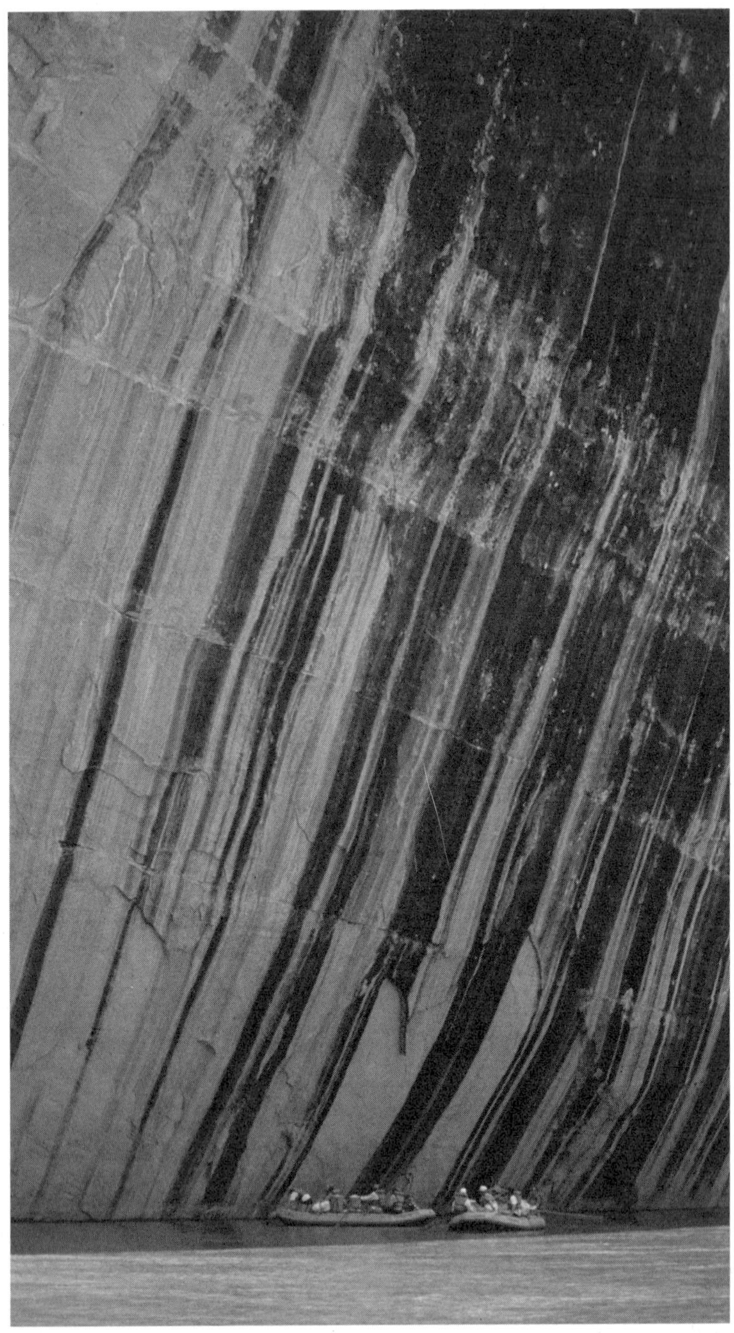

Tiger Wall, Yampa River.

Range lie the broad basin of North Park and the headwaters of the North Platte River; to the south are the rolling hills of Middle Park and the headwaters of the Colorado River. The range is named for the prominent stone "ears" of Rabbit Ears Peak, the eroded remnant of a volcanic plug that marks the west end of the range; Rabbit Ears Peak can be seen from the middle of North Park all the way south to near Kremmling, Colorado.

Parkview Mountain (12,296 feet) dominates the crest of the range, and several mountains—Radial, Elk, Gravel, and Little Gravel—exceed 11,000 feet in elevation. Muddy Pass (8,772 feet), at the western end of the range, is the lowest crossing of the Continental Divide in Colorado. During his 1844 expedition, John Charles Frémont was the first explorer to use this well-trodden buffalo trail, now the route of U.S. 40, linking North and Middle parks. Frémont was deeply impressed by Muddy Pass, noting in his journal that it was one of the most beautiful passes he had ever seen. In late May and early June, the soft green of newly emerged aspen leaves and the vibrant hues of avalanche lilies, chiming bells, and marsh-marigolds delight modern travelers. In summer, meadows resplendent with wild geranium, scarlet paintbrush, blue columbine, and corn lilies produce a firestorm of color. With the coming of winter, both Muddy and Rabbit Ears passes serve as gateways to some of the finest cross-country skiing to be found anywhere in the Southern Rockies.

Park Range and the Sierra Madre

The Park Range rises sharply from the gray-green sagebrush flats along the western edge of North Park. From its southern tip, near Rabbit Ears Pass, the rugged alpine ridge stretches northward for nearly thirty-five miles to the Colorado-Wyoming border. The range takes the name Sierra Madre as it continues into Wyoming, where it resembles the Medicine Bow Mountains to the east but lacks their broad upland surface. Except for a cluster of 12,000-foot peaks at the southern end of the Park Range, in the Mount Zirkel Wilderness Area, the landscape seems gentler than ranges to the south. The broad alpine uplands that characterize the crest of the Park Range are speckled with beautiful lakes: Luna, Bighorn, and Lake of the Crags. Along the western slope of the range, streams such as the South Fork and the Wolverine cascade through forests to join the Elk River and, ultimately, the Yampa.

The crystalline core of the Park Range is exposed only along the crest of the range, and in places sedimentary rocks extend to or across the crest. Valleys along both sides of the range head in steep-walled cirques and end in a rippled series of glacially deposited bouldery ridges. Along the eastern slope of the mountains, ridges of glacial rubble have dammed myriad small ponds and lakes. Along the western slopes of the range, the flat-floored Yampa River Valley is littered with enormous boulders flushed from glacial deposits upvalley by periodic flash floods. More than 150 hot springs issue from faults along the west side of the range. One of these springs—for which the town of Steamboat Springs is named—once made a rhythmic noise like the chugging of a steamboat.

Economically valuable mineral deposits are uncommon in the Park Range, except in the Hahns Peak area. John Hahn discovered placer gold in the 1860s near the peak that bears his name. By 1874, area gold-ore yields approached $5 million a year. North of the Colorado-Wyoming border, one of the earliest large-scale mining operations in Wyoming, the Ferris-Haggerty Copper Mine, led to the founding of the town of Encampment. Due to the absence of widespread mining activity, the Park Range and Sierra Madre lack the extensive backcountry road network found in so many areas of the Southern Rockies. The gravel road over Buffalo Pass is the only crossing of the range between the Wyoming border and Rabbit Ears Pass. Today, Steamboat Springs and other local communities depend largely on ranching and the extraordinary opportunities for four-season outdoor recreation. The development of a major downhill skiing facility at Steamboat Springs' Mount Werner attracts downhill skiers and other winter-sports enthusiasts in increasing numbers each year.

Elkhead Range

The low and rolling, eighteen-mile-long Elkhead Range rises just to the north of the Yampa River, west of the Park Range. Geologically, the east-west trending Elkheads are a by-product of the same violent volcanic eruptions that shaped the White River Plateau and the Flat Tops. With the exceptions of Welba Peak (10,801 feet), Bears Ears Peak (10,577 feet), and Mount Oliphant (10,670 feet), most summits in the Elkhead Range barely exceed 10,000 feet, providing a striking contrast to the many skyscraping ranges in the

Southern Rockies. Although considerably lower and drier than the nearby Park Range, the Elkheads receive sufficient moisture to nourish Yampa River tributaries such as the Elk and Little Snake.

Throughout prehistoric times, the Elkhead Range must have provided a welcome respite for early people, with good hunting and an escape from the semiarid badlands to the south and west. During the 1870s, the Elkhead Range provided one of the last refuges and a principal hunting ground for the Northern Utes. The peace was short-lived. Nathan Meeker, the imperious Indian agent assigned to the settlement of White River, vigorously pursued his dream of building an agricultural utopia at the base of the Elkheads populated, of course, by Utes "civilized" by his personal efforts. In 1879, goaded to violence by Meeker's attempts to force them to the plow, the Utes made a defiant stand against a unit of 200 soldiers at the mouth of Milk Creek. In the fierce battle that followed, now known as the Meeker Massacre, the Utes killed several soldiers and more than 250 packhorses. A war party sent to the Indian agency killed Meeker and several associates and took his wife, daughter, two small children, and their mother hostage. Sadly, public outrage over the incident led to the 1880 Ute Removal Act, which forced the deportation of Colorado's remaining Northern Utes to a reservation in Utah.

The Mountain Parks

Broad, treeless basins, a reflection of the rain shadows cast by the surrounding mountains, are a distinguishing feature of the Southern Rocky Mountain landscape. Although small intermontane basins are scattered throughout the mountains, the largest, North, Middle, and South parks and the San Luis Valley, are strung between the north-south-trending ranges like a string of pearls. Some might say that these sweeping, open expanses are as dramatic as the peaks that tower above them. Explorer and geologist John Wesley Powell was so impressed by the parklike character of these large basins that he identified the Southern Rockies as the Park Mountains on his regional map of the United States. The term *park* continues to be used to refer to any extensive basin or lowland that is essentially treeless and enclosed on all sides by well-defined groups of mountains, hence the naming of places such as Estes Park, Taylor Park, Woodland Park, and Saguache Park.

Novelist D. H. Lawrence once declared that the broad sweep of the Taos Valley, framed by the sunset-tinted backdrop of the Sangre de Cristos, was the most beautiful landscape he had ever seen in the world—not nation, world. Clearly, for many the surprise of open country invokes a sense of release and exhilaration, a landscape of promise, freed from the shadowed constrictions imposed by crag and canyon and washed with pure mountain light.

North Park

The rolling sagebrush country of North Park and its enclosing circle of snowcapped peaks epitomizes the dramatic beauty of the mountain parks. Spreading south from a series of low hills near the Colorado-Wyoming border, North Park extends for nearly sixty miles before disappearing into the choppy swells that lap against the flanks of the Rabbit Ears Range. This magnificent expanse is bounded on the east by the Rawah Peaks and along the west by the Park Range. High and windswept, the mean elevation of the basin floor exceeds 8,000 feet; areas of higher relief include the prominent landmarks of Owl Ridge, Peterson Ridge, Delaney Butte, Independence Mountain, and Pole Mountain. A seasonally accessible gravel road climbs the flanks of Independence Mountain, offering travelers an eagle's-eye view of the surrounding sagebrush sea. Just short of the summit, the road passes several boulder-dotted circlets: tepee rings. It's not difficult to imagine the significance that a spot like this, with its panoramic view, would have held for the Arapahos or the Utes. Tributaries of the North Platte River—the Canadian, Michigan, Illinois, Grizzly, Little Grizzly, and North Fork—form a meandering network before joining the North Platte near North Gate Canyon. Arapaho National Wildlife Refuge, situated in the heart of North Park, serves as an important link in the chain of refuges available to water-loving birds migrating along the Central Southern Rocky Mountain flyways.

When trappers and mountain men first arrived in North Park in the early 1800s, they shared the sage-dotted basin with Ute and Arapaho hunting parties. Herds of bison, deer, elk, and pronghorn were abundant. By the beginning of the twentieth century, however, professional hunters and North Park settlers had decimated wildlife populations to satisfy the booming meat trade in communities outside the park. During the

North Park from Independence Mountain.

1870s, Wyoming-bred English and Scottish cattle dominated cattle herds throughout North Park. However, a string of severe winters in the late 1880s contributed to the downfall of the English cattle empire throughout the Rocky Mountains. The harsh lessons learned those first winters were never forgotten. North Park ranchers replaced European cattle breeds with hardier white-faced Herefords and began harvesting wild hay and clearing large expanses of sage and willow to cultivate more hay. Now, each autumn, breadloaf-shaped haystacks dot the meadows: insurance against the long high-country winter. North Park old-timers still like to joke that the snow there never melts, it just blows around until it wears out.

Middle Park

Middle Park lies within an irregular eastward bend of the Continental Divide, enclosed by mountains: on the east by the Front Range, on the north by the Rabbit Ears Range, on the west by the Gore Range, and on the southwest by the Williams Fork Mountains. Though Middle Park lacks the expansive sweep of its northern and southern counterparts, its tumbling terrain reveals a patchwork of sagebrush shrublands intermixed with forests of aspen and pine. Lateral spurs from the surrounding mountains and the ragged remains of ancient lava flows disrupt the basin floor, compressing its stream valleys and partitioning its meadows. A dense thicket of cottonwoods, bright amber-gold in autumn, follows the course of the Colorado River as it snakes its way west across Middle Park to exit through the spectacular defile of Gore Canyon. Travelers taking advantage of the Colorado River Headwaters Scenic Byway can sample the scenic and historic ranching flavor of this unique region, with just enough time leftover for a soothing soak in the mineral pools at Hot Sulphur Springs.

By the late 1870s, Middle Park seems to have attracted the attention of every sort of adventurer: trapper, explorer, prospector, botanist, and government surveyor. Its relative seclusion ended with the construction of wagon roads over Rollins and Berthoud passes, linking Middle Park with Denver and other Eastern Slope communities. The summer of 1874 witnessed the beginning of real settlement in the area. The harsh, seemingly endless winters dashed the hopes and fortunes of all but the hardiest and most adaptive of ranching families. In those early years, ranchers often joined together each autumn to stage a cattle drive, chiefly over the alpine tundra of Rollins Pass, delivering their herds from the remote Middle Park rangeland to markets on the Eastern Slope.

Today, Colorado River water—liquid gold—is Middle Park's most sought-after commodity. The first plans for a transmountain water diversion from the North Fork of the Colorado to the semiarid Eastern Slope were proposed in 1889. By 1906, a major canal (the Grand Ditch) had been slashed across the slopes of the Never Summer Mountains, diverting a portion of the Colorado's water to the east-flowing Cache la Poudre River. These early diversions are dwarfed by the Colorado–Big Thompson Project, however, which remains one of the largest and most complex transmountain diversion projects ever undertaken by the Bureau of Reclamation. This massive project—an integrated network of dams, dikes, reservoirs, pumping stations, pipelines, tunnels, power plants, transmission lines, and substations—gathers water from the Colorado River and Willow Creek and channels it through the thirteen-mile-long Alva B. Adams Tunnel, an engineering marvel located nearly 4,000 feet beneath the Continental Divide in Rocky Mountain National Park. The Colorado–Big Thompson Project diverts approximately 260,000 acre-feet of water annually from the Colorado River headwaters on the Western Slope to the Big Thompson River, a South Platte River tributary on the Eastern Slope. The project provides supplemental water for irrigation of about 720,000 acres of land, municipal and industrial water for eleven Front Range communities, and sufficient hydroelectric power to meet the project's needs as well as those of customers in northern Colorado, eastern Wyoming, and western Nebraska. Concerns about the long-term environmental consequences of any large transmountain diversion, especially one the size and complexity of the Colorado–Big Thompson Project, loom like storm clouds on the horizon, and the future of an entire river system hangs in the balance.

South Park

To many people, South Park is the best known and most beloved of the mountain parks, a sweeping expanse of grassland encircled by rugged mountains and overarched by a turquoise sky. From the park's northern gateway, at Kenosha Pass, the smooth granite knobs of the Kenosha and Tarryall mountains angle off to the east, releasing the traveler from the twisting maze of canyons that breach the Front Range along Highway 285. In most places, the gently rolling floor of South Park lies well above 9,000 feet. Along its western edge, the Mosquito Range presents a formidable wall, the dramatic scallop of Horseshoe Cirque a prominent landmark south of Fairplay; along the eastern horizon, the low, forested ridges of the Rampart Range stretch south to the austere massif of Pikes Peak. The double summits of the Buffalo Peaks and a confusion of rough volcanic hills rise along the park's frayed southern edge. The South Platte and its upper tributaries meander eastward across the park, encountering the first of several reservoir impoundments before tumbling through Eleven Mile Canyon to meet the unquenchable thirst of Denver and other northern Front Range cities.

When the first American prospectors and settlers ventured into South Park during the mid-1800s, they called the broad valley Bayou Salado, a linguistic corruption of Valle Salado (Salt Valley), as it was known to the Spanish, and Bayou Salade (Salt Marsh), the name used by French trappers. The salt springs of Bayou Salado—the briny waters that bubbled up from deeply buried beds of ancient sea salt—were well known to the Utes and to other indigenous people in the region. The discovery of gold in 1858 lured a steady stream of prospectors and other colorful characters up the canyons of the South Platte and into Bayou Salado. It didn't take long for the newcomers to realize that they'd need a consistent, cheap supply of salt, a necessity for preserving meat, flavoring food, and a critical element in the new process being used to refine silver ore coming out of the mines at Leadville.

During those early years, the closest source of salt was Missouri, where it was sold by the wagonload and prohibitively expensive. In 1861, realizing the commercial potential of Bayou Salado's salt springs, a rancher built the first crude apparatus for processing salt from the briny springs on his ranch, aptly named the Salt Works Ranch. When Charles Hall bought the ranch and the salt operation, he began forcing the Utes to pay for the salt that they'd traditionally gathered for free. Colorado's fledgling territorial government was called in to intervene and to keep the peace. In 1864, Hall joined with two partners to form the Colorado Salt Works, a more ambitious venture that supplied all the salt Colorado needed until 1883. Today, the historic Salt Works Ranch, located at the base of Trout Creek Pass, just north of the junction of Highways 285 and 24, remains largely intact and is included on the roster of Colorado's Centennial Ranches.

The town of Fairplay, established in 1859, was by all accounts an unruly gold camp in the western tradition. Almost from the moment they arrived and set up shop along the boardwalks, enterprising boomtown businessmen set about supplying the prosperous mine owners with whatever luxuries they desired: everything from Steinway pianos to pressed-brick privies and vintage champagne. Fairplay was slow to give up its love affair with gold, maintaining placer operations until 1952; the last gold dredge still floats on its self-made pond a few miles south of town. Giant heaps and arcuate ridges of gravel—dredge tailings—provide a dramatic reminder of the boom days when gold fever held the Southern Rockies in its grasp.

Water has become the pivotal commodity in South Park, as it has in Middle Park and in the San Luis Valley. The sage-dotted floors of the mountain parks are characteristically dry, a reflection of their position in the rain shadow created by the moisture-robbing peaks that encircle them. The streams and rivers that meander across these basins, as well as the water-rich aquifer that hides beneath the surface, are nourished by snowmelt from the surrounding mountains. Faced with the grim economics of modern ranching, many of South Park's ranching families have been unable to resist the inflated prices their water rights bring in the Front Range urban marketplace. Many of the largest ranches, their irrigation water siphoned away to the eastern cities, are also losing the battle against the proliferation of five-acre ranchettes. Dusty and overgrazed fields are replacing the lush mountain grasslands that once held so much promise. The future prospects for South Park's historic ranches remain troubled, a traditional way of life hanging in the balance.

At the 1,200-acre High Creek Fen Preserve, The Nature Conservancy has sought to protect one of South Park's most extraordinary wetlands: a relict plant community (or fen) consisting of rare, cold-loving species that have persisted since the retreat of glaciers. Biologists studying this unique complex of wetlands are just beginning to understand how changes in the hydrologic integrity—either natural or human wrought—of the 15,000-acre watershed that lies directly to the west of the preserve are impacting an ecosystem that has persisted for thousands of years. The lessons learned in South Park as biologists struggle to provide long-term protection for High Creek Fen and other unique sites highlight the inherent challenges conservationists face in protecting the water and watersheds on which all ecosystems depend.

San Luis Valley

The San Luis Valley is truly a land apart, a mosaic of dune and high desert landscapes bordered along their eastern edge by the haze-blue wall of the Sangre de Cristo Range and, nearly sixty-five miles to the west, by the rugged, snowcapped massifs of the San Juan Mountains. The Sangre de Cristos and San Juans meet along the valley's northernmost edge at Poncha Pass, which provides a welcoming route through the maze of choppy swells that divides the Pacific and Atlantic watersheds. Uncompromisingly flat and nearly three times the size of Delaware, the San Luis Valley sweeps south from Poncha Pass for more than 150 miles to straddle the Colorado–New Mexico border north of the Taos Plateau. Along the valley's eastern edge, in an otherwise unremarkable *rincón* created by three low notches in the imposing barrier of the Sangre de Cristos, a giant dune field, Great Sand Dunes, rises to nearly 750 feet above the valley floor. Situated in the long rain shadow cast by the San Juans, the San Luis Valley receives less than ten inches of precipitation a year. With the exception of the Rio Grande, streams flowing into the valley along its margins sink into the sand and gravel of the valley floor to nourish the San Luis Valley Aquifer, one of the largest underground reservoirs in the West.

The human history of the San Luis Valley spans nearly 12,000 years, an extraordinary saga that begins with the first Paleo-Indian mammoth and bison hunters. Although more than a thousand archaeological sites have been recorded in the valley, only a small number have been excavated. Several that have—Linger, Zapata, Stewart's Cattle Guard, and Black Mountain—rank among the oldest and most important Paleo-Indian sites anywhere in the Rocky Mountain region. Several indigenous groups, such as the Puebloans, the Navajo, and the Utes, link various aspects of their creation mythology to sacred places in the San Luis Valley. Some Puebloans claim that their ancestors emerged from a lake in the San Luis Valley, possibly San Luis Lake. The Utes—the Blue Sky People—regard Indian Spring, located along the northwestern edge of Great Sand Dunes National Park, as their sacred site. The Navajo place their spiritual homeland within boundaries whose compass points are delimited by four sacred mountains; Blanca Peak is considered to be the Sacred Mountain of the East.

Spanish exploration and conquest left an indelible imprint on the land and the indigenous people of the Southwest. By 1600, Spanish territory, Nueva España, stretched from Mexico northward into the Southern Rockies as far as the Arkansas River, encompassing all of the San Luis Valley. From Puebloan villagers along the Rio Grande, the Spaniards learned that there were vast herds of bison and other game to be hunted in a broad valley to the north, today called the San Luis Valley. The journals of the Spanish adventurers provide the first written observations of the nomadic Utes and the village-based cultures of the various Puebloan groups along the Rio Grande. By the 1800s, as a result of the burgeoning Missouri–New Mexico fur trade, American and French trappers were ranging north from Santa Fe and the nearby Sangre de Cristos to the San Luis Valley and beyond. For the Spanish, whose fortunes had waxed and waned in the far-flung corners of Nueva España for nearly 200 years, dreams of empire were beginning to fade. In 1807, rumors reached Santa Fe of a new threat: a small U.S. Army contingent had succeeded in crossing the Sangre de Cristos from the east and had built a fort in which to spend the winter. Tracking Lieutenant Zebulon Pike and his men to their winter quarters in the San Luis Valley was a simple matter for the Spaniards, who arrested the men and took them to Santa Fe where they were briefly detained as political prisoners.

Fearing continued encroachment by the United States, the New Mexican territorial government renewed its efforts to encourage settlement throughout their northern frontier, from Taos to the Arkansas River, adopting a unique system of land grants and other incentives. Hispanic settlers began arriving in the San Luis Valley in significant numbers in the 1840s and 1850s, with more than 2,000 making their homes in the valley; the first permanent settlement, San Luis, was established in 1852. San Luis and other early communities—Costilla, San Pablo, Guadalupe, and Conejos—were patterned after New Mexican territorial settlements. Individual farmsteads, most made of adobe and log, were strung out like beads along the rivers at the valley's edge. At least forty irrigation ditches, including Colorado's first water right (the San Luis People's Ditch), were dug to bring water to the arid bottomlands of the valley to improve agricultural opportunities. Today, the San Luis Valley continues to be an important agricultural area; hundreds of artesian wells tap into the San Luis aquifer to supplement a complex network of irrigation ditches and canals, the lifeblood of modern agribusiness. When viewed from the air, a vast checkerboard pattern of center pivots—more than 2,000 quarter-mile circles of potatoes, malt barley, lettuce, and alfalfa—stretches across the central portion of the valley and provides a dramatic contrast to the adjacent expanses of native vegetation.

The battle for San Luis Valley water has dominated regional politics for more than fifty years. Finding a long-term solution to the continuing threat of water exportation from the San Luis aquifer required turning a battleground into common ground. Balancing human needs with those of natural landscapes and biological communities necessitated a unique conjoining of efforts by citizens of the San Luis Valley, The Nature Conservancy and other environmentalists, a bipartisan coalition of state and federal government leaders, and people from across the state of Colorado and the nation. In a deal brokered by the Conservancy, the federal government's purchase of the 100,000-acre Baca Ranch (one of the original

Mexican land grants) for inclusion in Great Sand Dunes National Park and to create Baca National Wildlife Refuge ended speculation concerning the fate of the last private land holding in the valley large enough to support a major groundwater exportation project.

Public lands offer a wealth of opportunities for exploring the San Luis Valley. Considered by many to be one of the "crown jewels" of our National Park System, Great Sand Dunes National Park and Preserve encompasses a stunning diversity of ecosystems, ranging from the dunes and shrublands of the valley floor to the alpine tundra of 14,000-foot mountain peaks. National wildlife refuges at Monte Vista, Alamosa, and the Baca encompass more than 100,000 acres of marshland and desert shrublands and provide critical migratory and nesting habitat for waterfowl and shorebirds. With the coming of spring, the San Luis Valley's wetlands welcome tens of thousands of northbound avian travelers: sandhill cranes, white-faced ibis, Canada and snow geese, and many species of ducks, grebes, shorebirds, and songbirds of every stripe. Monte Vista National Wildlife Refuge is the main stopover, a "refueling" stop for migrating sandhill cranes en route between their wintering ground at Bosque del Apache Refuge in New Mexico and their nesting areas in the Rocky Mountain valleys, such as the Yampa River Valley in northwestern Colorado and at Grays Lake, Idaho.

The Sangre de Cristos provide a dramatic counterpoint to the smooth sweep of the San Luis Valley.

CHAPTER TWO

Landscape Evolution: A Geologic Introduction

Driving west across the Great Plains, one barely notices as the road begins to climb—1,000, 2,000, 5,000 feet—on debris shed from the Rockies and spread across the floors of long-departed oceans. Rising like a wall out of these out-fanning sediments, the Southern Rocky Mountains form a succession of north-south-trending, folded and faulted uplifts cored with ancient crystalline rocks and interspersed with volcanics. The sedimentary rocks that once spread across this entire region have largely been eroded, their broken ends forming a hogback escarpment along the flanks of the mountains that displaced them. Broad basins between the ranges form a distinctive chain of high mountain valleys, the parks described by John Wesley Powell in his geologic survey of the region.

Compared to mountain ranges such as the Appalachians, the Southern Rockies are geologic newcomers. They began their rise from the bed of an ancient sea only 70 million years ago, during the last 2 percent of the Earth's history. The entire story of the Southern Rockies, however, spans nearly 3 billion years and encompasses a complex series of changing environments. Here, mountain ranges have risen time and again, only to be buried in their own debris. Shallow seas swept across the land, lapping at beaches edged by lush subtropical forests. Volcanoes erupted, searing the land with lava and filling the air with white-hot ash. While volcanic fires were still smoldering, rivers of glacial ice sculpted the higher mountains and scoured great U-shaped valleys.

Generalized Geologic History of the Southern Rocky Mountains

Era	Period	Epoch	Age (Ma)	Geologic Events in the Southern Rockies
CENOZOIC	Quaternary 1.8 Ma–Present	Holocene	11,800 BP–Present	End of conditions favoring full-scale glaciation; growth and decay of Little Ice Age glaciers. Active mass-wasting; development of periglacial features; stream erosion. Evidence from the Colorado Front Range suggests that Paleo-Indian hunters were making seasonal use of high-altitude valleys by at least 8,500 years ago. Development of present topography throughout the Southern Rockies.
		Pleistocene	1.8 Ma–11,800 BP	Climatic fluctuations result in the growth and decay of Ice Age ice sheets and valley glaciers; the glacial record is represented by three major glaciations (pre–Bull Lake, Bull Lake, Pinedale); glacial erosion and deposition processes create the U-shaped valleys and other landscape features typical of glaciated mountains. Dune fields develop in several areas at the close of the Pleistocene. Widespread mammalian extinctions.
	Tertiary 65–1.8 Ma	Pliocene	5.33–1.8 Ma	Regional uplift continues. Widespread erosion and canyon cutting; development of modern drainage patterns. Late Cenozoic (Pliocene and Pleistocene) volcanism results in the massive flow-on-flow basaltic rocks that cap mesas and plateaus in north-central Colorado and many other areas.
		Miocene	22.9–5.33 Ma	Broad regional uplift (as much as 5,000 ft. in some areas) and local block-faulting exhume the Laramide uplifts and redefines the structural basins along their flanks. The Rio Grande Rift develops along the crest of the uplift dome and is accompanied by intense volcanic activity in the Jemez volcanic field and elsewhere.
		Oligocene	33.9–22.9 Ma	Catastrophic volcanic eruptions occur repeatedly and are believed to correspond to the emplacement of a massive, near-surface batholith beneath the San Juan Mountains and the region that extends northeast from the Elk Mountains and the Sawatch Range to the Rocky Mountain front; explosive volcanism produces enormous calderas, massive floods of lava, and extensive ash falls.

Generalized Geologic History of the Southern Rocky Mountains				
Era	**Period**	**Epoch**	**Age (Ma)**	**Geologic Events in the Southern Rockies**
CENOZOIC	Tertiary 65–1.8 Ma	Eocene	54.8–33.9 Ma	Post-Laramide erosion and basin development prevail throughout much of the region. Fossil plants and animals indicate a warm temperate to subtropical climate.
		Paleocene	65–54.8 Ma	The continuation of Laramide Orogeny is associated with the emplacement of igneous plutons and mineralization along the trend of the Colorado Mineral Belt. Many economically important ore bodies are emplaced as crack and fissure fillings in Precambrian age rocks during this time.
MESOZOIC	Cretaceous		145–65 Ma	The subtropical climate sets the stage for the explosive development of the flowering plants. Geologic events reflect the interplay of global changes in sea level and tectonic forces; shifting shorelines of the Western Interior Seaway result in sequences of rocks (Pierre Shale, Dakota Formation, Mancos Formation, Mesaverde Formation, and many others) representative of both deep- and shallow-water marine environments as well as nonmarine settings; economically important coal-bearing rocks develop in many areas. The long history of subsidence and deposition came to an end about 70 million years ago with the onset of the beginning of Laramide Orogeny. **K-T Boundary 65 Ma**—At the close of the Cretaceous, an immense asteroid impact causes worldwide extinctions and brings an end to the Age of Dinosaurs, beginning the Age of Mammals. The K-T boundary is represented by a thin, ashy-colored layer in several south-central localities in the Southern Rockies.
	Jurassic		200–145 Ma	The earliest Jurassic rocks (Wingate, Navajo, and Entrada formations) represent coastal dune deposits of enormous proportions that developed along the leading edge of the Sundance Sea as it spread south along the north-south-trending Western Interior Basin. The geologic record corresponds to the cyclic transgression and regression of the sea; the sea's final withdrawal during the late Jurassic is represented by the fossil-rich interbedded shales and sandstones of the Morrison Formation. Morrison sediments yield one of the richest dinosaur faunas in the world.

Generalized Geologic History of the Southern Rocky Mountains

Era	Period	Epoch	Age (Ma)	Geologic Events in the Southern Rockies
MESOZOIC	Triassic		253–200 Ma	Geologic events reflect the beginning of the breakup of the supercontinent Pangaea. The fine-textured sandstones and shales that characterize the distinctive redbeds of the Triasssic were deposited under semiarid to arid conditions in mudflats, on alluvial plains, and in dune fields adjacent to the eroding highlands of the Ancestral Rockies. Conifers flourish in moister sites, joined by tree ferns, cycads, and scouring rushes. Dinosaurs dominate the land toward the close of the Triassic.
PALEOZOIC	Permian		300–253 Ma	Fossil-poor, coarse-textured redbeds record the continued erosion of the Ancestral Rockies, largely completed by the middle Permian, when shallow seas invade the region from the west and east. Dune fields form along the western margin of Uncompahgria (represented by the Weber Formation) and along the northern flanks of Frontrangia (represented by the Lyons Sandstone). By the close of the Permian, the continents have coalesced to form the supercontinent Pangaea, giving rise to semiarid and arid conditions worldwide.
	Pennsylvanian		318–300 Ma	Tectonic quiescence ends with the progressive collision-suturing of continental plates and the rise of the Ancestral Rockies. Mountain-building activity is concentrated along two main belts: Frontrangia and Uncompahgria. Shallow seas invade the region along the Central Colorado Trough during the early stages of uplift; thick sequences of evaporates (gypsum, anhydrite, and halite) form in the trough's center as the seaway evaporates. Thick sequences of sediments eroded from the uplifts consolidate to form colorful redbeds in many areas (Fountain, Maroon, Sangre de Cristo, and Cutler formations).

Generalized Geologic History of the Southern Rocky Mountains

Era	Period	Epoch	Age (Ma)	Geologic Events in the Southern Rockies
PALEOZOIC	Mississippian		360–318 Ma	Widespread submergence characterizes the Southern Rockies during this period. Shallow-water carbonate sedimentation results in the formation of massive gray limestones such as the Leadville Limestone Formation. Toward the end of the Mississippian, tectonic activity begins along the Transcontinental Arch, and in the wake of the retreating seas the surface of the limestone undergoes extensive solution weathering.
	Devonian		418–360 Ma	At the start of the Devonian, the region lies only slightly above sea level and is situated close to the equatorial zone. By late Devonian time, embayments of a western seaway spread across the central Southern Rockies, and the rock record is dominated by soft shales, fossiliferous limestones, and quartz-rich sandstones.
	Silurian		443–418 Ma	The most widespread submergence of North America occurred during the Silurian. Silurian-age rocks are exceedingly rare in the Southern Rockies as a result of subsequent erosion; the only evidence of the region's submergence comes from blocks of fossiliferous limestone preserved in later volcanic tubes (containing kimberlite).
	Ordovician		489–443 Ma	Seas deepen locally throughout the region, continuing a pattern of cyclic transgression and regression. A scattering of islands persists along the trend of the Transcontinental Arch. Ordovician limestones and sandstones (Harding Sandstone, Frémont Limestone, etc.) contain a diversity of marine organisms.
	Cambrian		545–489 Ma	At the beginning of the Cambrian, the largely eroded Precambrian ranges are part of the emergent North American continental platform. Ocean basin displacements resulting from plate tectonics cause seas to spread from west to east across the region. By the late Cambrian, highlands along the northeast-trending upwarp known as the Transcontinental Arch persist only as islands.

Generalized Geologic History of the Southern Rocky Mountains			
Era		**Age (Ma)**	**Geologic Events in the Southern Rockies**
PRECAMBRIAN	Proterozoic Eon	Late 1,600–545 Ma	Late Precambrian history is highlighted by two intervals of igneous intrusion resulting in the emplacement of batholiths such as the Pikes Peak Granite, the Laramie Anorthosite, the Sherman Granite, the Silver Plume Granite, and others. During the final years of the Precambrian (the Lipalian Interval), much of the region was eroded to a nearly featureless plain.
		Early–Middle 2,500–1,600 Ma	Evidence suggests that the region encompassing the present-day Southern Rockies was joined to the southwestern edge of the ancestral North American craton during the period 1,800–1,600 Ma. as a result of tectonic accretion. A lull in tectonic activity at this time resulted in the deposition of sediments in oceanic troughs along the edge of the Wyoming Province. The onset of intense regional metamorphism, intermittent erosion and sedimentation, and two intervals of massive igneous intrusion punctuate the remainder of the middle Precambrian.
	Archean Eon	Archean 4,500?–2,500 Ma	The oldest Precambrian rocks in the Southern Rockies, dated at more than 2,500 Ma., are found along the southern margin of the Wyoming Province (part of the Archean nucleus of North America); these rocks are separated from the younger Proterozoic rocks that comprise the remainder of the present-day Southern Rockies by a northeastern-trending zone of faults and fractures known as the Cheyenne Belt.

Landscape evolution is generally measured in thousands or even millions of years. The expansion of geologic knowledge resulting from the advent of radiometric dating has provided a measure of the vastness of geologic time and has allowed geologists to develop a reasonably well-dated chronology of the Earth's history. To understand the modern geologic landscape of the Southern Rockies, we must view these landscapes within the framework of geologic time, deciphering clues left behind by forces that create mountains as well as those that wear them down. The five chapters that follow this brief introduction to rocks and landscape processes describe the changing geologic environments that have shaped the face of the Southern Rockies during nearly 3 billion years.

Raw Materials of the Southern Rockies

The geologic history of the Southern Rockies is written in its rocks and landforms. Geologists recognize three basic types of rocks: igneous, sedimentary, and metamorphic, each type characterized by the process that formed it. The next time you are hiking in the mountains, pick up a rock that interests you and examine it closely, taking note of its color, texture, and any clues that might tell you how it formed. For the naturalist interested in deciphering the geologic story of any landscape, the ability to recognize differences in the origins of certain rocks is far more important than remembering their scientific names. Earth stories written in the rocks reveal glimpses of deep time, a geologic saga of epic proportions and enduring fascination.

Igneous Rocks

Igneous rocks are formed by the crystallization of a molten, liquid material called magma. Because magma develops deep within the Earth, it is normally extremely hot, sometimes exceeding 2,000 degrees Fahrenheit. Geologists define two broad classes of igneous rocks, based on the environment of their formation: plutonic (intrusive) and volcanic (extrusive). Plutonic rocks form when magma cools and crystallizes beneath the Earth's surface. Volcanic rocks form whenever magma erupts at the surface as lava or as airborne ejecta. Rocks in each group are given specific names (for example, granite) that precisely describe their mineralogy and texture.

Though plutonic and volcanic rocks are chemically similar, they differ markedly in color, texture, and general appearance. The proportion of light and dark minerals in an igneous rock determines its color. Light-colored (felsic) igneous rocks are derived from magmas that are rich in silicon, sodium, and potassium, the elements that make up late-crystallizing minerals, such as quartz and feldspar. Dark-colored (mafic) igneous rocks result from magmas rich in iron and calcium, the elements that make up early crystallizing minerals, such as hornblende, the pyroxenes, and the darker colored feldspars.

The texture of an igneous rock reflects the rate at which the magma cooled. The slower the rate of cooling, the larger the resultant crystals. Plutonic rocks, insulated during their formation by the preexisting rock into which the molten magma intruded, tend to cool slowly, resulting in a medium- to coarse-grained texture, with the individual minerals easily visible to the naked eye. Volcanic rocks tend to be fine grained or glassy because eruption at the Earth's surface brings about more rapid cooling. Geologists refer to an igneous rock having crystals of two markedly different sizes as a porphyry. Porphyries form when the magma undergoes two cycles of cooling, the first at depth, which permits the growth of large crystals (called phenocrysts), and the second when the magma moves to shallower depth, increasing the cooling rate and resulting in a matrix of smaller crystals.

Volcanic eruptions generally produce variable quantities of lava. The diversity of landscape features produced by volcanic eruptions reflects the chemistry of the lava and the degree to which volatile gases are encapsulated in the lava. The silica content of magma plays a critical role in landform development. Silica-rich (rhyolitic) lavas are generally so viscous that they flow with difficulty, producing landforms that increase in size by gradual accumulation or by mounding. Shield volcanoes, such as San Antonio Peak in the San Luis Valley, were formed in this way. In contrast, iron-rich basaltic lavas tend to flow freely across the landscape, often resulting in large, tabular-shaped topographic features; the basalts that cap Grand Mesa and the Flat Tops were produced in this way. When basalt lavas cool, they tend to crystallize from the outside to the inside, which causes the lava to contract dramatically and develop a distinctive columnar joint pattern. When viewed in a long section, columnar jointed basalt resembles a stockadelike wall of hexagonally shaped columns. Superb examples of columnar jointing are relatively common in the Southern Rockies; some of the best include the basalt cliffs along the Rio Grande in northern New Mexico, Wagon Wheel Gap (near Creede), Grand Mesa (near Lands End), and east of Cochetopa Pass (Colorado 114).

Lava that is heavily charged with gas may explode from a surface vent or fissure, producing a shower of porous rock fragments and ash. The term *pyroclastic* refers to volcanic rocks that form as a result of explosive ejection. When ash cools and hardens into rock, geologists refer to it as tuff. Pyroclastic agglomerates, breccias, and ash-fall tuffs, common on the Pajarito Plateau and in the West Elk and San Juan mountains, are formed from the consolidation of nonsorted ejecta—volcanic bombs, pumice, cinders, and ash—collected from the site of the eruption by mudflows or other types of fluid-driven transport mechanisms. Castlelike outcrops of West Elk Breccia, with its distinctive mixture of angular blocks, can be seen in the palisades along the Gunnison River. Ash-fall tuffs form as a result of the accumulation and consolidation of ash and other small-scale ejecta that have welded to varying degrees based on the temperature of the ash at the time of its deposition. A welded tuff forms when the ash fall is so hot that it fuses (or welds) into hard rock almost immediately. Examples of welded tuffs include Lava Cliffs in Rocky Mountain National Park, the 1,200-cubic-mile Fish Canyon Tuff just southwest of South Fork (U.S. 160), the "castles" of Wall Mountain Tuff near Castle Rock, and the fabulous cliffs into which the prehistoric residents of Bandelier National Monument carved their dwellings and ceremonial chambers. In contrast, ash-fall tuffs that undergo only minimal welding in the aftermath of the eruption are easily eroded; the spectacular spires and hoodoos of Wheeler Geologic Area (near Creede) result from the erosion of hundreds of feet of poorly consolidated ash fall tuff.

Mountain-Building Blocks: Plutons, Batholiths, Laccoliths, Stocks, Dikes, and Sills

The ability of magma to move upward through the Earth's crust is one of the most important forces in mountain building. These massive bodies of magma, which are known as plutons, melt their way upward through the overlying host rock, assimilating whatever rocks they intrude and often traveling along zones of weakness in the preexisting rock layers. Characteristically, plutons are composed of granitic rocks and come in many shapes and sizes. The largest pluton is called a batholith; by definition, a batholith must exceed forty square miles in area. The distinctive granitic massif of Pikes Peak is part of a 1,300-square-mile batholith that marks the southern end of the Colorado Front Range. The batholith surrounding Estes Park, which includes the well-known landmarks of Old Man Mountain and the Twin Owls, covers more than 600 square miles.

Smaller plutons come in a variety of shapes, depending on the manner in which the host rock was intruded, each with its own name. A stock is smaller than a batholith, roughly cylindrical in shape, and cuts across the bedding trend of the host rocks. Plugs, such as those that form Needle Rock (east of Crawford) and Huerfano Butte (north of Walsenburg), resemble "necks" of solidified igneous rock exposed by the erosion of the rock into which they were intruded. Laccoliths are typically large mushroom-shaped plutons that spread out laterally once they are emplaced, conforming to the structural trend of the host rock; with the addition of more magma, the laccolith grows in size and causes an up-doming in the overlying rock. The Southern Rockies were the first place where laccoliths were recognized and studied. The most famous of these include Mount Sopris, south of Carbondale; Chair Mountain, near Crested Butte; Gothic Mountain, in the West Elks; and Tater Heap, located south of Needle Rock. The sedimentary rocks into which these laccoliths were intruded can still be seen along their flanks.

Dikes are sheetlike bodies of rock that cut across the bedding (foliations) in the host rock, whereas sills are intrusions that travel between, and parallel to, the layers of the host rock. Along Colorado 9, near the Green Mountain Dam, light-colored dikes and sills intrude dark layers of shale; at one time, these intrusive conduits fed the thick laccolith that lies atop the shales. The famous Painted Wall at Black Canyon of the Gunnison National Park is a sheer, steel-gray cliff—an artist's canvas—crisscrossed with spectacular white dikes.

Sedimentary Rocks

Sedimentary rocks form when sediments—rock fragments, chemical precipitates and evaporites, or organic matter—consolidate on land or in the water under temperature and pressure regimes typical of the Earth's surface. Geologists separate sedimentary rocks into three general groups: clastic, nonclastic, and organic. Many sedimentary rocks are gradational between these simplified groups, while others may have a composite origin.

Clastic sedimentary rocks consist of fragments, or grains, of preexisting rocks that have undergone compaction and cementation to form new rocks. They are classified according to grain size into the following general categories: conglomerate (gravel- and cobble-sized), sandstone (sand-sized), siltstone (silt-sized), and shale (laminated clay- and silt-sized particles). For example, sandstone is formed by the cementation of sand-sized grains, usually quartz, and has been used as a building stone for homes and public buildings throughout the Southern Rockies.

If you look closely at a clastic sedimentary rock, you can learn a great deal about the environmental factors that played a role in its formation. Sediments are typically transported from one place to another by wind, water, ice, or gravity. The size and sorting of particles reflect the original size of the weathered grains, the character of the transporting medium, the energy characteristics of the environment in which the sediments are deposited, and any postdepositional changes that have occurred in this environment. Silt- and sand-sized particles are transported by both water and wind. The presence of cobbles, gravel, or sand generally implies a high-energy depositional environment, such as you would encounter in a stream channel or along a marine beach; sediments associated with beach, stream, and sand dune environments are often distinctly rounded and may appear etched or frosted. Fine particles, such as silt and clay, typically settle out in quiet water or from air and are associated most commonly with lake, deep-ocean, estuarine, or swamp environments.

Many clastic sedimentary rocks are conspicuously layered, each layer representing an episode of deposition, such as a windstorm or a flood event. Layers may be several feet thick or paper thin, depending on the character and duration of each depositional event. Boundaries between successive layers may be identified by looking for subtle changes in grain size or color, or distinct changes in rock type. Sedimentary structures, such as ripple marks, cross-bedding, mud cracks, raindrop impressions, and the tracks or other signs of animals, may pattern the surfaces of certain layers. Wherever wind or water currents have swept sediment into bars, dunes, or ripples, we are able to determine the direction of current flow or, in the case of cross-bedding relationships, changes in the current direction within the depositional environment.

Nonclastic sedimentary rocks (such as dolomite, rock gypsum, and rock salt) are derived from sediments that either precipitate out of water or are produced through the evaporation of water containing dissolved solids. Cherts are nonclastic rocks that consist largely of silica and are formed either from chemical precipitation or by silica replacement of plant or animal material; agates, jasper, and some petrified wood are examples. Secondary segregations, such as nodules, concretions, and geodes, are often found in sedimentary rocks and result from the orderly precipitation, or segregation, of mineral matter in the sediment after deposition. Organic sedimentary rocks are derived from the accumulation and consolidation of plant or invertebrate remains; most limestones (formed from coral reefs or shell fragments) and coal are examples.

The color of a sedimentary rock provides information on the mineralogy of the parent material as well as the oxygen levels present in the original depositional environment or the chemistry of waters flowing through the sediments after burial. In most cases, the mineral pigments we see are by-products of chemical weathering and later alteration of the sedimentary grains in place. Light colors prevail in sedimentary rocks in which the mineral grains or rock fragments and the cementing material are dominated by quartz or calcite. Darker colors are generally produced by the chemical alteration of iron-bearing minerals in the sediments. Buff, brown, salmon, and red hues result from the presence of ferric oxide (hematite) and are often associated with oxygen-rich depositional environments or groundwaters. The green, gray, or blackish hues associated with shale reflect an oxygen-poor environment in which organic decay was limited. Certain dark-colored rocks, such as coal, owe their color largely to the amount of organic carbon present. Glauconite (potassium iron silicate) grains in sufficient quantity are responsible for the greenish hues prevalent in certain sandstones, such as the Sawatch Sandstone of central Colorado.

Geologists identify sedimentary rocks that exhibit a relatively consistent, thick, and geographically extensive distribution by giving them a two-part name that provides both a geographic and a geologic identity; for example, Leadville Limestone is the name given the massive, cliff-forming limestone formation that outcrops throughout central Colorado. Because sedimentary rocks often contain fossils, they provide not only a record of past life-forms, but allow geologists to correlate specific intervals of geologic time from one area to another. Based on their knowledge of modern plant and animal habitat requirements and distributional patterns, paleontologists have been able to reconstruct many of the ancient environments of the Southern Rockies.

Metamorphic Rocks

Metamorphic rocks (*meta* means "change," *morph* means "form") are produced by subjecting preexisting igneous and sedimentary rocks to extremes of heat and pressure deep beneath the Earth's crust. The dramatic recrystallization, or metamorphism, that occurs in response to intense heat may result from contact with magma, radioactive decay, deep burial, or exposure to hot, chemically active solutions. The high heat and intense directed pressure of the metamorphic environment may cause the constituent minerals in the parent rock to form parallel layers, or folia. Geologists separate metamorphic rocks into two groups: foliated and nonfoliated. The bands in foliated rocks commonly consist of dark-colored concentrations of biotite mica and hornblende. In metamorphic rocks such as schist and gneiss, which are associated with the intense deformational stresses of mountain building, the folia may be spectacularly bent and folded. An amazing cross section of metamorphic rocks, principally gneisses and schists, can be seen by travelers along I-70 between Golden and Copper Mountain. Nonfoliated metamorphic rocks, such as marble, develop from rocks that are relatively homogeneous in terms of their mineralogy and were subjected only to the heat of an intruding magma and not to any directional stresses.

Two types of metamorphism are important in the Southern Rockies: regional and contact. Massive intrusions such as those that formed the cores of many of the mountain ranges of the Southern Rockies were slow to cool and often gave rise to large-scale regional metamorphism. Rocks such as schist and gneiss are produced by regional metamorphism and are associated with the axes of the large mountain ranges where deformational pressures have been particularly intense. Contact metamorphism, which occurs along the margins of small igneous intrusions such as dikes and sills, is initiated by the heat of the intruding magma and produces mostly nonfoliated rocks. Because small plutons cool more rapidly than do large ones, contact metamorphism tends to form relatively thin, nonfoliated sheaths, seldom exceeding a few feet in width. The famous Yule Marble, quarried in central Colorado for use in the Lincoln Memorial and other famous monuments, resulted from contact metamorphism of a thick bed of Leadville Limestone.

Mountain Building 101

Seismic studies show that the Earth is made up of three major zones arranged in concentric layers of differing densities: an extremely dense molten metallic core, a moderately dense, iron-rich mobile mantle, and an outermost layer, the so-called crust, which consists of relatively low-density materials. This differentiation by density is the most fundamental structural feature of the Earth and is crucial to our understanding of the geologic events that have shaped the face of the Southern Rockies.

Geologists use the term *tectonics* to refer to all deformation of the Earth's crust. These crustal movements may range from minor disruptions that affect small bodies of rock to the folding and faulting that produce mountain ranges and, on a global scale, to the forces that cause continents to move and seafloors to split. The causes of crustal deformation are complex. Geologists believe that large-scale tectonic activity is generated by the development of huge convection cells below the mobile zone that underlies the crust and includes at least the upper region of the mantle.

Plate Tectonics and the Southern Rockies

The theory of plate tectonics provides us with a broad outline of the forces that create mountains and initiate volcanic eruptions but few details to explain the events that have occurred in the Southern Rockies. The general model for plate tectonics embodies the idea that the Earth's crust is broken into several rigid plates that move at varying speeds over the underlying mantle. Plate boundaries do not correspond to standard geographic units but extend through continents, along the edges of continents, and down the middle of oceans. The Earth's plates include two types of crust: continental crust and oceanic crust. Continental crust consists largely of lightweight, silica-rich (felsic) rocks; oceanic crust consists primarily of dense, iron-rich (mafic) rocks. Radioactive heating within the mantle together with a small heat flow from the core induce an upward circulation of relatively buoyant mantle material; conversely, the outer layers of the mantle cool, become denser, and sink. Both these density contrasts lead to convection cells on a scale of thousands of kilometers. Defined by the surface boundaries of these cells, continental and suboceanic surface layers form the plates of plate tectonics. Because continental crustal material is much lighter than that of the mantle, it resists being dragged down (subducted) and floats as a kind of deformed scum where it can preserve Earth's oldest rocks.

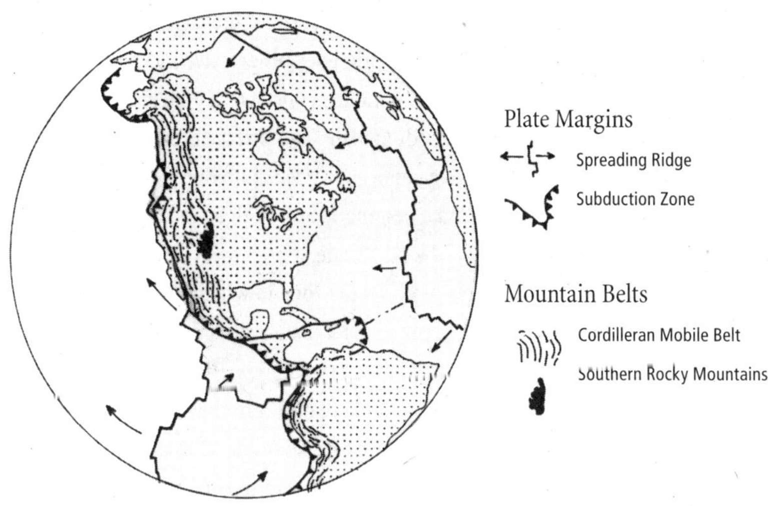

Generalized map of the major plates of the Western Hemisphere. Arrows indicate direction of plate movement. Courtesy of Emmett Evanoff

The North American continent includes two major tectonic features. A large, tectonically stable platform, or craton, encompasses much of the present-day continental interior and is underlain by Precambrian-age granitic and metamorphic rocks. The craton is characterized by subdued topography and low elevations. Tectonic disturbance of this stable platform occurs by broad, gentle upwarping, with only the craton's edges participating in the violent creation of mountains. The long, narrow, and generally arc-shaped zones of structural instability that form along the leading edges of a moving craton are called mobile belts. These belts are the loci of volcanoes, granitic batholiths, regional metamorphism, and earthquakes and are characterized by thick sequences of sedimentary and volcanic rocks that have been folded, metamorphosed, and intruded by plutons.

The Southern Rockies are unique in that they overlap the southwestern portion of the craton as well as the Cordilleran mobile belt that extends along the west coast of North, Central, and South America.

Mountain building, or orogeny, occurs as a result of mobile-belt disturbances along the zone where two plates converge. When an oceanic and a continental plate collide, the leading edge of the oceanic plate, being denser and less buoyant, plunges beneath the margin of the continental plate by a process called subduction. There it undergoes progressive melting. The zone of intrusive and volcanic activity along the continental plate margin indicates the trajectory of this descending plate. The surface expression of a subduction zone is delineated by an oceanic trench on one side and a curvilinear line of volcanoes, called a magmatic arc (both island arcs and intracontinental volcanic arcs), on the other side.

The axis of the oceanic trench marks the zone in which sediments from both the oceanic plate and the continental plate are accumulating. Deep-ocean sediments—fine clay and ooze—that have settled to the ocean floor are carried along on the moving oceanic plate. From the continent, terrestrial sediments—sand and mud—are carried to the shore by streams and then swept into deep-ocean waters by currents. In the bottom of the trench, sediments from both sources are mixed and then deformed as the subducting oceanic plate drags them downward. In this way, the continental margin is built outward and new continental crust is created by the addition (accretion) of these metamorphosed sediments.

Most of the world's great mountain belts lie along the margins of continents and fit neatly into the framework of the plate-tectonic model. But the Southern Rockies are located in the interior of the continent, far from the current boundaries between colliding plates. The actual mechanism behind their final rise during the Cenozoic era remains enigmatic, only partially explained by the modern plate-tectonic paradigm. Some scientists suggest that the episodes of mountain building that produced the Southern Rockies were an intraplate response to the collision of the North American and East Pacific plates. Whatever the answer, it seems probable that episodes of intense regional orogeny in the Southern Rockies were initiated at times when the geographic positions of convergent plate boundaries were different from those we see today.

CHAPTER THREE

Opening Scenes: Precambrian Landscapes

The dramatic opening scenes of the Precambrian era began with the Earth's formation some 4.5 billion years ago and ended with the appearance of the first shell-bearing animals about 545 million years ago. Precambrian mountain ranges of vast dimensions appeared repeatedly across the region of the present-day Southern Rockies, only to be worn away and engulfed by the advancing seas of the Paleozoic. Today, the uncovered, uplifted roots of these ancient ranges, the largest exposures of Precambrian crystalline rocks to be found anywhere in the western United States, lie at the heart of some of our most spectacular scenery.

In describing the events of the Precambrian, we tend to compress the uncompressible, consigning 90 percent of Earth's history to a single, lucid chapter. Geologists tell us that Precambrian landscapes were stark and barren, not unlike the most recently exposed mountain ranges of the Antarctic. The land owed its color to the rocks and its textural diversity to topography and the whims of gravity. There would have been no vegetation to slow the ravages wrought by a harsh, unforgiving climate. A network of braided rivers, clogged with rock debris eroded from highlands tipped beyond the angle of repose, would have flowed across a moonscape of bare rock, unimpeded in their rush to the sea.

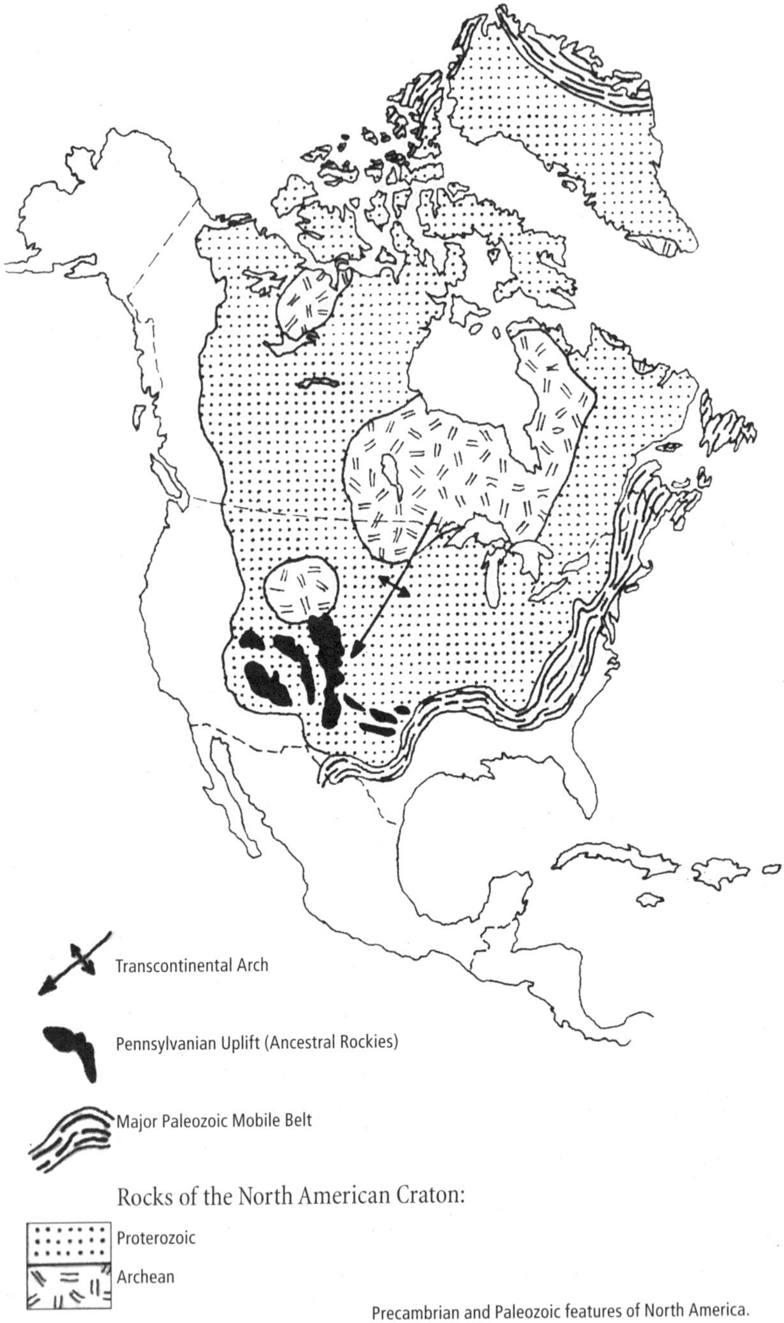

Transcontinental Arch

Pennsylvanian Uplift (Ancestral Rockies)

Major Paleozoic Mobile Belt

Rocks of the North American Craton:

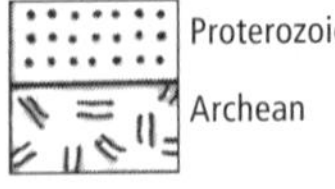

Proterozoic

Archean

Precambrian and Paleozoic features of North America. Courtesy of Emmett Evanoff

Precambrian Rock Provinces

Precambrian rocks form the foundations, the so-called basement rocks, of the continents. In many areas, these basement rocks are blanketed by later strata; outcrops of these ancient rocks are visible only in a few deep canyons, such as the Grand Canyon of the Colorado and the Black Canyon of the Gunnison, or in the cores of deeply eroded mountain ranges, such as the Colorado Front Range and the Park Range. The Precambrian basement rocks that make up the continents are subdivided into distinct regions, or provinces, based on rock ages. Radiometric dating of rock has shown that the North American craton can be divided into seven provinces, each distinguished by characteristic rock assemblages of differing rock ages and by generally similar deformational trends that have been preserved in the rocks; adjacent provinces have different deformational trends and appear to be separated by abrupt metamorphic boundaries known as orogenic fronts. Radiometric dates of rock samples taken from deep wells and scattered exposures of Precambrian rocks in western Canada, the United States, Mexico, and Greenland have enabled geologists to develop models that help to explain the growth of the North American continent during the Precambrian.

The Early Precambrian: Archean History (4.5 Billion to 2.5 Billion Years Ago)

Details of the Precambrian history of the Southern Rockies are slowly unfolding after nearly a century of study. Geologists who study deep time divide the Precambrian into two eons, the Archean, which spans the interval from 4.5 to 2.5 billion years ago, and the Proterozoic, which begins 2.5 billion years ago and ends at the start of the Paleozoic era. The oldest rocks found in the Southern Rockies are actually meteorites that fell from space and may well be older than Earth itself. The oldest, or Archean-age, Earth rocks are the garnet-bearing rocks (peridotites) that formed as the interior of the planet cooled and segregated into the core and mantle; these rocks were brought to the surface from 100 miles deep in the mantle by the diamond-bearing kimberlite pipes that outcrop near today's Colorado-Wyoming border. Rocks dated at nearly 2.7 billion years—a complex of gneisses, granites, and quartzites—are found in the Medicine Bow Mountains and the Sierra Madre Range of southern Wyoming and in extreme northwestern Colorado. These crystalline basement rocks form the southern margin of the Wyoming Province, part of the Archean nucleus of the North American craton. They provide the most complete and best-exposed record of Archean and early Proterozoic events in the western United States. Correlated in age with rocks of the southern Superior Province of Canada, the rocks of the Wyoming Province reflect widespread deformation, granitic plutonism, and volcanic activity.

A broad northeast-trending zone of faults and fractures known as the Cheyenne Belt separates the rocks of the Wyoming Province from a distinctly younger, Proterozoic basement complex to the south. This well-defined shear zone extends through the Sierra Madre, Medicine Bow, and Laramie mountains just north of the Colorado-Wyoming border. South of the Cheyenne Belt, in the Proterozoic province that encompasses the remainder of the Southern Rockies and much of the Southwest, the oldest basement rocks are dated at about 1.8 billion years. Some geologists have suggested that the Cheyenne Belt defines the southern margin of the Archean continental nucleus, a zone shaped by converging plates, the development of offshore island arcs, and crustal accretion (addition). According to this model, the juxtaposition of these two contrasting age provinces can be explained by the tectonic accretion of a 720-mile-wide band of Proterozoic crust to the Wyoming Province during the period 1.8 to 1.6 billion years ago. As a result of this dramatic suturing, the continental crust and the foundations of the modern-day Southern Rockies were finally in place.

Proterozoic History: The Middle and Late Precambrian (2.5 Billion to 545 Million Years Ago)

Geologists believe that by earliest Proterozoic time, the region encompassing most of the present-day Southern Rockies was joined—some use the term *welded*—to the southwestern edge of the ancestral North American craton. The beginning of the Proterozoic is marked by a lull in tectonic activity and by the deposition of thousands of feet of sediments in deep oceanic troughs along the southern margin of the Wyoming Province. The earliest

Proterozoic rocks in the Southern Rockies are the partially metamorphosed sedimentary rocks of the Snowy Pass Supergroup from Wyoming's Medicine Bow Mountains and the Sierra Madre Range. One of the best examples, a sparkling white quartzite called the Medicine Peak Quartzite, forms an impressive cliff in the Snowy Range of southern Wyoming. The quartzite is about 5,600 feet thick and is derived from the metamorphism of sediments deposited on a shallow marine shelf along the edge of the craton. Younger rocks in the same region, dated at about 2.4 billion years, contain stromatolites, the moundlike accumulations of calcium carbonate produced by reef-forming marine algae. Though outcrops of stromatolites are exceedingly rare, they are the only common fossil in Precambrian rocks and, along with other ancient stromatolites found in Australia and Africa, are thought to represent the oldest known evidence of life on Earth.

Fossil stromatolite outcrop near Snowy Range Pass, Wyoming.

The later portion of the middle Precambrian was characterized by intense regional metamorphism and deformation, intermittent erosion and sedimentation, and two intervals of massive igneous intrusion, on a scale far greater than in any subsequent time. Much of the metamorphic activity, including the alteration of the oceanic-trough-deposited sedimentary and volcanic rocks, was concentrated along the trend of the Colorado Lineament, a 100-mile-wide belt of Precambrian faults that can be traced from the

Grand Canyon northeast to the Rocky Mountain front, and possibly on beneath the northern midcontinent region to Lake Superior. Metamorphic rocks formed during this time were repeatedly folded and faulted into huge corrugated ridges. Metamorphic activity peaked in the region approximately 1.8 to 1.7 billion years ago, coinciding with diminished movement along the Colorado Lineament. This early deformation set the course of the Colorado River and, more important, initiated the fragmentation of the Precambrian basement of the Southern Rockies into a mosaic of fault blocks, which, when reactivated during the Cretaceous (Mesozoic), set the stage for the final rise of the Southern Rockies.

Large outcrops of early Proterozoic gneisses and schists dated at about 1.8 billion years are especially prominent in the walls of numerous mountain canyons and glacial cirques along the Colorado Front Range. These distinctive rocks, the first Precambrian rocks you see as you travel I-70 west from Denver, are easily observed along Trail Ridge Road in Rocky Mountain National Park and in Big Thompson Canyon (west of Loveland). Metamorphic rocks of this age group form the famous Keyboard of the Winds, a jagged ridge between Longs Peak and Pagoda Mountain in the park. At the southern end of the Colorado Front Range, metamorphic rocks are conspicuous in the Royal Gorge of the Arkansas (west of Cañon City). In Black Canyon of the Gunnison National Park, the 2,300-foot-high Painted Wall exposes a spectacular cliff of early Proterozoic gneiss interlaced with a series of younger, light-colored dikes.

South of the Cheyenne Belt shear zone, continent-island-arc collision produced the high-grade gneisses and schists typical of Colorado and northern New Mexico, as well as several other distinctive rock types. Outcrops of a dark greenish black metamorphic rock called amphibolite form striking cliffs along the Pecos River in New Mexico's Sangre de Cristos. Exposures of phyllite (metamorphosed shale), also common in the Sangre de Cristos, are the product of regional metamorphism and are easy to spot because of their silky sheen and crinkly foliation. Elsewhere in the Sangre de Cristos, middle Precambrian quartzites (metamorphosed sandstones) form Pecos Baldy, Chimayosos, and Truchas peaks.

White pegmatite dikes decorate the sheer face of the Painted Wall in Black Canyon of the Gunnison National Park, Colorado.

Fires in the Earth: The Late Precambrian (1.6 Billion to 570 Million Years Ago)

By the middle Precambrian, intensive episodes of metamorphism gave way to igneous intrusions of such magnitude that they dwarfed all previous events. The first wave of intrusions began about 1.7 billion years ago, with later episodes occurring during the late Precambrian and dated at around 1.4 and 1 billion years. With each episode of intrusion, mountains were built and subsequently eroded to near sea level. The great variety of shapes and sizes of these intrusions was determined by the structural characteristics of the host rocks into which they were intruded, the viscosity of the intruding magma, and the rate of its injection. Renewed metamorphism of the host rocks resulting from the thermal effects of the intruding magma accompanied each episode of intrusion.

Two of the most common "granitic" rocks associated with Precambrian-age batholiths and other large-scale intrusions.

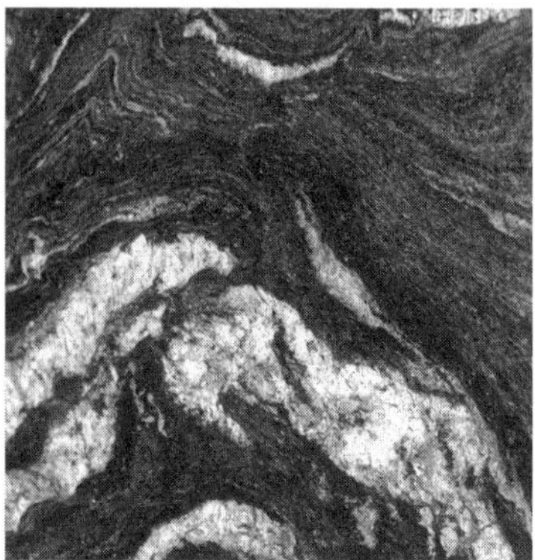

A classic example of gneiss, showing the distinctive banding and swirls that result from the intense deformational pressures associated with large-scale intrusions.

1.7-Billion-Year-Old Granites

The igneous rocks of this first intrusive episode consist of granite or gabbro (a dark-colored igneous rock) and occur as batholiths, stocks, dikes, and smaller lenticular bodies. The most well-known granite of this period is the Boulder Creek Granite, a dark blue-gray and faintly banded granodiorite. Outcrops of this small batholith are exposed west of Boulder in the central Front Range. A granite batholith of similar age makes up Mount Evans, one of the Fourteeners dominating the skyline west of Denver. In central Colorado, granite dated at 1.75 billion years can also be seen in the exposed core of the northern Sawatch Range. A period of major erosion is believed to have followed this first intrusive episode. Evidence of this erosive interval is limited, however, to the Needles Mountains in the San Juans, where an 8,000-foot-thick sequence of metamorphosed sedimentary rocks (quartzites, slates, and phyllites of the Uncompahgre Formation) overlies middle Precambrian granites and is, in turn, intruded by the Eolus Granite, a late Precambrian granite.

1.4-Billion-Year-Old Granites

Late Precambrian history in the Southern Rockies is highlighted by two intervals of igneous intrusion and concludes with a long period of erosion known as the Lipalian Interval. The first of the two intrusive periods began about 1.4 billion years ago and continued for almost 100 million years. Silver Plume Granite, locally exposed in the central Colorado Front Range, and Sherman Granite, conspicuous along the crest of the Laramie Range and in the Vedauwoo Rocks area of southern Wyoming, are the most representative granites of this second intrusive group. Most rock climbers are familiar with Silver Plume Granite because it forms the sheer wall of the Diamond on Longs Peak. Related in age to Sherman Granite is a batholith of anorthosite, an unusual igneous rock composed almost exclusively of greenish blue labradorite (a type of calcium-plagioclase feldspar). This unusual batholith is situated on the Cheyenne Belt where it crosses the Laramie Range and is cut by the northern margin of the Sherman Granite Batholith. Anorthosite plutons are rare on Earth but are very common on the moon, where they form light-colored lunar highlands.

Here and there, dikes of darker igneous rocks such as gabbro and andesite have intruded the 1.4-billion-year-old granites. Dikes of this type are especially common in the northern Front Range and the Sawatch Range. The forty-mile-long Iron Dike, which extends from just south of Boulder northwest across the Front Range, is believed to have been emplaced at this time. Road-cut and surface exposures of this dike are a conspicuous dark brown due to the dike's high iron (magnetite) content; the Iron Dike is easy to spot in a road cut about a mile west of Many Parks Curve in Rocky Mountain National Park.

1-Billion-Year-Old Granites

The emplacement of the Pikes Peak Batholith marked the final episode of granitic intrusion, the exclamation point at the end of a long and violent series of events. This isolated plume of granite has been difficult for geologists to explain because it was emplaced at a time when intrusive activity in the Southern Rockies had ended. The composition of the Pikes Peak Batholith is highly variable, but it is best known for massive, rounded outcrops of coarse-grained pinkish granite known as Pikes Peak Granite. Decomposition of Pikes Peak Granite into coarse, angular gravels (called grus), consisting mostly of feldspar and quartz, is conspicuous throughout the region. Bright green feldspar crystals, known as amazonite, are found in Pikes Peak Granite and are especially prevalent at Crystal Mountain, north of Florissant. A portion of the Pikes Peak Batholith forms the core of the Rampart Range, which extends north from Pikes Peak. Aeromagnetic surveys of the Pikes Peak area suggest that this enormous batholith may have fed a volcanic caldera.

The End of the Precambrian

The final years of the Precambrian are characterized by tectonic quiescence and widespread erosion. Between 600 and 400 million years ago, no rock record exists of mountain-building activity in the Southern Rockies. During this time, known as the Lipalian Interval, much of the region was eroded to a nearly featureless plain situated at or just above sea level. In most places, the erosion surface (geologists refer to this type of a gap in the rock record as an unconformity) separating the Precambrian basement from younger strata is smooth and somewhat beveled. Below the unconformity, tremendous thicknesses of granite or metamorphic rocks can be seen; above it are bedded sequences of younger sedimentary rocks. In some places, a thick fossil soil may also be present, such as the reddish, pebble-rich rock visible in a road cut on Flagstaff Mountain, just west of Boulder. Good exposures of the Upper Precambrian erosion surface can be seen in Glenwood Canyon near Glenwood Springs, at Box Canyon Falls near Ouray, and in the Williams Canyon–Cave of the Winds area west of Colorado Springs.

Missing pages of Earth history are marked by this angular unconformity at Box Canyon in Ouray. Note the erosional surface separating steeply dipping rock layers below from gently dipping, younger layers above.

CHAPTER FOUR

The Paleozoic: Mountain Islands and Desert Seas

Visualize the face of the Southern Rockies half a billion years ago, at the dawn of the Paleozoic era. The landscape is utterly barren. There are no plants to soften the contours, no animals except sea-dwelling invertebrates. At times, the land is emergent and marine waters spill only onto the continental margins. At other times, shallow seas sweep across the land, the few remaining highlands forming a chain of islands in the warm, tropical seas. In contrast to the spectacular deep-Earth fires that fueled the Precambrian, the story of the Paleozoic is revealed largely through its sedimentary rock record.

Geologists divide the Paleozoic into seven periods, each of which is associated with sedimentary rocks that reflect the environmental conditions at the time of deposition. In the Southern Rockies, widespread marine conditions, the deposition of predominately marine sediments, and a rapidly evolving marine fauna characterized early and middle Paleozoic time. The late Paleozoic witnessed the expansion of terrestrial life (land plants and animals); the rise of a major group of mountains, the Ancestral Rockies, in the region of the present-day Southern Rocky Mountains; and the formation of the supercontinent Pangaea. Differences in the Paleozoic sedimentary record from one area to another in the Southern Rockies reflect variations in the extent of the encroaching seas, changing depositional environments, and the effects of postdepositional erosion.

Cambrian Period (545 to 490 Million Years Ago)

At the beginning of the Cambrian period, the Southern Rockies were part of the emergent North American continental platform. The paleocontinents were dispersed around the globe in low tropical latitudes; there were no emergent landmasses above latitudes 60° north or south. In the Southern Rockies, the sea, which spread from west to east across the much-eroded Precambrian mountains, was beginning a series of advances, or transgressions. Each advance was punctuated by a retreat, or regression, of the sea from the land. This pattern continued intermittently throughout the Paleozoic and Mesozoic eras and is believed to have been the result of ocean-basin displacements associated with plate tectonics.

Geologists now relate the major sea level changes that occurred during the Paleozoic to the number, shape, and speed of spreading centers (places where tectonic plates move apart) in the ocean basins. Spreading centers, such as the modern Mid-Atlantic Ridge, allow magma to rise upward from the Earth's mantle, cooling and solidifying as oceanic crust and initiating a chain reaction that displaces seawater from the ocean basins and sends it flooding onto the continents. Although similar marine transgressions and regressions occurred during Precambrian time, Cambrian rocks provide the first clear record of these events.

Throughout early and middle Cambrian time in the Southern Rockies, emergent highlands persisted along a broad, northeast-trending upwarp known as the Transcontinental Arch, which extended from what is now modern-day New Mexico to Wisconsin. By the middle Cambrian, shallow seas had advanced to the crest of the arch from both the east and the west in a series of transgressive and regressive events. Most of the sediments laid down in the advancing seas were derived from the erosion of various highlands along the trend of the Transcontinental Arch. The western and eastern seas merged during the late Cambrian along an east-west-trending trough in the arch called the Colorado Sag; several portions of the highland landscape may have persisted as islands during this time.

In the Southern Rockies, Cambrian sedimentary rocks and fossils are restricted to certain portions of central Colorado, the San Juan region, and the northwestern edge of the Medicine Bow Mountains; no early Paleozoic sedimentary record exists for northern New Mexico. The Sawatch Sandstone (or Quartzite) of central Colorado is the most widespread Cambrian sedimentary formation in the region. Exposures of this ancient beach deposit overlie Precambrian rocks and can easily be identified by the presence of the minerals glauconite (green) and hematite (red), which give the formation a variegated appearance. Sawatch Sandstone can be seen along the flanks of the Sawatch Range (near Red Cliff and Minturn) and the Mosquito Range, the White River Plateau, in Williams Canyon (west of Manitou Springs), and in Glenwood Canyon (near Shoshone Dam). In the San Juans, the Cambrian Ignacio Formation (quartzite, conglomerate, and sandstone) can be seen along U.S. 550 south of Silverton and a few miles south of Coal Bank Pass (north of Durango).

Cambrian-age igneous dikes, some as many as ninety-eight feet thick and several miles long, occur along a west-northwest-trending tectonic zone believed to be related to a Paleozoic rift structure, or the zone of strike-slip faulting, that extended from southeastern Oklahoma through New Mexico and Colorado into Utah. Outcrops of these largely mafic dikes can be seen in the Sangre de Cristo Range in northeastern New Mexico, in Temple Canyon near Cañon City, at Black Canyon of the Gunnison, and in Unaweep Canyon west of Whitewater.

The Cambrian Explosion

The encroaching seas of the Cambrian witnessed the rapid evolution and adaptive radiation of most of the major phyla of invertebrate animals. The Southern Rockies lay astride the equator during the Cambrian, and the warm, shallow seas provided an ideal environment for the proliferation of marine life. Paleontologists refer to the extraordinary increase in species diversity and complexity that occurred during the first 10 to 20 million years of the Cambrian as the Cambrian Explosion. This burst of evolutionary activity was unprecedented, and nothing approaching it has occurred since. In the Southern Rockies, as in most areas where Cambrian fossils are found, the poor preservation of soft-bodied animals (such as jellyfish and worms) has biased the fossil record in favor of animals with hard parts; as a result, the fossil record provides only a sampling of the diversity of marine animals that existed in the Cambrian sea. Though not common, fossil trilobites, brachiopods, mollusks, and graptolites can occasionally be found in Cambrian rocks in Williams Canyon (near Cave of the Winds), at Baker's Bridge north of Durango, and in the Sawatch and Mosquito ranges. Of these, the well-armored trilobites were the most abundant and perhaps the most interesting. These pill bug–like bottom feeders, extinct since the late Paleozoic, are the first animals known to have possessed a compound eye. Fossil evidence indicates that the most complex trilobite eye may have contained 15,000 elements, each with its own lens of crystalline calcite oriented to transmit light most efficiently.

Ordovician Period (490 to 443 Million Years Ago)

During the Ordovician period, shallow seas once again swept across the Southern Rockies, continuing their cyclic invasion of the North American continent. Along the trend of the Transcontinental Arch, a scattering of islands protruded above the tropical seas; the occurrence of warm-water fossil faunas in the Ordovician deposits of the Southern Rockies suggests that the North American continent remained in a sub-equatorial position during the early Paleozoic. By mid-Ordovician time, marine waters were receding throughout much of the region and fossil-rich sediments were deposited either on top of Cambrian rocks or, in the absence of Cambrian sediments, directly on top of the Precambrian basement rock. Ordovician rocks are preserved primarily in the region of the Colorado Sag in central Colorado and are conspicuously absent from the San Juan Mountains, southern Wyoming, and the northern half of New Mexico.

In central and northern Colorado, the Ordovician is characterized by the deposition of thick sequences of limestone, dolomite, and sandstone. The fossils preserved in the Ordovician limestones and dolomites (carbonate-rich rocks) include stromatolitic algae (mound building), snails, echinoderms, sponges, crinoids, cephalopods (octopuslike), brachiopods, and trilobites. Manitou Limestone (a dolomitic limestone), named for its type locality near the town of Manitou Springs, is believed to have been deposited in vast subtidal mudflats that surrounded the emergent highlands of the Transcontinental Arch; the carbonate-rich sediments that made up these mudflats were produced largely by the bottom-dwelling organisms (benthos) that proliferated in the warm, shallow waters. Extensive exposures of this red to light-gray limestone form the lowermost portions of Cave of the Winds (near Manitou Springs) and can be seen on the fault-riddled slopes above Aspen, at the mouth of Trout Creek Canyon, and in canyons near the towns of Glenwood Springs, Wellsville, and Leadville.

Harding Sandstone, composed primarily of gray to reddish sandstone and layers of greenish brown shale, formed over a span of at least 35 million years and reflects receding seas and widespread erosion, probably in an estuarine environment. This formation is extremely fossil rich and has produced an astonishing diversity of marine animals. In 1887, the paleontologist Charles Walcott discovered the bony armor plates of a bottom-feeding fish (an *Astraspis*) in the Harding Quarry near Cañon City The jawless fishes (Agnathids), of which *Astraspis* is a member, are of particular importance because they are thought to be one of the Earth's first vertebrates. Tiny fossils called conodonts are also present in great quantities in Harding Sandstone. These brown, toothlike fossils come from the mouth region of an unknown marine animal, possibly resembling a lamprey eel, and are used by geologists as index fossils for stratigraphic correlation and as a tool for oil exploration. The best exposures of the Harding Sandstone can be seen at Phantom Canyon near Florence and at Crestone.

Following deposition of Harding Sandstone, the sea deepened locally and the massive amounts of Frémont Limestone were deposited. This gray, crystalline limestone formed during the most widespread submergence to which North America has ever been subjected. Frémont Limestone contains an amazing assortment of fossils, including hornlike cephalopods, giant ancestors of the modern chambered nautilus, which attained peak numbers during this time.

Silurian Period (443 to 417 Million Years Ago)

Sea levels rose dramatically in the Southern Rockies during the Silurian, but geologists believe that the rock record for this time was completely stripped away by erosion. The only known Silurian rocks, as well as the only evidence that seas covered the region during this time, are blocks of fossiliferous limestone preserved when gaseous explosions in a Devonian-age volcanic pipe (a diatreme) incorporated blocks of the overlying Silurian-age limestone in an erosion-resistant kimberlite breccia. These unique igneous rocks contain large fragments of Silurian limestone and are found only in the northern Colorado Front Range near the Wyoming border, the only known Silurian rocks for 300 miles in any direction.

Devonian Period (417 to 354 Million Years Ago)

By the early Devonian, the seas had largely withdrawn from the region of the Southern Rockies. To the east and west of North America's stable interior craton, mountain ranges developed along the continental margins as a result of tectonic activity associated with plate movement. For the first time since the Paleozoic began, sediments that had eroded from these uplifts were swept toward the center of the continent rather than away from it. During much of the Devonian, the Southern Rockies were situated just a little above sea level. By late Devonian time, however, embayments of a western seaway covered large portions of the central Southern Rockies. The changing climates and landscapes of the Devonian provided the impetus for the colonization of land by the vertebrates.

Interlayered beds of soft shales, fossiliferous limestones, and quartz-rich sandstones dominate the Devonian rock record in the Southern Rockies. Marine fossil assemblages in these rocks continue to reflect the region's proximity to the equatorial zone. In northern and central Colorado, the Devonian is represented by the Chaffee Group, which is subdivided into two well-defined units: Parting Sandstone and Dyer Dolomite. Parting Sandstone is recognized by the predominance of quartz and by the inclusion of thin layers, or partings, of shale. The distinctive Dyer Dolomite beds of the White River Plateau are highly fossiliferous and can be identified by their wavy laminations of dolomite and quartz sand; these dolomite beds offer some of the best fossil collecting to be found in the Southern Rockies. The thin-bedded limestone and shale of the Chaffee Formation can be seen at Deep Creek Canyon on the White River Plateau and near the eastern entrance of Glenwood Canyon, where the rock forms greenish gray slopes and ledges below the massive Mississippian-age Leadville Limestone.

In southwestern Colorado, Devonian strata are represented by the

Elbert Formation and the younger Ouray Limestone. The Elbert Formation, made up of sandstones, dolomites, and shales deposited in vast intertidal mudflats, can be seen along Elbert Creek between Coal Bank Pass and Rockwood (on U.S. 550); the shaley beds of the formation contain abundant evidence of stromatolites (fossil algal mounds) and evaporative salt crusts. The most spectacular exposure of Devonian sandstone overlies steeply dipping Precambrian strata in Box Canyon Park near Ouray (see page 78). Exposures of fossiliferous, burrow-riddled Ouray Limestone can be seen at the mouth of Canyon Creek on the outskirts of Ouray.

Mississippian Period (354 to 323 Million Years Ago)

Sea level peaked dramatically throughout the region of the Southern Rockies during the early Mississippian. For the first time since the start of the Paleozoic, tropical seas covered much of northern New Mexico, leaving the Precambrian quartzite highlands comprising Pecos Baldy, Truchas, and Chimayosos peaks (southern Sangre de Cristos) as islands in the advancing sea. A great diversity of marine animals—mollusks, corals, brachiopods, and crinoids—flourished in the clear, warm seas. The period has been called the Age of Crinoids because of the fossilized concentrations of these flowerlike animals in Mississippian limestone beds.

Throughout the Rocky Mountains, and from western and central Canada southwestward into Arizona, shallow-water carbonate sedimentation resulted in the formation of massive, cliff-forming beds of gray limestone. In the Southern Rockies, the most important and widespread of these Mississippian limestones are collectively referred to as the Leadville Limestone Formation; this formation can be traced into the subsurface of the Paradox Basin (in southwestern Colorado and southeastern Utah), the Four Corners region (where Colorado, Utah, Arizona, and New Mexico meet), and in the Grand Canyon, where it is known as Redwall Limestone.

In the Southern Rockies, good exposures of Leadville Limestone can be seen at the Rockwood Quarry north of Durango (along U.S. 550), at the eastern entrance to Glenwood Canyon (along I-70), on the slopes of West Aspen Mountain at Aspen, in the Eagle Park area north of Tennessee Pass (along U.S. 24), near Trout Creek Pass (on U.S. 285), east of Monarch Pass

(U.S. 50), along the South Fork of the White River, in Arkansas Canyon (near Wellsville), and in Rifle Box Canyon near Rifle (Colorado 325). The greatest concentration of caves in Colorado is found in the Leadville Limestone layer of the White River Plateau; Groaning Cave, located near Deep Creek Canyon, is thought to be the most extensive cave in the state, with an estimated twelve miles of passageways.

Elsewhere in the Southern Rockies, Mississippian limestones include Madison Limestone in northern Colorado and southern Wyoming, Williams Canyon Limestone near Colorado Springs, Hardscrabble Limestone and Beulah Limestone along the eastern flank of the Wet Mountains and the southern Front Range, the Tererro Formation in the Sangre de Cristos near Santa Fe, and the Arroyo Penasco Formation in the Nacimiento Mountains. Tererro Limestone can be seen in the bluffs along the Pecos River near the town of Tererro; a cave in the limestone cliff opposite the Tererro post office figures prominantly in Pecos Pueblo legends and may also be the cave referred to by Willa Cather in her novel *Death Comes for the Archbishop*.

During the late Mississippian, renewed tectonic activity along the Transcontinental Arch resulted in the reemergence of highlands in the Southern Rockies. Erosion intensified with the recession of the seas, and much of the rock record for the late Mississippian seems to have disappeared. The climate was humid, and the surface of the Leadville Limestone underwent extensive solution weathering, resulting in a cavernously pitted and channeled erosion surface; geologists use the term *karst* to refer to this type of erosional weathering in limestone. Distinctive karst topography is visible along the upper surface of Leadville Limestone in Glenwood Canyon, in Rifle Box Canyon, and at a number of localities in central Colorado and northern New Mexico. Weathering of the limestone has caused a rich red soil to develop, accumulating to depths of up to seventy-five feet on the karst surface in certain areas. Remnants of this fossil soil, called the Molas Formation, are best preserved in southwestern Colorado and are conspicuous in road cuts near Molas Lake in the San Juan Mountains (along U.S. 550), where the highway crosses the karst surface; the formation can also be seen along the rim of Rockwood Quarry north of Durango. Geologists suggest that Molas Lake and several nearby ponds actually fill hollows in the karst surface.

Pennsylvanian Period (323 to 290 Million Years Ago)

The Pennsylvanian period began with the return of shallow seas to the land, but the first rumbles of mountain building were just beginning to be felt in the Southern Rockies. While the rest of the North American continent experienced rising sea levels along its margins, tectonic activity intensified in the Southern Rockies during middle Pennsylvanian time, culminating in the uplift of two north-south-trending mountain ranges, the Ancestral Rocky Mountains, about 300 million years ago.

The Rise of the Ancestral Rockies

The origins of the Ancestral Rockies, like the present-day Southern Rockies, are enigmatic in terms of plate-tectonic theory because they were located in the middle of the North American craton, nearly 900 miles from plate margins. The tectonic quiescence that characterized the central portion of the craton throughout the early Paleozoic ended dramatically with the first of a series of continental collisions along the southern margin of the North American Plate; these collisions concluded, ultimately, with the formation of the Permian supercontinent Pangaea. Geologists currently believe that the rise of the Ancestral Rockies was triggered by the collision of the North American Plate with the South American–African Plate along the southern margin of North America. The progressive collision-suturing of these

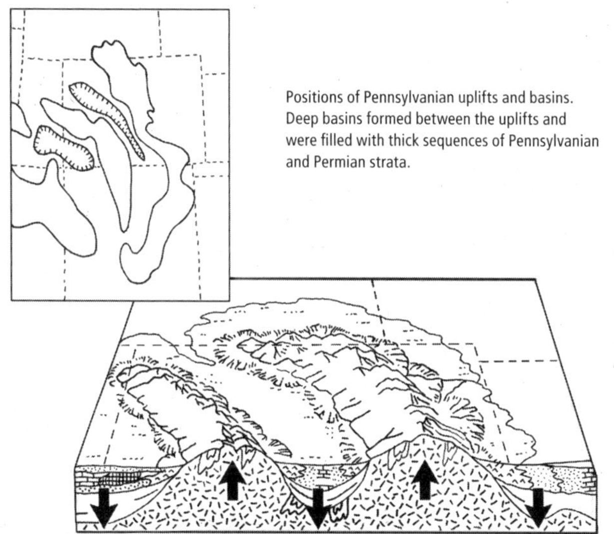

Positions of Pennsylvanian uplifts and basins. Deep basins formed between the uplifts and were filled with thick sequences of Pennsylvanian and Permian strata.

continental plates is believed to have sent waves of tectonic activity northwestward to encompass a southwestern peninsular projection of the North American craton; this region, which includes much of northwestern Texas, New Mexico, northeastern Arizona, Colorado, and southeastern Wyoming, was subsequently wrenched, pushed northwestward, and intensely deformed as the collision progressed.

In the Southern Rockies, Pennsylvanian events included dramatic block-fault mountain building and the development of actively subsiding basins, or down-dropped blocks, between the rising mountain blocks. In certain areas, mountain-building activity resulted in as much as 10,000 feet of relief. The uplifts that created the Ancestral Rockies were concentrated along two main belts. The eastern belt of uplift, called Frontrangia, essentially parallels the present-day Front Range, but was offset to the west of the modern mountain front by some thirty to fifty miles. The northern prong of Frontrangia extended into Wyoming, where it is known as the Pathfinder Uplift. The southern end of the uplift extended into New Mexico, where it is known as the Sierra Grande Uplift. The western belt of uplift, called Uncompahgria, extended from the present-day Nacimiento Mountains northwest along the western edge of the San Luis Valley to Colorado National Monument, including the area of the Black Canyon of the Gunnison and the Uncompahgre Plateau. The ranges of the Ancestral Rockies are roughly coincident with the modern or Cenozoic features of the Front, Gore, Park, Sawatch, southern Mosquito, and northern Sangre de Cristo ranges, the Wet Mountains, Las Animas Arch, and the Uncompahgre, Apishapa, and Sierra Grande uplifts.

During the early stages of tectonic activity, shallow seas invaded the region from the southeast and northwest, depositing marine sediments into the basins that adjoined the mountain uplifts. The most important of these basins, a deep and narrow trough known as the Central Colorado Trough, extended from northwestern Colorado to south-central Colorado between the major mountain belts. Between 10,000 and 20,000 feet of Pennsylvanian and Permian strata of both marine and nonmarine origins accumulated within the trough, recording a long history of marine transgression from the northwest. Pennsylvanian-age basins were roughly coincident with the following present-day basins: Paradox, Denver, Piceance, Sand Wash, South

Park, Antero, Currant Creek, Wet Mountain Valley, Raton, and the San Luis–Rio Grande Valley.

The earliest basin-deposited sediments of the Pennsylvanian are the marine-transitional black shales and sandstones of the Glen Eyrie Formation (outcropping near Colorado Springs) and Belden Formation of the Central Colorado Trough. Exposures of Belden Formation can be seen in Arkansas Canyon (near Wellsville), near Trout Creek Pass, in Glenwood Canyon (along I-70), between Tennessee Pass and Minturn (on U.S. 24), and in road cuts south of Antero junction (on U.S. 285). The variegated gray, green, and brown strata of the Minturn Formation overlie the Belden Formation and represent a complex sequence of marine, transitional, and nonmarine sediments deposited in the trough and along the western edge of Frontrangia; excellent exposures of the Minturn Formation (such as the 200-foot-high banded cliffs near Minturn) can be seen between Tennessee Pass and Minturn and in Arkansas Canyon (near Wellsville). A Pennsylvanian algal "reef" forms the Lionshead above Minturn. The Madera Formation, extending from south-central Colorado into northern New Mexico and correlative with the Minturn Formation, consists largely of gray-green sandstones and interbedded black shales, reflecting the cyclic deposition of marine and nonmarine sediments in a coastal mudflat or delta; exposures of this formation are prominent in the northern Sangre de Cristo Range near Orient and at Crestone.

Within the center of the Central Colorado Trough, between the towns of Avon and Gypsum, thick sequences of interbedded gypsum, anhydrite, halite, black shale, and siltstone are well exposed in bluffs along the Eagle River. These evaporite rocks formed in a warm, arid climate and are derived from thousands of feet of gypsum, salt, and potash precipitated from the brackish waters left behind by the evaporation of a narrow seaway. The most extensive concentration of gypsum and other evaporites anywhere in the Southern Rockies is a deposit totaling 7,500 feet near the town of Gypsum. The evaporite rocks of the Central Colorado Trough have undergone extensive deformation, as is visible along the Eagle River west of Gypsum; landforms developed in these areas are characterized by bedding that has been highly contorted and folded, largely because of gypsum's ability to flow in a solid state. Soils derived from the weathering of gypsum-rich shales create a growth environment that is extremely hostile to most plants.

Along the flanks of the Ancestral Rockies, sediments eroded from the granitic mountain blocks filled valleys and created braided alluvial (water-deposited) debris fans and cone-shaped alluvial fans known as bajadas. Thick sequences of nonmarine gravels and sand, from 7,000 to 12,000 feet in some areas, consolidated to form colorful "redbeds" in many areas of the Southern Rockies. Because of the association of these redbeds with extensive sand dunes and evaporite rocks, geologists suggest that a warm and probably arid climate prevailed at the time of their formation.

The Pennsylvanian redbeds of the Southern Rockies include the colorful Fountain, Maroon, Sangre de Cristo, and Cutler formations. High-energy white-water rivers and streams flowing off the east slope of Frontrangia were undoubtedly the source of sediment for the feldspar-rich (arkosic) sandstones and conglomerates of the Fountain Formation; outcrops of this formation are well exposed in several scenic landmarks, including Boulder's Flatirons, Red Rocks Park (near Denver), and the Garden of the Gods (near Colorado Springs). The bright red shales and sandstones of the Maroon Formation, derived from sediments washed from Uncompahgria during Pennsylvanian and Permian time, are prominent along Maroon Creek and form the scenic Maroon Bells (Fourteeners located in the Elk Mountains); these sediments were deposited in a vast mudflat subjected to alternating wet and dry periods. In south-central Colorado and northern New Mexico, the dark red and grayish green sandstones, conglomerates, and shales of the Sangre de Cristo Formation were deposited on sunbaked mudflats crisscrossed by braided, sand-choked stream channels. A conglomeratic unit of the formation, the Crestone Conglomerate, forms the Crestone Needle and extends to Eureka Mountain; other outcrops can be seen at La Veta Pass (U.S. 160), Huerfano Park, and along the serrated ridge east of Blanca Peak. In southwestern Colorado, the Pennsylvanian-Permian Cutler Formation of the Hermosa Group was deposited along the western flank of Uncompahgria; outcrops form the cliffs along the Animas River Canyon and the striking redbeds just beneath the rhyolite cap of Engineer Mountain (along U.S. 550 at Coal Bank Pass).

Permian Period (290 to 251 Million Years Ago)

Lower Permian sedimentary rocks record the continued erosion of the Ancestral Rockies and their subsequent burial in their own debris. The fossil-poor, arkosic redbeds laid down during this time are similar to those of the Pennsylvanian, making determination of the stratigraphic boundary between the Pennsylvanian and Permian difficult. Moving away from the uplifts, finer-textured units of the Fountain, Sangre de Cristo, Cutler, and Maroon formations continued to accumulate in stream channels, ephemeral lakes, and intertidal environments. Basin sediments are predominately carbonate and evaporite rocks, reflecting a continued trend toward aridity and stagnating seas.

By middle Permian times, terrestrial sedimentation had slowed and shallow seas once again invaded the region from the west and the east. Coastal dune fields built of sand swept south from the Wyoming Arch (central Wyoming) spread along the flanks of the eroded uplifts, stabilizing in front of the advancing Permian sea. One of these ancient dune fields formed along the northwestern margin of Uncompahgria and is preserved as the Weber Formation; outcrops of this massive sandstone are especially prominent in Dinosaur National Monument, on the White River Plateau, and near the towns of McCoy and Wolcott. Several large dune fields developed along the northern flanks of Frontrangia and are preserved as part of the Lyons Sandstone, which is named for its type locality near the city of Lyons. This beautiful buff to reddish quartz-rich sandstone outcrops in a number of localities along the northern Front Range and has been widely used as a building stone by the University of Colorado at Boulder and by a great many commercial contractors and home builders.

By the end of the Permian period, all the continents had coalesced to form the supercontinent Pangaea. Lasting for nearly 150 million years, this grouping of continental blocks stretched from pole to pole and was surrounded by an enormous interconnected ocean. Arid and semiarid conditions prevailed, decimating the tropical jungles that had prospered in certain localities since the Mississippian. These radical changes exerted adaptive pressures on inhabitants of both land and sea. Amphibians were forced to give way to the reptiles, whose adaptability to dry, terrestrial environments foreshadowed their coming days of grandeur during the Mesozoic. Large, carnivorous pelycosaur reptiles such as *Sphenacodon* or the sail-back "lizard" *Dimetrodon* represent the most common genera collected from Permian deposits in New Mexico. The appearance of these therapsid reptiles during the Permian is important because it is from this stock that mammals eventually evolved.

Permian Extinctions

The explosion of life at the start of the Paleozoic contrasts sharply with the mass extinctions of the late Permian, the most profound of several mass extinctions that occurred over the last 600 million years. At least half the known families of both marine and terrestrial animals died out within the span of a few million years. The victims of the Permian extinctions were primarily marine organisms, including the trilobites, all ancient coral species, all but one lineage of ammonites, all fusulinid foraminifera, and most bryozoans and crinoids. By the close of the Permian, 75 percent of the amphibian families and more than 80 percent of the reptile families had disappeared. Paleontologists now suggest that widespread habitat destruction resulting from the coalescing of the continents to form Pangaea and the associated withdrawal of shallow seas greatly reduced ecological space and sentenced species unable to adapt to changing conditions to extinction.

Outcrops of Weber Formation delineate the giant meanders of the Yampa River in Dinosaur National Monument, Colorado.

CHAPTER FIVE

The Mesozoic: Rising from the Sea

When the Mesozoic began, the seas had withdrawn from large areas of the continents, and a desert climate prevailed over much of the Earth. The Mesozoic era embraces three distinctly different periods: the Triassic, Jurassic, and Cretaceous. Widely known as the Age of Dinosaurs, the Mesozoic witnessed the triumph of the ruling reptiles (Archosauria)—birds, dinosaurs, and crocodilians—and their adaptive radiation into every ecological niche available to advanced vertebrates. The Mesozoic fossil record of the Southern Rockies is world famous and startling in its diversity. Of the fourteen reptilian orders present during the Mesozoic, only four survive today, and only two of these, the order Testudines (turtles) and the order Squamata (snakes and lizards), are found in the region's modern ecosystems.

Triassic Period (251 to 206 Million Years Ago)

Triassic geologic history reflects the beginning of the breakup of the supercontinent Pangaea. Throughout much of the period, Pangaea lay above sea level, resulting in persistent warm, dry climatic conditions and land-based rather than marine sedimentation. By the middle of the Triassic, continental drift had resulted in a more equal distribution of the Earth's continents between the Northern and Southern hemispheres. In fact, many of the climatic shifts that have occurred since Triassic time can be explained by plate motions and the changing configuration of lands and seas.

In the Southern Rockies, the Triassic palette is rich in the hues of red, maroon, and pink. The soft, fine-textured sandstones and shales that characterize the Triassic redbeds were deposited in mudflats, on alluvial plains, and in dune fields adjacent to the eroding highlands. Formation names differ from one area to another—Chugwater, Lykins, Moenkopi, Dolores, Chinle—but the sediments deposited throughout much of the Triassic are remarkably similar in composition and easy to identify.

Triassic through Jurassic stratigraphic sequence north of Abiquiu, New Mexico. The uppermost gray layer is Todilto Limestone; the paler layer directly below is Entrada Sandstone; the lower, interbedded sandstones and shales are Triassic-age Chinle Formation.

In southern Wyoming, the redbeds of the Triassic Chugwater and Jelm formations can be seen west of Laramie along the eastern flank of Centennial Valley (along Wyoming 130). Triassic redbeds are well exposed at several localities along the western edge of the Southern Rockies. In the San Juan Mountains, the stream-deposited reddish brown shales and interbedded sandstones of the Dolores Formation are prominent just north of Durango (along U.S. 550), between Dolores and Rico (along Colorado 145), west of Telluride (along Colorado 145), and approximately five miles north of Ouray (along U.S. 550). In north-central New Mexico, west of the Sangre de Cristos, the stream- and lake-deposited sandstones and shales that constitute the Chinle Formation are overlain by the dune-deposited, cliff-forming Wingate Sandstone (Jurassic-age); exposures of these formations can be seen at several localities north of Abiquiu (along U.S. 64/84). To the northwest, rocks of the Chinle Formation contribute to the spectacular scenery of Colorado National Monument, Unaweep Canyon, and the canyon of the Dolores River.

By the end of the Triassic, the archosaurs had given rise to the two great orders of dinosaurs: the Saurischia (lizardlike pelvic structures) and the Ornithischia (birdlike pelvic structures). Skeletons of one of the earliest of the Triassic dinosaurs, a small birdlike predator called *Coelophysis*, were first discovered in the red shales of the Chinle Formation at Ghost Ranch near Abiquiu, in northern New Mexico; the fossils are unique in that the dense concentration of skeletons at the site represents every stage of growth, from juvenile to adult. Weighing less than fifty pounds and with an upright stance, hollow, birdlike bones, and long, slender tail, *Coelophysis* filled somewhat the same niche as the modern roadrunner of the Southwest deserts. The dryland environment in which *Coelophysis* lived supported nearly 400 species of plants. Conifers flourished in the moister sites, joined by tree ferns, cycads, true ferns, and scouring rushes. Primitive twelve-foot-long crocodile-like reptiles prowled the waterways, and amphibians and mammal-like reptiles sought cover in the weedy understory and floodplain ponds.

At the close of the Triassic, the suture zones holding Pangaea together weakened and then failed, allowing several of the continents to pull apart; Africa and South America remained joined until Cretaceous time, but South America separated from North America during the Jurassic. North America–Europe moved in a northwesterly direction, the western margin of North America becoming the leading edge of the westward-drifting plate. From the late Triassic onward, the physical evolution of the continents and ocean basins has been influenced by tectonic events associated with plate collisions and rifting initiated by the progressive breakup of Pangaea.

Jurassic Period (206 to 144 Million Years Ago)

The Jurassic rocks of western North America record geologic events initiated by the separation of the North American and European plates and by a major shift in the direction of plate motions. The divergence of these two plates occurred along a rift that eventually evolved to form the Atlantic Ocean. Seafloor spreading along the trend of this ancient rift zone, now part of the Mid-Atlantic Ridge, intensified the westward movement and clockwise rotation of the North American Plate. Similar seafloor spreading occurred in the Pacific, along the East Pacific Rise, sending the eastern Pacific Plate (the Farallon Plate) scudding eastward on a collision course with the westward-moving North American Plate. The western margin of North America underwent massive deformation and volcanism as the two plates collided, the oceanic plate diving (or subducting) obliquely beneath the overriding continental plate. Wave after wave of tectonic activity swept eastward from the western continental margin. The mountain building that resulted from these compressional tectonic movements, known collectively as the Cordilleran Orogeny, occurred almost continuously from the late Jurassic into the early Cenozoic.

East of the present-day Sierra Nevada Range of California, the basic geologic framework of the north-south, asymmetrical Western Interior Basin had developed by earliest Jurassic time. In the Southern Rockies, the first of four transgressions by the Ancestral Arctic Ocean entered the region from the north, along the trend of the basin. This Jurassic seaway, known as the Sundance Sea, was limited in its southern and eastern extent by persistent highlands that paralleled the former Transcontinental Arch and the Uncompahgria region of the Ancestral Rockies. The pattern of these uplifts influenced the overall distribution of Jurassic sediments throughout the region. Full marine conditions were never uniformly widespread in the Southern Rockies during the Jurassic, and the sedimentary record for this period reflects the cyclic transgression and regression of the Sundance Sea. A gradual change to a maritime climate accompanied the advances of the Ancestral Arctic Ocean.

The earliest Jurassic rocks of the Southern Rockies—the Wingate, Navajo, and Entrada—were formed from enormous dune deposits. Exposures of these cross-stratified, sometimes salmon-colored sandstones form smooth cliff faces: the slickrock scenery for which the Colorado Plateau is so famous. In the Southern Rockies, these formations are typically paler in color than those of the Colorado Plateau and interfinger with marine or saline-lake sediments such as the Todilto Limestone of southwestern Colorado and northwestern New Mexico. Striking exposures of the Todilto Limestone can be seen north of Abiquiu and Ghost Ranch (U.S. 64/84), where the limestone forms a gray cap above the buff-colored Entrada Sandstone and the reddish sandstones and shales of the Triassic Chinle Formation (see photo page 94). Conspicuous bands of the Entrada can be seen at Colorado National Monument, in Unaweep Canyon, south of Ridgway (along U.S. 550), between Lizard Head Pass and Rico (along Colorado 145), and north of Durango (along U.S. 550).

The final withdrawal of the Sundance Sea from the Western Interior Basin occurred in late Jurassic time and is best represented by the widespread, fossil-rich Morrison Formation of Wyoming, Utah, Colorado, and New Mexico. The thick sequences of mudstones, shales, and sandstones that make up this fine-textured formation were laid down on broad floodplains and in shallow lakes that developed following the sea's retreat. The distinctive variegated gray, green, and maroon colors of the Morrison are the result of both the reduction and oxidation of iron under conditions of poor drainage and by postdepositional alteration of the sediments by groundwater on better-drained sites.

The climate during the late Jurassic is believed to have been warm and seasonally dry. Plant fossils are abundant in the Morrison Formation and include the unusual conifer *Araucaria* (an ancient relative of the monkey puzzle tree found today in the southern Andes), ginkgos, cycads, tree ferns, club mosses, and some flowering plants. Exposures of the Morrison Formation can be seen at the interpretive geologic site at the I-70 road cut just west of Denver, near Morrison between Red Rocks Park and the Dakota Hogback, in Colorado National Monument, west of Glenwood Springs along I-70, at Como Bluff in Wyoming, and in the quarry exhibit area at Dinosaur National Monument.

Morrison sediments have yielded one of the richest dinosaur faunas in the world. The first discoveries of dinosaurs in the Morrison were made in 1877 near the towns of Morrison and Cañon City, attracting the attention of the world's paleontologists. Dinosaurs representing fifteen genera were subsequently collected and described from Morrison strata. The most common and famous of these were *Stegosaurus*, *Diplodocus*, *Apatosaurus* (formerly known as *Brontosaurus*), *Camptosaurus*, and *Camarasaurus*; giant predators *Ceratosaurus* and *Allosaurus* dominated the top of the Morrison pecking order. At Como Bluff, in southeastern Wyoming, Yale paleontologist O. C. Marsh made a second major discovery of Jurassic dinosaurs in the Morrison in 1878. Today, the most accessible of the Morrison dinosaur localities are those at Dinosaur National Monument. There, inside the Quarry Visitor Center, the ongoing excavation of a dinosaur-bone-rich cliff attracts thousands of visitors each year. In the Picketwire Canyonlands, along the Purgatoire River south of La Junta, paleontologist Martin Lockley and his fellow trackers have identified North America's largest assemblage of dinosaur trackways in an exposed limestone layer of the Morrison Formation; the Picketwire Dinosaur Tracksite comprises more than 1,300 tracks and 100 trackways. The U.S. Forest Service offers guided auto tours of Picketwire Canyonlands, including visits to the dinosaur tracksite as well as to many of the unique prehistoric, historic, and natural features of the canyons.

Sauropod trackway, Picketwire Dinosaur Tracksite.

Cretaceous Period (144 to 65 Million Years Ago)

The Cretaceous geologic history of the Southern Rockies reflects the interplay of tectonic forces and global changes in sea level. The uplift and igneous activity that characterized much of western North America at the close of the Jurassic intensified during the Cretaceous, progressing eastward in a more or less continuous wave of deformation through time. Geologists recognize three distinct belts of Cordilleran tectonism based on differences in timing and in the type of mountain building that occurred in each area: the Nevadan Orogeny (Jurassic) in California and western Nevada, the Sevier Orogeny (late Jurassic-Cretaceous) in western Utah and adjacent regions, which migrated eastward to encompass the present-day Basin and Range Province, and the Laramide Orogeny (Cretaceous-Tertiary), which encompassed the mountain areas of Montana, Wyoming, Colorado, and New Mexico.

Paleogeography of the Western Cretaceous Seaway.
Courtesy of Emmet Evanoff, after Kauffman, 1977

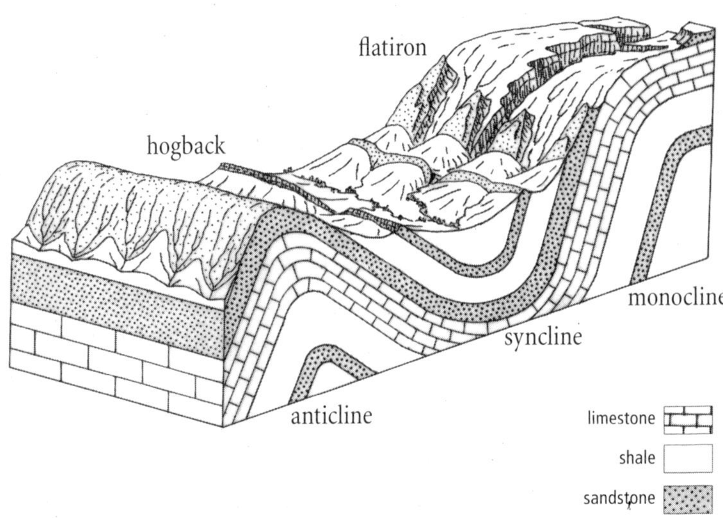

Folds and associated landforms in the Southern Rockies. Limestones are resistant to weathering in the dry climate and form steep canyon cliffs. Courtesy of Emmett Evanoff

Mountains rose in the Sevier orogenic belt to the west of the Southern Rockies, and sediments derived from these uplifts were carried eastward, accumulating in the Western Interior Basin. As the basin subsided, a vast cratonic seaway spread southward from the present-day Arctic Ocean to merge with the warm waters of the Gulf of Mexico. By late Cretaceous time, the Western Interior Seaway essentially divided North America into two large landmasses; at its maximum extent, the seaway was more than 600 miles wide. The seaway was generally oriented in a north-south direction, the shoreline shifting widely from east to west in concert with changes in sea level or in sediment influx. Cretaceous rocks were deposited in constantly changing marine and nonmarine settings, the dominance of one of these over the other alternating through time.

Throughout the region of the Southern Rockies, subtropical climatic conditions prevailed, nourishing forests that included conifers, fig, eucalyptus, ebony, palm, cycad, magnolia, and cypresslike trees. Better-drained highlands supported hardwood forests of oak, walnut, ash, sassafras, and birch, with lush understories of grape, bayberry, and ivy. The explosive development of the flowering plants is well documented during this time; although flowering plants are rare in lower Cretaceous strata, they make up at least 90 percent of the late Cretaceous plant fossils. Not surprisingly, these plants provided food for many groups of animals, including, in their first appearances, bees, wasps, and butterflies.

The oldest Cretaceous rocks in the Southern Rockies belong to the widespread and economically important Dakota Group. Rocks of this group are found in Utah, Montana, Wyoming, Colorado, New Mexico, North and South Dakota, Nebraska, Kansas, and the prairie provinces of Canada. The Dakota Group includes a complex series of clastic sediments derived under a warm-temperate to subtropical temperature regime, first from riverine, delta, and sand-beach environments and then from shallow-marine environments. Today, sandstones of the Dakota Group form a spectacular hogback ridge that can be traced along the eastern flank of the Southern Rockies for some 200 miles. Good viewpoints of these hogbacks are abundant along the Eastern Slope of the Colorado Front Range. One of the most interesting is Skyline Drive, which traverses a section of the Dakota hogback west of Cañon City.

Sandstones of the Dakota Group are often quite porous and permeable, serving as excellent reservoirs for oil and gas. Dakota rocks in the San Juan Basin of northeastern New Mexico and in the Four Corners area of Colorado continue to produce economically important quantities of petroleum. The basal layers of the Dakota Group include a distinctive chert-pebble conglomerate. Silica, derived from the alteration of the chert, has firmly cemented the sand grains together in some parts of the unit, forming a fine-grained gray to buff quartzite that was once highly prized by prehistoric peoples because it could be flaked into high-quality stone implements. The famous Spanish Diggings prehistoric stone quarries near Glendo, Wyoming, are located in a probable Dakota equivalent.

With the deepening of the seaway during the late Cretaceous, fine-textured limestones and shales were deposited in a wide variety of marine environments. Maximum inundation of the Western Interior Basin is marked by the deposition of Greenhorn Limestone, which reaches its greatest thickness in north-central Colorado; the depth of the water along the eastern margin of the seaway during the deposition of the Greenhorn has been estimated at approximately 1,000 feet. Between Pueblo and Walsenburg, gently tipped mesas, called cuestas, are capped by this resistant limestone and interbedded with darker layers of shale. Along the eastern portion of the seaway, the chalky shales and limestones of the Niobrara Formation were deposited in a shallow-water environment characterized by warm, tropical currents from the Gulf of Mexico. Typical Niobrara fossils include large corrugated-shelled clams, ammonites (related to modern octopi and chambered nautili), and small oysters in dense colonies.

In the deepest waters of the Western Interior Seaway, several thousand feet of marine mud accumulated on the seafloor. The distinctive marine deposits of the Pierre Shale, which are as much as a mile-and-a-half thick along the eastern flanks of the modern-day Southern Rockies, are typical of the Cretaceous shales that formed under these conditions. Pierre Shale is easy to recognize because of its gray-brown color and extremely fine texture. Good exposures are relatively rare because the shale tends to weather quickly. In some areas, the lower units of Pierre Shale are considerably darker and fossils of marine invertebrates are uncommon, suggesting that deep-water barren zones occurred periodically in response to sea-level changes. In most other units of Pierre Shale, fossil clams and ammonites, as well as the bones of fossil fish (sharks) and swimming reptiles, are abundant. Just north of Kremmling, a resistant sandstone unit caps towering bluffs of Pierre Shale. The Kremmling Cretaceous Ammonite Locality (administered by the BLM) may well be the most outstanding marine-fossil locality in the Southern Rockies; some fossil specimens of the giant ammonite *Placenticeras meeki* are two feet in diameter, and many retain the lustrous mother-of-pearl lining of the original shell. The diversity of marine fossils at the site includes more than a hundred species of mollusks, crabs, lobsters, and vertebrates such as fish and marine reptiles; the fossils of straight-shelled ammonites (baculites) may be found at the base of the bluffs. East of I-25, between Colorado Springs and Pueblo, hundreds of conical hills of resistant limestone, known as the Tepee Buttes, rise above the broad, gently undulating expanse of the Pierre Shale. These low hills are rich in marine fossils and appear to have formed as reeflike mounds on the muddy floor of the Cretaceous seaway.

Bluffs of Pierre Shale form a dramatic backdrop near Kremmling, Colorado.

Along the western margin of the Southern Rockies, the shales and sandstones of the Mancos Formation form grayish yellow, poorly vegetated badlands. The widespread Mancos Formation, deposited during roughly the same time interval and under the same circumstances as the Pierre Shale, is characterized by a variable sequcnce of interbedded silty to sandy shales and thinly bedded sandstones dotted with occasional nodules of limestone. Some of the best exposures of this formation can be seen near Grand Junction (along I-70) and surrounding the towns of Cortez, Mancos, and Durango, Colorado, and Cuba, New Mexico. Swelling clays in the Mancos Formation cause it to expand when wet, making it an unsuitable substrate for roads or buildings.

With the onset of tectonic activity during the late Cretaceous, marine waters receded to the north and east. Along the western margin of the Southern Rockies, sediments of the nonmarine Mesaverde Group were deposited in sandy beach, river delta, and swamp environments. Mesaverde Group sandstones often intertongue with the marine, fossil-bearing Mancos Formation; Mesaverde sandstones are fairly easy to recognize because of their tan color and tendency to develop honeycomblike weathering cavities. A spectacular ridge of Mesaverde Sandstone called the Grand Hogback extends along the southern margin of the White River Plateau; just as the Dakota Hogback creates the eastern margin of the Southern Rockies, the Grand Hogback delineates the western boundary of the Southern Rockies and the beginning of the Colorado Plateau.

Extensive deposits of low-sulphur bituminous coal are widespread in the Mesaverde Group and result from the accumulation of organic matter in the marshes and lagoons that formed behind the sand-barrier islands paralleling the shores of marine embayments. Good exposures of coal-bearing Mesaverde strata can be seen along the trend of the Grand Hogback, along the Colorado River near De Beque, near Oak Creek, south of Hayden, and near Redstone. Along the eastern margin of the retreating sea, sand beach and bar deposits formed the distinctive Fox Hills Sandstone and the overlying, interbedded sands and coal units of the Laramie Formation. This pattern of clastic deposits and interbedded coal units characterizes late Cretaceous rocks throughout the Rocky Mountains. Coal deposits in the San Juan, Raton, Piceance, Uinta, North Park, and Green River basins rank among the most economically important in the West.

Laramide Orogeny and the Rise of the Southern Rockies

Beginning approximately 70 million years ago, the long history of subsidence and deposition that had characterized the Western Interior Basin came to an end with the Laramide Orogeny and the rise of the Southern

Rockies. To the west, the Sevier Orogeny was drawing to a close. What, then, triggered this final phase of Cordilleran Orogeny so far inland from plate margins? Theories abound, but the facts remain elusive. Some geologists propose a plate-tectonic origin, suggesting that the Laramide orogenic phase was coincident with, and probably caused by, a long interval of high-speed convergence of the Pacific seafloor and North American plates. Their argument is supported by a well-documented increase in the rate of spreading along the Mid-Atlantic Ridge during this time, which would have greatly accelerated the westerly movement of the North American Plate and increased the velocity of its impact with the northeast-moving Pacific Plate. This acceleration is postulated to have caused a flattening of the angle by which the seafloor plate subducted beneath the continent. As a result, the tectonic effects of the impact were redirected along a more horizontal trajectory, ultimately triggering the eastward-moving wave of deformation that would envelop the Rocky Mountain region. In response to this new wave of tectonism, the Colorado Plateau, acting as a discrete unit of the continent and largely undeformed by the Cordilleran Orogeny, is believed to have rotated slightly in a clockwise direction and moved northward, exerting additional compression and shearing stress along its eastern boundary with the Southern Rockies.

The intense structural deformation that characterized the Laramide Orogeny produced mountain uplifts and deep bordering basins from Montana to northern Mexico along the entire Rocky Mountain chain. In the Southern Rockies, the Laramide uplifts rose vertically as narrow, mostly north-south-trending anticlines (upfolds) transfigured by block faulting and elevating the once flat-lying layers of sedimentary rock like rippled blankets across the Precambrian basement. Down-dropped blocks and synclines (downfolds) developed concurrently between the mountain uplifts and were rapidly filled with sediments eroded from the rising folds. Igneous intrusions and volcanic activity occurred in conjunction with the uplifts along a northeast-trending zone that essentially defines the Colorado Mineral Belt. Once begun, uplift and igneous activity, accompanied by intense periods of erosion, continued well into the Cenozoic era.

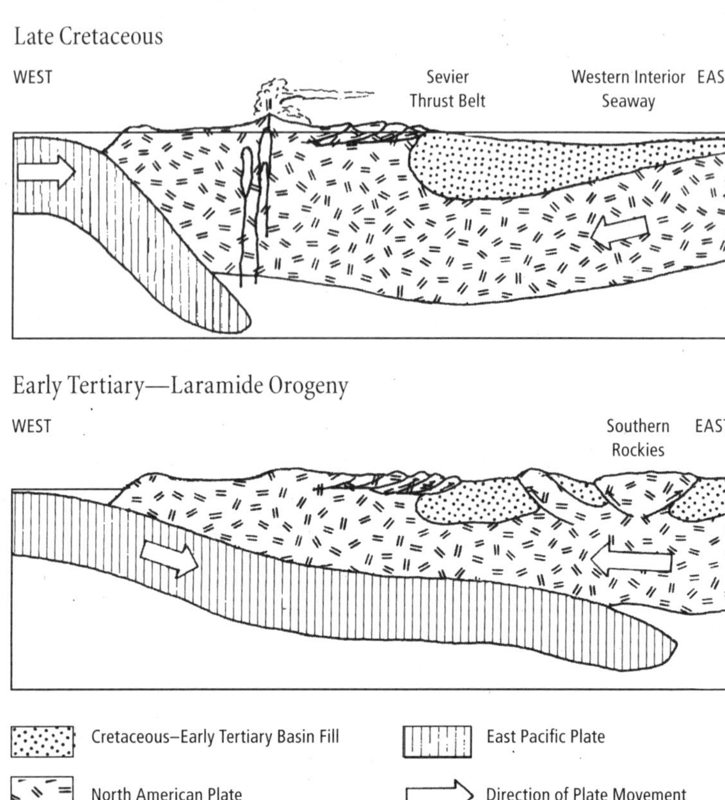

Plate tectonic model for Laramide Orogeny. Courtesy of Emmett Evanoff

Laramide tectonism was not synchronous throughout the Southern Rockies. The earliest uplift activity began in the Sawatch–San Luis highland and the Wet Mountains and spread outward as an irregular orogenic "front." Rejuvenation of the late Paleozoic Front Range highland followed, producing the Front, Park, and Gore ranges and the Medicine Bow Mountains. North, Middle, and South parks formed as structural sags in the former Front Range highland. The locations and orientations of the Laramide uplifts reflect preexisting Precambrian and Paleozoic tectonic features and in many cases correspond to the trend of the major Precambrian fault systems. The only major uplifts in the Southern Rockies that lack a pre-Laramide expression are the Sangre de Cristo Range, the White River Plateau, and the

Needle Mountains, all of which lie along the trend of the Paleozoic Central Colorado Trough.

Erosion kept pace with the Laramide uplifts, and sediments deposited in basins such as the Denver, Raton, San Juan, and Piceance provide geologists with a detailed record of the sequence of Laramide events. Older and older sedimentary layers were successively stripped from the crests of the anticlines until their Precambrian cores were exposed. The Gore Range is unusual in that fragments of some of the sedimentary rocks that once arched across the Precambrian core of this uplift can still be seen along the crest of the range. The Dakota and Grand hogbacks are representative of the steeply upturned sedimentary rocks that form the sides of the Laramide anticlines. At the close of the Cretaceous, the major uplifts and basins of the Southern Rockies were largely in place, awaiting their exhumation and finishing touches during the Cenozoic.

The K-T Boundary and Late Cretaceous Extinctions

For decades, the world's geologists pondered the origin of a thin, discontinuous layer of iridium-rich claystone: the K-T boundary layer. This distinctive sedimentary anomaly occurs at scattered locations around the world and marks the end of the Cretaceous (abbreviated as K) and the beginning of the Tertiary (T), the end of the Age of Dinosaurs and the start of the Age of Mammals. Below the K-T layer, the fossil record details a remarkable diversity and abundance of plant and animal species; above the K-T boundary, species diversity and abundance drop off sharply, and dinosaurs disappear from the fossil record altogether. Roughly 50 percent of all plant and animal genera disappeared from the land and from the oceans. What could have triggered a mass extinction of such colossal magnitude?

In the 1940s, the first exposure of the K-T boundary layer was discovered and described on South Table Mountain (west of Denver), and the race to solve one of the great geologic mysteries of all time was underway. Geologists shifted their attention to southern Colorado and to the ancient coal swamp deposits near Trinidad (Raton Basin), believing that conditions favoring the preservation of the iridium-rich clays would be optimal in the swamps and quiet backwaters along the Cretaceous Interior Seaway. In fact, samples collected from the Trinidad K-T boundary site contain the highest concentration of iridium ever measured in continental rocks. Geologists have subsequently located exposures of this iridium-rich claystone in scattered sites around the world, wherever late Cretaceous sediments accumulated under conditions favoring optimal preservation of the iridium clays.

In the Southern Rockies, a dozen or so K-T boundary sites have been identified in southern Colorado and northern New Mexico; the Smithsonian Institution collected a two-and-a-half-ton sample from the K-T site south of Trinidad to put on display in Washington, DC. The best place to see the K-T layer in situ is at an interpretive stop along the Long Canyon Trail in Trinidad Lake State Park.

Iridium is a rare element in terrestrial rocks, but it's exceedingly common in meteorites (asteroids). How did finely pulverized rock from deep space end up in a Cretaceous-age swamp? And where did it come from? Microscopic examination of the K-T claystone from the Trinidad site and others around the world has revealed that the constituent minerals exhibit the telltale signs of having been "shocked," subjected to the extreme heat and pressure of a shock wave resulting from an explosion or from the movement of a supersonic body. In a 1980 paper in the journal *Science*, Luis Alvarez and his colleagues proposed that approximately 65 million years ago, an asteroid-sized object, a meteorite, struck the Earth and produced a molten ejecta cloud that circled the globe like a firestorm. According to the Alvarez theory, the global nature of the K-T boundary layer provides irrefutable evidence of the magnitude of the catastrophe and its potential impact on all life-forms.

Scientists have scoured the world looking for a meteorite impact crater of suitable size and age that would support Alvarez's extraterrestrial hypothesis. The search may finally be over, with scientific attention currently focused on a 90-mile-wide subsurface crater centered on the northwest coast of Mexico's Yucatán Peninsula. Geologists believe that an extraterrestrial body calculated to be at least six miles in diameter created the Chicxulub impact crater. It is difficult to imagine the devastation and the enormous clouds of pulverized rock debris that would have been launched into the Earth's atmosphere by an immense meteorite traveling at 50,000 to 100,000 miles per hour. The ejecta cloud produced upon impact would most likely have circled the globe, blocking out the sun, loading the atmosphere with sulfur aerosols (acid rain), baking the Earth's surface as a consequence of surging carbon dioxide levels, and sparking global wildfires. The far-reaching ecological effects of such a catastrophe, perhaps even intensified by later meteorite strikes, provides the best scenario to explain the Cretaceous-Tertiary extinctions.

The K-T boundary layer appears as a pale-colored, thin layer of iridium-rich claystone in this outcrop near Trinidad, Colorado.

CHAPTER SIX

The Cenozoic: The Age of Mammals

The Cenozoic era, coming just after the Cretaceous extinction and extending to the present day, is the best-known span of geologic time because so much remains on Earth of Cenozoic worlds. By the beginning of the Cenozoic, 65 million years ago, the last vestiges of the great inland seas had disappeared from the Rocky Mountain region. With the demise of the dinosaurs, mammals such as camels, rhinoceros, saber-toothed tigers, and mammoths were starting to fill previously occupied ecological niches. The Laramide Orogeny still rumbled across the land and would do so for another 25 million years. The stage was set for high geologic drama, an action epic with a complex script, unusual special effects, and numerous scene changes.

The Tertiary Period: Landscapes in Upheaval (65 to 1.8 Million Years Ago)

The Cenozoic era is divided into two very unequal periods, the Tertiary and the Quaternary; the Tertiary includes five epochs—the Paleocene, Eocene, Oligocene, Miocene, and Pliocene—and embraces all but the last 1.8 million years of the Cenozoic (the Quaternary). Much of the topography of our modern world—the outlines of the continents, the mountain ranges, and most of the major drainage patterns—reflect Tertiary events. The plants and animals that evolved during the Tertiary are the ancestors of our modern flora and fauna.

Geologic Map of the Southern Rockies

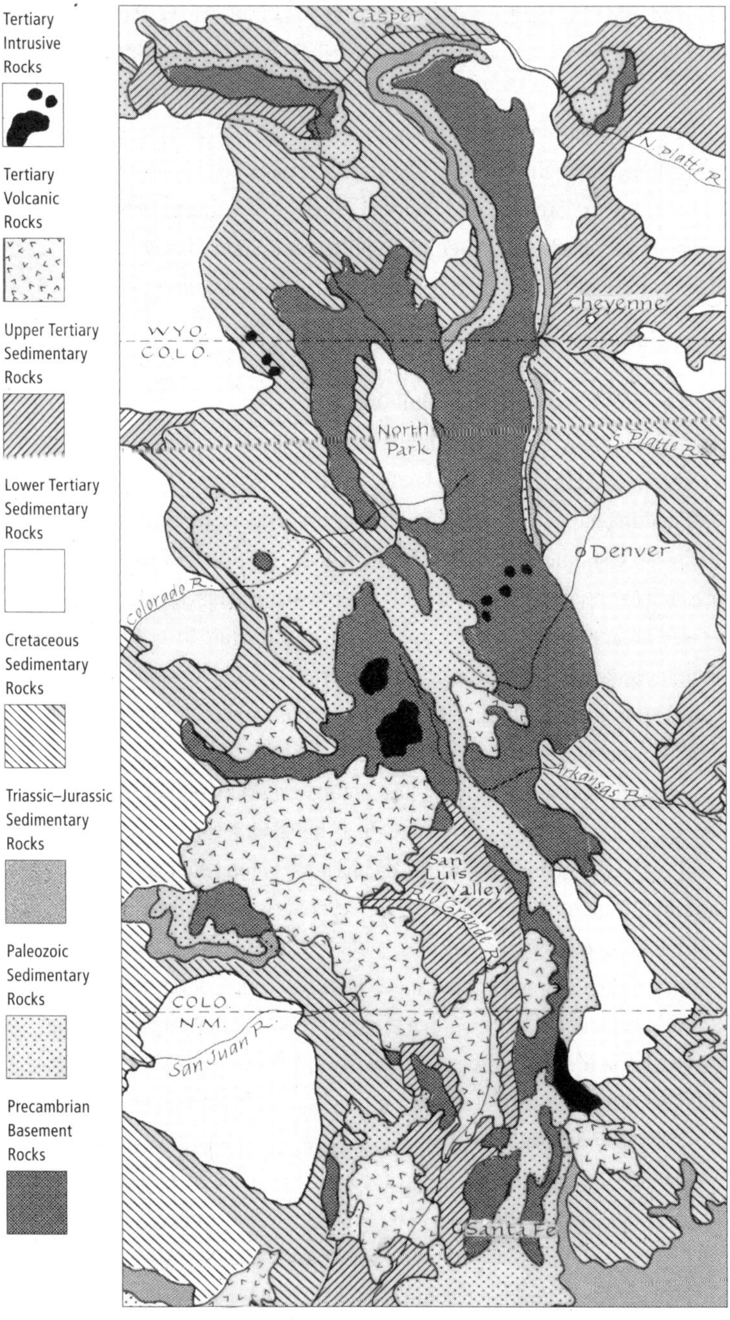

Tertiary Intrusive Rocks

Tertiary Volcanic Rocks

Upper Tertiary Sedimentary Rocks

Lower Tertiary Sedimentary Rocks

Cretaceous Sedimentary Rocks

Triassic–Jurassic Sedimentary Rocks

Paleozoic Sedimentary Rocks

Precambrian Basement Rocks

In the Southern Rockies, Tertiary geologic history can be conveniently divided into three stages: (1) early Tertiary Laramide events (Paleocene and Eocene epochs), which included mountain uplifts, pluton emplacement along the Colorado Mineral Belt, basin development, and erosion; (2) middle Tertiary post-Laramide events (late Eocene, Oligocene, and Miocene epochs), which were highlighted by tectonic quiescence and volcanism; and (3) late Tertiary events (Miocene and Pliocene epochs, extending into the Holocene), which included large-scale regional uplift, erosion and canyon cutting, development of the Rio Grande Rift, and late Cenozoic volcanism.

Laramide Events

Uplifts and Mountain Building

Evidence of the intensity and influence of Laramide tectonism is written in dramatic detail in the modern landscape. In the Southern Rockies, folding and faulting have acted singly and in concert to create the landforms we see today. For example, the majority of the region's north-south-trending ranges are faulted anticlines, linear uplifts whose structural fabric exhibits folding as well as faulting. In contrast, uplifts such as the White River Plateau, San Juan Mountains, and West Elks are comparatively simple domal uplifts cored with Laramide-age intrusive rocks and covered with a veneer of Oligocene and Miocene volcanics.

In the Southern Rockies, the amount of movement that has occurred along faults varies from a few inches to as much as several miles. In ranges such as the Colorado Front Range, displacement along fault zones is commonly measured in thousands of feet; a massive overthrust fault (where older rocks move horizontally over younger strata) delimits the southeastern margin of the Colorado Front Range, extending from Cheyenne Mountain to just north of Monument. Along this zone, Pikes Peak Granite and other Precambrian rocks have been thrust eastward, in some places for nearly a mile, over the Cretaceous sedimentary rocks of the Colorado Piedmont.

Fault zones, clusters of more or less parallel faults, have played a crucial role in landscape evolution and, in many areas, have controlled the development of valleys and determined the courses of certain rivers, such as the Colorado, Laramie, Rio Grande, and Arkansas. Most of the hot springs found in the Southern Rockies, such as those at Manitou Springs,

Glenwood Springs, Steamboat Springs, and Jemez Springs, emanate along major fault systems. Additionally, many of our mountain passes, such as Berthoud and Loveland, lie along fault zones that traverse the mountain crest. Recent fault-zone activity can be seen along the eastern margin of the San Luis Valley, where fault movement during the last few thousand years has produced a prominent fault scarp in the alluvial fans that flank the Sangre de Cristo Range; between Villa Grove and Great Sand Dunes National Park, erosion has caused this fault scarp to be segmented into a series of triangular facets, each with its base aligned parallel to the fault trace.

Igneous Intrusion and the Colorado Mineral Belt

Igneous intrusion and volcanism were closely associated with Laramide tectonism in the Southern Rockies. The joints and fractures that developed as a result of mountain building permitted mineral-rich solutions to move upward from magma sources deep within the Earth. During the early Tertiary, a series of pipelike intrusions (stocks) were emplaced along a northeast-southwest-trending zone that cut diagonally across the mountain uplifts extending from Durango to the eastern flank of the Colorado Front Range north of Boulder. These Laramide-age stocks are believed to be an expression of an underlying batholith or string of batholiths. Mineralization associated with these stocks and their associated dikes and sills was concentrated along a ten- to sixty-mile-wide zone known as the Colorado Mineral Belt.

Nearly all of the economically important gold, silver, lead, and zinc ore deposits in the Southern Rockies are located within the Colorado Mineral Belt. The only significant ore deposits located outside this mineralized zone are those of the Cripple Creek, Westcliffe–Silver Cliff, and Creede gold districts and the western Colorado vanadium and uranium districts. The famous mining districts and towns of Telluride, Silverton, Aspen, Leadville, Crested Butte, Fairplay, Breckenridge, Georgetown, Central City/Black Hawk, Jamestown, and a great many smaller towns, ghost towns, and mining camps are located along this productive belt.

The majority of ore deposits of the Colorado Mineral Belt can be placed into one of five basic categories: (1) Laramide-age and younger crack-and-fissure fillings in Precambrian rocks (like those in the Central City Mining District); (2) Tertiary vein, karst-fill, and replacement deposits in Paleozoic and younger sedimentary rocks (such as those in the Leadville Mining District); (3) molybdenum mineralization associated with mid-Tertiary porphyritic stocks (as found at the Climax Mine); (4) vein deposits in Tertiary volcanic rocks (such as those in the San Juan Mountains); and (5) placer-type deposits in Quaternary glacial and stream gravels (such as those at Fairplay and Breckenridge).

Though the quest for gold and silver dominated the early years of mining along the Colorado Mineral Belt, many of these same mines later gained a worldwide reputation for the gem-quality mineral crystals associated with the ore bodies, such as rhodochrosite, amazonite, and aquamarine. Exquisitely beautiful specimens of Colorado's state mineral, rhodochrosite, and the state gem, aquamarine, have attracted collectors and gemologists from around the world. Red rhodochrosite crystals from the Sweet Home Mine, near the town of Alma in central Colorado, are highly prized and have commanded prices up to $100,000. Ironically, miners during silver's heyday threw away or crushed many fine rhodochrosite crystals because the mineral fouled up the silver processing machinery at the mills. In addition to the Sweet Home, the best rhodochrosite specimens have come from mines south of Central City, the Henderson and Urad mines near Berthoud Pass, the Climax Mine near Leadville, and the American Tunnel Mine near Silverton. The best collecting localities for aquamarine, a clear, blue variety of beryl, are located at around 13,000 feet on Mount Antero and nearby Mount White.

Laramide Erosion and Basin Development

During Eocene time, coalescing alluvial (water-deposited) fans, or bajadas, formed along the margins of basins bordering the larger ranges of the Southern Rockies. Remnants of these debris aprons are preserved today as coarse-textured sedimentary rocks. Along the Eastern Slope of the Front Range, rivers and streams leaving the mountains and flowing across the eastern plains deposited vast quantities of erosional debris. These lowland-river and alluvial-fan deposits make up the Denver and Dawson formations and are as thick as 2,000 feet in some areas.

The Dawson Arkose, a coarse-grained sedimentary rock, formed from weathering products of the Pikes Peak batholith and, like other arkosic rocks, reflects the character of its granitic parent material. Good exposures of Dawson Arkose can be seen near the U.S. Air Force Academy in Colorado

Springs and in the nearby Black Forest area. In the Black Forest, the formation is of ecological interest because it supports an unusual eastern outlier of ponderosa pine that grows preferentially in the gravelly, feldspar-rich soils developed on the arkose. North of this area, a locally prominent Oligocene rock, the Castle Rock Conglomerate, forms the castle-shaped hill that gives the town of Castle Rock its name. This unusual conglomerate is a remnant of the broad valley fill cut into the Dawson Arkose and deposited by the Ancestral South Platte River where it emerged from the Rampart Range.

In south-central Wyoming, Eocene-age sediments derived from the Medicine Bow, Shirley, and Laramie mountains form a series of maroon-hued claystone beds in the Laramie and Shirley basin areas. Along the western flank of the Laramie Mountains, this distinctively variegated claystone contains deeply weathered cobbles and boulders of Sherman Granite, the 1.4-million-year-old granite that forms the core of the range. Near the Medicine Bow Mountains, the Eocene-age conglomerates contain cobbles of Medicine Peak Quartzite; this conglomerate forms massive outcrops near Kennaday Peak, on the north flank of the Medicine Bows, and in a series of well-defined hogbacks along the eastern flank of the range.

Along the western edge of the Southern Rockies, the shales that make up the Eocene-age Green River Formation formed in an immense lake-dotted basin that covered much of northeastern Utah, southwestern Wyoming, and northwestern Colorado. The Green River system accumulated such vast quantities of plant and animal detritus that the resultant shales constitute one of the world's largest oil shale reserves. The name *oil shale* is geologically misleading: the rock is actually classified as an organic marlstone (a mixture of clay and calcium carbonate), and the "oil" is actually kerogen, a precursor to oil. In the 6,000-square-mile Piceance Basin in northwestern Colorado, geologists estimate potential oil production from oil shale to be about 500 billion barrels, which is more than double the proven reserves of Saudi Arabia. Despite nearly a century of interest in using oil shale to produce oil, the development of an economically efficient extraction technology that minimizes the amount of water needed, reduces potential groundwater pollution, and also manages the volume of post-production waste remains elusive.

In addition to oil shale, the Piceance Basin contains one of the nation's most enormous reservoirs of natural gas. The U.S. Potential Gas Committee, an academic and industry-led group based at Colorado School of Mines, suggests that the Piceance Basin could well be the biggest natural gas field in North America, with total reserves of about 31 trillion cubic feet. As with many petroleum fields, extraction technology for natural gas is an evolving science frought with challenges created by the geologic character of the reservoir. The Piceance is no different. Conservationists caution, however, that rising oil and gas prices may drive development in the region before stringent environmental controls are in place. Energy industry players such as Shell Oil, Williams Energy, and Marathon Oil are already converging on the Piceance Basin in ever-increasing numbers. The infrastructure (roads, drill pads, etc.) required for exploration and extraction has already caused significant habitat fragmentation in many areas. The environmental costs to the once-pristine landscapes of the Piceance Basin hang in the balance.

Fossil animals and plants associated with the Green River Formation indicate warm-temperate to subtropical conditions, in sharp contrast to the desertlike climate that prevails in the area today. During the height of Eocene basin filling, the fauna of the Green River's marshy lowlands included crocodiles, alligators, boa constrictors, soft-shelled turtles, and subtropical fish; the Green River fossil flora suggests that lowland forests were dominated by deciduous trees and subtropical species such as bald cypress, palm, and hibiscus, while the higher elevations were covered by pine forests.

The main mammal-bearing deposits of the early Tertiary are found in the structural basins of the Rocky Mountains: the Denver, Huerfano, Middle Park, and northern San Juan basins. A single locality in the Denver Basin has produced more than 400 specimens of the earliest Tertiary mammals known. Along the San Juan Basin, the variegated clays of the San Jose Formation have yielded an early Tertiary bestiary that includes a hippolike animal (*Coryphodon*), a rhinoceroslike herbivore (*Uintatherium*), a flightless bird (*Diatryma*), five species of primates, and the first true carnivorous mammals. To the east of this area, in the Huerfano Basin, Eocene deposits contain some of the earliest known horse remains, skeletons of a collie-sized animal known as the dawn horse (*Hyracotherium*, formerly *Eohippus*). During the Oligocene and Miocene we see a dramatic shift toward a more modern fauna, with increasing numbers of grazers and the appearance of saber-toothed cats. The first appearance of many of the modern mammalian families occurred in the Southern Rockies during this time.

Middle Tertiary Events: Tectonic Quiescence and Volcanism

Awash in Debris: Post-Laramide Erosion

The end of Laramide mountain building was marked by a renewal of widespread erosion, reducing the rugged uplifts of the Southern Rockies to a series of rounded hills and ridges. The magnitude of post-Laramide erosion is documented by the cutting of a relatively flat, high-level erosion surface across the region's uplifts and by the accumulation of thick sequences of Tertiary sediments in the basins between the ranges. Although large portions of the post-Laramide erosion surface have been disrupted by Miocene-Pliocene uplift and faulting and dissected by modern streams, examples of this surface can still be seen in a number of localities. Remnants of the surface are well preserved only on the broader ranges, such as the Rampart Range and the northern Colorado Front Range; narrow ranges, such as the Sangre de Cristos, have lost nearly all traces of the erosion surface.

Fire in the Sky: Oligocene Volcanism

Catastrophic volcanic eruptions occurred repeatedly in the Southern Rockies between 40 and 25 million years ago. Oligocene volcanic activity is believed to reflect the emplacement of large near-surface batholiths beneath the San Juan Mountains and the region that extends northeast from the Elk Mountains and Sawatch Range to the Rocky Mountain front. Widely scattered volcanoes spewed lava and ash over hundreds of miles, with volcanic centers eventually coalescing to form a giant volcanic field that covered large portions of the southern and central Southern Rockies; individually named volcanic fields, such as the San Juan or West Elk fields, are merely the much-eroded remnants of this larger composite field. The southern segment of the Oligocene volcanic field covered all of south-central Colorado and adjacent New Mexico, and the northern segment extended from central Colorado to the eastern mountain front; the two segments were linked along the trend of the Colorado Mineral Belt. Local volcanic centers existed north of the Colorado Mineral Belt in the Never Summer Mountains and in the Park Range.

The Oligocene volcanoes of the Southern Rockies produced lavas with a high proportion of quartz and feldspar—andesite (a grayish, feldspar-rich rock), rhyolite (the volcanic form of granite), and quartz latite—which reflected the presence of shallow batholiths beneath the volcanic piles. Dark-colored rocks of basaltic (mafic) composition are rare in Oligocene volcanic assemblages and are more commonly associated with late Cenozoic volcanism related to the development of the Rio Grande Rift, a major intracontinental rift extending from central Colorado to northern Mexico. Because andesitic and rhyolitic magmas are less fluid than basalt, they tend to trap gases within the volcanic vent, resulting in more explosive eruptions, much like when the cork on a bottle of champagne is popped. This phenomenon resulted in the development of large craters, called calderas, and in the accumulation of tremendous thicknesses of pyroclastic rocks (sedimentary rocks produced by explosive eruptions).

At Wheeler Geologic Area, near Creede, a fairyland of spires and other fanciful shapes has been eroded from more than eight different layers of volcanic tuff and ash-flow deposits.

The largest ash-flow deposits, and most of the calderas, formed in the San Juan Mountains. Recent estimates suggest that as much as 5,400 cubic miles of ash and other ejecta were erupted during the height of volcanic activity in the San Juans. In comparison, the fateful 1980 eruption of Mount St. Helens, in Washington, is estimated to have produced only .25 cubic mile of ash, a minor volcanic event by San Juan standards.

The successive lava flows of the first phase of volcanic activity in the San Juans, between 35 and 30 million years ago, formed a shieldlike volcanic field approximately 100 miles in diameter. Many of the high peaks of the San Juan Mountains are carved from the welded ash-flow tuffs and fine breccias produced by these eruptions. The distinctive San Juan Tuff, conspicuous in several exposures between Ouray and Silverton, is easily eroded and has slumped and flowed in many areas. The most famous and recent of these slumps is the Holocene-age Slumgullion Earthflow that dams San Cristobal Lake, near Lake City.

A second eruptive phase began in the San Juan Mountains around 29 million years ago and is represented by at least eight layers of lava, ash-flow tuff, and welded tuff, and by an interval of widespread caldera formation. One of the second-phase volcanic domes, reaching a height of more than 2,000 feet, was centered near the modern town of Creede. Following an intense series of pyroclastic eruptions, the dome collapsed into the magma chamber, creating a caldera nearly ten miles in diameter. The fine, ashy sediment that accumulated in the caldera's lake preserved a diversity of middle Tertiary plants and insects. Spectacular Wheeler Geologic Area, near Creede, is a fairyland of lavender-and-white spires and hoodoos eroded from the volcanic tuff associated with these eruptions.

A final phase of eruptions, which began about 26 million years ago, bore little resemblance to the previous volcanic eruptions. Volcanic fissures erupted massive floods of black basalt all along the central and eastern portions of the San Juan volcanic field, coincident with the development of the Rio Grande Rift. Basaltic lavas are common along the western edge of the San Luis Valley, and are particularly well exposed at Wagon Wheel Gap, where the columnar jointing of the basalt gives the appearance of a log stockade.

Along its northern periphery, the San Juan volcanic field merged with another volcanic center in the West Elk Mountains. The thickening volcanic cover in this region, which is known as the West Elk Breccia, consisted primarily of streams of molten rock and fragmental debris. Remnants of this breccia, its original volume estimated at more than 150 cubic miles, are common along the southern half of the West Elks and make up the Dillon Pinnacles near Blue Mesa Reservoir and Castle and Cathedral peaks southeast of Crawford. In certain areas, thin layers of heat-welded tuff cap the less-resistant breccia pinnacles, creating a variety of fanciful shapes. Elsewhere, deposits of loosely consolidated pumice and ash-flow tuff produced by a later sequence of eruptions form light-colored, easily eroded foothills.

Columnar jointing near Wagon Wheel Gap, San Juan Mountains.

Breccia pinnacles and hoodoos near Blue Mesa Reservoir, Colorado.

Along the eastern margin of the San Juan volcanic field, a nearly continuous sheet of mid-Tertiary volcanic rocks once linked the San Juan Mountains with the Wet Mountains and the Spanish Peaks. Today, at places such as Cuchara Pass, we can see the resistant, wall-like dikes that formed as the magma forced its way into the network of vertical cracks that developed in the surrounding sedimentary rocks.

In the southern Front Range, Oligocene volcanic activity was concentrated around the cluster of volcanoes that make up the Thirty-Nine Mile volcanic field. The southwestern perimeter of the field closes off the basin of South Park and merges westward with the volcanic Arkansas Hills and the San Juan volcanic field. The most interesting event associated with the Thirty-Nine Mile volcanic field is the formation of ancient Lake Florissant, today the site of Florissant Fossil Beds National Monument. Nearly 35 million years ago, lava and mudflows dammed an ancient valley near the present-day community of Florissant and created a sickle-shaped lake that was nearly twelve miles long and two miles wide. Towering sequoia, white cedar, and numerous deciduous species lined the ancient lakeshore. Intermittent volcanic activity showered the lake with ash and pumice, and on shore, mudflows and volcanic ash buried the trees and low-growing vegetation. Bit by bit, successive layers of ashy mud buried plants and animals that had washed into the lake, creating the most extensive fossil record of its kind in the world. Since their discovery in 1874, the lake beds have provided scientists with the exquisitely detailed fossils of more than 1,100 species of insects, more than 140 species of plants, and several kinds of fish, birds, and small mammals.

To the west of Florissant, beyond the low volcanic hills of the Thirty-Nine Mile volcanic field, the dark mass of the Buffalo Peaks rises from the floor of South Park. The Buffalo Peaks and the flows capping several small buttes nearby are all that remain of the many thick layers of andesitic lava and volcanic ash that accumulated in this basin from sources in the southern Sawatch Range. Volcanic activity in the southern Sawatch Range was probably triggered by the mid-Tertiary emplacement of the Mount Princeton batholith, which fed a major volcano or cluster of volcanoes along the crest of the Collegiate Range.

North of the Colorado Mineral Belt, volcanic activity was concentrated in the Never Summer Mountains and the Rabbit Ears Range. In the Never Summer Mountains, multiple layers of silica-rich lava and ash-flow material were erupted from volcanic centers near Mount Richthofen and from Lulu, Lead, and Specimen mountains. Light-colored layers of volcanic ash and pumice can be seen in numerous road cuts along the western half of Trail Ridge Road in Rocky Mountain National Park. The ash-flow deposits from these and other volcanic centers filled deep canyons along the west side of the park. Welded ash-flow tuff, possibly the same as that at Specimen, can be seen in the 500-foot-high cliff above Iceberg Lake, along Trail Ridge Road.

The Rabbit Ears Range, an east-west-trending ridge of mid-Tertiary volcanic rocks, connects the Park Range with the Front Range, separating North Park from Middle Park. Rabbit Ears Peak, formed of the same reddish volcanic breccia that makes up most of the range, is the much-eroded plug of an Oligocene volcano. Just to the south, the pointed summit of Whitley Peak is capped with basalt that shows well-developed columnar jointing.

By the early Miocene, deposits of windblown volcanic ash originating from volcanoes in the Southern Rockies as well as from those in Wyoming and Montana blanketed large portions of the eastern plains. The widespread Oligocene White River Formation, extending from north-central Colorado to South Dakota, is characteristic of the alternating layers of volcanic ash and coarse erosional debris that accumulated during this time. Outcrops of the White River Formation can be seen in North Park, at Pawnee Buttes in northeastern Colorado, and near Bates Hole along the western flank of the Laramie Range.

The White River Formation has yielded a rich assemblage of Tertiary mammals, including the rhinolike brontotheres, ancestral horses, and a gazellelike camel. This suggests an open woodland environment. The Miocene Creede fossil flora is allied to genera living within a radius of 100 miles of the Creede area today. When compared with the Oligocene-age Florissant fossil flora, the evidence supports a sharp decline in the number of warm-temperate deciduous species. Regional uplift and changes in climate caused by the tremendous volumes of ash produced by Oligocene volcanoes may have been responsible for the changes in vegetation.

Late Tertiary Events

Raising the Roof: Miocene-Pliocene Uplift

The last major episode of tectonic and volcanic activity in the Southern Rockies began at the close of the Oligocene and continued to the end of the Tertiary. Unlike the Laramide Orogeny that preceded it, Miocene-Pliocene uplift was characterized by the domal upwarping of the entire Rocky Mountain and Great Plains region. This broad regional uplift triggered widespread block faulting and, along the crest of the uplift dome, basalt volcanism coincident with the development of the Rio Grande Rift. Block faulting rejuvenated and exhumed the Laramide uplifts and redefined the structural basins along their flanks. By the end of the Tertiary, the Southern Rockies had risen at least 5,000 feet; summits over 9,000 feet became Fourteeners, and the western plains were lifted to an elevation of 6,000 feet.

Development of the Rio Grande Rift

The Rio Grande Rift is one of the most amazing structural features to form during the late Tertiary. Segments of the rift can be traced for nearly 500 miles, beginning near Steamboat Springs and trending south through New Mexico and west Texas to end in northern Mexico. Structurally, the Rio Grande Rift consists of a series of interconnected grabens (down-dropped blocks) bounded on one or both sides by fault-block mountains; the best developed of the rift valleys include the Blue River Valley from Kremmling to Silverthorne, the Upper Arkansas River Valley from Leadville to Salida, and the San Luis and Rio Grande valleys of southern Colorado and north-central New Mexico. Adjacent to the valleys, major mountain blocks such as the Williams Fork, Mosquito, and Sangre de Cristo ranges rose along the east flank of the rift; the Gore, Tenmile, and Sawatch ranges appeared along the rift's west flank. As the mountain blocks rose, erosion intensified and the adjoining basins filled with thousands of feet of rock debris. The geometry of faulting along the rift indicates a pattern of crustal extension or spreading, a style characteristic of much of the western United States during late Cenozoic time. Basaltic volcanism has occurred repeatedly along the trend of the rift since its inception about 26 million years ago. The rift, which continues to be geologically active, is characterized by abnormally high heat flow, the presence of shallow magma bodies, crustal thinness, and high seismicity.

The Rio Grande Rift is deepest and broadest in the San Luis Valley, where subsidence of the rift's northern segment occurred simultaneously with the beginning of basalt volcanism in the San Juan Mountains. Basalt flows form an impressive plateau north of Taos and are as thick as 650 feet in exposures in Rio Grande Gorge. Just to the north of this area, a cluster of twelve volcanic cones and the larger domed volcanoes of San Antonio Peak and Los Mogotes dominate the otherwise flat valley floor. Turquoise, produced by hydrothermal alteration of copper minerals in the volcanic rock, was once mined in the basalt-capped hills near Manassa.

The turbulent geologic history of the central portion of the Rio Grande Rift is reflected in the development of the Jemez Mountains of northern New Mexico. This diverse assemblage of volcanic domes, craters, and interbedded ash and lava flows occurs where the Rio Grande Rift is offset eastward from the Albuquerque Basin to the Espanola Basin. The Jemez Mountains are part of the Jemez volcanic field, which covers an area of 2,000 square miles centered on Valles Caldera, one of the largest calderas in the world. Eruptions within the Jemez volcanic field spanned a time period from 10 million to 400,000 years ago.

The earliest eruptions, beginning about 10 million years ago, produced distinctly banded domes and composite volcanoes, such as St. Peter's Dome and Boundary Peak. These volcanoes, now much eroded, were high enough to stand well above the ash flows that later swirled around their flanks. During the period from 7 to 3.5 million years ago, silica-rich lava flows formed the massive rounded peaks that mark the skyline of the Jemez Mountains as seen from Santa Fe and Espanola. By about 3 million years ago, volcanism had shifted to the central portion of the Jemez volcanic field, culminating in the violent ash-flow eruptions that created the Pajarito Plateau.

The catastrophic ash-flow eruptions of 1.4 and 1.1 million years ago were the most important events in the history of the Jemez volcanic field. The volume of silica-rich pumice and ash erupted during these two episodes is estimated to have been at least 100 times greater than that produced by the 1980 eruption of Washington's Mount St. Helens. The collapsed craters of Valles Caldera and the remnants of the earlier Toledo Caldera provide ample testimony to the violence of these eruptions. Pyroclastic flows filled preexisting valleys and canyons along the flanks of the volcanic field and eventually formed the gently sloping surface of the Pajarito Plateau. The orange-brown to light tan pyroclastic rocks associated with these eruptions are collectively referred to as the Bandelier Tuff. Thick layers of Bandelier Tuff dominate the Pajarito Plateau and are prominent in Bandelier National Monument.

Late Cenozoic Volcanism

A southwest-trending belt of Pliocene and Pleistocene volcanism cuts across the Rio Grande Rift from the High Plains of northeastern New Mexico, through the Cimarron Range and the Jemez Mountains, to the southeast margin of the Colorado Plateau. Within this region, basalt flows cap a number of prominent mesas, such as Oak Canyon, Johnson, Barella, Raton, and Black mesas, and Mesa de Maya. At Capulin Volcano National Monument, just east of Raton, the well-preserved cone of a volcano active as recently as 10,000 years ago rises more than 1,000 feet from base to rim.

Another area of intense late Cenozoic volcanism was centered in north-central Colorado. Repeated eruptions, beginning about 25 million years ago, spread layer after layer of basalt lava across the White River Plateau, parts of the Gore, Park, and Sawatch ranges, the Elk Mountains, and Grand Mesa; basalt flows on Grand and Battlement mesas are 650 feet to nearly 3,000 feet thick in some exposures. In the Flat Tops, more than 1,300 feet of flow-on-flow basaltic rocks have been carved by erosion to form such landmarks as Trappers Peak.

The Exhumation of the Rockies: Pliocene Erosion and Canyon Cutting

By the end of the Pliocene, the northern ranges of the Southern Rockies were almost buried in erosional debris. Streams flowing eastward from the Park–Sierra Madre Range spread across the nearly submerged summits of the Medicine Bow and Laramie mountains depositing a vast apron of debris across the High Plains. A narrow, ramplike portion of this debris apron is still preserved along the eastern flank of the Laramie Range, west of Cheyenne. This geologic landmark, known as the Gangplank, forms a natural bridge between the High Plains and the top of the steeply dipping rocks flanking the Laramie Range. In 1869, the gentle approach of the Gangplank was chosen as the route of the nation's first transcontinental railroad across the Rockies. Elsewhere along the eastern front of the Southern Rockies, features analogous to the Gangplank are nonexistent. Along the Colorado Front Range, a broad valley called the Colorado Piedmont separates the High Plains from the eastern mountain front. Most geologists believe that the South Platte and the Arkansas rivers and their tributaries removed or greatly modified the debris apron that once lapped against the mountain front.

West of the mountain front, intermontane basins were inundated with erosional debris washed from the rising mountains. In the San Luis Valley, interbedded layers of Tertiary erosional debris and volcanic deposits accumulated to depths of 10,000 feet in certain areas. Groundwater resources in the arid San Luis Valley are uniquely tied to these alternating layers of gravel, clay, and lava. Water, entering the trough-shaped valley from the mountains to the north, east, and west, flows underground along the permeable gravel layers, confined between the impermeable layers of lava or clay. By the time the water reaches the center of the valley, it has developed considerable artesian pressure and can rise to the surface without the aid of mechanical pumps.

With the acceleration of regional uplift during the Pliocene, moist air masses moving eastward from the Pacific were forced upward and robbed of their moisture by the newly risen mountains. Rain shadows developed along the leeward side of the ranges, encouraging the development of a more drought-resistant shrub-and-grassland vegetation in these areas. In the mountains themselves, altitudinal differences in temperature and precipitation resulted in a more zonal distribution of forest vegetation, similar to what we see today. The increase in precipitation in the mountains was sufficient to sustain large perennial rivers and streams. As local gradients increased, streams that once wandered aimlessly across the crests of buried ranges began to straighten, rush, and cut their way through the mountain uplifts.

Ever since John Wesley Powell's epic journey down the Colorado River more than a hundred years ago, geologists have debated the origins of the rivers that flow across the structural grain of the mountains. Some geologists suggest that the major river systems in the Rocky Mountain region became established in their present positions prior to Miocene-Pliocene uplift and simply continued downcutting as uplift accelerated around them. Others hypothesize that the modern drainage systems of the Southern Rockies are relatively young, the product of increased precipitation resulting from Miocene-Pliocene uplift. These geologists propose that the major drainage systems, or at least sections of these drainage systems, have been superimposed onto a pre-Miocene landscape, downcutting through thousands of feet of erosional debris as the region underwent uplift. In support of this view, geologists studying the upper Colorado River and its tributaries have found that this drainage system had its beginnings near the end of the Miocene, about 10 million years ago; downcutting was rapid until about 8 million years ago, when rates of uplift decreased. Whatever the ultimate conclusion to this debate, water, in both its liquid and crystalline state, would come to assume a dominant role in landscape evolution during the Quaternary.

Mitten Park Fault, Dinosaur National Monument.

CHAPTER SEVEN

Finishing Touches: The Quaternary

Arapaho Glacier, Indian Peaks, Colorado Front Range.

The finishing touches that distinguish the modern landscape of the Southern Rockies—the jagged peaks, ice-carved basins, and U-shaped valleys—reflect the dramatic climatic changes of the Quaternary. Encompassing only the last 1.8 million years, the Quaternary period includes the comparatively short Pleistocene epoch, popularly known as the Ice Age, and the Holocene epoch, beginning roughly 10,000 years ago and continuing to the present day. In the Southern Rockies, Pleistocene climatic fluctuations resulted in the growth and retreat of enormous ice sheets and valley glaciers, producing distinctive changes in the mountain landscape and controlling the distribution and survival of many plants and animals.

Pleistocene glaciers once covered as much as 32 percent of the Earth's land surface. Continental ice sheets extended more than 2,500 miles across the northern conterminous United States and stretched as far south as the Missouri and Ohio rivers. In the Rocky Mountain region, alpine ice caps and valley glaciers formed as far south as south-central New Mexico (latitude 33° north). In the Southern Rockies, alpine glaciers formed in all major ranges; most were valley glaciers, but ice caps developed in areas of higher precipitation, such as the San Juan Mountains, Grand Mesa, and the White River Plateau. Today, though perennial snowfields persist in many alpine areas of the Southern Rockies, true glaciers are found only in the Colorado Front Range.

We know a great deal about the geologic, climatic, and biological changes that shaped the Southern Rockies during Quaternary time. The story is far from complete, however, and researchers representing a variety of disciplines—geology, paleontology, paleobotany, dendrochronology, archaeology, physics, and climatology—are continually adding to our knowledge of Quaternary environments. To develop a paleoclimatic history for the Quaternary, the geologist must work backward by examining deposits left behind by Pleistocene and Holocene glaciers or other climatic change events, dating these deposits wherever possible, and then reconstructing the climatic scenario that might have produced them.

Chronologies of Quaternary events, as well as correlations of events within and beyond the Southern Rockies, continue to be a work in progress and have been established by using an array of absolute (numerical-age) and relative (correlated- and/or calibrated-age) dating methods. The most commonly used absolute dating method focuses on changes in isotopic (carbon-14) composition in response to the amount of radioactive decay the organic material to be dated has undergone; radiocarbon dating is used to obtain dates on charcoal, wood, or other organic materials based on their carbon-14 content. For example, the radiocarbon age of peat (the decomposed remains of sphagnum moss) represents the time since the peat was deposited. In the absence of carbon-14, radiogenic methods, such as thermo-luminescence and fission-track dating, provide a numerical-age date by measuring the cumulative non-isotopic effects of natural radioactive decay on minerals.

Relative dating techniques include a variety of chemical, biological, and geomorphic methods—lichenometry, rock weathering, obsidian hydration, the amount of rock varnish (a biochemical alteration), tree-ring analysis, palynology, and many others—that are based on time-dependent chemical or biological processes or some combination of both. In most cases, relative dating methods track progressive changes over time that can be compared with, and correlated to, a material or substrate of known age in a similar environment. For example, the technique of lichenometry is based on the measurement of lichens (mostly of the lichen genus *Rhizocarpon*) growing on exposed, stabilized rock surfaces as a means of estimating the age of a geologic feature, such as a glacial moraine or a rock glacier; lichenometry is also used to date archaeological features, such as the rock walls and hunting blinds built by prehistoric hunters.

Glacially striated bedrock in the Indian Peaks Wilderness Area.

Reading the Evidence: Glacial Erosion

The advance and retreat of Quaternary glaciers led to a distinctive pattern of landform development that can be seen in every major mountain range in the Southern Rockies. Pyramidal peaks, amphitheater-like basins, hanging valleys, and U-shaped valleys are all trademarks of mountain glaciation. Glaciers modify the landscape primarily through the erosive processes of abrasion and plucking. Abrasion results from the presence of rock and rock fragments embedded in the base and sides of the moving glacier. Study of the striations (grooves) produced by glacial abrasion can provide information about glacier movement. Good examples of glacially striated bedrock can be seen in Rocky Mountain National Park along the Old Fall River Road (west of Chasm Falls) and in the Glacier Gorge area, east of Independence Pass in the Sawatch Range, and near Molas Pass in the San Juans.

Plucking, in contrast to glacial abrasion, involves the lifting and incorporation of loose rock material as part of the bed load of the glacier as it moves downslope. Frost-aided weakening and quarrying of the bedrock in contact with the glacier greatly enhances the subaerial removal of rock from the headwall and sidewalls of the glacier basin. The combined effects of abrasion and plucking can be seen in the streamlined bedrock landforms commonly observed on the floors of glaciated valleys; these features, known as whalebacks, or *roches moutonnées*, are abrasion-smoothed and often striated on their upvalley sides and roughened in response to glacial plucking on their downvalley sides. Good examples of *roches moutonnées* can be seen in the Glacier Gorge and Moraine Park areas of Rocky Mountain National Park and are common in the Indian Peaks Wilderness Area south of the park.

The most conspicuous landforms associated with glacial erosion are found in the glacier's source area and result largely from the headward quarrying of rock by the glacier. The names given to these features—cirque, tarn, arête, col, and horn—were first used in Europe and are in the lexicon of every mountaineer. The term *cirque* refers to the semicircular basin the glacier creates at its head; in longitudinal profile, a typical cirque exhibits a steep, quarried headwall, a circular or elongated basin below the headwall, and an abraded bedrock lip, or threshold. In many cases, the threshold serves to enclose the basin, allowing water to collect to form a cirque lake, or tarn, such as Chasm Lake at the base of Longs Peak and Frozen Lake at the head of Glacier Gorge (both in Rocky Mountain National Park). There are hundreds of cirques in the Southern Rockies, and many are visible from the major mountain highways; good examples can be found in Rocky Mountain National Park, in the Indian Peaks Wilderness Area (Colorado Front Range), at Horseshoe Mountain in the Mosquito Range, along the eastern slope of the Sangre de Cristo Range, and in the Elk Mountains.

The artistry of ice is apparent when two cirques develop on opposite sides of a bedrock ridge, eroding the ridge between them to create a high saddle, or col. A narrow, sawtoothed ridge consisting of a series of cols and intervening ridge segments forms an arête. Where two or more cirques intersect, a pyramidal peak, or horn, may persist above the general level of the sawtoothed divide. Good examples of horns are abundant in the Southern Rockies and include peaks such as Wetterhorn and the Matterhorn in the San Juans, Lone Cone in the San Miguel Range of the San Juans, and Lone Eagle on the western edge of the Indian Peaks in the Colorado Front Range.

Valleys that have been heavily glaciated usually have a characteristic U shape when viewed in cross section, in contrast to the V shape typical of unglaciated drainages. Good examples of U-shaped valleys are common throughout the Southern Rockies and include the Animas Valley in the San Juans, the Roaring Fork Valley near Aspen, and both Horseshoe and Moraine parks in Rocky Mountain National Park. The upper end of a glaciated valley sometimes appears stepped in long profile, each step fronted by a cross-valley ledge of more-resistant rock and often dotted by a chain of small lakes (as can be seen at Gorge Lakes, viewed from Forest Canyon Overlook in Rocky Mountain National Park). Hanging valleys, small glaciated valleys perched high above the main valley floor, mark the junctions where tributary glaciers joined the main trunk of a valley glacier; streams draining these tributary valleys often form waterfalls as they cascade to the main valley floor. Hanging valleys are common features in the Colorado Front Range and are especially prominent in the San Juan Mountains.

Depositional Landforms

A glacier, in contrast to a perennial snowfield, is a moving body of ice formed by the accumulation, compaction, and recrystallization of snow. Glaciers are able to transport enormous quantities of erosional debris beneath, within, and on the surface of the ice. Geologists use the term *glacial drift* to refer to all erosional debris—boulders, cobbles, pebbles, sand, silt, and clay—transported and deposited by glaciers or their associated meltwater streams. The word *till* refers to the unsorted, nonstratified debris that is picked up, transported, and deposited directly by the glacier without being reworked by meltwater streams. Glacial drift that has been transported by meltwater streams is called outwash; unlike till, outwash may be stratified or layered as a result of size-sorting of the sediment by the transporting stream.

Landforms constructed of glacial drift, though less spectacular than those sculpted by glacial erosion, are distinctive and often of impressive size. Most glacial deposition takes place as the ice melts and retreats, providing the geologist with a detailed record of the movement of glaciers that have long since disappeared. Like a giant conveyor belt, the glacier delivers much of its load of rock debris to its terminus, or snout, with lesser amounts deposited along the sides and bottom of the glacier. Geologists refer to these jumblelike deposits of till as moraines, and they may appear ridgelike or somewhat amorphous and hummocky in general appearance. Those that form around the glacier's snout are called terminal moraines. The smaller, cross-valley ridges of till that mark the various stages as a glacier recedes are known as recessional moraines. The long ridges of till that parallel valley walls along the sides of the glacier are called lateral moraines. The term *ground moraine* refers to the low, relatively rolling accumulations of till that forms a veneer on the floors of many glaciated valleys. Terminal and lateral moraines, such as those that enclose Moraine Park in Rocky Mountain National Park, can be enormous, reaching heights of 1,000 feet or more.

Pleistocene Glacial History in the Southern Rockies

Major glaciation events in the Southern Rockies correspond in a general way to worldwide patterns of Quaternary climatic change. It is important to remember, however, that specific intervals of climatic change were neither synchronous nor of similar intensity in all areas. In contrast to the midcontinent region of North America, which was mantled with continental ice sheets throughout much of the Pleistocene, all evidence of glaciation in the Southern Rockies appears to be restricted to the middle to late Pleistocene and the Holocene. In the Southern Rockies, the onset of glaciation is believed to correspond to a sharp drop in temperature coupled with an increase in precipitation, resulting in the deepening and expansion of large perennial snowfields throughout the higher ranges.

During the maximum extent of Pleistocene glaciation, the highest elevations of the Southern Rockies were nearly covered by glacial ice, and massive rivers of ice flowed down most of the major valleys to around

8,000 feet. One ice field in the San Juan Mountains was sixty miles wide and reached a thickness of more than 3,000 feet. In other areas, valley glaciers were as thick as 2,000 feet, creating the classic U-shaped valleys we see today as well as the lofty moraines that delineate former ice margins.

The Pleistocene glacial sequence for the Southern Rockies is represented by at least three major glaciations: (1) pre-Bull Lake, (2) Bull Lake, and (3) Pinedale. The names for these glaciations are derived from localities in the Wind River Range of central Wyoming, where Pleistocene glacial deposits of similar ages were first identified and studied. Evidence of multiple intervals of glacial advance, called stades, are reported for both the Bull Lake and Pinedale glaciations; each of the major glaciations was separated from its successor by an interglacial period in which the glaciers withdrew substantially or melted altogether. Glacial geologists continue to refine the existing chronology of glaciations, and they consider their results a work in progress.

Pre-Bull Lake Glaciation

The Pre-Bull Lake Glaciation, essentially middle Pleistocene in age, is the earliest recognized glaciation known for the Southern Rockies. Unfortunately, precise dating of the Pre-Bull Lake Glaciation has been difficult due to the paucity of deposits and because it lies beyond the time range of radiocarbon dating. Limited chronological control provided by oxygen-isotope dating suggests that at least two or more advances of pre-Bull Lake glaciers occurred between 300,000 and 700,000 years ago. Deposits of these isolated, sheetlike, and deeply weathered tills have been reported in the Colorado Front Range, from Grand Mesa, in the San Juan Mountains, and in the Sawatch and Sangre de Cristo ranges. In the Colorado Front Range, examples of possible pre-Bull Lake till can be seen just east of the Fall River entrance to Rocky Mountain National Park and in road cuts along Colorado 7 in the Tahosa Valley, just east of Longs Peak.

Bull Lake Glaciation

Evidence of Bull Lake ice caps and valley glaciers is found in nearly every glaciated range in the Southern Rockies. The Bull Lake Glaciation consisted of at least two distinct advances of glacial ice separated by a major withdrawal of ice, and has been dated as occuring between 300,000 and 130,000 years ago. Bull Lake valley glaciers were generally more extensive than later

Pinedale glaciers and in many areas were as thick as 2,000 feet in their upper portions. At Grand Mesa, for example, a Bull Lake ice cap covered the entire surface of the mesa, and tongues of ice extended into the surrounding drainages to an elevation of 5,800 feet.

Bull Lake moraines can generally be distinguished from those of Pinedale age by their broad crests and gently sloping sides. Moraine surfaces are less bouldery than Pinedale and Holocene moraines, have well-developed soils, do not exhibit the pronounced hummockiness or the undrained depressions characteristic of Pinedale moraines, and typically support a mature forest or sagebrush cover. Where Bull Lake moraines cross major valleys, most have been breached by later stream erosion. Examples of Bull Lake moraines can be seen along Glacier Creek in Rocky Mountain National Park and west of the Beaver Meadows entrance to the park, at the Home Moraine Geologic Site in upper Cache la Poudre Canyon, on Grand Mesa near Lands End, along the upper Laramie River Valley, and on the east slope of the Sawatch Range near Lake Creek and Twin Lakes.

Pinedale Glaciation

The Pinedale Glaciation was the last major Pleistocene glaciation event in the Southern Rockies. Radiocarbon dating and relative-age criteria suggest that the Pinedale Glaciation began about 30,000 years ago and that Pinedale glaciers were near their maximum lengths at least once, and perhaps twice, prior to 20,000 years ago. At Devlin Park in the Colorado Front Range, a radiocarbon date of 23,000 years relates to the last advance of a Pinedale glacier close to its terminal limit.

In the northern and central Southern Rockies, Pinedale glaciers occasionally exceeded twenty miles in length and were as thick as 1,500 feet in their source areas. To the south of this area, Pinedale glaciers were considerably shorter, stopping well above the maximum of Bull Lake ice. In southern Wyoming, Pinedale ice sheets accumulated around the flanks of the Snowy Range and spread across the post-Laramide erosion surface, overtopping passes and enveloping the major stream valleys of Libby Creek, French Creek, Rock Creek, Brush Creek, and the Medicine Bow River. In the Colorado Front Range, glaciers flowed both east and west from well-developed cirques along the crest of the range. Along the western slope of the range, glaciers grew to such enormous thicknesses that several overflowed their valleys to form a complex network of ice streams. Glaciers flowing eastward from cirques in the Never Summer Mountains merged with glaciers flowing westward from the Continental Divide to form the longest Pinedale glacier in Rocky Mountain National Park: the twenty-mile-long Colorado River Glacier.

To the south and west of the Colorado Front Range, Pinedale glaciers formed along the crests of most of the major ranges. In the San Juans, Pinedale ice caps and valley glaciers formed some of the largest ice bodies in the Southern Rockies. An enormous ice cap overflowed the divide between the Animas and the Uncompahgre rivers to form two spectacular rivers of ice: the Animas Glacier, flowing south for nearly forty miles down Animas Canyon, and the Uncompahgre Glacier, flowing north for more than twenty miles along the Uncompahgre Valley. From the rolling, glaciated terrain around Molas Lake, just south of Red Mountain Pass, it is easy to envision a virtual sea of ice, with only the summits of Mount Sneffels, Engineer Mountain, and a number of other peaks protruding above the level of the slow-moving ice.

The retreat of Pleistocene glaciers left behind broad U-shaped valleys at higher elevations throughout the Southern Rockies. This one, in Rocky Mountain National Park, was carved by the Cache la Poudre Glacier.

Large, forested Pinedale moraines are conspicuous features of most glaciated valleys in the Southern Rockies. Pinedale moraines can be distinguished from Bull Lake moraines by their steep sides and sharp crests, which tend to be somewhat hummocky and may contain small ponds. On the whole, Pinedale moraines are more bouldery and less weathered than deposits of Bull Lake age. Easily recognizable examples of Pinedale moraines include those flanking the eastern edge of the Park Range, those near Animas City and Bakers Bridge in the San Juans, and the extremely large moraines bordering the basins of Horseshoe Park, Moraine Park, and Glacier Basin in Rocky Mountain National Park. In cases where Pinedale terminal moraines formed temporary barriers to glacial meltwater streams, lakes were created, such as Grand Lake (west of Rocky Mountain National Park), Twin Lakes (near Leadville), Lake Marie (in the Snowy Range), and Lake Katharine (in the southern Sangre de Cristo Range).

In most areas of the Southern Rockies, Pinedale glaciers began receding from their outermost positions between 15,000 and 13,000 years ago, with glaciers in the southern portion of the Southern Rockies beginning their retreat by around 19,000 years ago. At Lake Emma and Molas Lake, in the San Juan Mountains, a series of radiocarbon ages obtained for the lowermost lake sediments suggests that Pinedale glaciers had all but disappeared from this region by 15,000 years ago. North of the San Juans, radiocarbon dates obtained for Pinedale deglaciation in the Colorado Front Range and the Park Range suggest that the last of the valley glaciers were in full-scale retreat by 14,000 to 13,500 years ago and that most were confined to their cirques by at least 12,000 years ago.

The effects of Pinedale glaciation extend well beyond the limits of glacial ice. Meltwater torrents deepened and scoured canyons along both the eastern and western slopes of the mountains: Royal Gorge, Clear Creek, Big Thompson, Cache la Poudre, and the Black Canyon of the Gunnison, to name just a few. In the higher valleys and intermontane basins, downcutting by meltwater-enriched streams removed tons of glacial outwash, leaving the remnants as terraces above the new stream levels. In some valleys, several Pleistocene terrace levels can be seen along the sides of streams and rivers. The upper Arkansas River Valley, near Buena Vista, is noted for the steplike Pleistocene terraces that flank both sides of the river.

Late Pleistocene Dune Fields

Spectacular dune fields developed in several areas of the Southern Rockies during the late Pleistocene. Those at Great Sand Dunes and along the eastern edge of North Park (near Cowdry) are still active and attract thousands of visitors each year. At Great Sand Dunes National Park, the main dune mass covers thirty square miles and towers 750 feet above the valley floor—the tallest dunes in North America. Deciphering "the story behind the scenery," how the dunes formed, how old they are, and how they change over time, remains a work in progress.

Geologists have been forced to work backward through the geologic record to determine the source areas for the sand that makes up the dunes. The diversity of rock types represented, a quartz-rich mixture of volcanic and metamorphic rock fragments, can be traced to sources in both the San Juan Mountains and the Sangre de Cristos. Current research suggests that rivers swollen by melting glaciers played a critical role in transporting massive amounts of sand to the valley floor, especially to the portion of the valley that lies north of the present-day floodplain of the Rio Grande, the so-called Closed Basin.

The Ute name for Great Sand Dunes is *sowapophe-uvehe*, "the land that moves back and forth." Though less poetic and succinct, studies of the shapes and orientation of the dunes indicate that the predominant south-westerly winds once carried trillions of tons of sand across the arid expanse of the northern San Luis Valley, funneling it into a natural sand trap formed by three low passes in the Sangre de Cristos: Music, Medano, and Mosca. As these winds slam into the towering wall of the mountains, the alcove created by the three passes produces additional turbulence, forcing the winds to lose energy and to drop their load of sand. Geologists believe that an additional 200 to 300 feet of sand lies buried beneath the main dune complex. Reverse storm winds roaring down from the northeast periodically blow dune crests back to the west, contributing to their great height and keeping them away from the mountain front. In spring and summer, Sand and Medano creeks transport immense quantities of sand from the eastern and northern perimeters of the dune field, carrying it back toward the valley floor. These streams eventually disappear into the sand along the western edge of the dunes, allowing the transported sand to dry and to be blown back toward the dune field, completing the circle of *sowapophe-uvehe.*

Mysteries surrounding the precise age of the Great Sand Dunes have long challenged geologists. Dates for the dune deposits have been elusive until recently, with the advent of optically stimulated luminescence dating of buried sand. This dating technique provides an estimate of how long sand grains have been in complete darkness. Dating of the sand 200 feet below the surface of Medano Creek provided an age estimate of 18,000 years, near the end of the last Ice Age. A sand sample collected from 200 feet below the crest of Star Dune, the tallest of the dunes, dated at approximately 750 years, a time of prolonged drought throughout the Southwest.

Along the eastern edge of the Southern Rockies and extending into the High Plains, Pleistocene dune fields have largely stabilized and become obscured by their vegetation cover. Deflation hollows, or blowouts, are common features of these dune fields, resulting from renewed wind scour in areas where the vegetation has been disturbed by fire or grazing. Big Hollow, an inactive blowout near Laramie, ranks as one of the largest in North America, measuring three miles wide, nine miles long, and almost 150 feet deep.

Pleistocene Extinctions

For nearly a century, paleontologists have debated the causes of the great wave of mammalian extinctions that occurred at the end of the Pleistocene. With few exceptions, all of the mammals that became extinct were large-bodied species: mammoths, camels, ground sloths, saber-toothed cats, and giant bison. Numerous theories have been proposed to explain their demise, including climatic change, disease, poor synchronization of breeding habits with climate, and overkill by Paleo-Indian hunters. It seems probable that the answer to the Pleistocene extinction puzzle lies in some combination of causal factors rather than in the effect of a single predator, such as man.

Holocene Glacial History in the Southern Rockies

In the Southern Rockies, the beginning of the Holocene epoch marks the end of climatic conditions favoring full-scale glaciation. There is growing paleoclimatic evidence that summer solar radiation had increased markedly in the Northern Hemisphere by 10,000 years ago. Several hypotheses have been proposed to explain the glacial-interglacial transition between 15,000 and 10,000 years ago, each relying on a different causal agent: changes in the Earth's orbit, sunspot cycles, volcanic activity, solar-lunar tidal forces, differences in atmospheric circulation patterns, and changing carbon dioxide levels in the atmosphere. Indeed, some combination of these factors may ultimately provide a framework for understanding Holocene climates.

In the absence of full glacial conditions, the development and survival of Holocene glaciers in the Southern Rockies depended to a large degree on wind-redistributed snow and favorable cirque orientation. Even the largest of the Holocene glaciers, measuring around a mile in length, were minuscule compared to the Pleistocene valley glaciers and ice caps that preceded them. At least four, and possibly more, Holocene ice advances have been reported for the Colorado Front Range, the Medicine Bow Mountains, and the Park Range. Ice advances in these northern ranges were confined to high-elevation cirques and to north-facing valley walls above present tree line. In the San Juan Mountains, where enormous glaciers flourished under Pleistocene conditions, there is no evidence of Holocene glaciation younger than about 9,000 years.

Holocene Glaciation in the Colorado Front Range

Much of what we know about Holocene glacial history and climatic change in the Southern Rockies is the result of extensive research in the Indian Peaks region of the Colorado Front Range by geologist and archaeologist Jim Benedict. Data derived from mapping of the glacial deposits, numerical and relative dating, archaeological excavations, and pollen and vegetation studies provide us with a continually evolving record of climatic change. In most cirques, the sequence of terminal moraines suggests multiple glacial advances separated by intervals of near-total disappearance of glaciers. The extent to which this sequence can be extrapolated to other ranges in the northern and central portions of the Southern Rockies remains to be determined.

The oldest of the post-Pinedale cirque-glacier advances occurred around 12,000 to 10,000 years ago; this advance just precedes the formal Pleistocene-Holocene boundary. Terminal moraines deposited by these glaciers are generally found within a mile of cirque headwalls, near present timberline; they are typically well vegetated, supporting trees and a shrub understory in certain situations. By 10,500 to 10,000 years ago, valley glaciers had completely disappeared and timberline had risen to at least its modern altitude. For several thousand years (approximately 10,000 to 8,000 years ago) the existing evidence suggests that relatively warm, moist conditions prevailed. Archaeological evidence from several high-altitude sites in the Indian Peaks Wilderness Area indicates that Paleo-Indian hunters were making seasonal use of the high valleys and alpine uplands by at least 10,000 years ago, enjoying the warmer conditions that followed this earliest of the Holocene glaciations.

This rock-rimmed hunting blind is part of a prehistoric game-drive system on Flattop Mountain, in Rocky Mountain National Park.

During the middle Holocene, a period of relative warmth and episodic drought, known as the Altithermal or Hypsithermal, impacted large areas of western North America. Glaciers and perennial snowbanks disappeared from the high mountains, and lowland areas underwent severe drought stress. The most catastrophic of the droughts may have culminated at around 5,500 years ago. Archaeological evidence indicates an extraordinary increase in human occupation of the cool, moist mountain environments during the Altithermal, in sharp contrast to the apparent decline in human populations in drought-susceptible areas of the Great Basin, Colorado Plateau, and Great Plains. Clearly, the mountains offered refuge to early peoples as well as to the large game animals on which they depended for food. More than forty prehistoric game-drive systems, consisting of low stone walls and rock-rimmed blinds, have been located in the Colorado Front Range; these game-drive systems are similar to those used in the Arctic by both prehistoric and modern peoples to hunt caribou and musk oxen. Archaeological evidence indicates that game-drive hunting became important above timberline in the Colorado Front Range by at least 8,000 years ago and continued until hunting from horseback supplanted traditional techniques. The youngest radiocarbon evidence of game-drive hunting in the Indian Peaks is a date of about 255 years.

The rebirth of glaciers following the Altithermal, from about 5,000 to 150 years ago, assumed the same pattern of intermittent advance and retreat, but on a much smaller scale. Moraines deposited by post-Altithermal ice advances do not extend far from the cirque headwalls; they appear fresh and unweathered and are only sparsely vegetated. The last of these ice advances, those of the Little Ice Age (or Neoglacial), began in the Colorado Front Range around 300 years ago and ended in the middle of the nineteenth century with the start of a global warming trend. Most cirques that still contain glaciers or large perennial snowbanks, such as the Andrews and Tyndall cirques in Rocky Mountain National Park, also contain small ice-cored moraines representing this last advance.

Present-day glaciers in the Southern Rockies are restricted to north- and east-facing cirques in the Colorado Front Range. Glaciers persist in these areas only because they are sheltered from the direct rays of the sun and receive large accumulations of windblown snow. Given the dire predictions concerning the scope of global warming, the future of these tiny glaciers seems grim indeed. Our evolving understanding of the impact of global warming on these perennial ice features has taken a new turn with the discovery and dating of ancient bison remains recently recovered from the margins of a melting glacier and two ice patches. Radiocarbon dates obtained from bison horn sheaths and bones span the period from 3,270 to 210 years ago, providing indisputable evidence that bison frequented the alpine uplands of the Colorado Front Range during much of the late Holocene. These bison remains have survived for more than 3,000 years in a virtual deep-freeze, which implies that recent environmental change exceeds that of the preceding two millennia. Though a few scientists still regard these changes as consistent with short-term climatic fluctuations, most researchers agree that we are entering an accelerating warming phase, or super-interglacial period, resulting from human-induced impacts on world climatic regimes.

Beyond Glacier Margins: Periglacial Landscapes

In mountain environments, frost action and gravity are the critical variables in the algebra of erosion. Geologists use the term *periglacial* to refer to any past or present near-glacial environment in which frost processes (freezing and thawing of water in rock or soil) have dominated weathering and landform development. The results of these geomorphic processes—rock glaciers, talus cones, blockfields, and various types of large- and small-scale patterned-ground features—are common above timberline throughout the Southern Rockies. During the Pleistocene, permafrost (perennially frozen ground) was widespread in the frigid, windswept uplands of the Southern Rockies. Permafrost probably formed during the first major glaciation, and may have formed and disintegrated several times during subsequent glacial and interglacial intervals. Though the prognosis for the persistence of permafrost seems grim given present-day climatic conditions in the Southern Rockies, isolated patches of permafrost may still exist at elevations above 11,500 feet.

Frost action causes change and instability through the processes of frost wedging, frost heave and thrust, frost cracking, and the development of needle ice. For example, the coarse, angular rock that mantles alpine summits and slopes in the Southern Rockies is thought to result primarily from the action of frost wedging, which occurs when joints and cracks in bedrock are penetrated by surface water that freezes, generating sufficient pressure to shatter the rock into angular blocks. Frost wedging in nearly flat terrain can result in the development of extensive blockfields; the German word *felsenmeer*, meaning "sea of rocks," is often used to refer to these features.

Frost heave is the major cause of disruption and upheaval of soil and rock in mountain environments and is a critical factor in the development of patterned-ground features. The combination of silty soils, saturated conditions, and slow, deep freezing promote heaving. As ice nuclei form in the soil during the fall freeze-up, free water migrates toward these nuclei, dewatering adjacent sediments and encouraging the development of layers or lenses of clear ice, generally oriented parallel to the soil surface. As these ice bodies grow, the ground expands vertically and may be accompanied by the ejection of rocks from depth. Differential frost heaving, the result of local variations in soil texture, moisture availability, or insulation of the freezing surface by snow or vegetation, creates a blistered or bubbled effect. The trouble spots that develop along paved mountain roads at the end of winter are often due to differential heaving. Earth hummocks, common features in alpine and subalpine wetlands in the Southern Rockies, owe their origins to frost-heave phenomena.

Needle ice consists of delicate filaments of ice an inch or less in length that develop at or near the soil surface in response to daily freeze-thaw cycles. The needles may be as densely packed as the bristles of a brush or scattered loosely throughout the soil. Soil surfaces affected by needle-ice development often appear somewhat frothy. In alpine areas where the vegetation cover has been disturbed and bare soil exposed, needle-ice development can uproot plant seedlings and discourage natural revegetation.

Patterned Ground

The patterning of rocks, soil, and vegetation into various geometric shapes as a result of frost action occurs widely in alpine areas of the Southern Rockies. The floors of ephemeral ponds or areas that receive meltwater from persistent snowbanks are especially susceptible to frost action. Actively forming patterned-ground features are restricted to areas with permafrost, but nonactive examples of these unique landforms may be found wherever permafrost existed in the past. Patterned-ground features—earth hummocks, sorted and nonsorted circles, polygons, nets, steps, and stripes—are classified according to their shape and the amount of sorting of fine and coarse materials that has occurred during their formation. The slope of the surface on which the pattern forms ultimately controls its shape.

Earth hummocks are most common in subalpine and alpine wetlands, where winter snow is deep enough to provide protection from wind erosion but shallow enough to permit deep frost penetration. Nonsorted circles (such as frost boils) tend to form primarily in snow-free zones. Relict or

Stone stripes on Niwot Ridge, Indian Peaks Wilderness Area.

inactive polygons, up to thirty feet in diameter, are common on windswept knolls and in dry saddles, reflecting times when climatic conditions were moister and colder than at present. Arctic-type "fossil" ice-wedge polygons, ranging from thirty to eighty feet in diameter, have been reported at a single locality at the base of Sawtooth Peak in the Colorado Front Range and in a number of localities in the Laramie Basin of Wyoming. One of the best places to see both active and inactive patterned ground features is along the alpine portion of Trail Ridge Road in Rocky Mountain National Park.

Landforms Produced by Mass-Wasting

Mass-wasting refers to the downslope movement of soil and rock on slopes in response to gravity. Many types of mass-wasting processes are at work in the mountain environment, each exerting a profound influence on landscape development. The processes can be imperceptibly slow, as in frost creep, producing effects visible only when accumulated over a long span of time; moderate, as in solifluction; or catastrophic, as in rockfalls and mudflows.

Frost Creep

Frost creep, an important process in alpine environments, involves the downslope movement of frost-heaved soils, often in large quantities. Over time, the effects of frost creep can be seen in the development of small steps, or terracettes. These miniature terraces, typically aligned approximately parallel to the contour of the slope, are influenced by wind and by the restraining effect of the vegetation cover.

Solifluction

Solifluction (soil flow) occurs in areas where bedrock, permafrost, or seasonal ground ice prevents the downward percolation of water. As the upper soil layer becomes increasingly saturated due to seasonal thawing, it tends to lose its cohesive strength and deform downslope as a viscous mass. Solifluction lobes and terraces frequently resemble large tongues of soil banked along their fronts by piles of rock or vegetation; they may coalesce to form scalloped, lobate terrace complexes extending for considerable distances across a slope. Solifluction features frequently have meltwater pools on their surfaces in summer, and patterned ground may develop on inactive lobes where vegetation cover is limited. Downslope movement rates vary depending on local conditions; rates of nearly two inches per year have been reported for the Colorado Front Range.

During the Pleistocene, solifluction was the most important soil movement process on all but the driest of alpine slopes. Under present climatic conditions, frost creep is the most important process, and active solifluction is restricted to areas where the water table remains high enough during the fall freeze to permit development of thick ice-lenses. Both inactive and active solifluction features can be seen in most alpine areas of the Southern Rockies; good examples are easily observed from Trail Ridge Road in Rocky Mountain National Park.

Earthflows and Mudflows

The terms *earthflow* and *mudflow* are applied to types of mass-wasting that are similar to solifluction but involve more rapid movement. An earthflow characteristically exhibits a spoon-shaped sliding surface, a crescent-shaped cliff at its upper end, and a tongue-shaped bulge at its lower end. The Slumgullion Earthflow, near Lake City in the San Juans, is the most famous example of this type of mass movement in the Southern Rockies. This spectacular earthflow began in supersaturated, strongly weathered volcanic rocks at an altitude of about 11,400 feet and flowed downvalley to an altitude of 8,200 feet, where the flow dammed the valley above the present community of Lake City and formed San Cristobal Lake. Where Colorado 149 crosses the Slumgullian Earthflow, the bumpy pavement provides some indication of continuing movement. Mudflows are more liquid than earthflows, tend to create steep-walled channels flanked by ridges of debris in the form of levees, and terminate in debris fans. Evidence of both young and old mudflow activity is common throughout the Southern Rockies.

Talus and Scree

Along the bases of steep slopes, accumulations of frost-wedged rocks commonly form apronlike deposits called talus if they are composed chiefly of large blocks or scree if they are made up of smaller-sized rocks. In certain volcanic ranges, most notably the San Juan Mountains, rapid scree development in closely jointed volcanic rocks has produced spectacular rock streams and debris mantles.

Rock Glaciers

Rock glaciers are lobate or tongue-shaped accumulations of unsorted rock debris that resemble ice glaciers in many ways. Active rock glaciers are ice cored or ice cemented, which accounts for their glacierlike movement. Most rock glaciers head in cirques or are located at the bases of steep-walled cliffs, where they receive a continual supply of frost-riven rock. Depending on local conditions, rock glaciers may be active or inactive and vary in length from a few hundred yards to more than a mile. The fronts of active rock glaciers tend to be steep, fresh-appearing, and unstable; evidence of past or present movement is apparent in the arcuate flow ridges that pattern their surfaces. Movement rates for active rock glaciers in the Southern Rockies are quite variable, ranging from less than eight inches per year in the Colorado Front Range and the Sawatch Range to as many as twenty-four inches per year in the Elk Mountains.

Rock glaciers can form in several ways. Some are simply ice glaciers that have been buried by rock debris, whereas others originate from the accumulation of massive quantities of frost-riven rock and the development of an internal ice core. Active and inactive rock glaciers are common in many areas of the Southern Rockies that have long been abandoned by glacial ice. On Mount Sopris, in the Elk Mountains, both types, some more than a mile long, fill all major valleys. Some of the most spectacular rock glaciers in the world are located in the San Juan Mountains; the best examples can be seen in the Imogene, Pierson, Silver, American, and Hurricane basins. Rock glaciers are also common in the Colorado Front, Sawatch, and Sangre de Cristo ranges.

CHAPTER EIGHT

Climate and Weather in the Southern Rockies

This mountain wave cloud marks a ripple in the airflow over the Continental Divide in the Colorado Front Range.

The climate of the Southern Rockies is a mosaic, with the differences from one area to another clearly imprinted on the shape and texture of the mountain landscape. An hour's drive into the mountains is generally all it takes to trade the scorching heat of a lowland summer's day for the crisp delight of an alpine snowfield. Every mountain range, basin, and canyon exhibits a climatic pattern as unique as a signature, one influenced by the interplay of topographic differences and regional climatic controls such as latitude, continentality, altitude, orientation of the main ranges, prevailing wind direction, and storm tracks. These regional climatic controls ultimately determine the distribution of solar radiation, temperature, precipitation, and local winds: the dependent meteorological variables that interact to produce our daily weather phenomena.

To a hiker caught above timberline in a sudden thunderstorm or snow squall, the behavior of the atmosphere may appear random, capricious, and even malevolent. In mountain environments, sharp contrasts often occur within short vertical and horizontal distances, as well as within short time spans. Although the interactions that determine day-to-day weather phenomena may seem complex, they conform to predictable patterns and characteristics common to all mountainous areas.

Regional Climate Controls

The term *climate* integrates all of the long-term, variable characteristics of the atmosphere in a particular region: temperature, precipitation, wind speed and direction, radiation, sunshine, cloudiness, and evaporation. Climate, to a large degree, determines the natural environment. It sets the stage upon which all physical, chemical, and biological processes operate. Weather, in contrast to climate, reflects short-term fluctuations in atmospheric conditions and describes, in both quantitative and qualitative terms, the state of the atmosphere at a given time and place.

Latitude and Continentality

The Southern Rockies are located in the middle latitudes, where seasonal differences in the angle of the sun above the horizon and in day length account for substantial variations in temperature from summer to winter. Middle-latitude mountains receive a greater proportion of incoming solar radiation than do lowland areas, both because the atmosphere is thinner at higher elevations and because the sun's rays strike slopes oriented toward the sun at a higher angle than they do level surfaces. In the Southern Rockies, latitudinally controlled differences in incoming solar radiation result in a decline in temperature from south to north; the effects of this gradient can be seen in the changing composition of forest communities and in the decreasing elevation of timberline as you move northward along the Rockies.

One of the major climatic controls affecting the Southern Rockies is their midcontinent location, far from the moderating influences of moist maritime air masses. The region is dominated by a highland continental climate and consequently experiences larger diurnal and seasonal differences in temperature, lower humidity, more sunshine, less cloudiness, and less precipitation than coastal mountain ranges. Eastward-moving storms originating in the Pacific Ocean lose a substantial quantity of their moisture as they pass over mountain ranges to the west of the Southern Rockies, further intensifying the effects of continentality.

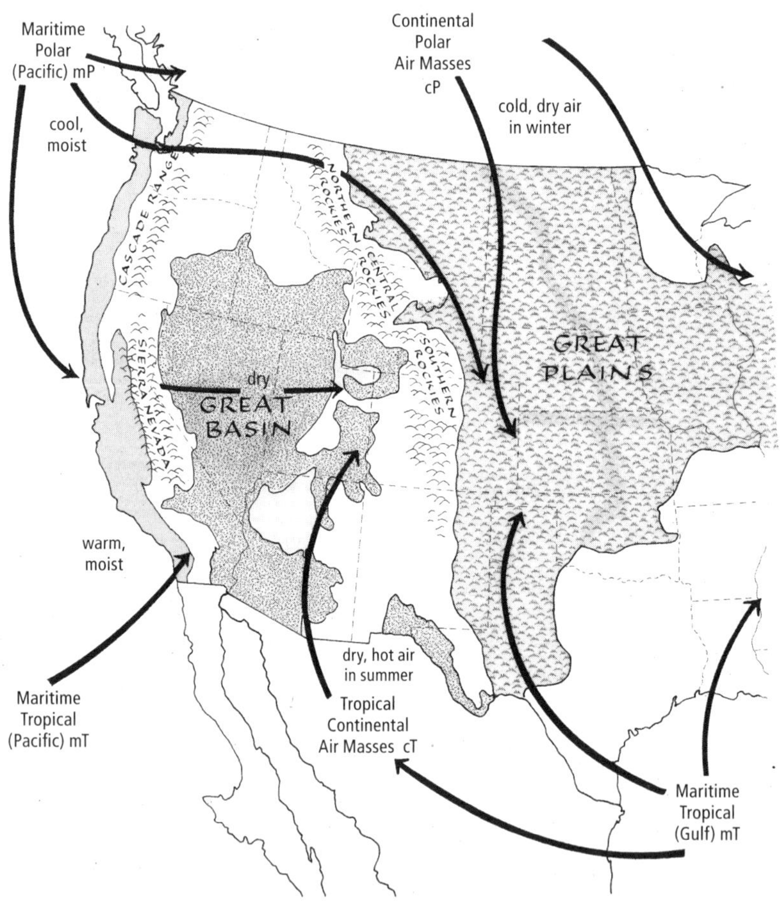

Air mass source areas affecting the Southern Rocky Mountains.

Air Mass Source Areas

Day-to-day weather depends primarily on the temperature, stability, and moisture content of the air masses that continually pass overhead. Air masses are classified according to area of origin and moisture content into two basic types: maritime and continental. Maritime air masses develop over an ocean and are characterized by high water-vapor content and high condensation potential. Continental air masses evolve over the dry interior of a continent and are characterized by low water-vapor content and low condensation potential. Three maritime source areas and two continental source areas influence the climate of the Southern Rockies: (1) maritime polar (cool Pacific, from the Pacific Northwest); (2) maritime tropical (warm Pacific, from the Baja area of southern California); (3) maritime tropical (from the Gulf of Mexico); (4) continental tropical (from Mexico); and (5) polar continental (from north-central Canada).

The Altitude Factor

Temperature and Altitude

When summer temperatures in Denver soar into the nineties, those atop nearby Mount Evans (14,264 feet) may only register in the sixties. This altitudinal variation in air temperature, called the lapse rate, is the result of a never-ending balancing act going on in the mountain atmosphere. The Earth absorbs the majority of incoming solar radiant energy in vegetation, soil, rocks, and water and then returns a portion of this energy to the atmosphere in the form of kinetic energy (as heat). As the air in contact with the surface is warmed, it expands and becomes less dense, which causes it to rise; this process is called convection. Heat is lost as a result of the kinetic energy of expansion, leading to a decrease in air temperature at the average rate of about 3.5°F for every 1,000-foot gain in elevation. It is important to remember that the lapse rate is influenced by the amount of incoming solar radiation, the slope aspect, winds, and the amount of moisture in the air.

Air Density and Altitude

The heat-holding capacity of air is determined by its density and composition. At sea level, the weight, or density, of the air (the standard atmospheric pressure) is expressed as 29.92 inches of mercury. As elevation increases, atmospheric pressure decreases at the rate of about one inch per 1,000 feet.

At higher altitudes, the molecules in a given parcel of air are spaced farther apart, so there are fewer molecules to receive and hold heat. Water vapor and suspended particulate matter are important heat-absorbing and radiating constituents in the atmosphere. More than half of the water vapor in the atmosphere occurs below an altitude of 8,000 feet; above this elevation, the amount of water vapor diminishes rapidly and is barely detectable at altitudes above 12,000 feet. In the mountains, temperatures tend to drop off sharply after sunset because of the limited ability of the high-altitude atmosphere to hold heat. The orientation of a given slope with respect to the sun exaggerates these effects, and great differences may occur between sunny and shaded slopes, wet and dry slopes, and windward and leeward slopes.

Most visitors to the mountains quickly notice the lower oxygen content of the air. As the density of the air decreases, there are fewer molecules of oxygen per unit volume, and consequently, above 8,000 feet most people begin to experience some shortness of breath. At 10,000 feet, a hiker must take in approximately a third more air to receive the same amount of oxygen as at sea level. Visitors to high elevations are encouraged to allow sufficient time for acclimatization (two to three days are recommended) before undertaking vigorous physical activity. Failure to do so may result in the unpleasant and sometimes life-threatening symptoms of acute mountain sickness (AMS): difficulty in sleeping, fatigue, persistent headache, nausea, and, in severe cases, pulmonary or cerebral embolism.

Atmospheric Circulation: Westerlies, Jet Streams, and Air Masses

Air Pressure and Winds

Atmospheric convection is the driving force behind the movement of air. When air is heated, it increases in volume and rises because of its greater buoyancy. These vertical air currents rob the surface of some of its air, thus creating regions of slightly lower pressure at the bottom of the rising air column. As air is forced to move from areas of higher pressure toward the newly created low-pressure area, a horizontal pressure gradient develops. These air movements vary in size and in their significance for climate, ranging from local winds, such as dust devils and valley winds, to large-scale air currents in the upper levels of the atmosphere.

The largest-scale wind patterns, the winds aloft, are initiated by pressure systems set up by latitudinal variations in incoming solar radiation. In the Northern Hemisphere, the winds aloft are deflected to the right by the Earth's rotation, spiraling counterclockwise around the lows and clockwise around the highs. Meterologists refer to centers of low pressure as cyclones; centers of high pressure are called anticyclones. As a result of the Coriolis force, large-scale air motions move perpendicular to the pressure gradient, that is, around regions of low and high pressure but not directly to or from them. These large-scale pressure patterns, and the winds aloft they generate, play a critical role in shaping the climate of the Southern Rockies.

Winds Aloft: The Westerlies and the Jet Stream

If we could look down on the atmosphere from above, we would see a broad current of air, the upper-air westerlies, moving generally from west to east around the globe in the midlatitudes. Frequently, atmospheric disturbances in the circumpolar flow of the westerlies produce large, wavelike undulations known as Rossby waves. Rossby waves develop along a narrow zone, called the polar front, which marks the contact between cold polar air (the polar easterlies) to the north and warm tropical air to the south. A trough (characterized by low pressure and cyclonic flow) and an adjacent ridge (characterized by high pressure and anticyclonic flow) constitute a wave. Rossby waves vary in number and position, but generally five such waves link to encircle the Earth.

Traveling with the Rossby waves, and coinciding with the polar front, is a zone of high-speed flow called the polar front jet stream. The position of the polar front jet stream is affected by major topographic features and by variables such as changes in land and sea surface temperatures. The Rocky Mountains, which are oriented almost perpendicular to the prevailing west-to-east airflow pattern, impose disturbances of all scales on upper-air circulation, ranging from the initiation of meanders in jet stream systems to the large-amplitude vertical waves that generate windstorms along the eastern slope of the Rockies. Large meanders or displacements of the polar front jet are responsible for some of the recent weather anomalies in the United States. Although the polar front jet stream is the most important jet affecting weather in the Southern Rockies, the eastward-moving subtropical jet stream, one of the strongest and most consistent winds in the world, also supplies energy to mid-latitude storms, and explains how thunderstorms in the tropics of Indonesia and South America can shape Western weather.

The sharp north-to-south temperature gradient that exists in the Northern Hemisphere during the winter months causes the upper-air westerlies to intensify seasonally and with increasing altitude. Consequently, winds in the Southern Rockies are nearly twice as strong in winter as in summer. Another important characteristic of the upper-air westerlies is that their location shifts latitudinally with the seasons in response to seasonal differences in the global pressure regimes. During the summer, when westerly airflow is comparatively weak, the main air current and its associated polar front jet stream stay far to the north, over Canada. By winter, however, the westerlies and the main axis of the polar front jet are frequently positioned over the Southern Rockies, guiding Pacific storm systems through the region at fairly regular intervals. As the main belt of westerlies migrates northward in the spring, the windy storms of winter give way to the calmer weather of summer. During those occasional winters when a large ridge in the upper atmosphere keeps the polar front jet along or to the north of the Canadian border, the Southern Rockies may experience a lack of snow, severe drought, and unseasonably warm weather.

Air Masses, Fronts, and Wave Cyclones

The storms that buffet the Southern Rockies are actually small wave disturbances, called wave cyclones, embedded in and traveling through the Rossby waves. Sharp contrasts, such as those encountered along the polar front, give rise to a procession of wave cyclones (cyclonic storms), each wave delineated by a vortex that forms, intensifies, and then dissolves as it travels east along the polar front. What we experience at the surface is a migration of cyclones and anticyclones, each disturbance initiated and steered by the winds aloft and then dragged along beneath the core of the polar front jet stream. Traveling cyclones may be mild in intensity, their passage marked by little more than a period of cloud cover and minimal precipitation, or, when pressure gradients are great, they may develop into powerful storm systems.

Pacific Influences: El Niño Events and Global Warming

Vasco Nuñez de Balboa's first glimpse of the Pacific Ocean, in 1513, was from a hill above present-day Panama City. Long acquainted with the stormy spirit of the Atlantic, Balboa gazed down on an ocean swept smooth as glass by the calming winds we now know to be typical of the equatorial doldrums. The peaceful appearance, or pacificity, of this largest of all oceans inspired Balboa to give it the name Pacific and to claim the entire ocean for Spain. We now know that the Pacific Ocean spawns more storms than any other ocean and that a large number of these affect North America, either directly or indirectly. In fact, two storm-generating phenomena that occur well offshore in the Pacific play an indirect but long-lasting role in shaping weather events in the Southern Rockies: the El Niño and the Pacific Decadal Oscillation.

El Niño is the name given by the fisherman of coastal Peru and Ecuador to an extremely warm ocean current that occurs periodically along the Pacific coast of South America. The arrival of an El Niño current can warm coastal waters by ten degrees or more, sufficient warming to interrupt or turn back the normal cold-water current that sweeps northward from the Antarctic and is responsible for triggering the amazing nutrient-loaded upwelling that occurs immediately offshore. This upwelling has historically made Peruvian and Ecuadorian coastal waters among the richest fishing grounds in the world. El Niños, in combination with overfishing, have become increasingly disastrous for the fishing industry, not to mention the fish themselves and the birds and other animals that depend on them for food. A La Niña event, the inverse of an El Niño, is associated with colder-than-usual sea surface temperatures. The shift from El Niño conditions to La Niña and back again takes about four years. Climatologists and meteorologists have only begun to understand this irregular oscillation and its consequences for global climate. In recent decades, the deployment of fixed, unmanned ocean buoys in the Pacific Ocean and orbiting satellites that transmit the data these bouys collect has enabled scientists to make great strides in understanding the intricate dance of ocean and atmosphere.

What does an El Niño portend for weather in the western United States? When the warm water of an El Niño spreads westward across the tropical Pacific and northward along the west coast of Mexico toward

California and Oregon, as it has most recently in the spectacular El Niños of 1982–83 and 1997–98, the worldwide climatic impacts can be catastrophic. The effects of an El Niño or a La Niña can also be felt far inland, even deep within the heart of the Southern Rockies, where the two snowiest winters in the late twentieth century coincided with the 1982–83 and 1997–98 events, the strongest El Niños of the last century.

Most evidence suggests that El Niño–related weather anomalies in the United States result primarily from the shifting positions of the seasonal storm tracks. The degree of certainty with which meteorologists are able to make long-range predictions concerning the potential impacts of an El Niño remains elusive, largely because the patterns of warming and cooling, as well as the timing, duration, and strength associated with an El Niño, differ substantially from one event to the next. Scientists from the National Center for Atmospheric Research, in Boulder, suggest that the pool of warm water in the Pacific that fuels an El Niño may be growing larger and that global warming and the El Niño phenomenon may be reinforcing each other in their impact on the environment and society, primarily through their combined effects on the hydrologic cycle and on water supplies. Though we have no way of knowing what the Pacific-based phenomena of El Niño and the Pacific Decadal Oscillation will do in the future, or, for that matter, what sunspot cycles, ocean currents, carbon dioxide levels, or volcanic eruptions will do, most meteorologists concur that any one or several of these factors have the capacity to exert an indirect, though long-lasting impact on the climate of the Southern Rockies.

Understanding Mountain Climates

Solar Radiation

Mountains experience the most extreme and variable radiation climate on Earth. We know that incoming solar radiation, predominately in the form of ultraviolet (short-wave) energy, increases in intensity with height above sea level. Research in the Colorado Front Range shows a 26 percent increase in ultraviolet radiation between the elevations of 5,500 feet and 14,000 feet on a cloudless summer day. There is little doubt that the greater intensity of ultraviolet radiation in mountainous areas has special significance for all life and for biological processes. Skin sunburns rapidly at high elevations because of the intensity of ultraviolet radiation. In recent years, the high incidence of skin cancer in individuals living and working outdoors at high altitudes has received widespread attention. Many plants growing at high altitudes exhibit a wide range of adaptations, such as protective pigments and surface hairs, that serve to reduce the damaging effects of high ultraviolet transmission.

Describing the color of the sky on a clear day challenges our imaginations and invokes an artist's palette of hues: cerulean, azure, cobalt, turquoise, sapphire, robin's egg, and aquamarine. Most people have no trouble describing the "color" of sunlight as white or pale yellow, though we know that sunlight is actually a mixture of all the wavelength colors, from blue to green, yellow, orange, and red. The light waves that travel through our atmosphere consist of electric and magnetic fields that tend to behave much like water waves when they encounter an obstacle, bending and rippling around the object and deflecting (or scattering) in various directions, depending on the amplitude of the wave. In the case of light waves, these obstacles are molecules of air. Light waves have mathematically precise lengths, each wavelength color corresponding to a specific set of electromagnetic parameters. Blue light has a shorter wavelength than red light, so when a sunbeam travels through the air molecules above our heads, blue light is scattered the most and red light is scattered the least and continues on a relatively straight path. When you look at the sky, away from the sun, the color blue is what you see because those wavelengths are subjected to greater scattering than are the red, yellow, or green wavelenths. Most people have noticed how much bluer the clear sky looks in the mountains than at lower elevations. This intensity of color results from a decrease in molecular scattering, which primarily affects wavelengths in the short-wave, or blue, end of the spectrum, and the greater availability of short wavelengths at higher elevations because of this decreased scattering.

Slope Differences

Differences in the duration and intensity of incoming solar radiation are among the key determinants of microclimate, the highly localized climate at or near the ground surface. The angle of the slope and the orientation of the slope with respect to the sun profoundly influence the amount of solar radiation available at the ground surface. Topographically controlled differences in energy income are reflected in soil and air temperatures, snow-cover duration, and soil moisture. In the Southern Rockies, south-facing slopes are measurably warmer and drier than north-facing slopes, resulting in slope-specific differences in the duration of winter snow cover, evapotranspiration rates, the plant species represented, and the types of habitats available to wildlife. Geologic processes such as frost shattering, soil creep, and rock exfoliation, each an important agent in landscape development, are controlled by variations in incoming solar radiation and the associated moisture conditions at the site.

Temperature

Mountains tend to heat up rapidly as a result of the higher levels of incoming solar radiation they receive but are quick to lose their heat by radiative cooling, producing a steep temperature gradient in the surrounding air. The Southern Rockies are characterized by strong diurnal and seasonal temperature gradients. At most elevations in the Southern Rockies, the diurnal temperature range is broad, generally between 30° and 40°F. Nocturnal cooling begins shortly before nightfall, reaching maximum rates just before midnight and continuing at a diminishing rate until shortly after sunrise. Summer nights with little or no cloud cover tend to be cool or cold because the clear night skies permit rapid radiative heat loss. Overcast conditions flatten the diurnal temperature curve by blocking incoming solar radiation in the daytime and retarding radiative heat loss at night.

Temperature Inversions

Temperature inversions are a common phenomenon in mountainous areas. During a temperature inversion, temperatures are lowest in the valley and increase upward along the mountain slope, a situation clearly at odds with the normal lapse rate rule. Temperature inversions develop best when skies are clear, permitting rapid heat loss to the atmosphere, especially when there is no wind to mix and equalize temperatures. As the higher ground surface becomes colder than the overlying air, the air immediately above the surface begins to lose heat to the surface (by conduction and turbulence) as a result of downward heat flux. Eventually the cool air flows downslope, sliding beneath the warm air along the valley floor and displacing it.

If the valley is open, with no topographic impediment to the free flow of air, there may be continuous downvalley movement, or cold air drainage. The magnitude of cold air drainage can range from a cool breeze in a narrow stream valley to a substantial flow, such as that experienced along the Rio Grande Valley in north-central New Mexico. If the valley is encircled by mountains, as is true of the Gunnison Valley, the cold air will tend to "pool" because cold air is heavy and tends to hug the ground in situations where the topography impedes cold air drainage. Similar conditions are responsible for the low temperatures associated with mountain basins such as the San Luis Valley and North and Middle parks, where diurnal temperature ranges of 50°F are common. The lowest recorded winter temperature in the Southern Rockies, a reading of -61°F at Maybell, in northwestern Colorado, was produced by a closed-basin temperature inversion. During the winter months, temperature inversions developing over the Denver metropolitan area, in the natural bowl formed by the South Platte River Valley and the Colorado Front Range, exascerbate air pollution problems by trapping dangerous levels of carbon monoxide.

Growing Season

The growing season is determined by the length of the frost-free period, the span of time bracketed by the last occurrence in spring and the first in fall of a temperature of 32°F or below. In alpine areas of the Southern Rockies, the growing season is no more than forty days, about half that of Alaska's Yukon Valley. Above 9,000 feet, freezing temperatures are possible any night during the year. At Leadville (10,158 feet), the highest city in the Southern Rockies, the growing season averages between sixty and eighty days. Lower elevations fare little better. Red River (8,676 feet), in the southern Sangre de Cristos, averages eighty-three days; Estes Park (7,522 feet), in the Colorado Front Range, averages fewer than 100 days. Along the eastern edge of the mountains, Denver's growing season is about 170 days, and nearby Colorado Springs averages 148 days. Grand Junction (4,586 feet), famous for its peach and apple orchards, has perhaps the longest growing season in the Southern Rockies, with a range of 160 to 190 days.

Precipitation: Orographic Effects, Cyclonic Storms, and Convection

Condensation of water vapor into cloud droplets occurs when large quantities of air—individual parcels, entire layers, or air masses—are forced upward and cooled to the saturation point. Three types of lifting mechanisms cause air to rise: frontal wedging associated with cyclonic storms, convective air currents generated by differential heating of the ground surface, and mechanical lifting resulting from orographic (topographic) impediments to horizontal wind flow. The highly variable precipitation pattern that characterizes the Southern Rockies results from differences in elevation, slope orientation, seasonal storm tracks, and the trajectories of air masses delivering precipitation.

Orographic Precipitation

Orographic effects dominate any discussion of precipitation in mountainous areas. The steeper and more exposed the slope, the more rapidly air will be forced to rise. During its forced ascent, the air is cooled by expansion. As the air cools, it loses its capacity to hold water vapor; clouds form as the excess moisture condenses, and if moisture and temperature conditions are suitable, precipitation will occur. Orographic lifting is most effective when the mountains are oriented, as the Southern Rockies are, perpendicular to the prevailing winds. In the Southern Rockies, as in all mountainous areas, orographic lifting serves to intensify cyclonic and convectional precipitation.

Orographic precipitation accounts for a significant percentage of the winter snowfall in the Southern Rockies. How much snow falls is determined largely by how moist the air is and how fast it is moving. The stronger the winds, the more rapidly the air will be forced to rise, producing greater amounts of precipitation in areas west of the Continental Divide. During periods of strong westerly airflow, a massive, wall-like cloud, or crest cloud, is commonly observed over the divide, while leeward slopes and other locations where the air is descending (such as into mountain basins) generally remain clear and receive little precipitation. In contrast, when moisture-laden Gulf of Mexico air is pumped northward along the Eastern Slope of the Southern Rockies under upslope conditions, the eastern foothills and plains may receive substantial precipitation. In the absence of a significant storm system, a stratiform cloud layer may form over lowland areas, leaving higher elevations basking in sunshine. Upslope fog is a frequent phenomenon in the mountains, occuring when moist air near the saturation point is forced upward along a sloping plain or steep mountain slope.

Cyclonic Precipitation

During a cyclonic storm, the upward spiral of air from the center of the low-pressure system produces clouds and rain as the air cools and ultimately reaches saturation. A typical cyclonic storm, intensified by orographic lifting along the Western Slope of the Southern Rockies, delivers the greatest amount of precipitation to the windward slope of the mountains, while a marked decrease in precipitation occurs on the leeward side. Where the ranges tend to be in echelon, the first mountain range usually receives the largest amount of precipitation and succeeding ranges downwind receive progressively less. As the air descends the leeward side of the mountains, it is compressed and warmed, making further precipitation unlikely and producing a distinctly dry area, or rain shadow, immediately to the lee of the higher ranges. The major intermontane basins of the Southern Rockies—North Park, Middle Park, South Park, and the San Luis Valley—are situated in rain shadows cast by the mountains that flank their western borders.

Convectional Precipitation

During the summer months, convection storms generate most of the precipitation received by the Southern Rockies. Daytime solar heating of the ground warms the adjacent air, producing an unstable air layer that may extend upward to a height of 3,000 feet or more. As the air is warmed, it begins to rise, setting up organized thermals, columns of upward-moving air that are sought by hang-glider pilots and soaring birds alike. If the moisture content of the air is sufficient and if the air rises high enough, the cooling caused by expansion of the rising air will lead to condensation and to the formation of small cumulus clouds. Continued heating of the ground will intensify the rising air currents, causing the clouds to increase in size. As the day proceeds and heat input from the sun decreases, the driving force for convection diminishes, resulting in clearing skies by late afternoon or early evening.

During the summer, cumulus clouds typically develop over the mountains by late morning and, if sufficient moisture is present, produce widely scattered rain showers and thunderstorms by midafternoon.

Although the frequency of afternoon showers in the mountains is relatively high, most are of brief duration, producing highly localized precipitation, lightning, and small hail in the higher elevations before drifting eastward with the prevailing winds. With enough heat and moisture, cumulus clouds can mushroom into colossal anvil-topped thunderheads. At their worst, the cloudbursts associated with these awe-inspiring thunderheads may spawn locally violent winds in combination with rain, lightning, thunder, and hail at higher elevations; along the Eastern Slope, a second peaking of thunderstorm activity in the early evening hours often marks the eastward passage of these towering cumulous clouds as they move across the High Plains.

Mountain Winds: Mountain Waves, Chinooks, and Local Winds

Mountain Waves

Mountain ranges are windier than nearby lowlands because they intercept the fast-traveling winds aloft and because they are able to generate their own localized wind systems. The Rocky Mountains are the longest north-south mountain barrier in the world. When the upper-air westerlies produce a strong, deep flow of air across the Rockies, the peaks along the Continental Divide create ripples in the air currents, in much the same way that a rock in a streambed produces ripples in the surface of the water. Once initiated, these wavelike undulations, known as mountain waves, develop over and to the lee of the mountains before settling back into a relatively horizontal flow pattern over the Great Plains. This orographically induced flow pattern is superimposed on the upper-air Rossby wave patterns and smaller wave disturbances that are already in place. Mountain waves with vertical air movement reaching fifty miles per hour can result in the kind of clear-air turbulence feared by both commercial airlines and private pilots.

Distinctive, lens-shaped clouds known as mountain wave clouds are a common sight in the mountains during the winter months. These lenticular clouds, sometimes appearing as caps above individual peaks, provide the best evidence that mountain-wave conditions are present in the upper air. Mountain wave clouds form near the crest of the range because the air there, expanding and cooling as it is forced upward by the peaks, chills sufficiently to condense some of its water vapor; lee wave clouds form downwind from the crest and may occur as far as 200 miles downwind from the mountains.

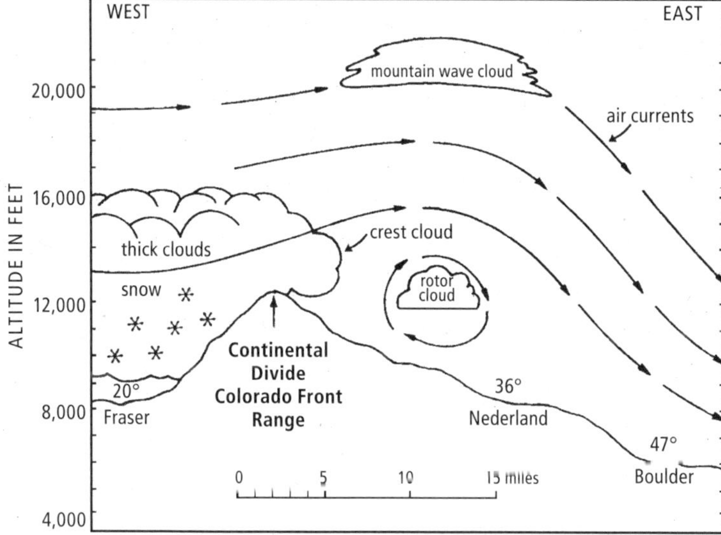

Schematic diagram illustrating the characteristic weather phenomena associated with a chinook. The transect extends from Fraser, on the Western Slope of the Colorado Front Range, eastward across the mountains to Boulder. Note the differences in temperature along the transect, especially at Fraser and at Nederland. (After Hansen, Wallace R., John Chronic, and John Matelock. "Climatology of the Front Range Urban Corridor and Vicinity, Colorado." U.S. Geological Survey Professional Paper no. 1019. Washington, DC.: U.S. Government Printing Office, 1978.)

The smoothly contoured base of a mountain wave cloud is determined by the altitude at which condensation occurs; the rounded top corresponds to the undulating shape of the airstream.

Chinook Winds

When a low-pressure system is situated to the lee of the mountains, the westerly airflow, after passing over the mountain barrier, is forced to accelerate downward along the mountains' leeward slopes. The downslope wind that results is known as a chinook, an Indian word that means "snow eater." Chinooks are characterized by several distinctive weather phenomena: persistent and often gusty winds, high temperatures, low humidity, and the development of a relatively stationary, cumuliform cloud, known as a crest cloud, along the windward slope of the mountains.

When viewed from the leeward side of the mountains, the shape of a crest cloud may be distinctly wall-like, its top planed horizontally by high winds, or it may be somewhat billowy, with a wind-tattered top. Crest clouds form when moist Pacific air is forced up the windward side of the mountains where it undergoes cooling and condensation; as the air descends the leeward slopes, it warms up and the clouds evaporate. When the winds are strong and persistent, crest clouds may last for several days and total precipitation may be significant. During most chinooks, considerable precipitation may occur along the windward slopes of the Southern Rockies, where the air is forced to rise, while the leeward or eastern slopes of the mountains receive little or no precipitation. The amount of moisture contained in a crest cloud is highly variable. Gray, ominous-appearing crest clouds are associated with moisture-laden Pacific air masses; these "wet" crest clouds deposit a great deal of snow along the higher elevations and windward slopes of the Colorado Front Range, spilling over as downslope storms along leeward slopes to elevations of 9,500 to 9,000 feet. White, "dry" crest clouds, on the other hand, generally contain minimal moisture and produce little or no precipitation on either the windward or leeward slopes of the mountains.

A crest cloud towers above Sawtooth Peak west of Boulder. Note the smooth-topped, wall-like shape compared to the snow plumes that envelop the summit area.

The rapid rise in temperature associated with the onset of a typical chinook is due to heating of the air by condensation processes on the windward side and by compression, or adiabatic heating, on the leeward side of the mountains. Although periodic chinooks may reduce the snowpack at lower elevations along the eastern slope of the mountains, maintaining large areas of snow-free winter range for grazing by elk, mule deer, and cattle, the low relative humidity of these winds, often below 10 percent, can also wick away valuable moisture from vegetation and exposed soil.

Destructive Windstorms

Chinook winds attain hurricane force several times each year, with gusts exceeding 100 miles per hour. These destructive windstorms develop when unstable conditions over the crest of the range initiate extreme amplification of the mountain wave patterns. Where the wave dips sharply downward along the Eastern Slope of the Southern Rockies, especially between the Front Range cities of Colorado Springs and Fort Collins, the resulting lee windstorms routinely damage roofs, shatter glass, and litter the streets with branches and trash. Wind velocities during these windstorms are usually highest close to the eastern mountain front and near the mouths of major canyons. Boulder, at the mouth of Boulder Canyon, has recorded wind velocities in excess of 143 miles per hour, nearly twice the strength of minimum hurricane-velocity winds. Lee windstorms are most common during the winter months, particularly during January.

Local Winds: Slope Winds and Mountain and Valley Winds

Local winds are small-scale, short-lived phenomena generated by topographic differences in surface heating. They are best developed under clear skies and in the presence of a weak high-pressure system. When such conditions prevail, the air above a mountain slope warms and begins to rise, producing vertical convection currents. Because the warm air is less dense, it moves upward along the slope. Cooler air from nearby areas flows in to replace the heated air, and a small-scale circulation pattern develops. Meteorologists recognize two types of local winds: slope winds and mountain and valley winds.

Slope winds are thin layers of air that flow up the slope during the day and down at night. Upslope flow begins shortly after sunrise, as the mountain slopes begin to warm, reaching maximum intensity around noontime. By late afternoon, the upslope wind has abated, and within half an hour of sunset, is replaced by a downslope wind that develops as the slopes and the adjacent air layer begin to cool; because of its increased density, the cool air flows rapidly downslope, displacing warm air in the valley bottom.

Mountain and valley winds blow upvalley during the day and downvalley at night, traveling essentially at right angles to the slope winds. Although controlled by similar thermal responses, mountain and valley winds involve greater thermal contrast and a larger air mass than slope winds. During stormy or windy weather, however, the daily pattern of slope winds and mountain-valley circulation may be highly modified or even nonexistent. Valley winds, blowing from the valley toward the mountain, begin shortly after sunrise, reaching a maximum around midday and diminishing by sunset. After sunset, as the pool of cold air in the valley bottom begins to build, valley winds are replaced by a mountain or downvalley wind. The cold air drainage typically associated with mountain winds may significantly delay the budding and flowering of trees and herbaceous plants that lie in the path of the cold air.

Seasonal Weather Patterns

Winter

Winter climate in the Southern Rockies is influenced by storm systems originating over the Pacific Ocean and by high pressure centering over the Great Basin. In most areas, the seasonal snowpack above 10,000 feet begins to accumulate in late October and reaches its maximum depth in mid-April. During most winters, frequent storms produce moderate amounts of dry, powdery snow. Consequently, the mountain resort developments of the Southern Rockies rank among the top destinations in North America for downhill and cross-country skiers and snowboarders. More important, however, the mountain snowpack is the lifeblood of the watersheds of the Rio Grande, the Colorado, the Canadian, the Pecos, the North and South Platte, and the Arkansas rivers, specifically because of its depth and water content.

Winter storm patterns affecting the Southern Rockies correspond largely to differences in the orientation of the jet stream and in the air mass source areas and trajectories. Meteorologists recognize four main winter storm patterns, designated here by source area and route of passage: (1) cool Pacific, tracking from the northwest; (2) cool and warm Pacific, tracking from the west; (3) warm Pacific, tracking from the southwest; and (4) Gulf of Mexico, the air mass but not the storm system tracking from the south.

Storm Systems Tracking from the Pacific Northwest

A high percentage of early and midwinter snowfall is generated by migrating cyclonic storms that originate over the cool Pacific Ocean (in the Pacific Northwest) and follow a southeasterly route that parallels the Columbia River Valley on the border between Oregon and Washington and the Snake River area of southern Idaho before sweeping south across the Wyoming Basin. This route coincides with the zone of maximum westerlies and the main axis of the polar jet stream, at a latitude of about 40° north. Precipitation associated with this flow tends to come in relatively frequent storms that drop light to moderate amounts of snow. In general, the amount of precipitation delivered by these storms increases with elevation on the windward slopes of the mountains, usually reaching a maximum slightly windward of the mountain crests; the leeward slopes, especially those east of the Continental Divide, receive comparatively little precipitation from these storms. Storm systems tracking southeast from the cool Pacific deliver their heaviest snows to the Flat Tops and the Park Range. Average annual snowfall at Steamboat Springs, at the western edge of the Park Range, is 166 inches; at Buffalo Pass (10,180 feet), just short of the crest of the Park Range, average annual snowfall is nearly twice that reported for Steamboat.

Storm Systems Tracking from the West

When the main axis of the winter jet stream crosses the Southern Rockies from the west or southwest, Pacific air is channeled across California, often pumping large quantities of moist, unstable air into the region. With strong westerly flow, air masses originating over both the warm and cool Pacific source areas penetrate the continent with sufficient moisture to produce substantial snowfalls in the Southern Rockies before continuing east. Some of the most intense winter storms occur when the jet stream plunges southward west of the mountains and loops northward once again just east of the mountain front. Under these conditions, a low-pressure center often forms in western Colorado or northwestern New Mexico, moving slowly eastward and producing substantial snowfall on the Eastern Slope as well as in the central and southern mountains.

Storm Systems Tracking from the Southwest

Air masses originating over the warm Pacific generally enter the Southern Rockies from the southwest and are capable of transporting larger quantities of moisture than those originating over the cool Pacific. Considerably fewer of these systems, however, reach the Southern Rockies. For these storms to successfully penetrate the region, their trajectory must angle northwest across Arizona and New Mexico, lingering long enough to draw up large quantities of tropical Pacific air. Maximum winter precipitation from these storms occurs in the San Juan Range, the first major barrier to storm systems tracking from the west and southwest. Snowfall along the windward side of the San Juans often exceeds thirty feet; during the winter of 1978–79, Wolf Creek Pass received nearly seventy feet of snow, establishing a Southern Rocky Mountain record for the greatest snowfall in one season.

Storm Systems Nourished by Moisture from the Gulf of Mexico

Major snowstorms occur along the eastern slope of the Southern Rockies as the result of upslope winds laden with moisture carried northward from the Gulf of Mexico. This influx of Gulf air masses is generated by the counterclockwise flow of air around low-pressure areas moving across New Mexico and southern Colorado; the presence of a stalled, cutoff low (known locally as an Albuquerque low) can produce heavy snowfalls as the Gulf air is forced to rise up the eastern flanks of the Southern Rockies. If the low-pressure system is slow to migrate eastward, upslope conditions can persist in the region for several days. Generally, however, upslope conditions are surprisingly shallow; the moisture-laden air being swept toward the Rockies may be only 2,000 to 3,000 feet thick. People looking down on an upslope storm from higher elevations in the mountains often view a sea of clouds swirling in slow motion as they break against the mountain front like waves on a beach. At times, even a low ridge such as the Palmer Divide, located at 7,500 feet, between Colorado Springs and Denver, can arrest a north-moving upslope, leaving Denver basking in sunshine while Colorado Springs remains overcast.

Cold polar air masses are occasionally able to spread south over the High Plains, east of the Rockies, causing a sudden drop in temperature along the eastern mountain front and effectively blocking the passage of cyclonic storms tracking from the Pacific. This situation can produce severe and dangerous blizzard conditions wherever the southern edge of the cold, dry air mass meets warm, moist air moving north from the Gulf of Mexico. These storms ordinarily move in a northeasterly direction, blanketing the

High Plains with several inches of snow, but they tend to be too shallow to push westward over the mountains. Consequently, the High Plains and Eastern Slope experience severe winter storms while the mountains and western valleys west of the Continental Divide remain clear and settled.

Spring

Springtime in the Southern Rockies tends to be wet, windy, and unpredictable, a capricious release from winter's cold. The months of March, April, and May have a distinct character that sets them apart from the winter months. From about the time of the vernal equinox (toward the end of March) through the first two weeks in June, large quantities of moisture periodically stream into the region, especially along the Eastern Slope. The diminished strength of the westerlies allows Gulf air masses to push their way northward into the Great Plains with increased frequency, resulting in heavy spring precipitation (snow or rain) both west and east of the Continental Divide. In 1921, a spectacular April upslope storm produced seventy-six inches of snow in a single twenty-four-hour period at Silver Lake in the Colorado Front Range, the largest twenty-four-hour snowfall ever recorded in North America. At nearby Berthoud Pass, the total snowfall received during the first two weeks of April that same year was nearly ten feet. During a four-day snowstorm in March of 2003, a rare combination of meteorological conditions produced more than seven feet of snow in some areas of the northern and central mountains of Colorado and as little as a few inches in others.

Throughout the higher elevations of the Southern Rockies, the snowpack generally reaches its maximum in April then declines steadily, disappearing almost entirely from lower and mid-elevation areas by mid-June. Temperatures climb rapidly, with about a 10°F increase in the mean occurring between April and May. In the mountains, skiers in shirtsleeves revel in the sunshine, carving graceful arcs through beds of fine spring, or corn, snow.

Summer

Toward the end of June, the zone of strong midlatitude westerlies shifts northward to Canada, taking with them the cyclonic storms and strong winds of autumn, winter, and early spring. The Bermuda High (situated over the western Atlantic) is now able to produce a strong northerly flow of moist air from the Gulf of Mexico and the tropical Pacific (off the west coast of Mexico) toward the mountains. Climatologists refer to this phenomenon as the Arizona Monsoon or Southwest Monsoon because of its impact on the climate of Arizona and surrounding regions. During the months of July and August and in early September, surges of moist air spread across the southern, southwestern, and eastern portions of the Southern Rockies under the influence of the Bermuda High. Consequently, greater summer precipitation occurs in southern ranges such as the San Juans, Sangre de Cristos, and Wet Mountains than in more northern ranges such as the Elk Mountains and the Park, Sierra Madre, and Colorado Front ranges. These northern ranges typically remain under the influence of comparatively dry air masses that must flow east across the arid western interior (Nevada and Utah).

Summer thunderhead builds over Sawtooth Peak in the Colorado Front Range.

Throughout the summer months, influxes of Gulf moisture fuel the afternoon convective showers and thunderstorms that rumble through the mountains. Occasionally, rainy spells lasting two or three days occur when a persistent tongue of moist air positions itself over the region. Because orographic lifting of warm, moist air amplifies the processes of convection, severe thunderstorms and flash flooding can occur under certain conditions. When the moist air masses withdraw from the region, cloud buildup may occur, but afternoon convection showers become rare and are comparatively light. Thunderstorms can pose a distinct hazard to the above-timberline hiker and climber: lightning-caused deaths are not uncommon in the Southern Rockies. Hikers should abandon ridges and summit areas when thunderstorms threaten.

Autumn

By mid-September, the Bermuda High has begun its annual migration toward the equator, reducing the amount of Gulf moisture being channeled toward the Southern Rockies. Because the westerlies are not yet ensconced over the Southern Rockies, they guide only occasional storms across the mountains. Thus begins what many residents feel is the Southern Rockies' most beautiful time of the year: Indian summer. The blue of the sky intensifies, and the rich hues of autumn leaves paint the landscape in a brilliant wash of color.

During the months of September and October, more than 50 percent of the days are bright and sunny. In most areas, temperatures are often forty degrees higher in the afternoon than at dawn. Nighttime temperatures above 9,000 feet average below freezing on about half the nights in September, on most of the nights in October, and on every night in November. Passing storms begin to dust the higher mountains with snow in September. By the end of October, winter has gained a firmer foothold at higher elevations. At lower elevation and in the southern portion of the Southern Rockies, precipitation may continue through October as rain rather than as snow. During most years, the westerlies are firmly positioned over the Southern Rockies by December, tracking Pacific storm systems through the region at regular intervals until the following June.

CHAPTER NINE

The Winter Landscape

Rime crystals produced by supercooled fog coat the needles and branches of a ponderosa pine.

With a thunderous roar, the catastrophic release of massive slabs of snow, an avalanche, instantly transforms everything in its path. Towering trees splinter like saplings against the onslought, willows flatten in mute supplication, the entire tumbling mass erupting in a blast cloud of sparkling white. Just a few feet away from the trajectory of devastation, on the valley floor, a smooth and undisturbed blanket of snow softens the land's contours and provides protective insulation for the plants and animals overwintering beneath the snow. Perhaps even more baffling is the realization that the same changes in snowpack structure that caused the snow to weaken and fail on the steeper, avalanche-prone slope offer greatly improved living conditions for small mammals moving about beneath the snow in more habitat-protected locations.

Snow is a critical component—and force—in shaping mountain ecosystems. In the Southern Rockies, topographic and climatic diversity combine to produce a complex regional snowfall pattern. Above 9,000 feet, snow may cover the ground more or less continuously for as long as nine months; above timberline, in certain alpine basins, snow may persist from one year to the next. Variations in the depth, duration, and other physical characteristics of the mountain snowpack influence landscape processes, control the distribution and composition of plant and animal communities, and determine plant and animal adaptations.

Snow Crystals

All precipitation starts as water vapor in the atmosphere. For snow crystals to form, the air at upper levels in the atmosphere must be at or below freezing and must contain minute particles, called freezing nuclei, around which ice crystallization can occur. Bacteria, as well as clay minerals, dust, minute crystals of sea salt, and even splinters of ice from a shattered, previously formed snow crystal, can serve as nuclei for ice-crystal growth. The embryonic ice crystal is a hexagonal prism, its shape determined by the orderly arrangement of water molecules within the crystal; the lattice of a single snow crystal may contain as many as 100 million water molecules.

The ultimate shape and size of a snow crystal depend on the temperature and the amount of moisture in the cloud in which it forms. In general, large, intricate crystals form at relatively warm cloud temperatures when ample water vapor is present; small, less-intricate crystals form at low temperatures when the air holds less moisture. Most snow crystals follow a hexagonal pattern; the most common is the stellar crystal, a flat, star-shaped crystal with delicate, branching arms. Less common are columnar crystals, which form in very cold clouds with limited moisture supplies; these hollow crystals are responsible for producing the colored halos you sometimes see around the sun or the moon. Needle crystals are produced when the air temperature during a snowstorm is near the freezing point. When a snow crystal evolves in or travels through a cloud composed of supercooled water droplets, it collects a coating of rime. Riming tends to obscure the hexagonal form of the parent crystal, giving it a distinctly whiter and more opaque appearance. When riming continues to such an extent that the original crystal form is unrecognizable or nearly so, the result is a grainlike crystal called graupel, or soft hail; many mountain rainshowers consist of melted graupel.

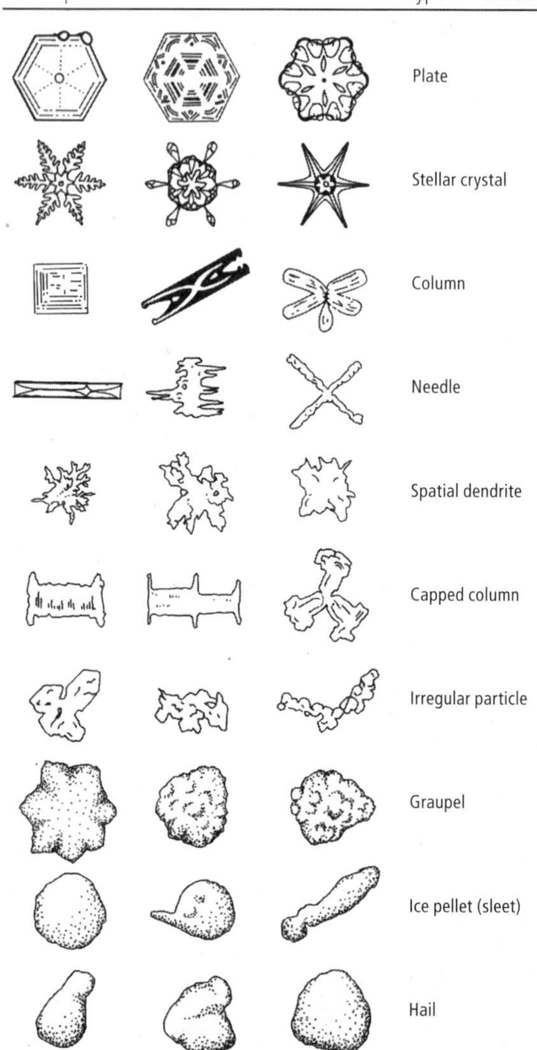

Ten basic forms of solid precipitation as summarized in the International Snow Classification system. (After La Chapelle, Edward, R., *Field Guide to Snow Crystals*. Seattle: University of Washington Press, 1969.)

Most of the snow crystals we see have been modified to some degree during their journey to Earth. Turbulent winds or violent updrafts tend to break off the branches of stellar crystals, or crystals may strike others as they fall and become attached to them. The term *snowflake*, often used erroneously to refer to a single snow crystal, refers to an assemblage of individual snow crystals, typically stellar crystals that have collided and remained hooked together during their fall through the atmosphere. A fresh deposit of snow dominated by stellar crystals tends to be fluffy and relatively cohesive because of the way the branches of the crystals interlock with one another. This cohesion produces spectacular snow canopies on tree branches, fence posts, and other exposed objects.

Snowpack Structure

A snowpack consists of many individual layers of snow, each representing a distinct storm or depositional interval. The accumulation of snow on the ground is in many ways analogous to the formation of a sedimentary rock, with each layer reflecting the nature of its origin. Differences between layers may be well defined or almost indistinguishable. Typically, thick layers are deposited by prolonged snowfalls or by wind transport. Thin layers may reflect events that occurred at the snow surface between storms, such as a brief interval of wind redistribution or the development of an ice crust resulting from melting and refreezing. Thin layers of brownish dust in the snowpack provide evidence that fine particles from a distant sandstorm, perhaps originating in the desert Southwest or in far-off Mongolia, have been transported by the fast-moving winds aloft.

During most of the winter, a temperature gradient exists within the snowpack as a result of differences in the heat energy budget at the snow surface and in the amount of heat flowing into the pack from the ground. In most cases, the temperature gradient reflects the thickness of the pack and the mean snow-surface temperature. Under spring conditions, when the snowpack warms to the melting point throughout, temperature gradients vanish and the snowpack becomes isothermal (the same temperature throughout).

Snow Metamorphism

Unlike most natural substances, snow exists quite close to its melting point. Newly fallen snow is especially unstable. A few days after deposition, it is virtually impossible to identify the original crystalline components of a new storm layer. In contrast to glacial ice, the typical snowpack is both porous and permeable, an emulsion of ice, air, water vapor, and, sometimes, liquid water. These important characteristics allow air and water vapor to circulate freely through the ice skeleton of the snowpack, transferring water molecules from one area to another. As a result, the changes that began when the snow crystal formed continue within the snowpack after deposition. Just as geologists use the term *metamorphism* to describe the recrystalization of a preexisting rock as a result of heat and pressure, snow scientists use it to describe changes in snow texture caused by pressure and temperature conditions. Two types of metamorphism, equi-temperature (ET) and temperature-gradient (TG), occur in a dry, seasonal snowpack; a third type, called melt-freeze, takes place when snowpack temperatures reach 32°F throughout.

Equi-Temperature Metamorphism (ET)

Equi-temperature metamorphism occurs only in snow layers that are essentially the same temperature throughout. Common in a newly fallen snow layer, the beginning stages of ET metamorphism require anywhere from a few hours at warm temperatures to a few days at cold temperatures; it proceeds most rapidly at temperatures close to the freezing point. Newly fallen snow crystals, especially finely branched stellar crystals, are thermodynamically unstable. The most stable shape for a snow crystal to assume in its new environment on Earth is that of a sphere. To achieve this, water vapor molecules must be transferred from crystal corners and dendritic branches toward the center of the crystal. The result of this transfer of water vapor is a progressive rounding of the original snow crystal, which reduces the ratio of surface area to volume and nearly obliterates the original crystal shape.

The predominant grain size of ET crystals is about .04 inches. The reduction in space occupied by each crystal, as well as the pressure exerted by subsequent snow layers, causes the snowpack to compact, or settle. As the density of the snow increases, individual ice grains tend to become bonded together along their points of contact. This process, known as sintering, greatly enhances the mechanical strength of the snow layer. During the final stages of ET metamorphism in a seasonal snowpack, the snow assumes the fine-grained texture typical of old snow; the powder snow favored by skiers is a transitional stage between new and old snow. In alpine areas, where portions of the snowpack may persist from one year to the next, periodic melting and refreezing of old snow results in firn, or névé: dense snow at least one year old.

Temperature-Gradient Metamorphism (TG)

In contrast to ET metamorphism, temperature-gradient, or TG, metamorphism occurs in response to a strong temperature gradient in the snowpack. In a moderate climate, snow layers near the ground are usually warmer than those near the surface of the snowpack because of the heat given off by the Earth. As snow accumulates, the temperature gradient generated by the upward flow of stored heat causes water vapor to flow from warmer snow layers to colder snow layers. Water vapor transfers from warm crystals to colder crystals throughout the snowpack until the entire mass of snow has passed through the water-vapor stage and has been redeposited in the form of completely new crystals. The new crystals bear no resemblance to the original precipitated snow or to the rounded ice grains produced by ET metamorphism. The large, fragile TG crystals are characterized by a distinctly layered or steplike structure, by alignment in vertical growth columns that reflect the direction of vapor diffusion in the snowpack, and by the virtual absence of sintering (bonding).

Angular crystals, layering has not begun

Small and poorly layered crystals

Well-developed depth hoar with prominent layering

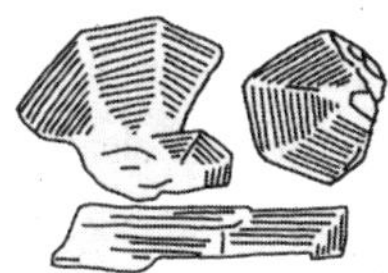

Progressive stages in the development of depth hoar. (After La Chapelle, Edward, R., *Field Guide to Snow Crystals*. Seattle: University of Washington Press, 1969.)

The net result of TG metamorphism is a general weakening of the snowpack. Snow layers in which TG metamorphism is well advanced tend to collapse into a cohesionless mass of crystals at the slightest disturbance: the weight of a skier or an animal moving across the snow, the destabilizing chain reaction caused by a structural failure of the snowpack immediately upslope, or even the impact of a large amount of snow falling from tree branches. Because TG metamorphism proceeds most rapidly in warmer snow layers, the process generally begins along the base of the snowpack. Climatic conditions in the Southern Rockies provide an ideal setting for the formation of TG layers, or depth hoar, because the snow cover is relatively thin and because ambient air temperatures are cold, resulting in steep snow-temperature gradients. Optimum conditions for TG metamorphism are found on north-facing slopes and in deep, shaded gullies; the probability of forming a TG layer is highest early in the winter when the snowpack is relatively thin and unconsolidated. TG layers more than three feet thick have been observed in Colorado.

Melt-Freeze Metamorphism

The third type of metamorphism is controlled by the presence of free water in the snowpack. Melt-freeze metamorphism dominates during occasional midwinter warm periods and during the spring thaw, when the snowpack is essentially isothermal. With the presence of free water in the snowpack, either from melting snow or from rainfall, temperature gradients and their effects all but vanish. Solar heating of the snow surface is the primary cause of melting; newly fallen snow may reflect 80 to 90 percent of the incoming solar radiation, while old granular snow may reflect as little as 40 percent.

The largest amounts of free water will be found adjacent to exposed rocks or trees, terrain features that act as efficient absorbers of radiation and therefore increase the rate of melt. When temperatures are low, ice grains freeze together along their points of contact to form large, multigranular units. Occasionally, meltwater freezes at the surface of the snowpack to form thin sheets of clear ice. These thin ice sheets act like glass in a greenhouse to trap heat underneath and promote further snowmelt.

In melt-freeze metamorphism, the mechanical strength of the snowpack increases during the freeze portion of the cycle and decreases rapidly with the onset of warmer temperatures. This cyclic increase and decrease of snowpack strength is a familiar phenomenon to the spring skier or early summer hiker who has traversed the ice-crusted snow of morning only to sink knee deep in midday slush. Under some conditions, melt-freeze metamorphism can also trigger avalanches. Wet snow instability should be expected after late spring snowstorms when buried ice layers often serve as gliding surfaces for the overlying snow.

Snow in Motion

The beautiful, bannerlike plumes of snow unfurling from peaks and ridges after a fresh snow are a familiar sight for most winter travelers. Blizzard and white-out conditions, on the other hand, are disorienting and can make highway or backcountry travel an extremely hazardous undertaking. Of all the external forces affecting snow in the Southern Rockies, few are as important as wind. Snow crystals falling to Earth under calm conditions accumulate as a delicate, fluffy mass. Light winds deflect snow in a horizontal direction, driving it against the windward sides of trees or other obstacles. Subjecting a fragile stellar crystal to strong winds is like putting it in a rock polisher. Wind processing shatters the delicate crystals, sorting the fragments by size before depositing them in firm, slablike layers.

The amount of snow transported by the wind depends upon the character of the snow, the nature of the snow surface, and the speed of the wind. The largest amounts are transported during or immediately after storm periods, since newly fallen snow is especially susceptible to wind erosion. Wet snow, on the other hand, resists movement by wind. The density of wind-deposited snow averages two to four times that of snow that falls in a wind-protected site. As a result, wind-drifted snow exhibits amazing strength; well-developed wind slab can fully support the weight of a person on skis or a small oversnow vehicle. The strength of wind-deposited snow is also a factor in the stability and longevity of the drifts that form to the lee of terrain obstacles: clumps of shrubs or trees, rocks, buildings, or other types of obstructions.

The distribution of snow in the mountain landscape is largely controlled by wind. Mountain terrain is highly irregular, disrupting the free flow of air and exerting a variable frictional force on the wind, which causes it to scour snow from one area and redeposit it in another. Snow is generally eroded from areas where wind speed is increasing and redeposited in areas where the wind is forced to decelerate because of surface obstructions. Wind-transported snow tends to accumulate in localized zones instead of spreading out evenly across the landscape. Accumulation areas are usually depressions bounded by rock outcroppings or groups of trees. The deepest accumulations typically occur in gullies and bowls, along the leeward flanks of mountain basins, and along the headwalls of alpine cirques. Small-scale surface features such as rocks, bushes, and fallen trees can also force the wind to decelerate, producing a variety of beautiful drift forms to the lee of the obstacle.

Wind Sculpture

Sastrugi

In many alpine areas of the Southern Rockies, beautiful beveled drifts form wherever windblown snow accumulates. These drifts are called sastrugi, a word first applied by the Russians to similar wavelike drift forms in the Arctic tundra. Sastrugi form ridges parallel to the prevailing winds with an abrupt, scoured edge pointing into the wind, a shape that often resembles the curl of a breaking wave. Because of the durability of wind-packed snow, sastrugi often continue to develop throughout the winter months as wind scour and sublimation rework the original drift patterns.

Sastrugi on Niwot Ridge in the Colorado Front Range.

Cornices

Wherever snow accumulates along ridge crests and other sharp breaks in slope, a distinctive, wavelike drift called a cornice may develop when suitable wind and snow conditions persist. Cornices can occur at any elevation and are formed when the prevailing winds pull snow over the top of a ridge and pack it on the leeward slope in a concave curl that mimics the shape of the eddying air current. Successive snow layers are added to the cornice during each period of snow transport, each layer extending out over the cornice face as a cantilevered sheet. A cornice may extend as far as fifty feet upward and outward from the point where it forms. Given sufficient time, the cornice may grow to resemble a massive wave of frozen surf and can be quite spectacular. Throughout its life, the cornice deforms steadily outward and downward over the slope, its cantilevered projections in an increasingly precarious balance with the forces of gravity. Collapsing cornices or even falling cornice blocks occasionally trigger avalanches; avalanche patrols at ski areas routinely destroy potentially dangerous cornices that develop at the tops of ski runs. Hikers and backcountry skiers should exercise extreme caution around cornices and remember that these formations can break a considerable distance back from their leading edge.

Cornices in Rocky Mountain National Park.

Snow Avalanches

Few natural hazards in the Southern Rockies are more frightening, or more common, than the avalanche. In Colorado, a storm that lasts four or five days can result in more than 500 avalanche reports. Powerful and awe-inspiring in equal measure, a large avalanche can transport as much as 100,000 tons of snow and can produce a horizontal thrust that ranges between five and fifty tons per square meter; a force of three tons per square meter is all that is required to destroy wood-frame structures and uproot mature Engelmann spruce trees. Professional avalanche forecasters play a critical role in helping predict and manage avalanche danger along mountain highways, at ski areas, and in popular backcountry recreational areas. In Colorado, a network of some forty snowpack observation sites are operated by the Colorado Avalanche Information Center, one of the most effective avalanche forecasting systems in North America. These sites provide avalanche forecasters with valuable field data and daily updates from November to April, a snapshot of current snowpack conditions that enables forecasters to issue location-specific avalanche hazard assessments. The highways that traverse Red Mountain and Wolf Creek passes (in the San Juan Mountains) and Loveland and Berthoud passes (in the Colorado Front Range) are notorious for the travel hazards posed by avalanches. More than twenty named, active avalanche chutes threaten the narrow, winding road over Red Mountain Pass. One of the most compelling reasons for the construction of the Eisenhower Memorial Tunnel under the Continental Divide was to provide a safe detour for I-70 around Loveland Pass, particularly because of the heavy traffic between the Eastern Slope metropolitan areas and the mountain ski resorts. Avalanche sheds, similar to those used in the Cascades of Washington and in Europe, now shelter the most dangerous stretches of all-season highway in the San Juans.

Understanding the key factors that trigger avalanches and learning to recognize the landscape features that predispose a slope to avalanching are the responsibility of every winter backcountry traveler. In simplest terms, avalanches occur whenever the gravitational or external forces acting on a snow slope overcome the forces that tend to keep the snow in place. In the Southern Rockies, avalanches start most frequently on slopes with gradients of thirty to forty-five degrees; the average gradient for the entire avalanche path, however, is much less, as little as fifteen degrees in some cases. The slope in the avalanche runout zone is often very gentle and sometimes completely flat. Avalanche tracks in forested areas are conspicuous, appearing as vertical or curving swaths cut through the forest; many begin above timberline, tracking downward through spruce and fir, with runout zones in grassy or brushy areas at the base of the slope. Frequent avalanche activity along the same path will prevent the regrowth of conifers along the slide route but may allow other types of vegetation, particularly pioneer species such as aspen and willow, which can regenerate from their roots, to colonize the avalanche chute. Plants that colonize an avalanche chute must be able to absorb the impact of small slides and adapt to the environmental changes characteristic of the open, sunny track.

Loose-Snow Avalanches

Fluffy, new-fallen snow on steep slopes is highly unstable. With little internal cohesion to hold the snow in place, a slight disturbance in equilibrium is all that is necessary to get small masses of snow moving downslope. The exact angle of repose for a new snow layer depends on the temperature, wetness, and shape of the snow crystals. Wet snow, for example, has very little strength for its weight and can avalanche off slopes as gentle as fifteen degrees. New-fallen, dry snow generally has enough cohesion to cling to a thirty-degree slope but exhibits increasing instability on steeper slopes. Once in motion, an avalanche of loose, dry snow can reach a velocity of nearly 140 miles per hour.

Most loose-snow avalanches take the form of small, shallow slides called sluffs. These events occur with regularity throughout the winter, and many small slides may take place during a single snowstorm. Most begin from a single starting point, spreading out to form a fan-shaped snow deposit. In some cases, loose-snow avalanches can have a stabilizing influence on the mountain snowpack, since frequent small sluffs on the steepest slopes force a continual adjustment in the snow and may prevent major slides from developing. Although few deaths have been associated with loose-snow avalanches, caution should always be excercised in traversing steep slopes shortly after a fresh snowfall.

Slab Avalanches

During a slab avalanche, the snow breaks away as a unit, with enough internal cohesion to release a large, slablike region of the snow slope at the same moment. Slab avalanches can originate in any type of snow, from old to newly fallen and from dry to wet. A smooth, wall-like fracture line, called a crown, marks the starting zone of the avalanche. Fast and deadly, release fractures in the snowpack can propagate as rapidly as 350 feet per second. Once released, the slab breaks into smaller blocks that tumble and collide with one another as they roar down the avalanche track. The size of the blocks depends on the cohesiveness of the original slab and the roughness of the terrain over which the avalanche travels. When a slab avalanche finally comes to rest, the fine particles and the larger blocks sinter rapidly to form an amazingly cementlike mass.

The mechanics of slab failure are complex. In most cases, slab failure is initiated when shear stress exceeds shear strength at the bed surface, the main sliding surface of the slab. Slab failures are most likely to start on slopes in the thirty- to forty-five-degree range. In the San Juan Mountains, for example, 72 percent of the slab avalanches occurring during a four-year period had starting zones located between thirty and forty-five degrees; the range of the total sample was twenty-five to forty-eight degrees. Several situations may set the stage for slab failure: the loading of an avalanche-prone slope by wind redistribution of older snow, a high-intensity snowfall, rapid impact (cornice collapse, explosive blast, etc.), the added load of one or more skiers traversing the slab, weakening of the bed surface by temperature-gradient metamorphism, or weakening of the bed surface due to melting.

Hard slabs, prevalent on the Eastern Slope, are composed of snow that has undergone extensive aging and compaction or has been deposited by strong winds; slides composed of these massive blocks are capable of causing tremendous damage. Soft slabs, on the other hand, tend to break into smaller chunks and may lose their initial character entirely as they tumble about on their journey downhill. Many of the massive avalanches west of the Continental Divide are of the soft-slab type. Wet slabs, initiated by intense spring melting or by rainfall, flow downhill as a fluid mass of chunks and smaller particles.

Avalanche Safety

Avalanches pose a serious threat to backcountry travel. Deaths from avalanches have occurred with increasing frequency as winter use of the mountains has grown over time. Each year about eighteen people are killed in avalanches in the United States; Colorado generally accounts for at least a third of those deaths. In areas where avalanches are a possibility, each member of a group should continually evaluate the terrain for high-risk areas and should carry a basketless ski pole or a sectional avalanche probe to help in locating victims in the event of a slide; brightly colored avalanche cords or electronic transceivers are also highly recommended for each member of the party. Because changes in weather often provide the best clues to when and where avalanches are likely to occur, backcountry travelers should consult regional weather services or the Colorado Avalanche Information Center for up-to-date information and hazard assessment. Roughly 50 percent of all avalanches occur during a storm interval or within twenty-four hours after its passage. Snow is a complex material; there is no substitute for exercising caution in choosing destinations and routes for winter backcountry travel. Snow recreationists are encouraged to refer to the excellent references on snow and avalanches listed in the bibliography.

A June snow, Trail Ridge Road, Rocky Mountain National Park.

Snow and Life

Snow and winter climatic conditions pose a variety of stresses for plants and animals. Plants must respond to environmental extremes through morphological and physiological adaptations. Most cold-blooded animals—insects, reptiles, amphibians, and fish—cope with environmental extremes by escaping them through hibernation or dormancy. Many warm-blooded animals choose to avoid the rigors of winter through migration. Those animals that overwinter acclimatize to seasonal environmental change by a combination of behavioral and physiological mechanisms. Behavioral mechanisms include the use of advantageous microclimates, adjustments in daily activity patterns, nest building, and communal nesting; physiological mechanisms include periodic torpidity, body-weight reduction, increased insulation, adjustments in the basal metabolic rate, and a variety of forms of thermogenesis, or metabolic heat production. Certain animals, such as the snowshoe hare and the white-tailed ptarmigan, also exhibit morphological adaptations that allow them to cope with, and to some degree even exploit, the winter snowpack.

With regard to life, the most important property of snow is its ability to insulate the ground, not only against low minimum temperatures but also against drastic fluctuations in temperature. It is this property that protects plants, cold-blooded animals, and small mammals from the harsh environment above the snow surface. With the approach of winter, the ground surface cools and then begins to freeze. If there is little or no snow cover, air temperatures at ground level fluctuate diurnally and the ground will continue freezing to considerable depths. Small mammals such as shrews, mice, voles, and pocket gophers have little physiological capability to withstand environmental extremes for long periods of time. Once the snow accumulates to a depth of about six inches, however, small mammals are able to construct tunnels and runways along the base of the snowpack, where they are protected by the moderating influence of the snow.

For those mammals small enough to utilize the subnivean (under-snow) environment, life follows an easy rhythm of sleeping, feeding from a supply of cached food, and foraging along snow tunnels for new sources of food (roots, buds, bark, fungi, etc.). The fear of predation is somewhat lessened, although coyotes and weasels still zigzag over the snow surface listening for faint squeals and scratchings, sounds they can hear through ten to twelve inches of snow. Communal nesting, a behavioral thermoregulation mechanism, is common for many small mammals. In areas where the snow cover lingers into early summer, some mice and voles may even breed beneath the snow. The southern red-backed vole, an animal characteristic of the subalpine forest in the Southern Rockies, begins breeding in late March beneath a continuous snow cover up to 100 inches thick.

Throughout much of the winter, the subnivean environment is dark and virtually silent. A twelve-inch snow cover transmits only 8 percent of the sunlight reaching the snow surface; midwinter snow depths of twenty inches transmit no light at all. The air beneath the snow is also surprisingly moist. Gaseous by-products produced by continuing bacterial decay at the soil surface are transported upward through the snowpack with the rising water vapor. Carbon dioxide, being relatively heavy, tends to settle into depressions along the base of the snowpack. To avoid concentrations of this gas, voles frequently construct ventilation shafts to the snow surface. These distinctive little holes are common during early winter but become less common after January. It is possible that the development of extensive zones of depth hoar may increase air space along the base of the pack and thus improve subnivean air quality as the winter progresses. As spring approaches, melt-freeze metamorphism destroys the insulative capacity of the snow and increases the amount of light transmitted to the ground surface. This increase in light transmission is believed to play a role in triggering subnivean reproductive behavior in many small mammals, so that breeding can take place during or immediately after snowmelt.

Mammals and birds unable to utilize the subnivean environment must cope continually with changes in the distribution, depth, and character of the snowpack if they are to survive. For mule deer, the energetic costs of moving about and foraging in deep snow are high. Severe winters can cause massive die-offs. Studies in Middle Park have shown that mule deer abandon all areas where snow depths exceed eighteen inches. In some areas, snow may limit usable winter range for deer to less than 1 percent of their normal summer range. A deep, persistent snow cover can impose drastic changes in diet by forcing deer to eat a higher percentage of less-digestible browse, a shift that results in a decrease in the digestive bacteria necessary to process food effectively. Deer faced with such a diet may starve, their stomachs full of undigestible plant fiber. With their longer legs, elk and moose can tolerate deeper snows but will generally migrate to lower elevations to avoid it. Similarly, when snow blankets the high valleys and alpine basins of the Southern Rockies, bighorn sheep confine their midwinter wanderings to areas sometimes no more than half a mile across; wind-scoured uplands, south-facing slopes, and steep, broken cliffs become preferred habitat during such times.

The snowshoe hare is the undisputed master of deep snow with its camouflage-white coat and its broad, snowshoe-shaped feet. The white-tailed ptarmigan, like the snowshoe hare, changes to a white winter coat in late fall and it also grows stiff mats of feathers on each toe. Lack of sufficient snow when ptarmigan are undergoing the molt from brown to white, however, can subject them to higher levels of predation than at other seasons. Molting of the white winter plumage in early spring, although largely controlled by day length, is apparently also affected by the amount of snow cover present in tundra breeding areas.

Most jumping mammals, such as rabbits and hares, support themselves on all four feet at once and have a distinct advantage in deep snow over predators such as coyotes and foxes, which use the walk-jog-trot-run mode of travel. A coyote can walk easily in six inches of new snow, but when the snow is much deeper, they must expend more energy to move and are less effective in catching prey. Smaller predators, such as a weasel or a marten, bound easily across the snow, initially supported on the two front feet, with a quick and efficient transfer of the hind feet into the prints of the front feet. For flying predators, such as owls and hawks, the snow is a fresh, white canvas; the unwary rabbit scampering across the snow surface provides an effortless target. Deep snow can also immobilize a fleeing deer and make it easy prey for a coyote or mountain lion.

White-tailed ptarmigan. Courtesy of Jim Benedict

How readily an animal is able to cope with metamorphic changes in the snowpack depends on the weight of the animal and the structure of its legs and feet. Small and medium-sized mammals continue to maintain their advantage over larger ones. Recognizing the usefulness of compacted snow, rabbits, hares, tree squirrels, and mice will often reuse trails between feeding areas. White-tailed ptarmigan, on the other hand, move away from areas where the snow has been compacted by wind or glazed by ice crusts, in order to find soft snow in which to construct their roosting burrows. Under some conditions, the snow surface may be so firm that a hunting coyote is unable to dig through it to catch small mammals. Wind slab and ice crusts can also prove deadly for elk, deer, and pronghorn. Because their body weight exceeds the bearing surface of their hooves, these animals sink readily into soft snow and will break through most crusts, which can be extremely costly in terms of the amount of energy expended in the winter environment.

CHAPTER TEN

Landscape Patterns

The first sighting of the Southern Rockies, rising miragelike along the western horizon, is an unforgettable experience. Approaching the foot of the mountains, the haze-blue peaks resolve into a kaleidoscope of multihued stripes and patches of grassland, shrubland, and forest, a landscape pattern that ends where the first snowfields begin. As you drive into the mountains and the road begins to climb, the forest changes with every turn in the road, from juniper to pine to aspen and, finally, to spruce and fir. These changes, from grassy steppe through woodland and forest to alpine meadow, clearly reflect a shifting suite of environmental variables. Mountains are unique in that they extend vertically into different environmental regimes within short horizontal distances. Consequently, as you climb in elevation, you encounter distinct changes in environmental conditions: decreasing mean temperatures, progressively shorter growing seasons, increasing rainfall, increasing wind speeds, and so on. All these factors influence the distribution of plants and animals.

Life Zones

In the Rocky Mountains, elevation sets the stage. It is the single most important factor in determining what species of plants or animals you can expect to see in any given area. In 1889, biologist C. Hart Merriam traveled to the San Francisco Peaks area in northern Arizona to study the patterns of plant and animal life at various elevations. Based on the results of his pioneering research, Merriam introduced the concept of "life zones" to describe the elevational zonation of vegetation in western North America.

Though Merriam's life zone system marked a great stride forward for the fledgling science of plant ecology and remained in common use through the 1960s, the theoretical basis for the system failed to recognize that vegetation responds not to a single physical factor such as temperature but to an array of environmental variables. For example, one of the most conspicuous features associated with the zonation of vegetation with increasing elevation in the Rocky Mountains is the presence of both an upper and a lower tree line. Trees are largely excluded from the lowest elevations by drought and from the highest elevations by cold temperatures and strong winds.

Biologists attempting to apply Merriam's life zone system along the entire length of the Rocky Mountains soon realized that the limits of elevation given for each life zone varied considerably from north to south along the mountains according to latitude. Treelimit at the northern end of the Canadian Rockies occurs at 5,000 feet; in the Southern Rockies, treelimit occurs at about 11,500 feet, a difference of 6,500 feet from north to south. Life zones are also seldom stacked in neat horizontal sections. In the Rockies, the distributions of the major plant species by which we recognize these zones tend to overlap broadly and often respond to highly localized differences in microclimate, especially moisture. For example, it is relatively easy to see the vegetation differences between north- and south-facing slopes. North-facing slopes receive considerably less direct sunlight than south-facing slopes and are consequently cooler, lose less water by evaporation, hold snow longer, and have a shorter frost-free season. These differences are significant enough to allow north-facing slopes to support plant species more typical of higher elevations than those on nearby south-facing slopes. In addition, boundaries between adjacent life zones or the ecosystems that comprise them are rarely sharply defined. Biologists use the term *ecotone* to refer to the mixture of plant and animal species that often occurs between two adjacent ecosystems.

Ecosystems and Ecoregions

Every habitat harbors a unique combination of plants and animals. The term *ecosystem* refers to the physical environment and all the organisms in a given area. Because plants are the most conspicuous ecosystem components, ecosystems are generally named for their dominant plant species (e.g., aspen forest ecosystem). Ecosystems may be of any size, from the bacteria that populate the gut of a porcupine to a spruce-fir forest covering several thousand acres. Ecologists use the term *community* to describe all the plants and animals found in a particular place. The community tends to be dominated by one or more prominent species or by some physical characteristic. For example, we speak of a sagebrush community or a pond community. Used in this way, community is spatially defined and includes all the populations of plants and animals within its boundaries.

Beginning in the 1990s, largely through the advent of computerized ecosystem mapping, ecologists began to recognize the conservation and management benefits inherent in dividing the landscape into broad climatic and physiographic units, called ecoregions, that transcend geopolitical boundaries and complex jurisdictions. The ecoregions covered by this book include the Southern Rocky Mountain ecoregion and adjacent portions of the Wyoming Basin ecoregion, the Central and Southern Shortgrass Prairie ecoregions, the Colorado Plateau ecoregion, and the Utah High Plateaus ecoregion.

Succession and Climax

In the West, towns were established—incrementally—by the efforts of a few hardy pioneers. The analogy of the pioneer is a useful one when we look at how vegetation communities develop and change over time. Ecologists use the term *succession* when describing the sequence of changes in plant species on a newly exposed site (i.e., where a glacier or perennial snowfield has melted) or an area that has undergone some sort of site-altering disturbance due to natural events (i.e., flood or fire) or human activities (i.e., logging). To a certain degree, the progression of species is predictable based on our knowledge of the ecological amplitude of the principal colonizing plant species. The final association of species achieved as a result of these successive changes is called a climax. For example, a plant community that is partially destroyed by fire and eventually replaces itself through a succession of intermediate vegetation types is considered to be the climax vegetation type for that region.

Biologist E. O. Wilson once described pioneer species as sprinters and climax species as long-distance runners, suggesting that a new marathon is always beginning somewhere in the natural world. Change essentially brings all the species—briefly—to the same starting line. Succession tends to work in one direction. Good colonizers exhibit rapid growth and a high tolerance for the sorts of environmental extremes associated with disturbed or newly exposed sites. These hardy pioneers are gradually replaced by slow-growing species with superior competitive adaptations that serve them well over the long haul. Successional plant species alter the environment by their physiognomy (growth form) and by their adaptations or physiological processes, often to their own detriment and to the benefit of other species. Some ecologists view succession as leading inexorably toward an ultimate expression of plant development, the climax community. A climax community is defined as one in which the species composition and population status of the community (or ecosystem) remains relatively stable over time (at least for centuries), with a balance between the addition of new individuals by reproduction and the loss of individuals as a result of death.

Ecologists continue to debate the idea that a region can have only one true climax. Most recognize that communities are essentially dynamic, open systems whose composition varies at any one locality depending on site-specific environmental conditions. Many factors determine the potential climax community for a given area, including climate, soil, topography, fire, and the activities of humans or other animals. Mosaic patterns of vegetation types are common to any climax community where the death or removal of certain individuals alters the environment, creating openings that are then invaded by seral (successional) species within an otherwise stable community.

Understanding the Ecosystem Concept

The unique life-forms that we see around us took millions of years to evolve. These organisms, in one form or another, have weathered environmental extremes and coped with both abundance and scarcity over evolutionary time, encoding their "responses" to these survival challenges in their genetic makeup. Each species of plant or animal has a genetic program that specifies a range of environmental conditions necessary for its survival. This species-specific range of tolerances defines the organism's ecological amplitude, which in turn is characterized by a minimum, a maximum, and an optimum. For most species, survival and reproduction (the ultimate test of a species' fitness in a particular environment) are most favorable within a relatively narrow set of conditions ranging around the optimum. At either extreme of its range of tolerance, a given species may be forced to yield the competitive advantage to another species with a different optimal range.

At Great Sand Dunes, dune-adapted plant species such as scurfpea, Indian ricegrass, blow-out grass, and prairie sunflower cope with the environmental challenges posed by shifting sands.

Some plant and animal species, the so-called generalists, have exceedingly broad ecological amplitudes and can be found in a great variety of habitats because of their adaptability. The coyote and the ubiquitous deer mouse are perhaps the best-known generalists in the Southern Rockies. In contrast, specialists such as the pika, a species restricted to high-elevation talus, and the Abert's squirrel, a strikingly beautiful squirrel that occurs only in ponderosa pine forests, have comparatively narrow ecological amplitudes. In fact, certain associations of plants and animals are so closely tied to a specific community type that they are considered indicator species for that ecosystem. Biologists and land managers often use the presence or absence of certain key indicator species as a means of evaluating the environmental health or degree of disturbance occuring within a given ecosystem. Not surprisingly, we are learning that specialists such as the pika may be as vulnerable to the perturbations of climatic change as they are to habitat loss or fragmentation.

When we examine the structure of natural communities, we find them to be mixtures of plants and animals with different ways of life. Within a given community, species evolve toward differences in habitat and niche (the organism's ecological role within the community) as a means of reducing competition. Habitat and niche are closely related aspects of the species' total adaptation to the environment. A given ecological niche is occupied by a single species. Where broad overlap occurs, such as might exist if two species were to utilize the same resources at the same time and space, one species will eventually displace the other or force changes in behavioral patterns that allow coexistence without direct competition. For example, competitive overlap between the great blue heron and the black-crowned night heron, which often nest in proximity to one another, appears to be eliminated by the lifestyles of the two species. The great blue heron is active by day, standing motionless in shallow water or in marshy upland sites and waiting for its preferred prey—fish, amphibians, and small mammals—to come within striking range. The black-crowned night heron, on the other hand, is largely nocturnal and prefers to stalk its prey in shallow water.

Maintaining the ecological balance in any natural community is a challenge. Eliminate one species from the equation, and another increases in number to take its place. Eliminate several species, and the ecosystem in question begins to degrade visibly. Even in a degrading ecosystem, life goes on, and though it may look superficially the same in the early stages of alteration, the species that will eventually dominate the reconstituted ecosystem tend to be those found in similarly degraded habitats elsewhere. The tragic spread of invasive plant species, such as cheatgrass and Canada thistle, is the result of the accidental introduction of species whose competitive adaptations and opportunistic reproduction and dispersal strategies allow them to colonize disturbed ecosystems with comparative ease.

The Role of Biodiversity

Biological diversity, or biodiversity, is the ultimate expression of countless mutations and recombinations across the immense span of evolutionary time. It's amazing to consider that 99 percent of all the species that ever lived on Earth are now extinct. The plants and animals we see today are the remarkable survivors that were able to chart a course through all the radiations and extinctions in geologic history. We know that the number of plant or animal species, which is expressed as species diversity, appears to increase in any given habitat over time in response to the productivity and structural heterogeneity of the vegetation. In the most immediate sense, biodiversity is the insurance policy that enables a community to remain ecologically resilient. As a species' population (plant or animal) decreases to a few individuals, local extinction often results due to genetic deterioration. When species are lost due to human activites or to environmental extremes that exceed natural perturbations, the community's ability to restore itself is threatened, sometimes irreversibly. If similar population declines occur throughout the species' range, than the future is grim indeed.

Ecologically speaking, the Southern Rockies can be thought of as an archipelago. Many of the same ecological processes that operate on islands are also important here, setting the stage for evolutionary change. The ecoregion is well known for its high species richness in butterflies and moths, mammals, birds, and several plant groups. Excluding Alaska, only southeast Arizona has a higher species' diversity rank for invertebrates, particularly moths and butterflies, than the lower foothills of the Colorado Front Range. In addition, the relative ecological isolation, the significant climate changes that have occurred in the recent geologic past, and the region's complex topographic and geologic features have resulted in a high degree of endemism. Species that are native to only one geographical region and are found nowhere else in the world are considered to be endemic to that region. Scientists have identified at least 184 species and subspecies of plants and animals that are known to be endemic to the Southern Rocky Mountain ecoregion. The known endemics include 118 plants, 51 invertebrates, 12 mammals, 2 birds, and 1 amphibian. Examples of endemic animal species include the Uncompahgre fritillary, Great Sand Dunes tiger beetle, Goat Peak pika, Jemez Mountains salamander, and brown-capped rosy finch. Several other species, such as the Greenland primrose, are disjunct circumboreal species occurring well south of their normal geographic distribution.

The Biodiversity Balance Sheet

Although many Southern Rocky Mountain landscapes remain largely intact, a number of plant and animal species are either extinct or have been extirpated at the hands of man. Since European settlement, seven mammal species—the grizzly bear, gray wolf, wild bison, black-footed ferret, lynx, wolverine, and river otter—have been extirpated in the Southern Rockies. Recent reintroduction efforts have focused on the black-footed ferret, lynx, and river otter and have been only moderately successful to date. In the Southern Rockies, the U.S. Fish and Wildlife Service currently lists twenty-three species as threatened or endangered. At least 100 species are ranked as globally imperiled, including the Gunnison sage grouse and the Great Sand Dunes tiger beetle. Another 283 species are of special concern because they are endemic, especially vulnerable to habitat loss or fragmentation, experiencing a significant population decline, or are considered to be a disjunct species in the ecoregion (e.g., greater sage grouse, northern leopard frog, and round-leaf sundew).

The Vegetation Zones Used in This Book

In the 1960s, University of Colorado plant ecologist John Marr developed an eminently workable vegetation classification for the Colorado Front Range that corresponds to the altitudinal zonation of the vegetation but is based on regional ecosystems and employs the ecological concepts of climax and succession. Although Marr's classification system remains extremely useful in explaining many of the vegetation patterns that we see in the Southern Rockies, readers should keep in mind that vegetation classification systems are continually being refined as our understanding of ecosystem processes improves. The system adopted for this book is modified from that of Marr and includes five distinctive zones: Grassland/Semidesert, Foothills, Montane, Subalpine, and Alpine. Each zone within this user-friendly system designates a region of more or less uniform climate in which distinctive types of climax vegetation occur. Various successional communities occur in each zone, and in some places may be even more common than the potential climax vegetation.

The **Grassland/Semidesert zone** is characterized by short- and mixed-grass prairie at elevations below 6,000 feet along the eastern edge of the Southern Rockies and by semidesert shrub ecosystems dominated by saltbush, greasewood, or sagebrush between 6,000 and 7,000 feet in the arid valleys west of the Continental Divide. On some sites, such as in the San Luis Valley, semidesert shrublands may even reach 8,000 feet under certain conditions. Watercourses occurring within this zone are characterized by lowland riparian ecosystems consisting of broad-leaved cottonwoods, willows, or box-elder.

The **Foothills zone** (or Submontane) marks the transition between the grassland/semidesert ecosystems and the mountain forests. It is characterized by mountain shrublands (Gambel's oak or mountain mahogany) and by woodlands consisting of piñon pine and various species of juniper. The elevation of this zone is quite variable and ranges between 6,000 and 8,000 feet. Ponderosa pine and Douglas-fir forests often occur in this zone, as they do along the Eastern Slope of the Colorado Front Range, but are at their lower limits of distribution.

Aspen forest.

The **Montane zone** occurs between 8,000 and 9,500 feet and is characterized by ponderosa pine ecosystems on drier, warmer sites and by Douglas-fir forests on moister, cooler slopes. Open stands of limber pine are typical of exposed ridges. Aspen and lodgepole pine ecosystems are common where fires or other types of disturbances have occurred. Mountain meadow and grassland communities are found in locations with suitable moisture and soils. Watercourses are numerous and delineated by distinctive assemblages of mountain riparian forest and shrub communities.

The **Subalpine zone** is found between 9,500 and 11,400 feet and is dominated by dense forests of Engelmann spruce and subalpine fir. Limber pine or bristlecone pine form open forests on exposed ridgetops within this zone. Aspen and lodgepole pine may be present in certain areas that have undergone disturbance. Throughout these dense forests, lush meadows, ponds, and various types of wetlands are common. The upper margin of the subalpine forest marks the forest-tundra ecotone, which occurs at higher and higher elevations from north to south along the mountains; at the southern end of the mountains, the forest-tundra ecotone may extend to more than 12,000 feet. Trees growing in the forest-tundra ecotone are small and stunted, often forming shrubby patches that extend into the alpine meadows above.

The **Alpine zone** begins at treelimit, which ranges from 12,200 feet in northern New Mexico and southern Colorado to 11,400 feet in northern Colorado and southern Wyoming, and extends to above 14,000 feet. Dwarf willows and a distinctive assemblage of herbaceous plants adapted to cold temperatures and a short growing season characterize this highest life zone.

Avalanche lily blooms at the edge of the melting snowfields.

The chapters that follow describe the most common ecosystems of the Southern Rockies, beginning with the shortgrass prairie and ending with the alpine tundra. Each ecosystem is portrayed in terms of its environmental setting, principal plant and animal species, and community characteristics. The Latin names for the plant and animal species used in this book generally conform to those used by the leading authorities on the flora and fauna of the Southern Rockies. These references are noted in the Bibliography. Readers should be aware, however, that certain scientic and common names may differ from one guidebook to another and can cause confusion. Though by no means comprehensive, this guidebook is intended to provide a thorough introduction to the most common plants and animals in each ecosystem.

CHAPTER ELEVEN

Land within the Rain Shadow: The Shortgrass Prairie

Shortgrass prairie in northeastern Colorado.

Within the long shadow cast by the Rockies, drought and wind have fashioned a beautiful but uncompromising landscape. Plains Indians called this vast ocean of grass the *waho*, "the great circle of the horizon." French fur traders referred to these grasslands as *un prairie*, a lyrical name that seems, in the mind's eye, to soar like a hawk above a world of never-ending promise and verdure. The first Euro-American explorers and naturalists had no experience with such a sweeping landscape. The immensity of the prairie was overwhelming, daunting to people used to the comforting embrace of forests. Many of the earliest travelers—Daniel Webster, John James Audubon, Rufus Sage, and countless others—sent bleak, disparaging reports home, describing the Great Plains as an uninhabitable wasteland. Others, such as explorers John Charles Frémont, Edwin James, and George Catlin, spoke to the beauty of a landscape that seemed, at first glance, nothing but grass and light as far as the eye could see.

Ecological Distribution

Native grasses define the soul of the prairie, their diversity across the immensity of the grassland landscape born of differences in climate, topography, and soils. The Great Plains Grassland Biome, which encompasses large portions of the central United States and spans the Canadian border to include parts of Alberta, Saskatchewan, and Manitoba, consists of three main ecoregional types arranged in irregular north-south belts that succeed one another primarily along a west-to-east gradient of increasing moisture: shortgrasses in the west, mixed short- and tallgrasses in the middle, and tallgrasses to the east. The mixed-grass prairie, which includes portions of Alberta, Saskatchewan, Montana, Wyoming, North Dakota, South Dakota, Nebraska, Kansas, Oklahoma, and a sliver of Texas, essentially marks a broad transition between tallgrass, midheight, and shortgrass prairie types, defining a zone within which the rain shadow effect of the Rockies diminishes. West of this zone, which includes the most sun-frazzled portions of Alberta, Montana, Wyoming, Colorado, New Mexico, Texas, and extreme southwestern Nebraska, Kansas, and Oklahoma, precipitation declines dramatically as one approaches the Rockies, and sod-forming shortgrasses dominate the landscape. Just as the overall distributional patterns of grasslands reflect large-scale climatic patterns, the patchiness of vegetation types that we see on the ground is a response to local variations in microclimate. Every wrinkle on the landscape, each butte, each arroyo, each riverine bottomland, provides its own variation on the theme. Too easily obscured by the dramatic scenery of the mountains, the shortgrass prairie offers visitors willing to spend time exploring its special places a wilderness world of subtle diversity but endless fascination.

Western history, as writer Wallace Stegner once pointed out, "is a series of lessons in consequences." Native grasslands rank among the most imperiled ecosystems in the world. Only fragments of the great American grassland biome remain, as little as 5 percent of the original tallgrass prairie and about half of the original mixed-grass and shortgrass prairies. The greater the agricultural potential of a given area, the less native prairie remains. Even within the rain shadow of the Southern Rockies, the vulnerable heart of the shortgrass prairie, roughly 30 percent, has been plowed, developed, overgrazed, and abused in ways too numerous to count. The true symbols of prairie wilderness, the bison, gray wolf, and black-footed ferret, have long since disappeared. Grassland birds such as the mountain plover and the lark bunting, both indicator species of healthy grassland ecosystems, are disappearing as quickly as the habitats they depend on.

Where to See Shortgrass Prairie

Visiting the shortgrass prairie on a spring day, when the sweet, slurred songs of horned larks and the melodious "falling-leaf" displays of chestnut-collared longspurs choreograph the morning, is to give in to the subliminal seduction of open spaces. Exploring the shortgrass prairie is as easy as consulting a good regional map (essential!), selecting one of several excellent guidebooks, and choosing the best time of the year for what you want to see. Fortunately, two of the best examples of shortgrass prairie, Pawnee National Grassland and Comanche National Grassland, are on public lands administered by the U.S. Forest Service. Depending on the season, camping is highly recommended, and established sites exist in both areas. A limited number of gravel roads (beware when wet!) and self-guided nature trails provide good access and introduce the visitor to the unique natural and human history of this remarkable landscape.

Physical Environment

The climate of the shortgrass prairie, like that of the alpine tundra, is one of extremes. Hail, blizzards, tornadoes, parching winds, and dust storms are not unusual. The most significant feature of this semiarid grassland, and what shapes its character, is low precipitation: the shortgrass prairie averages between ten and sixteen inches a year. Most precipitation comes during the growing season, May through July, with a conspicuous increase in storm activity during June. Spectacular to watch, prairie thunderstorms are visible from miles away, black clouds churning, thunder rumbling, lightning flashing, and rain falling in a slanting torrent.

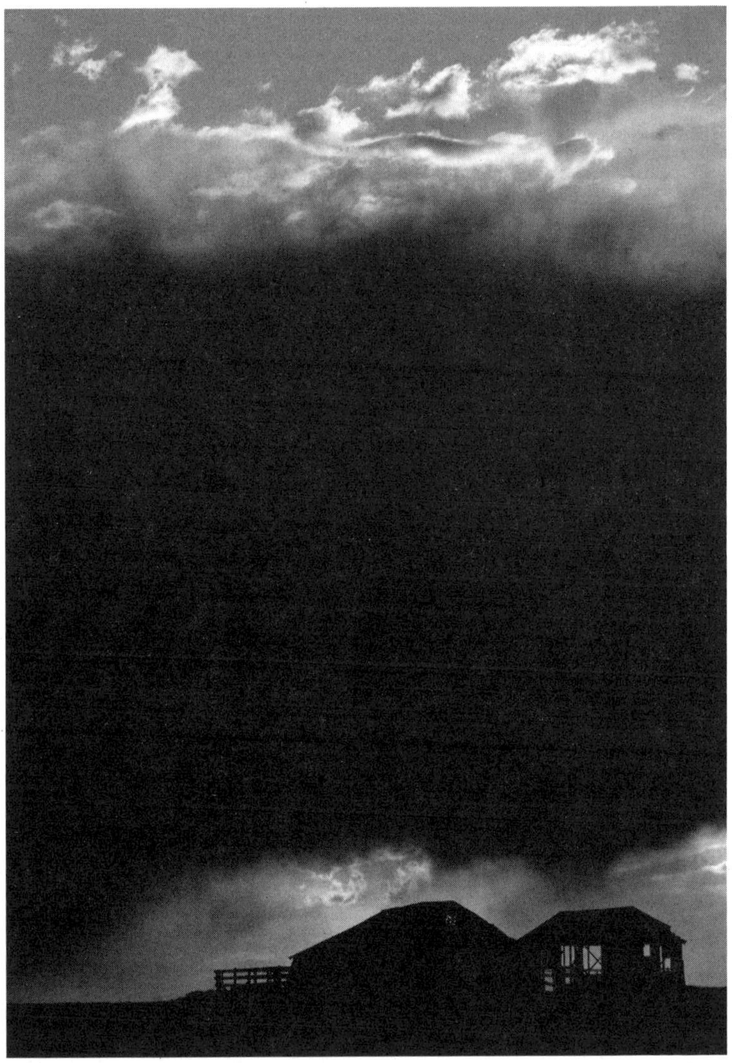

A prairie storm hides the sun as it sweeps across an abandoned farmstead near Grover, Colorado.

On a summer's day, heat shimmer obliterates the horizon line and the sun becomes a tangible weight to be endured. Temperatures in the shortgrass prairie fluctuate enormously, not only from season to season, but also from day to day. Winter minimums typically hover in the low teens, but may drop to a bone-chilling -20°F when cold polar air spreads across the plains. The highest temperatures in the region also occur here; summer daily maximums hover in the 90s and temperatures in excess of 100°F are becoming increasingly common.

Wind is a constant presence in the shortgrass prairie. Winter blizzards can transform the prairie into a stark, white moonscape. Throughout the winter, chinook winds—"snow-eaters"—roar down from the mountains, melting the snow, speeding evaporation, and robbing plants and soil of critical moisture reserves. By late spring, tornadoes and violent, wind-driven hailstorms begin striking the High Plains with alarming frequency. In especially dry years, the torrid winds of summer dessicate everything in their path, withering even the native vegetation and laying waste to promising croplands. Dust devils pivot and dance with every rising thermal, chasing each other across acre after acre of cactus-dotted grassland. Where the prairie sod has been plowed or overgrazed, high winds fuel the dust storms so characteristic of the area from Limon, Colorado, south to Las Vegas, New Mexico. The "black blizzards" of the 1930s were of spectacular proportions, sweeping their fury across thousands of acres of shortgrass prairie and forcing farmers and herdsmen to declare defeat by the hundreds.

Community Characteristics

Burnished with autumn light, the shortgrass prairie is a mosaic of verdigris and gold, enduring and subliminal in its appeal. In the midst of winter, the prairie presents an unwelcoming and somewhat stark countenance to travelers speeding westward along the major highways that cross the region. By May or June, if spring moisture arrives in sufficient quantity and at frequent enough intervals, the landscape undergoes a remarkable transformation, a greening so verdant it defies description. The native plants that grow here are tuned in to the climate, adjusting their metabolism downward when conditions are unfavorable for growth or speeding them up when the weather suits their needs. To see the shortgrass prairie in its full glory, when every aspect—rain, sunshine, and soil—is in perfect alignment, is to witness a grassy miracle begun more than 60 million years ago in the African region of the ancient supercontinent Pangaea.

More than two centuries after the first settlers crossed the oceanlike swells of the midcontinent, Western society has still not come to terms with the shortgrass country. Countless acres of shortgrass prairie have been overgrazed; others have been lost to center-pivot irrigation and urban sprawl. Despite these losses, however, much of what remains is uncultivated and supports an assortment of native and introduced perennial grasses. On suitable sites, two native shortgrass species share dominance: buffalo grass and blue grama. In years with average precipitation, a mixture of these two grasses forms a dense gray-green turf over hundreds of square miles, often making up nearly 80 percent of the native-grass cover.

Various midheight grasses, such as little bluestem, needle-and-thread, western wheatgrass, sideoats grama, and galletagrass, are also present to varying degrees, depending on topographic differences, grazing pressures, and soil moisture conditions. There can be considerable variation in the dominance of certain species from year to year and from place to place in response to changing environmental conditions. During wet years, for example, shimmering fields of needle-and-thread grass tend to obscure the ever-present understory of shortgrass species. Wherever the range has been grazed conservatively, midheight grasses become increasingly abundant.

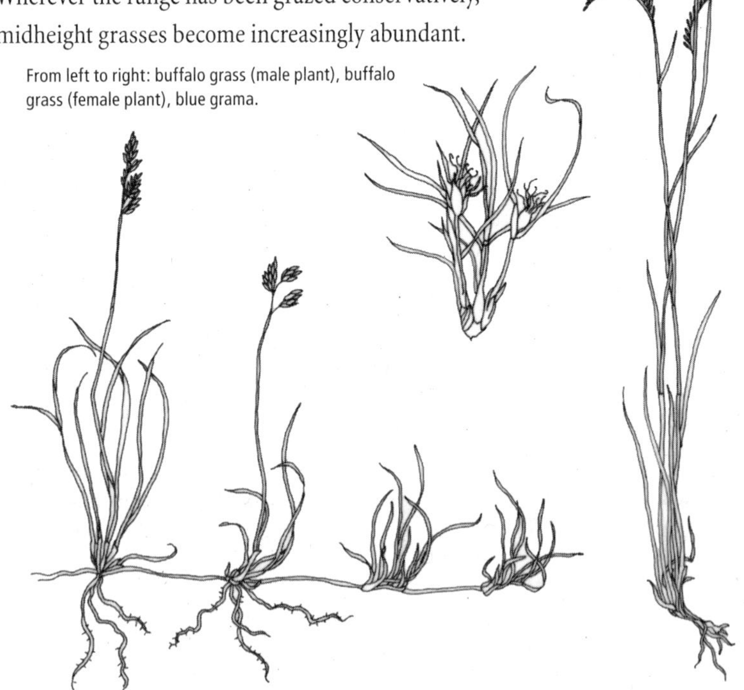

From left to right: buffalo grass (male plant), buffalo grass (female plant), blue grama.

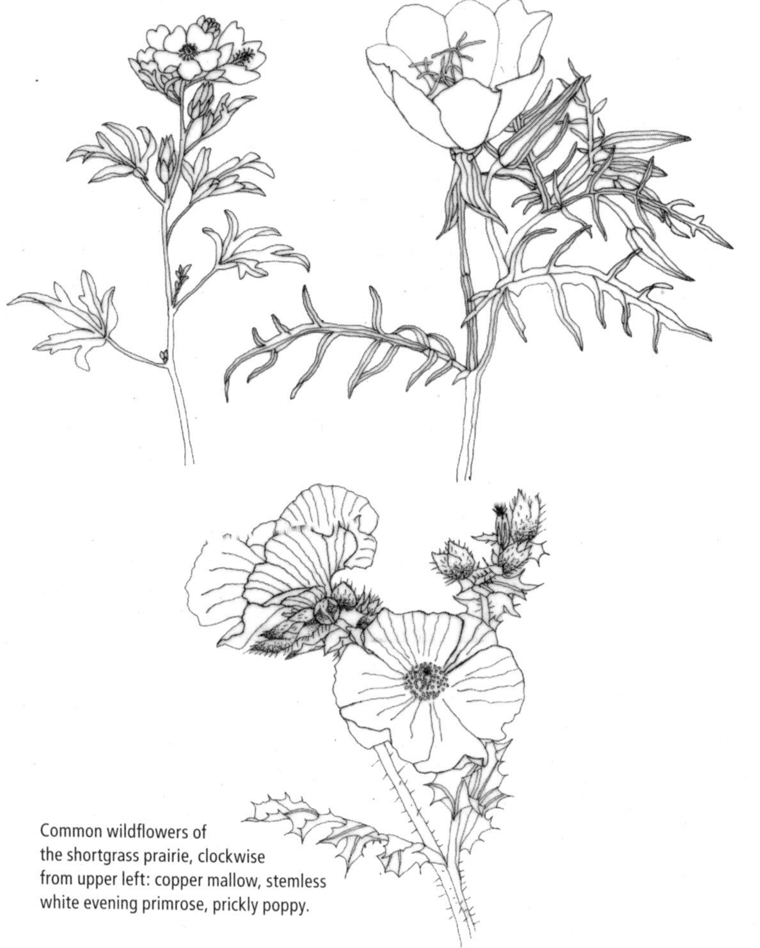

Common wildflowers of the shortgrass prairie, clockwise from upper left: copper mallow, stemless white evening primrose, prickly poppy.

The shortgrass prairie is made up of a patchwork of plant communities. Boundaries between communities may be quite sharp and often reflect differences in moisture availability and other microclimatic variables. On dry uplands, communities of buffalo grass and blue grama may form a durable turf interspersed with bare ground and cacti. Bunchgrasses such as little bluestem and Junegrass thrive in areas that have not been overgrazed and where deep soils ensure an adequate moisture supply. Moist swales and watercourses that are protected from desiccating winds favor taller grasses such as big bluestem and switchgrass. Concentric bands of desert saltgrass and foxtail barley encircle intermittent ponds and alkaline depressions. Sand-hill areas tend to be dominated by sand-tolerant grasses such as sand reed, red three-awn, and sand bluestem. Throughout the prairie, in disturbed sites such as around prairie dog burrows and harvester-ant mounds, clumps of sand dropseed, squirreltail, and Indian ricegrass are abundant. Cheatgrass, an exotic from Eurasia, is an aggressive colonizer of overgrazed or disturbed sites and forms large, monotonous stands in many areas.

During years with above-average precipitation, a bewildering variety of showy wildflowers lend their colors to the grassland. Local moisture conditions, grazing pressure, competition with grasses, and seed availability clearly influence patterns of species abundance and dominance. Drought years may cause an overlapping or telescoping of seasonal aspects, mixing the typical forbs of spring, summer, and autumn in rapid succession. The earliest wildflowers, palest lavender townsendias, magenta locoweeds, sand lilies, wild onions, and birdfoot violets, make their appearances in late April or May. In years with heavy spring rainfall, drifts of white evening primrose may cover the prairie like new-fallen snow. By late spring, the prairie is patterned with the variegated colors of blue penstemon, prairie larkspur, copper mallow, silky sophora, and many others. On the windswept tops of isolated buttes, cushion-forming plants such as phlox, sandwort, and mat vetch are common, their compact growth identical to that of species found on alpine summits. Wherever the land has been overgrazed, the yellow and apricot-pink flowers of prickly pears and the elegant cream-colored spikes of yucca dot the landscape. In the southern portions of the shortgrass prairie, the purple-red blooms of shrubby cholla provide bright bursts of color in an otherwise tawny-colored landscape.

By mid-July, the yellow composites—common sunflowers, butterweed, gumweed, snakeweed, golden asters, and prairie coneflower—become conspicuous. Sky-blue lupine and purple prairie clover mix with the silvery green foliage of sand sage. Along roadsides and in disturbed sites, the showy flowers of prickly poppy intermingle with lavender-flowered thistles. In sandy areas, clumps of white sand verbena, purple-flowered morning glories, and the carmine-colored, fleshy flowers of sand begonia are widespread. With the coming of autumn, the magenta flowers of blazingstar give way to the vibrant sun-gold of rabbitbrush and to white, woolly clumps of winterfat.

North and west of the Laramie Mountains, shortgrass prairie merges with the sagebrush-steppe and forms a distinctive understory. From Cheyenne south to Colorado Springs, blue grama, needle-and-thread, and western wheatgrass intermingle with ponderosa pine along the mountain front to form a savannalike transition zone. In southern Colorado and northern New Mexico, shortgrass borders piñon-juniper and oak woodland, which extends far to the east along the Colorado–New Mexico border. South of the Platte-Arkansas Divide, the shrubby chollas become conspicuous, and as temperature and aridity intensify, blue grama is joined by dryland species such as galletagrass and sideoats grama.

Plant Adaptation: Designs for Survival

In the shortgrass prairie, water conservation is the key to survival. The dominant plant species have evolved a variety of adaptations that allow them to take in water through their roots and to conserve water efficiently. Grasses are characterized by small, inconspicuous flowers, narrow, parallel-veined leaves, hollow, jointed stems, and fibrous root systems. The narrower leaves typical of most shortgrasses minimize water loss through evaporation. In addition, ranks of special hinge cells parallel the central vein of the leaf, allowing it to fold or roll inward to reduce surface area further. Species such as blue grama, Junegrass, and western wheatgrass roll up the edges of their leaves during times of drought to reduce evaporative loss. In many species, a protective, waxy coating called cutin covers the leaves; in others, fine hairs entrap a layer of moist air along the leaf surface to insulate the leaf from excessive heat or desiccating winds.

The ultimate master gardener, natural selection, has rewritten genetic programming in myriad ways, finely tuning each species or subspecies to local conditions. Like most plants, grasses lose water vapor to the atmosphere through tiny mouth-shaped valves, or stomata, in their leaves. The stomata are critical to plant respiration and remain open under most conditions to enable plants to take in carbon dioxide from the air. Strategic scheduling allows the plant to maximize carbon dioxide uptake during the cool of the evening and to close the stomata during the heat of the day. Consequently, prairie grasses are partially nocturnal; they do most of their growing at night or in the early morning hours.

The larger the surface area of the leaf, the more stomata it bears and the greater the potential for evaporative loss and subsequent water stress. Because intense sunlight increases the heat and water stress on plants in arid and semiarid environments, a further reduction in heat load is achieved by orienting photosynthetic tissue (leaves and stems) parallel to the sun's rays during the hottest time of the day. This vertical leaf and stem arrangement is typical of grasses, sedges, yuccas, and some cacti (e.g., prickly pear). The flattened stems (pads) of prickly pear cactus, for example, are noticeably more vertical than horizontal in hot, dry environments.

The ability to absorb moisture from several soil layers is especially important in arid and semiarid environments. The proportion of above- and belowground biomass in the typical bunchgrass is similar to that of an iceberg: between 60 and 80 percent of the plant's biomass lies beneath the surface of the ground. Long, vertical roots may reach a depth of six feet or more, tapping moisture reserves in the deeper soil layers. Nearer the surface, a multibranched network of fine rootlets spreads laterally to make use of the ephemeral moisture produced by brief showers. Grasses respond to prolonged drought by transferring their most valuable resources, sugars and proteins, the products of photosynthesis, to their root systems. The aboveground portion of the plant withers and may appear dead, while the root system is living frugally, drawing on its stored supplies and biding its time until conditions improve.

Prairie grasses are not uniformally capable of coping with the physiological stresses of drought. Tallgrass species, such as big bluestem and switchgrass, require the most moisture, while shortgrass prairie grasses are best adapted to drought. Midheight grasses, including needle-and-thread grass and western wheatgrass, fall somewhere near the midpoint along the moisture gradient. With its extensive root system, blue grama is one of the most drought resistant of all prairie grasses, exceeding even buffalo grass in durability. During times of severe drought, both species are able to remain physiologically dormant and to recover quickly after long periods without water. In the case of the amazingly resilient blue grama, the species can revive from dormancy, green up, and begin growing with as little as .2 inches of rainfall.

Many perennial shortgrasses have evolved elaborate methods of vegetative reproduction that allow them to propagate when conditions are unfavorable for sexual reproduction. The continuous mat of stems and roots so characteristic of buffalo grass is formed by modified stems known as stolons; these creeping runners spread over the ground surface and produce new plants by developing roots and shoots along the prostrate stem joints. Many other prairie grasses, such as galleta and western wheatgrass, produce horizontal underground stems, called rhizomes, that bear scalelike leaves and send up new plants from underground nodes. Under the right conditions, a single plant can produce enough rhizomes to carpet the area around it with dozens of new plants. Some species, such as galletagrass, produce large, woody rhizomes that may spread laterally for up to six and a half feet.

Bison have long been considered agents of natural selection in the shortgrass prairie, encouraging the evolution of plant features that enable grasses to withstand the grazer's activities. Whereas most plants grow from their tips, each grass leaf grows from its base. Thus when the tip of the blade is eaten or broken by trampling, growth continues from the base and the leaf is able to regenerate. Intermittent grazing also tends to encourage the production of side shoots, called tillers, which arise from nodes near the root crown; these ensure that grassland grazed frequently but not excessively will produce thick, bushy growth. Bison once moved freely from place to place across the prairie and were able to digest a wide variety of vegetation, leaving the land with ample time to recover after the animals moved on. More recently, domestic cattle and the fences that control their movements have dramatically changed the character of the shortgrass prairie in areas where grazing has been allowed to outstrip vegetative regeneration.

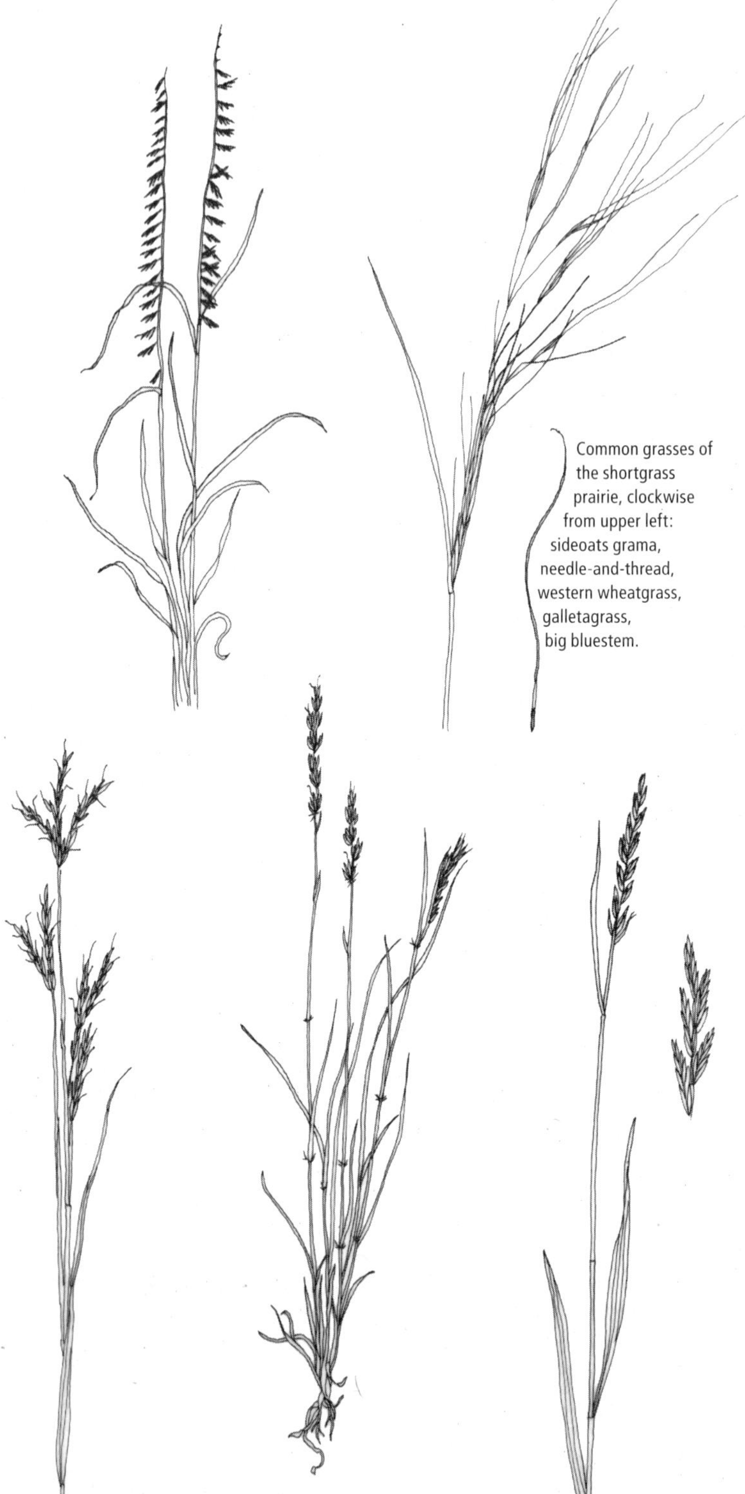

Common grasses of the shortgrass prairie, clockwise from upper left: sideoats grama, needle-and-thread, western wheatgrass, galletagrass, big bluestem.

Descriptions of Common Plants

Grasses

Buffalo Grass, *Buchloë dactyloides.* This native, warm-season shortgrass is easily distinguished by its sod-forming, stoloniferous growth habit. Wiry, gray-green leaves are produced in clusters at the nodes of the stolons and measure one to six inches in length. Male and female flowers are generally borne on separate plants, the flaglike male flowers on short, upright stems and the burlike female flowers enclosed in the leaves near the base of the plant.

Blue Grama, *Bouteloua gracilis.* This native bunchgrass is taller than buffalo grass and can be identified by its arched, comblike flowering spike and its wiry, blue-green leaves. The flowering stem, arising from a dense cluster of basal leaves, ranges in height from six to twenty-four inches. Blue grama is a warm-season grass, beginning growth in May or June.

Galletagrass, *Hilaria jamesii.* This native midgrass grows in scattered stands and is distinguished by the cluster of three spikelets that arises from each node along its spike; the spikelets are conspicuously hairy at their bases. The flowering stem, twelve to twenty inches in height, has a ring of soft hairs present at each joint. Though resembling a bunchgrass, the species has scaly rhizomes that spread out laterally for as much as six feet just beneath the soil surface. Galletagrass is a warm-season grass, beginning growth in summer after sufficient rain.

Sideoats Grama, *Bouteloua curtipendula.* This native midgrass is readily identified by its inflorescence, a one-sided raceme bearing ten to fifty spikelets. The length of the flowering stem is variable, depending on growth conditions, but heights of eighteen inches are not uncommon. Leaf blades may be up to twelve inches long, with scattered long hairs along the margins. A warm-season bunchgrass, sideoats grama begins growth in early spring and flowers from July to September; it reproduces by seed, tillers, and rhizomes.

Needle-and-Thread Grass, *Hesperostipa* (formerly *Stipa*) *comata.* The flowering stems of this elegant midgrass average about two feet in height and are tipped with multiple spikelets, each having a pointed, needle-like base and a long, threadlike awn. When a seed lands on the ground, the ability of the awn to twist and untwist in response to changing moisture conditions may help to position the seed for optimal germination. Needle-and-thread grass is a cool-season species, beginning growth in early spring or when moisture is available.

Western Wheatgrass, *Pascopyrum* (formerly *Agropyron*) *smithii.* This native, sod-forming midgrass is identified by its symmetrically arranged, imbricated spikelets. Western wheatgrass reproduces by seed or rhizome, its flowering stems ranging between one and two and a half feet in height. A cool-season species, growth begins when daytime temperatures are above 50°F; a period of dormancy is common in summer.

Wildflowers

Easter Daisy, *Townsendia exscapa.* This low, stemless composite is one of the earliest flowering species in the shortgrass country. The narrow, lance-shaped leaves are basal, subtending the one-and-a-half-inch-wide, daisylike, white to pinkish flower heads. This perennial herb arises from a branched rootstock and a deep taproot.

Sand Lily, *Leucocrinum montanum.* Blooming in earliest spring, this fragrant, ground-hugging little lily has a long white floral tube opening to six petals (botanists call these *tepals* because they are indistinguishable from the sepals). The leaves are basal and grasslike. This species is unusual in that the floral tube and the ovary lie beneath the ground surface throughout the growing season. The flower buds of the next season will push the elongated ovary of the previous season above the surface, allowing it to scatter its seeds.

Prairie Evening Primrose, *Oenothera albicaulis.* The spectacular white "drifts" that distinguish a shortgrass-prairie spring are generally attributed to this short, erect, annual herb. The simple leaves are somewhat spatula shaped and have distinctively wavy margins. The flowers are large, single, and arise from the bases of the upper leaves.

Downy Paintbrush, *Castilleja sessiliflora.* This is the only paintbrush species restricted to prairie grassland. Easily distinguished by its greenish white flowers, five-lobed greenish calyx, and green or pinkish green basal bract. The floral spikes are erect, and the clumped stems, with their linear and alternately arranged leaves, are densely covered with soft hairs.

Copper Mallow (or Cowboy's Delight), *Sphaeralcea coccinea.* In years with good moisture, this orange-flowered, five-petaled perennial herb is a conspicuous element of the prairie flora. Also known as cowboy's delight, this beautiful wildflower has star-shaped hairs on its finely divided, gray-green leaves.

Common Plants of the Shortgrass Prairie

Trees

Cottonwood, plains, *Populus deltoides* ssp. *monilifera*
Hackberry, *Celtis reticulata*

Shrubs

Plum, wild, *Prunus americana*
Rabbitbrush, *Chrysothamnus nauseosus*
Sage, prairie, *Artemisia ludoviciana*
  sand, *A. filifolia*
  silver (or fringed), *A. frigida*
Sagebrush, big (or Great Basin sagebrush), *Seriphidium* (formerly *Artemisia*) *tridentatum*
Saltbush, four-wing, *Atriplex canescens*
  silverscale, *A. argentea*
Sumac, three-leaf (or Skunkbrush), *Rhus aromatica* ssp. *trilobata*
Snakeweed, broom, *Gutierrezia sarothrae*
Snowberry, western, *Symphoricarpos occidentalis*
Winterfat, *Krascheninnikovia* (formerly *Ceratoides*) *lanata*
Yucca (or Spanish bayonet), *Yucca glauca*

Grasses

Barley, foxtail, *Critesion* (formerly *Hordeum*) *jubatum*
Bluestem, big, *Andropogon gerardii*
  little, *A. scoparius*

sand, *A. hallii*

Buffalo grass, *Buchloë dactyloides*

Cheatgrass, *Anisantha* (formerly *Bromus*) *tectorum*

Cordgrass, *Spartina pectinata*

Galletagrass, *Hilaria jamesii*

Grama, blue, *Bouteloua gracilis*

sideoats, *B. curtipendula*

hairy, *B. hirsuta*

Indiangrass, *Sorghastrum avenaceum*

Junegrass, *Koeleria macrantha*

Muhly, ring, *Muhlenbergia torreyi*

alkali, *M. asperifolia*

Needle-and-thread, *Hesperostipa* (formerly *Stipa*) *comata*

Needlegrass, green, *Nassella* (formerly *Stipa*) *viridula*

Ricegrass, Indian, *Achnatherum* (formerly *Oryzopsis*) *hymenoides*

Sacaton, alkali, *Sporobolus airoides*

Saltgrass, *Distichlis stricta*

Sandreed, *Calamovilfa longifolia*

Squirreltail, *Elymus elymoides* (formerly *Sitanion hystrix*)

Switchgrass, *Panicum virgatum*

Three-awn, *Aristida purpurea*

Wheatgrass, western, *Pascopyrum* (formerly *Agropyron*) *smithii*

Wildflowers

Aster, white prairie, *Virgulus* (formerly *Aster*) *falcatus*

Begonia, sand or wild, *Rumex venosus*

Bindweed, field, *Convolvulus arvensis*

Blazingstar, plains, *Nuttallia* (formerly *Mentzelia*) *nuda*

Broomrape, *Orobanche* spp.

Cactus, cholla (or Candelabra Cactus), *Cylindropuntia imbricata*

green-flowered, *Echinocereus viridiflorus*

pincushion (or ball), *Coryphantha vivipara*

prickly pear, *Opuntia polyacantha* and *O. macrorhiza*

Chicory, common, *Cichorium intybus*

Coneflower, prairie, *Ratibida columnifera*

Evening primrose, prairie, *Oenothera albicaulis*
white stemless, *O. caespitosa*
yellow stemless, *O. howardii*
Fleabane, *Erigeron bellidiastrum*
Gaura, scarlet, *Gaura coccinea*
Gayfeather, *Liatris punctata*
Gumweed, curlycup, *Grindelia squarrosa*
Larkspur, prairie, *Delphinium carolinianum*
Locoweed, Colorado, *Oxytropis lambertii*
Rocky Mountain, *O. sericea*
Lupine, Nebraska, *Lupinus plattensis*
Mallow, copper (or cowboy's delight), *Sphaeralcea coccinea*
Milkvetch, groundplum, *Astragalus crassicarpus*
Missouri, *A. missouriensis*
painted, *A. ceramicus*
Milkweed, green, *Asclepias viridiflora*
showy, *Asclepias speciosa*
Morning glory, bush, *Ipomoea leptophylla*
Onion, sand, *Allium textile*
Paintbrush, plains (or downy), *Castilleja sessiliflora*
Penstemon, narrow-leaved, *Penstemon angustifolius*
white, *P. albidus*
Peppergrass, *Lepidium densiflorum*
Phlox, moss, *Phlox hoodii*
Plantain, woolly, *Plantago patagonica*
Poppy, prickly, *Argemone polyanthemos*
Poppymallow, purple, *Callirhoë involucrata*
Prairie clover, *Dalea enneandra*
Puccoon, narrow-leaved, *Lithospermum incisum*
Ragweed, western, *Ambrosia psilostachya*
Sand lily, *Leucocrinum montanum*
Sand verbena, *Abronia fragrans*
Sophora, silky, *Sophora nuttalliana*
Spiderwort, *Tradescantia occidentalis*
Sunflower, common, *Helianthus annuus*

Thistle, Russian, *Salsola australis*
prairie, *Cirsium canescens*
Townsend Daisy (or Easter Daisy), *Townsendia hookeri* and *T. exscapa*
Violet, birdfoot or prairie, *Viola pedatifida*

Environment and Adaptation: Animals of the Shortgrass Prairie

High on a bluff, with the wind at full throttle, you can almost believe you are hearing the muffled thunder of a bison herd on the move. Any minute you'll see a billowing dust cloud on the horizon and the bison herd rolling effortlessly across the prairie swells. Within the long shadow cast by the Southern Rockies, hunting, agriculture, and urbanization have taken their toll on the prairie's animals. Despite these impacts, however, a remarkable diversity and abundance of wildlife remain. Pronghorn still number in the thousands. With the wolf gone from the open prairies, the adaptable coyote has proliferated, occasionally at the expense of the more vulnerable swift fox. The reappearance of black-tailed prairie dog colonies in areas where they were once eradicated by poisons or decimated by plague attracts large wintering populations of ferruginous and rough-legged hawks and an ever-growing number of bald eagles. Burrowing owls stake their claims to the abandoned burrows of prairie dogs and badgers. With the coming of spring, the prairie belongs largely to its nesting birds; the courtship rituals of long-billed curlews, mountain plovers, lark buntings, horned larks, and vesper sparrows fill the air with music and grace.

A Diet of Grass

A magnificent variety of large grazing animals—camels, horses, mammoths, bison, and pronghorn—roamed the grasslands during the Pleistocene. Many ecologists believe that the spread of grasslands and the evolution of grazing animals proceeded together. Unlike most other herbaceous plants, grasses secrete minute grains of silica between their cells; this plant sand abrades the teeth of animals that depend on a grass diet. The first grazers evolved with high-crowned (*hypsodont*) cheek teeth equipped with crescent-shaped ridges of hard enamel on the grinding surface of each tooth. Hypsodont teeth are not only resistant to abrasion, but they are able to compensate for wear by rising within the gum and exposing successive increments of the crown.

A grass diet is especially rich in cellulose, a structural carbohydrate found in the walls of plant cells. Cellulose is impervious to all vertebrate digestive enzymes and acids and is a source of food energy only for animals with very specialized digestive systems. To solve this problem, some large grazing species evolved a digestive system in which several large-capacity storage and fermentation chambers precede the true stomach. The first and largest of these, the rumen, serves as the principal fermentation site, where the plant food and saliva mixture is exposed to a variety of microorganisms (bacteria and protozoans). These organisms are able to break down the cellulose, reducing it to nutritionally useful metabolites and allowing access to the vital substances housed within the plant cells. Any undigested fibrous materials are partially regurgitated and remasticated and then swallowed once again to undergo a second round of fermentation. This process, known as rumination, allows the animal to graze quickly through an area and move on, digesting the food at leisure in a more protected spot, thereby minimizing the length of time the animal is exposed to predators. Pronghorns, for example, alternately feed and bed down throughout the day and night, with ruminating dominating almost 80 percent of bedding time.

Hares and rabbits have adopted another strategy to solve the challenge of digesting cellulose: they process their food twice. During the first round of cellulose digestion, food passes rather rapidly through the digestive system and a group of soft, greenish pellets forms in a pouchlike organ called the caecum, which is attached to the intestine. These pellets are high in protein, water-soluble vitamins, and other nutrients but require further processing before they can provide any nutritional benefit to the animal. The pellets are then voided and reingested for a second round of digestion. This process, known as coprophagy, is critically important because it allows maximum utilitization of the diet's nutritional content. The round droppings typically associated with hares and rabbits represent the final waste product of the digestive process.

Built to Run

For many prairie animals, survival depends on the ability to run fast and far without tiring. Hares are built for the quick getaway, their powerful hind legs allowing them to virtually explode from absolute immobility and bound across the prairie at speeds up to forty-five miles per hour. A jackrabbit on the move is a marvelous sight, taking fifteen-foot bounds, skillfully shifting directions in midair, and executing a series of "spy-hops" to scan the terrain ahead. The pronghorn truly has the prairie in its blood. It is the quintessential running machine, the fastest animal in North America. The pronghorn's legs are unusually long and slender, and the heaviest muscles are bunched close to the body; combined, these modifications serve to reduce and redistribute the weight of the limbs, thus favoring rapid limb movement with a minimum expenditure of energy. While running, the body moves almost in a straight line; little energy is wasted in the up-and-down movements typical of most galloping animals. Enlarged lungs and heart combined with a large-diameter trachea enable the pronghorn to maintain high speeds for long periods of time. The pronghorn may cruise at thirty miles per hour for distances of up to seven miles, and individuals have been clocked at fifty to sixty miles per hour for several miles, often running with their mouths open and tongues hanging out to increase the supply of air to the lungs.

Burrowers Large and Small

In the shortgrass prairie, the diversity of habitats available for feeding and reproductive activities is severely limited. Not surprisingly, the shortgrass fauna is characterized by a preponderance of burrowing animals that are specially adapted to exploit both the herbaceous layer and the sheltering subterranean environment. Burrows are used to escape predators, avoid environmental extremes, sleep, breed, rear young, and store food. The larger rodents, such as the black-tailed prairie dog, plains pocket gopher, and thirteen-lined ground squirrel, are skillful burrowers, constructing complex underground chambers. Grassland predators such as the coyote, badger, and swift fox dig their own dens or reconstruct burrows abandoned by other animals. The small noctural mammals of the shortgrass prairie—the Ord's kangaroo rat and several species of pocket mice, for example—create networks of underground tunnels complete with predator-fooling dead ends and alternate entrances. They often plug the entrances to their nesting chambers when in residence.

Many reptiles and amphibians seek shelter in abandoned burrow systems or have variously modified appendages that allow them to excavate their own burrows or dig out their prey. The western box turtle and the spadefoot toad have appendages modified for digging; the spadefoot toad is named for the hard, spadelike tubercles on the hind feet that it uses to dig resting and hibernation burrows. The western hognose snake, a voracious toad-eater, detects its buried prey by smell and then uses its cornified, upturned snout to dig the toad from its burrow.

From upper right: western hognose snake, showing spadelike snout; plains spadefoot toad, with detail of spadelike tubercle on hind feet.

Grassland Birds

Visitors often marvel at the richly textured symphony of bird songs, the "dawn chorus," that graces a spring morning on the shortgrass prairie. As early as 3 A.M., western kingbirds will begin to declare their restlessness to start the day, chattering like gossips in a grove of plains cottonwoods. Mourning doves begin cooing softly, their gentle woodwindlike calls giving way to a full-voiced avian choir: meadowlarks, horned larks, longspurs, lark buntings, and vesper sparrows, to name just a few. Grassland bird species are unique, exhibiting adaptations in appearance, physiology, and behavior that differ strikingly from those of forest species. Male territorial and courtship displays, such as those of the prairie chicken and sharptail grouse, can be spectacular. With few exceptions, grassland birds sing on the wing, often rising several hundred feet in the air to deliver their territorial messages before fluttering or dropping quickly back to earth. The mountain plover and the longspurs are well known for their song flights. The male chestnut-collared longspur begins its magnificent aerial displays over its nesting grounds by mid-April. Song flights begin with a gradual rise into the air accompanied by singing, wings beating rapidly to the peak altitude of the flight. Then, circling briefly, the bird flutters to the ground like a leaf floating downward. Other species, such as the western meadowlark and the lark bunting, select some suitably conspicuous perch—a fence post, small shrub, or tall weed stalk—from which to deliver their courtship preambles or territorial songs.

Cryptic coloration, or camouflage, is a common strategy for birds and mammals living in open country. In many grassland species—burrowing owls, long-billed curlews, vesper sparrows, and others—the feathers are variously striped or streaked with shades of brown, regardless of sex, so that when the bird is motionless it tends to disappear against its background. During the nesting season, the long-billed curlew makes concealment a fine art, stretching its neck out along the ground while sitting on its nest, to avoid attracting predators. The bold, black bands on the white breast of the killdeer, known as disruptive coloration, serve roughly the same purpose as cryptic coloration by visually breaking up the outline of the bird into unidentifiable pieces. White outer tail feathers, a distinguishing feature of many grassland species, including vesper sparrows, lark sparrows, horned larks, and longspurs, are particularly conspicuous when flashed in flight, serving as a group warning mechanism. The white rump patch of the pronghorn serves a similar function.

Life Histories of Selected Animals

Mammals

White-tailed Jackrabbit, *Lepus townsendii.* This large, heavy-bodied hare is easily distinguished from the black-tailed jackrabbit (*L. californicus*) by its pale, buffy gray pelage and pure white tail; winter pelage is mostly white. Distribution is largely restricted to open country, and alpine tundra may be occupied in some areas. White-tailed jackrabbits are herbivorous, foraging primarily in the early morning and from late afternoon well into the night. During the day, the jackrabbit rests in a form (a shallow depression) dug into the ground. During winter, a snow burrow is often used for concealment. The breeding period extends from late February to mid-July. During courtship, male jackrabbits fight vigorously, kicking out with their hind feet. Ovulation is induced by copulation, with females producing multiple litters of one to nine precocial young (fully furred, eyes open). Juvenile hares are able to survive on their own at only two weeks of age.

Thirteen-lined Ground Squirrel, *Spermophilus tridecemlineatus.* This small, diurnal ground-dwelling squirrel is easily identified by its dot-and-dash color pattern. Thirteen-lined ground squirrels seldom occur in defined concentrations and are not colonial. The winding, shallow burrow systems are constructed in sandy soils on gentle slopes and have separate nesting and food storage chambers; the earth from tunnel excavation is scattered away from the burrow entrance. Thirteen-lined ground squirrels are active from April through October; hibernation begins in October, in a chamber sealed off from the rest of the burrow system by a plug of soil. Insects and the seeds of various grasses and forbs are preferred as food, but they will also eat fleshy roots, carrion, and the eggs and nestlings of ground-nesting birds when available. Females mate soon after emerging from hibernation; gestation requires about twenty-eight days, and the young are altricial (naked, eyes closed) at birth.

Thirteen-lined ground squirrel.

Black-tailed Prairie Dog, *Cynomys ludovicianus.* This ground-dwelling squirrel is identified by its robust size, buffy brown pelage, and black-tipped tail. Diurnal, herbivorous, and active year-round, prairie dogs are opportunistic feeders, mixing their grass diet with a wide variety of succulent forbs, cacti, carrion, and insects. Black-tailed prairie dogs have a highly organized social system; prairie dog towns are composed of a series of subunits called wards. Each ward houses several coteries; the coterie typically consists of one or two males, several females, and half a dozen young. The dominant male controls the patriarchal society of the coterie, and the mating system is polygynous (one male mates with several females). The communication system of the prairie dog is highly evolved and based on tactile, olfactory, visual, and vocal cues. The most common call is the nasal alarm or warning bark, usually accompanied by a flick of the tail. Mutual grooming reinforces the strong social bonds within the coterie. During the breeding season, from March until April, a litter of four to six altricial young is born after a gestation period of twenty-eight to thirty-three days; juvenile prairie dogs remain with the coterie until their second year.

Pronghorn, *Antilocapra americana*. Its tan or reddish upper body, white rump patch, belly, and inner legs, and alternating bands of white and tan across the throat make the pronghorn easy to identify. A black band from eye to snout and on the neck distinguishes males. Horn sheaths surround laterally flattened horn-cores that are unbranched and permanent. Horns are present in both sexes; the larger, branching horn sheaths of the males are shed shortly after breeding. Pronghorn have keen eyesight; the eyes are set in protruding sockets that allow for an extraordinary degree of wide-angle vision. At the first hint of danger, the pronghorn erects the white hairs of its rump patch in a heliographlike warning display that alerts other members of the herd. Pronghorn are gregarious, especially during winter. In spring and summer, bachelor herds and female-kid groups are common. The rut begins in September, continuing into the first week in October; pronghorn defend their territories with ritualized displays and occasional fights. Twin, precocial young are born in late May or early June, after a gestation period of 230 to 250 days. During the first few days of its life, the pronghorn kid is virtually odorless and will flatten itself against the grass, attracting as little attention as possible and rising only when its mother visits it for nursing. Within as few as four days after birth, pronghorn fawns can outrun a man and are able to keep pace with adults in the herd.

Birds

Burrowing Owl, *Athene cunicularia*. This small, diurnal owl is identified by its short tail, long legs, brown barring on the breast, rounded head (no ear tufts), and ground-dwelling habits. The species is migratory in the shortgrass prairie, arriving in mid-April either singly or paired and returning south in mid- to late October. The owl's diet consists of insects, small rodents, and occasional small birds, reptiles, and amphibians. Burrow entrances may be littered with regurgitation pellets containing fur, bone, and insect parts. Males return to the same burrow year after year; unpaired males display from their burrow locations by "bowing" and giving their double-noted "coo-coo" song throughout the night. When approached or flushed, both sexes give a sharp "chatter" call. Burrowing owls are often observed standing at the entrance to their burrows or perching on fence posts. Males feed females during pair formation, incubation, and brooding. Incubation takes about twenty-eight days, and the young are able to fly after forty-four to forty-eight days.

Swainson's Hawk, *Buteo swainsoni.* The chestnut bib, somewhat pointed wings, finely banded tail, and preference for open country distinguish this large, dark buteo. Swainson's hawks hunt primarily from perches such as fence posts and low trees, or from prominent knolls. Pairs are monogamous and arrive on their breeding ground in late March or in April, about a month before egg laying begins. Swainson's hawks migrate in enormous flocks, making use of thermals during their annual migratory journey to South America. The diet consists of small mammals and insects; migrating flocks sometimes hunt crickets and grasshoppers on the ground. Swainson's hawks build large, bulky stick nests in isolated trees or tall shrubs. Both sexes incubate and feed the young; fledging occurs after about thirty days.

Mountain Plover, *Charadrius montanus.* Despite its name, the mountain plover is largely restricted to shortgrass prairie that has been extensively grazed by livestock or where the vegetative cover has been cropped short due to the presence of a large prairie dog colony. It is identified by its shorebird-like appearance, sandy brown upperparts, creamy breast, and whitish wing stripe (visible in flight). This species frequently crouches low to the ground, well camouflaged by its protective coloring. Mountain plovers are migratory, arriving in the Southern Rockies in late March and often returning to their old territories. Males advertise their territory with calls and an aerial "falling leaf" display; they also practice "scraping," preparing several potential nest bowls in an established territory. Despite pair bonds formed early in the breeding season, some females will mate with new mates within two weeks of completing their first clutch, leaving their original mates to rear the first clutch. While nesting, the adult will defend the nest, using a "crippled-bird act" to lure away potential predators. Nesting occurs in May. Loss of suitable habitat has caused a 60 percent drop in the population, and numbers continue to slide.

Western Meadowlark, *Sturnella neglecta.* The black V on the upper breast and the bright yellow throat, breast, and abdomen identify this robin-sized songster; the outer tail feathers flash white in flight. Meadowlarks typically walk on the ground while feeding, often in pairs, or perch on fence posts, tall weeds, and shrubs while delivering their intense, flutelike song. This species is largely insectivorous but may occasionally be seen scavenging roadkills. Meadowlarks nest on the ground, their nests well hidden in grass clumps. The nest may have a canopy woven into the surrounding vegetation and a lateral entrance. The female incubates the eggs, but both sexes feed the young.

Lark Bunting, *Calamospiza melanocorys.* Male lark buntings are identified by their jet-black plumage, large, white wing patches, and white-tipped tails; females and males in winter plumage are brownish with dusky streaking and buff or whitish wing patches. Lark buntings are migratory, moving in large, gregarious flocks north along the Southern Rockies in March from their wintering grounds in Mexico and on the southern plains. Birds at the rear of the flock continuously leapfrog to the front, the flock appearing like an enormous wheel rolling over the prairie. Males tolerate each other during the nesting season, and pairs will often nest only 100 feet apart. Strong fliers, males sing from perches or will often shoot up into the air to deliver their rich, warbling advertisement song. The lark bunting builds its cup-shaped nest of grasses on the ground, usually in a shallow depression.

From left to right: horned lark, lark bunting.

Vesper Sparrow, *Pooecetes gramineus.* The vesper sparrow is named for its preference for evening singing. This small, inconspicuous brown sparrow is identified by its white outer tail feathers, evident only in flight, and by the absence of strong facial markings and breast spots. Vesper sparrows arrive in small flocks on the nesting ground in March or April. Males sing only from elevated perches, and the song is a mixture of paired opening notes and a descending series of rapid trills. Vesper sparrows forage along the ground and fly only when closely approached. This species is fond of dust baths; several may be observed dusting together in sandy patches on dirt roads. Vesper sparrows generally build their nests in depressions in the ground, typically under tall vegetation.

Amphibians and Reptiles

Plains Spadefoot Toad, *Scaphiopus bombifrons.* This small toad is largely restricted to sandy grasslands and sandhills and is identified by its vertical pupils, the wedge-shaped black "spade" on each hind foot, and the hard lump between the eyes. Spadefoots are active from May to September but spend much of their time underground in rodent burrows or in burrows excavated with the cornified spades on their hind feet. Rains of an inch or more and temperatures of at least 50°F are necessary to initiate breeding. Males emerge in response to these conditions and give their loud, snorelike calls while floating in the water. During mating, the male clasps the female with his forelegs while the two swim from place to place. Egg masses are laid by the female on submerged vegetation or other objects and are fertilized by the male; eggs hatch in two to three days. Tadpoles develop rapidly, and metamorphosis requires fewer than forty days.

Great Plains Toad, *Bufo cognatus.* The Great Plains toad is a large species with horizontal pupils, warty skin, and a somewhat symmetrical pattern of light-edged dark spots on the back; cranial crests and oval paratoid glands are especially prominent. This species is common in lowland habitats where soils are relatively soft. Largely nocturnal and active from May to September, the Great Plains toad spends much of its time in self-dug burrows, but becomes more conspicuous after heavy rains. Heavy rainfall and flooding initiate breeding activity, and the male's jackhammerlike trill can be heard anytime from May to July. Each female may lay up to 20,000 eggs encased in slender tubes of jelly; eggs hatch in two to three days, and tadpoles normally metamorphose within forty days of hatching.

Western Box Turtle, *Terrapene ornata*. The domed top shell, patterned with yellowish radiating lines and spots, identifies this small terrestrial turtle; males have a reddish iris and foreleg spots, and females have a yellowish iris and foreleg spots. Box turtles prefer dry, open grassland with sandy soils; the average home range is about five acres, and favorable habitat may support three to six turtles per acre. Box turtles are diurnal and active from April to October; most activity occurs in early morning and late afternoon in midsummer. Males reach breeding age after eight to nine years; females become sexually active at ten to eleven years. During mating the male climbs up on the shell of the female and grips her shell with his hind feet. Female box turtles deposit four to six eggs in an underground burrow in May, June, or July; eggs hatch after two months, but the young turtles are rarely observed above ground.

Lesser Earless Lizard, *Holbrookia maculata*. This common small lizard is typical in sandhills and open, sparsely vegetated grasslands and is distinguished by its smooth, granular scales, the black marks on either side of the abdomen, and the light-colored stripe that runs down the center of its back; there are no external ear openings. Lesser earless lizards are diurnal and active from March or April to October if temperatures are mild. This species seeks shade during midsummer and may hide in small rodent burrows or bury itself by plunging headfirst into the soil and wriggling frantically until covered. Lesser earless lizards breed in May, the eggs developing underground in June or July; hatchlings appear from late July through August.

Western Hognose Snake, *Heterodon nasicus*. The western hognose is a small snake identified by a stocky body that narrows abruptly at the tail, the upturned, spadelike snout, and the black belly. This diurnal species is largely restricted to grassland and sandhill areas. Most activity occurs in the morning and late afternoon from April to October. Hognose snakes dig out their buried prey, mainly toads and lizards, with their snouts. When frightened or disturbed, this snake seldom bites, but it is a magnificent bluffer, flattening its head and neck, hissing vigorously, and pretending to strike. If this tactic fails, it may resort to its famous "death-feigning" act, rolling over on its back, regurgitating, defecating, and hanging its tongue out of its open mouth. If the snake is righted, it will usually flip over again and expose its black belly. This behavior presumably repulses some potential predators. If left alone, the hognose will turn over after a few minutes and crawl away. Females breed their second year and then alternate years thereafter; eggs are laid underground in July and hatch after about two months.

Common Animals of the Shortgrass Prairie

Mammals

Badger, American, *Taxidea taxus*
Bat, big brown, *Eptesicus fuscus*
Cottontail, desert, *Sylvilagus audubonii*
Coyote, *Canis latrans*
Fox, swift, *Vulpes velox*
Jackrabbit, black-tailed, *Lepus californicus*
    white-tailed, *L. townsendii*
Kangaroo Rat, Ord's, *Dipodomys ordii*
Mouse, deer, *Peromyscus maniculatus*
    northern grasshopper, *Onychomys leucogaster*
    plains harvest, *Reithrodontomys montanus*
    plains pocket, *Perognathus flavescens*
    silky pocket, *P. flavus*
Myotis, little brown, *Myotis lucifugus*
Prairie Dog, black-tailed, *Cynomys ludovicianus*
Pocket Gopher, plains, *Geomys bursarius*
Pronghorn, *Antilocapra americana*
Shrew, least, *Cryptotis parva*
    masked, *Sorex cinereus*
    Merriam's, *S. merriami*

Skunk, striped, *Mephitis mephitis*
Squirrel, thirteen-lined ground, *Spermophilus tridecemlineatus*
Vole, prairie, *Microtus ochrogaster*
Weasel, long-tailed, *Mustela frenata*

Birds

Blackbird, Brewer's, *Euphagus cyanocephalus*
Bunting, lark, *Calamospiza melanocorys*
Crow, American, *Corvus brachyrhynchos*
Curlew, long-billed, *Numenius americanus*
Dove, mourning, *Zenaida macroura*
Eagle, golden, *Aquila chrysaetos*
Falcon, prairie, *Falco mexicanus*
Goldfinch, American, *Carduelis tristis*
Harrier, northern, *Circus cyaneus*
Hawk, ferruginous, *Buteo regalis*
  red-tailed, *B. jamaicensis*
  rough-legged, *B. lagopus*
  Swainson's, *B. swainsoni*
Kestrel, American (formerly Sparrow Hawk), *Falco sparverius*
Killdeer, *Charadrius vociferus*
Kingbird, eastern, *Tyrannus tyrannus*
  western, *T. verticalis*
Lark, horned, *Eremophila alpestris*
Longspur, chestnut-collared, *Calcarius ornatus*
  Lapland, *C. lapponicus*
  McCown's, *C. mccownii*
Magpie, black-billed, *Pica hudsonia*
Meadowlark, western, *Sturnella neglecta*
Nighthawk, common, *Chordeiles minor*
Owl, burrowing, *Athene cunicularia*
Phoebe, Say's, *Sayornis saya*
Plover, mountain, *Charadrius montanus*
Prairie-Chicken, greater, *Tympanuchus cupido*
Shrike, loggerhead, *Lanius ludovicianus*

Sparrow, Brewer's, *Spizella breweri*
grasshopper, *Ammodramus savannarum*
lark, *Chondestes grammacus*
Sparrow, vesper, *Pooecetes gramineus*
Swallow, barn, *Hirundo rustica*
Vulture, turkey, *Cathartes aura*

Amphibians

Salamander, tiger, *Ambystoma tigrinum*
Toad, Great Plains, *Bufo cognatus*
New Mexico, *Scaphiopus multiplicatus*
plains spadefoot, *S. bombifrons*
Woodhouse's, *B. woodhousii*

Reptiles

Bullsnake, *Pituophis melanoleucus*
Coachwhip, *Masticophis flagellum*
Garter Snake, plains, *Thamnophis radix*
Hognose Snake, western, *Heterodon nasicus*
Lizard, lesser earless, *Holbrookia maculata*
plateau, *Sceloporus undulatus*
Racer, *Coluber constrictor*
Racerunner, six-lined, *Cnemidophorus sexlineatus*
Rattlesnake, western, *Crotalus viridis*
Skink, many-lined, *Eumeces multivirgatus*
Turtle, western box, *Terrapene ornata*

Butterflies

Satyr, Ridings', *Neominois ridingsii*
Skipper, plains gray, *Yvretta rhesus*
simius, *Amblyscirtes simius*

CHAPTER TWELVE

The Shrubland Tapestry: Semidesert, Sagebrush, and Mountain Shrublands

Bathed in pure sunlight, the West's shrublands are generous with everything but water. On a summer's afternoon, rainsqualls dance across an expanse of sagebrush, never quite touching down. The scent of water on the wind intensifies the sweet-sharp aroma of the sage. Beneath the passing clouds, the shrubland resembles an embroidered, faded tapestry French-knotted in hues of verdigris and olivine. At day's end, the land saturated in lavendar twilight, the sharp edges return to rim the horizon. If you, like me, never get enough of open spaces, a sojourn in sagebrush country will bring the world back into focus, leaving you with nothing but a hunger for more space, more light. The shrubland ecosystems of the Southern Rockies form a distinctive and important component of the mountain landscape. In many parts of the Southern Rockies, the shrub-steppe (shrub-dominated, semiarid grassland) extends for tens of miles across the intermontane basins. More commonly, shrublands occur as small patches or as a discontinuous, somewhat narrow transition zone between grassland or meadow ecosystems and the mountain forests. The three principal types described here and in the chapters that follow include the semidesert shrublands (dominated by greasewood or saltbush), sagebrush shrublands (dominated by big sagebrush), and mountain shrublands (dominated by either mountain mahogany or Gambel's oak). This chapter provides a general introduction to the fascinating ecological and physiological adaptations that characterize these shrublands. The chapters that follow describe in greater detail the unique plants and animals associated with each ecosystem.

Plant Adaptation: Designs for Survival

Coping with Drought

On a midsummer's day, when heat shimmers obscure the crisp edge of the horizon, the phrase *sun-frazzled* seems the best adjective to describe the shrub-steppe. Hot summers, cool to cold winters, and low precipitation characterize the climate of the shrub-steppe. These high desert ecosystems are typical of sites where the ratio between annual precipitation and potential evaporation is transitional between that of drought-adapted woodlands, such as piñon-juniper, and grasslands and semidesert herbaceous communities. Water stress is the most critical factor influencing the adaptations of plants growing in arid and semiarid environments. The morphological and physiological adaptations that enable a plant to maximize its ability to absorb groundwater efficiently and to moderate the rate at which water loss occurs as a result of evaporation are of paramount importance. Below ground, most aridland shrubs increase water uptake by developing extensive root systems. Rapid and deep penetration by a plant's taproot is a common characteristic of many shrub species. The root system of big sagebrush, for example, consists of an extensive lateral network of shallow roots, which take advantage of short-term moisture supplies in the upper soil layers, and a cluster of coarse, penetrating roots, which are able to tap groundwater reserves at greater depth.

Belowground detail of root connection between tufted broomrape, shown on the left, and fringed sage, the parasitized host.

Root Parasites

Some herbaceous plants have solved the problem of water and nutrient stress by parasitizing the roots of other species. The most interesting of these parasitic species is broomrape. Broomrape lacks chlorophyll and is unable to manufacture food by normal photosynthetic means; consequently, broomrape must rely on other sources for the nutrients and water necessary for growth. When first established, the broomrape seedling quickly attaches its roots to that of a suitable host, typically a species of sage or buckwheat. Paintbrush, in contrast to the parasitic broomrape, is capable of photosynthesis, but is also known to parasitize the roots of other plants. In the case of paintbrush, root parasitism provides a second insurance policy, enabling this species to better withstand periods of drought and to expand its ecological range into areas with nutrient-deficient soils.

Root Nodules and Symbiotic Bacteria

In addition to being dry, shrubland soils are often deficient in nitrogen and other nutrients. Several shrub and herbaceous plants have evolved special structures on their roots that house nitrogen-fixing bacteria. The roots of mountain mahogany have nodules populated by filamentous bacteria known as actinomycetes. These single-celled organisms counteract the relative sterility of the soil by converting atmospheric nitrogen into water-soluble nitrate compounds, which can then be utilized by the plant. In return, mountain mahogany furnishes the bacterium with nutrients and water. Nodules on the roots of lupine, a common wildflower in sagebrush shrublands, harbor rhizobium bacteria and serve a similar function. During the early stages of this symbiotic relationship, the bacteria gain entrance to the root hairs and are entirely parasitic until nodule formation has been completed.

Leaf Design

The challenge for most aridland plants lies in reducing evaporative losses. Adaptations to water stress are most conspicuous in the anatomical modifications of the leaves, where water loss, as a function of transpiration, occurs through minute openings, called stomates, in the leaf surfaces. Stomates are critical to terrestrial plants because they permit the exchange of gases between the living protoplasm of the plant's cells and the atmosphere. Each species has solved its water-balance problem by its own unique combination of adaptive characteristics. The leaves of most dryland shrubs are smaller than those of species growing in areas where water is abundant. In addition, the leaf blades are somewhat thickened, and in certain species, such as mountain mahogany and big sagebrush, the leaf blades may change their orientation or even inroll during times of severe water stress so as to moderate the amount of leaf surface exposed to direct sun.

On a hot summer day, thermal breezes build as the earth warms, wicking moisture from every leaf and stem and sending dust devils dancing across the sun-baked hardpan. Control over water loss is achieved by the degree of protection that can be afforded to the leaf surface and to the stomates. The leaf surfaces of several species, such as Gambel's oak and chokecherry, are covered with a fatty substance, called cutin, which gives the leaves a shiny, waterproof appearance and also reflects a certain amount of incoming solar radiation. Leaf surfaces that are heavily cutinized are extremely effective in retarding water loss and in protecting the underlying plant cells from desiccation. In some species, such as big sagebrush and rabbitbrush, the leaves may be covered with fine hairs, which keep moisture-robbing air currents elevated well above the stomata and insulate the leaf surface from excessive heat or cold.

A deciduous growth habit, either seasonal or initiated by prolonged drought, is another efficient means of reducing losses due to transpiration. In contrast to the primarily nondeciduous shrub species that dominate the true chaparral of California and Arizona, the principal shrubland species of the Southern Rockies are winter-deciduous. The corky or waxy materials that cover the leafless branches further reduce transpiration.

The Water Balance: Coping with High Salt Concentrations

Water-soluble salts and a variety of other substances are produced from rocks as a result of normal chemical weathering. In a high-rainfall environment, leaching flushes these salts from the soil, lowering the pH and increasing the acidity. In arid or semiarid environments, however, saline and alkaline soils (those having a pH greater than 7) are common because excessive amounts of soluble salts and carbonate compounds accumulate in the soil due to evaporative concentration. Excess solute accumulations, often appearing as a white crust on the soil surface, are conspicuous in areas where evaporative concentration is enhanced by a high water table. In other areas, periods of above-average precipitation may cause surface salt accumulations to be washed from upland sites and to accumulate in shallow depressions.

High soil concentrations of soluble salts interfere with the osmotic balance necessary for normal water uptake by a plant's root system. Plants that are physiologically adapted to grow in salty or alkaline soils are called halophytes. Greasewood and saltbush are highly specialized halophytes, solving the problem of excess salt by absorbing it into their tissues so that the concentration of salt in their cell sap exceeds that of their soil-moisture supply. Under conditions of severe soil-moisture stress, the capacity for continual adjustment of internal salt concentration helps these species cope with increasing salinity. In certain situations, the concentration of salt in a plant's tissues functions as antifreeze during the winter months, protecting the plant from injury by limiting the development of ice crystals within the plant's cells.

Most halophytes, despite their high salt tolerance, must prevent the buildup of toxic levels of salt in their tissues. Salt dilution and salt extrusion are the two most common ways in which plants combat the salt challenge. The succulent leaves of greasewood are capable of storing large amounts of water, which provide a means of diluting the amount of salt present in the leaf cells as needed. Saltbush, on the other hand, reduces its salt load by transporting the excess to specialized salt glands or storage hairs on the leaf surface. The storage hairs, each consisting of a small stalk cell and a large bladderlike cell, function as reservoirs, filling with salt water until the bladder cell ruptures and releases its contents to the exterior of the leaf.

Reproduction and Growth

Dryland shrubs exhibit several adaptations that help to ensure their reproductive success. The small, inconspicuous flowers of mountain mahogany produce seeds that effectively plant themselves and can respond immediately to microclimatic conditions conducive to germination. Each small, hairy seed is tipped with a long, feathery plume, which functions in much the same way as a parachute, allowing the sharply pointed seed tip to reach the ground first. Changes in relative humidity cause the featherlike tails to coil or twist hygroscopically, drilling the seed directly into the soil so that it can germinate the following spring.

Reproductive versatility—the ability to reproduce by either sexual or vegetative (asexual) means—is an important advantage for many dryland shrubs. For Gambel's oak, such versatility is critical, for the plant must contend, at least in the northern portions of its range, with environmental conditions such as cold temperatures and insufficient moisture during germination that would otherwise inhibit successful completion of the sexual cycle. At the base of the trunk, specialized anatomical structures called lignotubers enclose hundreds of dormant buds, each capable of sprouting and growing out into a leafy shoot. In addition, a network of subterranean stems (rhizomes) lies just beneath the ground surface. Each rhizome has its own supply of incipient buds that remain dormant until some sort of environmental stress, such as damage to the tree's crown by fire or heavy browsing, ends the hormonal suppression that keeps the buds dormant. Consequently, a stand of oak typically consists of several spreading clones (genetically related plants originating from a single mother plant) that may persist for thousands of years through stress-related suckering.

Plant Defenses

Aridland plants rely on an impressive arsenal of defensive structures—spines, thorns, and glandular-tipped hairs, called trichomes—to deter herbivores. Chemical interactions also play a crucial role in the ecology of shrublands. Some species seem remarkably passive in their resistance to herbivory or competition, while others engage in sophisticated chemical warfare. Plants that synthesize or deploy chemical defenses generally do so in situations where basic resources are limited and each plant must compete with its neighbors in order to survive. The term *allelochemic* describes a large class of chemical interactions in which one species affects the well-being and growth of another by releasing chemical compounds into the environment. Allelochemic interactions may occur between different species of plants or between plants and animals.

The majority of chemicals involved in allelochemic interactions are produced as by-products of plant metabolism and belong to one of three major groups, phenolics, terpenoids, and alkaloids, or to one of a number of minor groups that include mustard oils and organic cyanides. All of these compounds are toxic or inhibitory to varying degrees and may be released to the environment either as volatile (airborne) substances or as water-soluble agents. For the most part, these compounds remain at low levels or are degraded by microbial action in the soil without producing effects detrimental to other organisms. In some cases, however, the concentrations of these secondary compounds in plants are such that substantial quantities are released into the environment, either from the living plant or by decomposition of plant litter. For example, the pungent odor of big sagebrush, especially aromatic after a rain, is produced by the emanation of volatile terpenes (camphor and cineole) from its leaves.

The term *allelopathy* refers to situations in which compounds produced by one plant species influence the germination and growth of another. In communities dominated by a single species, such as big sagebrush, the chemistry of the soil may reflect the influx of secondary compounds to such a degree that only those species that are tolerant of this chemistry can survive. Terpenes in the litter and fresh leaves of big sagebrush have been shown to inhibit the growth of blue grama, golden aster, and many other would-be competitors. The concentration of toxic compounds in the soil is greatest directly beneath the sagebrush canopy, frequently resulting in areas of bare, vegetation-free soil.

Some secondary compounds exhibit inhibitory effects on animal metabolism and digestion, while others may interfere with reproduction, produce cancerous growths in vital organs, or destroy the central nervous system. Coevolution on the part of many herbivores, however, has included numerous mechanisms that circumvent or counteract these detrimental effects. For example, the foliage of some succulent plant species, such as greasewood and prickly pear, contain large amounts of oxalic acid, a compound toxic to most animals. Animals that routinely utilize these plants for food and as a source of water—jackrabbits, pocket gophers, and pronghorn—have evolved a means of metabolizing oxalic acid and excreting the by-products without harmful side effects.

Environment and Adaptation: Shrubland Animals

Shrublands provide critical habitat for a great diversity of animal species. In fact, rocky shrubland habitats support more mammalian species than any other mountain ecosystem. For small and medium-sized animals, cover from predators is readily available. Many shrubland communities offer a rich harvest of seasonal foods: acorns, seeds, berries, foliage, insects and other invertebrates, small vertebrates, and eggs. Living space, though somewhat limited in terms of vertical differentiation, is less condensed than in purely herbaceous communities. The majority of animal species make use of shrubland ecosystems on a seasonal or occasional basis. Year-round residents are primarily small mammals, reptiles, some birds, and an enormous variety of invertebrates.

Adaptations to Water Stress

For all animals, the maintenance of water balance is essential for survival. Adaptations for water conservation can be seen in the timing of activity cycles, the kinds of food eaten, and a variety of behavioral, morphological, and physiological features. In environments where the availability of free water is largely limited to the rare instance of rain or snow, carnivorous and insectivorous animals primarily extract water from the body fluids of their prey. Many herbivorous animals obtain sufficient water from the tissues of plants they eat. Ord's kangaroo rat, the undisputed master of water conservation, can live indefinitely on a diet of dry seeds, without any water intake. Though low in moisture content, the seeds that comprise this species' diet are typically high in fats and carbohydrates, which yield a large amount of *metabolic water* as a result of the oxidation of hydrogen associated with digestion.

Evaporation is the most important cause of water loss in dry environments, especially when temperatures are high. Moist-skinned animals such as frogs and toads are particularly vulnerable to evaporative water loss through the skin and, as a result, are present in shrublands only in microhabitats with consistent water supplies. Birds and mammals must rely on their fur or feathers to reduce evaporative losses and to insulate their bodies from excessive heat. Lung-breathing animals regularly lose moisture to the atmosphere when they exhale. Ord's kangaroo rat has achieved a remarkable reduction in respiratory evaporation. This species can exhale air at a lower temperature than that of its body core because the convolutions of its nasal passages function as a countercurrent heat exchanger. When the kangaroo rat inhales, the walls of the nasal passages give off heat to the air flowing over them, causing the temperature of the nasal passages to fall below that of the air being inhaled. The inhaled air undergoes further warming and subsequent saturation in the lungs. On exhalation, this warm air passes over the nasal membranes cooled during inhalation and is forced to leave some of its moisture behind as condensation on the membranes. The system's effectiveness is enhanced by the kangaroo rat's highly efficient kidneys, nocturnal habits, and prolonged periods spent resting and feeding in the relatively humid environment of the burrow.

In arid environments, the ability of the kidneys to concentrate urine is an important adaptation for reducing water loss. The more concentrated the urine, the more economical the use of water for urine formation and the elimination of toxic wastes produced by metabolic processes. Kangaroo rat urine is roughly twice as dense as seawater and five times more concentrated than human urine. Consequently, in excreting comparable amounts of toxic metabolic wastes, the kangaroo rat uses one-fifth as much water as humans do.

Avoiding Heat Stress

All animals must avoid extremely high temperatures. A variety of physiological, anatomical, and behavioral adaptations allow animals to maintain a degree of constancy, or homeostasis, in their body temperatures. Cold-blooded animals, such as the rattlesnake or the plateau lizard, maintain optimal body temperature behaviorally, by shuttling between a warm, sunlit area and a cooler, shaded refuge. Mammals and birds that remain active above ground during the heat of the day must be able to withstand hours of exposure to an unrelenting sun. Many have pale-colored, reflective pelage or feathers, thus reducing the rate at which heat is absorbed from the environment. Others have evolved morphological features, such as large ears that dissipate heat in much the same way that a radiator does. The large ears of the desert cottontail and the black-tailed jackrabbit are crisscrossed with a network of tiny, pulsating blood vessels that give off heat to the air blowing over them.

In order to prevent overheating under conditions of high heat stress, warm-blooded animals may be forced to resort to evaporative cooling, a function of the respiratory organs or the sweat glands. Humans dissipate heat effectively through sweating. Coyotes, in contrast, have few sweat glands and must pant to produce evaporative cooling. Birds, lacking sweat glands altogether, increase evaporative cooling by panting or by the rapid oscillation of the throat, known as gular fluttering.

CHAPTER THIRTEEN

Living Dry: Semidesert Shrublands

Mancos Shale and mat saltbush badlands near Grand Junction, Colorado.

From a vantage point along the northern rim of the San Luis Valley, a threadbare tapestry of grayish green shrubs rolls out before me, fraying along the distant horizon. This is a landscape born, tough and enduring, at the heart of a rain shadow; it makes no apology for its aridity. Here and there, circlets of alkali hardpan remind us that this is what "living on the edge" really means.

Ecological Distribution

Considered an eastern outlier of the Great Basin Desert, semidesert shrublands occur below 7,500 feet in the upper Rio Grande Basin, from the San Luis Valley south into New Mexico, on broad valley floors in westernmost Colorado, in parts of the Shirley Basin in Wyoming, and as isolated stands near Pueblo, Cañon City, and Walsenburg. The most extensive communities are developed on a massive Cretaceous marine deposit known as the Mancos Shale. The Mancos Shale, where not protected by more resistant sandstones, erodes into undulating gray and yellow badlands characterized by swelling clays and by soils rich in gypsum and other salts. When spring moisture has been good, the Grand Valley area surrounding Grand Junction, both north and south of I-70 and west to the Utah border, is one of the best places to experience the sublime beauty of the semidesert shrublands.

Community Characteristics

Semidesert shrublands consist of two main community types, one dominated by greasewood and the other by various species of saltbush. In the San Luis Valley and the Gunnison Basin, large expanses of winterfat-dominated shrub-steppe can also be found on shaley soils and young alluvium deposits. Overall, species diversity tends to be quite low; in some shrublands, a single shrub species may constitute 90 percent or more of the total plant cover. In most cases, the shrubs are interspersed with drought-tolerant bunchgrasses and a few sturdy wildflowers; bare soil often exceeds 50 percent in the harshest sites. Because of the thin vegetation cover and deflation of the soil by wind scour, a "pavement" of wind-burnished stones is present in many areas.

Annual precipitation averages less than ten inches in the semidesert shrublands, most coming in the critical spring and summer period. During the summer, however, high daytime temperatures and low humidity conspire to produce high rates of evaporation. In the San Luis Valley and in shrublands along the Colorado River near Grand Junction, summer temperatures often soar above 100°F. Winter minimum temperatures, on the other hand, may drop below 0°F because of cold-air drainage from surrounding mountain slopes.

Soil factors, in combination with climate, determine which species of plants grow in the semidesert shrublands. Greasewood predominates in areas with either saline or alkaline soils and a consistently high water table. In the most alkaline bottomlands, greasewood may form single-species stands or may occur in association with saltgrass, alkali sacaton, desert wild rye, kochia, whiteweed, and marsh elder. In less alkaline situations, saltbush, big sagebrush, rabbitbrush, Russian thistle, and winterfat may also be common. Saltbush is most common in areas where the soils are generally drier and less saline or alkaline than those where greasewood grows. Typical associates of saltbush in these communities include copper mallow, galletagrass, Indian ricegrass, ring muhly, and both hairy and blue grama. Cacti are far less common in these communities than in the warm-temperate deserts of the Southwest.

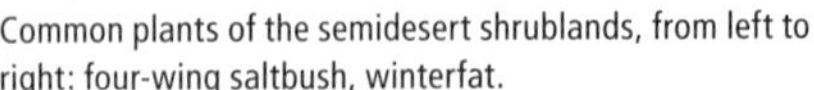

Common plants of the semidesert shrublands, from left to right: four-wing saltbush, winterfat.

Common plants of the semidesert shrublands, from left to right: Russian thistle, greasewood, with detail of fruit.

Descriptions of Common Plants

Shrubs

Four-wing Saltbush, *Atriplex canescens*. This densely branched shrub rarely exceeds four feet in height and is distinguished from other saltbush species by its narrowly oblong leaves, silvery leaf scales, and clusters of four-wing fruits; male and female flowers appear on separate bushes. The leaves and young shoots of four-wing saltbush are extremely palatable to browsing animals, and many small mammals and birds relish its fruits.

Shadscale Saltbush, *Atriplex confertifolia*. Shadscale, the dominant shrub of the Great Basin salt-scrub, is most common in the Grand Valley (near Grand Junction) and in other basins along the western margin of the Southern Rockies. This compact, moderately sized shrub ranges in height from one to three feet, depending on local conditions, and has rigid, spine-tipped branches. The leaves are broader and more oval in shape than those of four-wing saltbush, and its flat fruits have two parallel wings instead of four. At maturity, the fruit turns from pale green to a lovely deep pink.

Mat Saltbush, *Atriplex corrugata*. Its matlike growth and the succulent, oblong-to-ovate leaves identify this distinctive saltbush. Mat saltbush often forms single-species communities in extremely water-stressed environments such as the Mancos Shale badlands in the Grand Valley.

Greasewood, *Sarcobatus vermiculatus.* Greasewood is readily identified by its scraggly, much-branched growth form, spine-tipped branches, and dark green, rosemarylike leaves. The inconspicuous flowers of greasewood are unisexual, but both male and female flowers are typically present on the same shrub. Female flowers are pale green, borne in pairs or singularly within the axil of the leaf. The cone-shaped male flowers average about one inch in length and are clustered at the tips of leafy branchlets. The fruits develop in the axil of the leaf and are somewhat funnel shaped, consisting of an erect nutlet rimmed by a membranous wing that is characteristically tinged with red.

Winterfat, *Krascheninnikovia* (formerly *Ceratoides*) *lanata.* Winterfat is a low shrub, ranging in height from one to three feet, and is common throughout the arid West. Its leaves are slender and almost needlelike, with a dense covering of hairs and rolled-under leaf margins. The male and female flowers occur separately but are borne in terminal spikes on the same plant. Winterfat is most conspicuous in seed, when the fruits open and cloak the branches with woolly hairs.

Grasses and Herbaceous Plants

Russian Thistle, *Salsola australis.* This abundant tumbleweed, introduced from Eurasia, is distinguished by its stiffly spreading, prickly branches and by its alternate threadlike leaves. Though distinctly woody and often tinged with red when mature, this species is an annual. The flowers occur in the leaf axils and are subtended by two bracts; the fruits have five membranous white or pink persistent sepals.

Indian Ricegrass, *Achnatherum* (formerly *Oryzopsis*) *hymenoides.* This tall, graceful bunchgrass is identified by its multiple-branching inflorescence and solitary spikelets appearing at the ends of curved pedicels. The seeds of this native species are high in protein, favored by Ord's kangaroo rats, and were ground into flour by various Indian tribes.

Ring Muhly, *Muhlenbergia torreyi.* Ring muhly derives its name from the large, ring-shaped cushions that it forms on dry, sandy soils and blowout areas; the growth form is maintained because as the clump grows, the inner portion dies, leaving a ring of living grass. *M. pungens*, a common species on the Western Slope, assumes the same growth form as *M. torreyi*. The leaves of ring muhly are conspicuously curved and sharply pointed, contributing to the compact appearance of the cushion; the inflorescence is much branched, and the spikelets are solitary.

Ring muhly, showing typical growth form.

Common Plants of the Semidesert Shrublands

Shrubs

Greasewood, *Sarcobatus vermiculatus*
Horsebrush, shortspine, *Tetradymia spinosa*
Rabbitbrush, *Chrysothamnus nauseosus*
    small, *C. depressus*
    sticky-leaved, *C. viscidiflorus*
Sagebrush, big (or Great Basin sagebrush), *Seriphidium* (formerly *Artemisia*) *tridentatum*
Saltbush, four-wing, *Atriplex canescens*
    Gardner's, *A. gardneri*
    mat, *A. corrugata*
    shadscale, *A. confertifolia*
Snakeweed, broom, *Gutierrezia sarothrae*
Spiny Hopsage, *Atriplex grayi*

Winterfat, *Krascheninnikovia* (formerly *Ceratoides*) *lanata*

Grasses and Rushes

Cheatgrass, *Anisantha* (formerly *Bromus*) *tectorum*
Galletagrass, *Hilaria jamesii*
Grama, blue, *Bouteloua gracilis*
  hairy, *B. hirsuta*
Muhly, alkali, *Muhlenbergia asperifolia*
  ring, *M. pungens* and *M. torreyi*
Ricegrass, Indian, *Achnatherum* (formerly *Oryzopsis*) *hymenoides*
Rush, Baltic, *Juncus balticus*
Ryegrass, desert, *Leymus salina*
Sacaton, alkali, *Sporobolus airoides*
Saltgrass, *Distichlis stricta*
Spikerush, *Eleocharis palustris*

Wildflowers

Buckwheat, desert, *Eriogonum ovalifolium*
Cactus, prickly pear, *Opuntia polyacantha* and *O. macrorhiza*
Fleabane, desert, *Erigeron pulcherrimus*
Hyacinth, wild, *Androstephium breviflorum*
Mallow, copper, (or cowboy's delight), *Sphaeralcea coccinea*
Mariposa lily, desert, *Calochortus nuttallii*
Marshelder, *Iva axillaris*
Milkvetch, milkweed-flowered, *Astragalus asclepiadoides*
Oreocarya, desert, *Oreocarya* (formerly *Cryptantha*) *flavoculata*
Puccoon, long-flowered, *O. longiflora*
Scorpionweed, desert, *Phacelia splendens*
Skeletonweed, *Lygodesmia grandiflora*
Sunflower, common, *Helianthus annuus*
Thistle, Russian, *Salsola australis*

Desert mariposa lily.

Environment and Adaptation: Animals of the Semidesert Shrublands

Semidesert shrublands have long been mistreated and underappreciated, their subtle beauty and fascinating wildlife overlooked. These unique shrub ecosystems provide food and cover for a diversity of desert-adapted species. Where the soil is easily dug, the burrow mounds and foraging trails of Ord's kangaroo rat crisscross the landscape. Avoiding midday heat, desert cottontails and black-tailed jackrabbits rest in shallow scrapes beneath the shrubs. Coyotes prowl the brushy swales in search of prey, and a loggerhead shrike perches atop a tall shrub as it scans the ground for the unwary mouse. Swainson's and other open-country hawks ride the spiraling thermals while flocks of Brewer's sparrows forage for protein-rich seeds among silvery tussocks of ricegrass. In the sparse shade beneath a saltbush, a perfectly camouflaged short-horned lizard ambushes a harvester ant with a quick flick of its tongue.

Life Histories of Selected Animals

Mammals

Desert Cottontail, *Sylvilagus audubonii.* A medium-sized, buff-gray rabbit distinguished from other cottontails by its whitish underparts and large, sparsely furred ears. Water is obtained primarily from succulent vegetation or from the oxidation of food; the ability of the kidneys to concentrate urine surpasses that of other cottontails. Desert cottontails are largely solitary. Males occupy home ranges of up to fifteen acres and maintain strict territories against other males, while home ranges of females average about an acre in size and several females may coexist in a given area. Breeding begins by late April, with two or more litters of altricial young born in most years. Ovulation is normally induced by copulation, and gestation takes about one month. Young rabbits reach full maturity at about six to nine months; few individuals live longer than three years.

Black-tailed Jackrabbit, *Lepus californicus.* This somewhat dark- colored hare is easily distinguished from the white-tailed jackrabbit (*L. townsendii*) by its large, black-tipped ears, lack of whitish fur on the sides of the body, and black tail patch; there is no winter color change in this species. These jackrabbits prefer semiarid brushlands and grasslands below 7,000 feet. Usually solitary except during the breeding season, the black-tailed jackrabbit normally has a home range of less than 2,000 acres. Mating behavior is complex, involving long chases, jumping, and frequent fighting between males and females. Ovulation is induced by copulation, with one to four litters of precocial young born annually. Young hares are capable of moving about at birth and will be hopping quite well within two or three days; adult size is attained in about ten weeks.

Ord's Kangaroo Rat, *Dipodomys ordii.* Huge hind feet, short forelegs, and a long, bushy-tipped tail make this small mammal unmistakable, especially if you see it leaping across the road at night, framed in the glow of your headlights. Distinctively colored, the upper portion of the body is generally cinnamon-buff, shading to white below, and white stripes run along each flank to the tip of the tail. Fleet of foot, Ord's kangaroo rat is bipedal, with the hind feet providing power and the small forelegs carried close to the body; the tail is used for balance. The kangaroo rat is chiefly nocturnal and solitary. Burrow systems are dug in sandy soils, with an opening typically situated at the base of a shrub or one of the bunchgrasses. The kangaroo rat retreats by day into its burrow, plugging the entrance with soil to protect itself from predators and to maintain optimal temperature and humidity. The preferred diet consists mainly of seeds (a special favorite is Indian ricegrass), which are gathered with the forepaws, often by sifting the sand, and then carried to the burrow in capacious, fur-lined cheek pouches. Seed stores are kept in the burrow, occasionally in species-specific piles; kangaroo rats are known to pilfer the seed caches of harvester ants. Courtship is active and reciprocal; males engage in fighting, aerial kicks, hind-foot drumming, teeth chattering, and vocalizations. The female delivers her altricial young with her forepaws and incisors. Adult size is attained by five or six weeks of age.

Birds

Ferruginous Hawk, *Buteo regalis.* The ferruginous hawk is distinguished by its rufous brown upperparts, whitish breast, and white, unbanded tail; seen from below, the darkly barred legs form a conspicuous V against the white body and dark crescents mark the wrist of each wing. In flight, the wings are held in a V. Hunting is done from a perch, on the ground, while soaring, or in low, rapid flight; this hawk often soars in great circles. Ferruginous hawks utilize a variety of nest sites: trees, rock ledges, hillsides, and rocky pinnacles. Nests may be used repeatedly by the same pair, and aggressive protection of the nest against predators—red-tailed hawks, great horned owls, and coyotes—is common. Breeding occurs from March to July; incubation is by both sexes and averages twenty-eight days. The young fledge forty-four to forty-eight days after hatching. Ages of seventeen to twenty years have been reported for this species.

Loggerhead Shrike, *Lanius ludovicianus*. Often confused with the mockingbird, this robin-sized predator is identified by its black wings, dark gray upperparts, falconlike bill, and broad black mask extending through the eyes and over the bill; white patches flash prominently in flight. Solitary except during the breeding season, the shrike hunts from a conspicuous perch: the top of a shrub, a small tree, or a fence post. Mice, small birds, insects (especially large grasshoppers and crickets), and small reptiles provide the bulk of the diet; undigestible parts (fur, feathers, etc.) are regurgitated as pellets. Excess food items may be impaled on the tips of twigs or on barbed wire for later retrieval. The call of the shrike is short, harsh, and scolding, while the song consists of a repetitious, fluid series of two-syllable notes. Breeding occurs from April to July; both sexes incubate, and the young fledge within thirty-six days of hatching.

Brewer's Sparrow, *Spizella breweri*. This small, rather nondescript sparrow is distinguished from other clear-breasted sparrows by its slender shape, long, notched tail, whitish wing bars, and the lack of a rufous cap or strong head markings. In the Southern Rockies, the species is considered the dominant dryland sparrow in many areas. Brewer's sparrows are insectivorous in summer and granivorous in winter. On the winter range, this species forages in large, mixed flocks with other sparrows. On the nesting grounds, the male sings an elaborate, canarylike song from the end of a branch near the nest; many males may sing in chorus at dawn and at twilight.

Open-country birds of prey, from left to right, by row: (top row) rough-legged hawk, Swainson's hawk; (row two) ferruginous hawk, northern harrier, with detail showing white rump patch; (row three) red-tailed hawk, prairie falcon, American kestrel; (row four) golden eagle, with detail of white wing patch visible on immatures; (row five) turkey vulture. Silhouettes show wing position while soaring.

Reptiles

Short-horned Lizard, *Phrynosoma douglassii*. This small lizard is distinguished by its rounded and somewhat flattened midsection, spiny head and upper back, the fringe of thick spines that projects backward from the flattened head, and the enlarged row of pointed scales on each side of its body. Short-horned lizards are most often found in dry, sparsely vegetated grasslands and shrublands. Remarkably well camouflaged, the color of this species typically resembles the soil coloring of its habitat. Though the lizard's scaly, spiny skin significantly reduces evaporative losses, this species wears its suncreen internally, as a dark pigment that colors the peritoneum (body sac) and reduces the potential damage to internal organs from excessive solar radiation. Ants and beetles are dietary staples (and sources of water) for this insectivorous species. At night or on cool days, these diurnal lizards seek shelter in small rodent burrows or by burying themselves in the soil; activity extends from April to October. Short-horned lizards are relatively easy to catch and handle if treated gently; disturbed individuals may spurt blood from the corner of the eye as a defensive mechanism. Unlike all other lizard species in the Southern Rockies, females give birth to live young in underground burrows in July or August; average litter size is seventeen.

Western Rattlesnake, *Crotalus viridis*. This venomous snake is identified by its triangular-shaped head, the presence of a rattle (consisting of horny segments) on the end of its tail, and a body pattern highlighted by splotches of brown on a tan background. Though not generally considered aggressive, rattlesnakes will coil defensively when approached and may strike if harassed; vibration or buzzing of the rattle does not always occur prior to striking. Rattlesnakes are potentially dangerous to humans; any bite victim should be kept immobile and transported to medical facilities as quickly as possible. In the Southern Rockies, the western rattlesnake is typically found in dry terrain—grasslands, shrublands, and foothill woodlands—below about 8,200 feet; in recent years, there have been a limited number of reports of rattlesnakes occurring at higher elevations (at least to 9,000 feet). Rattlesnakes do not actively search out their prey, which include small mammals, nestling birds, toads, and lizards, but rely instead on their ability to ambush warm-blooded animals through the use of a special heat-sensing organ that produces an image of the prey in the brain; this radarlike organ also determines the strike range, even in total darkness. Rattlesnakes are largely nocturnal in midsummer, becoming active at dusk and retreating to an abandoned burrow, a rocky crevice, or the shade of a small shrub during periods of inactivity. Group hibernation chambers are common; emergence typically occurs in late April, with a return to den sites in mid-September through early November. Females give birth from late August to early October, producing an average of twelve precocial young.

Common Animals of the Semidesert Shrublands

Mammals

Badger, American, *Taxidea taxus*
Chipmunk, least, *Tamias minimus*
Cottontail, desert, *Sylvilagus audubonii*
Coyote, *Canis latrans*
Deer, mule, *Odocoileus hemionus*
Fox, gray, *Urocyon cinereoargenteus*
Jackrabbit, black-tailed, *Lepus californicus*
  white-tailed, *L. townsendii*
Kangaroo Rat, Ord's, *Dipodomys ordii*
Mouse, deer, *Peromyscus maniculatus*
  northern grasshopper, *Onychomys leucogaster*
  silky pocket, *Perognathus flavus*
Pocket Gopher, Botta's (or Valley Pocket Gopher), *Thomomys bottae*
  northern, *T. talpoides*
Prairie Dog, white-tailed, *Cynomys leucurus*
Pronghorn, *Antilocapra americana*
Skunk, striped, *Mephitis mephitis*

Birds

Eagle, golden, *Aquila chrysaetos*
Hawk, ferruginous, *Buteo regalis*
  red-tailed, *B. jamaicensis*
  rough-legged, *B. lagopus*

Swainson's, *B. swainsoni*
Lark, horned, *Eremophila alpestris*
Phoebe, Say's, *Sayornis saya*
Raven, common, *Corvus corax*
Shrike, loggerhead, *Lanius ludovicianus*
Sparrow, Brewer's, *Spizella breweri*
lark, *Chondestes grammacus*
vesper, *Pooecetes gramineus*
Towhee, canyon, *Pipilo fuscus*
Vulture, turkey, *Cathartes aura*

Reptiles

Bullsnake, *Pituophis melanoleucus*
Lizard, collared, *Crotaphytus collaris*
plateau, *Sceloporus undulatus*
sagebrush, *S. graciosus*
short-horned, *Phrynosoma douglassii*
Rattlesnake, western, *Crotalus viridis*
Skink, many-lined, *Eumeces multivirgatus*

Butterflies and Insects

Ant, harvester, *Pogonomyrmex* spp.
Beetle, darkling, *Eloedes* spp.
ten-lined June, *Polyphylla decemlineata*
Butterfly, saltbush sooty-wing, *Pholisora alpheus*
wood nymph, Great Basin, *Cercyonis sthenele*
Gall Midge, woolly stem, *Asphondylia floccosa*
Tarantula, *Aphonopelma* spp.

Ten-lined June beetle.

Heart of the Rain Shadow: Sagebrush Shrublands

Sagebrush. The very word conjures up images of wide-open spaces, a silvery green landscape rimmed by billowing clouds and azure skies. Enshrined and romanticized in countless American novels and cowboy movies, sagebrush is truly synonymous with the Old West. Its most famous admirer, Mark Twain, described sagebrush as "an imposing monarch of the forest in exquisite miniature." But to many people, a landscape dotted with sagebrush is a lonesome, charmless wasteland. To most westerners, however, these durable shrublands fill a special niche, a magical place where the eerie howl of a coyote can still be heard at dusk, where the stars seem close enough to touch, and where you can still wake up to sage grouse strutting on an ancient lek. Sagebrush country is perhaps the West's most enduring symbol, a place where the air is forever redolent of sage and sunbaked earth, where hawks and golden eagles soar endlessly on the spiraling thermals, and where pronghorns race the wind, white tail-flags flashing in the sunlight.

Ecological Distribution

Sagebrush shrublands cover vast areas of western North America, some estimates suggest as much as 150 million acres. More than a dozen species of woody sagebrush are found from British Columbia down to Baja California and as far east as Nebraska. Despite their abundance and ecological significance, sagebrush shrublands are seldom afforded the conservation protection they deserve. Two major types of sagebrush shrubland occur in the Southern Rockies: sagebrush-steppe and Great Basin sagebrush. Sagebrush-steppe is dominated by mountain sagebrush (*Seriphidium vaseyanum*); it is associated with basins and broad valleys in the northern half of the Southern Rockies and at elevations ranging from 7,000 to 10,000 feet and above. Sagebrush-steppe is best developed on the Western Slope and occurs sporadically on the Eastern Slope; it covers large expanses in the Shirley Basin and Laramie River Valley of Wyoming, the Yampa River Valley, the Little Snake River Valley, the western flanks of the Park Range, North Park, Middle Park, the upper Gunnison Basin, and the Beaver Meadows area on the eastern side of Rocky Mountain National Park. The existence of small and largely isolated stands of mountain sagebrush, such as those found in the Front Range, is difficult to explain. Some biologists believe that these stands persist as relicts of larger populations that flourished during a time when climatic conditions favored their development.

Great Basin sagebrush shrublands are dominated by big sagebrush (*S. tridentatum*) and adapted to slightly warmer semidesert environments. Big sagebrush is typical of lower-elevation plateaus and river valleys to nearly 8,000 feet. Great Basin sagebrush communities are well established in north-central New Mexico and in the Animas, Colorado, and lower Gunnison river drainages of Colorado. The understory in a Great Basin sagebrush community tends to be sparse as a result of the competition for available moisture. On the most arid sites, big sagebrush may grow in association with greasewood, various species of saltbush, black sagebrush, and winterfat.

Dry, relatively sandy soils typically support luxuriant stands of rabbitbrush. Where growth conditions are optimal and where livestock grazing has been controlled, stands of big sagebrush often include a showy display of rabbitbrush, broom snakeweed, spiny hopsage, and cottonthorn. Aridland bunchgrasses and wildflowers such as orange paintbrush, phlox, desert buckwheat, and desert sandwort may be especially common on such sites.

Community Characteristics

The coldest temperatures in the Southern Rockies are regularly reported from the sagebrush-covered basins of Middle Park, the Gunnison and Taylor Park area, and northwest Colorado. In sagebrush shrublands, the annual precipitation is highly variable and can range from ten inches in lowland sites to more than twenty inches at higher elevations. Soil moisture recharge in sagebrush ecosystems occurs primarily in the spring, when the snow melts, and is followed by a warm growing season with little precipitation.

In the Southern Rockies, sagebrush dominates sites where the soils are moderately deep, well drained, and only mildly alkaline. In order for sagebrush to outcompete other shrub species, the soils must be friable and unrestrictive, allowing root penetration to substantial depths and easy circulation of air and water. In contrast to the soils associated with semidesert shrublands, those supporting sagebrush have lower salt concentrations and a deeper calcium carbonate, or caliche, layer. Sagebrush-steppe communities often exhibit a greater diversity of herbaceous plants than are found in adjacent coniferous forests. Shrubs such as horsebrush, serviceberry, bitterbrush, wild rose, and snowberry may also be common. During years with above-average precipitation, a surprising abundance of wildflowers produces a firestorm of floral color. The most conspicuous species include larkspur, various species of lupine, balsamroot, mule's ears, penstemon, scarlet gilia, paintbrush, fleabane daisies, and buckwheat. Interspersed among the wildflowers, grasses such as blue grama, wheatgrass, Junegrass, needle-and-thread, and various species of fescue are typical of communities with limited grazing. With extreme grazing pressure, the herbaceous understory is quickly depleted and the living crust of mosses and soil lichens trampled beyond recovery; exotic species such as cheatgrass, an aggressive annual, and the classic tumbleweed, Russian thistle, are quick to invade overgrazed sites.

Crushing the richly aromatic leaves of sagebrush (a member of the sunflower family) produces a scent that some consider reminiscent of the culinary sages (*Salvia* spp.). Identifying sagebrush to species,

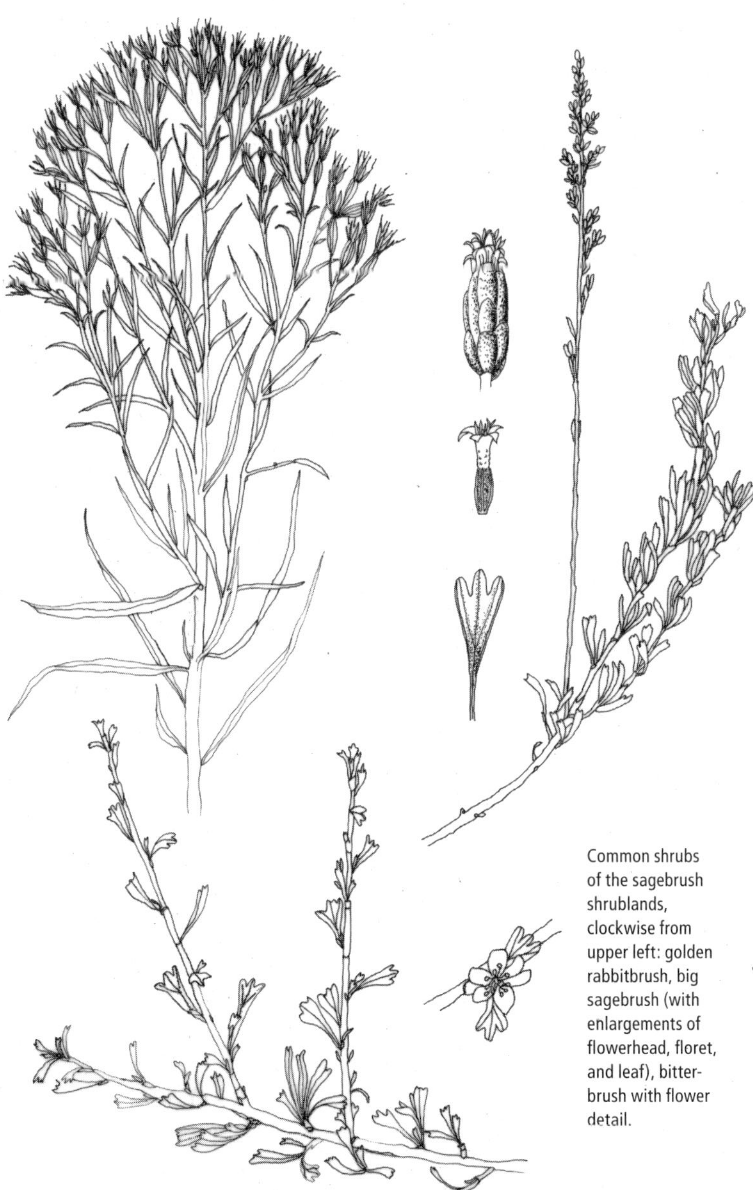

Common shrubs of the sagebrush shrublands, clockwise from upper left: golden rabbitbrush, big sagebrush (with enlargements of flowerhead, floret, and leaf), bitterbrush with flower detail.

however, can be challenging for even the most dedicated botanist. In most cases, sagebrush-steppe and Great Basin sagebrush communities can be distinguished on the basis of species-specific differences in growth form and preferred habitat. Big sagebrush (*S. tridentatum*) is a tall, robust shrub associated with deep soils and is especially common on gravelly floodplains and in arroyos. Mountain sagebrush (*S. vaseyanum*), on the other hand, seldom exceeds three feet in height and is associated with shallower soils and cooler, more moist habitats than big sagebrush. Wyoming sagebrush (*S. vaseyanum* ssp.), a subspecies of mountain sagebrush, occurs in northern Colorado and southern Wyoming and is typical of sites that are more arid than those occupied by mountain sagebrush. Dwarf sagebrush (*S. arbuscula*) is found in the mountain parks from Gunnison Basin northward. Black sagebrush (*S. novum*), as the name would suggest, is darker colored in mass effect than other sagebrush species and is a common component of the sagebrush-steppe at lower elevations and in areas with relatively shallow, calcareous soils. Hoary sagebrush (*S. cana*) is a tall species and is generally associated with moist meadow situations in the northern half of the Southern Rockies. Where communities dominated by different species of sagebrush occur in close proximity, community boundaries tend to be sharply defined.

In certain situations, sagebrush ecosystems represent a long-lived successional stage. In relatively moist environments, grasses and moisture-loving trees and shrubs such as aspen and willow tend to replace sagebrush in successional stands. Grazing and fire can dramatically alter normal successional patterns in sagebrush communities. Under heavy grazing, big sagebrush and other woody species increase in size and number at the expense of more palatable, herbaceous species. In contrast, fire selectively destroys sagebrush and favors the spread of grasses, an ecological reality that range managers often exploit to increase forage yields for livestock. Sagebrush must reestablish itself by seed after fire, so growth and recovery are slow. Following a range fire, the niche of the fire-intolerant sagebrush is often assumed by the proliferation of fire-adapted plants such as rabbitbrush and snakeweed, which sprout from their stumps in burned-over areas.

Descriptions of Common Plants

Shrubs

Big Sagebrush, *Seriphidium* (formerly *Artemisia*) *tridentatum*. The distinctively pungent, sagelike aroma and the leaves, which are silver-green, three-lobed, and wedge-shaped, make this an easy species to identify. This evergreen species produces two sets of leaves annually and is capable of performing photosynthesis at extremely low temperatures. Clusters of small, yellowish green flower heads appear during mid- to late summer and bear little resemblance to the flowers of more showy members of the sunflower family. Each flower head consists of numerous tubular florets; the multiple flower heads are arranged in numerous open panicles. Sagebrush flowers are wind pollinated. Big sagebrush is a taller and more robust species than its nearest relative, mountain sagebrush (*S. vaseyanum*). Under optimal conditions, big sagebrush often exceeds six feet in height.

Mountain sagebrush, *S. vaseyanum*. This sagebrush has a more compact growth form than that of big sagebrush, and its flowering stalks (panicles) are narrower and more densely branched. This species is more characteristic of highland sagebrush habitats than the similar black sagebrush (*S.novum*), which is found on stonier, poorer soils.

Rabbitbrush, *Chrysothamnus nauseosus*. Rabbitbrush, or chamisa, as it is known in New Mexico, is easily distinguished from big sagebrush by its narrow, nonlobed leaves and the absence of a sagelike odor. The branches are slender and flexible, and young twigs are covered with feltlike matted hairs. The pungent odor and unpalatable qualities of rabbitbrush are due to the presence of latex, a viscous fluid composed of terpenoid particles suspended in water; the latex has been investigated as a commercial source of rubber. Masses of narrow, clustered flower heads with about five tubular, chrome-yellow disk flowers per head begin to appear in August and build to a spectacular, golden climax in September.

Bitterbrush, *Purshia tridentata*. Bitterbrush is readily identified by its much-branched growth habit and small, three-lobed leaves, which superficially resemble those of big sagebrush but lack the conspicuous covering of fine hairs and the distinctive sagelike aroma. Like most members of the rose family, the fragrant, pale yellow flowers have five sepals, five petals, and multiple stamens. The single carpel ripens into a tapered, yellow-orange capsule containing numerous small black seeds; despite their bitter, quininelike taste, the seeds are a favorite of small mammals. In areas where browsing is severe, heavily pruned shrubs of bitterbrush are generally no more than two feet tall.

Wildflowers

Lupine, *Lupinus* spp. Lupines are among the most common wildflower associates of sagebrush and are distinguished by their palmately compound leaves and pealike blue flowers borne in elongated clusters (racemes). Each flower consists of five different petals: an upright or nearly upright petal known as the banner (or standard), two lower petals joined along one edge to form the keel, and two lateral petals, the so-called wings, one to each side of the keel. The stamens, generally ten in number, are enclosed within the keel and form a sheath around the carpel. Following fertilization, the carpel elongates to form a podlike fruit enclosing a single row of seeds and splitting open into two halves at maturity. Lupine pods contain poisonous alkaloids that can be extremely toxic to livestock, particularly sheep.

Common wildflowers of the sagebrush shrublands, from left to right: Indian paintbrush, with detail of flower, and larkspur.

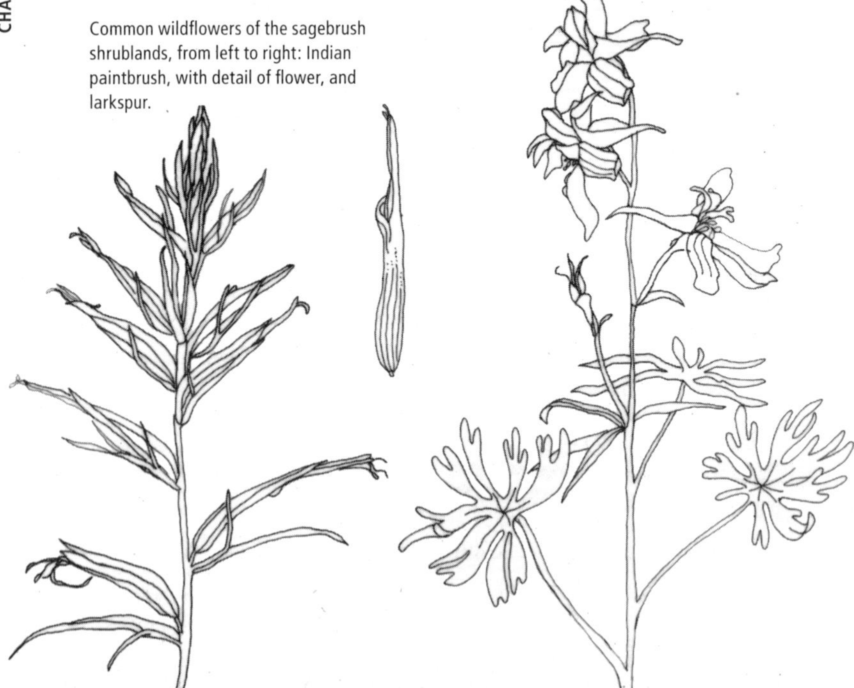

Mule's Ears, *Wyethia amplexicaulis*. Few species can match the spectacular floral display of this golden, sunflowerlike wildflower. Mule's ears is distinguished from a similar species, balsamroot (*Balsamorhiza sagittata*), by its leathery-textured, hairless leaves, its leafy flowering stems, and the presence of two or more flower heads per stem. Some hybrid populations in western Colorado may have pubescent (furry) leaves.

Indian Paintbrush, *Castilleja* spp. The striking colors associated with the paintbrushes—palest cream, yellow, pink, magenta, orange, and crimson—are due not to the flowers themselves, which are small and greenish, but to the brilliantly colored bractlike leaves and sepals that surround the flowers. The flower consists of a two-lipped corolla, with the upper lip (or galea) elongated like a beak and enclosing the four stamens. Paintbrush flowers are a favorite with nectar-seeking pollinators, especially hummingbirds.

Nutall's Larkspur, *Delphinium nuttallianum*. Its largely basal, narrowly palmate leaflets and its blue-purple flowers identify this distinctive wildflower. Larkspur flowers are bilaterally symmetrical, with the uppermost sepal elongated to form a conspicuous spur. The Latin name for this species

Common wildflowers of the sagebrush shrublands, from left to right: lupine, mule's ears.

is derived from the word *delphinus*, meaning dolphin, and refers to the flower's unusual shape.

Tufted Broomrape, *Orobanche fasciculata*. Broomrape is a small, easily overlooked plant identified by its clustered, coral-colored flowering stalks, each bearing a single penstemonlike flower, and its coral-colored, scalelike leaves. The flower petals are fused into a slightly arched tube with five lobes. Stems, leaves, and flowers are typically covered with sticky, glandular hairs. Broomrapes are root parasites; a single broomrape flower produces enormous numbers of small seeds, as many as 50,000 in some species, which can remain dormant in the soil for ten to fifteen years, or until suitable germination conditions occur.

Common Plants of the Sagebrush Shrublands

Shrubs

Bitterbrush, *Purshia tridentata*
Chokecherry, *Padus* (formerly *Prunus*) *virginiana* ssp. *melanocarpa*
Greasewood, *Sarcobatus vermiculatus*
Hopsage, spiny, *Grayia spinosa*
Horsebrush, *Tetradymia canescens*
Rabbitbrush, *Chrysothamnus nauseosus*
    flax-leaved, *C. linifolius*
    sticky-leaved, *C. viscidiflorus*
Rose, wild, *Rosa woodsii*
Sagebrush, big (or Great Basin sagebrush), *Seriphidium* (formerly *Artemisia*) *tridentatum*
    black, *S. novum*
    dwarf, *S. arbuscula*
    hoary, *S. cana*
    mountain, *S. vaseyanum*
    Wyoming, *S. tridentatum* ssp. *wyomingensis*
Saltbush, *Atriplex* spp.
Serviceberry, Utah, *Amelanchier utahensis*
    western, *A. alnifolia*
Snakeweed, broom, *Gutierrezia sarothrae*

Snowberry, roundleaf, *Symphoricarpos rotundifolius*

Grasses, Rushes, and Sedges

Cheatgrass, *Anisantha* (formerly *Bromus*) *tectorum*
Fescue, Arizona, *Festuca arizonica*
Idaho, *Festuca idahoensis*
Galletagrass, *Hilaria jamesii*
Grama, blue, *Bouteloua gracilis*
sideoats, *B. curtipendula*
Junegrass, *Koeleria macrantha*
Muttongrass, *Poa fendleriana*
Needle-and-thread, *Hesperostipa comata*
Ricegrass, Indian, *Achnatherum* (formerly *Oryzopsis*) *hymenoides*
Sedge, valley, *Carex vallicola*
Squirreltail, *Elymus elymoides* (formerly *Sitanion hystrix*)
Wheatgrass, *Pascopyrum* (formerly *Agropyron*) spp.
Wild Rye, giant, *Elymus cinereus*

Bitterroot.

Wildflowers

Aster, *Aster occidentalis*
golden, *Heterotheca villosa*
Balsamroot, *Balsamorhiza sagittata*
Bitterroot, *Lewisia rediviva*
Broomrape, tufted, *Orobanche fasciculata*
Buckwheat, desert, *Eriogonum ovalifolium*
sulphur flower, *E. umbellatum*
wild, *E. racemosum*
Flax, blue, *Adenolinum* (formerly *Linum*) *lewisii*
Fleabane, Eaton's, *Erigeron eatoni*
little, *E. pumilus*
Geranium, wild, *Geranium caespitosum*
Gilia, scarlet, *Ipomopsis aggregata*
Larkspur, Nuttall's, *Delphinium nuttallianum*
Lily, mariposa, *Calochortus gunnisonii*

Locoweed, Rocky Mountain, *Oxytropis sericea*
Lupine, Baker's, *Lupinus bakeri*
lodgepole, *L. parviflorus*
silky, *L. sericeus*
silvery, *L. argenteus*
spurred, *L. caudatus*
Milkvetch, silverleaf, *Astragalus argophyllus* var. *martinii*
Mule's Ears, *Wyethia amplexicaulis*
Paintbrush, Indian, *Castilleja chromosa, C. integra, C. linariifolia, C. miniata*
Penstemon, Colorado, *Penstemon linarioides*
grayleaf, *P. teucrioides*
mat, *P. caespitosus*
showy, *P. speciosus*
Watson's, *P. watsonii*
Phlox, *Phlox hoodii, P. longifolia,* and *P. austromontana*
Pussytoes, *Antennaria rosea, A. dimorpha,* and *A. rosulata*
Salsify, *Tragopogon dubius*
Sandwort, desert (or Hooker's sandwort), *Arenaria hookeri*
Sunflower, common, *Helianthus annuus*
Yarrow, *Achillea lanulosa*

Environment and Adaptation: Animals of the Sagebrush Shrublands

Sagebrush shrublands provide food, shelter, and breeding habitat for a diversity of wildlife species. Sagebrush obligates, creatures such as the sage grouse, sage sparrow, sagebrush lizard, and sagebrush vole, cannot survive without sufficient high-quality sagebrush habitat. Though domestic livestock find sagebrush unpalatable, this terpene-rich shrub is a critical food resource for animals such as the sage grouse, and an important supplementary food for pronghorn, mule deer, and elk, especially during the winter months when other forage is scarce. Pronghorn rely on sagebrush for nearly 90 percent of their diet. Sage grouse are almost totally dependent on sagebrush for food and cover, often moving long distances during the winter to find snow-free stands.

Dining on Sagebrush

More than forty years ago, shortly after moving to Colorado, I mistakenly substituted the leaves of big sagebrush for culinary sage (*Salvia*) in cooking a turkey for Thanksgiving—a misdaventure that taught me the true meaning of the word *unpalatable*. The bitter, acrid taste remains a lasting memory. So how do animals cope with this terpene-rich food source? To realize the nutritional benefits locked within the cellulose-rich twigs and foliage of big sagebrush requires prolonged bacterial fermentation to break down the cellulose, a process that relies on the presence of "cellulose-digesting" microbial organisms in the stomach. Research shows that a high intake of terpene-rich foods can seriously reduce the microbial population normally found in the herbivore digestive tract, rendering it largely ineffective in terms of cellulose digestion.

In mule deer and pronghorn, the initial bacterial processing, or fermentation, of cellulose-rich foods takes place in the rumen, the first and largest compartment of the multichambered stomach. Studies of mule deer suggest that these animals can tolerate up to 30 percent sagebrush in their diet without incurring significant inhibition of rumen bacterial activity. Feeding experiments have shown that mule deer, and probably other native ruminants as well, are selective in their browsing of sagebrush, choosing plants that have comparatively lower levels of toxic compounds and varying their total daily consumption of sagebrush in relation to other plant foods. These foraging behaviors appear to play a critical role in maintaining an adequate population of rumen bacteria for proper fermentation. The association of heavy deer mortality with excessive feeding on sagebrush, however, suggests that selective browsing may be inadequate when mule deer are forced to subsist primarily on sagebrush when other food resources are in short supply.

Birds that subsist on a cellulose-rich diet of sagebrush, such as the sage grouse, possess a pair of sacs known as the caeca, located toward the posterior end of the intestine. The caecum functions as a temporary storage chamber in which microbial fermentation can occur and is especially large in sage grouse: the combined length of the two sacs is roughly equal to that of the intestine. Sage grouse are able to concentrate and detoxify terpenoid compounds in the caeca, eliminating all indigestible and potentially harmful residues in the form of a caecal dropping. Caecal droppings are entirely unlike normal feces and are easy to identify because of their tarlike appearance and strong sage smell. There is no evidence that ruminants are able to isolate and detoxify harmful substances in the same way that sage grouse do.

Rites of Spring

Elaborate courtship and territorial displays are characteristic of many birds that breed in open country. Few are more impressive than those of the male sage grouse, the classic lek-forming species of North American grouse. From late March until May, males and females begin congregating at their traditional strutting grounds. Most leks consist of a small, windswept clearing in a stand of sagebrush, often on a knoll or other prominent area. During the peak of the breeding season, fifty or more males may be present at a single lek. With their tails fanned and their yellow air sacs inflated, the cocks strut and swoop, ending each display with an abrupt deflation of the air sacs. A single display sequence lasts a few seconds and is repeated frequently. Each male maintains distinct territory within the lek. Dominant cocks defend territories closest to the lek center, while the younger males remain on the periphery. Females appear somewhat passive during the display, gathering in the center of the lek to await copulation with a dominant male. Once copulation has been completed, the females leave the lek and proceed to the nesting grounds.

Male display postures, showing lateral view of strutting sequence.

Living in Sagebrush Country

Spring and summer are busy times in the sagebrush shrublands. Sagebrush and other shrubs provide perching areas, escape cover, and nesting sites for birds such as the sage thrasher, lark sparrow, and green-tailed towhee. The lush understory of some stands offers concealment for the runways and foraging activities of small mammals such as the northern grasshopper mouse and the sagebrush vole. The deep, friable soils are ideal for burrowing mammals: prairie dogs, northern pocket gophers, badgers, and several species of ground squirrels. Black-tailed jackrabbits and cottontails escape the heat of summer days in the shade beneath the shrubs, emerging only at dusk to forage. Unfortunately, the widespread use of herbicides, chaining, and fire to open up sagebrush habitat for cropland and grazing will continue to chart the futures of the animals that rely on the sagebrush shrublands.

Life Histories of Selected Animals

Mammals

Sagebrush Vole, *Lemmiscus curtatus.* This pale, ash-gray vole is identified by its whitish underparts and extremely short tail; color and sagebrush habitat distinguish it from other vole species. Sagebrush voles feed on the leaves of sagebrush, greasewood, and other shrubs. A lackluster climber, the vole depends on deer mice to scale the shrubs and clip off the foliage, whereupon the vole steals the fallen harvest. The sagebrush vole lives in small, social colonies; the burrow and runway systems of the colony form an interconnected cluster. Colonies are mobile, changing location seasonally and in response to changes in the distribution of the snow cover.

White-tailed Prairie Dog, *Cynomys leucurus.* This robust, buff-colored ground squirrel is identified by its white-tipped tail. **Gunnison's prairie dog** (*C. gunnisoni*) also has a white- or grayish-tipped tail but is considerably smaller in size. White-tailed prairie dogs are common in the drainage of the Laramie River, North Park, and the valleys of the Colorado River and its northern tributaries. Gunnison's prairie dog is common in mountain parks from central Colorado south into the upper Chama Valley and upper Rio Grande Valley of New Mexico. The white-tailed prairie dog is gregarious, and its vocal communication, consisting of shrill whistles and barks, is well developed. Daily activity in summer revolves around foraging, basking in the sun, and territorial behaviors. Animals enter hibernation in early fall and emerge in spring, when body fat stores have been depleted.

American Badger, *Taxidea taxus*. Grizzled gray coloring, a prominent black-and-white facial pattern, and a waddling gait distinguish this large member of the weasel family. The badger is a fast and powerful digger, literally sinking out of sight under a geyser of flying dirt. The neck and legs of this species are short and muscular; the front claws are extremely long. Conspicuous excavations, with entrance holes about eight to twelve inches in diameter, are the most common indication of badger activity. Badgers are carnivorous, their diet consisting mostly of small mammals and ground-nesting birds. Though largely nocturnal and active year-round, badgers may be seen at any time of the day. Badgers are solitary except during the breeding season, which occurs in late summer and fall.

Birds

Golden Eagle, *Aquila chrysaetos*. The large size (average adult wingspan is 6.5 feet), uniform brown coloring, and broad wings distinguish the golden eagle from smaller avian predators; golden neck feathers are inconspicuous except at close range. Juvenile eagles, when seen in flight from below, show white wing patches and a broad white tail band. Rabbits, hares, and small rodents comprise nearly 90 percent of the diet; carrion is utilized when available and may comprise as much as 60 percent of the winter diet. Golden eagles hunt from perches or while soaring, with wings held horizontally rather than in the V position typical of vultures; they will soar for hours over mountain ridges, sometimes diving with tremendous speed to capture prey or in presumed play. Courtship involves soaring and undulating flight displays; pairs may remain mated for life. Some pairs, as well as successive generations of eagles, may use the same nest site repeatedly. Nesting success is usually limited to one eaglet; human disturbance can cause nest abandonment. Though the female incubates, the male may help; incubation time is about forty-five days, and eaglets fledge at around seventy days.

Sage Grouse, *Centrocercus urophasianus*. The largest of all North American grouse species, the sage grouse is identified by its mottled gray-brown plumage, black belly, and stiff, pointed tail feathers; the male is distinguished by its greater size, yellow eye combs, black throat patch, and white breast. Sage grouse are relatively common in sagebrush habitat in the northern half of the Southern Rockies and are considered uncommon south of this area. This grouse is considered a bellwether species in evaluating the health of sagebrush-steppe ecosystems throughout its range. Sagebrush

foliage comprises the bulk of the sage grouse's diet; juveniles also eat insects and forbs during their first few weeks. Seasonal movements between sheltered wintering areas in dense sagebrush, traditional leks, and nesting and brooding habitats in more open sagebrush are common.

Sage Thrasher, *Oreoscoptes montanus.* Its gray-brown upperparts, strongly streaked breast, bright yellow eyes, and white-cornered, narrow tail distinguish this small, slender thrasher. The sage thrasher is a migratory species and is largely restricted to sagebrush shrubland and arid semidesert shrublands. The species forages for insects by running over the ground like a robin. Shy and difficult to approach closely, the male perches atop a shrub to deliver its rich, mockingbird-like song; males may also sing in flight. Sage thrashers construct a nest of coarse twigs and finer plant fibers in the lower branches of a small, densely branched shrub.

Green-tailed Towhee, *Pipilo chlorurus.* The smallest of the towhees is identified by its rufous crown, white throat patch with vertical dark stripes, gray sides, white belly, and olive green upperparts. This denizen of dense underbrush is often observed scratching and scuffing as it searches for seeds, berries, and insects on the ground. When disturbed, the towhee runs swiftly over the ground as it heads for cover. During the breeding season, males deliver their trilling song from a conspicuous shrub-top perch; the call is a catlike *puee.*

Reptiles

Sagebrush Lizard, *Sceloporus graciosus.* This small, spiny lizard is identified by the pale stripe along each side of its back; males have a blue-mottled throat and blue patches on each side of the body. Sagebrush lizards occasionally climb trees or bushes in search of insect prey. They emerge from winter chambers in large numbers in April; males typically emerge first. Adults are diurnal and active throughout the summer and into mid-September, juveniles until early October. Females generally lay two clutches of eggs, the first in early June and the second in early July; first clutch eggs hatch in August, second clutch eggs in mid-September.

Common Animals of the Sagebrush Shrublands

Mammals

Badger, American, *Taxidea taxus*
Chipmunk, least, *Tamias minimus*
Cottontail, desert, *Sylvilagus audubonii*
    Nuttall's, *S. nuttallii*
Coyote, *Canis latrans*
Deer, mule, *Odocoileus hemionus*

Ground Squirrel, Wyoming, *Spermophilus elegans*
Jackrabbit, black-tailed, *Lepus californicus*
white-tailed, *L. townsendii*
Kangaroo Rat, Ord's, *Dipodomys ordii*
Mouse, deer, *Peromyscus maniculatus*
northern grasshopper, *Onychomys leucogaster*
Pocket Gopher, northern, *Thomomys talpoides*
Prairie Dog, Gunnison's, *C. gunnisoni*
white-tailed, *Cynomys leucurus*

Pronghorn, *Antilocapra americana*
Vole, sagebrush, *Lemmiscus curtatus*
Weasel, long-tailed, *Mustela frenata*
Woodrat, bushy-tailed, *Neotoma cinerea*

Birds

Bluebird, mountain, *Sialia currucoides*
Eagle, golden, *Aquila chrysaetos*
Grouse, sage, *Centrocercus urophasianus*
Hawk, ferruginous, *Buteo regalis*
red-tailed, *B. jamaicensis*
rough-legged, *B. lagopus*
Hummingbird, black-chinned, *Archilochus alexandri*
broad-tailed, *Selasphorus platycercus*
Lark, horned, *Eremophila alpestris*
Raven, common, *Corvus corax*

Shrike, loggerhead, *Lanius ludovicianus*

Sparrow, Brewer's, *Spizella breweri*

lark, *Chondestes grammacus*

sage, *Amphispiza belli*

vesper, *Pooecetes gramineus*

Thrasher, sage, *Oreoscoptes montanus*

Towhee, green-tailed, *Pipilo chlorurus*

Reptiles

Bullsnake, *Pituophis melanoleucus*

Lizard, plateau, *Sceloporus undulatus*

sagebrush, *S. graciosus*

Rattlesnake, western, *Crotalus viridis*

Butterflies and Insects

Ant, velvet, *Dasymutilla* spp.

Beetle, carrion, *Heterosilpha* spp., *Nicrophorus* spp., *and Oiceoptoma*

Butterfly, blue copper, *Chalceria heteronea*

sagebrush white, *Pontia beckerii*

Cricket, Mormon, *Anabrus simplex*

Midge, sagebrush sponge gall, *Rhopalomyia pomum*

Tephritid, rabbitbrush cotton gall, *Aciurina bigeloviae*

sagebrush stem gall, *Eutreta diana*

Walkingstick, Colorado, *Parabacillus coloradus*

A Resilient Beauty: Mountain Shrublands and Gambel's Oak Woodlands

Gambel's oak woodlands near Steamboat Springs, Colorado.

The coming of autumn transforms the dull midsummer greens of the mountain shrublands and Gambel's oak woodlands with brushstrokes from an artist's palette: ochre, cinnabar, and persimmon. Sunwashed and backlit against a turquoise sky, the intricately feathered seeds of mountain mahogany lend a silvery hue to the canyonsides. The blaze of fiery orange and red that spreads across the oak woodlands like a firestorm each autumn lends its own magic. Our earliest written accounts of Gambel's oak, however, fail to appreciate the seasonal magic. They come from the journals of the Dominguez-Escalante Expedition as it charted a serpentine loop through the Gunnison River country in 1776. The rather taciturn Escalante was unimpressed with these impenetrable, gnarled woodlands; in his view, the "dwarf oaks" were an impediment to travel and nothing more. The adventuring priest might have taken a more favorable view had his expedition witnessed the spectacular rust-red foliage of Gambel's oak that cloaks the north rim of the Black Canyon of the Gunnison each autumn.

Ecological Distribution

Mountain shrublands and Gambel's oak woodlands vegetation occur throughout the foothills of the Southern Rockies. In the northern and eastern foothills, a rough tangle of mountain mahogany and three-leaf sumac dominates dry, rocky slopes between the grasslands below and the midelevation coniferous forests above. On the south-facing slopes of the sandstone hogbacks north of Lyons, Colorado, mountain mahogany frequently forms homogeneous stands.

Woodlands of Gambel's oak, or scrub oak, give a chaparral-like feeling to hillsides in the western and southern foothills of the Southern Rockies. In the southern foothills, stands of Gambel's and wavy-leaf oak form small, islandlike groves on gentle slopes and dense thickets on steeper slopes in a zone roughly transitional between that of the piñon-juniper woodlands and the ponderosa pine forests. To the north, along the Eastern Slope, stands of mountain mahogany begin to replace Gambel's oak in the foothills north of Denver and the Palmer Divide area. Gambel's oak reaches its northern limit along the Colorado Front Range near Morrison. Its conspicuous absence in the foothills north of this area suggests a major climatic boundary affecting oak seedling survival, possibly related to the increasing frequency of frost damage or to the probability of summer drought stress associated with the diminished influence of the Arizona monsoon in this region.

On the Western Slope, thousands of acres of scrub oak dominate the foothill shrub belt, reaching their greatest development between 7,000 and 8,500 feet. At their lower limit, oak brushlands adjoin piñon-juniper woodlands or sagebrush ecosystems; at their upper limit they merge with aspen, ponderosa pine, or lodgepole. Within this region, scrub oak is conspicuously absent from South, Middle, and North parks, perhaps as a result of cold air drainage in these basins. In the northwestern ranges of the Southern Rockies, dense thickets of Gambel's oak and sticky-laurel are common on steep slopes, while in other areas the shrubland consists almost entirely of serviceberry or littleleaf mountain mahogany.

Community Characteristics

In the mountain shrublands and oak woodlands, summer temperatures in the eighties and nineties are common. Winter temperatures, on the other hand, are more moderate because the majority of these communities occur on south-facing slopes and in other upland situations that avoid the extremes of temperature and wind associated with most basins. Annual precipitation is normally less than fifteen inches. Well-developed stands of Gambel's oak or mountain mahogany occur wherever microclimatic and soil conditions preclude the invasion of these habitats by trees. Communities developed on the most xeric sites, such as those dominated by mountain mahogany, generally consist of only one or two shrub species and a sparse understory of herbaceous plants. On more topographically diverse and less xeric sites along the East Slope, mountain mahogany may occur in association with three-leaf sumac, chokecherry, wild plum, and bitterbrush. On the Western Slope south of Grand Junction, these shrublands may include greenleaf manzanita, cliffrose, mountain spray, and squaw apple, as well as Gambel's oak.

On sites with deeper soils and more moisture, shrubland communities generally consist of several species of shrubs and a lush understory of herbaceous vegetation. Oak-dominated woodlands are typical of such sites, and the more common shrub associates include snowberry, serviceberry, chokecherry, big sagebrush, and wild rose. In the southern foothills, Gambel's oak forms dense stands in association with mountain mahogany, mountain spray, Apache plume, and New Mexican locust.

Fire and Gambel's Oak

Fire plays a critical role in maintaining oak woodlands throughout the West. Though Gambel's oak reproduces by seed, the ability to sprout from specialized swellings near the base of the trunk (lignotubers) as well as from underground rhizomes allows this species to form spreading clones of sprouts in response to crown damage due to fire or heavy browsing by wildlife. In the event of a fire or other severe stress, the hormonal suppression that would normally prevent the dormant buds in the lignotuber and the network of rhizomatous roots from sprouting is lifted. Aggressive vegetative reproduction by suckering allows Gambel's oak to take advantage of changing conditions for renewed growth. In north-central New Mexico, Gambel's oak has spread into large areas of the lower montane region in places where ponderosa pine has been burned or logged.

Gambel's oak.

Descriptions of Common Plants

Shrubs

Gambel's Oak, *Quercus gambelii.* This deciduous, thicket-forming scrub oak is easily recognized by its leathery, deeply lobed leaves. Newly emergent leaves are yellowish green, turning dark green in summer and deep reddish in fall, prior to shedding. Flowers appear in spring, shortly before or in conjunction with the growth of new leaves; male and female flowers are produced on the same tree. The fruits, or acorns, are borne singly or in clusters and mature in the fall. Acorns are a favorite food of black bears, squirrels, jays, wild turkeys, and band-tailed pigeons.

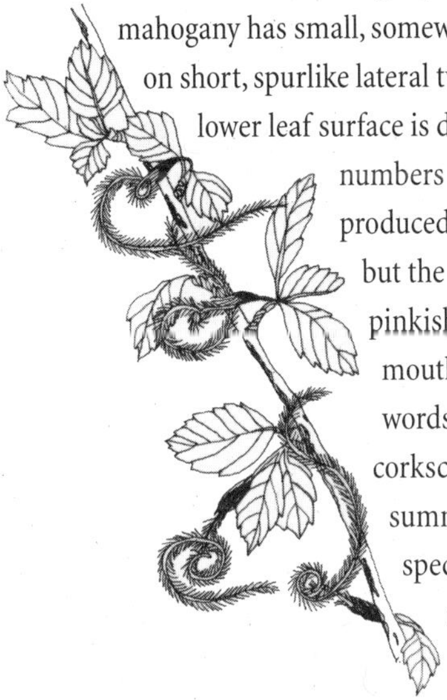

Mountain Mahogany, *Cercocarpus montanus.* Mountain mahogany has small, somewhat oval-shaped leaves arranged alternately on short, spurlike lateral twigs; leaf margins are toothed, and the lower leaf surface is densely covered with fine hairs. Large numbers of small, inconspicuous flowers are produced in early spring; the flowers lack petals, but the sepals form a greenish tube with flared, pinkish to reddish petal-like lobes rimming the mouth. The name *Cercocarpus,* from the Greek words for "tail" and "fruit," refers to the feathery, corkscrewlike fruits that grace this shrub in late summer and fall. This is an important browse species for deer. The Arapahos and Utes are reported to have used the largest mountain mahogany branches in making their hunting bows.

Western Serviceberry, *Amelanchier alnifolia.* Common names for serviceberry abound: saskatoon, Juneberry, sarvisberry, shadbush, and shadblow. Western serviceberry is a deciduous, thicket-forming shrub or small tree with an erect, rounded crown and multiple trunks. The leaves of this variable species are simple, alternate, oval to round in shape, and coarsely toothed, changing from hairy to smooth with age. Clusters of white, star-shaped flowers appear near the tips of the branchlets in early June; each flower has five strap-shaped, white petals and multiple stamens. In mid- to late summer, dark bluish purple fruits appear in small bunches. The foliage and twigs are heavily browsed during all seasons, and the fruit is a favorite with birds and small mammals.

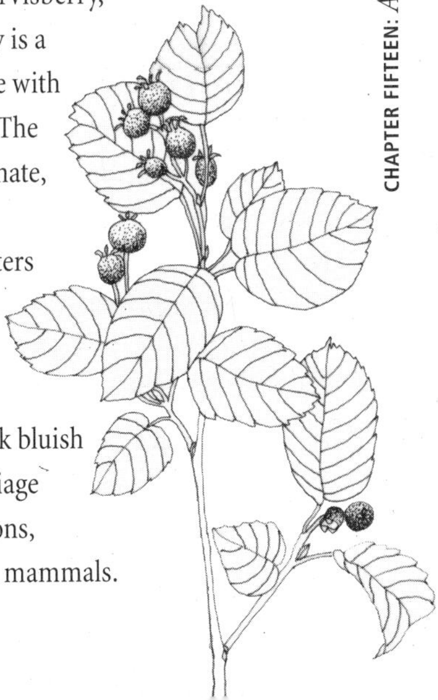

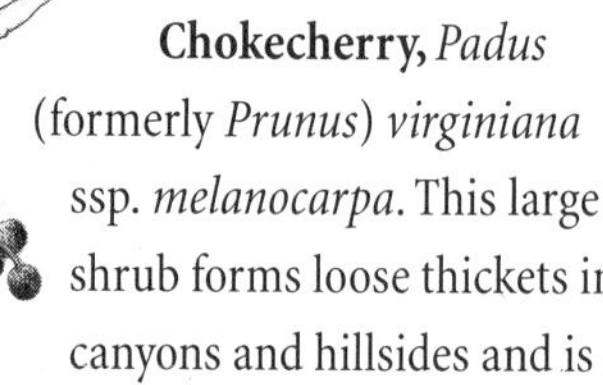

Chokecherry, *Padus* (formerly *Prunus*) *virginiana* ssp. *melanocarpa*. This large shrub forms loose thickets in canyons and hillsides and is readily distinguished by its broadly lanceolate leaves and cylindrical racemes of white, roselike flowers. The small, five-petaled flowers appear in June and are followed in late summer by mouth-puckering purple-black fruits. The large-pitted fruits are a favorite food of birds, small mammals, black bears, coyotes, and foxes, and make excellent jelly and wine.

Roundleaf Snowberry, *Symphoricarpos rotundifolius*. This small- to medium-sized shrub is a member of the honeysuckle family and is common in oak scrub and aspen forests from the foothills to the subalpine zone. Snowberry is distinguished by its small, oval leaves, paired tubular flowers (white to pinkish), and clusters of porcelain-white berries. This shrub reproduces largely by vegetative means, sending out a network of underground runners.

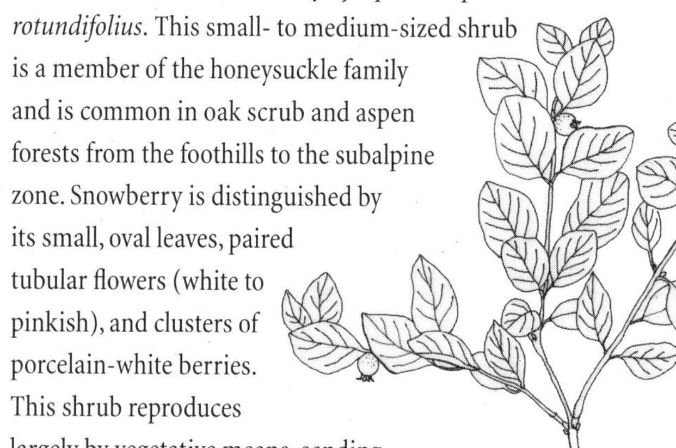

Three-leaf Sumac (or Skunkbush), *Rhus aromatica* ssp. *trilobata*. This much-branched, rounded shrub is identified by its compound leaves (each leaf divided into three scallop-margined leaflets) and by its clusters of reddish orange berries. The scent given off by the crushed foliage is produced by resinous oils housed in ducts in the leaves and branchlets. Flowering occurs in spring, with clusters of small, inconspicuous yellow flowers appearing before the leaves. The berrylike fruits, despite their covering of sticky glandular hairs, are sought after by birds and small mammals; a lemony tea can be prepared by steeping the ripe berries in boiling water. Some sumac species are toxic to humans, so care should be taken to ensure correct identification. The leaves of three-leaf sumac turn a rich red-orange prior to autumn leaf shed.

Common Plants of the Mountain Shrublands and Gambel's Oak Woodlands

Trees

Hawthorn, river, *Crataegus rivularis*
Locust, New Mexican, *Robinia neomexicana*
Pine, ponderosa, *Pinus ponderosa*

Shrubs

Apache Plume, *Fallugia paradoxa*
Bitterbrush, *Purshia tridentata*
Buckbrush (or New Jersey Tea), *Ceanothus fendleri*
Buffaloberry, Silver, *Shepherdia argentea*
Chokecherry, *Padus* (formerly *Prunus*) *virginiana* ssp. *melanocarpa*
Cliffrose, Mexican, *Purshia stansburiana* (formerly *Cowania mexicana*)
Current, golden, *Ribes aureum*
Fendlerbush, cliff, *Fendlera rupicola*
Gooseberry, whitestem, *Ribes inerme*
Mahogany, curl-leaf, *Cercocarpus ledifolius*
  littleleaf mountain, *C. intricatus*
  mountain, *C. montanus*
Mountain Spray (or Ocean Spray), *Holodiscus dumosus*
Oak, Gambel's, *Quercus gambelii*
  wavyleaf, *Q. undulata*
Olive, New Mexican, *Forestiera neomexicana*
Plum, wild, *Prunus americana*
Rabbitbrush, *Chrysothamnus nauseosus*
Rose, wild, *Rosa woodsii*

Sagebrush, big (or Great Basin sagebrush), *Seriphidium* (formerly *Artemisia*) *tridentatum*

mountain, *S. vaseyanum*

Serviceberry, Utah, *Amelanchier utahensis*

western, *A. alnifolia*

Snakeweed, *Gutierrezia sarothrae*

Snowberry, roundleaf, *Symphoricarpos rotundifolius*

Squaw Apple, *Peraphyllum ramosissimum*

Squaw apple.

Sumac, three-leaf (or Skunkbush), *Rhus aromatica* ssp. *trilobata*

smooth, *R. glabra*

Yucca (or Spanish bayonet), *Yucca glauca*

Grasses and Sedges

Fescue, Thurber's, *Festuca thurberi*

Grama, blue, *Bouteloua gracilis*

sideoats, *B. curtipendula*

Muhly, mountain, *Muhlenbergia montana*

Sedge, Geyer's (or Elk Sedge), *Carex geyeri*

Wildflowers

Aster, golden, *Heterotheca villosa*

Balsamroot, arrowleaf, *Balsamorhiza sagittata*

Blanketflower, *Gaillardia aristata*
Buckwheat, *Eriogonum subalpinum*, *E. umbellatum*, and *E. cernuum*
Fleabane, *Erigeron* spp.
Gaura, scarlet, *Gaura coccinea*
Geranium, wild, *Geranium caespitosum* and *G. richardsonii*
Gilia, scarlet, *Ipomopsis aggregata*
Lily, mariposa, *Calochortus gunnisonii*
Locoweed, Rocky Mountain, *Oxytropis sericea*
Lupine, *Lupinus* spp.
Paintbrush, Indian, *Castilleja linariifolia* and *C. chromosa*
Spring Beauty, western, *Claytonia lanceolata*
Tasselflower (or Bricklebush), *Brickellia grandiflora*
Vetch, American, *Vicia americana*
Yarrow, *Achillea lanulosa*

Environment and Adaptation: Animals of the Mountain Shrublands and Gambel's Oak Woodlands

The fauna of our mountain shrublands and woodlands is remarkably rich, an ecotonal assemblage of species transitional between lowland communities and mountain forests. Where brushy vegetation adjoins cliffs or other rocky areas, denning and nesting sites abound, providing habitat for wildlife species such as hawks, jays, marmots, ground squirrels, woodrats, foxes, bobcats, black bears, mountain lions, lizards, and snakes. The attractiveness of shrubland habitats for wildlife changes with the seasons. In most areas, mountain shrublands bustle with activity by early May, when the first leaves appear. The roster of bird species swells to its highest number as resident species, such as the spotted towhee and the scrub jay, are joined by an influx of summer breeders: wild turkey, lazuli bunting, Virginia's warbler, green-tailed towhee, blue-gray gnatcatcher, bushtit, house wren, and many others. Animals that have spent the winter underground, such as the rock squirrel, Colorado chipmunk, and plateau lizard, emerge to bask on sun-warmed boulders. Mule deer browse on the succulent new growth before beginning the journey to summer ranges at higher elevations.

By hot midsummer, the intense activity of spring has diminished, leaving the shrublands subdued, even silent, the air redolent of resinous foliage. With the exception of the resident species, many of the birds that nested in the shrublands have moved higher into the mountains or begun migrating south to their wintering areas. Small mammals and reptiles remain active but now restrict their activities to the cooler times of the day.

A bountiful supply of seeds and fruit in late summer coincides with the onset of fall bird migration, when high-energy foods must be eaten in large quantities to build the reserves of subcutaneous fat that will fuel the long flights to southern wintering grounds. Mountain shrublands and woodlands fill with noisy flocks of birds; residents and migrants alike feed on the fruits of serviceberry, chokecherry, and skunkbrush. Ripening acorns attract large numbers of scrub jays as well as black bears, desert cottontails, woodrats, rock squirrels, and chipmunks. Ground feeders, such as the spotted towhee and the wild turkey, search for fallen fruits and seeds under the protective cover of the shrubs.

In winter, mountain shrublands serve as a refuge for many species that have spent the summer at higher elevations. Escaping the deep snows of their summer ranges, mule deer return to favorite wintering areas. The tracks of the gray fox and the long-tailed weasel are frequently seen in the snow. Mice continue to forage over the ground for seeds and fruit, and the well-packed trails of hares and rabbits zigzag from shrub to shrub. Ground-dwelling squirrels retreat to underground nests and become torpid during long periods of severe weather. Overwintering birds, often in large flocks, forage on the ground for seeds or harvest the dry fruits that remain on the shrubs. Scrub jays search the branches and dead leaves of Gambel's oak for nymph-filled galls. Twig gleaners, such as the mountain and black-capped chickadees, scour the branches for dormant insects and eggs attached to the surface or under loose bark.

Of the forty-nine species of mammals reported to occur in the mountain shrublands, sixteen belong to the Chihuahuan Faunal Element, a fauna whose origins can be traced to the semiarid highlands and grasslands of Chihuahua, in north-central Mexico. Mammalogists suggest that this warmth-loving fauna was able to spread north into the Southern Rockies during the early Holocene, when the climate is believed to have been warmer and perhaps drier than at present. These Chihuahuan species, with their affinities for the desert Southwest, include many of our most interesting foothill mammals: Townsend's big-eared bat, desert cottontail, black-tailed jackrabbit, rock squirrel, rock mouse, Mexican woodrat, gray fox, and ringtail. In the Southern Rockies, the Chihuahuan fauna is narrowly restricted to the foothills zone. Along the Eastern Slope, species such as the Mexican woodrat, rock mouse, and rock squirrel reach the northern limits of their distribution just short of the Colorado-Wyoming border. With increasing elevation, Chihuahuan species are replaced by mammals with affinities for the boreal forests of northern Canada.

Life Histories of Selected Animals

Mammals

Colorado Chipmunk, *Tamias quadrivittatus.* The Colorado chipmunk is distinguished from the **least chipmunk** (*T. minimus*), the common chipmunk of higher elevations, by its larger size, less-animated behavior, and preference for rocky sites instead of wooded habitat. The bright cinnamon coloring of this species is similar to that of the least chipmunk, but the black-and-white stripes along the head and sides do not continue to the base of the tail. Most common at elevations below 8,000 feet, the species occurs at higher elevations (to 10,000 feet) in the southern portion of its range. Colorado chipmunks are solitary and live in burrows dug beneath rocks, shrubs, or the exposed roots of trees. Winter torpor alternates with consumption of food stores. Mating occurs in late April or early May, and females give birth to one litter of altricial young per year; the young are weaned at six to seven weeks of age.

Rock Squirrel, *Spermophilus variegatus.* The rock squirrel is identified by its ground-dwelling habit, bushy tail, and salt-and-pepper fur. The species is locally abundant in broken, rocky terrain to 8,200 feet; the northern limit of distribution occurs in Colorado near Meeker on the Western Slope and near Livermore on the Eastern Slope. Rock squirrels construct burrows beneath boulders and shrubs, occasionally in steep-sided arroyos. The diet of this semiarboreal squirrel includes acorns, seeds, and other fruits. Rock squirrels arc noncolonial, and communication is poorly developed; their call is an abrupt, moderately loud whistle. The annual cycle of activity consists of successive periods of fattening, cold-season torpor, warm-season foraging, and two breeding periods. The altricial young are born in a well-constructed nest and do not appear above ground until they are nearly two months of age.

Rock squirrel.

Mexican Woodrat, *Neotoma mexicana*. This woodrat (or packrat) is distinguished from the **bushy-tailed woodrat** (*N. cinerea*) by the presence of a dark ring around the mouth, the absence of pure white fur on the breast, and a sparsely furred rather than bushy tail. Locally abundant in rocky areas of the foothills to 8,500 feet, the Mexican woodrat prefers horizontal crevices in broken, sedimentary rock for denning; man-made structures may also be used when available. The diet consists mostly of foliage, which is clipped and stored during all seasons, but particularly in late summer and fall. Nocturnal and active throughout the year, the Mexican woodrat has a less developed collecting instinct than other woodrat species: dens contain only moderate amounts of sticks and collected debris. The food refuse pile, or midden, serves as a urination perch where plant fragments and fecal pellets are gradually cemented into hard masses that may be preserved for thousands of years. Females breed in March and bear altricial young in April.

Western Spotted Skunk, *Spilogale gracilis*. This small skunk has no dorsal stripes, but rather a distinctive checkerboard pattern of white spots on an otherwise black body. Spotted skunks are common in broken, shrub-covered terrain along the Western Slope and are uncommon on the Eastern Slope. Den sites are in rock piles, abandoned burrows, brush piles, hollow logs, and man-made structures. Home range is extremely limited, with as many as twelve spotted skunks per square mile in good habitat. Spotted skunks are nocturnal and omnivorous, taking a wide variety of animal and plant foods. They are solitary animals, except during the breeding season and during severe winter weather, when a communal den may hold six or more individuals. Breeding occurs in September, and females are spontaneous ovulators. Implantation of the fertilized egg in the uterus is delayed (six to seven months) until April; the altricial young are born in May. Young skunks are furred at three weeks, and eyes open between four and six weeks; full size is attained at about three months of age.

Mule Deer, *Odocoileus hemionus*. Mule deer are identified by their large, mulelike ears and somewhat narrow, black-tipped tails. Adults stand about three feet high at the shoulder and are about half the size of an elk; adult males, or bucks, average 250 pounds. Seasonal migrations between summer and winter range are common; mule deer tend to avoid dense forests, and snow depths in excess of eighteen inches are believed to preclude use of potential winter range by mule deer. Active primarily at dawn and dusk, mule deer are moderately gregarious but seldom form large herds. They are most dispersed during the spring fawning period, when the females (does) seek isolation and drive off any yearlings. Does give birth to precocial, spotted, and odorless young from June to early July; fawns are kept hidden, and does approach only to nurse. Does, fawns, and yearlings form small herds again in midsummer, remaining together through the winter. Socialization breaks down among bucks during the rut (November to December), when food intake declines and aggressive behaviors involving urine marking, thrashing and rubbing of the antlers in shrubs and trees, and sparring increase in intensity. Antlers are shed in February or March; new antler growth is completed by late summer.

Birds

Scrub Jay, *Aphelocoma coerulescens*. This slim-bodied, crestless jay is identified by its whitish throat, long tail, smoke gray back, and undulating flight; the head, wings, and tail are a rich blue, and a narrow white eye stripe is sometimes present. The scrub jay's diet consists of acorns, piñon nuts, wild and cultivated fruits, insects, eggs, nestlings, small mammals, reptiles, and amphibians; acorns are often buried for later retrieval. Conspicuous and noisy, the scrub jay is often seen perched atop a prominent shrub or hopping about on the ground or in shrubbery. Jay calls are typically harsh and raucous, but musical "whisper" songs by both sexes are not uncommon. Scrub jays are communal nesters; young jays leave the nest about eighteen days after hatching, remaining in loose family groups.

Rock Wren, *Salpinctes obsoletus.* The larger size, pale grayish color, buffy flanks, and bobbing gait as it walks or when alarmed distinguishes the rock wren from the more familiar **house wren** (*Troglodytes aedon*). Rock wrens are found from the foothills to the alpine tundra in suitably rocky habitat. The bird is extremely active, foraging among the rocks for insects. The call is a variety of trills on a single pitch (a ringing buzzy *pdzeeee*) often delivered from atop a rock. Though both the rock wren and the **canyon wren** (*Catherpes mexicanus*) may occur in the same habitat, the beautiful, descending whistle-song of the canyon wren bears no resemblance to the buzzy, trilled, ringing phrases produced by the rock wren. Nests are constructed in a rock crevice or in an abandoned burrow on a rocky slope; the entrance to the nesting cavity is often paved with small stones.

Virginia's Warbler, *Vermivora virginiae.* This small, gray and olive-yellow warbler has a white eye ring, whitish underparts, and a yellow breast patch; the reddish patch on the head of the male is seldom visible except during courtship or territorial displays. Virginia's warbler is a summer resident in the foothills to 9,000 feet. This somewhat shy warbler can be observed foraging for insects on the ground, in dense shrubbery, or catching insects on the wing. Males sing while foraging or from a conspicuous perch. Females construct a cup-shaped nest on the ground, slightly sunken in dead leaves or loose soil, and typically at the base of a shrub or clump of grass.

Lazuli Bunting, *Passerina amoena.* This small, brightly colored species is superficially similar to the western bluebird. Males have a turquoise-blue head, throat, back, and rump; upper breast and sides are a rich cinnamon, the lower belly is white, and the wings show two white wing bars. Females and immatures are grayish brown but have a hint of blue on the rump and tail. Lazuli buntings are resident here only during the breeding season, with males arriving on nesting areas first, singing from prominent perches and courting females with spread-wing displays. Females build a cup-shaped nest in low shrubs, often near water. Lazuli buntings are insectivorous, foraging on or near the ground or in shrubbery.

Spotted Towhee, *Pipilo maculatus.* The male spotted towhee is identified by its red eyes, black hood and back, conspicuous white spots on the wings, cinnamon-colored sides, white breast, and white-cornered black tail; female plumage is more washed out but otherwise similar. Nonmigratory and locally common in brushy habitats, towhees are often first detected by their noisy scratching as they forage for insects in the leaf litter. During courtship, males sing from prominent perches in the shrubbery and fan their tails. The song is a buzzy trill; the call resembles a monosyllabic *tweee* or *chweee*. The spotted towhee typically nests on the ground, and only occasionally in shrubs or small trees.

Reptiles

Plateau Lizard, *Sceloporus undulatus.* This small, variable lizard is identified by the presence of spiny scales on the back and keeled scales on the rear of the thigh. These insectivorous lizards follow a spot-and-pursuit style of hunting, sometimes leaping into the air to catch prey. Plateau lizards emerge from underground chambers in late March and April, remaining active until September or October. Most activity occurs in mid- to late morning and late afternoon; Plateau lizards retreat underground during the warmest times of the day. Males are polygamous, conducting "bobbing" courtship displays from May through early July. Females lay a clutch of eight to twelve eggs; hatching occurs from mid-July through early September. Longevity seldom exceeds four years.

Smooth Green Snake, *Opheodrys vernalis*. Its grass green coloring, slender body, and smooth scales easily identify this beautiful snake. Smooth green snakes are found in lush undergrowth and dry mountain shrublands, especially oak brushland, at elevations to 9,000 feet. This diurnal, shy, and quick snake is active from May to September, seeking shelter underground when not active. Smooth green snakes will climb into low herbaceous plants or shrubs in search of insect prey, and may also enter shallow water. Little is known of breeding; females lay six to seven eggs, which may hatch after as little as four days.

Common Animals of the Mountain Shrublands and Gambel's Oak Woodlands

Mammals

Badger, American, *Taxidea taxus*
Bat, Townsend's big-eared, *Plecotus townsendii* (C)
Bear, black, *Ursus americanus*
Bobcat, *Lynx rufus*
Chipmunk, cliff, *Tamias dorsalis*
    Colorado, *T. quadrivittatus*
    Hopi, *T. rufus*
    least, *T. minimus*
Cottontail, desert, *Sylvilagus audubonii* (C)
    Mountain (or Nuttall's), *S. nuttallii*
Coyote, *Canis latrans*
Deer, mule, *Odocoileus hemionus*
Elk (or Wapiti), *Cervus elaphus*
Fox, gray, *Urocyon cinereoargenteus* (C)
Jackrabbit, black-tailed, *Lepus californicus* (C)
Lion, mountain, *Felis concolor*
Marmot, yellow-bellied, *Marmota flaviventris*

Mouse, brush, *Peromyscus boylii* (C)
deer, *P. maniculatus*
Great Basin pocket, *Perognathus parvus*
northern rock, *Peromyscus nasutus* (C)
Myotis, small-footed, *Myotis leibii*
Porcupine, common, *Erethizon dorsatum*
Ringtail, *Bassariscus astutus* (C)
Skunk, western spotted, *Spilogale gracilis*
Squirrel, rock, *Spermophilus variegatus* (C)
white-tailed antelope, *Ammospermophilus leucurus*
Weasel, long-tailed, *Mustela frenata*
Woodrat, bushy-tailed, *Neotoma cinerea*
Mexican, *N. mexicana* (C)

***The (C) indicates that the species is associated with the Chihuahuan Faunal Element

Birds

Bushtit, *Psaltriparus minimus*
Chickadee, black-capped, *Parus atricapillus*
mountain, *P. gambeli*
Flicker, northern, *Colaptes auratus*
Flycatcher, dusky, *Empidonax oberholseri*
gray, *E. wrightii*
Gnatcatcher, blue-gray, *Polioptila caerulea*
Hawk, red-tailed, *Buteo jamaicensis*
Hummingbird, black-chinned, *Archilochus alexandri*
broad-tailed, *Selasphorus platycercus*
Jay, scrub, *Aphelocoma coerulescens*
Sparrow, Brewer's, *Spizella breweri*
Titmouse, juniper, *Baeolophus ridgwayi*
Towhee, canyon, *Pipilo fuscus*
green-tailed, *P. chlorurus*
spotted, *P. maculatus*
Turkey, wild, *Meleagris gallopavo*
Warbler, black-throated gray, *Dendroica nigrescens*
MacGillivray's, *Oporornis tolmiei*

orange-crowned, *Vermivora celata*
Virginia's, *V. virginiae*
Wren, house, *Troglodytes aedon*
rock, *Salpinctes obsoletus*

Reptiles

Bullsnake, *Pituophis melanoleucus*
Green Snake, smooth, *Opheodrys vernalis*
Lizard, plateau, *Sceloporus undulatus*
sagebrush, *S. graciosus*
short-horned, *Phrynosoma douglassii*
Rattlesnake, western, *Crotalus viridis*
Skink, variable, *Eumeces gaigeae*
Whiptail, plateau striped, *Cnemidophorus velox*

Butterflies and Insects

Butterfly, Aphrodite fritillary, *Speyeria aphrodite*
arrowhead blue, *Glaucopsyche piasus*
Colorado hairstreak, *Hypaurotis crysalus*

Colorado hairstreak, the Colorado state butterfly; upperside is an iridescent purple bordered with black and spotted with orange.

large wood nymph, *Cercyonis pegala*
tailed copper, *Tharsalea arota*
two-tailed swallowtail, *Pterourus multicaudatus*
Cicada, Putnam's, *Platypedia putnami*
Gall Wasp, oak leaf, (Family Cynipidae)
oak bulletgall, (Family Cynipidae)

Sun Forests: Piñon-Juniper Woodlands

From my rimrock aerie, I see an orderly profusion of piñon pine and Utah juniper stretching across the mesa to the distant horizon. The lizard-tough foliage, dark green against the buff-colored sandstone, smells like sun-warmed incense. These ancient woodlands with their short, gnarled, and round-crowned trees evoke the enduring spirit of the desert Southwest. Invariably, whenever I've hiked up a canyon in search of a secluded cliff dwelling I've found the sandstone portals of the ruin to be guarded by an elegant, silvered sentry tree: a venerable Utah juniper or a piñon whose memories of this place I can only imagine. Piñon-juniper woodlands have little in common with the verdure of the high mountain forests, an extravagant lifestyle they can ill afford. But to call them "pygmy forests," as some do, diminishes their extraordinary beauty and resilience. Piñon-juniper woodlands are perfectly suited to the vagaries of life in a drought-prone land.

Ecological Distribution

Piñon-juniper woodlands cover more than 75,000 square miles in the West, their distribution extending from west of the Pecos River in Texas to the Santa Ynez Mountains of Southern California and from southern Idaho deep into Mexico. Though species composition varies from place to place, the overall character of these woodlands remains much the same. In the Southern Rockies, piñon-juniper woodlands are dominated by piñon pine or, more commonly, by one of several species of juniper: Rocky Mountain juniper, Utah juniper, or one-seed juniper. Piñon-juniper woodlands occur along both sides of the Continental Divide and are best developed in a zone between 5,000 and 7,000 feet; patches of woodland can also be found at elevations as high as 9,000 feet on west- or south-facing slopes. Along their lower margins, piñon-juniper woodlands merge with semiarid grasslands or shrub communities. Near their upper limits, these woodlands interfinger with forests of ponderosa pine and Douglas-fir, or with Gambel's oak.

On the Eastern Slope, piñon-juniper woodlands are most common from Colorado Springs south along the foothills. Extensive woodlands can be seen along the western flanks of the Sangré de Cristo Range and in the vicinity of Great Sand Dunes National Park. At relatively low elevations, piñon pine and one-seed juniper dominate woodlands along the East Slope; Rocky Mountain juniper is seldom found below 6,500 feet, except in moist canyon environments. Scattered woodlands occur on canyon and mesa sides well out into the shortgrass prairie from Walsenburg to the southern terminus of the Southern Rockies. North of Colorado Springs, Rocky Mountain juniper replaces one-seed juniper and piñon pine becomes increasingly uncommon. At Owl Canyon, north of Fort Collins, an isolated stand of piñon pine marks the northern limit of piñon along the Eastern Slope. North of this area, Rocky Mountain juniper grows alone or in combination with ponderosa pine, Douglas-fir, or limber pine.

On the Western Slope, woodlands consisting of piñon pine and Utah juniper cover hillsides and mesa tops from the Colorado-Wyoming border south into New Mexico. Along the western edge of the Southern Rockies, Utah juniper may form pure stands in areas unfavorable for piñon. Rocky Mountain juniper typically replaces Utah juniper along the upper margin of Western Slope woodlands. Alligator juniper, so named because of the distinctive pattern of its bark, reaches the northern limit of its range in the woodlands of north-central New Mexico, where it grows alone or in small stands in the Jemez Mountains.

Physical Environment

Piñon-juniper woodlands occupy sites characterized by intense sunlight, hot summers, relatively low precipitation, high evapotranspiration, and moderately strong winds. Though daily and seasonal temperatures vary greatly, the frost-free period generally exceeds ninety days, the longest for any forest type in the Southern Rockies. Annual precipitation ranges between twelve and eighteen inches. Soil moisture recharge occurs primarily in the spring, when the snow melts. Summer precipitation occurs in cloudbursts, which result in a high percentage of runoff. Drought is common in these woodlands, and potential evaporation greatly exceeds precipitation during periods of prolonged drought.

Community Characteristics

Piñon-juniper woodlands often appear as evenly spaced as if they'd been planted by a xeriscape gardener intent on making the most of what moisture and soil was available, an economy born of necessity. Along the lower margin of the piñon-juniper zone, the trees tend to be widely spaced and rarely exceed twenty feet in height. With increasing elevation and moisture availability, piñon-juniper woodlands become dense and the tree canopy more forestlike. Even under optimal conditions, however, tree height rarely exceeds forty feet. Variations in resistance to drought and tolerance of cold temperatures determines whether piñon or one of several species of juniper will dominate a given woodland. Piñon pine is better adapted to cold temperatures and dominates higher-elevation woodlands, whereas the more drought-tolerant junipers are prevalent at lower elevations. Piñon is commonly associated with one-seed juniper or Utah juniper in areas receiving at least one-third of their precipitation during the summer months, and it is associated with Rocky Mountain juniper in areas where a spring precipitation maximum prevails. Soil factors are especially important in the distribution and character of individual stands. The best-developed woodlands tend to occur on rocky substrates characterized by coarse-textured, calcareous soils.

Shrubs dominate the understory vegetation in most piñon-juniper

Piñon-juniper woodland in Yampa Canyon, Dinosaur National Monument.

communities. Semidesert species such as greasewood and saltbush are common in low-elevation woodlands with strongly alkaline soils. Elsewhere, shrubs such as three-leaf sumac, rabbitbrush, bitterbrush, cliffrose, and mountain mahogany may assume local dominance. In the southern woodlands, wavyleaf oak, Apache plume, and candelabra cactus are important shrub associates. Big sagebrush is a common species in areas with unusually deep soils.

The total cover provided by herbaceous species is extremely low, and in many communities may be less than 1 percent. Herbaceous vegetation is most abundant where the overstory is open, for example on gentle slopes at both the lower and upper fringes of the woodlands, where the community may may have a savannalike appearance. Where livestock grazing has been extensive, the herbaceous understory is largely depleted. In the Southern Rockies, grasses such as blue grama, Indian ricegrass, and galletagrass tend to dominate the herbaceous layer. Broad-leaved herbaceous plants include such species as golden aster, gumweed, fleabane, bladderpod, copper mallow, and Colorado four-o'clock. Various species of cacti, such as prickly pear, claret cup, and the magenta-flowered hedgehog, may be common on rocky slopes with a southern exposure.

Plant Adaptation: Designs for Survival

Water Stress

The needlelike, wax-coated leaves of conifers are perfectly designed for water economy, whether the tree must cope with a hot, arid environment or a cold one in which groundwater supplies are largely unavailable during the winter months. Junipers, also known as cedars, have carried this versatile adaptation one step further than in other conifers, producing leaves so small and appressed to the stem that they are almost scalelike, an advantage that partially explains their ability to outcompete piñon along the drought-prone lower margin of the woodlands.

The root systems of piñon pine and juniper include long taproots that enable them to exploit rocky substrates and to plumb deep-seated moisture sources below the rooting zone of herbaceous plants. These taproots are capable of rapid elongation and are thus able to adjust to changing moisture conditions, an important adaptation during periods of prolonged drought. In addition to the taproot, a group of branching, lateral roots fans out into the upper horizons of the soil, competing with herbaceous plants for ephemeral moisture supplies produced by rain or snow.

Chemical Defenses

Plant chemical defenses play an important role in reducing herbivory and resource competition in piñon-juniper woodlands. Both juniper and piñon produce an arsenal of secondary compounds that, when released into the environment in sufficient quantities, may affect the growth and well-being of plants or animals that come into contact with them. Some defensive compounds simply taste bad; others inhibit digestion, alter reproduction, or interfere with development in various ways. Many of these compounds are volatile resins and are readily detected by their odor when they are released as a vapor. Volatile terpenes present in both the berrylike cones and foliage of juniper are what give gin its distinctive taste, and they lend their pungent aroma to the woodlands. The fragrance of woodlands dominated by piñon pine is produced by the volatization of ethyl caprylate, a chemical compound also found in Zinfandel grapes. This same compound is responsible for the intense, spicy-sweet woodsmoke that perfumes the air in towns such as San Luis and Santa Fe, or wherever fireplaces and woodstoves are fueled with piñon.

The concentration of chemical defenses in a given tree varies from season to season and also with age; it is often greatest in young foliage and developing reproductive structures. This strategy has obvious advantages in reducing predation on new growth. Though some animals eat resinous foliage, most defensive compounds are released into the environment through the roots or through the decomposition of plant litter. Recent studies have shown that, in addition to having antiherbivore action, many of these defensive compounds function as natural herbicides, inhibiting the growth of would-be competitors such as blue grama and golden aster. The concentration of toxic compounds tends to be greatest directly under the tree canopy, frequently resulting in areas of bare, vegetation-free soil. Furthermore, some of these compounds inhibit the growth of fungi, making the heartwood of piñon and juniper highly durable and resistant to decay.

Rocky Mountain juniper (upper left) and Utah juniper (right); piñon pine (below) shows mature cone with bracts spread to expose the seeds.

Descriptions of Common Plants

Trees

Colorado Piñon Pine, *Pinus edulis*. First described by Cabeza de Vaca in the early 1500s, the Colorado piñon is one of eleven species of piñon pine native to North America and the only species found in the Southern Rockies. It is thought that New World piñon pines evolved in central Mexico during the late Miocene and spread northward into suitable habitat. Biologists refer to the piñon as a "bird pine," a species that produces a heavy, wingless seed and relies on birds (such as jays and nutcrackers) for seed dispersal. The piñon pines as a taxonomic group are believed to have coevolved in association with primitive pine nut–harvesting jays. This hypothesis is supported by the discovery in Colorado of a fossil piñon jay–like corvid from Miocene-age rocks. The piñon is distinguished from other pines in our region by its low, rounded growth form and by its needles, which are arranged in bundles of two and are normally less than two inches long. The male and female cones occur on the same tree, appearing in early summer from buds formed the previous summer. The male, pollen-producing cones are small and crowded into reddish yellow clusters near the tips of the branches. The newly emerged female cones are pincushionlike and purplish, consisting of numerous spirally arranged, overlapping scales, each scale bearing on its upper surface two tiny ovules. At the end of the third growing season, the egg-shaped cone dries to a yellowish brown. Ripening completed, the cone scales open to reveal plump, paired seeds on the upper surface of each scale; these wingless and highly nutrious seeds (the delicious pine nuts of culinary fame), numbering about ten to twenty per cone, fall to the ground within a few weeks after the cones open—unless, of course, they've been harvested directly from the

cone by piñon jays or Clark's nutcrackers. Containing over 3,000 calories per pound, piñon nuts have long been an important food resource for humans and animals alike. A good piñon seed crop occurs about every fifth year. Cone production begins at about twenty-five years of age. Mature piñon pines vary from 75 to 200 years in age, with a maximum age of approximately 400 years.

Rocky Mountain juniper, *Sabina* (formerly *Juniperus*) *scopulorum*; **one-seed juniper,** *J. monosperma*; and **Utah juniper,** *J. osteosperma*. Some flora manuals use the genus name *Sabina* for the junipers, with the exception of common juniper (*Juniperus communis*). **Rocky Mountain juniper,** also known as western red cedar, can be easily identified by its small, scalelike leaves that overlap one another like shingles; slender and elongated branchlets; and small, bluish purple "berries" (female cones). This species tends to occur at higher elevations and in slightly moister habitats than either one-seed or Utah juniper. **Utah juniper** has stout branches and dry, rather than resinous, berries. **One-seed juniper** is distinguished by its Eastern Slope distribution pattern, resinous cones, and large berries. Except in Utah juniper, male and female cones are borne on the same tree. Male cones, small and cylindrical, are located inconspicuously at the ends of the branchlet. The female (seed-producing) cone is round and berrylike, its fleshy scales permanently fused to enclose the seeds. Male cones begin pollen production in late summer or early fall, and the pollen is shed the following spring. Following fertilization, the seeds ripen over one or two seasons; during maturation, the ripening cone changes from green to bluish purple in Rocky Mountain and one-seed juniper, and to reddish brown in Utah juniper. Once the seeds are released from the cone, a prolonged "after-ripening" period is required for the seed coat to break open and release the embryo from dormancy. Seeds that have been through the digestive tract of a fruit-eating bird (such as a Townsend's solitaire) or mammal tend to germinate faster than seeds that have not had this advantage. Good cone crops are produced at intervals of two to five years.

Shrubs

Apache Plume, *Fallugia paradoxa*. This attractive member of the rose family is distinguished by its white, apple blossom–sized flowers and its small, simple, and deeply lobed leaves. Apache plume tends to grow in clumps rarely exceeding six feet in height. Its slender branches are whitish, the bark becoming shreddy with age. The five-petaled flowers appear in May or early June and are followed by clusters of feathery-tailed fruits. When not in flower, the only shrub with which it might be confused is the cliffrose, whose flowers are smaller and cream-yellow in color and whose fruits have only five plumes per cluster.

Cliff Fendlerbush, *Fendlera rupicola*. Fendlerbush occurs in dry foothill canyons from central Colorado south into New Mexico. Though inconspicuous until it blooms, the opposite, lanceolate-shaped leaves and four-petaled white flowers readily distinguish fendlerbush from all other woodland shrubs except the littleleaf mock orange (*Philadelphus microphyllus*); the flowers of fendlerbush have eight stamens per flower, whereas the flowers of littleleaf mock orange have fifteen. The fruits of both shrubs are narrow, acornlike, and about half an inch long. Muledeer and bighorn sheep relish the small, one-inch-long leaves.

Mountain Spray (or Ocean Spray), *Holodiscus dumosus*. This attractive shrub is identified by its serrate, broadly ovate leaves and its pyramidal clusters of tiny white flowers. The inflorescence and seed heads usually remain on the shrub throughout the year. In the Southern Rockies, mountain spray is common along canyon walls and in rocky habitat from north-central Colorado southward.

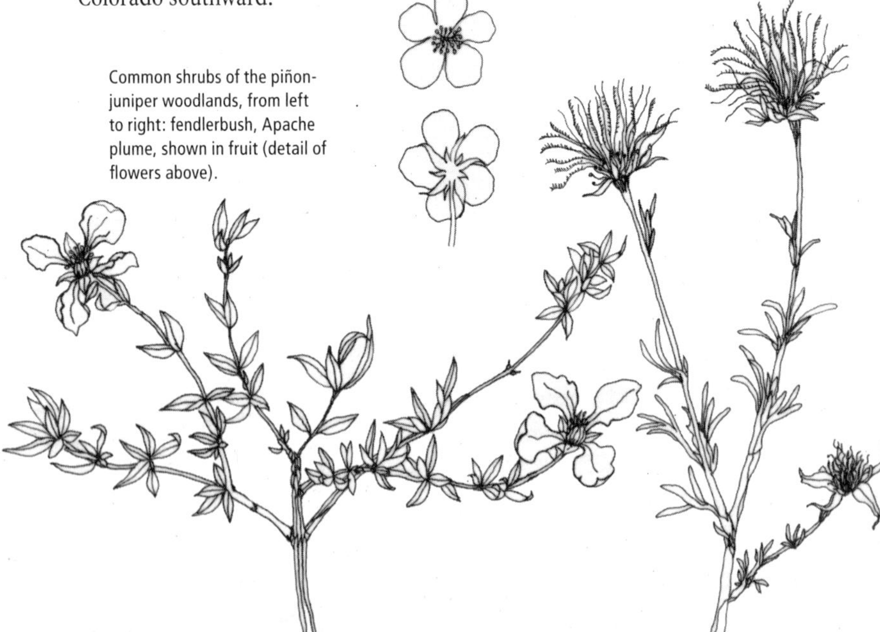

Common shrubs of the piñon-juniper woodlands, from left to right: fendlerbush, Apache plume, shown in fruit (detail of flowers above).

Flowers

Claret Cup Cactus, *Echinocereus triglochidiatus.* This exquisite cactus is identified during its blooming season (May to June) by the large scarlet flowers that appear along the sides of the numerous short stems. When not in bloom, the multistemmed character of the claret cup distinguishes this species from the solitary-stemmed, magenta-flowered hedgehog cactus (*E. fendleri*).

Claret cup.

Colorado Four-o'clock, *Mirabilis multiflora.* This robust and colorful wildflower is widely distributed on open canyonsides in the piñon-juniper zone. Colorado four-o'clock is identified by its erect or sprawling bushy growth form, its thick, dark green, and deltoid-shaped leaves, and its large, petunialike, magenta-purple flowers. The funnel-shaped flowers resemble morning glory blossoms, and several are clustered together within a papery floral cup (involucre). Bandelier National Monument is an excellent place to see this species.

Golden Aster, *Heterotheca villosa.* This common member of the sunflower family, with its woody, purplish green, sticky stems and yellow daisylike flowers, grows in bunches and rarely exceeds nine inches in height. The three-quarter-inch flowers, with their strap-shaped yellow ray flowers and orange disks, arise from multibranched stems.

Yellow Puccoon, *Oreocarya flava.* This showy wildflower is identified most easily by the dense clusters of yellow flowers and the stiff hairs that coat the lance-shaped leaves, the flower stems, and sepals. The five-petaled flowers flare open, and the petal edges are minutely ruffled.

Desert Beard-tongue, *Penstemon barbatus.* This beautiful, red-flowered penstemon is identified by its five-lobed tubular flowers; the two lobes that form the upper lip of the floral tube (corolla) project outward, and the three lobes that comprise the lower lip are reflexed backward. The only other red-flowered penstemon in the Southern Rockies, **Eaton's (or firecracker) penstemon** (*P. eatonii*), is a taller, more robust species with opposite, shiny, spear-point-shaped leaves that clasp the flower stalk and inch-long tubular flowers that do not flare at the mouth. The penstemons get their name from the Latin word for "five stamens"; most penstemons have only four fertile stamens and a single brush-tipped, sterile stamen. The brush-tipped stamen effectively keeps out the smallest of the nectar-seeking insects while serving as a guide to bees seeking nectar, thus the common moniker "beardtongue." The superficially similar **scarlet gilia** (*Ipomopsis aggregata*) has finely divided leaves and long-throated, trumpet-shaped red flowers in which the floral tube flares outward into points.

Rimrock Paintbrush, *Castilleja scabrida.* The genus *Castilleja* is named for Domingo Castillejo, an eighteenth-century Spanish botanist. This early blooming, intensely red-orange paintbrush hugs the ground or rimrock niche where it grows, and it seldom exceeds more than a few inches in height. The leaves are narrow, much incised, and covered with short, reflexed hairs. The only other species with which it might be confused, the **common paintbrush** (*C. chromosa*), is taller, more upright, and has a shorter corolla. To enhance their chances for survival, all paintbrush are partially parasitic on the roots of other plants, with specialized conducting tubes, known as haustoria, located along the plant's taproot that allow it to seek out the root system of a suitable host (often sagebrush or buckwheat).

Rimrock paintbrush.

Common Plants of the Piñon-Juniper Woodlands

Trees

Juniper, one-seed, *Sabina* (or *Juniperus*) *monosperma*
Rocky Mountain, *S. scopulorum*
Utah, *S.* (or *Juniperus*) *osteosperma*
Oak, Gambel's, *Quercus gambelii*
Piñon Pine, Colorado, *Pinus edulis*

Shrubs

Apache Plume, *Fallugia paradoxa*
Ash, singleleaf, *Fraxinus anomala*
Bitterbrush, *Purshia tridentata*
Cliffrose, *Purshia stansburiana* (formerly *Cowania mexicana*)
Fendlerbush, cliff, *Fendlera rupicola*
Mahogany, curl-leaf, *Cercocarpus ledifolius*
littleleaf mountain, *C. intricatus*
mountain, *C. montanus*
Mock Orange, littleleaf, *Philadelphus microphyllus*
Mormon Tea, *Ephedra viridis* and *E. torreyana*
Mountain Spray (or Ocean Spray), *Holodiscus dumosus*
Rabbitbrush, *Chrysothamnus nauseosus*
flax-leaved, *C. linifolius*
sticky-leaved, *C. viscidiflorus*
Sagebrush, big (or Great Basin sagebrush), *Seriphidium* (formerly *Artemisia*) *tridentatum*
Saltbush, *Atriplex* spp.
Serviceberry, Utah, *Amelanchier utahensis*
western, *A. alnifolia*
Sumac, three-leaf (or Skunkbush), *Rhus aromatica* ssp. *trilobata*

Grasses, Rushes, and Sedges

Cheatgrass, *Anisantha* (formerly *Bromus*) *tectorum*
Feathergrass, New Mexican, *Stipa neomexicana*
Grama, blue, *Bouteloua gracilis*

sideoats, *B. curtipendula*
Junegrass, *Koeleria macrantha*
Ricegrass, Indian, *Achnatherum* (formerly *Oryzopsis*) *hymenoides*

Wildflowers and Cacti

Aster, Tansy, *Machaeranthera grindelioides*
Aster, golden, *Heterotheca villosa*
Bee Plant, yellow, *Cleome lutea*
Bladderpod, double, *Physaria acutifolia*
Blue Star, Jones, *Amsonia jonesii*
Brickellia, *Brickellia* spp.
Buckwheat, desert, *Eriogonum ovalifolium*
Cactus, candelabra (or Cholla), *Cylindropuntia imbricata*
claret cup, *Echinocereus triglochidiatus*
hedgehog, *E. fendleri*
prickly pear, *Opuntia polyacantha* and *O. macrorhiza*
prickly pear, brittle, *O. fragilaris*
Fleabane, desert, *Erigeron pulcherrimus*
Four-o'clock, Colorado, *Mirabilis multiflora*
Galletagrass, *Hilaria jamesii*
Gilia, ballhead, *Ipomopsis* (or *Gilia*) *congesta*
prickly, *Leptodactylon pungens*
Lupine, *Lupinus* spp.
Mallow, copper (or cowboy's delight), *Sphaeralcea coccinea*
Milkvetch, painted, *Astragalus ceramicus*
Milkweed, spider, *Asclepias asperula*
Mustard, skeleton, *Schoenocrambe linifolia*
Muttongrass, *Poa fendleriana*
Paintbrush, desert, *Castilleja chromosa* and *C. scabrida*
Pincushion (or Dusty Maiden), *Chaenactis douglasii*
Puccoon, yellow, *Oreocarya* (formerly *Cryptantha*) *flava* and *O. flavoculata*
Rockcress, beautiful, *Boechera* (formerly *Arabis*) *pulchra*
Rock Jasmine, western, *Androsace occidentalis*
Sandwort, desert (or Hooker's sandwort), *Arenaria hookeri*
Scorpionweed, *Phacelia ivesiana*

Stonecrop, yellow, *Amerosedum* (formerly *Sedum*) *lanceolatum*
Sunflower, little, *Helianthella microcephala*
Townsendia (or Easter Daisy), *Townsendia hookeri* and *T. exscapa*
Yarrow, *Achillea lanulosa*

Environment and Adaptation: Animals of the Piñon-Juniper Woodlands

Walking through a piñon-juniper woodland on a summer morning, before midday heat stills the air, is a revelation, an introduction to a larder of almost infinite possibilities. Every ledge or rocky outcrop displays the remains of some seed or plant eater's banquet. A Hopi chipmunk chitters its displeasure before abandoning a sideboard dappled with the papery husks of ricegrass seeds. In an abandoned tree cavity beneath finely shredded juniper bark, a tidy pile of juniper seeds, each with a perfectly round hole gnawed into the surface, suggests the work of a piñon mouse. On a high, seemingly inaccessible ledge, the whitewash- and shiny-amberlike midden—the latrine of a bushy-tailed woodrat—is situated at the opposite end of the ledge from the entrance to a packrat's rocky fortress, which is strategically blocked by an imposing tangle of twigs and cactus pads and littered with small bits of freshly clipped greenery. In the soft sand along the trail, the diminutive tracks of a gray fox lead to a much-used overlook. The discovery of several fox scats along the way reveals a diet that runs the gamut from fruit to nuts, with a bit of mouse fur and tiny bones rounding out the omnivorous mix. Overhead, the low-pitched *ch-ch-ch-ch* calls of juniper titmice, the buzzy twitter of bushtits, and the nasal *chick-a-zee-zee-zee* of mountain chickadees heralds the arrival of a mixed-species foraging flock. The birds move quickly from branch to branch, gleaning tiny caterpillars and insects from the resinous needles of the piñon. The busy foragers are soon displaced by a raucous, *kawing* flock of piñon jays, which alight in a cone-laden tree and begin assaying the season's crop of piñon nuts. As the day heats up and the sun bears down like a hot iron, the woodland marketplace winds down, and the metallic staccato calls of cicadas announce the start of the afternoon siesta.

Many animals are year-round residents of the piñon-juniper woodlands, and the life histories of several species, such as the piñon jay and the piñon mouse, are intricately tied to these woodlands. The majority of animals, however, visit the woodlands on a seasonal basis, attracted by the diversity and abundance of nesting sites, the rich larder of plant foods, and the shelter these woodlands provide from the harsh winter climate typical of high elevations. The ample supply of seeds and fruits supports large populations of mice and chipmunks, prey species for hunters such as the gray fox and the ringtail. Overwintering herds of mule deer and small bands of bighorn, avoiding the deep snows typical of higher elevations, provide food for larger predators such as the mountain lion and coyote.

The Fine Art of Seed Caching

Seed caching and dispersal by birds and mammals are critical components of the natural history of piñon-juniper woodlands. Most coniferous trees in the Southern Rockies rely on the wind to disperse their winged seeds to suitable germination sites. Winged seeds are kept tightly sealed in their cones until maturity to protect them from birds and other seed predators. Piñon and limber pine, however, have evolved wingless seeds, which require seed-eating birds—pinavores—for effective dispersal. Wingless seeds tend to be larger than their winged counterparts, with a greater investment in stored energy and nutrients: attributes that are attractive to the seedeater but also serve to enhance seedling establishment and survival. Large seed size is considered to be an adaptation to dry environments, where competition for available resources is more intense than in other habitats.

At first glance, based solely on the sheer volume of piñon seeds consumed by small mammals and birds, it seems likely that seed predation would eventually impact the viability of piñon in an existing woodland and would reduce the potential spread of the species into new areas. So how does the relationship between the piñon pine and its avian seed predators actually work? The answer to this coevolutionary puzzle lies in the foraging behavior of the principal harvesters of pine seeds: the jays and the nutcrackers. Though piñon jays, Clark's nutcrackers, and Steller's jays harvest impressive numbers of piñon seeds in the fall, they do not immediately eat their autumn bounty. Instead, they bury much of the harvest in large communal caches, sometimes more than two or three times what the birds could consume over the course of the year. Seed caches serve as supplemental food stores during the winter, when other foods are in short supply. The advantages to the pines in this coevolved system derive from the failure of the birds to recover all the seeds they've cached. Carefully sequestered in a good seedbed, unconsumed seeds have a much better chance of germinating when conditions are right.

Piñon jays are a gregarious, highly colonial species. The flock, the critical social unit in piñon jay life, varies in size from small groups of birds to more than a hundred. Clamorous flocks of piñon jays are especially conspicuous in the piñon-juniper woodlands during the first golden days of autumn. When a new seed crop is ripe, piñon jays forage intensively for a period of two to three weeks. Excess seeds are communally cached—often several miles away—in the flock's traditional nesting area. The flock moves one to two miles per hour while foraging, with long-distance movements generated by some form of mutual stimulation within the flock. Distinct *kawing* vocalizations generally accompany foraging flights.

Partly because of the abundance of the food supply, there is virtually no aggression within the foraging flock. Individual jays take turns at sentry duty, remaining at good vantage points along the periphery of the foraging flock. The appearance of potential predators elicits warning calls and mobbing behavior from the sentries, the distraction allowing the flock to seek protective cover. Social organization within the flock is characterized by cooperative feeding of the young, the use of sentinels to watch for predators during foraging bouts, communal food caching, synchronization of reproductive activities, and a strong repertoire of group-cohesion behaviors. As long as the seed crop (or mast) remains good, a flock will occupy a foraging territory of about eight square miles, which it defends vigorously against other flocks. During poor seed years, flocks may band together as they wander over hundreds of miles in search of food. When a productive tree is located—a "hot spot"—the noisy, *kawing* flock descends in a swirl, and it is not uncommon to see as many as fifteen jays in a single tree.

Like the Clark's nutcracker, considered by some biologists to be the most proficient harvester of pine seeds, the piñon jay has a long, sharply pointed bill with which to chisel open the resin-sealed green cones. This bill gives the piñon jay a substantial head start over other pine nut eaters. Other jays lack this adaptation and must wait for the cones to open naturally before harvesting the seeds. The length of the piñon jay's bill also allows it to poke deep between the scales of the cone while keeping its facial feathers free of pitch. When harvesting seeds from green cones, the jay will remove the cone from the branch by twisting the cone stalk or by jabbing at it with its bill. Once detached, the piñon jay carries the cone to a nearby branch, wedging it into a snug crotch that serves the same function as a vise. With rapid, hammerlike strikes aimed precisely between the cone scales, the jay is able to extract the seeds with its long bill. After extracting a seed, the piñon jay "rattles" it in its bill, testing the seed's edibility by sound and weight. Inedible (undeveloped or insect-damaged) seeds are discarded, while edible (viable) seeds are transferred to the bird's expandable esophagus (or crop) for later transport to a caching site. Later in the fall, when the cones have opened on their own, piñon jays hop through the branches, visually scanning each cone for edible seeds; inedible, yellow-hulled seeds are left in the cones or dropped to the ground.

Though lacking the capacious sublingual (or gular) pouch of the Clark's nutcracker, the piñon jay is capable of transporting as many as sixty seeds at a time, more than double the quantity carried by other jays. For a single piñon jay, caching an average of 300 seeds per day, the total number of seeds cached during the ninety-day autumn harvest season exceeds 25,000 seeds. In years with a bumper cone crop, one researcher estimates that a single flock of jays can cache up to 4.5 million seeds over the course of the year. The capacity to carry food in such large quantities minimizes the energy expended in caching and in delivering food to the nestlings.

The reproductive cycle of the piñon jay is entrained in the seasonal rhythm of the woodland. Piñon jays choose their mates during the fall, sealing the bond with a ceremony in which the male feeds piñon seeds to his prospective mate. Breeding activities begin in earnest during February, when courtship behavior intensifies and mated pairs begin leaving the flock to feed separately. Nest building begins in March, with egg laying by the entire flock synchronized during a three- or four-day period. Nestlings and fledglings are cooperatively fed by their parents as well as by other adults. Family groups forage by themselves for much of the spring and summer, the large group flock reforming as the piñon harvest begins anew in late summer.

A Terpenaceous Larder

Juniper seeds, like the seeds of piñon, are wingless and depend on fruit- or seed-eating mammals and birds for reliable dispersal. To achieve this end, juniper seeds are presented in an abundant, easily accessible, and nutritious "berry" (actually a female cone) that attracts avian consumers in large numbers: Bohemian and cedar waxwings, Townsend's solitaires, and robins. These juniper-loving birds digest the calorie-rich pulp that surrounds the seeds, passing the seeds through their digestive tracts intact and ready for germination.

The relationship between the Townsend's solitaire and the juniper provides an elegant example of this mutually beneficial system. During the breeding season, Townsend's solitaires are found in cool, dense, north-facing forests at higher elevations and are largely insectivorous. With the coming of fall, solitaires migrate to wintering areas in the piñon-juniper woodlands or to mixed coniferous forests that include a high proportion of Rocky Mountain juniper, switching from an insect and fruit diet to one that consists almost exclusively of juniper berries. For the juniper to benefit from avian dispersal, the solitaire must select only ripe berries and must be able to digest the high-carbohydrate pulp without damaging the seeds. Fruit color provides a simple visual cue to ripeness. Unripe juniper berries are green, whereas ripe berries are blue or copper, colors that are known to attract fruit-eating birds. Furthermore, to help ensure that the developing berries escape predation during the two- to three-year ripening period, the pulp that surrounds the seeds is imbued with terpenoid resins, secondary chemical compounds whose toxic qualities serve as a deterrent to the would-be seed predator or fruit eater. When you cut a juniper berry in half, the translucent sacs in which these volatile, aromatic resins are contained are readily apparent to the naked eye. Terpene levels are consistently higher in immature berries and decline substantially as ripening proceeds, a fact reflected by the Townsend's solitaire's preference for mature fruit.

The Townsend's solitaire avoids the physiological hazards of a terpene-rich food resource by changing the way its digestive system functions. When insects are eaten, they are first routed through an outpocketing of the main digestive tract, called the gizzard, where they undergo mechanical grinding to release the digestible material from the indigestible chitin (the exoskeleton). This kind of processing would destroy the thin-shelled juniper seeds and would also break open the resin sacs, releasing harmful terpenoid compounds into the bird's digestive tract. Instead, juniper berries are shunted past the gizzard and into the main part of the digestive tract, where the calorie-rich pulp is digested without the seeds being harmed or the resin sacs breaking down. The solitaire excretes both seeds and resin sacs undamaged in the feces.

In contrast to the piñon jay, the Townsend's solitaire is anything but social, as its name suggests. On their wintering grounds, male solitaires aggressively defend individual feeding territories in prime juniper habitat. Territory size reflects the quality and abundance of the juniper berry crop, the number of solitaires utilizing the wintering grounds, and individual aggressiveness. Winter territorial defense includes an extensive repertoire of songs and calls, boundary patrols from conspicuous treetop perches, threat postures, pursuit of intruders (mostly other males), and physical confrontations. Females do not establish territories but move about the wintering grounds as nonterritorial "floaters," completely tolerated by the males.

Woodrat Middens: Archiving the Past

In their search for answers to the riddles of climate change through the millenia, paleoecologists have turned to an unusual source for information: the packrat, or woodrat, as it is more properly called. Woodrats maintain traditional denning sites in small caves and crevices in the walls of rocky canyons or in clifflike outcrops. The bushy-tailed woodrat, the most common species in the Southern Rockies, ranges widely from northern Canada to central Arizona and inhabits everything from alpine talus, spruce-fir forest, piñon-juniper woodland, sagebrush shrubland, shortgrass prairie, and semidesert shrubland—as well as your attic, if it can find access. Woodrats are notorious for their habit of keeping just about everything that interests them and storing these items in their bulky nests or in a refuse pile known as a midden, thus the moniker "packrat." The bushy-tailed woodrat is a dietary generalist, drawing widely from the smorgasboard of shrubs and herbaceous vegetation growing near its den. Woodrats also collect bones, carnivore scat, and owl pellets—a future treasure trove for paleontologists.

The best denning sites tend to be used by generations of woodrats for thousands of years; a well-protected midden can be up to 40,000 years old. Since the midden also functions as a privy, the fragments of plant and animal matter that accumulate over time become encased in amberlike crystallized urine. By studying these fossil middens, paleoecologists are able to identify plant remains and date them with carbon-dating techniques, providing an extraordinary opportunity to reconstruct past climates and vegetation changes through time.

Life Histories of Selected Animals

Mammals

Piñon Mouse, *Peromyscus truei.* This large, buffy brown, and distinctly long-eared mouse is distinguished from two similar deer mice found in piñon-juniper woodlands, the **brush mouse** (*P. boylii*) and the **northern rock mouse** (*P. nasutus*), by having ears longer than the hind foot and a tail usually no longer than the length of the head and body. The piñon mouse is largely restricted to piñon-juniper habitat and is found from southwestern Wyoming south to Oaxaca, Mexico; on the Eastern Slope, this species is found as far north as the Colorado Springs area. This surprisingly arboreal mouse nests above the ground in a tree cavity or in the hollow branch of a juniper; the nest consists of a ball of shredded bark with an opening on one side. Piñon mice are especially fond of juniper seeds, selecting mature berries, discarding the resinous pulp surrounding the seed, and chewing a small hole in the seed coat from which to extract the embryonic seedling. Breeding begins in April and continues through September, with two litters of altricial young produced during a single breeding season.

Bushy-tailed Woodrat (or Packrat), *Neotoma cinerea.* This beautiful, squirrel-sized rodent is distinguished from other woodrats by its grayish buff fur, bushy, squirrel-like tail, large ears, and fully furred hind feet. Bushy-tailed woodrats are widespread in the Southern Rockies from 5,000 feet to timberline. Extremely agile climbers, this species is normally found in rocky areas with vertical fissures or talus, or around abandoned, man-made structures that offer good denning sites. Woodrats are herbivorous, solitary, and largely nocturnal. The collecting instinct is well developed in this species, and most will accumulate a large pile of sticks, bones, and other debris to restrict predator access at the entrance to their den; denning areas occupied by woodrats for long periods contain sweet-pungent, urine-cemented accumulations (middens) of brown, oval-shaped fecal pellets, plant matter, animal remains, and the odd treasure. Females bear one or two litters of altricial young yearly.

Gray Fox, *Urocyon cinereoargenteus*. The gray fox is distinguished from its larger cousin, the red fox, by its silvery fur and black middorsal stripe, which extends down the back to the top of the tail, and whitish underparts. In the Southern Rockies, gray foxes prefer shrublands and brushy woodlands where the terrain is rocky or broken. Mostly nocturnal, the gray fox is secretive and inconspicuous over most of its range. The omnivorous diet includes small mammals, birds, eggs, and fruit (especially juniper berries). Gray foxes are adept at climbing trees to forage for fruit or nesting birds. Mating occurs in February, followed by a gestation period of about nine weeks; newborn foxes are blind but well furred. Male foxes deliver food to the vixen while the young are being reared. Family units break up in autumn, with the young dispersing and the parents going their separate ways until the next mating season.

Ringtail, *Bassariscus astutus*. The white-ringed eyes, long and distinctly ringed tail, and the absence of a black face mask identify this slender-bodied relative of the raccoon. In the Southern Rockies, ringtails are largely restricted to rocky terrain in the foothill shrublands and piñon-juniper zone. They are carnivorous, nocturnal, and active throughout the year. The species is secretive and rarely observed, though it may hunt in pairs or in extended-family groups. These animals are agile runners and daredevil rock climbers. Dens or daytime resting sites are typically among rocks or in tree cavities. Territories are marked with urine and accumulations of scat. Ringtail vocalizations include chirps, chittering, barks, and hissing. Breeding occurs in spring, with a litter of altricial young born in May or June.

Mountain Lion, *Felis concolor*. This unmistakable cat is distinguished by its large size, short, tawny fur, and long tail. Mountain lions, also called pumas or cougars, are mostly restricted to rugged areas of the foothills and higher mountains and may be surprisingly common in areas supporting large populations of their favorite food: mule deer. These fast and skillful predators will take both small to midsized mammals and, in rare instances, domestic animals; carrion is seldom utilized. Secretive and solitary, mountain lions hunt primarily at dawn and dusk. After killing a deer, a lion typically covers the leftovers with leaves or brush and will return to the kill over a two- to three-day period. Home range size is variable, depending on the age and sex of the lion, as well as on the season; males average about 48 square miles in winter and spring and nearly 120 square miles in summer and fall. Scrapes—pine needles, leaves, or dirt scraped into a pile with the hind feet—may be used to mark home range boundaries; they do not maintain a permanent den. Mountain lions are promiscuous breeders, mating for the first time at two or three years of age; females give birth to blind but well-furred young, alone, after a gestation period of about ninety-six days. Young lions (kittens) are weaned at six weeks or so but will stay with the female for up to two years. Mountain lions have become increasingly habituated to the presence of humans, and caution is advised whenever hiking in areas where lions have been reported; staying alert to your surroundings is always your best protection in lion country.

Birds

Piñon Jay, *Gymnorhinus cyanocephalus.* The piñon jay is a large blue to grayish blue bird with a short tail and a pale, streaked throat. In the Southern Rockies, the species occurs in piñon-juniper woodlands, and less commonly in oak woodlands and ponderosa pine forests. Piñon nuts are the preferred food of this jay, but fruit, insects, bird eggs, and the nestlings of small bird species are taken when available. Piñon jays are gregarious and maintain large, highly organized flocks; social organization focuses on the piñon nut crop and includes communal food caching. Adult jays maintain pair bonds from year to year; courtship between established pairs and pair-bond formation in young jays takes place during the winter. Like the Clark's nutcracker, piñon jays are among the earliest nesting birds in North America because they are able to draw on their seed stores to feed the nestlings; nesting begins as early as February or March. This moderately colonial species builds a bulky nest in a piñon, tall juniper, ponderosa pine, or Gambel's oak; typically there will only be one nest per tree in a communal nesting area. Though both sexes build the nest, only the female incubates the eggs; cold temperatures force the female to provide nearly continuous incubation (a period of about seventeen days) to prevent cold damage. Female piñon jays are fed by the male throughout the incubation and early nestling development stages; until fledging occurs (after about six weeks), the young jays are fed communally as the families merge into nursery groups.

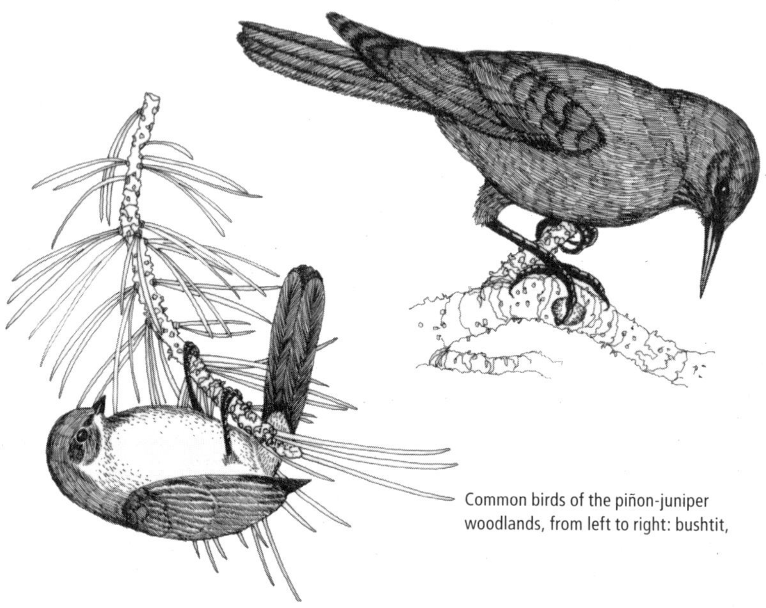

Common birds of the piñon-juniper woodlands, from left to right: bushtit,

Juniper Titmouse, *Baeolophus ridgwayi.* This small dull-gray bird is easily identified by its erect gray crest. In the Southern Rockies, the plain titmouse breeds, and occasionally winters, in the piñon-juniper woodlands and oak scrub of the central and southern mountains. The titmouse is insectivorous; when foraging, it mimics the twig-gleaning style of the chickadees and is often seen hanging upside down from branches. This nonsocial species rarely gathers in large flocks. Titmice roost in tree cavities. Mated pairs remain together for at least two years; males defend territories of several acres during the nesting season. The female selects a nest site in a tree cavity or old woodpecker hole, but the pair may also excavate their own cavity in the rotten portion of a living tree.

Bushtit, *Psaltriparus minimus*. One of the smallest birds, the bushtit can be recognized by its grayish brown plumage, long tail, rounded wings, and the absence of any crest; the Rocky Mountain race has brown patches on its cheeks, and the wings lack wing bars. In the Southern Rockies, bushtits are locally common in piñon-juniper woodlands, scrub oak, and mountain mahogany thickets from central Colorado southward. Like many species of "bush" birds, bushtits are highly acrobatic and insectivorous, twittering noisily while foraging. Bushtits tend to be sociable, forming small flocks of twenty or more individuals, except during the breeding season, when they remain alone or in pairs. In late April or early May, bushtits begin constructing their masterfully built, gourd-shaped nests, which they suspend from tree branches or a tall, sturdy shrub. Outside the breeding season, bushtits are often observed in mixed-species foraging flocks along with mountain chickadees and juniper titmice.

Blue-gray Gnatcatcher, *Polioptila caerulea*. This slender, bluish gray bird has a narrow bill, white eye ring, and a long, thin tail. The breeding range of the blue-gray gnatcatcher extends across the western United States and southward to Central America; in the Southern Rockies, blue-gray gnatcatchers are summer residents in piñon-juniper woodlands and scrub oak. They are often spotted foraging actively for insects in trees or in the brushy understory, making buzzy, insectlike vocalizations and conspicuously flicking or fanning the tail. Nesting occurs from April through May; the cuplike, lichen-covered nest is built on a horizontal branch or in the crotch of a tree and is often anchored to the branch with spider's silk. Both sexes incubate the eggs.

Reptiles and Amphibians

Collared Lizard, *Crotaphytus collaris*. This large, long-tailed lizard is identified by the twin black collars encircling the neck, the granular scales on the back, and the patterning of light dots on a darker background; during the breeding season, mature males are identified by their blue-green throat; the sides of breeding females are marked with orange spots or bars. In the Southern Rockies, the collared lizard is absent from Wyoming but occurs in Colorado and New Mexico, mainly from the Arkansas River south on the Eastern Slope and from the Roan Plateau south on the Western Slope.

Collared lizards are insectivorous and will sometimes capture other small lizards. This diurnal species emerges from hibernation in late March and April, remaining active throughout the summer; adults enter hibernation in early September, hatchlings in October. Males are highly territorial, threatening intruders with dramatic bobbing displays. Eggs are laid in June or July, with hatchlings first appearing in August.

Side-blotched Lizard, *Uta stansburiana.* This attractive lizard is identified by the numerous small light and dark dots that pattern the uniformly colored brownish topside; a dark blotch (sometimes blue-black in males) is found on either side of the chest, and the throat is bluish and edged with orange. Side-blotched lizards are active from April through October and are apt to begin their daily activities early in the morning, basking perpendicular to the sun's rays when they first emerge from their nighttime retreat. Male territorial displays include a series of push-ups with the back arched, the body compressed, and the throat lowered; low-amplitude vibrations are emitted at the summit of each push-up. Females may lay as many as three clutches of eggs, with the last clutch laid no later than July. Favorite foods include grasshoppers, beetles, leafhoppers, ants, termites, and insect larvae.

Common Animals of the Piñon-Juniper Woodlands

Mammals

Bat, pallid, *Antrozous pallidus*

Chipmunk, Colorado, *Tamias quadrivittatus*

  Hopi, *T. rufus*

  least, *T. minimus*

Cottontail, desert, *Sylvilagus audubonii*

  mountain (or Nuttall's), *S. nuttallii*

Coyote, *Canis latrans*

Deer, mule, *Odocoileus hemionus*

Fox, gray, *Urocyon cinereoargenteus*

Jackrabbit, black-tailed, *Lepus californicus*

Mountain Lion, *Felis concolor*

Mouse, brush, *Peromyscus boylii*

  deer, *P. maniculatus*

northern rock, *P. nasutus*
piñon, *P. truei*
Myotis, long-legged, *Myotis volans*
Porcupine, common, *Erethizon dorsatum*
Ringtail, *Bassariscus astutus*
Skunk, western spotted, *Spilogale gracilis*
Squirrel, rock, *Spermophilus variegatus*
Weasel, long-tailed, *Mustela frenata*
Woodrat, bushy-tailed, *Neotoma cinerea*
Mexican, *N. mexicana*

Birds

Bluebird, mountain, *Sialia currucoides*
western, *S. mexicana*
Bunting, lazuli, *Passerina amoena*
Bushtit, *Psaltriparus minimus*
Chickadee, mountain, *Parus gambeli*
Dove, mourning, *Zenaida macroura*
Eagle, golden, *Aquila chrysaetos*
Flicker, northern, *Colaptes auratus*
Flycatcher, ash-throated, *Myiarchus cinerascens*
gray, *Epidonax wrightii*
Gnatcatcher, blue-gray, *Polioptila caerulea*
Hawk, red-tailed, *Buteo jamaicensis*
Hummingbird, black-chinned, *Archilochus alexandri*
Jay, piñon, *Gymnorhinus cyanocephalus*
scrub, *Aphelocoma coerulescens*
Steller's, *Cyanocitta stelleri*
Nutcracker, Clark's, *Nucifraga columbiana*
Nuthatch, white-breasted, *Sitta carolinensis*
Phoebe, Say's, *Sayornis saya*
Raven, common, *Corvus corax*
Solitaire, Townsend's, *Myadestes townsendi*
Sparrow, chipping, *Spizella passerina*
Swift, white-throated, *Aeronautes saxatilis*

Titmouse, juniper, *Baeolophus ridgwayi*
Towhee, canyon, *Pipilo fuscus*
Warbler, black-throated gray, *Dendroica nigrescens*
orange-crowned, *Vermivora celata*
Virginia's, *V. virginiae*
Wren, canyon, *Catherpes mexicanus*
house, *Troglodytes aedon*
rock, *Salpinctes obsoletus*

Reptiles and Amphibians

Bullsnake, *Pituophis melanoleucus*
Lizard, collared, *Crotaphytus collaris*
plateau, *Sceloporus undulatus*
sagebrush, *S. graciosus*
side-blotched, *Uta stansburiana*
tree, *Urosaurus ornatus*
Rattlesnake, western, *Crotalus viridis*
Toad, Great Basin spadefoot, *Spea intermontana*
Treefrog, canyon, *Hyla arenicolor*
Whiptail, western, *Cnemidophorus tigris*
plateau striped, *C. velox*

Butterflies and Insects

Ant, honey, *Myrmecocystus mexicanus*
Beetle, piñon ips, *Ips confusus*
Cicada, *Platypedia putnami* and *Okanagana* spp.
Butterfly, juniper hairstreak, *Callophrys gryneus*
Great Basin wood nymph, *Cercyonis athenele*
Gall midge, piñon spindle, *Pinyonia edulicola*

CHAPTER SEVENTEEN

Music in the Pines: Ponderosa Pine Forests

Walking through a ponderosa pine forest is a sensual delight, the air redolent with the opiate essence of pine and the vanillalike aroma of the sun-warmed bark. The nineteenth-century naturalist John Muir once said, "Of all the pines, this one gives forth the finest music to the winds." Without doubt, ponderosa pine redefines the true meaning of "woodwind"—an ensemble of performers who weave their melodies from the soft whisper of pine needles. No other conifer in the Southern Rockies has needles as long—or as graceful. To walk in a sun-washed forest of old-growth ponderosa pine is to step back in time—to a place where the trees are of such generous proportions that you cannot encircle their trunks with your arms. Standing in a grove of these venerable pines, you are struck by the contrasts around you—the velvety black shadows that run between the trees, the burnt orange pillars of the trunks, and the sparkling, serpentine green of the needles. Muir also marveled at the "inviting openness" of ponderosa pine forests. Today, few ponderosa forests retain the parklike appearance and large, broad-crowned trees that figured so prominently in historic descriptions. These elegant old-growth forests are the progeny of recurrent and low-intensity fires—once a natural component of the ponderosa pine ecosystem throughout the West.

Ecological Distribution

The range of ponderosa pine essentially defines the American West. From Nebraska to California, and from southern British Columbia to northern Mexico, ponderosa pine is the dominant forest tree of the montane zone in western North America. Three chemically distinct races of ponderosa pine

have evolved as a result of the species' wide-ranging geographical distribution. The race present in the Southern Rockies is Rocky Mountain ponderosa pine (*Pinus ponderosa* var. *scopulorum*), a tree of less generous proportions than the so-called typical variety (*P. ponderosa* var. *ponderosa*) encountered in the Pacific Northwest or the race (*P. ponderosa* var. *arizonica*) found in Arizona and other parts of the Southwest.

In the Southern Rockies, ponderosa pine ecosystems occupy warm, dry slopes and gently rolling uplands from 5,600 to 9,000 feet on both sides of the Continental Divide. Along the Eastern Slope, forests dominated by ponderosa pine are common on south-facing slopes from the Wyoming border south to the southern end of the Sangre de Cristos, near Santa Fe. Near Colorado Springs, ponderosa pine can be found on scarps extending eastward into the shortgrass prairie; studies of these forest outliers attribute their presence to topography and to the unique water-holding capacity of soils developed on the Castle Rock Conglomerate.

North of the Wyoming border, ponderosa pine forests tend to be restricted to sheltered, low-elevation sites in the foothills. Though the species occurs sporadically on the Eastern Slope north of the Snowy Range, well-developed stands are largely confined to scarp woodlands located well east of the Rocky Mountains, such as in the Bighorn Mountains of northern Wyoming and in the Pine Ridge country and the Black Hills of South Dakota. The northward attenuation and eventual disappearance of both ponderosa pine and piñon-juniper woodlands along the Rocky Mountain front is thought to reflect the downward displacement of vegetational zones that occurs with increasing latitude.

On the Western Slope, ponderosa pine forests occupy a narrower elevational range and are not as extensive as those on the Eastern Slope. The species is largely absent from the western and northwestern mountains of Colorado, where Douglas-fir replaces it as the dominant conifer. South of this area, ponderosa pine forests are common from the Uncompahgre Plateau south to the Jemez Mountains of New Mexico. At higher elevations within this region, as well as in canyons and on north-facing slopes, mixed coniferous forests replace ponderosa pine forests. Below 7,500 feet, ponderosa pine forests are generally replaced by piñon-juniper woodlands throughout much of the southern portion of our range.

Physical Environment

Some might say that ponderosa pine forests strike the perfect balance when it comes to climate: not too hot, not too cold, not too wet, and not too dry. Ponderosa pine is best adapted to midelevation montane regions characterized by cold winters and warm summers with intense solar radiation and frequent short-term droughts. Summer temperatures rarely exceed 90°F; freezing temperatures can occur from mid-September until late May. The low temperatures typical of higher elevations in the Southern Rockies inhibit the growth of ponderosa pine, thereby determining its upper elevational limit. The average precipitation associated with this forest type varies from about sixteen inches in New Mexico and south-central Colorado to more than twenty-five inches in the Medicine Bow Mountains of Wyoming. A winter snowstorm seldom exceeds twelve inches in depth and typically melts within a few days.

Community Characteristics

Ponderosa pine forests may be of any size, from single-species stands that cover entire hillsides to small, single- or mixed-species stands. Along their lower altitudinal limits, ponderosa pine forests typically merge with piñon-juniper woodlands, grasslands, or various types of shrubland. Along their upper limits, these forests interfinger with Douglas-fir, Engelmann spruce–subalpine fir forests, or successional forests dominated by aspen or lodgepole pine. On ridges exposed to strong winds, ponderosa pine may occur with limber pine or bristlecone pine.

The character of a ponderosa pine forest reflects differences in elevation, degree of slope, exposure, soil, stand age, disturbance history, and the relative importance of associated species. South-facing slopes are generally dominated by open, variable-age stands of ponderosa pine or by mixed stands of ponderosa pine and Douglas-fir, with pine predominating on drier sites and Douglas-fir prevalent on the steepest slopes. Under the most moderate conditions, these stands are open and parklike, with numerous grassy clearings. Stands on north-facing slopes are dominated by Douglas-fir and have an almost closed canopy with a sparse understory of shrubs and herbaceous vegetation. Young stands of ponderosa pine, especially those on more mesic sites, can be very dense.

The amount of shrub and herbaceous understory is highly variable, depending on tree density and moisture availability. In the southern foothills, a well-developed shrub layer dominated by Gambel's oak or New Mexican locust may be locally common, especially in areas that have been cut over. Elsewhere, the shrub understory is typically sparse, consisting of species such as wax currant, kinnikinnik, common juniper, big sagebrush, mountain mahogany, and bitterbrush. On gentle slopes, grasses such as mountain muhly or timber oatgrass may form a luxuriant growth, particularly in areas where the soil is deep and fine textured.

Plant Adaptation: Designs for Survival

Coniferous trees—the gymnosperms, or "naked seed" trees—evolved from seed-ferns in the drier climates that prevailed during the late Paleozoic. For coniferous trees to evolve, survive, and compete successfully with herbaceous plants in these new habitats, however, they needed to have the structural strength to overtop their competitors. Today, the tallest trees on Earth are conifers: the sequoia and the California redwood. The evolution of woody tissue, a unique cellular fabric made up of interwoven cellulose fibrils bound by a chemical compound called lignin, made it possible for trees to finally exceed the six-foot ceiling that heretofore had kept most herbaceous plants tethered to the understory. Lignin is a complex linkage of three aromatic alcohols, coumaryl, coniferyl, and sinapyl, which fills in the spaces in the cell walls, often displacing water molecules and other nonstructural cell wall components. Woody tissues average about 65 percent cellulose and 35 percent lignin, with lignin serving much the same function as steel rebar does in cement. By binding the strong, light fibrils of cellulose, lignin adds structural stiffness to plant stems (trunks, branches, leaf stalks) and increases resistance to the pull of gravity. Furthermore, lignins allow plants to branch extensively, exposing many leaves or needles to sunlight, and to transport water and minerals (via the xylem) upward to great heights. The toughness of lignified tissues, especially in the inner bark, or cambium (the cylindrical layer of cells that adds girth to a tree or a shrub branch), also helps to deter herbivores and, in the event of injury, protects the wound site from further damage and speeds healing.

A tree's water and mineral transport tissue, the xylem, consists of highly lignified, spindle-shaped cells (called tracheids) arranged end on end like a series of perforated drinking straws. It is thought that evaporative losses in the tree's crown provide the driving mechanism that pulls water upward through the xylem to replenish the highest leaves or needles, effectively creating myriad, upward-flowing streams. On hot summer days, a large ponderosa pine may evaporate as much as 100 gallons a day. The photosynthetic products produced in the leaves, needles, and stems are transported downward to the roots and other tree tissues by another lignified system of conduits: the phloem. Impediments to the optimal functioning of a tree's "plumbing" system as well as a reduction in the numbers of leaves or needles available as sites for photosynthesis due to wind or other kinds of storm damage, insect infestations, excessive parasitism, and so forth can impact survival in a variety of ways. When a tunneling bark beetle punctures the xylem column, for example, air intrudes and the column will cease to lift water for the remainder of the tree's life. When infestations of bark beetles reach epidemic proportions, as they have periodically in many areas of the Southern Rockies, thousands of trees are killed.

The needles of ponderosa pine cope as well with the vagaries of mountain winters as they do with drought stress during spring, summer, or fall. In the piñon-juniper woodlands, we saw how a reduction in needle size and, in the extreme case of junipers, the evolution of tiny, scalelike leaves, helps to conserve water in an arid environment. Environmentally, ponderosa pine has a much easier time of it than most other conifers and can afford a slightly different design strategy to fine-tune its survival. The pine's extremely long needles substantially increase the amount of sunlight that can be captured for photosynthesis, which adds to the yearly carbon gain of the tree overall. As is true for other conifers, the openings for gas exchange (stomates) are sunken in pits on the underside of the heavily cutinized needle, greatly reducing moisture loss.

Competition for available moisture, nutrients, and sunlight is one of the major factors affecting the growth of ponderosa pine. Numerous studies have shown that wide spacing is essential for optimal growth in ponderosa pine. Mature pines have wide-spreading root systems consisting of deep taproots that can plumb water from depths of up to six feet in porous soils or up to forty feet in fractured bedrock; networks of lateral roots fan out through the surface soils for distances of up to 100 feet. Even a young seedling is quick to produce a long taproot. For example, a three-inch seedling may have a taproot two feet long, allowing it to gather moisture from below the rooting level of many herbaceous plants, conferring a competitive advantage.

The Mycorrhizal Connection

One does not usually associate mushrooms with sun-drenched ponderosa pine forests. Yet fungi are more prolific in these forests than you might imagine, and they are critical to the health and well-being of the pines. In mid-July, when the monsoon rains arrive to refresh the dry soils of the forest, the heady, resinous aroma of the pines is replaced by the earthy smell of mushrooms. Though only a few mushroom species in the ponderosa forest produce fruiting bodies that appear above ground, a rich mycoflora—the so-called false truffles (hypogeous basidomycetes)—is amazingly prolific beneath the soil surface. The "truffles" are potatolike fruiting bodies that mature and remain underground, thus the name *hypogeous*. When moisture conditions are suitable, these trufflelike fungi appear along a fibrous network of slender fungal strands called hyphae, which wind themselves around the roots of ponderosa pine. In fact, the hyphae and the roots of the pine are so interwoven that they are considered a single functional entity called a mycorrhiza (fungus-root). The rootlike mycorrhiza absorbs nutrients and water needed by both fungus and pine; in return, the mycorrhiza withdraws carbohydrates, a product of photosynthesis, which have been sequestered in the roots of the pine. Myccorhiza are the true masters of absorption, far more efficient than the pine's unassisted roots if left to their own devices. Mycorrhizal symbiosis is an obligate relationship for all conifers; that is, it is considered critical to the health and survival of both organisms.

Reproduction Challenges

Successful reproduction in ponderosa pines depends on an ample seed supply and sufficient moisture to ensure germination and early seedling survival. Ponderosa pine is intolerant of shade, and seedling success is poorest in forests with dense understory vegetation. Seeds germinate best on bare, moist mineral soils with unobstructed sunlight and little competition from other plants. In the Southern Rockies and throughout the Southwest, heavy seed production (an event that occurs at three- to five-year intervals) and higher-than-average moisture in spring and early summer provide optimal conditions for seedling establishment. This fortuitous pairing of events may happen only once every sixty years.

Fire and Ponderosa Pine

After centuries of wildfire, windstorms, and insect infestations, most old ponderosa pines have a story to tell. It is not uncommon to find a venerable old-timer with a lightning scar—a spiral stripe of charred wood or a distinctive triangular-shaped scar, called a cat-face—that extends for several feet up the trunk. Because pine forests occupy warmer, drier sites than those typical of the subalpine spruce-fir zone, wildfires occur with far greater frequency in the montane zone than they do elsewhere. Evidence from tree rings and historical sources suggest that low-intensity, lightning-initiated ground fires were a natural component of ponderosa pine ecosystems prior to settlement. Under a natural fire cycle, ground fires swept through the forests periodically, clearing away the litter of needles, thinning out dense stands of ponderosa seedlings, and enhancing the fertility of the soil. Most of the ponderosa pine forests that we see today, however, reflect human intervention, primarily fire suppression and logging.

Fire has clearly been a major force in shaping the character of pine forests throughout the West. The degree of thinning produced by low-intensity fires (fire ecologists call these fires "stand-maintaining") depends on the quantity of burnable fuel on the forest floor. The thick, fire-resistant bark of the ponderosa, functioning much like a suit of asbestos, helps to ensure that mature trees withstand all but the most severe fires. High-intensity, or "stand-replacing," fires typically occur at the height of summer or in early fall, when the forest is tinder dry and the humidity is low. During settlement, the expansion of logging activities throughout the West quickly removed most of the large, flameproof trees, and the forests began filling in with thick stands of young ponderosas. Since the early 1900s, the combination of wildfire prevention and selective logging has continued to allow ponderosa pine forests to regenerate at an alarming rate, increasing the competition for limited soil moisture and nutrients and setting the stage for high-intensity, destructive crown fires.

Forest Health

Overcrowded stands of ponderosa pine tend to be unhealthy and susceptible to diseases and insect infestations. Though the infamous mountain pine beetle (*Dendroctonus ponderosae*) has become a major predator of ponderosa pine throughout the West, evidence of the importance of the pine beetle as a selective force in the evolution of ponderosa pine can be traced to beetle galleries in petrified wood more than 225 million years old. During the past few years, thousands of acres of unhealthy ponderosa and lodgepole pine forests in the Southern Rockies have been devastated by infestations of mountain pine beetle. Today, despite the loss of trees to the beetle, it is important that we continue to view the pine beetle as an integral part of the ponderosa pine ecosystem, a natural thinning agent in overcrowded stands. Scientists suspect that though pine beetle epidemics are cyclical in nature, the outbreaks are triggered by an abundance of suitable host trees, weakened, unhealthy trees that cannot fend off the wood-boring beetles with chemical deterrents or by flushing the beetles from their tissues with pitch.

Descriptions of Common Plants

Trees

Ponderosa Pine, *Pinus ponderosa*. Ponderosa pine is the largest and most majestic conifer species in the Southern Rockies. In favorable locations, ponderosas may grow to be 150 feet in height and more than three feet in diameter. Ponderosa pine was named by the Scottish botanist David Douglas, who chose the species name *ponderosa* from the Latin word *Ponderosus*, which means heavy, weighty, significant—a suitable name for a tree of such grand proportions. The tree is readily identified by its long needles (up to seven inches in length), which are arranged in groups of two or three needles per bundle; a distinct white line made up of air pores, or stomata, runs the length of each needle. The bark of mature ponderosas is thick, orange-brown, and broken into large plates that give off a strong vanilla or butterscotch aroma when warmed by the sun; the bark of immature trees is brownish black, turning to yellow-brown or cinnamon with increasing age. The mahogany-colored cones are moderately large and globe shaped; the spine-tipped scales open at maturity to release dark brown, winged seeds. Ponderosa pines must be at least twenty-five years old before cone production can begin. Mature trees typically have rounded crowns; the more flattopped crowns of the oldest trees are conspicuous only in old-growth forests. The largest trees in a mature stand may be 300 to 500 years old. Younger ponderosas exhibit a more pyramidal crown and may be branched nearly to the ground.

Shrubs

Wax Currant, *Ribes cereum*. Wax currant is a common shrub of dry gulches, canyons, and hillsides from the lower foothills to the upper montane. Obtusely lobed leaves and pink, funnel-shaped flowers, which are among the first flowers to appear in the spring, distinguish this species. Broad-tailed hummingbirds visit the flowers as early as mid-April because they provide one of the few sources of nectar available to them when they arrive on their breeding territories each spring. Sticky hairs coat the surfaces of the translucent, orange-red berries. The fruits are eaten by birds (especially mountain bluebirds) and small mammals but have a rather insipid taste. Wax currants are often found growing beneath pines, where their seeds have been dispersed in the feces of fruit-eating birds.

Boulder Raspberry, *Oreobatus* (formerly *Rubus*) *deliciosus*. First collected by Edwin James (Long Expedition of 1820), boulder raspberry (also called Rocky Mountain thimbleberry in some guides) is a handsome shrub found on rocky slopes from the foothills to the montane zone. The species is especially common on the Eastern Slope; a smaller-flowered, smaller-leaved variety is found in Unaweep Canyon among granitic rocks. Identified by its bright green, more or less round-lobed leaves and its white, roselike flowers. Blooming in late May and June, the five-petaled flowers average about 1.5 inches in diameter and are followed by raspberrylike fruits that are bland and seedy but are relished by small mammals and birds.

Kinnikinnick, *Arctostaphylos uva-ursi*. First collected by Edwin James (Long Expedition of 1820), kinnikinnick is the most common evergreen

Common shrubs of the ponderosa pine forest, from top to bottom: waxflower, wax currant, boulder raspberry (with detail of flower), common gooseberry.

plant (outside the pines) found in the Southern Rockies. This trailing, woody species is a member of the heath family and is easily identified by its matlike growth form, the oval, bright green, and shiny leaves, its pink-and-white urn-shaped flowers, and the scarlet berries that appear each fall. The fruits and leaves are eaten by wildlife and were also used by indigenous groups, the fruits combined with dried meat and fat to make pemmican and the leaves smoked as a tobacco substitute.

Waxflower, *Jamesia americana.* Waxflower is a member of the hydrangea family and is encountered most frequently in rocky crevices or at the base of cliffs. This lovely shrub is easily identified by its ovate, opposite leaves, silky leaf undersides, peeling outer bark, and clusters of fragrant, cream-white flowers. *Jamesia,* named for Edwin James, botanist with the 1820 Long Expedition, is a unique genus of plants with an ancient lineage; fossils of a related species have been found in 35-million-year-old Oligocene-age deposits near Creede, Colorado.

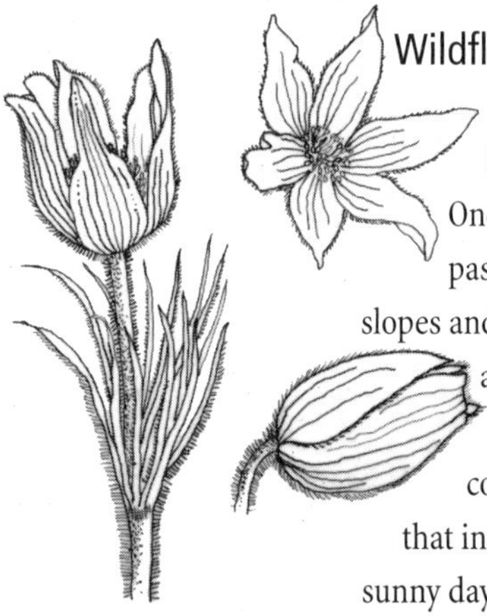

Wildflowers

Pasqueflower, *Pulsatilla patens.* One of the earliest flowers of spring, the pasqueflower is most abundant on open slopes and mesas, blooming first in the foothills and later in the higher mountains. Flower buds emerge in April and are conspicuous because of the woolly hairs that insulate the sepals; the buds open on sunny days to reveal crocuslike lavender flowers. In early summer, the pasqueflower is recognized by its ball of feathery-tailed seeds. A whorl of finely dissected leaves appears only after the blossoms fade.

Mountain Ball Cactus, *Pediocactus simpsonii.* Often overlooked, this small, pincushionlike cactus is found in grassy clearings in open pine forest from the foothills to the montane zone. In contrast to the flat pads of the prickly pear (*Opuntia* spp.), this species consists of a flattened ball two to six inches in diameter, its surface covered with spine-tipped tubercles. Pink, rose-scented flowers appear in spring and are clustered atop the cactus like a crown.

Sulphur Flower, *Eriogonum umbellatum*. This bright yellow flower, a member of the buckwheat family (Polygonaceae), is abundant on dry hillsides from the foothills to the subalpine. Sulphur flower is easily identified by its umbellate (umbrellalike) cluster of small, yellow flowers and by its simple, spatulate leaves; after blooming, the flowers persist and become papery and turn a dark apricot-rose.

One-sided Penstemon, *Penstemon secundiflorus*. This showy, robust wildflower is abundant on dry hillsides in the foothill and montane zones from late spring to early summer. One-sided penstemon is easily distinguished from other blue-flowered penstemons by its large size and by the arrangement of its blue-magenta flowers along one side of the flowering stalk; a sterile stamen, bearded with stiff, yellow hairs, is present and serves to brush the pollen from the abdomens of visiting bees.

Common wildflowers of the ponderosa pine forest, from left to right: sulpher flower, western wallflower, and one-sided penstemon.

Common Plants of the Ponderosa Pine Forest

Trees

Fir, Douglas, *Pseudotsuga menziesii*
Juniper, Rocky Mountain, *Sabina* (formerly *Juniperus*) *scopulorum*
Oak, Gambel's, *Quercus gambelii*
Pine, limber, *Pinus flexilis*
ponderosa, *P. ponderosa*

Shrubs

Bitterbrush, *Purshia tridentata*
Buckbrush (or New Jersey Tea), *Ceanothus fendleri*
Chokecherry, *Padus* (formerly *Prunus*) *virginiana* ssp. *melanocarpa*
Cinquefoil, shrubby, *Pentaphylloides floribunda*
Currant, wax, *Ribes cereum*
Holly Grape (or Oregon Grape), *Mahonia repens*
Juniper, common, *Juniperus communis* ssp. *alpina*
Kinnikinnik, *Arctostaphylos uva-ursi*
Mahogany, mountain, *Cercocarpus montanus*
Raspberry, boulder, *Oreobatus* (formerly *Rubus*) *deliciosus*
Sagebrush, big (or Great Basin sagebrush), *Seriphidium* (formerly *Artemisia*) *tridentatum*
Sage, silver (or Fringed Sage), *Artemisia frigida*
Waxflower, *Jamesia americana*

Grasses and Sedges

Dropseed, pine, *Blepharoneuron tricholepis*
Fescue, Arizona, *Festuca arizonica*
mountain, *F. saximontana*
spike, *Leucopoa kingii*
Grama, blue, *Bouteloua gracilis*
Junegrass, *Koeleria macrantha*
Muhly, mountain, *Muhlenbergia montana*
Oatgrass, Parry, *Danthonia parryi*
poverty, *D. spicata*

Sedge, aridland, *Carex xerantica*
sun, *C. pennsylvanica* ssp. *hellophila*

Wildflowers

Aster, *Aster laevis* and *A. foliaceous*
Blanketflower, *Gaillardia aristata*
Buckwheat, James, *Eriogonum jamesii*
Cactus, mountain ball, *Pediocactus simpsonii*
Candytuft, mountain, *Noccaea* (formerly *Thlaspi*) *montanum*
Chickweed, *Cerastium* spp.
Townsendia Daisy (or Easter Daisy), *Townsendia hookeri* and *T. exscapa*
Fleabane, trailing, *Erigeron flagellaris*
Geranium, wild, *Geranium caespitosum*
Groundsel, *Packera* (formerly *Senecio*) *neomexicana* and *P. fendleri*
Gumweed, curlycup, *Grindelia squarrosa*
Larkspur, Nuttall's, *Delphinium nuttallianum*
Lily, sand, *Leucocrinum montanum*
Miner's Candle, *Oreocarya* (formerly *Cryptantha*) *virgata*
Mistletoe, dwarf, *Arceuthobium vaginatum*
Parsley, whiskbroom, *Harbouria trachypleura*
Pasqueflower, *Pulsatilla patens*
Penstemon, one-sided, *Penstemon secundiflorus*
small-flowered, *Penstemon virens*
Pussytoes, *Antennaria rosea, A. parvifolia,* and *A. microphylla*
Spring Beauty, western, *Claytonia lanceolata* and *C. rosea*
Sulphur Flower, *Eriogonum umbellatum*
Sunflower, little, *Helianthella parryi*
Wallflower, western, *Erysimum capitatum*
Yarrow, *Achillea lanulosa*

Environment and Adaptation: Animals of the Ponderosa Pine Forest

From left to right: least chipmunk, golden-mantled ground squirrel.

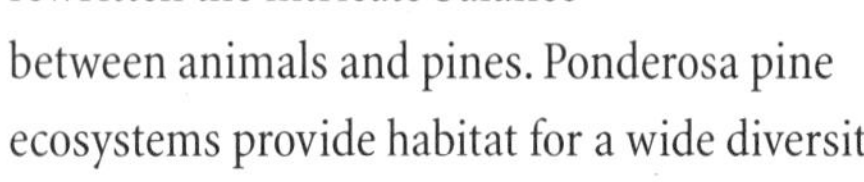

Paleontologists discovered the first known record of ponderosa pine in west-central Nevada, a fossil dated at around 600,000 years. In all the intervening years, ponderosa pine ecosystems have evolved and rewritten the intricate balance between animals and pines. Ponderosa pine ecosystems provide habitat for a wide diversity of forest animals; at least 57 mammals and 128 bird species occur in these forests. More than 200 species of insects are known to prey on ponderosa pine. The life histories and distribution patterns of several animal species, including Abert's squirrel, pygmy nuthatch, red crossbill, flammulated owl, and mountain pine beetle, are closely interwoven with that of ponderosa pine. Clearly these are relationships built of reciprocity, a coevolved system in which ponderosa pine has flourished for thousands of years.

Most of the ancient, elegant ponderosa pine forests are gone. Those that remain, whatever the size, are precious fragments, habitat islands in a race against time and reason. But even the most fragmented second-growth stands remain important to wildlife whose needs vary with the seasons. Mature and old-growth forests, typified by well-developed shrub and herbaceous understories, are favored by mule deer and elk as winter range. Porcupines can be found in these open woodlands throughout the year, eating herbaceous vegetation on the forest floor during spring and summer and savoring the nutrient-rich inner bark of the ponderosa in other seasons. Grassy clearings and rocky, shrub-covered hillsides amidst the pines provide optimal habitat for chipmunks, golden-mantled ground squirrels, Nuttall's cottontails, and deer mice. Bats will roost behind large plates of loosened bark.

Birds are an important and conspicuous component of ponderosa pine ecosystems throughout the Southern Rockies. The changing cast of characters includes year-round residents, such as pygmy nuthatches, chickadees, juncos, hairy woodpeckers, and Steller's jays, as well as breeding season arrivals, such as Williamson's sapsuckers, mountain bluebirds, western tanagers, pine siskins, and flammulated owls, that are attracted by the abundance of nesting sites and the diversity of food resources. Strong year-to-year fluctuations in the populations of species that depend on conifer seeds for food, such as the red crossbill, reflect the cyclical nature of the cone crop.

Niche Relationships in Old-Growth Pine Forests

Old-growth forests (forests that are older than 200 years) have unique qualities. The complex relationships that bind certain animal species to these old-growth habitats are just beginning to be understood. The presence or absence of certain animal species can tell us much about the disturbance history and structural complexity of a ponderosa pine forest. Old-growth forests exhibit the highest species diversity, largely because these forests tend to be open and have well-developed understories. Stands with trees of various ages are preferred to those in which a single age class predominates. For example, Abert's squirrel and the flammulated owl show a strong preference for old-growth, multiple-storied forests. With so many species dependent on the same food resources (conifer seeds and insects) specializations have evolved that limit interspecific competition. Significant differences in size and foraging behavior enable species to use slightly different resources and thus avoid intense competition. For example, the red-breasted nuthatch forages in the top one-third of a tree, effectively segregated from the white-breasted nuthatch, which forages mainly on the trunk and largest branches of the lower two-thirds of the tree, and from the pygmy nuthatch, which forages among the pine needles and smaller branches.

Unfortunately, the history of ponderosa pine forests throughout the West has been one of heavy use due to their high commercial value and year-round accessibility. In recent years, increases in logging activity and the proliferation of mountain home developments have resulted in the continued loss of habitat for species dependent on old growth, a situation that may eventually cause the disappearance of these species. The most obvious impacts are to cavity-nesting birds such as flammulated owls, flickers, woodpeckers, tree swallows, chickadees, nuthatches, house wrens, and mountain bluebirds, because of their vulnerability to forest management practices such as logging and fuel-wood cutting, which eliminate snags. Outside the breeding season, large cavities provide critical thermal cover and are often used as communal roosts by small birds such as pygmy nuthatches and brown creepers. One Colorado study reported more than fifty pygmy nuthatches sharing a single large cavity in a ponderosa pine. Woodpeckers—either the hairy or the downy woodpecker—are the primary cavity excavators; each nesting season, the smaller species, the so-called secondary cavity nesters, take over the holes abandoned by the woodpeckers. Cavity-nesting birds cannot establish themselves, however, in stands that lack snags of sufficient size.

Flammulated Owls

In the black velvet darkness of a June evening, the call of a flammulated owl, a low, soft-hooted *poot* or *pooip*, breaks the stillness just before the moon rises. More often heard than seen and small enough to fit in the palm of your hand, the flammulated owl may be the most abundant but also the most secretive raptor in old-growth ponderosa pine and Douglas-fir forests. Mature forests tend to have an abundance of snags and live trees with cavities, a necessity for this obligate cavity nester. In Colorado, radiotelemetry studies of this nocturnal, insectivorous owl have shown that it prefers to forage in these forests as opposed to any other forest type. In most cases, the home ranges of nesting flammulated owls include high proportions of old-growth pine forest. In fact, extensive stands of old growth support higher densities of nesting owls than are found in patchy habitat that includes small, disjunct stands of old growth. Furthermore, home ranges in continuous old-growth stands are more consistently reoccupied by owls returning in the spring than are ranges located in a mosaic of different forest types.

A fledgling flammulated owl "rests" after being banded by researchers.

The flammulated owl's affinity for old-growth ponderosa pine forests appears to be closely related to the owl's preferred diet, the structure of the forest, and the character of the individual trees where foraging activities occur. There are up to four times as many insect species in old-growth ponderosa pine and Douglas-fir forests than in other coniferous forest types. In fact, many of these insect species are host-plant specific and are therefore found only in association with ponderosa pine and Douglas-fir. The favored foraging techniques of the flammulated owl require open tree crowns where gleaning can occur while the bird hovers, or spaces between trees where the owl can "hawk" insects in the air. Research conducted over the past twenty-five years at Manitou Experimental Forest suggests that the future of flammulated owls depends on our ability to preserve sufficient acreages of old-growth ponderosa, as well as the key components of the habitat (such as nest cavities and foraging sites) that have proven to be critical to their survival.

Abert's squirrel.

Abert's Squirrels

In a fluid wave of motion, the most distinctive mammal of the ponderosa pine forest, the Abert's squirrel, leaps from branch to branch, leaving in its wake an image that seems all ears: two-inch-long exclamation points framing a face full of surprise. This magnificently silky, tassel-eared squirrel is found only sporadically in the Southern Rockies, in parts of the Colorado Plateau (the Chuskas, the La Sals, the Abajos, and the Santa Catalinas), on the Mogollon Rim and the Kaibab Plateau, and in the Sierra Madre in central Mexico. These widely disjunct islands of habitat have given rise to nine distinct subspecies, the West's version of Darwin's Galapagos finches. As you would imagine, there is tremendous variation in fur color among the subspecies, everything from the pale silver of the Kaibab squirrel to the inky blacks, henna-tinted browns, and steely grays of the Abert's in our region. Though fur color hints at genetic differences between the subspecies, the subtlest cues come from what these squirrels eat: the sweet, terpene-rich cambium (inner bark) of the ponderosa pine. The cambium in each isolated patch of pine forest presents a slightly different suite of terpenes (resinous chemicals in the tree sap). Abert's squirrels have evolved a taste—as discriminating as that of a wine sommelier—for the terpene cocktail produced by the population of ponderosa pines in their "home" habitat, and they reject the terpene recipe associated with other ponderosa stands as unpalatable. Recent studies of Abert's squirrels in the Colorado Front Range support this idea, suggesting that the squirrel's choice of trees in which to feed corresponds to the differential concentration of certain aromatic monoterpenes in the tree's resinous fluids.

Despite these differences, all subspecies of tassel-earred squirrels depend on mature forests of ponderosa pine for food, cover, and nesting habitat. Unlike most other tree squirrels, Abert's squirrels do not cache food. Beginning in late spring, the squirrels gorge on the ponderosa's male pollen-producing cones; from early summer until autumn, the squirrels shift their attention to the ripening crop of pine seeds. A single Abert's squirrel may consume the seeds from about seventy-five cones in the span of a day. During the winter and spring months, the succulent cambium of ponderosa pine twigs is consumed; heavily utilized trees are recognized by their cambium-stripped branches and by the piles of cone "cobs," needles, and peeled twigs at their bases.

During midsummer, the food item most relished by tassel-earred squirrels comes in a small, round, and fragrant package: a false truffle. Watching an Abert's squirrel as it zigzags across the forest floor is to watch a true connoisseur, a highly skilled truffle hunter at work. Stopping abruptly, going by scent, the squirrel begins digging in the soil, extracting and consuming its fungal prize on the spot before continuing the search. Because airborne spore dispersal is impossible in the world of hypogeous fungi, the so-called false truffles, just like their gourmet counterparts, the true truffles found in southern Europe, rely on fungi-loving small mammals for dispersal of their spores. The spores are passed still viable through the animals gut and then are spread far and wide in the squirrel's feces, ensuring the continued presence of this beneficial mycorrhizal symbiont in the ponderosa pine ecosystem.

Mountain Pine Beetle

No other insects inflict as much damage to conifers as the tiny bark beetle, which includes about eighty species in the Southern Rockies, each adapted to its coniferous host in myriad ways. Like the Abert's squirrel, the mountain pine beetle's (*Dendroctonus ponderosae*) survival and reproductive success depend on the nutrient-rich tissues of ponderosa pine. In recent years, environmental conditions appear to be tipping the balance in the pine beetle's favor. Let's look at the life history of the pine beetle—the intricate dance between beetle and pine—to better understand how this might occur.

The mountain pine beetle completes its entire one-year life cycle, except for a brief summer flight period following emergence, beneath a thick layer of pine bark. The ponderosa's bark, which is sometimes several inches thick in the oldest trees, provides the beetle with protection from cold winter temperatures, and the nutritious cambium provides a food source. Pine beetles mate in midsummer, following emergence, and eggs are laid (about seventy-five per female) in vertical galleries excavated beneath the bark by the parent beetles. Following egg hatch, the tunnels of the grublike larvae splay outward from their natal gallery, producing a distinctive mazelike pattern in the cambium as a result of their feeding activities. Survival of the beetle brood depends on lower-than-normal moisture content within the tree, which restricts the pine's ability to effectively "pitch-out" the invaders.

Maintaining an optimal environment for the developing larvae requires an unusual collaboration, or mutualistic relationship, between the adult beetle and species of *Ceratocysis* and *Trichosporum*, known collectively as the "blue-stain fungi." A close look at the head of the adult beetle reveals tiny openings—mycangial pits, or mycangia—that are filled with the spores of these fungi. In the course of tunnel excavation, the spores are spilled into the resin canals of the pine's sapwood. Before long, the sapwood becomes clogged with tangled strands of fungal hyphae, and the sap will cease to flow. Upon hatching, the hungry larvae are nourished by the fungal gardens that prosper within the nursery galleries until cold weather induces inactivity in the fall.

With the coming of spring, the pine beetle larvae resume feeding on the nutrient-rich tissues of the tree, undergoing a transformation from pupa to adult by early summer. The new adults begin to emerge as early as mid-July, but the majority emerge during the first two weeks of August. Prior to emergence, the beetle's mycangial pits will be replete with fresh new spores to be introduced into the pines that they will later attack. Following emergence, female beetles pioneer the assault on new host trees, followed by large numbers of males, and the cycle begins once again.

Evidence of a successful pine beetle infestation includes popcornlike masses of resin on the trunk, boring dust in bark crevices and around the tree's base, blue-stained sapwood, and browning of the tree's needles. Ponderosa pines that have been attacked by large numbers of pine beetles die almost immediately from the combined effects of the beetle's excavations and the physiological drought induced by the blue fungus.

Recent studies have shown that ponderosa pine, like most conifers, is not a passive recipient of the pine beetle's attack and has an arsenal of chemical compounds that serve as natural insecticides; these resins, consisting mostly of terpenes, are responsible for the ponderosa's aromatic bouquet. Trees that are successful in fending off a pine beetle attack do so by "pitching-out" the beetles as they burrow through the bark and into the cambium or by killing the beetles outright with their terpene-rich sap before they can become established. Tree tissues possessing high levels of the monoterpene limonene have been shown to be toxic or inhibitory to the pine beetle, effectively reducing the reproductive success of the beetle as well as the viability of its fungal symbiont. Studies indicate that trees that survive predation by pine beetles tend to have high concentrations of limonene, suggesting that predation by a specialist herbivore such as the mountain pine beetle would eventually result in directional selection for limonene in a ponderosa pine community.

Mountain pine beetles, on the other hand, have evolved adaptations that counter the pine's defenses and turn its chemical arsenal to their own advantage. In this case, the pine beetles utilize monoterpenes present to varying degrees in the tree's resinous fluids in both the selection and the colonization of host trees. For example, the female beetle requires high concentrations of the monoterpene myrcene in order to synthesize the chemical signal, the aggregating pheromone, which will encourage male beetles to follow her to an appropriate host tree. When beetle populations are excessively high, the female beetle may synthesize compounds from the monoterpene alpha-pinene to mask the attractiveness of her aggregating pheromone and redirect male beetles to adjacent host trees, a phenomenon that results in the clustering of infested trees in a ponderosa stand.

Life Histories of Selected Animals

Mammals

Abert's (or Tassel-eared) Squirrel, *Sciurus aberti.* This large, heavy-bodied squirrel is distinguished by its prominent ear tufts and its long, full tall; at least four color phases are reported for the Southern Rockies: salt-and-pepper, gray with a white belly, pure black, and dark brown. Abert's squirrels (*S. aberti ferreus*) are found in ponderosa pine habitat along the Eastern Slope from the Sangre de Cristos and Wet Mountain north along the Colorado Front Range to southern Laramie County, Wyoming. The subspecies (*S. aberti mimus*), found in the San Juan Mountains of southwestern Colorado and the Jemez Mountains of New Mexico, is slightly smaller than the one found in the northern and central mountains. Strictly diurnal, this squirrel remains active throughout the year. Abert's squirrels do not defend territories but maintain home ranges (often overlapping) averaging about twenty acres in size. Largely solitary, the species forms loose social hierarchies only during the mating season, when males compete for the opportunity to mate with an estrous female. Breeding occurs from late March to May, and one litter of altricial young is born annually. The ball-shaped nest is constructed of pine twigs with a lining of softer materials and is built in the crotch of a branch.

Golden-mantled Ground Squirrel, *Spermophilus lateralis.* Commonly mistaken for a large chipmunk, the golden-mantled ground squirrel can be distinguished from the latter by its shorter tail, dorsal stripes that run only from hip to shoulder, and the conspicuous absence of stripes on the head. This ground squirrel inhabits a broad elevational range and is most common in open forests and forest-edge communities. Though a brazen beggar in tourist areas, the golden-mantle normally prefers plant material: stems, leaves, flowers, seeds, and fruits; when available, fungi, insects, eggs, nestling birds, and carrion also provide nourishment. Diurnal and asocial, golden-mantles establish and maintain a dominance hierarchy with chases, fights, scent marking, teeth chattering, and other threat displays. These animals enter hibernation in late September or October, their torpidity facilitated by large reserves of body fat; they rouse from hibernation every few weeks to feed on cached food. Breeding occurs shortly after emergence in spring, producing a single litter of altricial young.

Least Chipmunk, *Tamias minimus*. This beautiful small mammal is distinguished from the golden-mantled ground squirrel by its smaller size, the presence of sharply defined head stripes, and its rapid, darting movements. Least chipmunks are found from the foothill forests and shrublands to the alpine tundra on both sides of the Continental Divide; the species is largely restricted to higher elevations in the San Juan and Jemez mountains and in the Sangre de Cristos, where the species' distribution overlaps with that of the Colorado chipmunk (*T. quadrivittatus*). The chipmunk's diet consists of seeds from conifers and herbaceous plants (especially those from the sunflower family), as well as fruit, insects, and carrion; food is cached for winter use. Least chipmunks are diurnal, with a peak of activity in the morning, and often forage in trees or shrubs. The species appears to be more social than golden-mantled ground squirrels; vocalizations and various tail displays are used to maintain social organization. Home ranges overlap broadly and vary in size from one to several acres. Least chipmunks enter torpor in October or November, retreating to a nest chamber within the burrow; chipmunks may rouse occasionally to feed on stored food or venture above ground during warm periods. Breeding occurs shortly after emergence, with a litter of altricial young born in early July.

Birds

Flammulated Owl, *Otus flammeolus*. This small, secretive, and strictly nocturnal owl breeds in western mountain forests, especially ponderosa pine, where it may be rare to locally common depending on the quality of the habitat. The flammulated owl is identified by its small size (six to seven inches in length), dark eyes (it's the only small owl with dark eyes), reddish (flamelike) facial disk, and short tail. Its diet consists of night-flying insects, especially moths, which it takes on the wing. Daytime roosts are well hidden by branches and are typically situated close to the trunk of a dense conifer. The flammulated owl is most easily located at night from May until July, when males sing on their territories. This species is an obligate cavity nester, selecting abandoned flicker or woodpecker cavities in a pine or an aspen adjacent to its foraging areas. Flammulated owls are a migratory species in the Southern Rockies, wintering from Mexico southward.

Williamson's Sapsucker, *Sphyrapicus thyroideus*. The male Williamson's sapsucker is dramatically colored, with a black back, white wing and rump patches, red throat, and yellow belly; the female is more cryptically colored, with a brown head and a brown-and-white barred body. A shy, somewhat secretive bird, the Williamson's drills rows of tiny holes in the bark of pine, fir, aspen, and other trees, from which it drinks sap and also eats the insects that become trapped in the sap; this species also eats ants, spruce budworm moths, and other insects when available. Males arrive on the breeding grounds by early May, establishing their territories by drumming and with threat displays. Both sexes excavate the nest cavity, and egg laying occurs shortly thereafter. Both sexes incubate the eggs, uttering a harsh *churring* call throughout the nesting period; the male sleeps with the eggs and the young.

Steller's Jay, *Cyanocitta stelleri*. The Steller's jay is identified by its dark blue body, black crest, and the conspicuous white flecking over the eye. The species is common in coniferous forests throughout western North America. Steller's jays are often bold near human habitation but may be difficult to approach in forest situations. Though somewhat less gregarious than other species, Steller's jays have an amazing repertoire of songs and calls, ranging from soft whisper songs and rolling click calls to more raucous, even hawklike, squawks and calls. These jays are omnivores, foraging on the ground and in trees for insects, seeds, acorns, and other plant foods; they also occasionally take carrion, snakes, and the eggs and young of other birds. Steller's jays build a bulky nest of twigs cemented together with mud, typically situated in a conifer.

Pygmy Nuthatch, *Sitta pygmaea.* The pygmy nuthatch occurs most frequently in open forests of ponderosa pine. This species is easily distinguished from other nuthatches by its gray-brown cap, blue-gray back, and buff underparts. Gregarious except during the nesting season, pygmy nuthatches travel in large, occasionally mixed-species flocks. Their call is a high, rapid *peep-peep.* Pygmy nuthatches are insectivorous and forage actively through the tops of pines, searching the needles, cones, and twigs for insects. During the breeding season, pairs of nuthatches excavate their own cavity nest or utilize an existing one; the young are born in June and leave the nest about twenty-two days after hatching. Pygmy nuthatches roost communally in large tree cavities during the fall and winter.

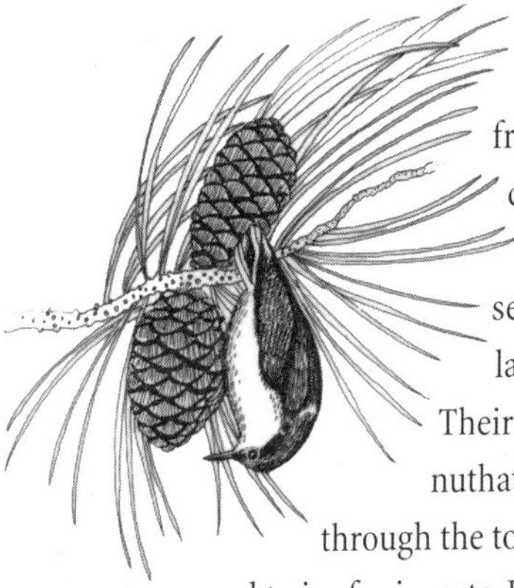

Western Tanager, *Piranga ludoviciana.* This unmistakable, brilliantly colored tanager is a common summer inhabitant of coniferous forests throughout western North America. The male has a red head and face and a yellow-and-black body; the female has grayish upperparts and a yellowish green breast. Upon arriving in the spring, the male perches for a long period in one spot while delivering its robinlike song. Western tanagers are insectivorous, gleaning insects from the branches and foliage and occasionally taking insects on the wing. The nest, built by the female on the outer branches of a pine, consists of a loose cup of plant materials.

Evening Grosbeak, *Coccothraustes vespertina.* This conspicuous grosbeak is identified by its conical bill, black tail and wings, and yellow body. Gregarious even during the nesting season, small flocks are often observed foraging for seeds, buds, small fruits, and insects; flocks roost in coniferous trees and are common visitors to bird feeders. Evening grosbeaks are fond of and can often be seen eating salty soil in areas where salt is spread on roads to melt ice. These grosbeaks frequently drink and bathe, eating snow and seeking ice-free stretches of streams during the winter months. During courtship, the male feeds the female and dances before her; both sexes sing during the nesting season. The nest is built by the female in a conifer tree, usually near the end of a branch.

Pine Siskin, *Carduelis pinus.* The breeding range of the pine siskin embraces the coniferous forests of North America. This species is easily identified by its small size, prominent streaking, diagnostic yellow patches at the base of the tail and flight feathers, and forked tail; undulating flight style and the light, twittery flight notes may help in long-distance identification. Unpredictably nomadic, flocks of these birds will appear one day and be gone the next. Pine siskins are gregarious throughout the year; nesting may occur in loose colonies, and breeding siskins may forage in small groups. During the winter months, siskins frequent open fields and may forage with goldfinches and red crossbills in mixed-species flocks. The diet of this species consists largely of seeds, especially conifer seeds, with buds and insects taken when available. Nesting occurs in high evergreens; nestlings are fed regurgitated masses of small seeds by the adults.

Common Animals of the Ponderosa Pine Forest

Mammals

Chipmunk, Colorado, *Tamias quadrivittatus*
    least, *T. minimus*
Cottontail, mountain (or Nuttall's), *Sylvilagus nuttallii*
Coyote, *Canis latrans*
Deer, mule, *Odocoileus hemionus*
Elk (or Wapiti), *Cervus elaphus*
Ermine (or Short-tailed Weasel), *Mustela erminea*
Marmot, yellow-bellied, *Marmota flaviventris*
Mountain Lion, *Felis concolor*
Mouse, deer, *Peromyscus maniculatus*
Myotis, little brown, *Myotis lucifugus*
    long-eared, *M. evotis*

Pocket Gopher, northern, *Thomomys talpoides*
Porcupine, *Erethizon dorsatum*
Shrew, dwarf, *Sorex nanus*
Squirrel, Abert's, *Sciurus aberti*
  golden-mantled ground, *Spermophilus lateralis*
Vole, montane, *Microtus montanus*
Weasel, long-tailed, *Mustela frenata*
Woodrat, bushy-tailed, *Neotoma cinerea*
  Mexican, *N. mexicana*

Abert's squirrel.

Birds

Bluebird, mountain, *Sialia currucoides*
  western, *S. mexicana*
Chickadee, mountain, *Parus gambeli*
Creeper, brown, *Certhia americana*
Crossbill, red, *Loxia curvirostra*
Dove, mourning, *Zenaida macroura*
Finch, Cassin's, *Carpodacus cassinii*
Flicker, northern, *Colaptes auratus*
Flycatcher, Pacific slope, *Empidonax difficilis*
Grosbeak, black-headed, *Pheucticus melanocephalus*
  evening, *Coccothraustes vespertina*
Hawk, red-tailed, *Buteo jamaicensis*
  sharp-shinned, *Accipiter striatus*
Hummingbird, broad-tailed, *Selasphorus platycercus*
Jay, Steller's, *Cyanocitta stelleri*
Junco, dark-eyed, *Junco hyemalis*
Magpie, black-billed, *Pica hudsonia*
Nighthawk, common, *Chordeiles minor*
Nutcracker, Clark's, *Nucifraga columbiana*
Nuthatch, pygmy, *Sitta pygmaea*
  red-breasted, *S. canadensis*
  white-breasted, *S. carolinensis*
Owl, flammulated, *Otus flammeolus*
  great horned, *Bubo virginianus*

northern pygmy, *Glaucidium gnoma*
northern saw-whet, *Aegolius acadicus*
Raven, common, *Corvus corax*
Robin, American, *Turdus migratorius*
Sapsucker, Williamson's, *Sphyrapicus thyroideus*
Siskin, pine, *Carduelis pinus*
Solitaire, Townsend's, *Myadestes townsendi*
Sparrow, chipping, *Spizella passerina*
Swallow, tree, *Tachycineta bicolor*
violet-green, *T. thalassina*
Tanager, western, *Piranga ludoviciana*
Vireo, plumbeous, *Vireo plumbeus*
Warbler, Grace's, *Dendroica graciae*
yellow-rumped, *D. coronata*
Woodpecker, downy, *Picoides pubescens*
hairy, *P. villosus*
Wood-pewee, western, *Contopus sordidulus*
Wren, house, *Troglodytes aedon*

Reptiles

Lizard, prairie and plateau, *Sceloporus undulatus*
Milk Snake, *Lampropeltis triangulum*
Skink, variable, *Eumeces gaigeae*

Butterflies and Insects

Beetle, ips, *Ips calligraphus, I. knausi, I. integer*
Beetle, mountain pine, *Dendroctonus ponderosae*
pine sawyer, *Monochamus* spp.
Butterfly, chryxus arctic, *Oeneis chryxus*
southern Rocky Mountain orangetip, *Anthocaris julia*
Elfin, western pine, *Callophrys eryphon*
white, pine, *Neophasia menapia*

CHAPTER EIGHTEEN

The Raven's Forest: Douglas-fir Forests

Douglas-fir branch and cone.

Douglas-fir forests provide a striking contrast visually and ecologically to the open pine forests that share their montane habitat. A tree of remarkable beauty, the Douglas-fir is one of the most widely distributed conifers in western North America. The species is found from British Columbia south to central Mexico, but does not occur east of the Rockies. Douglas-fir is divided into two major subspecies: Pacific coast Douglas-fir, which occurs along the Pacific coast, and the Rocky Mountain Douglas-fir, which is confined to the interior west of the continent. In the forests of the Pacific Northwest, Douglas-fir is surpassed in size and grandeur only by the coast redwood. In the Southern Rockies, however, forests of Douglas-fir bear only a fleeting resemblance to those mist-shrouded coastal forests. Rocky Mountain Douglas-fir's more modest stature reflects the climatic challenges it faces in the western interior: a shorter growing season, colder temperatures, and greater aridity.

Native American stories featuring plants and animals are common, especially those that teach children important values and life skills. Teaching stories have been used by generations of elders from every culture on Earth to inform all those who follow. One of the most intriguing stories tells how the Douglas-fir's cone got the three-pronged bracts that distinguish it from that of any other conifer. The story is a simple one, and a perfect choice for teaching children to identify the common trees of the Southern Rockies. What follows is just one of many variations.

When the world was very young, a beautiful tree began to grow in the forest. With every day that passed, the tree grew taller and taller. From its lofty place, the tree could look down on all the life of the forest, both the very small and the very large. It could see how difficult life was for the smallest animals: the mice, the rabbits, and the squirrels. The tree watched hawks and owls swoop through the forest every day, hunting the small animals and making them run for cover. Each day, the hawks and owls got better and better at hunting. This made the tree sad because it liked all the animals of the forest, even the hawks and the owls. One day, the tree watched a tiny mouse run from a hawk until it had run out of places to hide. The tree could see the mouse cowering amidst the cones that lay on the forest floor, bravely awaiting its fate. "Quick," said the tree, "make yourself as small as you can so that you can hide between the scales of one of my cones." The mouse did as it was told, squeezing its body under one of the cone's woody scales, with its tiny hind legs and tail just peeking out from beneath the scale. Frustrated, the hawk flew off and the mouse was safe, its life spared by the kindness of its tall friend. To this day, Douglas-fir cones have an unmistakable three-pointed bract between each cone scale, one that looks just like a little mouse in hiding and reminds us that we must always look out for others.

What's in a Name?

The strange odyssey involved in the naming of the Douglas-fir is one of the most interesting stories in North American botanical exploration. For more than a hundred years, botanists debated the taxonomic lineage of the Douglas-fir. Scientifically speaking, the species is a square peg in a round hole; it's not really a true fir or a spruce or a pine or a hemlock, which ultimately explains the hyphenation of its common name. The tree's scientific name, *Pseudotsuga menziesii*, doesn't help much either: *Pseudotsuga* means "false hemlock" and *menziesii* honors the tree's discoverer, Archibald Menzies. In 1792, Menzies, the Scottish botanist assigned to the Vancouver Expedition, collected the first specimens of this unusual tree.

Unfortunately, Menzies' botanical collections received little attention in the scientific community, quite probably because of the rancor that existed between Menzies and George Vancouver, the irascible captain of the HMS *Discovery*. In 1806, nearly fifteen years after Menzies' initial discovery, Meriwether Lewis collected specimens of the firlike conifer and described it in his expedition journal. Not surprisingly, the collections made during the Lewis and Clark Expedition captured the interest of many of the nineteenth century's leading botanists, on both sides of the Atlantic.

David Douglas, a young Scottish plant collector in the employ of the Royal Horticultural Society of London, was one of the most famous, certainly the most prodigious and ill-fated, botanical explorers of his day. Traveling to Philadelphia in 1823 to examine the collections brought back by Lewis and Clark, Douglas was immediately intrigued by Lewis's discovery. Returning first to Scotland to talk with an ailing Archibald Menzies, Douglas then enlisted the support of the Hudson's Bay Company in his quest to rediscover Menzies' tree. In 1825, after spending nearly a year aboard ship, Douglas collected a small specimen of the mystery tree near Fort Vancouver on the Columbia River, giving it the name Oregon pine. The Scottish-American naturalist John Muir added to the botanical confusion by calling it Douglas spruce, even though many of his contemporaries thought it to be a type of hemlock. In 1867, new discoveries in China and Japan resulted in a compromise, and the name *Pseudotsuga douglasii* was proposed by a French botanist. Nathaniel Britton, the founder of the New York Botanical Garden, entered the botanical debate at this point, overruling the French designation and giving it the name *Pseudotsuga taxifolia* because of its yewlike qualities. In scientific nomenclature, however, most names honor the original discoverer in some way. A final appeal from yet another botanist gave Douglas-fir the scientific name we know it by today because, quite simply, Archibald Menzies got there first. The common name honors David Douglas, who "rediscovered" the tree for science.

Ecological Distribution

In the Southern Rockies, Douglas-fir forests can be found from about 6,000 to 9,500 feet on both sides of the Continental Divide. At lower elevations, stands of Douglas-fir are largely confined to sheltered north-facing slopes and cool ravines, whereas in the upper montane zone, Douglas-fir may be found on all slope aspects, often in association with ponderosa pine. Along the Western Slope, in western and northwestern Colorado, Douglas-fir replaces ponderosa pine as the dominant montane coniferous species.

Physical Environment

Douglas-fir forests are adapted to cool, moist conditions. Due to the inclination of the sun, a north-facing slope in northern temperate latitudes receives less total insolation than a south-facing slope in the same region. Consequently, air and soil temperatures are cooler, the relative humidity is greater, and more moisture is available for plant life. In addition, the frost-free season is shorter and snow lingers longer than on south-facing slopes. The upper elevational limit of Douglas-fir, as is true for ponderosa pine, is determined by low summer temperatures; the lower limit depends on soil factors, especially moisture. In general, at their upper elevational limits, species tend to be present primarily on warm slopes or in successional stands; species at their lower limits tend to grow in mesic sites.

Community Characteristics

The correlation of tree species with exposure—Douglas-fir with steep, north-facing slopes and ponderosa pine with south-facing slopes and ridgetops—is most striking at lower elevations in the montane zone. Here, Douglas-fir and ponderosa pine forests interfinger in a complicated way, the relative abundance of the two species varying with the angle of slope and with soil conditions. White fir is a common codominant of Douglas-fir in these forests in the southern half of the Southern Rockies. At higher elevations in the montane zone, especially in the northern and western mountains, Douglas-fir dominates coniferous forests on all slope aspects. In transitional areas between forest types or on disturbed sites, Douglas-fir may be found in association with aspen, ponderosa pine, lodgepole pine, limber pine, blue spruce, Engelmann spruce, and subalpine fir.

The density of Douglas-fir forests is variable and highly dependent on moisture availability, with the most mesic sites supporting the densest forests. Young stands of Douglas-fir may be quite dense, becoming more open with maturity. Under optimal conditions, mature Douglas-fir forests on steep, north-facing slopes have an almost closed canopy; little sunlight penetrates to the forest floor. In the shadiest forests, a pale green, branching lichen known as old man's beard drapes the lower, light-starved branches. Understory vegetation is sparse in such forests and consists mostly of shrubs such as common juniper, mountainlover, kinnikinnik, and waxflower. Where moisture conditions are favorable, a rich moss and lichen flora patterns rock outcrops and rotting stumps.

As a result of logging and fire suppression, few Douglas-fir forests in the Southern Rockies retain their primeval character. Consequently, mixed conifer forests generally prevail in areas that were once dominated by Douglas-fir. These disturbed stands tend to be more open and are characterized by shrub and herbaceous species typically associated with drier ponderosa pine or mountain shrub ecosystems. While old Douglas-firs develop resistance to fire due to thick, corky bark, young trees are easily killed by fires. Trees in the oldest stands average about 400 years in age, although some trees have reached an age of 700 years. Fire suppression has altered the distribution and frequency of Douglas-fir in the Southern Rockies. Some forest biologists believe that pure stands of Douglas-fir historically were limited largely to the Roan Plateau/Piceance Basin region and the north-facing slopes and canyons in a narrow elevational belt along the Eastern Slope of the Colorado Front Range. Along with fire frequency and intensity, insect infestations (tussock moth, spruce budworm, and the Douglas-fir beetle) continue to shape the character of Douglas-fir forests throughout the region.

Plant Adaptation: Designs for Survival

Rocky Mountain Douglas-fir is relatively resistent to drought, far more so than the coastal subspecies. Like most other conifers, however, Douglas-fir enhances its ability to absorb water and nutrients from the soil by forming a symbiotic, and possibly obligatory, relationship with certain soil fungi. Mycorrhizal fungi confer extraordinary resilience on their host trees in the face of droughts, floods, high temperatures, a paucity of soil nutrients, low oxygen, and other possible sources of stress. To envision how this mutually beneficial system functions, it is necessary to understand something about the biology of fungi. Unlike higher plants, fungi reproduce by spores. When a spore lands in a suitable environment, it germinates and sends out long filaments, called hyphae, which spread through soil or wood. The hyphae grow and divide deep in the soil, producing a mass called a mycelium that constitutes the main portion or vegetative body of a fungus. When moisture and temperature conditions are right, the mycelium sends up the spore-producing, or reproductive, structure of the fungus: the varicolored mushrooms that we see poking through the forest litter.

Fungi are incapable of manufacturing their own food internally, since they have no chloroplasts, as green plants do. Though it may seem unlikely, fungi are far better at extracting the critical nutrients that the Douglas-fir needs from the soil, such as phosphorus and nitrogen, which the fungi trade to the tree in exchange for sugar. In the meantime, the hyphae liberate enzymes that digest dead roots, logs, cones, and other organic matter, providing additional nutrients for the fungus's growth. Fungi require carbohydrates for growth but, in contrast to green plants, can only obtain them by tapping into the roots of plants that produce their own food through photosynthesis. To do this, as in the case of Douglas-fir, fungal hyphae envelop the tree's rootlets in a filamentous shroud, with some hyphae penetrating the roots' outer tissues. The new structures that are formed are called mycorrhizae. Mycorrhizal absorption of water is more efficient than absorption carried on by the unaided root. Some mycologists estimate that the mycorrhizal gauze around a tree's roots connects the tree with as much as 1,000 times more soil area than the roots themselves. In the case of Douglas-fir, the increased absorption surface provided by the fungus is believed to counterbalance water lost through evaporation. Recent evidence suggests that the presence of mycorrhizae helps to prolong root life and may also serve as a natural "fungicide" in controlling the proliferation of parasitic fungi that attack tree roots.

Descriptions of Common Plants

Trees

Douglas-fir, *Pseudotsuga menziesii*. Botanists recognize two varieties of Douglas-fir: the Pacific coast Douglas-fir (*Pseudotsuga menziesii* var. *menziesii*) and the Rocky Mountain Douglas-fir (*P. menziesii* var. *glauca*), distinguished from the Pacific variety by the bluish "bloom" on the needles, the smaller cones, and the shorter stature. Douglas-fir is not a true fir, but belongs instead to an entirely different genus found only in western North America and in the mountains of China, Japan, and Taiwan. Douglas-fir is distinguished from other short-needled conifers by its flat, stalked, round-tipped needles, its sharp-pointed winter buds, and its female cones, which are unmistakable due to the three-pronged bract that protrudes from between each cone scale. The male (pollen-producing) cones of the Douglas-fir are small, oblong, and orange-red in color. Unlike the true firs, in which the female (seed-bearing) cones stand straight up on the branches, Douglas-fir cones hang down, falling from the tree intact at maturity. During the single growing season required to reach maturity, female cones change from garnet red to green and, finally, to a rich brown. The paired seeds are reddish brown and shiny and have a dark brown wing. Seed production begins when the tree is ten years old, with seed numbers increasing dramatically at twenty-five to thirty years and reaching maximum production when the tree is between 200 and 300 years old.

Shrubs

Mountainlover, *Paxistima myrsinites.* This small evergreen shrub is a member of the staff-tree family (Celastraceae), of which bittersweet is the best-known representative. In contrast to kinnikinnik, which it superficially resembles, the opposite leaves are oval in shape and have finely toothed margins. The reddish, four-petaled flowers are small and inconspicuous. Mountainlover is especially common in moist, montane forests on the Western Slope but may be found in suitable forest habitat throughout the Southern Rockies.

Wildflowers

Fairy Slipper Orchid, *Calypso bulbosa.* This small, lovely orchid is found in moist coniferous forests and is locally common on north-facing slopes. The fairy slipper is easily identified by its slender, rose-colored petals and whitish, slipper-shaped lip; the interior of the slipper is streaked with purple, and the lip sports a fringe of golden hairs and a spattering of purple dots. Look closely at the arrangement of the yellow fringe and the dots and you will see the face of a deer, thus its other common name, deer-head orchid. Fairy slippers bloom in late May or early June, depending on the elevation, and each four- to eight-inch stalk supports a single, fragrant flower; each flower stalk arises from a tuber and is paired with a solitary basal leaf that withers after the plant blooms in the spring. Small nectar-loving bees are the primary pollinators of this species. Attracted by nectar, the bee lands on the orchid's large, pouting lower lip, whereupon the upper lip closes, trapping the bee momentarily inside the floral pouch; as the bee struggles to escape, it collides with the anther and picks up a cap of pollen, which it then transfers to the next orchid it visits. Germination requires the assistance of symbiotic fungi to aid in seedling establishment.

Twinflower, *Linnaea borealis*. This tiny, bell-flowered plant, with its trailing stems and paired evergreen leaves, is named for the Swedish botanist Carl Linnaeus, who discovered it on a trip to Lapland. Twinflower is a member of the honeysuckle family (Caprifoliaceae) and is common in

From left to right: fairy slipper orchid, pipsissewa.

boreal forest situations throughout North America and Europe. It is identified by its prostrate and slightly woody stems, small size (less than four inches tall), and paired pink, funnel-shaped flowers. Twinflower is pollinated primarily by small, slender flies. Linnaeus was so fond of the twinflower that many of his portraits show him, in Lapland clothing, holding a sprig of it in his hands.

Heartleaf Arnica, *Arnica cordifolia*. This showy, yellow wildflower can be identified by its solitary, sunflowerlike flower head, measuring about three inches in diameter, its heart-shaped, opposite leaves, and the white hairs that envelop the stem and involucre. Blooming in late spring and early summer, heartleaf arnica provides a conspicuous floral display in moist coniferous forests of the montane and subalpine zones.

Lichens

Old Man's Beard, *Usnea hirta*. This pale green, fruticose lichen is common in Douglas-fir and Engelmann spruce–subalpine fir forests throughout the Southern Rockies. Readily identified by its branching and often pendant growth form, old man's beard is attached to bark or bare wood by a single holdfast. This lichen is especially prolific in dense forests, where it covers stumps and dead branches and sometimes drapes entire trees. Several reports indicate that elk and mule deer may eat old man's beard during the winter months, when other food resources are covered by snow. Because of its sensitivity to pollution, especially acid rain, this lichen is being used by researchers to monitor environmental degradation at several forest sites.

Common Plants of the Douglas-fir Forest

Trees

Douglas-fir, *Pseudotsuga menziesii*
Fir, white, *Abies concolor*
Juniper, Rocky Mountain, *Sabina* (formerly *Juniperus*) *scopulorum*
Pine, limber, *Pinus flexilis*
Lodgepole, *Pinus contorta*
Ponderosa, *Pinus ponderosa*

Shrubs

Baneberry, *Actaea rubra*
Chokecherry, *Padus* (formerly *Prunus*) *virginiana* ssp. *melanocarpa*
Juniper, common, *Juniperus communis*
Kinnikinnik, *Arctostaphylos uva-ursi*
Maple, Rocky Mountain, *Acer glabrum*
Mountain-ash, *Sorbus scopulina*
Mountainlover, *Paxistima myrsinites*
Ninebark, *Physocarpus monogynus*
Raspberry, wild, *Rubus idaeus* ssp. *melanolasius*
Raspberry, boulder (or Thimbleberry), *Oreobatus* (formerly *Rubus*) *deliciosus*
Rose, wild, *Rosa woodsii*
Thimbleberry, *Rubacer parviflorum*
Waxflower, *Jamesia americana*

Herbaceous Plants and Lichens

Arnica, heartleaf, *Arnica cordifolia*
Aster, smooth, *Aster laevis*
Blue-eyed Mary, *Collinsia parviflora*
Hawkweed, *Chlorocrepis albiflora* and *C. tristis*
Mistletoe, dwarf, *Arceuthobium douglasii*
Northern Coralroot, *Corallorhiza trifida*
Old Man's Beard (lichen), *Usnea hirta*
Orchid, fairy slipper, *Calypso bulbosa*
Pipsissewa, *Chimaphila umbellata*
Sedge, Geyer's (or Elk Sedge), *Carex geyeri*
Solomon's Seal, false, *Maianthemum* (formerly *Smilacina*) *stellatum*
Twinflower, *Linnaea borealis*
Twistedstalk, *Streptopus fassettii* (formerly *S. amplexifolius*)

Environment and Adaptation: Animals of the Douglas-fir Forests

No mammal or bird species is restricted to the Douglas-fir ecosystem. Open forests of Douglas-fir, especially those with a well-developed understory, provide food and cover for mule deer and elk. Dense, shady Douglas-fir forests attract mammals normally associated with coniferous forests at higher elevations. For example, boreal forest species such as the chickaree (or pine squirrel) and snowshoe hare are often encountered in dense stands of Douglas-fir, whereas the Abert's squirrel and Nuttall's cottontail are more likely to be found in open, mixed forests of Douglas-fir and ponderosa pine.

Birds are perhaps the most conspicuous residents of Douglas-fir forests. Woodpeckers and a variety of smaller birds—Cassin's finches, chickadees, nuthatches, and juncos—are found year-round. Townsend's solitaires and ruby-crowned kinglets are present during the breeding season. The blue grouse, though not common, is found in the densest forests, and on rare occasions you may catch a fleeting glimpse of one of the forest hawks—the sharp-shinned hawk or the larger Cooper's hawk—as it leaves a hunting perch.

Top: hairy woodpecker. Right: dark-eyed junco.

The Western Spruce Budworm

Douglas-fir is susceptible to several insect pests, the most significant being the western spruce budworm (*Choristoneura occidentalis*). The budworm is the most widely distributed forest defoliator in western North America. Though normally held in check by some combination of predators, parasites, and adverse climatic conditions, major outbreaks of western spruce budworm have occurred in the Southern Rockies during the past few years, the largest infestation encompassing more than 2 million acres. Defoliated stands are especially common along the Eastern Slope. Western spruce budworms may also attack Engelmann spruce, blue spruce, and subalpine fir, but Douglas-fir is by far their favorite host.

The adult form of the western spruce budworm is a small, mottled orange-brown moth. Following mating, which occurs from late June to early August, the female moths flutter about the crowns of infested trees looking for egg-laying sites on the undersides of the needles. Each female will lay a mass of some twenty-five to forty bright green eggs that hatch in approximately ten days. Once hatched, the budworm larvae do not feed but instead begin building the silken shelters under the bark scales (called hibernaculae) in which they will overwinter in a state of dormancy. In late April or May of the following year, the budworms emerge and begin feeding, moving from the older needles to enter the succulent developing needle buds. After the buds break open, the budworms loosely web the new needles and feed until most or all of the new growth is destroyed. If the branch of an infested tree is shaken, wriggling budworms will descend from the foliage on strands of silk. The larvae mature thirty to forty days after feeding begins in spring, and pupation occurs within the feeding webs, the adults emerging as a cryptically colored brown moth a week or so later, ready to begin the cycle anew.

Life Histories of Selected Animals

Birds

Great Horned Owl, *Bubo virginianus*. This large, nocturnal owl is a common resident of the montane forests of the Southern Rockies and is readily identified by its prominent, widely spaced ear tufts and its resonant hoot: *Whoo! Whoo-whoo-whoo! whoo! whoo!* The great horned owl roosts by day, usually in dense foliage; roosting owls are often harassed by noisy flocks of ravens, jays, and other birds. When hunting, great horned owls utilize a perch, wait, and pounce technique. Their diet is variable and consists of rabbits, hares, rodents, and birds of all sizes. These owls tend to use a feeding post near the nest site, leaving the ground nearby littered with regurgitated pellets of undigestible materials: bones, fur, feathers, and insect chitin. Though solitary outside the breeding season, the male begins territorial hooting in December or January, bonding with a female prior to egg laying, usually by February or March. Both sexes incubate the eggs and deliver food to the nestlings; young owls are able to leave the nest sixty-three to seventy days after hatching.

Hairy Woodpecker, *Picoides villosus.* This robin-sized, black-and-white woodpecker is distinguished from the similar **downy woodpecker** (*P. pubescens*), which shares most of its range, by its larger size and longer bill; both species have a conspicuous white patch on the back, and the males of each species have a red patch on the back of the head. Common in both coniferous forests and riparian woodlands, the hairy's presence is often detected by its loud *peek* call note or by its drumming signals. Both sexes use drumming—a series of raps on any resonating surface—as a signaling device. The hairy woodpecker tends to be noisier and more active than the downy, but is generally shier when approached. Resident year-round, adults maintain a large range that includes their nesting territory. Their diet consists mostly of wood-boring insects, which they probe for with their bills and extensible tongues. Both sexes excavate the cavity and incubate the eggs; the young fledge approximately thirty days after hatching.

Mountain Chickadee, *Parus gambeli.* This common chickadee, restricted to the mountain West, is easily distinguished from the similar **black-capped chickadee** (*P. atricapillus*) by the presence of a white stripe over the eye; note that this stripe is missing during late-summer molt. The call is a conspicuous *chickadee-dee-dee*; a whistled call of three or four notes, *fee-bee-bay*

From left to right: black-capped chickadee, mountain chickadee.

or *fee-bee, fee-bee* (scaled like the nursery song "Three Blind Mice"), is also common. Nesting habitat consists of coniferous forests in the montane and subalpine life zones; the species tends to winter at lower elevations, and may be especially common in riparian or open woodlands, its range overlapping that of the black-capped chickadee. Both species are gregarious and may travel during the fall and winter months in noisy, mixed-species flocks with brown creepers and golden-crowned kinglets. The diet of chickadees consists mostly of insects gleaned from needles, twigs, and bark; seeds of various types are taken when available. Nesting occurs in a natural cavity or in a cavity excavated by both sexes; incubation requires about fourteen days, and young leave the nest at approximately twenty days of age.

Dark-eyed Junco, *Junco hyemalis.* Four subspecies of juncos occur in the Southern Rockies on a seasonal basis: slate-colored, white-winged, Oregon, and gray-headed; all geographic races have white outer tail feathers that flash conspicuously in flight. Dark-eyed juncos breed in coniferous forests or mixed woodlands; in winter, birds travel in small flocks and may be encountered in a variety of habitats. The song is a musical trill, and a rapid twittering is often delivered in flight. The diet of these ground-foraging birds consists primarily of insects during the breeding season and seeds during the winter months. Winter flocks break up into pairs upon arrival on the nesting grounds. Nests are cup shaped and usually located on the ground; the female incubates the eggs, and young leave the nest eleven to thirteen days after hatching.

Cassin's Finch, *Carpodacus cassinii.* The male Cassin's finch is distinguished by its conspicuous crimson crown, which ends abruptly at the brown-streaked nape; in comparison to the house finch, the Cassin's red plumage appears paler in color, and the sides lack brown streaking. Female Cassin's lack red plumage and are identified by the strong brown streaking on the breast and back. The warbled song is more varied than that of other finches and is delivered by the males from a treetop perch or in flight. Outside the breeding season, Cassin's finches may travel in flocks, often with crossbills and evening grosbeaks; family groups are common in summer. This species forages for conifer seeds and buds in the tops of trees or on the ground; summer diet includes insects as well as fruits. Nests are constructed in large conifers, often near the outer end of a limb; females incubate the eggs.

Common Animals of the Douglas-fir Forest

Mammals

Chipmunk, Colorado, *Tamias quadrivittatus*
Least, *T. minimus*
Cottontail, mountain (or Nuttall's), *Sylvilagus nuttallii*
Coyote, *Canis latrans*
Deer, mule, *Odocoileus hemionus*
Elk (or Wapiti), *Cervus elaphus*
Hare, snowshoe, *Lepus americanus*
Mountain Lion, *Felis concolor*
Mouse, deer, *Peromyscus maniculatus*
Myotis, little brown, *Myotis lucifugus*
long-eared, *M. volans*
Shrew, masked, *Sorex cinereus*
montane, *S. monticolus*
Squirrel, Abert's, *Sciurus aberti*
Chickaree (or Red or Pine Squirrel), *Tamiasciurus hudsonicus*
golden-mantled ground, *Spermophilus lateralis*
Vole, southern red-backed, *Clethrionomys gapperi*
Weasel, long-tailed, *Mustela frenata*
Woodrat, bushy-tailed, *Neotoma cinerea*

Birds

Chickadee, black-capped, *Parus atricapillus*
mountain, *P. gambeli*
Creeper, brown, *Certhia americana*
Crossbill, red, *Loxia curvirostra*
Finch, Cassin's, *Carpodacus cassinii*
Flicker, northern, *Colaptes auratus*
Goshawk, northern, *Accipiter gentilis*
Grosbeak, black-headed, *Pheucticus melanocephalus*
evening, *Coccothraustes vespertina*
Grouse, blue, *Dendragapus obscurus*
Hawk, Cooper's, *Accipiter cooperii*

sharp-shinned, *A. striatus*
Jay, Steller's, *Cyanocitta stelleri*
Junco, dark-eyed, *Junco hyemalis*
Kinglet, golden-crowned, *Regulus satrapa*
ruby-crowned, *R. calendula*
Nutcracker, Clark's, *Nucifraga columbiana*
Nuthatch, pygmy, *Sitta pygmaea*
red-breasted, *S. canadensis*
white-breasted, *S. carolinensis*
Owl, great horned, *Bubo virginianus*
northern saw-whet, *Aegolius acadicus*
Raven, common, *Corvus corax*
Siskin, pine, *Carduelis pinus*
Solitaire, Townsend's, *Myadestes townsendi*
Tanager, western, *Piranga ludoviciana*
Thrush, hermit, *Catharus guttatus*
Swainson's, *C. ustulatus*
Warbler, yellow-rumped, *Dendroica coronata*
Woodpecker, downy, *Picoides pubescens*
hairy, *P. villosus*

Open Country: Mountain Grasslands and Meadows

Backlit Wyoming paintbrush on Buffalo Pass, Park Range.

Summer's arrival in the mountain grasslands and meadows of the Southern Rockies is a visual poem, richly embellished with luminous greens and the jewel-like colors of wildflowers. The lavish scent of damp soil, the greening that marks the upsurge of chlorophyll, and the burgeoning of new growth nearly overwhelm the senses. Our perception of color sharpens and takes on a whole new dimension with the season. The wildflower palette—the periwinkle-blue penstemons, the firecracker-red gilias, the rose-pink paintbrush, the ivory-hued mariposa lilies, and chrome-yellow sunflowers—seems almost gaudy, full-blown and drenched with light, reveling in summer's seductive embrace. For animals, too, this is a time of comparative ease and abundance. The air redolent with their musky scent, a small herd of cow elk and their calves lingers to graze in a secluded meadow. At the meadow's edge, a coyote stands, head cocked, listening to the faint scratching noises of a tunneling pocket gopher. Nearby, the staccato alarm calls of Wyoming ground squirrels protest the coyote's presence, their heads just visible above the entrances to their burrows. Overhead, a mountain bluebird hovers kestrel-like in search of insect prey, an arc of brilliant blue against the billowing clouds.

Ecological Distribution

Herbaceous ecosystems (vegetation communities defined by the dominance of herbs as opposed to shrubs or trees) are classified on the basis of size, moisture regimes, plant associations, and ecosystem history. Natural grasslands and meadows are scattered throughout the foothill, montane, and subalpine forests and are the predominant vegetation type in the intermontane basins and alpine uplands of the Southern Rockies wherever environmental conditions are unsuitable for tree growth but not so adverse as to preclude the development of a perennial herbaceous layer. These herbaceous ecosystems vary in size from small openings in the forest to more extensive communities covering several thousand acres. The principal ecosystem types described in this chapter include mountain grasslands and dry meadows, moist meadows, and successional communities. A discussion of herbaceous wetlands can be found in Chapter 20, and Chapter 26 focuses on alpine tundra ecosystems.

Mountain grasslands occupy large areas characterized by low precipitation, cold temperatures, and relatively fine-textured soils, all factors that discourage tree growth. In the Southern Rockies, mountain grasslands are primarily restricted to the semiarid intermontane basins: parts of the Shirley and Laramie basins (Wyoming), parts of North, Middle, and South parks, the Wet Mountain Valley, the perimeter of the San Luis Valley, parts of the upper Rio Grande Basin in Colorado, and the Moreno Valley in New Mexico. Natural meadow ecosystems are generally smaller in areal extent than the mountain grasslands, ranging in size from small patches to communities covering several hundred acres. The distribution of meadows, in contrast to that of the mountain grasslands, reflects localized differences in soil texture, depth, and moisture conditions rather than regional climatic patterns resulting from the rain-shadow effects associated with leeward sides of the major mountain belts.

Natural meadow ecosystems occur in topographic situations characterized by deep, fine-textured soils: floodplains, valley bottoms, old lake beds, and gently rolling uplands. Many of the larger mountain meadows, such as Moraine Park in Rocky Mountain National Park, are developed on glacier-derived sediments; this distributional pattern is repeated in glaciated valleys throughout the Southern Rockies. Dry meadow ecosystems are typical of well-drained soils; moist meadows predominate in areas with seasonally or permanently high water tables.

Successional herbaceous ecosystems are found on a wide variety of sites. Plant ecologists recognize two types of successional communities: primary and secondary. Primary successional communities occur in areas where physical changes in landscape features, such as the filling in of a pond or changes in the course of a river, have created a new soil surface and initiated the colonization of land that has not been previously vegetated. Secondary successional communities, on the other hand, are found wherever a natural or human disturbance, such as fire, windthrow, logging, overgrazing, cultivation, or irrigation, has altered or destroyed the preexisting vegetation.

Physical Environment

The climatic characteristics of mountain grasslands and meadows are highly variable. Differences in microclimate from one community to another can be correlated with altitude, topographic setting, moisture availability, and the degree of protection afforded by the surrounding vegetation. Lacking an overstory, herbaceous ecosystems are exposed repeatedly to the unmoderated influence of solar radiation and the desiccating effects of strong winds, remaining largely snow free during the winter as a result of wind scour. In a general sense, mountain grasslands tend to be associated with climatic conditions that are considered more severe than those typical of most meadow sites. The growing season is short, and frosts may occur at any time.

Annual precipitation in the intermontane basins averages less than fifteen inches; the driest conditions exist in the San Luis Valley, where the average is less than ten inches and summer drought is common in years when the Arizona monsoon fails to push deeply into the region. Winters tend to be very cold as a result of cold air drainage from the surrounding mountain slopes. Summers, except in the San Luis Valley, are also comparatively cool.

Community Characteristics

Images of lush, flower-filled mountain meadows are synonymous with the Southern Rockies. No two meadows ever appear quite the same: the patterns of floral color change constantly as the season progresses. Mountain grasslands and meadows exhibit great variability from one area to another. Species composition varies conspicuously with altitude, available moisture, geographic location, and in response to the disturbance history of the community. Unfortunately, nearly every herbaceous ecosystem in the Southern Rockies has been altered in some way as a result of grazing, agricultural activities, and/or fire suppression. Because these communities are so variable, only a general discussion of each type is possible within the scope of this book.

Mountain Grasslands and Dry Meadows

Mountain grasslands and dry meadows share several traits. The mineral soils typical of these ecosystems have limited water-storage capacity and are subjected to recurring drought at all times of the year. Bunchgrasses, rather than turf-forming species, predominate; each grass plant must spread its roots horizontally to tap peripheral moisture reserves, precluding the growth of other plants immediately adjacent to it. The narrow leaves of the bunchgrasses and similar plants present a reduced surface area from which evaporative losses can occur; additional water conservation is achieved by the waxy coating of cutin that protects the leaves. Many broad-leaved species, such as silver sage, also have fine hairs on the leaf surfaces that entrap a layer of moist air, insulating the leaf from excessive heat or dessicating winds. Most of the bunchgrasses found in the mountains are classified as cool-season grasses because they photosythesize most efficiently at

Common grasses of the mountain grasslands, clockwise from left: mountain muhly, Junegrass, foxtail barley, cheatgrass (alien).

moderate temperatures and light levels. These species tolerate drought quite well and simply become dormant when conditions are unfavorable.

Though wildflowers may be conspicuous in certain grassland and dry meadow communities, most fail to approach the floral display associated with moist meadows. Small pockets of moisture-loving species may occur in suitable microsites, but the vegetational zonation typical of many moist or wet meadow ecosystems is largely absent from these drier habitats. Bunchgrasses such as mountain muhly and several species of wheatgrass, as well as weedy species such as yarrow and fringed sage, tend to dominate at lower elevations. In late spring, especially on dry, gravelly grasslands in North Park, the large flowers of bitterroot transform an otherwise drab hill-side with splashes of bright pink. On relatively moist sites, wildflowers such as scarlet paintbrush, Colorado locoweed, western wallflower, penstemon, miner's candle, sulphur flower, and blanketflower lend their bright colors to many montane communities. Shrubs such as shrubby cinquefoil and wax currant may be present in certain areas, reflecting differences in soil characteristics or disturbance history. Subalpine grassland and dry meadow communities are often dominated by bunchgrasses such as Thurber's fescue and timber oatgrass. By midsummer, these communites are highlighted by the scattered colors of trumpet gilia, common harebell, whiskbroom parsley, orange sneezeweed, and subalpine buckwheat.

Miner's candle.

Mountain grasslands and dry meadow ecosystems are particularly susceptible to disturbance, either as a result of grazing or human activities. Prior to settlement, Thurber's fescue or Idaho fescue would have made up a large proportion of the bunchgrass communities in the northern and central portions of the Southern Rockies, with Arizona fescue most common to the south. In undisturbed grasslands it is still possible to find a fragile organic layer—a cryptogamic crust—that consists of soil lichens, mosses, liverworts, and cyanobacteria. The cryptogamic crust serves to stabilize the soil, restrict the establishment of weedy species, and helps retain moisture. Intense grazing pressure or human disturbance destroys this fragile crust, which may never recover its structure or function. Selective feeding by livestock also encourages the spread of less palatable species, both native and alien, and has greatly altered the species composition of many herbaceous ecosystems. In most areas of the Southern Rockies, invasive species such as Russian thistle, Canadian thistle, and cheatgrass are increasing in abundance at the expense of native bunchgrasses and broad-leaved herbaceous plants.

Moist Meadows

In areas where disturbance has been minimal, grasses such as the native bluegrasses, Junegrass, blue grama, foxtail barley, and timber oatgrass dominate moist meadows in the montane zone. Alien species such as redtop and timothy are now common wherever the land has been grazed or hayed. With sufficient moisture, spectacular displays of wildflowers such as Rocky Mountain iris, shootingstar, golden banner, black-eyed Susan, aspen-daisy, wild geranium, and fringed gentian create an ever-changing palette of color. Where soils are alkaline, such as in the San Luis Valley, salt-tolerant species such as saltgrass, arrowgrass, alkali grass, and glasswort predominate.

In the high meadows of the subalpine zone, the profusion of wildflowers spreads a blaze of color across the landscape like a firestorm. Species such as rose paintbrush, groundsel, bistort, wild onion, elephantella, subalpine daisy, and aspen sunflower create islands of rich color wherever you look. Grasses such is tufted hairgrass, spike trisetum, and Canadian reed-grass are conspicuous in many communities, often sharing dominance with sedges and rushes. Several species of willow and bog birch may also be common on moist sites.

Successional Ecosystems

Without careful observation, herbaceous ecosystems that have undergone disturbance may be difficult to distinguish from climax herbaceous communities. In the case of fire disturbance, communities that once had a tree cover can be identified by the presence of charred logs, cut stumps, or other evidence of a preexisting forest. Without further disturbance, the tree species that were originally present will eventually invade these communities. Aspen is well adapted for invading herbaceous ecosystems because the young saplings, which are root suckers, do not have to compete with the herbaceous vegetation for water or nutrients. Other tree species, however, may be slow to reinvade because of competition from herbaceous plants, the absence of shade protection for tree seedlings, or the lack of a nearby seed source.

Successional grasslands and meadows, especially those that have recently been disturbed, are characterized by a decrease in native perennial grasses and an increase in the abundance of annuals and weedy species such as common dandelion, Colorado locoweed, pussytoes, fringed sage, and silver sage. In communities where overgrazing has been a factor, aggressive annuals such as cheatgrass proliferate and may share dominance with native perennials such as gumweed, coneflower, wild geranium, false hellebore, and sticky cinquefoil. Intense grazing can turn a herb-dominated ecosystem into a shrubland by selectively eliminating the perennial grasses and allowing shrubs and cacti to establish themselves. At higher elevations, northern bedstraw, fireweed, pearly everlasting, and false dandelion predominate on disturbed sites. Fireweed and mullein are common species in areas that have been burned over. On subalpine slopes where avalanches have removed the forest cover, species such as avalanche lily, chiming bells, monkshood, and larkspur are especially common.

Plant Adaptation: Designs for Survival

Successful reproduction provides the critical measure of a species' ability to survive in a given environment. Each plant species has evolved its own repertoire of adaptations to enhance reproductive success. Grasses and sedges employ an efficient, seemingly effortless system of wind pollination.

The showy wildflowers of the mountain grasslands and meadows, as you might expect, are pollinated by insects or hummingbirds. The dazzling array of shapes, colors, and fragrances that distinguish these flowers has evolved for the sole function of attracting pollinators and maintaining the species' reproductive isolation. For services rendered, the pollinator's reward is food, in the form of nectar, pollen, or oil.

The mutualisms that we observe between flowering plants and their pollinators are the result of a long and intimate coevolutionary relationship. Animal pollinators exhibit distinct color, shape, and food-type preferences in the flowers they choose to visit. The pollinator is equipped with one or several anatomical features that maximize collection of pollen or nectar. Beetles have brushlike mouthparts for collecting pollen; hummingbirds have long, narrow bills and tongues for nectar gathering; bees have hollows, or pollen baskets, on their hind legs for storing pollen during foraging trips; and butterflies, moths, and flies have tubular, bristled proboscises for nectar drinking.

One-sided penstemon showing nectar guides.

The patches, streaks, and spots of contrasting color—called guide marks or nectar guides—that pattern the inner surfaces of some flowers are believed to direct the pollinator to the location of pollen or to the site of floral nectar glands. These guide marks are generally positioned so that the pollinator must brush against the sex organs of the flower on its way to the nectar or pollen source. Many guide marks are conspicuous, such as the yellow lines on the interior of some penstemon flowers, the brown spots of the wood lily, or the yellow eye typical of forget-me-not flowers. Other guide marks, produced by specialized plant tissues that strongly reflect ultraviolet light (UV), are visible only to the insect eye, which perceives ultraviolet light as a color. When flowers with UV-reflecting tissues, such as marsh-marigold and star gentian, are photographed using a filter that passes only ultraviolet light, a clear pattern of guide marks becomes apparent on what had seemed, to the human eye, an unpatterned corolla.

A plant's adaptations for attracting pollinators must be balanced against its need for defending itself against the invertebrate and vertebrate herbivores that abound in mountain grasslands and meadows. The anti-herbivore defenses evolved by flowering plants are as diverse as the animals that threaten them. The most obvious defenses are anatomical features such as spines or thick cuticles, but an array of chemical defenses (allelochemic agents) also make certain plants toxic, unpalatable, or simply less nutritious to herbivores. The harmful effects attributed to defensive compounds such as alkaloids, selenium, and phytoestrogens (hormone mimics) include irritation of mucous membranes, acute intoxication, nerve damage, fertility inhibition, congenital malformations, digestive disorders, cancers, and death. A great many poisonous plants are found in mountain grassland and meadow ecosystems. Some of the most common are false hellebore, death camas, lupine, locoweed, golden banner, larkspur, and orange sneezeweed.

In some plants, the levels of chemical defenses fluctuate seasonally, with the highest levels present during periods that are critical for plant reproduction or growth. Those that produce compounds that mimic animal hormones are able to combat insect herbivores by altering their natural pattern of metamorphosis. To understand the impact that phytoestrogens might have on small mammals, one fascinating study looked at variations in the production of phytoestrogens in certain grasses and how these differences might influence the breeding patterns of the montane vole. In late summer and fall, when high phytoestrogen levels coincide with the setting of seed by the grasses, vole reproduction rates are drastically reduced in response to the disruption of ovulation caused by a phytoestrogen-rich grass diet. The results of laboratory testing added another dimension to the story, strongly suggesting that the higher vole-reproduction rates in spring appear to be associated with plant chemicals that actually stimulate female ovulation and male testicular growth at that time.

Some plants, lacking chemical defenses, enlist the services of an "ant guard" to protect their flowers, seeds, or foliage from herbivorous insects. Although ant-plant mutualisms are quite common in the tropics, a fascinating temperate-region example has also been discovered in the Southern Rockies. The aspen sunflower, a showy species found in subalpine meadows, attracts and rewards its ant guardians (typically of the genus *Formica*) with extrafloral nectar that it produces in bracts encircling the base of its flower head. In return for a steady supply of nectar, which begins several weeks before the flowers open and ends just before the seeds are shed, the ants aggressively deter egg laying by any one of several species of flies whose life cycles are closely tied to these sunflowers and whose larvae would otherwise destroy the flower heads. Clearly, this mutualism is of critical importance to the sunflower; research suggests that seed loss to predators may be as high as 90 percent when no guard ants are present.

Aspen sunflower with its retinue of ant guards.

Descriptions of Common Plants

Grasses

Mountain Muhly, *Muhlenbergia montana.* This bunchgrass is a common dry-site species encountered on gentle slopes, grasslands, and in open forests of ponderosa pine. The culm (flowering stem) of this grass ranges in height from one to two feet. The inflorescence is a narrow, short-branched panicle ranging from two to six inches long.

Junegrass, *Koeleria macrantha.* This small, pretty bunchgrass is very common on meadows and slopes from the foothills to the subalpine. Maturing early in summer, the culm ranges in height from one to two feet; the inflorescence is a dense one- to five-inch spikelike panicle.

Parry's Oatgrass, *Danthonia parryi.* This beautiful bunchgrass, largely restricted to the Eastern Slope, is a common species of drier meadows, open parks, and open ponderosa pine forests from the upper montane to the subalpine. The culms range in height from four to twenty inches; the inflorescence is a spiky, mostly one-sided panicle. Parry's oatgrass is distinguished from **timber oatgrass** (*D. intermedia*), a species found in subalpine and alpine environments, by the hairs found on the back of the outer bract of the grass floret (lemma).

Thurber's Fescue, *Festuca thurberi.* This tall, robust bunchgrass is a common species from the montane to the subalpine and may form pure stands on suitable sites. The culms occur in dense tufts and vary in height from twenty to thirty-six inches; the inflorescence is a loose, slightly drooping four- to six-inch panicle. The outer bract of the grass floret lacks an awn but does have a sharp point.

Tufted Hairgrass, *Deschampsia cespitosa.* This luxuriant, medium to tall bunchgrass is found in moist meadows from the upper montane through the alpine; it is always associated with sites that maintain good winter snow cover. The culms are two to four feet in height; the leaves are stiff and pointed, pricking the palm of the hand when pressed against it. The inflorescence is an open, purplish panicle with a distinctly feathery appearance.

Wildflowers

Prairie Sage and Fringed (or Silver) Sage, *Artemisia ludoviciana* and *A. frigida*. These two species, with their silvery green, pubescent (hairy), and aromatic leaves, are common in dry grasslands and meadows from the foothills to the subalpine. Fringed sage, with its woody stem, is actually a very small shrub and is distinguished from the herbaceous prairie sage by its finely divided leaves; the leaves of prairie sage are large, lanceolate to deeply lobed, and coated with soft, white hairs. The inflorescence of prairie sage is an elongate cluster of small, pale-green flower heads, in contrast to the nodding, yellowish flower heads of fringed sage. Both species are quick to colonize overgrazed meadows and areas where the soil has been disturbed.

Yarrow, *Achillea lanulosa*. Yarrow is a common, widely distributed member of the sunflower family found in dry meadows and grasslands from the foothills to the alpine zone. Individual plants are approximately a foot in height and are easily identified by their finely dissected, fernlike, aromatic leaves and their flattopped cluster of small white flower heads.

Pussytoes, *Antennaria rosea*. This small sunflower-family member is typically encountered in dry to moist meadow situations from the foothills to the subalpine, where it may form a matlike ground cover in some areas. Pussytoes is readily distinguished by its clusters of white flower heads and their papery phyllaries (the bracts that surround each flower cluster); the phyllaries are often but not always tinged with pink. The leaves of all species of pussytoes are small, silvery green, and arranged in a basal rosette; stems range in height from four to ten inches.

Orange Sneezeweed, *Dugaldia hoopesii*. This tall, showy member of the sunflower family is found in open meadows and in sunny aspen forests from the montane to the subalpine; sneezeweed is common on the Western Slope but occurs only in the Pikes Peak region on the Eastern Slope. Orange sneezeweed is easily identified by the bright orange-yellow petals of its ray flowers and the darker orange of its interior circle of disk flowers; in most cases, the petals of the ray flowers droop and look slightly wilted. The species is highly poisonous, especially to sheep.

Subalpine Daisy, *Erigeron peregrinus*. A handsome member of the sunflower family, the subalpine daisy is common in moist subalpine and alpine meadows. The species is easily identified by its lavender or rose-violet ray flowers, yellow diskflowers, phyllaries in one series rather than shingled, and robust size; the petals of the ray flowers are approximately ⅛ inch wide. A similar species, the **aspen-daisy** (*E. speciosus*), is encountered in open meadows and aspen groves at lower elevations and is distinguished by the narrower petals of its ray flowers.

Aspen Sunflower, *Helianthella quinquenervis.* This tall, elegant sunflower is common in moist meadows, aspen groves, and avalanche tracks from the montane to the subalpine. The aspen sunflower is identified by its glossy, leathery leaves (each with five prominent veins) and by its large flower heads (three to four inches in diameter) made up of bright yellow ray flowers and yellowish green disk flowers; the flower heads dip slightly and usually face east. Check for the presence of ant guards at the leaf axils and on the green involucre that surrounds the flower head.

Golden Banner, *Thermopsis montana.* This showy member of the pea family is common in meadows and open aspen forests from the montane to the subalpine. Golden banner has an erect, lupinelike growth form, yellow sweetpealike flowers, palmately compound leaves with leaflets in groups of three, and straight pubescent seedpods. A similar species, *T. divaricarpa*, is more common on the Eastern Slope and produces pods that are curved and mostly hairless. Golden banner is toxic to humans and most other animals.

Colorado Locoweed, *Oxytropis lambertii.* This widespread member of the pea family is the most common locoweed in open, relatively dry meadows and grasslands from the plains to the subalpine. Locoweed has showy racemes of magenta flowers, an erect (rather than trailing) growth form, and pinnately compound leaves that appear silvery because of the coating of fine hairs. This species may hybridize with Rocky Mountain locoweed (*O. sericea*), forming striking variations in color and habit. Locoweeds tend to accumulate naturally occurring selenium from the soil, making all species toxic to animals, especially domestic livestock.

Scarlet Gilia, *Ipomopsis aggregata.* Scarlet gilia, skyrocket, and trumpet gilia are all colloquial names for this beautiful member of the phlox family. Gilia includes several subspecies, and one form or another can be found in midsummer meadows from the foothills to the subalpine zone. The plants are twelve to fifteen inches tall, with fernlike leaves and inch-long, trumpet-shaped, scarlet, pink, or white flowers; pink flowers are especially common on the high mesas of the Western Slope, such as Grand Mesa, the Flat Tops, and the Uncompahgre Plateau. Hummingbirds and long-tongued moths pollinate this species and seem undeterred by the skunky aroma of the foliage.

Western Shootingstar, *Dodecatheon pulchellum.* This spectacular wildflower, a member of the primrose family, is found in moist meadows and along stream courses from the montane to the subalpine zone. Shootingstar flowers most resemble those of the cyclamen, and are identified by the sharply reflexed, magenta petals and by the five brownish black anthers, which join to form a point; the flowers hang upside down from a slender stem like an umbrella turned inside out. Largely pollinated by bees, the lack of a landing platform forces the bee to cling to the pointed cone formed by the stamens. Flapping its wings to hold its position, the bee inadvertently dislodges pollen grains that land on its abdomen, and so it goes from one shootingstar to another. Shootingstars may be so abundant in some areas, as they are in South Park, that entire meadows may appear drenched in pink.

False Hellebore, *Veratrum tenuipetalum.* This tall, robust member of the lily family (also known as the cornhusk lily) is found in moist and often overgrazed meadows from the upper montane through the subalpine zone; false hellebore is especially common on the Western Slope and in the southern ranges of the Southern Rockies. It is easily identified by its height (three feet or more), by its pleated, upright leaves, and by the erect, plume-like inflorescence of greenish white flowers.

Common Plants of the Mountain Grasslands and Meadows

Shrubs

Birch, bog, *Betula glandulosa*
Cinquefoil, shrubby, *Potentilla* (or *Pentaphylloides*) *floribunda*
Currant, prickly, *Ribes lacustre*
Rabbitbrush, *Chrysothamnus nauseosus*
  sticky-leaved, *C. viscidiflorus*
Sagebrush, big (or Great Basin sagebrush), *Seriphidium* (formerly *Artemisia*) *tridentatum*
Sage, fringed (or Silver Sage), *Artemisia frigida*
  prairie, *A. ludoviciana*
Willow, *Salix* spp.

Grasses, Sedges, and Rushes

Arrowgrass, *Triglochin maritima*
Barley, foxtail, *Critesion* (formerly *Hordeum*) *jubatum*
Cheatgrass, *Anisantha* (formerly *Bromus*) *tectorum*
Fescue, Arizona, *Festuca arizonica*
  Idaho, *F. idahoensis*
  Thurber's, *F. thurberi*
Grama, blue, *Bouteloua gracilis*
Hairgrass, tufted, *Deschampsia cespitosa*
Junegrass, *Koeleria macrantha*
Muhly, mountain, *Muhlenbergia montana*
Needle-and-thread, *Hesperostipa* (formerly *Stipa*) *comata*
Needlegrass, green, *Nassella* (formerly *Stipa*) *viridula*
Oatgrass, Parry's, *Danthonia parryi*
  timber, *D. intermedia*
Redtop, *Agrostis gigantea*
Reedgrass, Canadian, *Calamagrostis canadensis*
Ricegrass, Indian, *Achnatherum* (formerly *Oryzopsis*) *hymenoides*
Rush, Arctic, *Juncus balticus*

subalpine, *J. mertensianus*
Saltgrass, *Distichlis spicata* ssp. *stricta*
Sedge, mountain-loving, *Carex oreocharis*
narrow-leaf, *C. stenophylla* ssp. *eleocharis*
thick-spiked, *C. pachystachya*
Squirreltail, *Elymus elymoides* (formerly *Sitanion hystrix*)
Three-awn, *Aristida purpurea*
Timothy, *Phleum pratense*
Trisetum, spike, *Trisetum spicatum*
Wheatgrass, crested, *Pascopyrum* (formerly *Agropyron*) *cristatum*
slender, *A. trachycaulum*
western, *Pascopyrum* (formerly *Agropyron*) *smithii*

Wildflowers

Bedstraw, northern, *Galium septentrionale*
Bergamot, wild (or Bee Balm), *Monarda fistulosa*
Bitterroot, *Lewisia rediviva*
Bistort, American, *Bistorta bistortoides*
Black-eyed Susan, *Rudbeckia hirta*
Blanketflower, *Gaillardia aristata*
Blue-eyed-grass, *Sisyrinchium montanum*
Buckwheat, subalpine, *Eriogonum subalpinum*
Buttercup, *Ranunculus* spp.
Camas, subalpine death, *Anticlea* (formerly *Zigadenus*) *elegans*
Cinquefoil, soft, *Potentilla pulcherrima*
Clover, red, *Trifolium pratense*
Columbine, Colorado blue, *Aquilegia coerulea*
Coneflower, black, *Rudbeckia occidentalis* var. *montana*

Top: trumpet gilia.
Bottom: shootingstar.

Daisy, showy, *Erigeron speciosus*
subalpine, *Erigeron peregrinus*
Dandelion, common, *Taraxacum officinale*
Elephantella, *Pedicularis groenlandica*
Gentian, bottle, *Pneumonanthe parryi*
fragrant, *Gentianopsis barbellata*
fringed, *G. thermalis*
green (or Monument Plant), *Frasera speciosa*
prairie, *P. affinis*
Geranium, wild, *Geranium caespitosum*
sticky, *G. viscosissimum*
white, *G. richardsonii*
Gilia, scarlet, *Ipomopsis aggregata*
Golden Banner, *Thermopsis montana*
Groundsel, Fendler's, *Packera* (formerly *Senecio*) *fendleri*
Gumweed, *Grindelia squarrosa, G. subalpina,* and *G. decumbens*
Harebell, common, *Campanula rotundifolia*
Parry's, *C. parryi*
Hellebore, false (or Cornhusk Lily), *Veratrum tenuipetalum*
Iris, Rocky Mountain, *Iris missouriensis*
Lily, avalanche, *Erythronium grandiflorum*
mariposa, *Calochortus gunnisonii*
Locoweed, Colorado, *Oxytropis lambertii*
Rocky Mountain, *O. sericea*
showy, *O. splendens*
yellow, *O. campestris* var. *gracilis*
Lupine, *Lupinus* spp.
Miner's Candle, *Oreocarya* (formerly *Cryptantha*) *virgata*
Monkshood, *Aconitum columbianum*

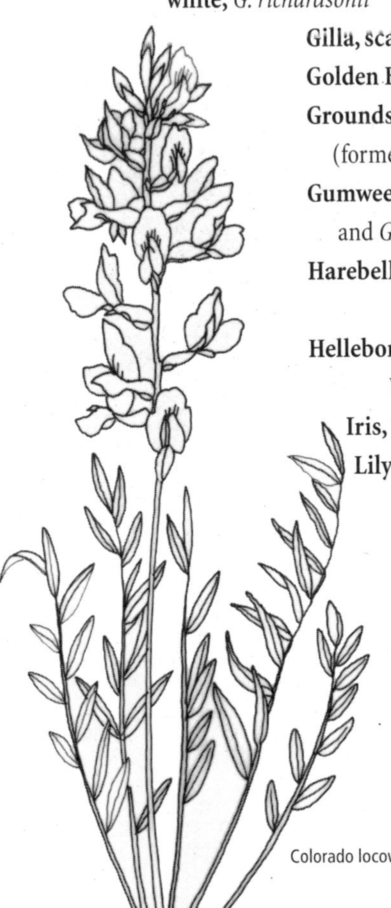

Colorado locoweed.

Mullein, *Verbascum thapsus*

Paintbrush, rose, *Castilleja rhexifolia*

scarlet, *C. miniata*

Wyoming, *C. linariifolia*

Penstemon, Rocky Mountain, *Penstemon strictus*

lavender, *P. virgatus*

Rydberg, *P. rydbergii*

sidebells (or One-Sided Penstemon), *P. secundiflorus*

small-flowered, *P. confertus* ssp. *procerus*

Whipple, *P. whippleanus*

Prairie Smoke, *Erythrocoma* (formerly *Geum*) *triflora*

Pussytoes, *Antennaria rosea* or *A. corymbosa*

Shootingstar, western, *Dodecatheon pulchellum*

Sneezeweed, orange, *Dugaldia hoopesii*

Orange sneezeweed.

Sulphur Flower, *Eriogonum umbellatum*

Sunflower, aspen, *Helianthella quinquenervis*

Thistle, Russian, *Salsola australis*

Wallflower, western, *Erysimum capitatum*

Yarrow, *Achillea lanulosa*

Environment and Adaptation: Animals of the Mountain Grasslands and Meadows

Animals adapted to open country face different challenges than do those that prefer forested habitats. The mountain grasslands and meadows of the Southern Rockies provide critical resources for a surprising diversity of animals. Some are cryptically colored while others, like the butterflies, are often as brightly colored as the wildflowers. The species richness of these ecosystems clearly reflects the influence of the edge effect: the increase in species diversity and in biological productivity that characterizes the transition zone, or ecotone, between two adjacent ecosystem types. A great many species that we normally associate with herbaceous ecosystems—elk, Nuttall's cottontail, least chipmunks, mountain bluebirds, savannah sparrows, and dark-eyed juncos, for example—are edge-loving species that rely on the juxtaposition of the protective cover provided by the forest and the greater productivity associated with herbaceous ecosystems.

The lack of an overstory limits the variety of habitats available for foraging and reproductive activities. Not surprisingly, the resident mammalian fauna is characterized by a preponderance of burrowing animals: northern pocket gophers, Wyoming ground squirrels, prairie dogs, montane voles, and badgers. Most other species utilize these ecosystems on a seasonal or occasional basis. The luxuriant growth of grasses and other herbaceous plants provides prime summer range for elk and pronghorn as well as for domestic grazing animals. Predators such as coyotes and red-tailed hawks are attracted by the abundance of small mammals. Broad-tailed hummingbirds time their breeding cycle to coincide with the flowering of their most important nectar sources: larkspur, trumpet flower, and paintbrush. Many other species, including mountain bluebirds, tree swallows, common nighthawks, and several species of bats, forage for insects over the meadows, returning to nest or roost within the protection of adjacent forests.

Burrowers Large and Small

The northern pocket gopher is one of the most highly evolved of all burrowing mammals. The body is tubular in shape and equipped with powerful neck and shoulder muscles that enhance its digging prowess.

In addition, sensitive whiskers surrounding the mouth and nose assist in tunnel navigation. The forefeet have long, sharply curved claws, and the lips close behind the upper incisors, enabling the pocket gopher to gnaw roots and to use the incisors for tunnel excavation without packing the mouth with soil. Perhaps the most unusual of the pocket gopher's adaptations, however, are the capacious, outward-folded, fur-lined cheek pouches that carry the food items obtained while foraging. Pocket gophers are herbivores, and though they spend most of the year underground, they will emerge on summer nights to clip, eat, and cache vegetation.

During the excavation of their extensive tunnel systems, pocket gophers loosen dirt with their long front claws and, when necessary, use their large, chisel-shaped incisors as excavating tools. In some cases, the gopher may also use its upper incisors to anchor its body in place while digging. Excavated dirt is pushed backward under the body and then directed toward the surface or into a burrow that is no longer being used. Mounds of freshly excavated dirt, with a small plug of soil blocking the entrance hole, are often conspicuous in mountain grasslands or meadows and indicate recent pocket gopher activity. Networks of cylindrical soil casts, called gopher eskers, or garlands, are produced when tunnels in the snow along the ground surface are packed with soil brought up from below ground as a result of winter foraging activities. Abandoned burrow systems, in turn, provide shelter for a variety of other small mammals, tiger salamanders, toads, snakes, and insects.

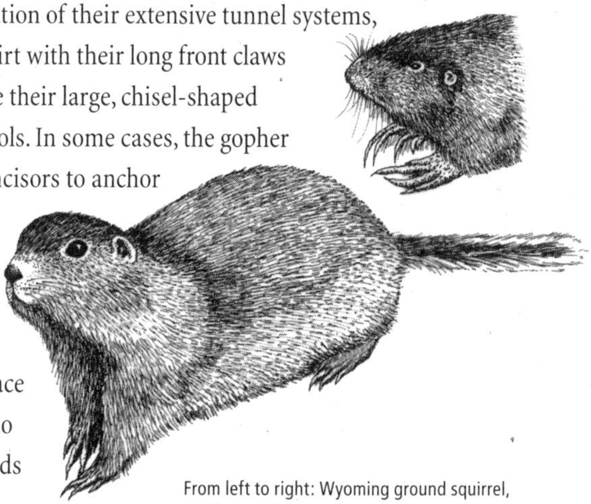

From left to right: Wyoming ground squirrel, northern pocket gopher.

The ecology of the montane vole, like that of the pocket gopher, reflects the grass-dominated ecosystems in which it evolved. Both the montane and the long-tailed vole subsist primarily on grasses and are equipped with evergrowing incisors, allowing them to eat silica-rich, abrasive plant material; as the teeth wear down, they continue to grow from the roots. Additionally, the problem of digesting the complex carbohydrates (cellulose and hemicellulose) found in grasses is solved by microorganism-driven fermentation in a rumenlike foregut, an anatomical adaptation unique to voles but similar to that found in grazing or browsing animals such as elk, deer, and mountain sheep.

Grazers

Historically, mountain grasslands and meadows supported enormous herds of bison, pronghorn, and elk, the true aficionados of open country. The last bison in the Southern Rockies was shot in South Park in the late 1800s. There is increasing evidence that bison made use of alpine tundra as well prior to that time. Pronghorn are much less common in the mountains than on the High Plains, although small bands are often seen in the San Luis Valley and in both Middle and North parks. The great herds of elk reported by explorers such as John Frémont were largely extirpated by market hunters prior to the 1900s, but reintroductions and hunting restrictions have reestablished populations in most areas of the Southern Rockies. In Rocky Mountain National Park, where the winter resident elk population has soared to more than 2,000 animals, population control in the absence of natural predation has become a chronic problem. In other areas of the Southern Rockies, elk must compete with domestic livestock for grazing space and are further restricted by the appropriation of former elk habitat for residential developments and recreational use.

The ruminant digestive system has played a critical role in the evolutionary success of mountain ungulates (hoofed mammals). Because of it, these species are able to rapidly harvest large amounts of forage and then retreat to suitable cover or to the relative safety of the herd, where the real work of digestion can begin. While the animal rests, partially digested food is regurgitated, chewed more thoroughly, shunted to a compartment of the stomach (the omasum) for further mechanical reworking, and then passed to another compartment of the stomach for bacterial processing. Elk, in contrast to mule deer, are primarily grazers rather than browsers. Grasses and other herbaceous plants dominate the elk's diet during the spring and summer, with shrubs and aspen bark supplementing herbaceous forage during fall and winter. Grass provides substantially more energy, while winter browse plants are a better source of protein. Consequently, by consuming both grass and browse, elk are able to obtain a more nutritionally complete diet than if they were restricted to a single forage type.

During the winter months, the forage available to elk seldom provides sufficient nutrients to meet the metabolic requirements of traveling and foraging in deep snow and withstanding winter temperatures. Fat stores accumulated while the animals were on their summer ranges must be utilized to meet these demands, resulting in substantial weight loss over the course of the winter. The ability to survive winter stresses depends to a large degree on the nutritional quality and digestibility of the forage consumed by elk on their summer ranges. Thus, the maintenance of healthy elk populations depends on the quality and availability of good summer and winter range—and the maintenance of a healthy microflora in the rumen to assist digestion.

Birds of a Feather

The birds that inhabit open country exhibit adaptations in physical appearance and behavior that differ markedly from those of forest species. Cryptic or camouflage coloration is common in many species such as the common snipe, Lincoln's sparrow, vesper sparrow, savannah sparrow, horned lark, and water pipit. These species forage and nest on or near the ground, and their cryptic coloration enables them to blend in with the background vegetation. In much the same way that herd formation benefits grazing animals, flocking behavior provides critical group protection for birds foraging in open environments. Additionally, the white outer tail feathers that distinguish several flocking species, including vesper sparrows, horned larks, and juncos, flash conspicuously in flight and serve to maintain visual contact as the birds move from area to area.

Good vision and finely tuned flight capabilities are critical to the success of many open-country predators. Hawks of the genus *Buteo*, such as the red-tailed hawk, probably have the keenest eyesight known; a red-tailed hawk is believed to be able to detect a mouse from one-third to one-half mile away. The broad, blunt wings typical of *Buteos* and golden eagles provide high lift, allowing them to take off at low speeds, often with heavy prey, and to maintain soaring flight as they hunt; these species often use the natural updrafts (thermals) that develop over open country to stay aloft for long periods. The northern harrier combines keen eyesight; a sound-concentrating, owl-like facial disk; and a somewhat rocking, close-quartering flight style when searching for prey. Northern harriers have been reported to pluck vole nests from the ground and shake them in midair, catching the tiny mammals as they tumble out.

Insectivorous birds, such as the common nighthawk and all species of swallows, are equipped with wings that narrow abruptly at the tip, providing high speed and maneuverability for capturing insects in flight; these species also have bristlelike feathers encircling their bills that help to funnel insects toward their mouths. Some species, such as the insectivorous mountain bluebird and the loggerhead shrike, which feeds on small mammals, birds, and large insects, have perfected a wait-and-watch style of hunting; these birds typically hunt from a suitable perch—a fence post or shrub top—at the meadow's edge, fluttering kestrel-like in the air as they search or swooping down quickly when they spot prey.

Flower-filled meadows are critical to the survival of the broad-tailed hummingbird, the most common hummingbird in the Southern Rockies. Hummingbirds most likely evolved in the South American tropics, where flowers bloom throughout the year. Of the eighteen species of hummingbirds that occur in the western United States and Canada, all are nectar feeders with extremely high metabolic rates (the fastest of any bird) but with only limited storage capacities for nectar in their crops and livers. Each day, the average hummingbird must consume about half its weight in food, primarily nectar, but in the absence of flowers, hummingbirds will eat large quantities of tiny insects (gnats, flies, mosquitos, and aphids) and spiders. To cope with the chilling

Broad-tailed hummingbird (male).

climate and uncertain nectar production associated with most mountain habitats, hummingbirds have become energy conservation specialists. Soon after arriving on their mountain breeding territories in spring, male broad-tails stake out choice feeding territories where nectar-producing flowers are clustered, often restricting females to less productive areas. The situation is further complicated in late July and early August by the arrival of aggressive rufous hummingbirds migrating south, initiating fierce competition for the available nectar. For the female broad-tail, who must meet not only her own energy requirements but also those of her eggs and nestlings, any decline in food supplies, either through competitive exclusion, drought, or inclement weather, necessitates drastic measures to maintain the energy balance. Short-term energy crises occur frequently, but in most cases the female is able to achieve considerable energy conservation through careful insulation of her nest and by lowering her body temperature and energy demands and entering a brief state of semihibernation, or torpor, between foraging bouts; hummingbirds do not enter torpor every night but make use of it as a contingency measure. Torpor rarely exceeds eight hours in length; when their body temperatures warm up to about 86°F, they are able to resume flying. In the most extreme situations, when adverse conditions do not abate, female hummingbirds are forced to abandon their nests and fend for themselves in order to survive.

Life Histories of Selected Animals

Mammals

Masked Shrew, *Sorex cinereus.* This medium-sized shrew is distinguished from voles and mice by its long, pointed snout, its tiny eyes, and the dark, reddish black pigmentation on the tips of its pointed teeth. Masked shrews are common year-round in moist habitats throughout the Southern Rockies. Highly active, shrews forage with rapid, darting movements above ground or burrow through loose litter to locate invertebrates and other prey. Predators apparently find shrews to be unpalatable because of their odiferous glandular secretions. Female shrews bear several litters of four to ten young each year in nests hidden in cavities of old stumps or logs, under rocks, or in the abandoned burrows of other small mammals. Newborn shrews are blind and helpless, but attain self-sufficiency at three to four weeks of age.

Big Brown Bat, *Eptesicus fuscus.* Widely distributed in North America, the big brown bat is distinguished from other brown bats by its large size (only the hoary bat is larger), membranous black ears and wings, and strong, direct flight. This species is a beetle specialist, emerging at dusk to forage on flying insects; individuals may chatter audibly during foraging flights. Big brown bats are most commonly observed over grasslands and meadows, but are also seen in ponderosa woodlands. Big brown bats exhibit a predilection for using man-made structures such as porches, eaves, bridges, attics, and mine structures for diurnal roosts; natural rock crevices are also used. These bats spend the winter alone or in small colonies (up to several hundred individuals) in a protected hibernaculum near the summer roosting area. Breeding occurs prior to hibernation, but fertilization and implantation of the embryo are delayed until spring. Females generally give birth to one nearly hairless young in mid-June. Development is rapid, and young bats can fly within three to four weeks of birth. Big brown bats are long-lived: a record age of nineteen years has been reported.

Mountain (or Nuttall's) Cottontail, *Sylvilagus nuttallii.* This medium-sized rabbit is distinguished from the eastern and desert cottontails by its smaller size, shorter ears, dark dorsal color, and habitat preference for forest edge and sagebrush; the desert cottontail prefers open, semiarid grassland and foothill shrub communities and is most consistently found at lower elevations than the mountain cottontail. The diet varies with availability and season, ranging from succulent forbs to woody plants. Cottontails are largely nocturnal, making use of forms (unlined depressions) or other sheltered spots for resting during the day. Like most rabbits, the mountain cottontail is typically solitary, but groups may be found foraging close together in grassy clearings bordered by brush. This species breeds throughout the warmer months, giving birth to altricial young in a protected, fur-lined nest.

Wyoming Ground Squirrel, *Spermophilus elegans.* Resembling a diminutive prairie dog in appearance, the Wyoming ground squirrel is identified by its brownish gray coloring, cinnamon nose, and the absence of striping. In the Southern Rockies, the species reaches its southern limits in the Gunnison Basin, but it is believed to be actively expanding its range. Wyoming ground squirrels are common in open grasslands, meadows, and sagebrush stands, at elevations of 6,000 to 12,000 feet. Diet is variable, consisting mostly of grasses, forbs, and some shrubs; carrion is eaten when available. The species is diurnal and highly colonial, with dominance hierarchies, vocalizations, and territorial maintenance circumscribing individual movements and social interactions within the colony. Wyoming ground squirrels begin accumulating fat reserves for hibernation in midsummer, retreating to their burrows in late August or early September. Mating takes place soon after emergence from hibernation, in late April, and females bear a single litter of altricial young; young squirrels first appear above ground in early June.

Northern Pocket Gopher, *Thomomys talpoides.* This small, snub-nosed rodent is easily identified by its long, curved claws, prominent yellowish orange incisors (always in view because the lips close behind them), and external fur-lined cheek pouches. In the Southern Rockies, northern pocket gophers occur from the foothills to the alpine zone and are mostly encountered in sites with well-drained, relatively fine-textured soils. Active year-round, this solitary animal maintains tunnel systems that can be extensive and are distinguished by loose mounds of soil or by sinuous, pipelike soil castings. Mating occurs in April or May, and a single litter of altricial young is born in late spring.

Montane Vole, *Microtus montanus.* This small rodent is distinguished from the more familiar deer mouse by its dark grayish brown fur, small eyes, inconspicuous ears, and pale gray underparts. In the Southern Rockies, montane voles are common in moist meadows and in open aspen woodlands, wherever a dense cover of grasses and forbs permits these herbivores to construct their elaborate network of runways. Active year-round and typically nocturnal, the montane vole may begin breeding activity beneath the snowpack. Altricial young are born in a ball-shaped grass nest after a three-week gestation period; the young voles develop rapidly, and females of the first litter may breed during their first summer of life.

Coyote, *Canis latrans.* This handsome German shepherd–sized canid takes its name from the Aztec word *coyotl* and is distinguished from a fox by its larger size, buffy gray fur, and black-tipped tail, which points downward when the animal runs. These highly adaptable animals are encountered in nearly every habitat type, but they prefer open country. The amazing repertoire of coyote vocalizations includes yips, a trailing howl, and serenades of group yip-howling. Most active at sunrise and sunset, the coyote hunts small prey but will also consume carrion and fruit when available.

Coyotes are less social than wolves; the basic social unit consists of an adult male, a female, and their young. Solitary individuals or a mated pair generally follow a habitual hunting trail; cooperative hunting occurs only when food is abundant. Courtship behavior begins two to three months prior to the onset of estrus, which takes place between January and March. Coyotes rarely mate for life, but pairs may remain together for several years. Dens are often located near water. A male provisions the female and their five to seven offspring until the pups are about eight weeks old. Longevity is usually fewer than ten years.

Elk (or Wapiti), *Cervus elaphus.* The American elk is easily identified by its large size, coarse brown fur, dark mane, straw-colored rump patch, and inconspicuous tail. Mature bulls stand five feet tall at the shoulder and weigh 750 pounds or more. Grazing occurs mostly just after dawn and at dusk; elk retreat to forest cover during daylight and at night, and the same trails and bedding areas are used repeatedly. Elk are gregarious; wintering herds tend to be quite large, with anywhere from twenty-five to several hundred animals of mixed sexes and ages. Bulls are first to leave the wintering herds, following the retreating snow line to higher elevation meadows. Cows and calves eventually follow the bulls to summer range and remain there until fall. Breeding begins in mid- to late September with the onset of the rut, which involves the bull's flutelike vocalizations (bugling), swelling of the chest and neck, antler rubbing and thrashing, wallowing, and ritualized battles with other bulls to assert authority over the harem bands of cows, calves, and yearlings that each has assembled. Once dominance has been asserted, typically by bulls of four or more years in age, cows are bred, each giving birth to a single precocial calf in late May or June (near the wintering range or during migration to the summer range).

Birds

Red-tailed Hawk, *Buteo jamaicensis.* This common hawk is distinguished from other raptors by its large size, broad wings, brick-red tail, brown patagial stripe on the leading edges of its wings, crescent-shaped wrist patches, and the diffuse band of brown streaks across its pale breast; plumage can be extremely variable. The call of the red-tail is distinctive: a harsh, descending *kee-e-e-e.* Red-tailed hawks still-hunt from high perches (the tops of trees, utility poles, or rocky outcrops) or while soaring. Consummate soarers, red-tailed hawks are often seen making wide, lazy circles on thermals over open country or riding the deflection air currents along ridgelines. When soaring, the wings are held flat and the body does not tilt to and fro as with turkey vultures. Red-tails are thought to mate for life. Pairs remain faithful to their territories year after year. Courtship flights can be spectacular and consist of a series of steep dives and climbs. Nests are built of sticks and are typically in the tops of tall trees, on ledges on the sides of canyons, or on rocky outcrops; fresh greenery is brought to the nest throughout the nesting season. Females incubate the eggs, which they lay in late winter or earliest spring; males deliver food to the female while she is on the nest. The young are able to fly after forty-five days; the juveniles try to elicit food deliveries from the adults with loud, shrill begging calls for weeks after fledging occurs.

Northern Harrier, *Circus cyaneus.* Formerly called the marsh hawk, this slender-bodied hawk is distinguished from other medium-sized raptors by its long, narrow wings, owl-like facial disk, and white rump patch; females have brownish upperparts, while males are gray or gray-brown. Northern harriers are conspicuous as they search for prey because of their acrobatic, close-quartering flight. The northern harrier has a facial disk and large ear openings that collect the squeaks and scampering noises of its prey; when a harrier detects prey, it may hover briefly and then execute a corkscrew drop to the ground. Courtship flights, consisting of dives, swoops, and wingovers, are spectacular and often occur within a hundred feet or so of the ground. Harrier nests are located on the ground in dense cover. The female harrier incubates the eggs alone, but the male supplies her and the nestlings with food; the male passes the food to the female while both are in flight.

Broad-tailed Hummingbird, *Selasphorus platycercus.* The male broad-tail is easily distinguished by its metallic-green crown, rose-red gorget, and cricketlike "trilling" sound produced by the wings in flight; the female and juvenile birds both lack the red gorget and have a wash of reddish brown along the flanks. The only other hummingbird commonly seen foraging in the mountain grasslands and meadows of the Southern Rockies during the summer months is the **rufous hummingbird** (*S. rufus*), an iridescent orange-red species that enters the area only during its migration to and from its breeding range in the Northwest; competitive interactions between these two species can be spectacular. Male broad-tails arrive on the breeding grounds before the females. The display flights of the male are conspicuous, with a pendulumlike pattern consisting of a series of U-shaped power dives. Like most hummingbirds, this species nectars at flowers, at sap wells excavated by sapsuckers, and will take small insects when available. The female builds a tiny lichen-covered nest, typically a few feet or more above the ground in a tree or tall shrub; she attaches the nest to the branch with spider webbing. Female broad-tailed hummingbirds incubate the eggs and rear the two young without assistance from the male; the male's reproductive strategy is to mate with as many females as possible during the breeding season. This species overwinters from central Mexico to Guatemala.

Mountain Bluebird, *Sialia currucoides.* The male mountain bluebird is sky blue, with the darkest blue on the upperparts, wings, and tail; the female is a brownish blue overall. Mountain bluebirds are insectivorous, foraging from perches, by flycatching, or by hovering kestrel-like over the ground. This species prefers forest-edge habitats close to piñon-juniper woodland, open ponderosa pine, and aspen forests that provide suitable cavity trees for nesting. The mountain bluebird nests in tree cavities or in nest boxes; the loss of suitable cavity-nesting sites has reduced bluebird populations in many areas. Nesting can occur as early as mid-April, shortly after the birds return from their wintering areas, or as late as early July at high-elevation sites. The female lines the tree cavity with fine plant materials and proceeds to incubate the four to six eggs; incubation takes about thirteen days. The male feeds the female who, in turn, feeds the nestlings in the first few days after hatching; both sexes will eventually take turns feeding the young until fledging occurs. Family groups flock together in late summer and are a common sight in high-elevation meadows.

Savannah Sparrow, *Passerculus sandwichensis.* This small, common sparrow inhabits open, moist grasslands and meadows with dense cover. Savannah sparrows are distinguished from other sparrows that frequent open country by their prominent allover brown streaking, notched tail, and pink legs and feet; a breast spot is generally present. In the Southern Rockies, this species is a common summer resident and migrant. Savannah sparrows forage on the ground for insects, exhibiting a hopping style and sometimes double-scratching to locate food. When approached, this species runs rapidly through the grass with its head carried low, or it may fly short distances to drop quickly into vegetation cover. Males arrive on the breeding grounds before females, establishing territories and giving their buzzy trill from prominent perches.

Common Animals of the Mountain Grasslands and Meadows

Mammals

Badger, American, *Taxidea taxus*
Bat, big brown, *Eptesicus fuscus*
  silver-haired, *Lasionycteris noctivagans*
Chipmunk, least, *Tamias minimus*
Cottontail, mountain (or Nuttall's), *Sylvilagus nuttallii*
Coyote, *Canis latrans*
Deer, mule, *Odocoileus hemionus*
Elk (or Wapiti), *Cervus elaphus*
Fox, red, *Vulpes vulpes*
Jackrabbit, white-tailed, *Lepus townsendii*
Kangaroo Rat, Ord's, *Dipodomys ordii*
Marmot, yellow-bellied, *Marmota flaviventris*
Mouse, deer, *Peromyscus maniculatus*
  northern grasshopper, *Onychomys leucogaster*
  silky pocket, *Perognathus flavus*
  western harvest, *Reithrodontomys megalotis*

western jumping, *Zapus princeps*
Myotis, little brown, *Myotis lucifugus*
Pocket Gopher, northern, *Thomomys talpoides*
Botta's (or Valley Pocket Gopher), *T. bottae*
Pronghorn, *Antilocapra americana*
Sheep, bighorn, *Ovis canadensis*
Shrew, masked, *Sorex cinereus*
montane, *S. monticolus*
Squirrel, golden-mantled ground, *Spermophilus lateralis*
Wyoming ground, *S. elegans*
Vole, long-tailed, *Microtus longicaudus*
montane, *M. montanus*
Weasel, long-tailed, *Mustela frenata*

Birds

Blackbird, Brewer's, *Euphagus cyanocephalus*
red-winged, *Agelaius phoeniceus*
Bluebird, mountain, *Sialia currucoides*
western, *S. mexicana*
Cowbird, brown-headed, *Molothrus ater*
Eagle, golden, *Aquila chrysaetos*
Falcon, prairie, *Falco mexicanus*
Goldfinch, American, *Carduelis tristis*
Grouse, sharp-tailed, *Tympanuchus phasianellus*
Harrier, northern, *Circus cyaneus*
Hawk, red-tailed, *Buteo jamaicensis*
rough-legged, *B. lagopus*
Hummingbird, broad-tailed, *Selasphorus platycercus*
rufous, *S. rufus*
Junco, dark-eyed, *Junco hyemalis*
Kestrel, American (formerly Sparrow Hawk), *Falco sparverius*
Kingbird, western, *Tyrannus verticalis*
Lark, horned, *Eremophila alpestris*
Magpie, black-billed, *Pica hudsonia*
Meadowlark, western, *Sturnella neglecta*

Nighthawk, common, *Chordeiles minor*
Owl, great horned, *Bubo virginianus*
Pipit, water, *Anthus spinoletta*
Raven, common, *Corvus corax*
Robin, American, *Turdus migratorius*
Shrike, loggerhead, *Lanius ludovicianus*
Snipe, common, *Gallinago gallinago*
Sparrow, Brewer's, *Spizella breweri*
chipping, *S. passerina*
lark, *Chondestes grammacus*
Lincoln's, *Melospiza lincolnii*
savannah, *Passerculus sandwichensis*
vesper, *Pooecetes gramineus*
white-crowned, *Zonotrichia leucophrys*
violet-green, *Tachycineta thalassina*

Reptiles and Amphibians

Frog, western chorus, *Pseudacris triseriata*
Garter Snake, western terrestrial, *Thamnophis elegans*
Lizard, short-horned, *Phrynosoma douglassii*

Butterflies

Arctic, chryxus, *Oeneis chryxus*
Checkerspot, anicia, *Occidryas anicia*
arachne, *Paladryas arachne*
Copper, blue, *Chalceria heteronea*
ruddy, *C. rubida*
Crescent, northern, *Phyciodes cocyta*
Crescentspot, pearly, *Phyciodes tharos*
Fritillary, Atlantis, *Speyeria atlantis*
Parnassian, phoebus, *Parnassius phoebus*
Rocky Mountain, *P. smintheus*
Ringlet, ochre, *Coenonympha ochracea*
Skipperling, garita, *Oarisma garita*
Sulfur, Queen Alexandra's, *Colias alexandra*

Streambank and Shoreline: Mountain Wetlands

Water is the one compound that binds all life together. The mingling of land and water is a theme repeated with endless variations in the Southern Rockies. In valleys washed with sunshine or in cool, shaded canyons, the lush tangle of vegetation and wildlife diversity associated with wetland habitats provides a striking contrast to adjacent upland communities. Though seldom extensive, wetland communities are among the most biologically productive ecosystems in the West.

Wetland ecosystems exist in a fragile balance; even subtle changes in the water table can cause irreversible damage. Throughout the Southern Rockies, as in most areas of the West, wetlands are in jeopardy, doomed to increasing fragmentation and dewatering from both climatic changes and a host of human activities. Severe drought can transform a lush oasis for life into a brittle, mud-cracked wasteland in a single season. Much of the human-wrought destruction is the result of transmountain and other water diversion projects, stream channelization, development dredge and fill, peat mining, and degradation related to agricultural activities. Because the region's economic development has been largely concentrated along mountain watercourses and floodplain corridors, ecosystems associated with streams and rivers have been especially hard hit. The future of many mountain wetlands remains uncertain, dependent on our wise stewardship of these important ecosystems.

Ecological Distribution

The term *wetland* is a catchall for lands that are transitional between aquatic and terrestrial ecosystems and where the water table is usually at or near the ground surface during all or part of the year. In the Southern Rockies, ecosystems associated with standing or flowing water are shaped by different ecological processes and form distinctly different communities. For simplicity, however, the mountain wetland ecosystems described in this chapter are broken down into three major types, based on the physiognomy, or growth form, of the dominant plants: (1) riparian forests, (2) shrub-dominated wetlands, and (3) herbaceous wetlands. Within these broad categories, differences in moisture availability, soil, nutrient characteristics, and plant associations are used to separate wetlands into ecologically distinct communities.

Riparian communities are associated with the banks and borders of bodies of water. Plant communities bordering flowing waters assume a linear configuration, extending as a somewhat continuous strand of distinctive vegetation through several life zones. Major riparian communities that form continuous strands include those along the Rio Grande, the Arkansas, the Platte, and the entire Colorado River system. Riparian communities associated with standing water or with high water tables are found along the shores of ponds and lakes, in ravines and gulches, in association with springs or other areas of groundwater seepage, or in situations where the local geology or topography traps moisture and maintains a high water table.

Most shrub-dominated and herbaceous wetlands persist only in topographic sites where moisture is available in abundance as a result of seasonal or permanent runoff. Such sites include well-watered depressions adjacent to streams, ponds, or lakes, the surfaces of solifluction terraces, and areas where late-lying snow has filled small basins. Successional wetland communities are typical of areas where a pond or lake has filled with sediment. Wetland biologists classify herbaceous and shrub-dominated wetlands on the basis of their soils. Organic soils are defined as having 20 percent or more organic carbon by weight; these soils, in contrast to the pale color and gravelly or sandy texture typical of most mineral soils, are generally dark colored and somewhat fibrous in texture because they contain partially decomposed plant materials. Wet meadows and marshes are herbaceous wetland ecosystems developed on sites with mineral soils; true bogs and fens, on the other hand, are herbaceous wetland ecosystems developed on organic soils. The term *carr* is used to refer to a shrub-dominated fen.

Herbaceous wetlands developed on mineral soils occur wherever alluvial sediments accumulate more rapidly than organic materials or where organic material is being lost through microbial activity or oxidation. Wetlands developed on organic soil are largely restricted to valley bottoms and natural depressions, wherever drainage is sluggish and where peat is accumulating in response to the incomplete decomposition of plant and animal remains. The term *bog* is frequently used incorrectly to refer to any soggy, peat-rich wetland. Wetland biologists, however, define a bog as a herbaceous wetland whose principal source of water is surface runoff. Bogs, then, are largely rain fed, or ombrotrophic, and tend to be nutrient poor, acidic, and characterized by a depauperate, highly specialized flora. Fens, on the other hand, are nourished by both surface runoff and groundwater sources, resulting in waters with a high nutrient content capable of supporting an extraordinary diversity of plants. Wetland ecologists believe that fens are widespread in the Southern Rockies and that true bogs are exceedingly rare in the Rocky Mountains south of Canada.

Physical Environment

Water is the primary factor controlling the environment and the associated plant and animal life of mountain wetlands. It is difficult to generalize about the climatic and environmental conditions that characterize these ecosystems because they traverse such a broad elevational range. In placing mountain wetlands within the broad framework of mountain climate, it is important to keep in mind that an increase in elevation is typically associated with a decrease in temperature and an increase in precipitation. Consequently, the linear configuration typical of many riparian communities results in conspicuous changes in the vegetation and associated fauna in relation to the elevation gradient. Though communities tend to intergrade continuously along environmental gradients, each community can be described according to a given range of temperature, humidity, type and amount of precipitation, growing-season length, amount and distribution of wind, and soils.

Climatic variables such as precipitation and temperature are strongly influenced by differences in slope and exposure. Precipitation patterns are modified by local conditions, such as whether the ecosystem is located on a west-facing or east-facing slope, and by the geographical position of the ecosystem with regard to regional precipitation regimes. Microclimatic contrasts resulting from variations in the amount of solar radiation received by south-facing slopes as opposed to north-facing slopes can be great. At lower elevations, these differences are often reflected in the character and species composition of the riparian community. Riparian communities located in valleys tend to be colder than communities on slopes or on ridgetops as a result of cold air drainage and the pooling of cold air that occurs in topographically enclosed basins. During the colder months, visual evidence of the effects of cold air drainage can be seen at dawn, when a zone of hoar frost often parallels a drainage system or delineates a valley bottom.

Community Characteristics

Mountain wetlands are unique in their combination of high species diversity, high species density, and high productivity. It is not uncommon for a mountain riparian community to contain two to three times the number of species, both plant and animal, as adjacent upland communities. Elevation and factors that affect water chemistry, such as nutrient content, salinity, acidity, and oxygen richness, play a critical role in determining the species composition of a particular wetland community. Most riparian forests, for example, consist of a mosaic of stands that differ in structure, age, and species composition, forming a continuum of change along altitudinal gradients.

Lowland and Foothill Wetlands

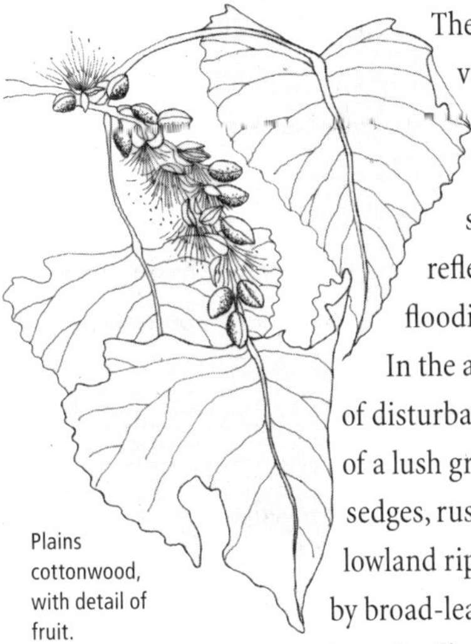

Plains cottonwood, with detail of fruit.

The riparian flora of the lowland valleys and foothill canyons is especially rich because of the mixing of lowland and mountain species. Each community type reflects differences in water availability, flooding history, and human disturbance. In the absence of grazing or other types of disturbance, the forest understory consists of a lush growth of shrubs, forbs, grasses, sedges, rushes, and climbing vines. Most lowland riparian communities are dominated by broad-leaved species of cottonwood, peach-leaved willow, and box-elder; plains cottonwood is most common on the Eastern Slope, while Frémont and Rio Grande cottonwoods dominate the western and southwestern valleys. Some lowland riparian forests contain an abundance of introduced species, such as Russian olive, green ash, and tamarisk (salt cedar). Dense gallery forests, such as New Mexico's beloved bosques, prevail on the broadest floodplains and consist of various combinations of the dominant riparian forest species and thickets of coyote willow, sandbar willow, and snowberry.

With increasing elevation, broad-leaved cottonwoods are replaced in most communities by narrowleaf cottonwood; lanceleaf cottonwood, a hybrid of plains and narrowleaf cottonwoods, may also be present. In the moist canyons of north-central New Mexico, species such as red-osier dogwood, wild privet (or forestiera), and New Mexican locust may be locally common. In Colorado and northward into southern Wyoming, community associates of narrowleaf cottonwood include shrub willows, mountain alder, and twinberry. Species such as netleaf hackberry, wild plum, chokecherry, and hawthorn are common in drier canyons and gulches. Cool ravines along the eastern foothills of the Colorado Front Range harbor Pleistocene relict populations of beaked hazelnut and wild sarsaparilla, tree species of the eastern United States; in the foothills near Boulder, North America's southernmost stand of paper birch occurs with beaked hazelnut.

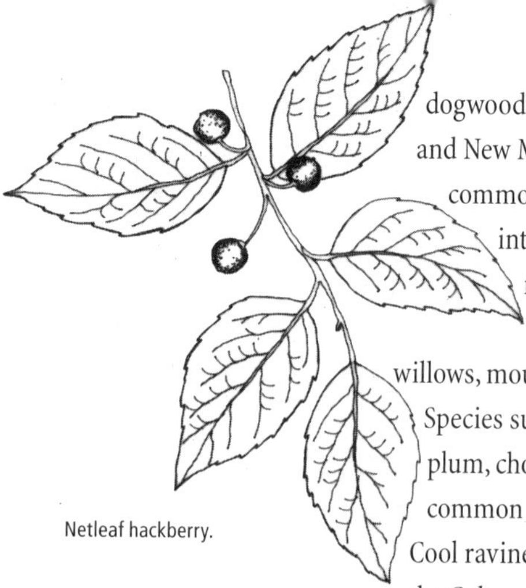

Netleaf hackberry.

In the more arid mountain parks and intermontane basins, such as Wyoming's Shirley Basin and Colorado's San Luis Valley, poor drainage and saline-alkaline soils support shrub wetlands dominated by greasewood and salt-tolerant species such as rabbitbrush, fourwing saltbush, cattails, Baltic rush, and saltgrass. The most lush and well-watered communities provide critical nesting habitat for waterfowl, both red-winged and yellow-headed blackbirds, marsh wrens, and sora rails.

Montane Wetlands

Montane riparian communities are dominated by discontinuous forests of narrowleaf cottonwood, mountain alder, and river birch. Colorado blue spruce and Douglas-fir are common in the cooler canyons and may occur with white fir in montane riparian forests from central Colorado south into New Mexico. One or several species of willow as well as shrubs such as red-osier dogwood, Rocky Mountain maple, twinberry, common gooseberry, red elderberry, and shrubby cinquefoil predominate in the understory. In some situations, aspen may form dense stands along the margins of certain wetlands; aspen-dominated communities are often characterized by lush understories of grasses and wildflowers such as cow parsnip and false hellebore.

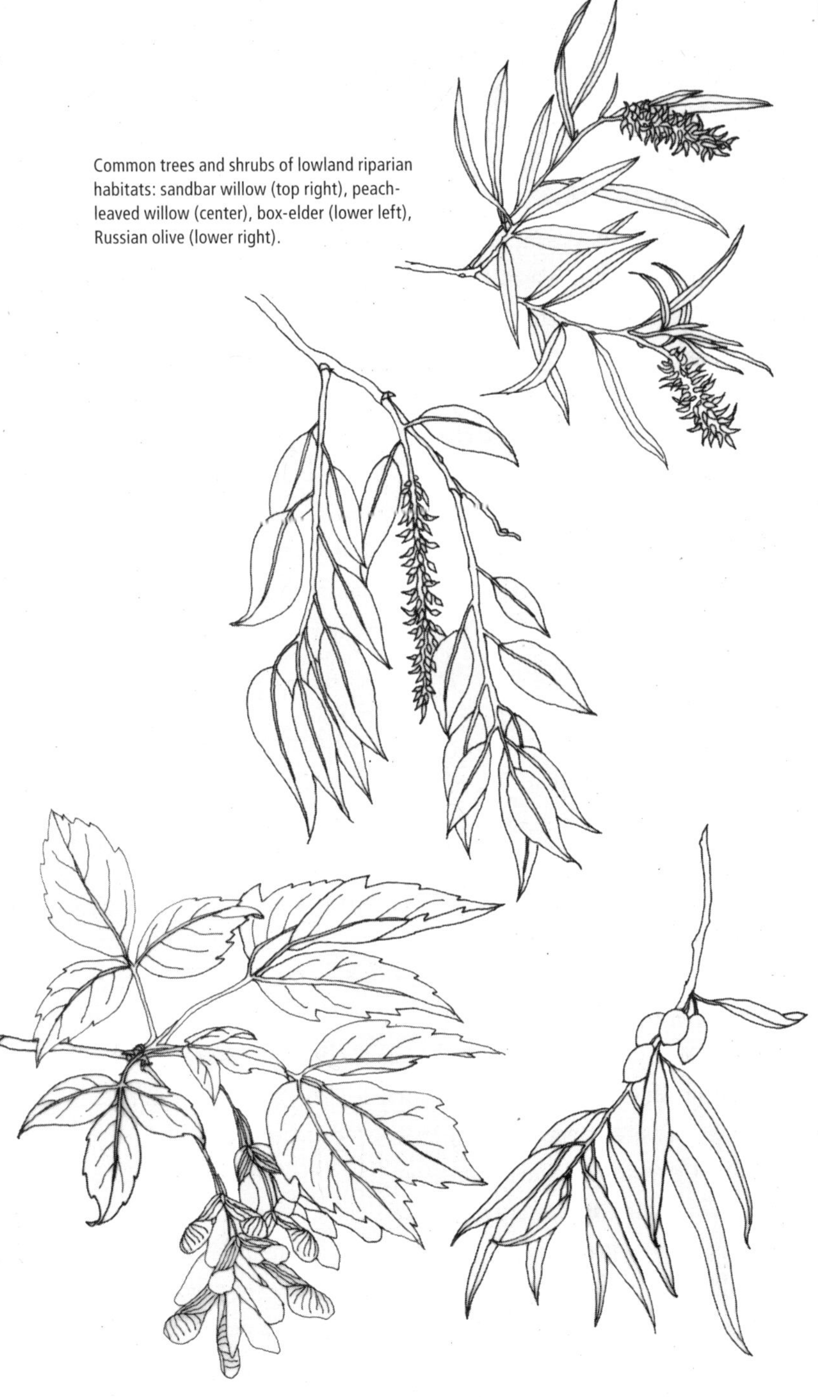

Common trees and shrubs of lowland riparian habitats: sandbar willow (top right), peach-leaved willow (center), box-elder (lower left), Russian olive (lower right).

Herbaceous and shrub-dominated wetlands are common in the montane zone throughout the Southern Rockies. Species diversity tends to be low in these communities, in contrast to most riparian forests or to drier herbaceous communities. Single-species stands are common and are often dominated by sedges, rushes, turf-forming grasses, or, less commonly, water-loving forbs. Where such a community encircles a lake, pond, or moisture-retaining depression, different species associations frequently form discrete bands, each reflecting changes in moisture conditions. In other situations, these communities may form "islands" within drier ecosystem types.

Shrub wetlands dominated by shrubby cinquefoil are common in valley bottoms and may form circular zones around willow-dominated shrub wetlands. The organic soils associated with abandoned stream meanders, floodplain depressions, and the borders of ponds and lakes provide suitable sites for the development of willow carrs and other types of shrub wetlands; the species typically found in these communities include mountain (or yellow-twigged) willow, Geyer willow, river birch, and grasses such as Canadian reedgrass.

Subalpine Wetlands

Subalpine riparian forests are dominated largely by coniferous trees. Blue spruce is the most common species throughout the Southern Rockies and, with few exceptions, is largely confined to floodplains, moist terraces, and shorelines associated with permanent water supplies. White fir is found with blue spruce from the central Southern Rockies south into New Mexico, and hybrids of blue spruce and Engelmann spruce are common throughout this zone. Deciduous species such as narrowleaf cottonwood, aspen, and mountain-ash extend from the montane into the subalpine zone in some areas; small stands of balsam poplar, a possible Pleistocene relict common in the Central and Northern Rockies, are found in scattered locations in the Southern Rockies is far south as Gunnison.

Herbaceous plants form a rank understory in many subalpine riparian forests. Along the rushing streams that grace the higher mountains, tall wildflowers such as cow parsnip, chiming bells, bittercress, twisted stalk, arrowleaf groundsel, larkspur, and monkshood produce a showy, waist-high display. Striking wildflowers such as Parry's primrose, yellow monkeyflower,

Common trees and shrubs of mountain riparian habitats, clockwise from upper left: Rocky Mountain maple, narrow-leaf cottonwood, planeleaf willow with detail of male catkins, mountain alder with detail of female catkins, western river birch.

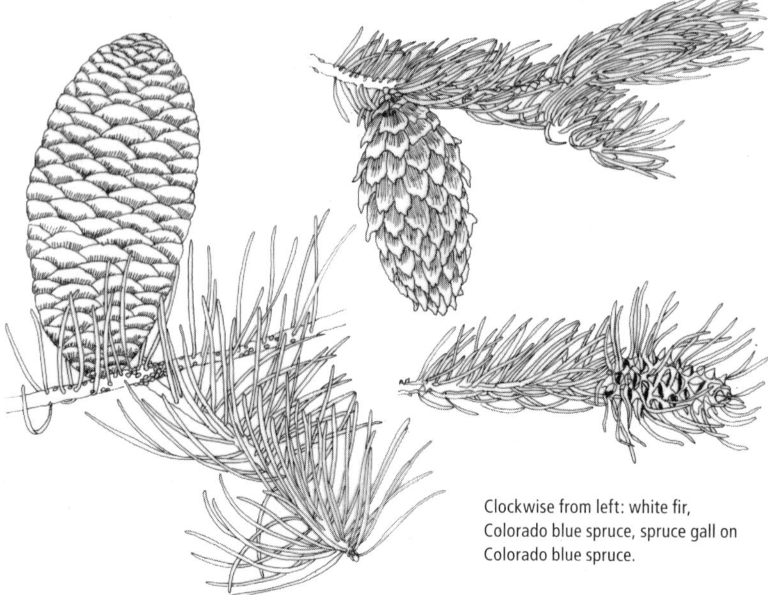
Clockwise from left: white fir, Colorado blue spruce, spruce gall on Colorado blue spruce.

globeflower, northern bog orchid, and marsh-marigold are common in many streamside and shoreline communities. The white rhododendron and the magenta Lewis's monkeyflower, species typical of the flora of the Northern Rockies and the Pacific Northwest, are restricted to moist habitats in the Park Range.

Shrub wetlands and carrs are especially conspicuous in the broad, glaciated valleys of the subalpine zone. Bog birch and several species of willow dominate these communities. Planeleaf willow is perhaps the most common species and is typical of willow carrs in the San Juans, the Sawatch Range, North Park, the Laramie River Valley, and many areas of the Colorado Front Range. In spots, shrub communities form a dense, almost impenetrable thicket of tough stems and branches. Along narrow streams, willows conspire with mountain alders to keep even the most ardent angler from a promising pool. In late winter and early spring, however, these willow and bog birch communities carry the first luminous hint of spring into the high country, their stems glowing red and golden against the lingering snows. With the arrival of fall, the orange-red leaves of bog birch and the ochre hues of the willows rival the autumn display of the aspen.

Herbaceous wetlands in the subalpine zone are dominated by sedges, rushes, grasses, or spikerushes. A moss layer may be well developed in some fens, but in contrast to bogs, it seldom includes *Sphagnum* spp. Fens with an especially high water table may consist of only one or two plant species; rhizomatous species of sedge such as *Carex utriculata* or *C. aquatilis* often form dense, continuous mats in these communities. In many communities, wildflowers such as marsh-marigold, rose crown, king's crown, white bog orchid, elephantella, and several species of buttercup are often conspicuous.

Successional Wetland Communities

Mountain wetlands are diverse, dynamic systems subject to frequent change and, in some situations, replacement by other ecosystems. Many montane and subalpine wetlands reflect a landscape in transition. For example, the typical successional progression from subalpine pond or lake to spruce-fir forest involves several distinct stages and begins with a pioneer phase dominated by floating and semiemergent species such as quillwort, pondweed, buttercup, and *Carex aquatilis*. As silt and plant debris build the level of the soil relative to that of the water, a herbaceous wetland, or fen, consisting of sedges, rushes, and arid grasses such as Canadian reedgrass and tufted hairgrass begins to encroach upon the remaining open water. Eventually, a willow-dominated shrubland colonizes the fen, persisting until sufficient soil develops to a level well above the water table and permits an invasion of the area by Engelmann spruce or subalpine fir. In some cases, cold air drainage, soil characteristics, or other factors may maintain the shrub wetland and deter the growth of trees.

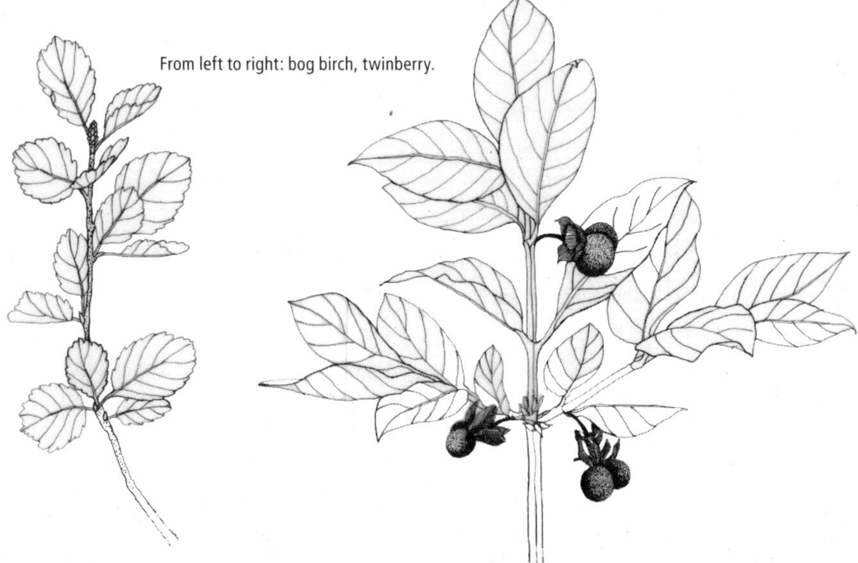

From left to right: bog birch, twinberry.

Plant Adaptation: Designs for Survival

Floodplain Strategies

Most of the principal tree and shrub species found in mountain wetlands are remarkably well adapted to sites that have higher levels of soil moisture than surrounding upland habitats. Willows and cottonwoods are obligate phreatophytes (literally "well plants") and can only survive if their root systems are in close contact with the water table. Some phreatophytes, such as the introduced tamarisk, are so successful at mining water that they can substantially lower the water table and have become the scourge of watercourses throughout the arid West. High concentrations of sodium chloride and other salts in the groundwater can reduce a plant's ability to absorb water through its roots by disrupting the osmotic balance. Willows and cottonwoods have a low salt tolerance and will grow only where the salt content of the groundwater is low. Tamarisk, on the other hand, has a high salt tolerance and proliferates, outcompeting native species, wherever the heavy use of fertilizers on adjacent agricultural lands is increasing the salinity of the groundwater.

Coping with Low Oxygen Levels

The availability of oxygen is essential to plants, just as it is to animals. Plants require oxygen for root respiration and for the active absorption of minerals by the root cells. Most terrestrial plants take in oxygen through their roots. Because oxygen diffuses many times faster in air than in water, species growing with their roots in waterlogged soils are at a distinct disadvantage. Aquatic plants solve the problem of oxygen deficiency by having within their tissues large gas-storage compartments, called lacunae, that create a continuous system of air passageways. For riparian trees and shrubs, saturated soils or prolonged intervals of flooding require unusual adaptations for coping with low levels of oxygen. The willow, for example, is stimulated when flooded to produce new, air-filled roots to replace those damaged by high-water events. Other species, such as the river birch and the mountain alder, increase the number and effectiveness of the tiny openings in their bark, called lenticels, that allow gas exchange with the atmosphere. The wettest sites are successfully occupied by narrowleaf cottonwood, mountain alder, and willows, species able to withstand flooding for portions of two growing seasons and still maintain good root growth. Species such as bog birch, Rocky Mountain maple, river birch, hawthorn, and Colorado blue spruce are able to tolerate flooding for most of a single growing season. No riparian species, however, are able to withstand flooding for periods exceeding two consecutive growing seasons.

Nitrogen Fixation

Of all the mineral elements required by plants, only nitrogen, critical for plant growth, must be obtained from the atmosphere rather than from the soil in which the plant grows. In areas that have not been previously vegetated, such as sandbars, colonization by nitrogen-fixing plants plays a critical role in primary succession. The process by which atmospheric nitrogen gas is converted into organic compounds that can be assimilated by the plant is called nitrogen fixation; this process is essential to successful colonization and is accomplished largely by certain free-living bacteria that consume organic matter in the soil, producing ammonia or nitrate as a by-product of their activities. Other types of nitrogen-fixing bacteria live in swellings, or nodules, within their host plant's roots; these specialized bacteria are involved in an ancient symbiotic relationship with their host, supplying fixed nitrogen in return for organic molecules secreted by the plant.

If you examine the roots of the mountain alder, you will see large numbers of spherical nodules that have formed as a growth response to the presence of the nitrogen-fixing, filamentous bacteria known as actinomycetes. Within these nodules, the bacteria take nitrogen from the air and transform it into nitrate compounds that are water soluble and transported throughout the tree's tissues. Alder leaves and other nitrogen-rich decaying tree tissues contribute significant amounts of nitrogen to riparian ecosystems. Trees and shrubs growing in association with mountain alder often exhibit a boost in growth resulting from the nitrogenous enrichment of their soils. In addition, the alder enhances the nutritive value of the water flowing past it, as well as the lakes, ponds, and rivers into which these waters flow.

Reproductive Strategies

Willows are finely tuned to life along rivers or streams. The reproductive cycle begins in early spring, and the seeds ripen at about the time that mountain streams and rivers are bank-full. The willow's multitudinous small seeds take to the air in clouds of silken fluff but rarely travel great distances, an advantage since they are short-lived and must land on moist soil and germinate within two to three days in order to survive. During the spring, it is common to see whitish mats of new willow seeds along the edges of gravel bars and on mudflats. Maintaining a waterside ecological niche requires resilience and the ability to resist small-scale perturbations and flood events by stabilizing the soil to prevent erosion. Both shrub and tree willows have the capacity to reproduce vegetatively, sending out a network of underground stolons and suckers as needed; even odd bits of broken stem can take root and sprout. Of course, following even the most thoughtful hiker through a dense thicket of willow saplings—or "willow slaps," as they've been nicknamed—is enough to remind us of the effectiveness of this colonization strategy.

Descriptions of Common Plants

Trees

Plains Cottonwood, *Populus deltoides* ssp. *monilifera.* There is no mistaking the broad, heart-shaped, and finely serrated leaves of the plains cottonwood; the leaves of the similar Frémont (*P. deltoides* ssp. *deltoides*) and Rio Grande cottonwoods (*P. deltoides* ssp. *wislizenii*), the subspecies found on the Western Slope, have slightly narrower, tapering tips; the fruiting capsules are distinctly egg-shaped in all populations. This massive-trunked tree, with its grayish brown, deeply furrowed bark, is the giant of the lowland riparian forests. Male and female flowers appear on separate trees in spring before the leaves appear; the ripened ovoid fruits on the female trees burst open in June to release their abundant cotton-tufted seeds. The downy seeds, carried far and wide by the wind, collect in soft drifts wherever they come to rest. This species hybridizes with the narrowleaf cottonwood along the upper margins of its range; hybrids exhibit considerable variability.

Narrowleaf Cottonwood, *Populus angustifolia.* The narrowleaf cottonwood is identified by its narrow lanceolate leaves and its large aromatic buds. In contrast to the buds of willows, which are enclosed by a single bud scale, cottonwood buds have overlapping scales. Flowering occurs in spring, before the leaves unfold; male and female catkins, which consist of pendant spikes of inconspicuous and usually unisexual flowers, grow on separate trees. When the female catkins burst open, they release masses of white cotton and numerous tiny seeds. The seeds remain viable for only a few days and must land on a suitably moist, sandy substrate in full sunlight to germinate successfully. This species hybridizes with the plains cottonwood along the lower margins of its range; hybrids exhibit considerable variety.

Peach-leaved Willow, *Salix amygdaloides*. Named for the resemblance of its narrow lanceolate leaves to those of the common peach, the peach-leaved willow is the only native tree-sized willow in the Southern Rockies. The male and female flowers of this short-lived, fast-growing species appear with the leaves in spring. The cone-shaped fruits mature about a month after flowering and contain numerous tiny seeds.

Box-elder, *Acer negundo*. The box-elder is a member of the maple family and is distinguished from the cottonwoods and willows by its compound, three-part leaves and its two-winged, maplelike fruits (samaras). Male and female flowers appear on separate trees in early spring; the fruits mature by autumn and are a favorite food for fox squirrels, evening grosbeaks, and mice. The box-elder grows quite rapidly for its first fifteen to twenty years and then slows, living a maximum of seventy-five to a hundred years.

Netleaf Hackberry, *Celtis reticulata*. This small, somewhat irregularly shaped tree is typical of drier sites along intermittent streams and rocky riverbanks. Netleaf hackberry is distinguished from other species by its thick, simple leaves with conspicuous netlike veins on the lower surface and orange-red, globe-shaped fruits. The species flowers in early spring, with male and female flowers appearing on the same tree.

Mountain Alder, *Alnus incana* ssp. *tenuifolia*. Mountain alder often forms large, spreading clumps of gray-barked stems and is identified by its double-toothed, obovate leaves and, in winter, by the small woody cones that decorate its slender, reddish branches. Male and female flowers are produced in separate catkins on the same tree; male catkins are slender and drooping, and female catkins are conelike (woody), clustered, and persist on the branches through the winter months.

River Birch, *Betula fontinalis*. This small tree, seldom exceeding thirty feet in height, is identified by its oval and sharply pointed leaves, its nonpeeling, coppery red bark, and the nonwoody character of its female catkins. Male and female flowers are borne in separate catkins, but on the same tree. Male catkins develop during the summer, remaining on the tree throughout the winter and into the following spring, when they become limp and pendulous, shedding clouds of pollen. Female catkins emerge in spring and, following pollination, elongate to form conelike structures that consist of numerous three-lobed scales, each scale enclosing a tiny winged seed.

Colorado Blue Spruce, *Picea pungens*. Blue spruce seldom occurs in large stands and is most common in small groves or as scattered trees in moist habitats. This species is easily distinguished from other conifers by its narrow, pyramidal growth form, four-sided and sharp-tipped needles, smooth rather than hairy branchlets, and brown, furrowed bark. The degree of "blueness" of Colorado blue spruce is highly variable; some trees may not be blue at all except in the new growth of the season. Male and female cones are produced on the same tree; the female cones are papery when mature, cylindrical, and have wavy-edged scales. Distinctive brown, conelike galls created by the abnormal growth of shoots infested with spruce gall aphids tip many branchlets. Blue spruce are long-lived, sometimes reaching 600 to 800 years of age.

White fir, *Abies concolor*. White fir is largely restricted to the central and southern portions of the Southern Rockies. This beautiful conifer is distinguished from subalpine fir (*A. lasiocarpa*) by the broadly pyramidal crown, the frosted appearance of the long, flat needles, and the large, upright greenish yellow cones that adorn its crown. The needles are typically two to three inches long and have a whitish cast due to the heavy coating of epidermal wax. Female and male cones are produced on the same tree; the female cones are somewhat barrel-shaped and are borne at the top of the tree. Cone production does not begin until a tree is approximately forty years old; on average, heavy seed crops are produced every fifth year.

Shrubs

Shrub Willows, *Salix* spp. A great many species of willow occur in wetland habitats, but only a sampling of the most common can be described here. Sandbar (*S. exigua*) and Plain's sandbar willow (*S. interior*) have extremely narrow leaves and are typical of lowland valleys and foothill canyons. Planeleaf willow (*S. planifolia*), a subalpine species, is distinguished by its larger, smooth-surfaced leaves, purplish black or reddish brown twigs, and hairy capsules. Mountain willow (*S. monticola*) is identified by its erect growth form, yellow-colored branches, and relatively narrow, pointed leaves. Blue willow (*S. drummondiana*) occurs from the upper montane to the subalpine and is distinguished by the silky-hairy lower surfaces of its leaves and by the dark blue-green, smooth appearance of the upper leaf surfaces. The male and female catkins of all shrub willows occur on separate plants; the male catkins, because of their silky hairs, tend to be most prominent. Willows reproduce by both sexual and vegetative (asexual) means.

Bog Birch, *Betula glandulosa*. This low, somewhat robust shrub is a member of the birch family. This species is common in the Arctic and is distributed widely throughout the high mountain areas of North America. Bog birch is identified by its thick, roundish, serrated leaves and by the warty, resinous glands found along its young twigs. Male and female catkins are borne on the same plant; the catkins for the next growing season form during late summer.

Rocky Mountain Maple, *Acer glabrum*. Noteworthy for its rich autumn color, this attractive and somehat airy shrub is identified by its three- to five-lobed, maplelike leaves and its two-winged fruits (samaras); the deep green leaves, attached to the twigs by long slender stalks, contrast beautifully with the reddish hue of the twigs, buds, and samaras. Crimson feltlike blotches on the upper surfaces of the leaves are caused by the galls of eriophyid mites. Clusters of yellowish green flowers appear in early spring, coincident with the leaves; in some cases, male and female flowers are borne on separate plants. At maturity, the two-winged fruit splits in two, each wing enclosing a single seed.

Twinberry (or Bush Honeysuckle), *Distegia* (formerly *Lonicera*) *involucrata*. This shrub is identified by its dark green oval leaves and paired yellow flowers. Twinberry seldom exceeds three feet in height. Individual flowers are somewhat pendant and borne in pairs on a long stalk. Each pair of flowers is enclosed by four fused bracts, which enlarge and turn reddish as the fruits, paired purplish berries, mature. The fruits are considered poisonous.

Wildflowers

Cow parsnip, *Heracleum sphondylium*. This tall, robust member of the parsley family is identified by its three-lobed, coarsely toothed compound leaves, its enormous, flattopped umbel of white flowers, and the sheathing petiole that envelops its stem leaves. The stems are hollow, and the flowers mature into large, flat seeds. In suitably moist sites, this species grows to a height of six feet.

Chiming bells, *Mertensia ciliata*. This graceful wildflower (also known as bluebells or mertensia) is identified by its pendant clusters of bell-shaped blue flowers and by its bluish green, smooth-edged lanceolate leaves. The flowers hang from slender stems that arise from within the leaf axil; pinkish blue hues, especially in the buds, are common. Chiming bells often grow in dense sprays along streams and rivulets, from the upper montane through the subalpine zone.

Chiming bells.

Monkshood, *Aconitum columbianum*. The monkshood, once thought to be a member of the buttercup family (Ranunculaceae), is now included in the hellebore family (Helleboraceae), along with the columbines, the larkspurs, the marsh-marigold, and the globeflower. The blue-purple flowers of monkshood appear along a tall stalk and are easily identified by the unusual way in which the uppermost sepal (bluish) arches over the other floral parts to form a hood. The common name of this species is derived from the resemblance of the hood to that worn by a medieval monk. Another superficially similar wildflower found in moist habitats, the **larkspur** (*Delphinium barbeyi*), lacks the hood; in this case, the fifth sepal (also bluish) is drawn backwards to form a spur. All parts of the monkshood and the larkspur contain poisonous alkaloids and are considered toxic, especially to livestock.

Bittercress, *Cardamine cordifolia*. Bittercress, also known as brook-cress, is a member of the mustard family and is identified by its white, round-topped racemes of four-petaled flowers and its heart-shaped, toothed leaves.

Yellow Monkeyflower, *Mimulus guttatus*. This lovely wildflower grows around springs and along streambanks and cascades. It is identified by its bright yellow snapdragonlike flowers; each flower has a sprinkling of red spots on the lip of the floral tube, a closed throat, and is usually less than an inch in length. The leaves are broadly ovate in shape and are arranged opposite each other. The spectacular, red-flowered **Lewis's monkeyflower** (*M. lewisii*), named for Meriwether Lewis, is a species of the

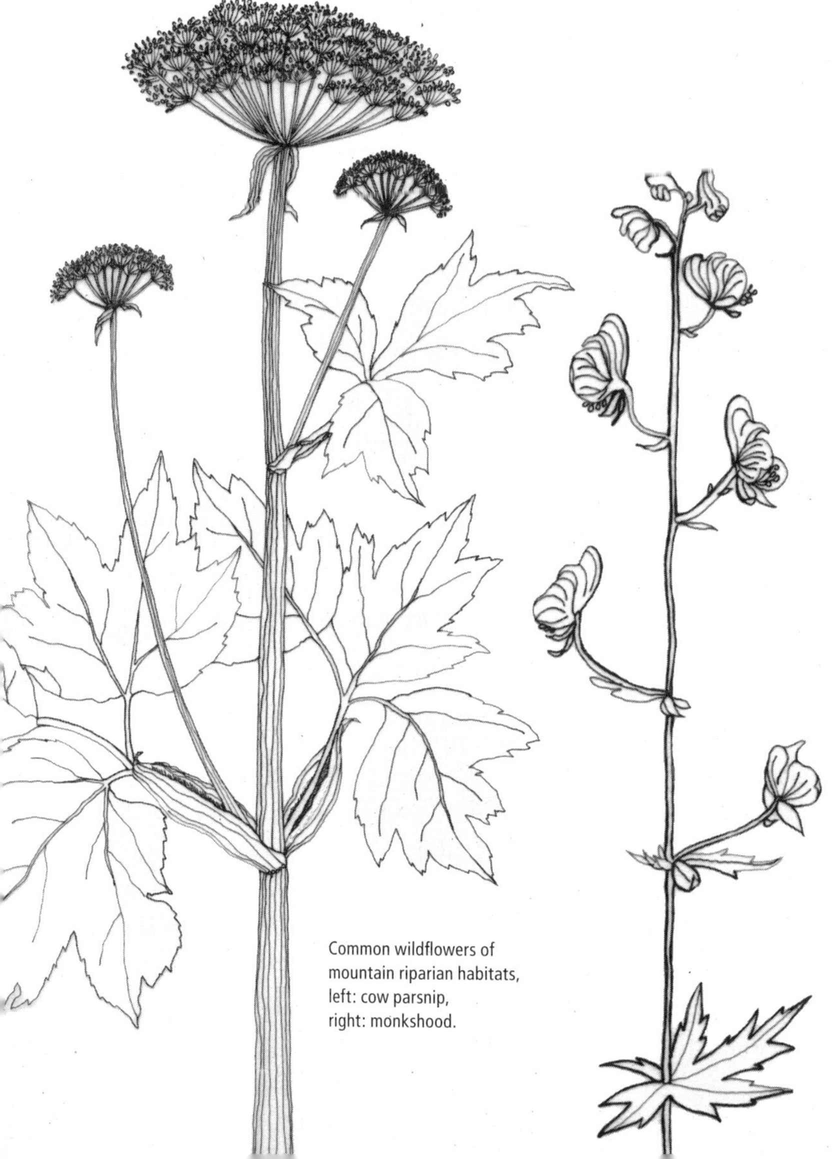

Common wildflowers of mountain riparian habitats, left: cow parsnip, right: monkshood.

Pacific Northwest and in the Southern Rockies is found only in Routt County (northwestern Colorado).

Arrowleaf Groundsel, *Senecio triangularis.* Arrowleaf groundsel is identified by the following combination of characters: an unbranched stem, toothed and narrowly triangular leaves, and an open but somewhat round-topped raceme of small, yellow sunflowerlike flower heads. Each flower head consists of a ring of yellow ray flowers and a tightly packed cluster of tubular disk flowers, encircled from beneath by a bell-shaped single series of narrow green bracts.

Northern Bog Orchid, *Limnorchis* (formerly *Habenaria*) *hyperborea.* This small-flowered orchid is frequently found along moist streamsides from the foothills to the subalpine zone. All bog orchids are alike in that their flowers are somewhat crowded together along a stout, erect stalk and their strap-shaped leaves are distributed along the length of the stem. The northern bog orchid is identified by the green color of its flowering spike and the small spur at the base of the lip of each flower. A similar species, the white bog orchid (*L. dilatata* ssp. *albiflora*), bears a slender stalk of pure white, fragrant flowers and is found in more open subalpine environments, such as in fens or along the shores of ponds.

Common Plants of the Mountain Wetlands

Trees

Alder, mountain, *Alnus incana* ssp. *tenuifolia*
Ash, mountain, *Sorbus scopulina*
Aspen, quaking, *Populus tremuloides*
Birch, river, *Betula fontinalis*
Box-elder, *Acer negundo*
Cottonwood, Frémont, *Populus deltoides* ssp. *deltoides*
    plains, *P. deltoides* ssp. *monilifera*
    Rio Grande, *P. deltoides* ssp. *wislizenii*
    lanceleaf, *P.* × *acuminata* (hybrid)
    narrowleaf, *P. angustifolia*
Douglas-fir, *Pseudotsuga menziesii*
Fir, white, *Abies concolor*

Hackberry, netleaf, *Celtis reticulata*

Locust, New Mexican, *Robinia neomexicana*

Pine, Mexican white, *Pinus strobiformis*

Poplar, balsam, *Populus balsamifera*

Spruce, Colorado blue, *Picea pungens*

Engelmann, *P. engelmannii*

Willow, peach-leaved, *Salix amygdaloides*

Shrubs

Birch, bog, *Betula glandulosa*

Chokecherry, *Padus* (formerly *Prunus*) *virginiana* var. *melanocarpa*

Cinquefoil, shrubby, *Pentaphylloides floribunda*

Currant, golden, *Ribes aureum*

Dogwood, red-osier, *Swida sericea* (formerly *Cornus stolonifera*)

Elderberry, red, *Sambucus microbotrys*

Forestiera (or Mountain Privet), *Forestiera pubescens*

Gooseberry, whitestem, *Ribes inerme*

Greasewood, *Sarcobatus vermiculatus*

Hawthorn, *Crataegus erythropoda*

Maple, Rocky Mountain, *Acer glabrum*

Plum, wild, *Prunus americana*

Serviceberry, Utah, *Amelanchier utahensis*

Serviceberry, western, *Amelanchier alnifolia*

Twinberry (or Bush Honeysuckle), *Distegia* (formerly *Lonicera*) *involucrata*

Willow, Bebb, *Salix bebbiana*

blue, *S. drummondiana*

bluestem, *S. irrorata*

sandbar, *S. exigua*

geyer, *S. geyeriana*

mountain, *S. monticola*

planeleaf, *S. planifolia*

Plain's sandbar, *S. interior*

subalpine, *S. brachycarpa*

wolf, *S. wolfii*

Vines

Grape, wild, *Vitis riparia*
Virginia Creeper, *Parthenocissus inserta*
Virgins Bower, *Clematis ligusticifolia*

Grasses, Sedges, and Rushes

Arrowgrass, *Triglochin palustris*
Bulrush (or Tule), *Schoenoplectus lacustris* ssp. *acutus*
Cottongrass (or Cottonsedge), *Eriophorum angustifolium*
Hairgrass, tufted, *Deschampsia cespitosa*
Mannagrass, *Glyceria* spp.
Reedgrass, Canadian, *Calamagrostis canadensis*
Rush, scouring (or Horsetail), *Equisetum* spp.
Rush, subalpine, *Juncus mertensianus*
Spikerush, *Eleocharis* spp.
Woodrush, common, *Luzula parviflora*

Wildflowers

Angelica, giant, *Angelica ampla*
Bishop's Cap, *Mitella pentandra*
Bittercress, *Cardamine cordifolia*
Buttercup, *Ranunculus* spp.
Chiming bells, *Mertensia ciliata*
Cow Parsnip, *Heracleum sphondylium*
Elephantella, *Pedicularis groenlandica*
Gentian, star, *Swertia perennis*
Globeflower, *Trollius albiflorus*
Grass-of-Parnassus, *Parnassia parviflora*
  fringed, *P. fimbriata*
Hollyhock, mountain, *Iliamna rivularis*
Larkspur, *Delphinium barbeyi*
Marsh-marigold, *Psychrophila* (formerly *Caltha*) *leptosepala*
Monkeyflower, Lewis's, *Mimulus lewisii*
  yellow, *M. guttatus*

Elephantella.

Monkshood, *Aconitum columbianum*
Orchid, northern bog, *Limnorchis* (formerly *Habenaria*) *hyperborea*
white bog, *L.* (formerly *Habenaria*) *dilatata* ssp. *albiflora*
Pondlily, yellow, *Nuphar lutea*
Pondweed, *Potamogeton* spp.
Primrose, Parry's, *Primula parryi*
Saxifrage, brook, *Saxifraga odontoloma*
Senecio, arrowleaf, *Senecio triangularis*
Shootingstar, western, *Dodecatheon pulchellum*
Trefoil, marsh (or Water Buckbean), *Menyanthes trifoliata*
Twistedstalk, *Streptopus fassettii* (formerly *S. amplexifolius*)
Willowherb, *Epilobium* spp.

Environment and Adaptation: Animals of the Mountain Wetlands

Framed in moonlight, a beaver swims a steady course across the pond, towing a freshly cut willow sapling. Swooping low over the water, a little brown bat forages on the wing for insects. Nearby, a cow elk grazes in the sedge meadow that encircles the shoreline. With the coming of dawn, the rattling call of a belted kingfisher can be heard as it flies upvalley to a morning fishing perch. From a spray-slick boulder, a dipper dives beneath the frothy torrents to poke among the rocks for larval insects. In the tangle of willows and alders along the streambank, chrome-yellow Wilson's warblers flutter from branch to branch gleaning insects. These images exemplify the wilderness spirit inherent in mountain wetlands.

Mountain riparian forests and shrublands, with their unique mixture of terrestrial and aquatic resources, provide abundant food and protective cover for a diversity of resident and nonresident animals. Some species prefer an aquatic or semiaquatic lifestyle; others concentrate their foraging and breeding activities at different levels in the shrubs and trees; still others forage in the lush understory or seek shelter in the litter of the riparian forest floor. A high rate of net primary productivity, the amount of organic matter created or energy bound by green plants, provides the foundation for these species-rich ecosystems. Species diversity also depends, however, on a critical factor known as niche space, a term that refers to the total resource space available within a given community. In essence, diversity creates and sustains diversity. The greater the number of niches available, the greater the variety of species that an ecosystem can support. In the case of most riparian forests, the multistoried structure of the vegetation and the proximity to water provide a multitude of habitat and feeding possibilities. To coexist in this richly stratified community, each species must appropriate a specific niche space, either by using different resources or by using resources that must be shared by several species at different times of the day or year to avoid competition.

Woodcutter, Dam Builder, and Hydrologic Engineer

Adaptations for an aquatic lifestyle are common among many species associated with mountain wetlands. For example, though the beaver is less than graceful on land, it has achieved a supreme mastery of the water through a variety of adaptations: webbed hind feet, a waterproof coat, a paddlelike tail, nostril and ear valves that close during submersion, small eyes with a transparent inner lid designed for unimpeded underwater vision, and special controls on heart rate and breathing, which permit extended dives. Whereas many animals are capable of modifying their immediate environment, the beaver is able to create its own habitat and then manipulate that habitat to suit its needs.

Beaver sign.

Beavers generally create their own pond by impounding a stream with a dam constructed of logs, sticks, rocks, and mud. Within the pond, the beaver builds a conical lodge of sticks and mud, complete with an underwater entrance. Beavers living along larger streams or rivers do little dam building and make use of bank burrows rather than lodges. The pond not only protects the beaver from most predators, it ensures the proliferation of the beaver's preferred plant foods, provides an all-weather transportation route and a means of floating the harvest home, and, as side benefit, creates additional stillwater habitat for muskrats, fish, frogs, ducks, and shorebirds.

Long, curved incisor teeth make short work of the beaver's woodcutting tasks, allowing it to cut a willow sapling in seconds and fell a six-inch-diameter aspen in a matter of minutes. The problem of a cellulose-rich diet of bark, roots, and other plant materials is efficiently solved by a gland along the digestive tract that secretes enzymes into the stomach to soften woody tissues. The inner bark of aspen and willow is rich in salicylic acid (the active ingredient in aspirin); this same compound is also the main constituent of castoreum, an oil the beaver secretes from oblong scent glands within its cloaca and uses to waterproof its fur and mark its territory.

Water Sprite and Angler

The birds we associate with shoreline and streambank exhibit a host of adaptations that enable them to exploit their watery habitat. Lured by an abundance of aquatic insects, the American dipper (or water-ouzel) has developed the amazing ability to walk underwater as it forages among the rocks for aquatic insects. The dipper uses its rather stubby wings to get to the bottom of a stream and then, using a combination of downward and rearward strokes, is able to overcome its natural buoyancy and move nimbly across the streambed, often traveling against the rushing current. Dippers are equipped with large preen glands, at least ten times the size of those of any other passerine species, which provide the oil needed for rewaterproofing feathers. Additionally, a movable flap over the nostril seals out water during dives and an extra, transparent eyelid allows the dipper to use its eyes underwater and also provides protection from waterborne particles in the swift current. In keeping with a semiaquatic lifestyle, the dipper's nesting period coincides with the hatching of many aquatic insect species, especially the stonefly, which it harvests in large numbers.

Naturalist John Muir was captivated by the dipper, a bird that often kept him company on his rambles through the West's mountains. His lyrical description of a dipper foraging along a rushing mountain stream captures the essence of this water sprite and remains one of the finest pieces of evocative natural-history writing from a long and distinguished career:

> The ouzel alone of all the birds dares to enter the white torrent. The vertical curves and angles of the most precipitous torrents he traces with the same rigid fidelity, swooping down the inclines of cascades, dropping sheer over dizzy falls amid the spray, ascending with the same fearlessness and ease. His flight is solid and impetuous, without any intermission of wing-beats—one homogeneous buzz like that of a laden bee on its way home.
>
> (From "The Water Ouzel," Chapter 13, *The Mountains of California* by John Muir, 1894)

Another water-adapted species, the belted kingfisher, prefers to do its hunting from a comfortable perch overhanging the water. A skillful angler, the kingfisher is able to see fish through the mirrored surface of the water, thanks to tiny droplets of red oil that coat the cones of its eyes, reducing glare and distortion. Scanning the water from its perch, the kingfisher may hover briefly before diving headlong into the water, often remaining underwater for several seconds before emerging with a fish or other suitable prey in its beak. Returning to its perch, the kingfisher first kills the fish and then throws it into the air to be swallowed headfirst. Kingfishers never stray far from their favorite fishing stream or river, preferring a room with a view: a snug burrow in a cut-bank in which to rear their brood.

Room to Nest

Mountain riparian communities generally have higher densities of breeding birds than other mountain ecosystems due to the rich variety of available nesting sites and the abundance of food. The dipper chooses its nest site, nearly always near water, with a keen eye toward predator inaccessibility.

This master builder constructs a ball-shaped nest of grass and mosses on a streamside ledge, in a rock crevice tucked safely behind a cascading waterfall, or set neatly amidst the steel girders beneath a bridge. The belted kingfisher excavates its long, tunnel-like burrow near the top of a steep earthen bank adjoining a favorite stream, river, or pond. The lush riparian tangle provides cover for ground-nesting species such as the Wilson's warbler, Lincoln's and song sparrows. MacGillivray's and yellow warblers build their nests in the shrub layer, taking advantage of dense willow and alder thickets. Green-winged teals, mallards, ring-necked ducks, common snipe, soras, and shorebirds such as the spotted sandpiper exploit sedge tussock islands in the more secluded mountain ponds, lakes, and wetlands.

Common snipe (top), American dipper (bottom).

A room with a view is preferred by several species: herons, flycatchers, chickadees, warbling vireos, swallows, robins, and many others. Most great blue and black-crowned night herons nest colonially in aggregations known as rookeries, generally located in tall cottonwoods. In some areas, black-crowned night heron rookeries may occupy the lower branches of trees already appropriated by great blue herons. Competitive overlap appears to be eliminated by the lifestyles of the two species. The great blue heron is active by day and is often observed standing motionless in shallow water, waiting for prey to come within striking range of its sharp bill. The black-crowned night heron, on the other hand, is largely nocturnal and fishes by alternately stalking and standing motionless.

Amphibians and Reptiles

Mountain riparian communities harbor several species of amphibians and reptiles, including the mountain toad, western chorus frog, northern leopard frog, western terrestrial garter snake, and smooth green snake. Most amphibians and reptiles cannot live in a cold environment, but three species, the striped chorus frog, the mountain toad, and the tiger salamander, have been found above 12,000 feet in the Southern Rockies. These species are well adapted to cold temperatures, utilizing a combination of behavioral and physiological adaptations that enable them to remain active from spring through fall under a wide range of conditions. For example, western chorus frogs, sometimes called "penny frogs" due to their small size, may begin breeding as early as March in foothill locations and as late as early June at high elevation sites. Mountain populations may remain active well into September, even after the first September snowstorms. Diurnal and nocturnal activity patterns appear to be related to the seasonal progression of temperatures; diurnal activity is common in spring and fall, when cooler temperatures force these animals to be active whenever opportunities occur for basking, while nocturnal activity dominates the warmer summer weeks, especially at lower elevations. Winter environmental extremes are avoided by making use of underground hibernacula, either in natural cavities or in the abandoned burrows of other animals.

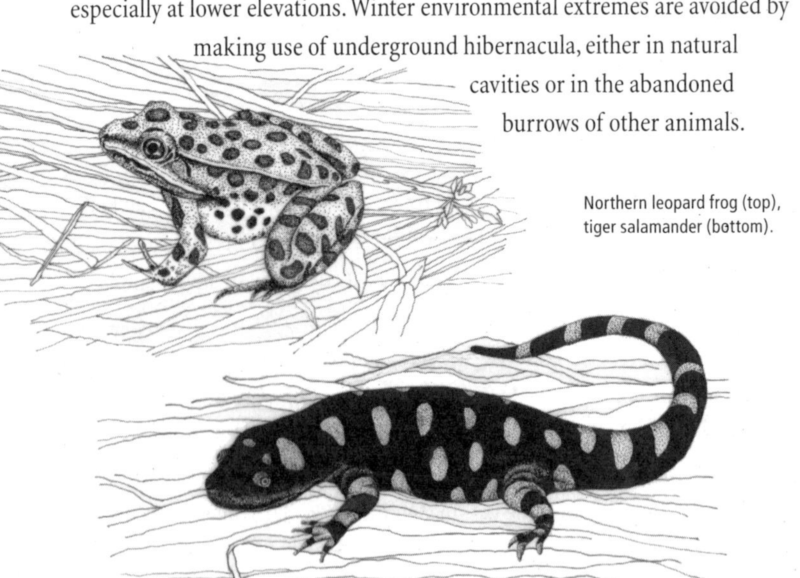

Northern leopard frog (top), tiger salamander (bottom).

During the past decade, a sharp decline in populations of mountain toads and northern leopard frogs has been reported. Once very common in the Southern Rockies, the mountain (or boreal) toad began to decline over much of its range as early as the 1970s and is now a candidate for federal protection under the U.S. Endangered Species Act. Long-term studies are currently underway to determine the degree to which habitat destruction and degradation, the impacts of increased levels of ultraviolet (UV-B) light, the anthropogenic acidification and heavy-metal contamination of the waters in traditional breeding habitats, increased predation by nonnative trout and other fish, or the introduction of pathogenic diseases in populations already coping with suppressed immune system function may be contributing to this rapid decline. Likely, multiple factors are involved.

Life Histories of Selected Animals

Mammals

Water Shrew, *Sorex palustris.* This is the largest shrew found in the Southern Rockies and is easily distinguished by its size (total length of adults averages six inches), dark gray-black upperparts, silvery gray belly, and the fringe of stiff hairs on the hind feet. Water shrews are found along cold mountain streams with overhanging ledges, boulders, and exposed root systems, which provide cover. Masterful swimmers, water shrews are often observed skimming across the surface of the water propelled by the fringed hind feet or swimming and foraging underwater. Active year-round and both night and day, the water shrew forages energetically for insects, small fish, carrion, and other animal foods. Water shrews are short-lived, seldom surviving their second winter of life.

Little Brown Myotis, *Myotis lucifugus.* This common, medium-sized bat is identified by its dark, glossy coloring and its erratic, zigzagging flight style. Most often observed over water, this species begins its foraging at dark and continues intermittently until dawn. The diet of the little brown myotis consists mostly of flying insects (midges, craneflies, wasps, and mosquitos), which it locates by sonar; beetles, water boatmen, and true bugs will also be taken when available. Mating begins in fall, and sperm are stored within the uterus of the female throughout hibernation, which typically occurs in a cave or abandoned mine; fertilization is delayed until the females emerge from hibernation in the spring. Upon returning to the summer range, pregnant females establish nursery colonies, which may include several dozen individuals; maternity colonies numbering in the thousands have also been reported. After a gestation period of less than two months, each female gives birth to a single altricial young in May, June, or July; the pup dines only on mother's milk during the first eighteen days of its life. Young bats begin flying and foraging on their own by about three weeks of age; there is apparent dietary and habitat partitioning between juveniles and adults during the flight-learning stage of development. The little brown myotis is a long-lived species, and individuals have been reported to exceed thirty years in the wild.

Beaver, American, *Castor canadensis.* Its paddlelike tail, webbed hind feet, and rich brown fur identify this large and mostly nocturnal rodent. Beavers occur wherever permanent streams of moderate grade and a sufficient food supply of aspen, willow, alder, and aquatic plants provide suitable habitat. Active throughout the year, the beaver stores cut saplings and other plant foods underwater for use during the winter. Beaver social life revolves around the mated pair, the yearlings, and the young (called kits). Breeding occurs within the den in January or February; fully furred and open-eyed kits are born in April or May. Beavers are long-lived animals, with many individuals living for fifteen years or more.

Muskrat, *Ondatra zibethicus.* This medium-sized rodent is identified by its slender and hairless tail, diminutive ears, and partially webbed hind feet. The mink (*Mustela vison*) is more weasel-like in appearance and has a fully furred tail. Muskrats are more common at middle and lower elevations, especially in areas with past or present beaver activity. Though not the skilled architect the beaver is, muskrats build small, dome-shaped lodges consisting of piles of herbaceous vegetation and equip them with underwater entrances; some individuals utilize bank burrows rather than lodges. The diet of the muskrat is more cosmopolitan than that of the beaver, including virtually any type of aquatic or semiaquatic plant and occasionally very small animals. Muskrats are promiscuous, and breeding occurs in spring and summer. Females produce two or three litters a year; newborn muskrats are altricial, but the young develop quickly and are largely independent of the female after one month.

Raccoon, *Procyon lotor*. Raccoons are identified by the black facial mask and the alternating rings of yellowish buff and black on the bushy tail. Chiefly nocturnal, the raccoon is an opportunist when it comes to diet, taking amphibians, small mammals, fish, fruit, and other foods as available. Raccoons are promiscuous breeders, the females becoming receptive to males in February or March. Young raccoons are born in early spring, and the female cares for the young alone. Adult size is achieved after two years; a life span of ten to twelve years is common.

Striped Skunk, *Mephitis mephitis*. The striped skunk, with its jet black coat, white stripes, and odiferous scent glands, requires little introduction. Chiefly nocturnal, skunks forage for insects, amphibians, ground-nesting birds and their eggs, and fruit. Though active year-round, striped skunks avoid cold, snowy weather by sleeping, relying on stored fat. Mating occurs in March or April and is accompanied by complex courtship behaviors. The altricial young are born in May or June and may remain with the mother their first winter.

Red Fox, *Vulpes vulpes*. This small, beautiful canid is distinguished by its normally rust orange upperparts, whitish underparts, and black feet, muzzle, and backs of ears; all color morphs of the red fox have bushy, white-tipped tails. Home range size is variable, averaging between one and three square miles. The red fox is largely nocturnal and solitary, except during the breeding season. The diet is omnivorous, consisting of rabbits, small mammals, birds, fish, amphibians, fruits, and insects. A den, usually

a renovated burrow or an enlarged natural cavity, is used mostly during inclement weather and becomes the center of activity during the breeding season. Pair bonds are formed in December or January; a single litter of four to five pups is born blind but furred in early spring. The pups remain within the den until they are about five weeks old; they are weaned at two months and begin joining the parents on hunting trips. The family unit breaks up in autumn, and the young foxes disperse to new territories.

Birds

Great Blue Heron, *Ardea herodias.* The great blue heron is identified by its large size, bluish gray plumage, serpentine neck, and long legs. The **black-crowned night heron** (*Nycticorax nycticorax*) is considerably smaller, with a black back and crown, pale gray wings, and white underparts. Male great blue herons conduct ritualized courtship displays as soon as they arrive on the breeding territory in early spring, often returning to the same rookery used in previous years. The male selects the nest site, but the female constructs the nest with materials delivered by the male. Pair bonds are solidified by passing twigs, locking bills, and mutual preening. Both parents rear the young.

Common Merganser, *Mergus merganser.* This fish-eating, diving duck is identified by its thin red bill, streamlined and loonlike appearance, and rounded, shaggy crest; the male has a clear white breast and flanks and a dark green head during the breeding season; female mergansers have a brownish red head and show little white except on the neck and chin and a rectangular patch on the wing (prominent during flight). Common mergansers prefer clear rivers and streams but can also be found on large mountain lakes and reservoirs. Good breeding populations are reported throughout the Colorado River headwaters system, and especially along the Yampa River. Mergansers begin nesting in May, and suitable nest sites include large tree cavities, broken snags, streamside deciduous trees, and streamside ledges. Incubation averages about thirty days, and clutch sizes vary widely (averaging seven to fifteen young). The fledglings exhibit remarkable swimming and diving skills, foraging alongside their mother and hitching a ride on her back as she cruises along a river.

Green-winged Teal, *Anas crecca.* This crow-sized, surface-feeding duck is identified by the chestnut head, large green ear patch, and vertical white bar that extends through its gray-streaked breast; the female is a nondescript speckled brown, but both sexes have a green speculum on the wing, visible in flight. When foraging for aquatic insects, teals probe, or "dabble," with their bills poking into the mud. Arriving shortly after the ice melts, the green-winged teal selects a secluded nest site in a clump of grass or sedges. Eight buff-colored eggs are laid in early summer.

Spotted Sandpiper, *Actitis macularia.* This is the only sandpiper that breeds in the Southern Rockies, and it is found along rivers, streams, and mountain lakes and ponds. Spotted sandpipers are identified during the breeding season by their brown-spotted breast, plain brown back, orange bill and legs, and the distinctive habit of constantly "teetering" (bobbing its hindquarters); nonbreeding season birds are all brown above and have a white breast. When moving along the shore, spotted sandpipers fly low, with short bursts of stiff, shallow wingbeats. To raise more broods in a season, this sandpiper practices polyandry (the female mates with more than one male), forming pair bonds within minutes but remaining monogamous only until the first clutch of eggs (typically four) is laid. The female then leaves the male with all the incubation duties and moves on to the next and repeats the process all over again; depending on the availability of males, female spotted sandpipers have been reported to lay up to twenty eggs (five four-egg clutches) in a single seven-week egg-laying season. This type of breeding behavior is physiologically and energetically costly for the female sandpipers; consequently, their life spans average only 3.7 years, the shortest of all North American shorebirds.

Common Snipe, *Gallinago gallinago.* This secretive, robin-sized bird is identified by its brown-dappled body, short legs, sandpiperlike appearance, and long bill. On the breeding grounds, the snipe's circling displays, performed by both sexes, can be spectacular; during the shallow dives associated with this display, air vibrations along the fanned tail produce an eerie winnowing sound. Most displays occur at twilight or at dawn. The ground call, often delivered in the vicinity of the nest, is a whistled, slow *wheek-a-wheek-a-wheek-a.* Largely crepuscular (active at dusk and dawn), the snipe forages along the ground, probing with its bill for insects in the mud; the bill is extremely sensitive, with an upper mandible that can be raised and curved to extract worms and clinging larvae. The female selects the nest site, making several scrapes on the ground before choosing one, and incubates the eggs alone. Shortly after hatching, as soon as the young are dry, both parents lead the brood away from the nest.

Belted Kingfisher, *Ceryle alcyon*. This pigeon-sized bird is identified by its large, crested head, spear-shaped bill, blue-gray upperparts, and white breast with horizontal breast band. Its distinctive call, a reverberating rattle, is delivered from a fishing perch or in flight. The kingfisher is an agile angler, preying on fish, amphibians, and small reptiles. Solitary except during the breeding season, the pair selects a suitable burrow site in a sandy or gravelly stream or riverbank within the male's territory. An average of six to seven eggs are laid, and hatching occurs after a period of about three weeks; time to fledging is believed to be at least three weeks.

American Dipper, *Cinclus mexicanus*. Dippers, or water ouzels, are identified by their slate gray coloring, rounded shape, stubby tail and wings, large feet, and underwater foraging style. Common along mountain streams and rivers during the summer, the dipper abandons these watercourses during the winter in favor of lower-elevation, ice-free waters. When flushed, dippers give a rapid, musical *bzeet* call as they fly low over the water to a new area of the stream. Dippers are often observed bobbing up and down as they perch on a boulder or partially submerged log. The sites dippers choose for secreting their ball-shaped grass nests tend to be inaccessible to most predators: a crevice in a sheer ledge within the spray zone, a log jam in the middle of a stream or river, or the steel beam beneath a bridge. Solitary except at nesting time, the female dipper incubates the eggs, but both sexes feed the squawking, demanding young.

Wilson's Warbler, *Wilsonia pusilla*. The male Wilson's warbler is identified by its olive upperparts, yellow face and breast, and small black cap;

females are similar in coloring but lack the black cap. A similar species, the **common yellowthroat** (*Geothlypis trichas*), has a broad black facial mask rather than a cap. Wilson's warblers actively forage for insects in dense shrub thickets, often twitching their tails and flicking their wings in a nervous manner. The song of the male is a hurried, staccato chatter dropping in pitch at the end; the call is a flat *chuff*. This species builds a somewhat bulky nest on the ground, often sunken in moss or sedges; Wilson's warblers are subject to nest parasitism by the brown-headed cowbird.

Red-winged Blackbird, *Agelaius phoeniceus*. Male red-winged blackbirds are identified by their black plumage and red shoulder patches (epaulets); the epaulets can be exposed during displays or concealed during times of danger. Female blackbirds are dark brown with mottled breasts. The song of the male is a liquid, gurgling *conk-ka-ree*; the common call is a *chack*. The male is strongly territorial during the breeding season, defending an area of marsh within which up to a dozen females may nest. Both sexes become less conspicuous and somewhat secretive in late summer as they undergo molt.

Bullock's Oriole, *Icterus galbula*. This is the only common oriole in the Southern Rockies. The male is identified by its fiery orange underparts, rump patch, and outer tail feathers; the wings are black with white wing patches, and the orange head is highlighted by a black crown and eye stripe. The female oriole is an inconspicuous grayish yellow. Orioles are insectivorous, but will take fruit or nectar at flowers. Male orioles arrive on the breeding territory in late spring; the song is a series of rich, flute-like whistles. Both sexes participate in nest building, territorial defense, incubating the eggs, and rearing the young. In riparian areas with an ample food supply, orioles enforce typical songbird territories; when their foraging opportunities are more limited because of insufficient cover, orioles may nest semicolonially. The deep, somewhat pendant nests are built of plant fibers and the inner bark of willows or junipers; nests are most easily seen when the tree (often a cottonwood) sheds its leaves in the fall. Orioles can identify the eggs of the brown-headed cowbird, a notorious nest parasite, and will remove these eggs by piercing them with their beaks and carrying them from their nest.

Lincoln's Sparrow, *Melospiza lincolnii*. Lincoln's sparrow is distinguished from two other species that share its habitat, the **fox sparrow** (*Passerella iliaca*) and the **song sparrow** (*M. melodia*), by its slimmer body shape, muted brown streaking, and lighter gray eyebrow stripe and ear coverts. Though relatively common, the Lincoln's sparrow is a shy skulker through brushy habitat, but it can sometimes be attracted by making squeaking noises. When approached or surprised, this species may twitch and elevate its crown feathers. Lincoln's sparrows forage on the ground for insects and seeds and may engage in double-scratching to locate food items. The song of the male on the breeding territory is a rapid, bubbling trill; the call note is a low, hard, oft-repeated *tsup*. During courtship, the male Lincoln's (like the song sparrow) pounces on its mate in response to the female's behavioral and vocal invitation.

Amphibians and Reptiles

Tiger Salamander, *Ambystoma tigrinum*. This pugnacious-appearing salamander is identified by its stout body and legs, costal (body) grooves, laterally flattened tail, and broad head. The color pattern of tiger salamanders varies considerably: some have yellowish spots or bars on a dark background while others have dark spots on a light background; larval forms are brownish or greenish and lack spots. Adults may be seen in or out of the water; the larval stage has gills and is aquatic. Metamorphosed tiger salamanders are largely terrestrial and are found in a wide variety of moist habitats at elevations up to 12,000 feet. This species requires the presence of a body of still water nearby for breeding purposes. Tiger salamanders leave their underground winter chambers and migrate to the breeding ponds anytime from April to July, depending on when the ice melts. Eggs are laid in ponds, and hatching occurs within two to five weeks. The length of the aquatic larval phase is variable; some may metamorphose within two to five months, others after a period of one or two years, whereas some larvae may never metamorphose at all. Metamorphosed salamanders eat snails and aquatic insects, as well as the eggs and larvae of other amphibians; cannibalism occurs frequently among salamander larvae.

Northern Leopard Frog, *Rana pipiens*. This beautiful frog is identified by the large dark spots that pattern its green or brown back and the prominent dorsolateral folds and midline; the iris of the eye is golden.

Leopard frogs emerge from their winter retreats (usually the bottom of a pond) in early spring and may remain active through October, depending on local conditions. Breeding areas are in shallow, still bodies of water (beaver ponds, glacial kettle ponds, and shallow marshes). The distinctive call of the male is a prolonged snore followed by a series of croaks. Females are more secretive and begin laying eggs a few days after the males begin calling; egg masses are attached to vegetation in relatively warm shallows (three to ten inches) and hatch in four to seven days. Populations of northern leopard frogs are in decline throughout their range, due primarily to predation by nonnative bullfrogs and habitat loss. Factors impacting populations of western toads may also play a role in the decline of this species.

Western Chorus Frog, *Pseudacris triseriata.* This tiny frog, also known as the striped chorus frog, is distinguished from other frogs by its size (usually under two inches), the stripe that extends through its eye to its groin, and the absence of distinct hind toe webbing. The color patterning of the striped chorus frog is highly variable, with background colors of green, red, or brown. This species occurs to nearly 12,000 feet and can be found in or adjacent to any still body of water. Chorus frogs emerge from their underground hibernaculurn in late spring, remaining active until September or October. Breeding occurs in both temporary and permanent bodies of water. Males begin their chorus, a slow, staccato trill, soon after emergence in the spring, attracting females to the breeding ponds. During mating, the male clasps the female and eggs are released; the tadpoles of this species metamorphose during their first summer, reaching adult size in about seventy-eight days.

Western Terrestrial Garter Snake, *Thamnophis elegans.* This nonpoisonous snake is distinguished by its darkish, largely patternless body, the keeled brownish scales on its back, the pale yellowish stripes that run the length of its body, and its smooth tail. The western terrestrial garter snake is most common below 11,000 feet. Garter snakes emerge from their underground winter chambers in late spring and remain active at moderate elevations through October; these snakes may emerge from their winter chambers to bask in the sun on warm days from February onward into the spring. The diet of the western terrestrial garter snake includes small invertebrates, fish, larval and metamorphosed amphibians, very small birds and nestlings, and small mammals. Like other garter snakes, this species does not lay eggs but gives birth to live young. Though normally quite docile, when handled roughly, this garter snake may expel a foul-smelling liquid from its anal glands.

Common Animals of the Mountain Wetlands

Mammals

Bear, black, *Ursus americanus*
Beaver, *Castor canadensis*
Chipmunk, least, *Tamias minimus*
Cottontail, mountain (or Nuttall's), *Sylvilagus nuttallii*
Coyote, *Canis latrans*
Deer, mule, *Odocoileus hemionus*
Elk (or Wapiti), *Cervus elaphus*

Bull elk grazing on water plants. Courtesy of Jim Benedict

Fox, red, *Vulpes vulpes*
Mink, *Mustela vison*
Mouse, deer, *Peromyscus maniculatus*
western jumping, *Zapus princeps*
Muskrat, *Ondatra zibethicus*
Myotis, little brown, *Myotis lucifugus*

long-legged, *M. volans*
Raccoon, *Procyon lotor*
Shrew, montane, *Sorex monticolus*
water, *S. palustris*
Skunk, striped, *Mephitis mephitis*
Vole, long-tailed, *Microtus longicaudus*
montane, *M. montanus*
Weasel, long-tailed, *Mustela frenata*

Birds

Avocet, American, *Recurvirostra americana*
Chat, yellow-breasted, *Icteria virens*
Chickadee, black-capped, *Poecile atricapillus*
mountain, *P. gambeli*
Coot, American, *Fulica americana*
Crane, sandhill, *Grus canadensis*
Cuckoo, yellow-billed, *Coccyzus americanus*
Dipper, American, *Cinclus mexicanus*
Duck, ring-necked, *Aythya collaris*
Eagle, bald, *Haliaeetus leucocephalus*
Flicker, northern, *Colaptes auratus*
Flycatcher, Cordilleran, *Empidonax occidentalis*
willow, *E. trailii*
Harrier, northern, *Circus cyaneus*
Hawk, Cooper's, *Accipiter cooperii*
Heron, black-crowned night, *Nycticorax nycticorax*
great blue, *Ardea herodias*
Hummingbird, black-chinned, *Archilocus alexandri*
broad-tailed, *Selasphorus platycercus*
Ibis, white-faced, *Plegadis chihi*
Killdeer, *Charadrius vociferus*
Kingbird, western, *Tyrannus verticalis*
Kingfisher, belted, *Ceryle alcyon*
Magpie, black-billed, *Pica hudsonia*
Mallard, *Anas platyrhynchos*

Merganser, common, *Mergus merganser*
Oriole, Bullock's, *Icterus galbula*
Osprey, *Pandion haliaetus*
Owl, great horned, *Bubo virginianus*
  northern saw-whet, *Aegolius acadicus*
  western screech, *Otus kennicottii*
Phalarope, Wilson's, *Phalaropus tricolor*
Phoebe, Say's, *Sayornis saya*
Plover, snowy, *Charadrius alexandrinus*
Robin, American, *Turdus migratorius*
Sandpiper, spotted, *Actitis macularia*
Snipe, common, *Gallinago gallinago*
Sparrow, fox, *Passerella iliaca*
  Lincoln's, *Melospiza lincolnii*
  song, *M. melodia*
  white-crowned, *Zonotrichia leucophrys*
Stilt, black-necked, *Himantopus mexicanus*
Swallow, bank, *Riparia riparia*
  cliff, *Hirundo pyrrhonota*
  northern rough-winged, *Stelgidopteryx serripennis*
  tree, *Tachycineta bicolor*
  violet-green, *T. thalassina*
Swift, black, *Cypseloides niger*
  white-throated, *Aeronautes saxatilis*
Teal, green-winged, *Anas crecca*
Thrush, Swainson's, *Catharus ustulatus*
Vireo, warbling, *Vireo gilvus*
Warbler, MacGillivray's, *Oporornis tolmiei*
  Wilson's, *Wilsonia pusilla*
  yellow, *Dendroica petechia*
  yellow-rumped, *D. coronata*
Waxwing, cedar, *Bombycilla cedrorum*
Woodpecker, downy, *Picoides pubescens*
  Lewis's, *Melanerpes lewis*
Wood-Pewee, western, *Contopus sordidulus*

Wren, canyon, *Catherpes mexicanus*
marsh, *Cistothorus palustris*
Yellowthroat, common, *Geothlypis trichas*

Amphibians and Reptiles

Bullsnake, *Pituophis melanoleucus*
Frog, northern leopard, *Rana pipiens*
Frog, western chorus, *Pseudacris triseriata*
Garter Snake, western terrestrial, *Thamnophis elegans*
Green Snake, smooth, *Opheodrys vernalis*
Salamander, tiger, *Ambystoma tigrinum*
Toad, mountain (or Boreal Toad), *Bufo boreas*
Woodhouse's, *B. woodhousii*

Butterflies

Admiral, Weidemeyer's, *Limenitis weidemeyerii*
Alpine, common, *Erebia epipsodea*
Blue, greenish, *Plebejus saepiolus*
Fritillary, northwestern, *Speyeria hesperis*
Mourning Cloak, *Nymphalis antiopa*
Orangetip, *Anthocharis* spp.
Swallowtail, pale, *Papilio eurymedon*
Tortoiseshell, Milbert's, *Nymphalis milberti*
White, spring, *Pontia sisymbrii*

Riffle, Pool, and Tarn: Aquatic Ecosystems

Small lake flanked by subalpine spruce-fir forest, Park Range.

Liquid, vapor, ice: the presence of water, in all its forms, shapes the world we know. From the tiniest trickle emanating from a melting snowbank to the sunlit riffles of a mountain stream, the presence of water creates a mosaic of habitats for plants and animals. Water, the elemental combination of two atoms of hydrogen and one of oxygen, has served as evolution's crucible for more than 3 billion years. The powerful affinity of the hydrogen bond is the liquid embrace that holds the world together. A closer look at the aquatic ecosystems around us reveals layer upon layer of complexity and interconnectivity, the result of ancient collaborations we are only just beginning to understand. Our absolute dependency on water, as well as that of every living organism, must be balanced against the technological skills that allow us to intervene at every level, to capture every free-flowing river or to tap subterranean aquifers that are millions of years old.

Aquatic ecosystems are found throughout the Southern Rockies, ranging in elevation from 4,000 to more than 14,000 feet. These ecosystems are divided into two general groups: flowing-water, or lotic, habitats and standing-water, or lentic, habitats. Lotic ecosystems range in size from seeps and springs to streams and rivers. Lentic ecosystems include both lakes and ponds as well as a variety of transitional wetland habitats in which the surface of the land is covered, at least seasonally, with shallow water. Both types of ecosystems are described in this chapter. A discussion of the physical and biological features that shape each ecosystem is included to provide an introduction to the complex relationships that govern aquatic communities.

Lotic Ecosystems: Mountain Streams and Rivers

Physical and Biological Features

The physical and biological characteristics of a stream vary markedly as you move downstream from its source. Changes in the structure and function of the stream's biological communities are closely correlated with changes in physical characteristics: the source of the water, the slope of the streambed (gradient), the volume and velocity of the water being moved, the width of the channel, the depth of the channel, water temperature, the character of the streambed, and the water's turbidity (clear, cloudy, or muddy). Biologists recognize three broad zones that bracket the ecological changes that occur in a flowing-water system from its source to its mouth: (1) headwater streams, (2) intermediate-sized streams or small rivers, and (3) large rivers. Each zone is characterized by a different assemblage of organisms specifically adapted to the food resources and living conditions found within that zone. Significant changes in one or more physical variables anywhere upstream tends to exert a ripple effect downstream, altering the stream's physical characteristics and associated biotic communities.

Stream Animals

To the plants and animals that live in moving waters, the current brings food, oxygen, and all the other nutrients they need for survival. Change, however, is a constant force to be reckoned with in the dynamic life of a stream or river. Too drastic a change, such as a natural flood or a dam release, can sweep these organisms downstream into drastically different habitats where they will not survive. Animals that live in flowing water are classified into the following groups according to the way in which they feed: shredders, collectors, scraper-grazers, and predators. Shredders (such as case-building caddisflies, crane fly larvae, and herbivorous mayfly nymphs) are adapted to feed on coarse plant detritus that enters the stream from surrounding terrestrial ecosystems; plant fragments that have been colonized by microscopic decomposers such as bacteria and aquatic fungi are preferred food items. Shredders play an important role in breaking organic material down into finer particles, which are then available to other animals in the food chain.

Collectors (such as net-spinning caddisflies and black fly larvae) capture fine particles of organic matter produced by the feeding activities of the shredders or fragments broken down by mechanical action within the stream. These fascinating animals obtain their food, fragmented, microbe-conditioned organic particles and feces produced by the shredders, by filtering or sieving fine particles carried in suspension by the current or by gathering particles, vacuum-cleaner fashion, from the bottom sediments. Common adaptations for filter feeding include mouth brushes, head fans, and sieve nets fashioned from silk secretions. Most collectors select their food on the basis of particle size rather than food quality, opportunistically ingesting all manner of fine detritus.

The scraper-grazer group includes a diverse array of animals (including snails, caddisfly larvae of the genus *Glossosoma*, and clinging mayflies of the genera *Ephemerella* and *Rhithrogena*) that have mouthparts with rasplike teeth specialized for shearing off diatoms and other microalgae attached to rocks or other surfaces. Other adaptations, such as a streamlined, flattened body and the suckerlike gills of the mayfly *Ephemerella*, enable these organisms to withstand considerable current.

The predator group includes all animals (such as stonefly nymphs, water striders, water boatmen, and trout) adapted specifically for the capture of live prey. Though members of other groups may ingest live prey in the course of their feeding, true predators engulf their prey. Some rove from stone to stone, using their large eyes and, in the case of the stonefly nymph, their sensitive antennae to detect prey. Others, such as some dragonfly and damselfly nymphs, ambush their prey, responding to the stimulus of the prey touching an antenna or other receptor. Larger predators, particularly fish, are capable of rapid bursts of speed in pursuit of a prey item. Mammals such as the river otter and the mink as well as a diverse array of avian predators including bald eagles, osprey, common mergansers, herons, dippers, and kingfishers, are highly skilled at exploiting the abundant food resources found in streams and rivers.

Lotic Environments: Community Characteristics

Headwater Streams

A cascading, boulder-strewn stream, drifts of pink Parry's primroses and white marsh-marigolds edging a plunge pool, and the close-quartering flight of a dipper skimming the crest of a waterfall: these scenes capture the magical essence of an alpine headwater stream in the Southern Rockies. Headwater streams, with the exception of those flowing through alpine meadows, are narrow and have steep gradients, alternating series of rapids and pools, high levels of dissolved oxygen, cold and relatively constant temperatures, reduced light levels, a paucity of vascular

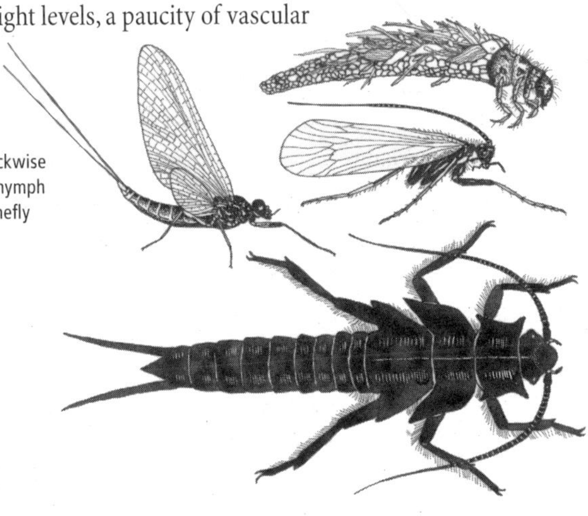

Common stream insects, clockwise from upper right: caddisfly (nymph in case), adult caddisfly, stonefly nymph, mayfly.

aquatic plants, and substrates that consist of rock rubble of various sizes. Mountain streams typically contain two different habitats: the turbulent riffle and the quiet pool. Riffles are characterized by the periodic growth of attached algae (periphyton) on the streambed during favorable periods and by the algae's subsequent removal, or scouring, during high water events. Anyone who has tried to cross from one slippery rock to another in a mountain stream has experienced an algal bloom of diatoms firsthand. Alternating with riffles are pools, where the current slows and organic materials settle out. In contrast to riffles, pools serve as sites of decomposition and free carbon dioxide production during summer and fall. This alternation of habitats acts like a conveyor belt, delivering dissolved gases, minerals, sand, silt, and organic materials to downstream reaches. The decomposition of plant tissues by bacteria and fungi along the streambed, however, also consumes oxygen. Consequently, streams and rivers are constantly depleting their oxygen, and constantly, unless they are dammed, replacing it.

The majority of the stream's animal inhabitants live in the oxygen-rich environment of the riffles, on the undersides of rocks, or in gravel, where they are sheltered from the effects of the current. Characteristic riffle insects include the nymphs of mayflies, caddisflies, true flies, and stoneflies, which depend on flowing water to aid their respiration and bring them food. Most riffle animals exhibit adaptations that protect them from the current's destructive power: hydrodynamically shaped bodies, suckers or holdfasts, grapplelike appendages, and protective cases constructed of fine gravel or organic debris. In the pools, the dominant insects are the skilled predators: dragonfly and damselfly nymphs, diving beetles, and water striders. Some animals, such as trout, move between riffle and pool at will, selecting the first environment for food, the other for shelter.

Riparian vegetation—the fallen leaves of cottonwoods, willows, aspen, and alders—plays a critical role in headwater streams, supplying both shade and organic input. Invertebrate collectors and scraper-grazers, mayflies being the most abundant of these, dominate streams above 10,000 feet. Populations of insects of other orders fluctuate in response to local conditions, with stoneflies often more abundant than caddisflies as elevation increases. Insects belonging to the shredder or predator groups make up only about 20 percent of the fauna of the typical high-altitude stream. With decreasing elevation, species richness increases dramatically, and shredders and predators assume greater importance. For example, a single riffle may provide habitat for at least six species of the caddisfly genus *Rhyacophila*. Since the major influx of organic matter occurs during autumn leaf drop, shredder life cycles, such as those of the stonefly *Nemoura*, are keyed to this food supply; eggs of most shredders are laid and hatch in the fall, and growth is completed by spring.

The phenomenon known as invertebrate drift is an integral part of headwater stream ecosystems and consists of bottom-living invertebrates washed downstream by the current. There are two main types of drift: voluntary and involuntary. In the former, the animal voluntarily lets go of the substrate and is transported downstream, where it can colonize new sites. Voluntary drift may be triggered by a decline in flow, changes in current patterns, or high population densities within the existing habitat. Predators such as trout, which time their feeding to coincide with times of maximum drift, dawn and dusk, successfully exploit invertebrate drift. Fisheries biologists suggest that a good trout stream should be about evenly divided between riffles and pools. First and foremost, however, a good trout stream must be a good insect stream, a haven for algae, fungi, and bacteria, a prime repository for dead leaves, and a superior reservoir of oxygen and calcium.

Midreaches: Intermediate-sized Streams and Small Rivers

Downstream from the frothy white cascades that distinguish the headwaters region, a noticeable shift in the character of aquatic communities occurs in response to changes in physical setting and the coalescing of tributary waters. The most important of these changes include progressive increases in channel width and depth, a reduction in gradient, a decrease in the rate of flow, an increase in flow volume (highest during spring runoff), a reduction in terrestrially derived organic matter, an increase in the amount of in-stream primary production, an increase in solar input, and warmer, more variable water temperatures. Oxygen levels are typically lower than those found in headwater streams. The streambed consists of boulder- to cobble-sized rubble, gravel, or silt producing a mosaic of habitats for plant and animal life.

Streams and rivers in this size class, such as the Roaring Fork and

Cache la Poudre rivers, exhibit higher species diversity than that found in either headwater or big-river habitats. With the decreasing velocity, warmer waters, and greater accumulation of bottom sediments, animals adapted to life in swift currents are found only in areas with riffles. Shredders are less abundant because of the decline in coarse particulate organic matter entering the stream from terrestrial sources. Collectors, however, are well represented because of the greater concentration of fine sediments produced by the coalescing of headwater streams. Scraper-grazers are also abundant because of the proliferation of attached algae and, to a lesser extent, vascular aquatic plants. Foraging predators such as trout and dragonfly nymphs and bottom feeders such as minnows and suckers are common in most intermediate-sized streams.

Large Rivers

The Southern Rockies is justifiably famous for its rivers. The Yampa River, in northwestern Colorado, is one of the premier wilderness rivers in North America. Arising as a tumbling snowmelt cascade in the Flat Tops, the Yampa still dances to its ancient seasonal rhythms, free of any significant dam impoundments in its upriver reaches. From its alpine headwaters, where it runs fast and crystal clear, to its final looping meanders through the spectacular sandstone canyons of Dinosaur National Monument, the Yampa flows through a constantly changing array of geologic settings before joining the Green River at Echo Park. It is typical of large rivers in their lower reaches, such as the Rio Grande, the Yampa, and the Colorado, to be turbid with sediments gathered from their coalescing tributaries, especially during the spring runoff. The riverbed is usually covered by mud and silt, except where rocks in the channel create turbulent flow. Depending on the local geology, deep pools may alternate with stretches of rapids. Flow velocity in large rivers is highest during spring runoff and declines markedly by fall, with a corresponding drop in turbidity (suspended silt and organic material).

Primary production (photosynthesis) is generally low in large rivers, and is limited largely to planktonic organisms. Biological diversity is also significantly lower in large rivers than in upstream waters. Rubble-dwelling insect larvae are replaced by species adapted for burrowing in soft sediments. The prevalence of fine particulate organic matter supports large numbers of collectors specifically adapted to the warmer temperatures and lower dissolved oxygen levels of the river environment, as well as bottom-feeding fish such as the fathead minnow and the bluehead sucker. In the shallows along the banks and in backwater areas, river animals are similar to those found in ponds or lakes: water boatmen and diving beetles are common, and emergent plants provide microhabitats for animals such as pond snails and water mites. A scoop of mud reveals filter-feeding aquatic earthworms and leeches and a variety of other organisms that thrive in low-oxygen habitats.

The presence of impoundment dams and water diversion projects in the midreaches of most of the major rivers in the Southern Rockies have dramatically altered normal hydrologic regimes as well as the assemblages of animals and plants that depended on these ancient flow patterns for survival. Not surprisingly, the Yampa River remains one the last strongholds for the endangered native fish of the Upper Colorado River basin: the northern pike minnow (Colorado squawfish), razorback sucker, bonytail, humpback chub, bluehead sucker, and the flannelmouth sucker. These endangered fish species have lived for millions of years in the Colorado River system and nowhere else in the world, their unique life histories rivaling those of the Pacific Northwest's legendary salmon.

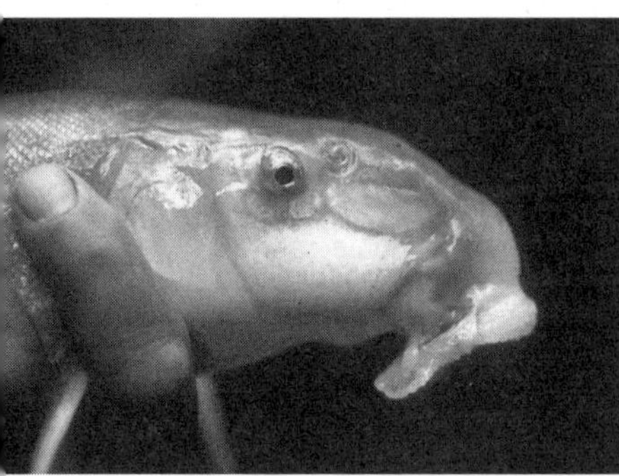

The flannelmouth sucker, easily identified by its large, overhanging mouth and golden-green coloring, is disappearing from the larger streams and rivers of the Colorado River System as a result of competition from introduced species and cold-water reservoir releases.

Lentic Ecosystems: Marsh, Pond, and Lake

Marshes, ponds, and lakes are scattered throughout the Southern Rockies. These bodies of water, nourished by streams, groundwater, or runoff, are either natural or man-made, and most are found in well-defined depressions, in valleys where beavers are active, as spring-fed pools, or behind man-made impoundments. Marshes develop in poorly drained areas and are characterized by a mosaic of emergent, submergent, and floating plant communities interspersed with areas of open water. Natural lakes and ponds are most common in the glaciated portions of the higher mountains, where water collects in basins at the foot of melting snowfields or behind moraines deposited by retreating glaciers. Lakes and ponds are generally distinguished on the basis of size and depth; ponds tend to be considerably smaller and shallower than lakes and have waters that are relatively uniform in temperature.

Pond lily.

Physical Features of Lentic Ecosystems

Light Penetration

The diversity, distribution, and abundance of life in lentic ecosystems is influenced by the penetration of light, seasonal and daily temperature regimes, oxygen levels, and nutrients. Solar radiation provides the primary energy source in such environments. In marshes and shallow ponds, light penetrates to the bottom. In deeper waters, light penetrates only to a certain depth, depending on the turbidity of the water. Most lakes can be divided horizontally into two layers on the basis of light penetration: the upper layer, known as the trophogenic zone, in which there is sufficient light for photosynthesis, and the lower layer, called the tropholytic zone, where light penetration is so low that photosynthesis cannot occur and where decomposition is most active. There is increasing evidence that the combined effects of higher ultraviolet (UV-B) radiation, as well as excess nitrogen deposition and metal pollution (from air pollution or historic mining) are causing a significant decline in the populations of zoo- and phytoplankton that form the all-important base of the aquatic food chain. Though the long-term impacts to aquatic ecosystems are difficult to predict, researchers suggest that we need to intensify the focus of our scientific concern and conservation efforts on these vital ecosystems if we are to preserve them.

Temperature

Patterns of thermal stratification and circulation develop in bodies of water as a result of seasonal changes in temperature, and they strongly influence community structure. During the summer months, thermal stratification in shallow ponds or lakes is largely diurnal and of short duration, with only slight differences in temperature between the surface and the bottom. Deep-water lakes in the Southern Rockies, on the other hand, experience two thermal overturns, one in spring and one in fall. Thermal overturns are triggered by convection currents set in motion by density differences created by the heating and cooling of the water. These overturns are of critical importance in replenishing the oxygen supply available to organisms in the deepest waters and in mixing nutrients throughout the lake.

Oxygen

Oxygen enters the aquatic environment by diffusion from the atmosphere and from the photosynthetic activities of aquatic plants. The oxygen content of pond or lake water is relatively low compared to that of flowing waters because only a small proportion of the water is in direct contact with the air. In general, the amount of oxygen in ponds and lakes is greatest near the surface and decreases sharply with depth, due in part to the respiration of aerobic bacteria and other microbes involved in decomposition. The decomposition of organic matter on the bottom of a pond or lake produces a black, oxygen-poor (anaerobic) mud that smells strongly of hydrogen sulfide. When large quantities of organic matter are decomposing, the oxygen in a pond or shallow lake may decline to such a low level that animals cannot survive.

Sunlight triggers high levels of photosynthetic activity in aquatic plants, especially algae, resulting in the production of significant quantities of oxygen. Oxygen levels are highest in the late afternoon and lowest just before sunrise. In a weed-filled pond on a sunny day, streams of bubbles can be seen rising to the surface when plants release oxygen as a by-product of photosynthesis. In deep water, except in lakes so clear that light penetration permits the growth of phytoplankton even at great depth, oxygen levels are lower than those found in shallow waters. Only during the spring and fall overturns, when oxygen is transferred downward and nutrients brought upward, is life abundant in the tropholytic zone.

Biological Features of Lentic Ecosystems

Ecological zonation in aquatic ecosystems is correlated with photosynthetic activity. Moving out from the shoreline, the trophogenic zone can be divided into two subzones. The first of these is the littoral (shallow-water) zone, where light penetrates to the bottom and aquatic life is richest and most abundant. Beyond the littoral zone, which extends to the limit of rooted plant growth, lies the limnetic (open-water) zone. This zone is inhabited by plant and animal plankton, as well as by free-swimming organisms such as fish; the limnetic zone is typically absent from marshes and other shallow-water habitats. Beneath the limnetic zone, below the depth of effective light penetration, lies the profundal zone. The abundance and diversity of life in this zone is extremely limited due to reduced oxygen availability and cold temperatures. The bottom of the marsh, pond, or lake, extending from shore to shore, is called the benthic zone.

Adaptations for Living in Water

Aquatic Plants

Aquatic plants, in contrast to land plants, lack cuticles (the noncellular external waterproof coating) and absorb nutrients over their entire surfaces directly from the surrounding water. Consequently, aquatic plants have little need for elaborate root systems or for the well-developed conductive tissues found in most terrestrial species. Water provides the supporting medium for the plant, reducing the need for the structural tissues necessary for life on land. Buoyancy is achieved by the presence of large, intercellular air spaces within the plant's tissues; these air spaces may link together to form a continuous passage for the circulation and storage of oxygen produced by photosynthesis. To avoid supersaturation, aquatic plants are often covered with a layer of mucilage.

Aquatic Animals

Aquatic organisms, whether they live on the water's flexible, tough surface, in the organic muck of the bottom, or in the liquid space in between, are faced with a variety of challenges. Like all animals, they require oxygen, obtaining it in one of two ways. The first method is to collect a supply of air at the surface, stay below until it is exhausted, then quickly resurface to replenish it. Animals that depend on scuba-style procurement include the diving beetles and water scavenger beetles, which carry large bubbles of air beneath their wing cases; the water boatmen, which trap layers of air within the fringes of hairs on their bodies; and the snails, which crawl along upside down beneath the surface film, taking air into the mantle chambers within their shells. The second method of obtaining oxygen involves anatomical adaptations that enable the animal to draw its oxygen directly from the surrounding water, either through the use of gas-exchanging gills, such as those found in many aquatic insect larvae (mayfly and stonefly nymphs, and dragonfly, damselfly, and caddisfly larvae, for example), or by diffusion over the entire thin walled body surface (as in aquatic earthworms, planaria, and leeches).

The way in which aquatic animals move about in water is linked to the way in which they obtain oxygen. Those that extract oxygen directly from the water are generally denser than water and move by crawling, either on the bottom or on submerged plants. Animals that collect air from the surface tend to be strong swimmers; most of these species are lighter than water and naturally bob to the surface like corks, unless they keep swimming or are able to cling to submerged plants. Animals that move about on the surface film of the water, such as the water strider, have water-repellent waxy hairs on their legs and claws that keep them from piercing the surface film.

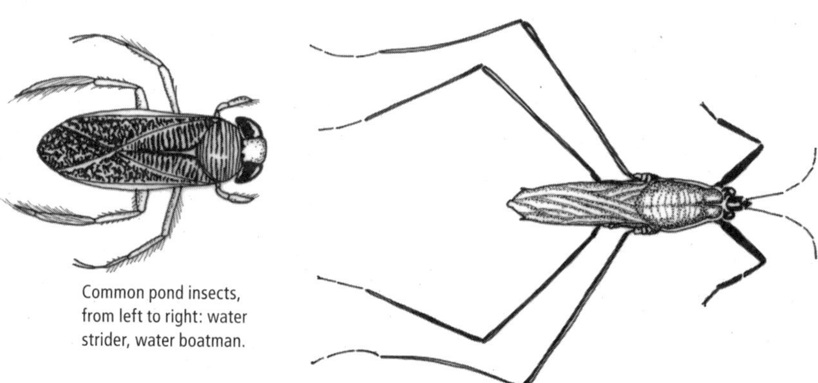

Common pond insects, from left to right: water strider, water boatman.

Community Characteristics

Life in the Shallows: The Littoral Zone

The littoral zone is found around the edges of most lakes and usually throughout marshes and ponds. Within this zone, aquatic life varies with water depth, and a distinct ecological zonation can be observed extending from the shoreline to the deeper waters of the limnetic zone. Closest to shore, in the shallowest water, are emergent and floating-leaf vegetation, plants whose roots and lower stems are immersed in water but whose upper stems and leaves float on or project above the water. Many of these plants produce at least two different types of leaves: the submerged leaf, typically finely dissected; and the emergent leaf, which is conspicuously broader. Common emergent plants include water crowfoot, water smartweed (or bistort), marestail, pondweed, and yellow pondlily.

Submerged and free-floating aquatic plants are typical of the deeper waters of the littoral zone. Submerged plants are rooted in mud, and most species, such as water moss, water starwort, and water milfoil, have thin, finely dissected or ribbonlike leaves. Free-floating plants occur at or just below the water surface, where they can obtain the light necessary for photosynthesis, and include a great variety of microscopic species (such as green and blue-green algae and diatoms), as well as many higher plants. Some free-floating species, such as duckweed, have thin roots that dangle into the water but do not touch bottom, while others, such as great bladderwort, lack true roots but have evolved bladders on their leaves that serve as insect traps, providing energy through carnivory. Free-floating plants are often found over very deep water and can sometimes form extensive carpets across the surfaces of ponds or shallow lakes.

Many aquatic animals find food and shelter in the diverse microhabitats of the littoral zone. The shimmering surface film is exploited by a specially adapted group of organisms, the neuston, which includes the water strider and the marsh treader, as well as certain spiders and springtails. On the underside of this film, pond snails and planarian flatworms crawl along in search of algae and other minute plants on which to feed. Here and there, hydras hang upside down from the floating leaves of plants, capturing water fleas and other tiny crustaceans with their stinging tentacles. Beneath the floating-leaf canopy, swarms of single-celled protozoans, rotifers, water fleas, copepods, and fairy shrimp swim freely through the submerged vegetation. Releasing their hold on submerged plants, diving beetles and backswimmers dart swiftly after their tiny prey, rising to the surface occasionally to replenish their oxygen supply. The littoral bottom receives a constant rain of dead plants and animals from the waters above, supporting a great variety of decomposers and detritus feeders. Because of the abundance of life, the littoral zone serves as the principal hunting ground for both small and large predators: larval insects, fish, larval tiger salamanders, and frogs.

Open Water: The Limnetic Zone

Minute suspended plants and animals—phytoplankton and zooplankton—populate the limnetic zone. Phytoplankton, which include the diatoms, desmids, and filamentous green algae, are the photosynthetic base on which the rest of limnetic life depends. Swimming and drifting with the phytoplankton are the zooplankton: rotifers, copepods, volvox, water fleas, and various protozoa. Most limnetic zooplankton are light-colored or translucent, while species found in littoral waters are darker in color, ranging from light yellowish brown to reddish brown, grayish, or almost black. Zooplankton living in high-altitude waters, such as *Daphnia longispina* and *Diaptomus* copepods, have even higher levels of the dark pigment melanin to help block harmful ultraviolet radiation. Fish, such as trout, are common visitors to the linmetic zone, their distribution influenced mostly by food supply, oxygen levels, and temperature.

Most zooplankton are filter-feeders, sieving their food, including bacteria, algae, detritus, and other smaller zooplankton, from the nutrient-rich soup that surrounds them. Some species, such as the rotifers, have a circlet of moving cilia, which they fan to create a current that carries food particles toward the mouth and also serves to propel the animal through the water. When put into motion, the circlet of cilia resembles a turning wheel, thus the species' name, which comes from the Latin word *rota*, meaning wheel. Water fleas, typically the most common crustacean found in ponds or lakes, create a constant current with their bristle-edged legs, filtering out food particles that are then directed forward through a ventral groove to the mouthparts. Another group of tiny crustaceans, the copepods, have mouthparts adapted either for seizing food (as in the *Cyclops* spp.) or for filtering; the hairs of the filter are so fine and close together that they can remove an individual bacterium.

The degree to which light is able to penetrate sets the lower limit at which phytoplankton can exist; the depth at which various species live is determined by the optimum conditions for their growth and development. Phytoplankton are more abundant during spring and summer, when nutrient levels, available light, and water temperatures are highest. Since zooplankton depend on phytoplankton for food, these animals often concentrate in surface waters and tend to be most numerous in productive waters where food is plentiful. In contrast to phytoplankton, which depend largely on the mixing action of currents to move them about, most zooplankton are capable of independent movement, exhibiting both diurnal and seasonal migrations to avoid predation and in response to changing conditions; it is believed that the primary stimulus for vertical migrations is the daily cycle of subsurface illumination.

Planktonic organisms have evolved a number of highly specialized adaptations that allow them to overwinter or withstand adverse environmental conditions. Many small crustaceans, such as water fleas, produce two kinds of eggs: one type that develops quickly when the habitat is favorable and another, a thick-shelled resting egg that is laid in autumn and during times of environmental stress. The resting egg typically remains dormant, sometimes for several years, until favorable conditions return. Other animals, such as certain protozoa and the copepod *Cyclops*, form cysts or cocoons composed of secreted organic membrane and an enveloping mass of detritus. These adaptations tend to be multipurpose, the same device being used to overwinter or as an estivation mechanism to avoid drying, low oxygen levels, high or low temperatures, or changes in water chemistry.

Dark Waters: The Profundal Zone

The profundal zone lies below the depth of effective light penetration. Consequently, photosynthetic plants, except for benthic algae and some bacteria, are absent. The animals found here, particularly fish, water fleas, and opossum shrimp, rely on the rain of organic materials from upper layers for food. Other zooplankton may occupy the profundal zone as part of their daily migrations. Only during the spring and fall overturns, when currents deliver oxygen and organisms from the surface to the deeper waters, is life abundant in this zone. Large deep-water lakes tend to support more life in the profundal zone because the productivity of the limnetic zone is low in comparison to the volume of water, and decomposition in the benthic zone does not deplete the oxygen supply available for profundal animals.

Life on the Bottom: The Benthic Zone
Layers of organic and inorganic sediments at the bottom of a lake or pond constitute the benthic zone. Here, detritus feeders eat the remains of plants and animals that have been decomposed by aquatic fungi and bacteria. In the shallow waters of marshes and most ponds, the littoral bottom extends from shore to shore and is inhabited by a diverse assemblage of aquatic insects, known collectively as benthos. In lakes and ponds with deeper waters, the benthic zone includes both the littoral bottom and the biologically impoverished profundal bottom. For the most part, the fauna of the profundal bottom is not unique to that zone but includes only those representatives of the larger littoral bottom fauna that can tolerate severe stagnation.

On the littoral bottom, benthic animals are most abundant in areas with emergent vegetation, which provides surfaces for attachment and cover from predators. Many organisms, including species of blue-green algae, diatoms, freshwater sponges, and colonies of bryozoans, attach themselves to the submerged substrate, forming a crustlike growth on stones, logs, and other bottom materials. Burrowing into and living within this living crust are numerous associated animals; rotifers, hydras, copepods, insect larvae, and a wide variety of protozoans. Some benthic animals, including scavengers such as water boatmen and predators such as damselfly nymphs, caddisflies, and various beetle larvae, roam freely over the surface of the ooze, while others burrow into the organic-rich sediments. The burrowers include tiny fingernail clams, segmented worms, roundworms, flatworms, and a host of diminutive crustaceans.

Succession and Aquatic Ecosystems

Most ponds, lakes, and marshes are temporary features on the landscape, undergoing changes through time that result in their eventual transformation into terrestrial ecosystems. The continual addition of mineral and organic matter gradually reduces water depth, allowing emergent plants to proliferate from shore to shore. With time, as the bottom rises above the groundwater level, the emergent plants are replaced by sedges, rushes, grasses, and, eventually, shrubs such as willow and bog birch or moisture-loving trees such as aspen.

Common Plants of Aquatic Ecosystems

Bladderwort, great, *Utricularia vulgaris*
  small, *U. minor*
Bulrush, *Scirpus pallidus* and *S. microcarpus*
Burreed, *Sparganium* spp.
Buttercup, birdfoot, *Ranunculus pedatifidus*
  floating, *R. hyperboreus* ssp. *intertextus*
  heart-leaved, *R. cardiophyllus*
Cattails, *Typha* spp.
Coltsfoot, sweet, *Petasites sagittata*
  yellow-flowered, *Ranunculus gmelinii* var. *hookeri*
Crowfoot, small-flowered, *Ranunculus abortivus* ssp. *acrolasius*
  water, *Batrachium* (formerly *Ranunculus*) *trichophyllum*
Duckweed, *Lemna* spp.
Mannagrass, *Glyceria* spp.
Marestail, *Hippuris vulgaris*
Milfoil, marsh, *Myriophyllum sibiricum*
Pond Lily, yellow, *Nuphar lutea*
Pondweed, *Potamogeton* spp.

Marsh trefoil.

Quillwort, *Isoetes bolanderi*
Rushes, *Juncus* spp.
Sedges, *Carex* spp.
Smartweed (or Water Bistort), *Persicaria amphibia*
scarlet, *P. coccinea*
Spearwort, *Ranunculus reptans*
Spikerush, *Eleocharis* spp.
Starwort, water, *Callitriche* spp.
Trefoil, marsh, *Menyanthes trifoliata*
Tule (or Bulrush), *Schoenocrambe linifolia* ssp. *acutus* (formerly *Scirpus acutus*)
Water Moss, *Fontinalis* spp.

Life Histories of Selected Animals

Insects, True Bugs, and Other Invertebrates

Mayflies, Order Ephemeroptera, Family Baetidae. The adult mayfly is easily identified by its delicate gossamer wings and by the two or three long, segmented filaments that project from the end of its slender abdomen. A swarm, or "hatch," of these lovely insects is often observed fluttering over a mountain stream, attracting predators such as trout and fly-catching birds. Mating occurs in the air, and females deposit large numbers of eggs in the water; hatching occurs within a few days. Once hatched, mayflies spend the majority of their lives as dull-colored, aquatic nymphs (naiads) and are distinguished from other aquatic larvae by the paired tracheal gills along the abdominal segments and by the long, fringed caudal filaments at the tip of the abdomen. Nymphs are essentially herbivorous, feeding on plant detritus or algae. When ready to emerge, the mayfly nymph floats to the surface or crawls out of the water onto rocks or vegetation. The mayfly is unique among insects in that it has two winged stages in its life cycle. The first of these, called the subimago, sheds its nymphal skin, flies upward, and alights on vegetation. Within minutes or hours, the subimago sheds an exocuticle from its whole body, including the wings, and the adult mayfly is revealed in all its delicate beauty.

Caddisflies, Order Trichoptera, Family Rhyacophilidae and Family Hydropsychidae. At least nineteen families of Tricopterans (caddisflies) occur in the Southern Rockies; the two most common and representative families are noted above. Caddisflies are closely related to butterflies and moths; the wings of the mothlike, terrestrial adult caddisfly are thickly covered with hairs that do not rub off, unlike the scales of a moth's wing. Caddisfly larvae and pupae are aquatic and may be found in both lotic and lentic ecosystems; the larval stage lasts nearly a year, the pupal stage only a few weeks, and the adult form thirty days or less. Caddisfly larvae somewhat resemble caterpillars, with tough, brown heads, soft, pale bodies, and long, thoracic legs. Most larvae are either case-building or net-spinning; a few species are free-living, building a case only when entering pupation. The case-building caddisfly (Rhyacophilidae) constructs a portable or fixed tubelike case by attaching materials such as sand grains, conifer needles, small stones, twigs, and plant fragments to an inner silken lining spun by the larva; each case is built according to a species-specific pattern and provides excellent camouflage from predators. Prior to pupation, larvae seal both ends of their cases, leaving only a small hole to allow entry of water and oxygen. When the pupa-adult is fully formed, it cuts an opening in the case, swims to the surface, and crawls out of the water onto a rock or log; as soon as it is capable of flight, the adult flies off to seek a mate. No matter the material used to build the case, a close look with a hand lens will reveal the handiwork of a master architect. Net-spinning species (Hydropsychidae), in contrast to the case builders, weave delicate silken nets between stones in a stream, each net having a tunnel leading off to one side and ending in a shelter of stream debris; the larva lives in the shelter, crawling out occasionally to scrape off food particles intercepted by the net.

Water Boatmen, Order Hemiptera (true bugs). Water boatmen are distinguished from other aquatic bugs and beetles by their fringed, oarlike hind legs and their diminutive forelegs; they are usually less than half an inch in length and have conspicuously flattened and mottled bodies, large eyes, and mouthparts fused into their rounded heads. A surface breather, the water boatman envelops its body in a layer of air and stores air beneath its wings. Water boatmen swim, headfirst, in a quick, darting manner, propelled by oarlike movements of the hind legs; most species are also strong fliers and take off easily from the surface of the water. These insects are largely bottom feeders and are the only Hemiptera not wholly predaceous. During courtship, the males of most species produce shrill, chirping noises. Eggs are onion-shaped and attached to the stems of aquatic plants; there are five nymph stages in the life cycle.

Fairy Shrimp, Order Anostraca. Fairy shrimp are found in shallow ponds and lakes, but are most common in temporary pools and slightly alkaline waters. These delicate, ethereal-looking animals lack the shieldlike, chitinous carapace of their larger relatives and vary in color from translucent whitish to blue, green, orange, or red. The fairy shrimp is remarkably graceful as it alternates between drifting and fast darts, swimming usually on its back, beating its many long, leaflike gill feet. This filter-feeder brings its food, bacteria, rotifers, and fine detritus, forward to its mouth by the beating of its legs. Female fairy shrimp are usually more abundant than males; when males are present, they are typically paired with females. The eggs of the fairy shrimp are produced by parthenogenesis or by fertilization and are carried in a brood sac; two types of eggs are produced, thin-walled summer eggs and thick-walled winter (resting) eggs, and are released in clutches at intervals of two to six days, with 10 to 250 eggs per clutch. The thick-walled resting eggs are able to withstand prolonged periods of desiccation and winter cold.

Fish

Trout, Family *Salmonidae*, Genera *Salmo* and *Salvelinus*. Trout are distinguished from other freshwater fish by their tiny scales (more than 100 scales in each lateral line), the presence of an adipose (fatty) dorsal fin, and well-developed teeth. Color patterns vary, not only with species, but also with habitat, size, and, during the breeding season, by sex. When young, all trout have a series of dark blotches along their sides that disappear with age. Young trout feed largely upon insects and other small invertebrates; as they increase in size, trout may feed on larger organisms and other smaller fish. Some trout spawn in spring and early summer and others in the fall and winter. All species deposit their eggs in gravel, usually near the head of a riffle; the female prepares the cavity for the eggs while the male defends the territory from other fish until the eggs hatch several weeks later. Nonnative trout species, introduced for the multimillion-dollar recreational fishery, have outcompeted and decimated populations of native trout throughout the Southern Rockies.

Cutthroat Trout, *Salmo clarki.* In general, cutthroat trout (both native and nonnative races) are distinguished by the reddish or orange streaks in the folds beneath the lower jaw and by the prominent but sparse pattern of black spots dispersed over the upper body; males in breeding colors may have blood red or orange lower sides. Cutthroats spawn in spring or early summer. Nonnative cutthroat are common as a result of introductions. Pure populations of Colorado cutthroat are largely restricted to northwestern Colorado and southwestern Wyoming; extremely small populations of greenback cutthroat are found in western Boulder and Larimer counties, and transplant populations inhabit certain streams in Rocky Mountain National Park.

Brook Trout, *Salvelinus fontinalis.* This beautiful trout is native to eastern North America and the only species lacking black spots; back and sides are patterned with light spots (reddish or yellowish) and wavy lines on a dark background. Brook trout are found only in small, cold headwater streams and cold lakes. Spawning occurs in the fall.

Brown Trout, *Salmo trutta.* This trout is a native of Europe and is distinguished by the blackish spots (few or none on the tail fin) and small orange or reddish spots that speckle its greenish brown or olive body; the adipose fin is tipped with orange. Spawning occurs in the fall.

Rainbow Trout, *Salmo gairdneri.* This trout has been introduced from the West Coast and differs from the cutthroat in that it has a shorter upper jaw; there is usually a diffuse band of rosy scales along the sides and a greater number of black spots. Rainbows spawn in spring.

Common Animals of Aquatic Ecosystems

Fish

Brook Stickleback, *Culaea inconstans* (nonnative)
Chub, boneytail, *Gila elegans* (native)
  humpback, *G. cypha* (native)
  roundtail, *G. robusta* (native)

Rio Grande, *G. pandora* (native)
Dace, longnose, *Rhinichthys cataractae* (native)
speckled, *R. osculus* (native)
Minnow, fathead, *Pimephales promelas* (nonnative)
Pikeminnow, Northern, (formerly Colorado Squawfish), *Ptychocheilus lucius* (native)
Sculpin, Mottled, *Cottus bairdi* (native)
Shiner, red, *Notropis lutrensis* (nonnative)
Sucker, bluehead, *Catostomus discobolus* (native)
flannelmouth, *C. latipinnis* (native)
longnose, *C. catostomus* (nonnative)
razorback, *Xyrauchen texanus* (native)
white, *C. commersoni* (nonnative)
Trout, brook, *Salvelinus fontinalis* (nonnative)
brown, *Salmo trutta* (nonnative)
cutthroat, *S. clarki* (nonnative)
greenback cutthroat, *S. clarki stomias* (native)
rainbow, *S. gairdneri* (nonnative)

Invertebrates

Back Swimmer (Order Hemiptera, Family Notonectidae)
Beetle, riffle (Order Coleoptera, Family Psephenidae)
water scavenger (Order Coleoptera, Family Hydrophilidae, *Tropisternus sublaevis*)
whirligig (Order Coleoptera, Family Gyrinidae)
Caddisfly (Order Trichoptera, Family Rhyacophilidae and Hydropsychidae, *Arctopsyche* spp.)
Clam, fingernail (Order Pelecypoda, Family Sphaeriidae)
pea (Family Sphaeriidae, *Pisidium casteranum*)
Copepods (Order Cyclopoida, *Cyclops* spp.)
Damselfly (Order Odonata)
Dragonfly (Order Odonata, Family Anisoptera, *Ophiogomphus severus*)
Earthworms, aquatic (Order Oligochaeta)
Flatworm (or Planaria, (Order Tricladida, Family Planariidae)
Fly, crane (Order Diptera, Family Tipulidae)

Dobson (Order Megaloptera)

Leeches (Order Hirudinea)

Marsh Treader (Order Hemiptera, Family Hydrometridae)

Mayfly (Order Ephemeroptera, Family Baetidae and Family Ephemerellidae, *Drunella* spp.)

Midge (Order Diptera, Family Chironomidae, *Chironomus* spp.)

Mosquitoe, (Order Diptera, Family Culicidae, *Drosophila* spp.)

Mussel, freshwater (Family Unionidae)

Pondsnail, marsh (Order Gastropoda, *Lymnaea* spp.)

Rotifers (Order Ploima)

Shrimp, fairy (Order Anostraca)

opossum (*Mysis* spp.)

Snail, hot spring (or Physa snail), Order Gastropoda, *Physa cupreonitens*)

Sponge, freshwater (Family Spongillidae)

Stonefly (Order Plecoptera, Family Pteronarcyidae, *Pteronarcys californica*)

Water Boatmen (Order Hemiptera, Family Corixidae)

Water Fleas (Order Cladocera, *Daphnia* spp.)

Water Strider (Order Hemiptera, Family Gerridae)

Worms, horsehair *Gordius robustus*

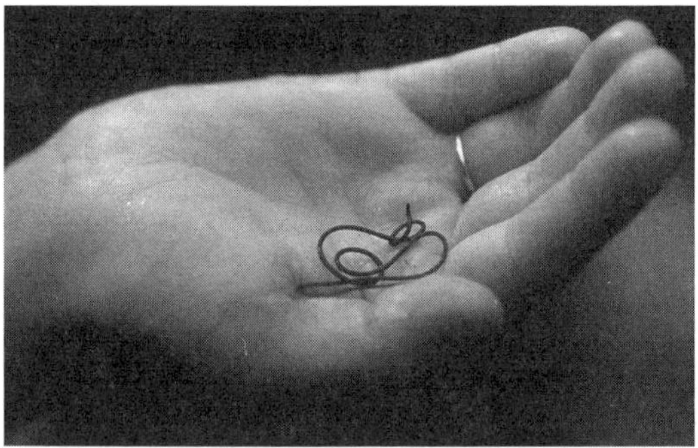

The threadlike horsehair worm (phylum Nematomorpha) is found in warm, shallow ponds, ephemeral pools and puddles, and livestock watering troughs. Larval worms develop as parasites in the body cavities of insects and emerge as adults when their terrestrial host comes in contact with water.

Leaf Dance: Aspen Forests

From their first greening in spring to the golden crescendo that symbolizes autumn in the Rockies, aspen forests occupy a special place in the hearts of westerners. With snow still lingering in the high country of Colorado's Park Range, meltwater rivulets nurture a carpet of avalanche lilies, spring beauties, and chiming bells, resplendent against a frieze of ivory-hued aspen trunks and the first flush of new leaves. In a landscape dominated by the somber hues of conifers, the silvered trunks and apple-green leaves of aspen brighten the monochromatic majesty of the forest palette. During the summer, with their hip-high profusion of wildflowers and rich assortment of cavity-nesting birds, aspen forests have an almost tropical quality. With September's arrival, the green of summer dissolves in a blaze of golden light. The soft rustling of the leaves and the sweet, tannin-rich aroma of aspen dust fills the air. The leaves themselves appear impossibly luminous, miniature lanterns powered by distilled sunshine. The autumn wind riffles through the branches, releasing a meteor shower of amber leaves to pattern the forest floor. Even in winter, the black eyelike knots patterning the trunks and the branches swaying in unison to the wind, aspen forests have a curiously animate and welcoming quality.

Ecological Distribution

Quaking aspen (*Populus tremuloides*) is the most widely distributed native tree species in North America. This amazingly adaptable tree occurs from the Brooks Range of Alaska south to the Sierra Madre of Mexico and from the shores of the Atlantic west to the Pacific. Many of the common names for this slender, graceful tree: quakies, quaking aspen, popple, trembling poplar, and, in Spanish, *alamo blanco* and *alamo temblon*, as well as the Latin epithet *tremuloides*, refer to the tendency of the leaves to flutter and shimmer in the slightest breeze. In the Southern Rockies, aspen is found in relatively moist environments from the foothills through the subalpine zone on both sides of the Continental Divide. Though the most extensive aspen forests are found on the Western Slope, the species also occurs in small groves, along riparian corridors, in transitional belts between coniferous forests and open meadows or shrublands, and as scattered individuals in coniferous forests.

Aspen is one of the few plant species that can grow in every ecological zone except alpine tundra. It reaches its lower limits in foothill ravines, where cooler temperatures prevail and channelized seepage from higher elevations provides sufficient moisture. From north to south along the mountains, aspen is generally found at progressively higher elevations. In southern Wyoming, the upper limit of aspen occurs at about 10,000 feet. In the mountains of north-central Colorado, krummholz (crooked, stunted) stands of spruce and fir in the timberline ecotone occasionally include dwarfed, gnarled aspen. In the San Juan Mountains of southwestern Colorado, aspen forms extensive forests between 8,500 and 10,500 feet. At the southern end of the Southern Rockies, in the Sangre de Cristos and the Jemez Mountains, aspen forests can be found between 7,500 and 11,500 feet, with aspen taking the place of lodgepole pine as the dominant successional tree species on many middle-elevation slopes.

The persistence, health, and survival of aspen forest ecosystems throughout the West depends on aspens' ability to cope with the changing environmental conditions associated with global warming. In a broad spectrum of habitats across the Intermountain West, aspen forests appear to be in serious trouble. In many areas of the Southern Rockies, trees are dying and aspen stands are experiencing massive diebacks, with no discernible pattern or apparent cause. Recent investigations by forest biologists have shown that the primary root systems of the affected aspen are dying, a critical and life-threatening problem for a tree that reproduces in the West primarily by vegetative means (new sprouts arise from the roots). Historically, aspen have been able to withstand droughts, blights, insect infestations, grazing, and other pressures without massive die-offs. Can the problem be blamed on air-fall pollutants and acidification, global warming, fire suppression, a decline in genetic vigor, or some deadly combination of several of these factors? No one knows for sure, and the ripple effect could be devastating for the plant and animal species that depend on aspen forests for their own survival.

Physical Environment

The broad altitudinal and ecological range of aspen attests to its ability to adapt to wide variations in climate. Aspen can tolerate relatively cold temperatures and late-lying snow but cannot withstand high temperatures or prolonged moisture deprivation. Sites that support large, healthy stands of aspen receive more than twenty-five inches of precipitation annually, experience moderately cold and snowy winters and warm summers, and have reasonably long growing seasons. Large-scale air movements and precipitation patterns in the Southern Rockies tend to maximize precipitation on windward slopes, creating optimal growing conditions for aspen in many areas of the Western Slope. Spring temperatures (from April to June), especially critical because of their influence on the beginning of annual growth and the length of the growing season, increase from north to south along the Southern Rockies. The longer growing season and the additional precipitation associated with the Arizona summer monsoon provide the most likely explanation for the more majestic proportions of aspen in the West Elk, San Juan, and Jemez mountains.

Aspen is a fragile species especially susceptible to windthrow and damage from snow. Snow damage to aspen saplings is a common phenomenon on mountain slopes with deep snowpacks. As the snowpack builds over the course of the winter, it tends to deform downhill, bending the bases of young aspen in the downslope direction and producing the pistol-butted lower trunks so often exhibited by aspen in deep snow areas. Avalanching on steep, aspen-covered slopes is common at higher elevations in many ranges, periodically scouring the larger trees from active avalanche chutes and encouraging the development of thickets of even-aged saplings.

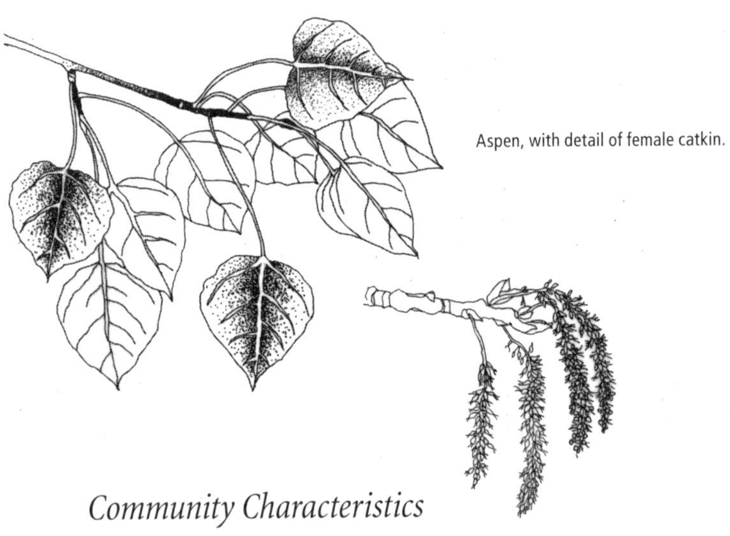

Aspen, with detail of female catkin.

Community Characteristics

Aspen forests are highly variable, the composition and character of each community determined by differences in local environmental conditions (such as soil moisture), the age structure of the forest, stand history, tree density within the stand, adjacent vegetation types, and composition of the understory. In many ways, the diversity of these communities results from the occurrence of aspen in successional communities as well as in stable, self-perpetuating stands. Aspen is an aggressive pioneer species, invading sites where the preexisting vegetation has been destroyed by fire or some other type of disturbance. In the Southern Rockies, the majority of aspen-dominated forests are successional (seral) to other types of vegetation. Stable aspen communities, though considerably less common than seral stands, occur in areas where soil conditions are favorable to aspen and where the dense understory discourages invasion by coniferous species.

All aspen forests can be described as multilayered, but the number of layers and the composition of the understory vegetation vary greatly from one stand to another. Under optimal soil and moisture conditions, aspen are often tall and robust and the understory is a lush tangle of shrubs and herbaceous vegetation. On sites with less than optimal growing conditions—limited moisture, poor soils, or strong winds—aspen stands are characterized by smaller and occasionally stunted trees and by a less luxuriant understory. In an aspen forest with a long history of livestock grazing, the understory is represented by fewer species and by the competitive dominance of the least palatable species.

The high organic-matter and nutrient content of the soils associated with most aspen communities contrasts markedly with those in coniferous forests. Though aspen are capable of growing in a wide variety of soils, their very presence in any forest stand greatly improves the quality of the soil. Because aspen leaves and herbaceous plant material decay more rapidly than conifer needles, the return of nutrients to the soil in an aspen community is relatively quick. More important, however, aspen serves as an efficient nutrient pump, enriching the surface soil layers by withdrawing large quantities of available nutrients from the entire rooting depth and incorporating those nutrients into the upper soil layers where they become available for other plants.

Successional Communities

Successional (seral) communities are best identified by the active replacement of the aspen overstory by conifers. The presence of an uneven-aged coniferous understory is considered a strong indicator of seral status. In a successional aspen community, the tree canopy is usually dominated by aspen for as long as 150 years, or until the slower-growing conifers are able to overtop the aspen. Once the conifers penetrate the aspen canopy, the reduction in light reaching the forest floor limits aspen regeneration because of the species' intolerance for shade, resulting in a gradual decline in the abundance and vigor of the understory.

In most cases, the aspen overstory in successional communities tends to be single-aged because of the rapidity and uniformity with which aspen regenerates disturbed stands or expands local populations through vegetative reproduction. Some stands may have a domelike appearance, with the oldest trees in the center of the stand and progressively younger and shorter trees occupying the outer, expanding edge. Two-storied stands consisting of trees representing two age classes are often found in areas where grazing, either by wild or domestic animals, has been reduced or eliminated after a long period of overuse.

In most seral communities, conifers such as Engelmann spruce, Colorado blue spruce, subalpine fir, white fir, ponderosa pine, and Douglas-fir make up an increasing proportion of the canopy as succession progresses. On certain sites, lodgepole pine, another aggressive colonizer, may share dominance. Where successional communities are being replaced by grass- or shrublands, an absence of young trees indicates a gradual deterioration of aspen clones resulting from suckering suppression or from heavy browsing by wildlife or livestock. Some seral communities occupy an ecotonal position, incorporating understory species that reflect the composition of an adjacent community as well as those more typical of aspen forests.

The understory in most seral communities is luxuriant when compared to the understories of adjacent coniferous forests. At the dry end of the moisture gradient, the aspen understory is dominated by a herbaceous layer consisting mostly of grasses, with a scattering of wildflowers and medium-sized shrubs. Grasses typical of such communities include purple oniongrass, Thurber's fescue, slender wheatgrass, native blue-grass, and blue wild rye. Dryland sedges such as Geyer's sedge may be common in some communities, and the assortment of wildflowers includes white geranium, northern bedstraw, common harebell, mountain parsley, and yarrow. The shrub layer, where present, consists of widely spaced, medium-sized shrubs such as common juniper and shrubby cinquefoil. With increasing moisture, wildflowers become more conspicuous and may include meadowrue, golden banner, arnica, mariposa lily, lupine, paintbrush, orange sneezeweed, showy daisy, lovage, and Colorado columbine. Common shrubs in such stands include snowberry and wild rose.

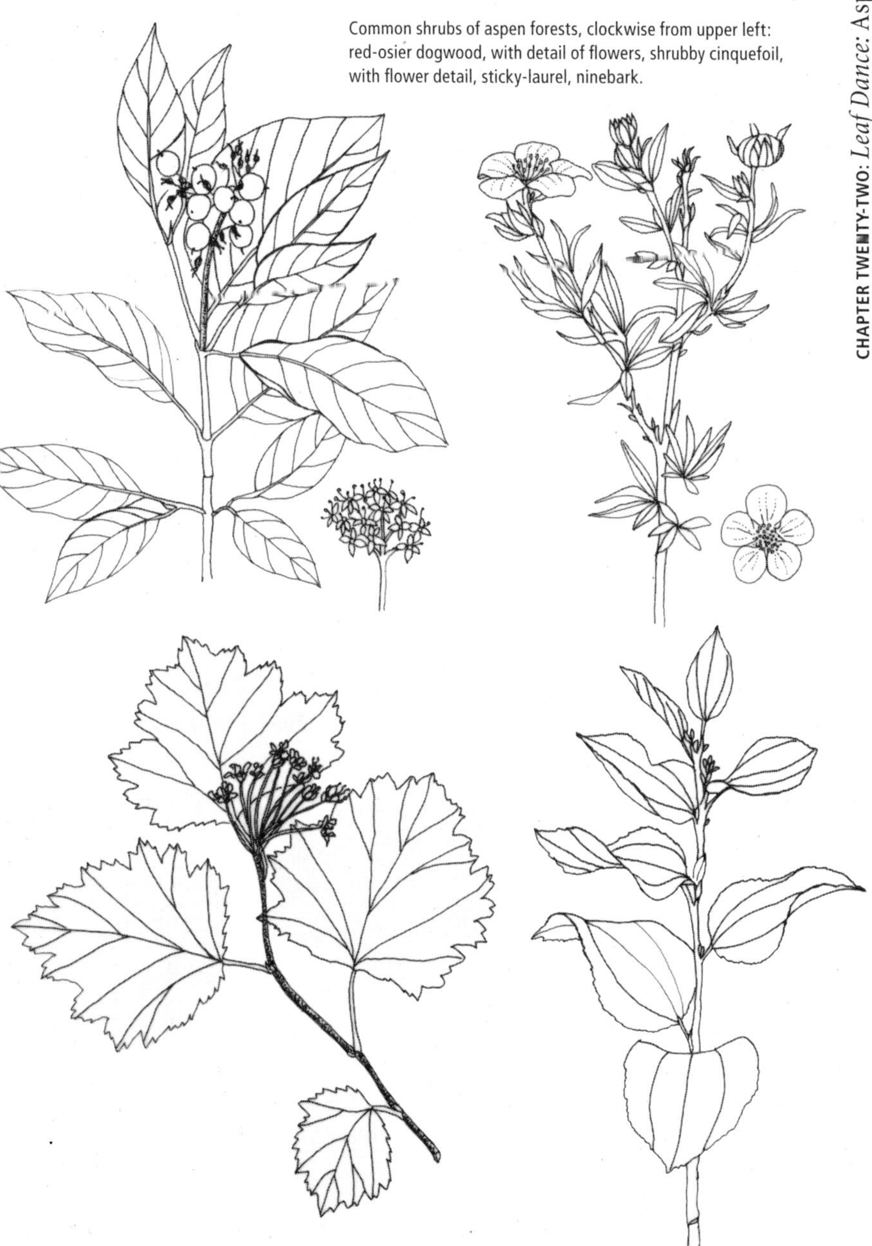

Common shrubs of aspen forests, clockwise from upper left: red-osier dogwood, with detail of flowers, shrubby cinquefoil, with flower detail, sticky-laurel, ninebark.

Stable Communities

Forest biologists are only beginning to understand the environmental conditions that encourage the establishment and maintenance of stable or long-lived aspen forests. Stable communities, in contrast to seral stands, may persist for several centuries and exhibit three main characteristics: an uneven-aged structure of the aspen overstory, lack of evidence of successional change in the understory, and an absence of tree species more shade-tolerant than aspen. In the Southern Rockies, stable aspen communities are most common at midelevations and on southerly exposures. Whether or not these communities represent a true climax forest remains uncertain.

Stable forests are generally characterized by a multilayered shrub and herbaceous understory, although in some, the shrub layer may be nonexistent. Scattered conifers may be present, but there is no evidence of conifer reproduction. In certain stands, especially those on south-facing slopes and at lower elevations, tall shrubs form a distinctive layer from six to twelve feet in height. Species typical of this layer include serviceberry, ninebark, and chokecherry. A layer consisting of a mixture of medium-sized shrubs such as snowberry, red-osier dogwood, boulder raspberry, common gooseberry, sticky-laurel, and bush honeysuckle may also be present or may take the place of the tall shrub layer in some stands.

A two-tiered herbaceous layer is common in many stands. The tall herb layer consists of a wide variety of species, including monkshood, cow parsnip, false hellebore, black coneflower, lovage, lousewort, orange sneezeweed, aspen sunflower, Rocky Mountain columbine, and bracken fern. In addition to or instead of the tall herb layer, species such as golden banner, meadowrue, fleabane daisy, wild geranium, Canada violet, bedstraw, and aster may form a continuous carpet of wildflowers across the forest floor. Several vining plants, including white-flowered peavine and American vetch, use the lush undergrowth as a trellis.

Plant Adaptation: Designs for Survival

Though millions of aspen seeds are produced, successful germination and seedling survival is a rare event in the West, the exception rather than the rule. How, then, was aspen able to spread successfully into so many habitats?

Seedling success requires a persistently moist seedbed, soil temperatures that are warm but not too hot, and soils that are well-drained, loamy, and high in nutrients. The seedbed must be free of destructive soil fungi and have no surface leaf litter to snuff out the light for the sun-loving seedlings. In the West, drying out of the seedbed is the most common cause of seedling mortality. Though a certain number of seedlings can usually be found in areas where fires have occurred, in garden plots, and in clear-cuts, seedling survival is tenuous at best. In fact, some researchers have suggested that conditions favoring widespread seedling establishment may occur only once every 200 to 400 years.

At one time, suitable growth conditions must have been more widespread, allowing aspen to increase its distribution. The discovery of fossil leaves similar to those of modern quaking aspen suggests that aspen have florished throughout western North America for the last 15 million years, since middle Miocene time. The advance and retreat of the Laurentide and Cordilleran ice sheets during the Pleistocene is believed to be responsible for the present-day distribution of aspen. Once the glaciers retreated, patches of quaking aspen persisted wherever cool, moist conditions prevailed and where sunny, newly exposed seedbeds provided optimal conditions for germination and growth. With the onset of warmer, drier conditions during the Holocene, the incidence of forest fires, both lightning and human caused, increased dramatically across the West. The ecological stage was set for any species that could adapt its reproductive strategies to withstand the vagaries of climatic change and the catastrophic impact of fire.

Quaking aspen, as is true for many pioneering tree species, hosts a diverse community of mycorrhizal fungi that appear to be essential for seedling establishment and survival. The intricate mutualistic association between plant roots and fungi no doubt played a critical role in the spread of aspen forests across North America. In the case of aspen, the fungi are predominately "ectomycorrhizal," which means that the fungal hyphae form a layer over the aspen root tips and surround, rather than penetrate, the aspen root cells. The fungal mycelium proliferates in the soil, essentially extending the tree's functional root system and enhancing the uptake of inorganic nutrients, primarily phosphorus and nitrogen. In return, the fungi subsist on carbohydrates produced by the tree, which are then converted to fungal sugars. The types of ectomycorrhizal fungi associated with aspen are determined by soil type, age of the aspen stand, geographic region, and other edaphic and historical factors. Many of these species are familiar to readers due to their distinctive, aboveground reproductive structures (the mushroom) and include several species of *Amanita*, *Russula*, *Lacterius*, and *Boletus*.

In Praise of Clones

Aspen are capable of reproducing both sexually and asexually. Though reproduction from seed is important in initial establishment, the regeneration or expansion of existing aspen forests in the Southern Rockies is achieved by clonal growth, a type of asexual (or vegetative) reproduction to which this species is superbly adapted. In the case of aspen, the clone is defined as a group of genetically related individuals, known as ramets, which arise vegetatively from the root system of a single "parent" seedling, or ortet. During its first year, the ortet produces a multibranching lateral root system. In subsequent years, especially after a fire or other competition-reducing disturbance, ramets arise from buds along the ortet's root system. Each newly formed ramet depends on the parent root for nutrients and water, with the degree of dependency diminishing gradually as the ramet develops its own root system. In a mature aspen, each lateral root may contain thousands of budding sites, up to 600 per eighteen-inch section of root. It is not uncommon for the lateral root system of the "parent" tree to have spread out for 100 feet or more. The sprouting, or suckering, potential of an aspen root system is astronomical; aspen ecologists have reported close to a million aspen suckers per acre in one regenerating stand in Colorado.

What triggers such fecundity? Auxin, a growth regulating hormone, is continually being produced in the crown of an aspen tree and shunted to the roots, where, in the absence of disturbance, it serves to inhibit suckering. In an undisturbed aspen stand, suckering remains moderately suppressed. When the tree's crown is destroyed or otherwise damaged by fire, avalanching, windthrow, harvesting by beaver, girdling, disease, defoliation, or logging, auxin flow to the roots stops and the roots become instant sprout factories. Cytokinin, a growth-stimulating hormone synthesized in the tips of the roots, quickly rewrites the hormonal equation. With the hormonal balance shifted in the direction of vegetative reproduction, suckers begin proliferating at previously dormant budding sites along the lateral roots. Studies suggest that aspen suckers grow very rapidly and that some may become independent of their parental root system by the end of their first growing season. In fact, most aspen suckers will have established independent root systems at approximately twenty-five years of age.

Through expansion of the ramet root system and additional suckering, the clone may proliferate over time to cover 100 acres or more. The abundance of light along the leading edge of the expanding clone enhances the survival and proliferation of new ramets, often resulting in the development of a somewhat symmetrical, islandlike stand of aspen. Clones of this type often have a "fairy ring" of younger trees around their edges and are especially common in high mountain basins such as South, Middle, and North parks.

The ability of aspen to regenerate or expand a preexisting stand by clonal growth clearly gives the species a competitive advantage. Reliance on the parent rootstock permits rapid initial growth and provides superb insurance against drought during the critical seedling stage. Because of the durability of the rootstocks, the species is able to maintain a suppressed but viable population through long periods of time, even hundreds of years; these persistent rootstocks survive low temperatures, surface fires, and many other types of environmental disturbances, enabling aspen to recolonize a newly disturbed site through the stimulation or reinitiation of vegetative propagation.

The typical aspen forest consists of a single clone—a specific genotype—or a mosaic of clones. The boundary between two adjoining clones is often abrupt; distinguishing individual clones within a stand is especially easy in the fall, when the genetically controlled timing of color change and leaf fall within a clone sets it apart from other clones in the stand. The following list of characteristics is useful in distinguishing individual clones within a stand: (1) sex: all trees within a clone are either female or male; (2) synchronized timing of flowering and leaf development in spring; (3) leaf color, onset of color change, and leaf drop in fall; (4) similarities in the shape and size of the leaves; (5) the degree of leaf serration; and (6) the degree of pubescence of dormant buds.

Withstanding Adversity

Avoidance of environmental stress is critical to the survival of aspen. During times of moisture stress, water storage in the aspen's woody tissues, which include trunks and branches, provides a reserve supply from which transpiring leaves can draw, an alternative to relying solely on translocation from the roots. Water content of the aspen's trunk and branches is consistently higher during dormancy than when the tree is leafed out; during prolonged drought, aspen trunks shrink in diameter as their water reserves are tapped. The presence of chloroplasts in aspen bark enables the trunk and branches, unlike those of most tree species, to carry on photosynthesis whenever conditions permit. When insolation is high, the contribution made by bark photosynthesis, while not at net photosynthetic levels, may sufficiently meet the tree's respiratory requirements when leaf photosynthate production is severely reduced as a result of a late spring freeze or insect defoliation.

A whitish layer of cells called the periderm overlies the green, photosynthetic bark and forms a powderlike, protective layer so thin that you can scrape it off with a fingernail. In winter, high-altitude sunlight can cause extensive sunscald damage to unprotected trees, especially those at the outer edge of a grove. Whiter periderm tissues mean higher reflectance levels and reduced vulnerability to heat damage as well as to the kinds of temperature fluctuations that can cause cell breakage in the sap-conducting tissues, or cambium.

Autumn Color

During the spring and summer, aspen leaves serve as the primary factories for photosynthesis. In addition to chlorophyll, aspen leaves contain three pigments that, in differing gene-based combinations, produce the colors that define the chromatic amplitude of a Rocky Mountain autumn: the purest yellow is produced by the pigment xanthophyll, gold and orange hues come from carotene, and the rarer reds are the result of anthocyanin. These pigments are almost completely masked by chlorophyll during the spring and summer months. When temperatures begin to drop and the days get shorter with the approach of autumn, the trees stop food production in the leaves and begin withdrawing sap into the trunks and roots for the coming winter. With the halt in circulation to the leaves, the chlorophyll in the leaves breaks down, the green color disappears, and the vivid hues of the other pigments move to center stage. Crisp, sunny days and cool nights when temperatures drop below 45°F (but not below freezing) are necessary to bring about the most spectacular displays of autumn color. When these conditions prevail they serve to inhibit the withdrawal of sugars from the leaf, a situation that favors the accumulation of pigments. While all these changes are taking place, a hormone at the base of the aspen leaf is working to weaken the link between leaf and branch, producing a separation layer. Once this process is complete, the leaf will be ready to separate from the tree with the first fretting breeze.

Descriptions of Common Plants

Trees

Quaking Aspen, *Populus tremuloides.* This medium-sized deciduous tree is distinguished from other members of the willow family by its smooth, pale greenish to ivory-colored bark, ovate and finely serrated leaves, flattened petioles (leaf stalks), and conical buds. Each petiole acts as a pivot for the leaf blade, causing it to flutter in the slightest breeze, giving the entire tree the appearance of trembling, hence the common names quaking aspen and quakies. Male (pollen-producing) and female (seed-producing) flowers are called catkins and appear on separate trees in early spring (April or May), just prior to the leaves. Though seed production may be prolific, successful reproduction in western North America is largely by asexual (vegetative) propagation. The best fall color occurs during autumns characterized by crisp, sunny days, cool nights, and an absence of hard frost.

Shrubs

Red-osier Dogwood, *Swida sericea.* Common in aspen groves and in mountain riparian communities from the foothills to the subalpine zone, red-osier dogwood is easily identified by its slender red branches and by its opposite, lanceolate leaves, flattopped clusters of white flowers, and white, berrylike fruits. The flowers consist of four small sepals, four white petals, and four stamens perched atop an ovary (pistil).

Ninebark, *Physocarpus monogynus.* This medium-sized shrub is common in aspen stands and occasionally on dry, rocky hillsides from the foothills to the subalpine zone. A member of the rose family, ninebark is distinguished by its three- to five-lobed, toothed, simple leaves, white to pale rose flowers arranged in an umbrellalike head, and the distinctive peeling and shedding of its outer bark. Each flower has five rounded petals borne on the edge of a small cup. The fruit is an inflated capsule, which splits open at the tip during dry weather to release the seeds but closes during wet weather.

Shrubby Cinquefoil, *Pentaphylloides floribunda.* This common small shrub, a member of the rose family, is found in open aspen and pine forests and mountain meadows from the montane to the subalpine zone. Shrubby cinquefoil (sometimes called potentilla) is identified by its small, pinnately compound leaves, golden yellow flowers, and shreddy brown bark. The leaves are green on top, their undersides muted by the presence of gray, silky hairs. The roselike flowers have five petals borne on the edge of a shallow cup and are arranged individually along the branches. Flowering begins in June and may continue throughout the summer.

Sticky-laurel, *Ceanothus velutinus.* This medium-sized shrub, a member of the buckthorn family (Rhamnaceae), is found in open forests and in clearings from the foothills to the subalpine zone; the species is especially common on slopes that have been burnt over or otherwise disturbed. Sticky-laurel, also known as snowbrush, is identified by its balsam-scented, oval, evergreen leaves and by the dense clusters of small white flowers that appear near the ends of its branches in early summer. During dry or cold weather, the edges of the leathery, sticky-surfaced leaves roll under. The roots are dotted with nodules that contain symbiotic, nitrogen-fixing bacteria.

Wildflowers

Mariposa Lily, *Calochortus gunnisonii.* This lovely wildflower is a member of the *Calachortaceae*, a monotypic family is restricted to western North and Central America. The mariposa lily, or sego lily, is found in open aspen woodlands and in mountain meadows from the foothills to the lower alpine tundra. The flower is identified by its tuliplike appearance, white or pale lavender color, yellow petal hairs, and the distinctive purple-bearded zone on the inner petals. The leaves are strap-shaped and parallel-veined.

Common wildflowers of aspen forests, clockwise from upper left: showy daisy, heartleaf arnica, common harebell, mariposa lily.

Common Harebell, *Campanula rotundifolia*. This member of the bellflower family (Campanulaceae) is common in open aspen woodlands and mountain meadows from the foothills to the lower alpine tundra. As its name suggests, the common harebell is distinguished by its blue-violet bell-shaped flowers, which hang from multiple stems. The stems are extremely slender, with narrow lanceolate leaves.

Fendler Meadowrue, *Thalictrum fendleri*. This delicate wildflower, a member of the meadowrue family (Thalictraceae), is abundant in shaded ravines and aspen forests from the montane to the subalpine zone. Meadowrue is identified by its greenish nodding flowers and by its small, three-lobed leaves, which resemble diminutive columbine leaves. The somewhat inconspicuous flowers of the meadowrue have minute green sepals but no petals. Male and female flowers are borne on separate plants; the male flower is distinguished by the tassel-like appearance of the numerous pointed stamens and the female flower by the several curved ovaries clustered on the receptacle.

Colorado columbine.

Colorado Blue Columbine, *Aquilegia coerulea.* This spectacular member of the hellebore family (Helleboraceae) is the Colorado state flower and was designated as such by a special referendum proposed by the state's schoolchildren. Other names for this distinctive species include Rocky Mountain columbine and blue columbine. The Colorado blue columbine is easily identified by its large (two- to three-inch) flowers, each consisting of five periwinkle-blue sepals and five funnel-shaped white petals with long purplish spurs; a spray of yellow stamens protrudes from the center of each flower. Some high-altitude populations may have mostly white flowers (very rarely all blue). The leaves of this species have deep, rounded lobes and arise mostly from the base of the plant; the Colorado blue columbine can grow to three feet in height. A beautiful red-and yellow-flowered species, the **western red columbine** or **shooting star columbine** (*A. elegantula*), can be found on both sides of the Continental Divide and is especially common in the southern and western portions of the Southern Rockies. Hummingbirds and bumblebees are especially fond of columbine nectar; short-tongued bees also "rob" nectar by chewing a hole in the tip of the petal spur and drinking the nectar, thus cheating the flower of its services as a pollinator.

Heartleaf Arnica, *Arnica cordifolia.* Heartleaf arnica, a low-growing, showy member of the sunflower family (Asteraceae), is common in relatively dry aspen and coniferous forests from the foothills to the subalpine zone. This arnica is easily dentified by its heart-shaped, opposite leaves and by its large (2- to 2.5-inch), yellow sunflowerlike flower heads.

Showy Daisy, *Erigeron speciosus.* This beautiful member of the sunflower family (Asteraceae) is conspicuous in moist aspen forests and in meadow-edge habitats from the foothills to the subalpine zone. Showy daisy, with its lavender ray flowers and yellow disk flowers, is distinguished from other superficially similar species by its mostly hairless, narrowly lanceolate leaves, multiple narrow ray flowers, and the two even rows of green bracts that make up the cup that subtends the ray and disk flowers; the flowering stems are little branched, and the flower heads appear singularly at the terminus of each flowering stem.

Black Coneflower, *Rudbeckia occidentalis* var. *montana.* This tall and somewhat unusual member of the sunflower family is found in open aspen forests and moist meadows from the montane through the subalpine zone.

Black coneflower is easily identified by its size (up to three feet in height) and by its elongated, conical flower heads. The flower heads of this species are distinctive, consisting solely of disk flowers, and are a dark brownish purple. **Black-eyed Susan** (*Rudbeckia hirta*) is distinguished from the coneflower by its bright yellow rayflowers and dark brown disk flowers.

Wild Geranium, *Geranium caespitosum.* This member of the geranium family (Geraniaceae) is abundant in aspen forests and mountain meadows from the foothills to the subalpine zone. Common wild geranium is identified by its five-petaled pinkish lavender flowers, multibranched flowering stems, and palmately compound, lobed leaves. A similar species, the white geranium (*Geranium richardsonii*), has white, somewhat paired flowers and fewer flowering stems. Another pink-flowered geranium, *G. viscosissimum*, has stems and leaves with a glandular pubescence that makes them sticky to the touch. As the five-parted fruits of the geranium dry, the sections curl upward and fling their seeds into the air.

Porter's Lovage, *Ligusticum porteri.* This moderately tall member of the parsley family (Umbelliferae) is abundant in aspen forests and moist mountain meadows from the foothills to the montane zone. Lovage (also known as osha) is easily identified by its fernlike leaves, white flower clusters borne in compound umbels, and the carrotlike aroma of its crumbled leaves.

Gray's Lousewort, *Pedicularis procera.* This tall member of the figwort family (Scrophulariaceae) is common in moist forests from the montane to the subalpine zone. Gray's lousewort is distinguished by its size (up to three feet in height), fernlike leaves, and terminal spike of yellow flowers. The flowers are yellowish and streaked with red; the petals of each are fused to form two lips, the upper lip forming an arched, pointed hood (the galea) and the lower lip two-lobed. A similar species, **fernleaf lousewort** (*P. bracteosa*), has yellow flowers without red streaking.

Common Plants of the Aspen Forests

Trees

Aspen, quaking, Populus *tremuloides*
Fir, subalpine, *Abies lasiocarpa*
Oak, Gambel's, *Quercus gambelii*
Pine, lodgepole, *Pinus contorta*
Spruce, Engelmann, *Picea engelmannii*

Shrubs

Blueberry, *Vaccinium* spp.
Chokecherry, *Padus* (formerly *Prunus*) *virginiana* ssp. *melanocarpa*
Cinquefoil, shrubby, *Pentaphylloides floribunda*
Dogwood, red-osier, *Swida sericea* (formerly *Cornus stolonifera*)
Gooseberry, whitestem, *Ribes inerme*
Juniper, common, *Juniperus communis* ssp. *alpina*
Kinnikinnik, *Arctostaphylos uva-ursi*
Maple, Rocky Mountain, *Acer glabrum*
Mountainlover, *Paxistima myrsinites*
Ninebark, *Physocarpus monogynus*
Raspberry, wild, *Rubus idaeus* ssp. *melanolasius*
Rose, wild, *Rosa woodsii*
Sagebrush, big (or Great Basin sagebrush), *Seriphidium* (formerly *Artemisia*) *tridentatum*
Serviceberry, western, *Amelanchier alnifolia*
Snowberry, roundleaf, *Symphoricarpos rotundifolius*
Sticky-laurel, *Ceanothus velutinus*
Thimbleberry, *Rubacer parviflorum*
Twinberry (or Bush Honeysuckle), *Distegia* (formerly *Lonicera*) *involucrata*

Grasses and Sedges

Bluegrass, *Poa* spp.
Fescue, Thurber's, *Festuca thurberi*
Junegrass, *Koeleria macrantha*

Oniongrass, purple, *Bromelica spectabilis*
Sedge, Geyer's (or Elk Sedge), *Carex geyeri*
Wild Rye, blue, *Elymus glaucus*

Wildflowers

Arnica, heartleaf, *Arnica cordifolia*
Balsamroot, *Balsamorhiza sagittata*
Bedstraw, *Galium* spp.
Black-eyed Susan, *Rudbeckia hirta*
Chiming bells, *Mertensia ciliata*
    southwestern, *M. franciscana*
Cicely, sweet, *Osmorhiza* spp.
Cinquefoil, *Potentilla* spp.
Columbine, Colorado blue, *Aquilegia coerulea*
    western red, *A. elegantula*
Coneflower, black, *Rudbeckia occidentalis* var. *montana*
Cow Parsnip, *Heracleum sphondylium*
Daisy, showy, *Erigeron speciosus*
Dandelion, common, *Taraxacum officinale*
Fireweed, *Chamerion angustifolium*
Golden Banner, *Thermopsis montana*
Harebell, common, *Campanula rotundifolia*
    Parry's, *C. parryi*
Hellebore, false (or Cornhusk Lily), *Veratrum tenuipetalum*
Geranium, wild, *Geranium* spp.
Larkspur, *Delphinium* spp.
Lily, avalanche, *Erythronium grandiflorum*
    mariposa, *Calochortus gunnisonii*
    wood, *Lilium philadelphicum*
Lousewort, Gray's, *Pedicularis procera*
    Canadian, *P. bracteosa* ssp. *paysoniana*
Lovage, Porter's, *Ligusticum porteri*
Lupine, *Lupinus* spp.
Meadowrue, Fendler's, *Thalictrum fendleri*
Monkshood, *Aconitum columbianum*

Mule's Ears, *Wyethia amplexicaulis*
Paintbrush, *Castilleja* spp.
Parsley, mountain, *Pseudocymopterus montanus*
Peavine, white-flowered, *Lathyrus leucanthus*
Pussytoes, *Antennaria* spp.
Sage, prairie, *Artemisia ludoviciana*
Sneezeweed, orange, *Dugaldia hoopesii*
Strawberry, wild, *Fragaria* spp.
Sunflower, aspen, *Helianthella quinquenervis*
Valerian, *Valeriana* spp.

Lupine and sunflowers.

Vetch, American, *Vicia americana*
Violet, Canada, *Viola rydbergii*
Windflower, *Anemone multifida*
Wintergreen, green-flowered, *Pyrola chlorantha*
Yarrow, *Achillea lanulosa*

Fungi

Amanita (or Grisette), *Amanita vaginata*
Boletus, peppery, *Boletus piperatus*
Bracket, violet-pored, *Trichaptum biforme*
Conk, aspen, *Phellinus tremulae*
Lacterius, white, *Lacterius controversus*
Russula, yellow, *Russula aeruginea*

Environment and Adaptation: Animals of the Aspen Forests

Naturalists can sample only a small portion of the diversity of life in any forest. Aspen forests are especially rich because of their broad elevational range and inherent variability, providing critical habitat for an amazing array of resident and nonresident animal species. Elk and aspen forests are almost synonymous throughout the Southern Rockies. Elk and deer, as well as moose, feed on the new shoots, strip leaves from the lower branches, and scrape sweet bark from the trunks with unabashed gusto. Beaver, too, rely on aspen for a good portion of their diet; these able tree cutters require about two to four pounds of aspen bark a day, which amounts to an estimated 1,500 pounds annually. Wherever aspen trees are newly scarred or where boring beetles or red-napped sapsuckers have penetrated the bark tissues, fungal infections find ready entry. The most devastating of these infections, white heartrot (*Fomes igniarius*), produces the distinctive hoof-shaped conks (the fungal fruiting body) and lays waste to the tree's vital conducting tissues, eventually attracting cavity-drilling birds (such as sapsuckers) that, in turn, provide nest holes for the secondary cavity nesters. It's not surprising that nearly 50 percent of the breeding birds associated with aspen forests are cavity nesters, and insect eaters. Insects seem to be everywhere in the aspen forest; you can almost hear them chewing. When you walk through an aspen grove, the evidence of insects hard at work is all around you: a sawdust-rimmed hole and rivulets of ambered sap are the work of a poplar-borer beetle, a curious spider-shaped track on a nearby trunk is the result of a bark-mining fly, a leafy branchlet in the tree's crown wrapped in a gossamer web encloses a wiggling mass of tent-caterpillar moth larvae, and the serpentine maze that winds through the epidermis of a leaf reveals the feeding trail of the tiniest caterpillar of all, the larval stage of a leaf-miner moth. And this is just the handiwork of four insect species, a small sampling of the thirty-four species of insects whose life histories are intimately intertwined with quaking aspen.

Resource Partitioning

Within the aspen community, resource partitioning enables each species to appropriate suitable niche space and avoid competition with other species. The similarities between aspen forests and mountain riparian communities can be striking, both in terms of the species found in each and the range of food resources and habitats available. Not surprisingly, faunal diversity is greater in moist, mature aspen stands than in dry, sparsely stocked forests or in a dense, brushy monoculture of young trees. The differential use of space is best illustrated by the high breeding-bird diversity and density associated with many aspen ecosystems. Birds, in contrast to ground-dwelling animals, are able to partition the aspen forest habitat by selecting different vertical strata, whether ground, shrub understory, tree trunk, or the high canopy, in which to concentrate their foraging and/or nesting activities. Diet and foraging style, as well as location, permit the general grouping of aspen forest birds into a series of feeding guilds: (1) ground, or low-level, foragers that eat seeds, fruit, or nectar, (2) ground foragers that feed on insects, (3) shrub or tree foliage gleaners that feed on insects, (4) fly-catching or on-the-wing foragers that feed on insects, (5) wood borers that feed on sap and/or insects, and (6) predators that eat small- to medium-sized mammals and birds.

To the casual observer, the ways in which resources are partitioned may seem somewhat subtle. For example, both Hammond's and Cordilleran flycatchers breed and forage for insects in aspen forests, apparently avoiding competitive interaction through vertical separation of foraging niches and by taxonomic differences in the composition of their respective diets. The Hammond's consistently forages at higher levels in the forest than does the Cordilleran flycatcher, exhibiting a distinct dietary preference for beetles rather than for the moths and butterflies favored by the Cordilleran flycatcher.

A more obvious example of niche partitioning can be seen in the diurnal-nocturnal hunting patterns and prey preferences of the owls and hawks that use aspen forests. Six species of owls, ranging in size from the diminutive flammulated owl to the great horned owl, are known to occur in this forest type, in itself a testimony to the ecosystem's biological diversity. Among the small, cavity-nesting owls, competition is limited primarily by foraging time and diet. For example, the northern saw-whet owl is a nocturnal predator of small mammals and roosting birds, whereas the flammulated owl is a nocturnal predator of insects, chiefly moth species associated with adjacent ponderosa forests. The northern pygmy owl, on the other hand, is a diurnal hunter, preying upon small mammals and birds.

Cavity Nesters

Aspen is highly susceptible to fungal diseases that weaken and decay its heartwood, resulting in the development of natural cavities and inviting the excavation of nesting holes by woodpeckers, flickers, and sapsuckers. In fact, cavity-nesting birds make up a large proportion of the breeding-bird species in mature aspen communities. Those species that excavate their own holes, the so-called primary cavity nesters, typically abandon their holes after a single season, making them available as nesting habitat for a still-larger group of birds, the secondary cavity nesters, which includes the flammulated owl, northern saw-whet owl, northern pygmy owl, tree and violet-green swallows, house wren, brown creeper, mountain bluebird, pygmy nuthatch, and mountain chickadee. Cavities are almost always at a premium as a result of natural attrition due to windfall, excessive rot, and other causes. Consequently, it is common for a tree with several good cavities to provide "condominium" housing for two or three different species. The sharp decline in cavity trees that is occurring throughout the West as a result of fuel-wood cutting, residential and resort development, and intensification of logging cannot fail to have a serious impact on cavity-dependent species.

The Herbivore's Larder

Aspen forests provide excellent habitat for a varied group of herbivorous mammals. The smallest of these, several species of mice, voles, and the northern pocket gopher, are most abundant in forests where the lush understory provides protective cover and a diversity of food resources. These small rodents, with the exception of the western jumping mouse, are winter-active but avoid the exigencies of the winter environment by foraging and living beneath the snowpack. During severe winters, patches where bark has been gnawed from lower aspen trunks and from shrubs may be common when populations are abnormally high. In many aspen forests, the beaver may be the most important consumer of aspen. The winter diet of the beaver consists mostly of aspen and willow cut and stored the previous autumn. Though beaver can cut an aspen of almost any diameter, they prefer young trees in the two- to six-inch-diameter range, harvesting an average of about twenty medium-sized aspen a year.

The lush shrub and herbaceous understory provides abundant, high-quality forage as well as protective cover for elk and mule deer. During the spring, cow elk and their calves linger in secluded aspen stands and adjacent meadows before resuming their migration to summer range at higher elevations. The elks' consumption of aspen and associated understory vegetation is comparatively light during the summer, when most herds are at higher elevations. Where palatable herbaceous forage is in short supply, or when the snowpack exceeds twenty inches on the winter range, aspen leaves, shoots, and bark may become a major component of their diet. In contrast to elk, mule deer are primarily browsers; aspen ranks among the top eight browse plants for this species throughout the year but is especially important during summer and fall. In areas with high concentrations of elk or mule deer, as is common on some wintering grounds or along seasonal migration routes, these animals can have a serious impact on aspen forest ecosystems. Deformed aspen trunks are typical of young trees in which the leader, or primary shoot, has been repeatedly nipped by elk and regrowth has occurred from lateral branches; black scarring on the trunks resulting from bark scraping is especially conspicuous in areas with high elk populations.

A "bear register" tree.

Black bears are common in aspen forests, feeding on aspen buds, catkins, and new leaves in the spring and returning in fall to take advantage of the berry crop produced by the understory shrubbery. Because bears tend to select den sites near their fall feeding areas, dens are often located within or adjacent to aspen and mixed aspen-coniferous communities. Bears are good tree climbers, and their distinctive claw marks, known as "bear registers," are often preserved in the soft bark of the aspen trunk and are easily distinguished from marks made by elk canines; bear claw marks persist for the life of the tree and often provide a record of repeated climbs of a favorite tree. Black bears are omnivores, occasionally climbing aspen trees to rob bird nests and even ripping open cavity nests to get at the eggs or nestlings within.

Miners and Tent Builders

Insect populations in aspen ecosystems tend to be quite high because of aspens' palatability to a great many species. Few insect infestations are severe enough, however, to affect the aspen host significantly. The silvery-colored calligraphy that sometimes appears on an aspen leaf is made by the larval stage of the aspen leaf-miner moth. Leaf miners usually spend the entire larval stage within a single leaf, the proof of their residency revealed by the persistent trails created by their feeding activities as they tunnel through the leaf's spongy tissue dining on chlorophyll. In fact, the larvae of several small moths, flies, beetles, and wasps have coevolved this way, each species creating a distinctively shaped mine within the leaf. Despite the obvious constraints, leaf mining offers several adaptive advantages: protection from the elements and some predators and, possibly, a way of avoiding the defensive chemicals that coat the leaves of some plants and are intended to deter herbivores. When the larvae finish feeding, most either pupate within the mine or cut their way out of the leaf, dropping to the ground to pupate externally.

Another fascinating insect, the western tent caterpillar (*Malacosoma* spp.), forms large cooperative colonies and is often the culprit responsible for the periodic defoliation of aspen in many parts of the Southern Rockies. Serious infestations have occurred in the Pikes Peak area, the San Juans, and the Sangre de Cristos of northern New Mexico. The tent caterpillar begins its life cycle and overwinters as a fully formed individual encapsulated within an egg, one of a large mass of eggs deposited by a rather small, nondescript moth. The eggs hatch in early spring, and the emerging caterpillars, often as many as 200 or 300 from a single egg mass, venture out en masse to feed on aspen buds and new leaves. Within a few days of hatching, the caterpillars construct a silken tent to protect the colony and to serve as a base from which to launch feeding forays. To maximize feeding efficiency, foraging tent caterpillars create a chemical trail system to guide fellow colony members to good foraging areas and away from areas that have been exhausted by feeding. When tent caterpillar populations are high, defoliation drastically reduces the ability of aspen to photosynthesize and reduces stand vigor; infestations attacking the same aspen stand repeatedly over several years may kill entire trees and top-kill others.

Defensive Strategies

Aspen are not passive hosts to the onslaught of herbivorous browsers, leaf-miners, and wood-borers. The chemical, or allelopathic, defenses employed by aspen consist of variable quantities of phenolic glycosides (salicylates) and condensed tannins, which are both found in leaf, bark, and root tissues, and coniferyl benzoate, which occurs only in flower buds. The presence of each of these compounds, all of which may be potentially toxic or inhibitory to herbivores, varies tremendously from tree to tree in response to clone-specific genetic factors, phenology (seasonal changes), and environmental conditions. In numerous studies of aspen-feeding insects, for example, concentrations of phenolics glycosides were shown to negatively impact insect feeding, reproduction, development, and overall survival during times of moderate infestation. Severe infestations, on the other hand, appear to overcome the tree's chemical defense system. Much less is known about the influence of these same allelopathic compounds on mammalian herbivores such as beaver or elk. In the case of beaver, the research suggests that juvenile growth stages of aspen exhibit the highest concentrations of phenolic constituents and that beavers avoid these chemically defended tissues whenever more mature growth forms are available.

Life Histories of Selected Animals

Mammals

Silver-haired Bat, *Lasionycteris noctivagans.* This extremely handsome, medium-sized bat is distinguished by its silver-tipped black fur, slow flight, and its habit of foraging just a few feet above the level of woodland ponds and streams. The silver-haired bat is considered a forest-dwelling species and is rare in extensive open country. Only males are summer residents in the mountain forests of the Southern Rockies; females generally migrate farther north along the Rockies, although both males and females may be present during spring and fall migration. These solitary bats roost mostly in trees, taking advantage of natural cavities in rotting snags, flaps of loose bark, abandoned cavity nests, or the dense tree canopy, emerging after dark to begin their slow, low-flying foraging flights for moths and other flying insects. Mating occurs in the fall; the female stores sperm in her reproductive tract during hibernation. The young (usually twins) are born on the female's summer range; young bats generally fly at three to four weeks of age and are sexually mature at the end of their first summer.

Western Jumping Mouse, *Zapus princeps.* The western jumping mouse resides in moist forest and meadow habitat and is identified by its long, nearly naked tail (which is much longer than its body), yellowish gray back (adults have a blackish mid-dorsal patch), large hind feet, and bipedal jumping gait. Mostly nocturnal, the western jumping mouse feeds on seeds, some foliage, and occasional insects. In summer, the species constructs a small ball-shaped nest of fine grasses and other plants in rank vegetation. It accumulates fat in preparation for the eight- to nine-month hibernation period that begins in September and lasts until late spring. Once in the hibernaculum, the jumping mouse securely plugs the burrow entrance with soil. Emergence from hibernation may be triggered by a sustained increase in the temperature of the soil surrounding the nest chamber; individuals with insufficient fat reserves may fail to rouse from hibernation or may rouse when environmental conditions limit survivorship. Males emerge first, from mid-May to mid-June, and mating occurs shortly thereafter. Gestation takes less than three weeks, with the young born in June or July. Following birth, the altricial young are dependent on the mother for at least a month. Western jumping mice are relatively long-lived, surviving four years or longer.

Black Bear, *Ursus americanus.* This unmistakable mammal is identified by its large size, blackish, dark chocolate brown, or cinnamon-red fur, stubby tail, and flat-footed gait. The scat of these large omnivores resembles that of humans and often consists of remains of a single kind of food: beetle wings, ants, vegetation, undigestible seeds, etc. Black bears are essentially solitary, except during the breeding season and when the females are rearing cubs. Primarily nocturnal and crepuscular, black bears wander several miles while foraging but will spend daylight hours in a shallow resting den. Black bears are surprisingly agile runners, able tree climbers, and good swimmers;

they will use mud wallows to cool off or to rid themselves of insect pests. Mating occurs in early summer, but implantation of the fertilized eggs is delayed until November. Black bears do not hibernate but instead induce a deep sleep during which they rely on body fat accumulated during the previous summer. The sow gives birth to two or three highly altricial young while still within the winter den. The cubs spend their first summer with their mother and disperse their second spring. Maximum longevity ranges between twenty and twenty-five years.

Birds

Northern Goshawk, *Accipiter gentilis*. This large forest-loving hawk is identified by its conspicuous "eyebrow," fluffy undertail coverts, rounded wings, and relatively long, white-tipped tail. Immature goshawks have brown backs and sides and buff, vertically streaked breasts; adult coloring (appearing during the second year) is bluish gray on the back and sides, and the eye stripe is more prominent. In the Southern Rockies, the northern goshawk prefers mixed aspen and coniferous forest habitat above 7,000 feet. This somewhat secretive species perch-hunts for birds and small- to medium-sized mammals utilizing a quick plummeting or gliding flight to surprise and confuse intended prey. The goshawk begins its nesting cycle in mid- to late March, building a bulky nest of branches thirty to fifty feet above the ground in an aspen or conifer; nests are situated quite close to the trunk. Incubation takes approximately thirty days, and after hatching, the young goshawks are able to fly within six to seven weeks.

Red-naped Sapsucker, *Sphyrapicus nuchalis*. Red forecrown, red chin, and black-and-white facial striping distinguish the male red-naped sapsucker from the Williamson's sapsucker (*S. thyroideus*), which has a black back, red chin patch, and yellow belly. This species returns from migration in late spring to its preferred habitat in aspen groves or mixed aspen-coniferous forests. Red-naped sapsuckers drill small holes in aspen and other trees, drinking the sap that collects in these wells with their short, brush-tipped tongues. In addition to sap, the sapsucker feeds on the soft cambial tissue beneath the bark; insects are obtained by gleaning and fly-catching. Red squirrels, warblers, hummingbirds, woodpeckers, and several kinds of insects take advantage of sapsucker wells. Upon arrival on the nesting

Red-naped sapsucker feeding nestling .

ground, the female sapsucker returns to the nest site of the previous year or, if she does not have a site to return to, selects a temporary territory in which to begin signal drumming (a steady, drumlike roll punctuated at intervals by loud taps). Eventually a male—either her mate from last year or a male returning to a previous nest site—hears her and responds with drumming. During courtship, both sexes engage in bobbing displays as well as in continued drumming. Red-naped sapsuckers are primary cavity nesters, often excavating new cavities in previously used trees. Both sexes excavate the nest hole, incubate the eggs, and feed the young. Young sapsuckers fledge twenty-five to twenty-nine days after hatching.

Tree Swallow, *Tachycineta bicolor.* This swallow is the earliest of the swallows to move north from its wintering grounds, arriving in the Southern Rockies by April in most areas. Tree swallows are identified by their blue-black backs, pure white underparts, and swooping-gliding style of flight. A similar species, the **violet-green swallow** (*Tachycineta thalassina*), has a white cheek patch that extends over the eye and white flank patches that extend almost over the rump. Tree swallows are insectivorous, coursing back and forth over meadows and bodies of water to catch flying insects on the wing. Though not colonial in their nesting habits, tree swallows often forage together in large groups. During courtship, the male pursues the female with aerial acrobatics.The female, occasionally with the help of her mate, constructs a grassy nest within a preexisting tree cavity or bird box. Both sexes bring food to the young, which are able to fly within sixteen to twenty-four days after hatching.

House Wren, *Troglodytes aedon*. This wee, almost mouselike wren is distinguished by its upright tail and brown-checked plumage. The house wren is a migratory species, returning to deciduous woodlands and brushy habitats in early spring. The loud, exuberant, cascading song of this species belies its small size. House wrens are insectivorous, foraging close to or on the ground in dense underbrush, often emitting a buzzy *chek-chek-chek* rattle as they move from place to place when feeding or disturbed. The house wren is aggressive in securing nesting cavities, often harassing or evicting other species from desired sites. Both sexes feed the young; fledging occurs twelve to eighteen days after hatching.

Warbling Vireo, *Vireo gilvus*. The melodious warbling cantata of this small, gray-green bird provides much of the background music in the spring and early summer aspen forest. The warbling vireo is identified by its gray-green back and wings, whitish underparts, absence of wing bars, dusky eyeline, and pale-white eyebrow. A similar species, the **Plumbeous vireo** (*V. plumbeus*, formerly called the solitary vireo), has prominent wing bars and a white eye ring. The warbling vireo is migratory in the Southern Rockies, arriving on its nesting grounds in May or early June, as soon as the aspen have leafed out. This species is highly insectivorous, gleaning insects from branches and leaves in the forest canopy. Male warbling vireos are persistent singers, even in the heat of the day or while taking a turn on the nest. The warbling vireo nest is an exquisitely woven cup of fine grasses suspended from a forked branch by spider webs and plant fibers. Both sexes incubate the eggs and then feed the young; the young fledge about twelve to fourteen days after hatching.

Yellow-rumped Warbler, *Dendroica coronata*. This lovely warbler, often called Audubon's warbler in the West, is easily identified by its yellow throat, yellow rump patch, yellow crown patch, and bluish gray back and wings. Yellow-rumped warblers are largely migratory in the Southern Rockies, returning to their nesting grounds in aspen groves and mixed aspen-coniferous forests by early May. This species may be abundant and conspicuous during migration, both in spring and fall. The yellow-rumped warbler gleans insects from the canopy foliage as well as from vegetation a few feet from the ground; the species may also fly-catch from a perch and is often observed circling outside the canopy when changing foraging positions. The cup-shaped nest is usually built on a horizontal limb and may be found at various heights above the ground. Both sexes incubate the eggs and feed the young.

Common Animals of the Aspen Forests

Mammals

Bat, silver-haired, *Lasionycteris noctivagans*
Bear, black, *Ursus americanus*
Chipmunk, least, *Tamias minimus*
Cottontail, mountain (or Nuttall's), *Sylvilagus nuttallii*
Coyote, *Canis latrans*
Deer, mule, *Odocoileus hemionus*
Elk (or Wapiti), *Cervus elaphus*
Ermine (or Short-tailed Weasel), *Mustela erminea*
Hare, snowshoe, *Lepus americanus*
Moose, *Alces alces*
Mouse, deer, *Peromyscus maniculatus*
    western jumping, *Zapus princeps*
Myotis, long-legged, *Myotis volans*
Porcupine, common, *Erithizon dorsatum*
Shrew, masked, *Sorex cinereus*
    montane, *S. monticolus*
Squirrel, chickaree (or Red or Pine Squirrel), *Tamiasciurus hudsonicus*
    golden-mantled ground, *Spermophilus lateralis*
Vole, long-tailed, *Microtus longicaudus*
    montane, *M. montanus*
Weasel, long-tailed, *Mustela frenata*

Birds

Bluebird, mountain, *Sialia currucoides*
Chickadee, black-capped, *Parus atricapillus*
  mountain, *Parus gambeli*
Flicker, northern, *Colaptes auratus*
Flycatcher, Cordilleran, *Empidonax occidentalis*
  dusky, *E. oberholseri*
  Hammond's, *E. hammondii*
Goshawk, northern, *Accipiter gentilis*
Grouse, blue, *Dendragapus obscurus*
Hawk, Cooper's, *Accipiter cooperii*
  red-tailed, *Buteo jamaicensis*
  sharp-shinned, *A. striatus*
Hummingbird, broad-tailed, *Selasphorus platycercus*
  rufous, *S. rufus*
Jay, Steller's, *Cyanocitta stelleri*
Junco, dark-eyed, *Junco hyemalis*
Magpie, black-billed, *Pica hudsonia*
Nuthatch, red-breasted, *Sitta canadensis*
  white-breasted, *S. carolinensis*
Owl, flammulated, *Otus flammeolus*
  great horned, *Bubo virginianus*
  northern pygmy, *Glaucidium gnoma*
  northern saw-whet, *Aegolius acadicus*
  western screech, *Otus kennicottii*
Robin, American, *Turdus migratorius*
Sapsucker, red-naped, *Sphyrapicus nuchalis*
  Williamson's, *S. thyroideus*
Sparrow, song, *Melospiza melodia*
Swallow, tree, *Tachycineta bicolor*
  violet-green, *T. thalassina*
Vireo, plumbeous (or Solitary Vireo), *Vireo plumbeus*
  warbling, *V. gilvus*
Warbler, yellow-rumped, *Dendroica coronata*

Woodpecker, hairy, *Picoides villosus*
Wood-pewee, western, *Contopus sordidulus*
Wren, house, *Troglodytes aedon*

Amphibians and Reptiles

Garter Snake, western terrestrial, *Thamnophis elegans*
Green Snake, smooth, *Opheodrys vernalis*

Butterflies and Insects

Butterfly, Weidemeyer's Admiral, *Limenitis weidemeyerii*
Crescentspot, silvery, *Charadrius nycteis*
Swallowtail, anise, *Papilio zelicaon*
western tiger, *P. rutulus*
Caterpillar, forest tent, *Malacosoma disstria*
Leafminer, aspen blotch, *Phyllonorycter tremuloidiella*

CHAPTER TWENTY-THREE

The Fire Forest: Lodgepole Pine

Lodgepole pine forest with an understory of blueberry.

Viewed from a distance, olive green forests of lodgepole pine provide a striking contrast to the darker green of Engelmann spruce and subalpine fir. In the Southern Rockies, lodgepole pine is the archetype of the fire forest, the undisputed master of reforestation in the aftermath of fire. The scientific name for this familiar pine, *Pinus contorta*, seems an anomaly in the Rockies, where the species almost invariably grows tall and straight. In fact, the common name, lodgepole pine, dates back to the journals of the

Lewis and Clark Expedition and refers to the widespread use of the sapling pines as tepee poles by indigenous people throughout the Rocky Mountains. The Latin epithet *contorta*, and the source of our confusion, dates back to the intrepid Scottish botanist David Douglas, who made the first collections of this species as well as five other western conifers while under the employ of the Royal Horticultural Society. Douglas seemed especially surprised by the number of new pines he kept finding, writing to his botanical mentor, William Hooker, "You will begin to think that I manufacture pines at my pleasure." The type specimen of *Pinus contorta* that Douglas collected in 1830, sending branches and seeds back to the society's taxonomists in London, came from a windswept coastal promontory near Cape Disappointment, at the mouth of the Columbia River. Douglas's written desciption of this new species corresponded precisely to what he saw. This pine was anything but ramrod straight; it was stunted and gnarled like all the others around it, a pine utterly at home along the windswept coast of the Pacific Northwest.

We now know that lodgepole pine is one of the most widely distributed of the New World pines. The species occurs from coastal southeast Alaska and the Yukon Territory south to the mountains of southern California and east across the Rocky Mountains to the Black Hills of South Dakota. Because of its wide geographic distribution, the species is also highly variable and has been separated into three geographic varieties based on growth form and other characteristics. Douglas's type specimen is *Pinus contorta* ssp. *contorta*; the common name for this variety, shore pine, reflects its bonsailike growth form—suggested by the Latin epithet *contorta*—and the wind-exposed, coastal, and muskeg habitats where the species thrives in Southeast Alaska, British Columbia, and coastal Washington. A second variety, the Sierra lodgepole pine (*Pinus contorta* ssp. *murrayana*), is found in the Cascade Mountains of southwestern Washington and western Oregon, the Sierra Nevada of central California, and south to Baja California, and is decidedly more lodgepole than *contorta*. The variety found throughout the Rocky Mountains and in the Black Hills of South Dakota is Rocky Mountain lodgepole pine, *Pinus contorta* ssp. *latifolia*; the varietal epithet *latifolia* refers to the distinctively curved core of the woody, female cones.

Ecological Distribution

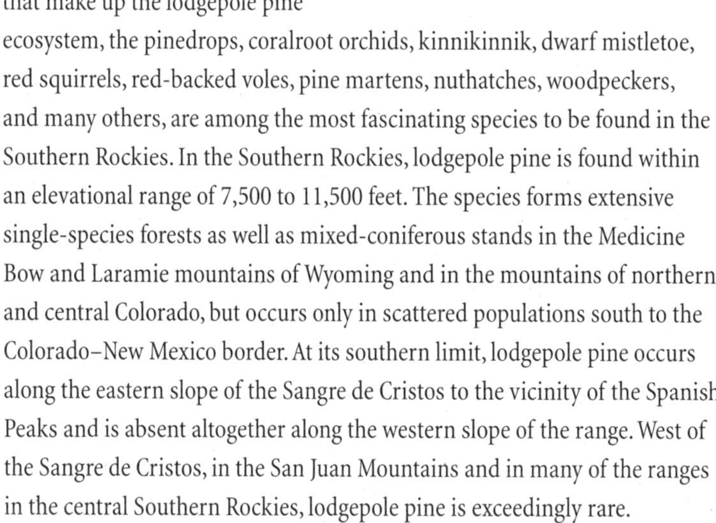
Lodgepole pine.

These monochromatic and seemingly uniform forests are sometimes described as "biological deserts" by forest biologists, an unfortunate label that belies the beauty inherent in the lodgepole's geographic amplitude and its ability to take advantage of environmental adversity. The plants and animals that make up the lodgepole pine ecosystem, the pinedrops, coralroot orchids, kinnikinnik, dwarf mistletoe, red squirrels, red-backed voles, pine martens, nuthatches, woodpeckers, and many others, are among the most fascinating species to be found in the Southern Rockies. In the Southern Rockies, lodgepole pine is found within an elevational range of 7,500 to 11,500 feet. The species forms extensive single-species forests as well as mixed-coniferous stands in the Medicine Bow and Laramie mountains of Wyoming and in the mountains of northern and central Colorado, but occurs only in scattered populations south to the Colorado–New Mexico border. At its southern limit, lodgepole pine occurs along the eastern slope of the Sangre de Cristos to the vicinity of the Spanish Peaks and is absent altogether along the western slope of the range. West of the Sangre de Cristos, in the San Juan Mountains and in many of the ranges in the central Southern Rockies, lodgepole pine is exceedingly rare.

In the northern and central ranges of the Southern Rockies, lodgepole pine reaches maximum development in the upper montane and lower subalpine zone, dominating sites between 8,500 and 10,500 feet that have a history of repeated fires. Below 9,000 feet, lodgepole pine forests are most common on northern and eastern exposures; high-elevation lodgepole stands may be found on all slope aspects. At its southern distributional limit, lodgepole pine is largely confined to sheltered, north-facing slopes in a narrow zone between 9,000 and 10,000 feet.

Physical Environment

The climate generally associated with lodgepole pine forests is slightly cooler and moister than that of ponderosa pine–Douglas-fir forests but more moderate than that of the subalpine spruce-fir forests. Summers tend to be warm and subject to intermittent drought. Most precipitation is received as snowfall, and the best growth of lodgepole occurs in areas that average or exceed twenty inches of annual precipitation; the snowpack is consistently deeper and more persistent in lodgepole pine forests at higher elevations. Soils supporting stands of lodgepole are highly variable, but most stands occur on coarse-textured soils that are considerably less fertile than those associated with aspen. Lodgepole pine attains maximal growth on soils that are moist but well drained, gravelly-loamy in texture, and only moderately acidic.

Community Characteristics

The character of forests dominated by lodgepole pine varies with their age, stand history, tree density, and degree of species diversity. Lodgepole pine is considered an aggressive pioneer or successional species in the Southern Rockies. Wherever catastrophic fires, insect infestations, or logging have destroyed large areas of the preexisting climax forest, lodgepole pine regenerates vigorously, producing a dense, homogeneous, even-aged forest. On other sites, lodgepole may occur in uneven-aged mixed-species stands or as small patches in other forest types. Occasionally, lodgepole pine may invade seral aspen communities or even preempt aspen on sites that have experienced high-temperature crown fires.

At lower elevations, under normal successional processes, lodgepole pine is replaced on cool, somewhat moist sites by Douglas-fir and on warm, dry slopes by ponderosa pine. At higher elevations, lodgepole pine is seral to Engelmann spruce and subalpine fir. The time required for a successional lodgepole forest to be replaced by climax forest species is variable and depends on the type and intensity of the initiating disturbance as well as any changes in the microclimate of the forest floor that might influence the reproductive success of the climax forest species for that site.

Young lodgepole pine forests colonized as a result of fire or some other type of disturbance are typically even-aged and single-storied, their density and homogeneity giving them the appearance of a tree farm. Limited light penetration beneath the canopy causes the foliage of the lower branches to die, resulting in an interlacing network of dead branches that enhances the impenetrable quality of these forests. A thick layer of acidic pine-needle litter accumulates on the forest floor, resulting in the leaching of nutrients from the soil. This is in striking contrast to the direct enhancement of soil nutrients and nutrient cycling that occurs in aspen forest soils. Lodgepole forest understory is sparse or absent because the trees use most of the forest's resources. Consequently, very few other plant species occur with lodgepole pine in these ecosystems. As trees die from lack of sufficient light and nutrition, understory vegetation increases in response to the opening of the forest.

Lodgepole pine forests tend to form stable, persistent communities where repeated disturbances have disrupted normal successional patterns, where fires or other large-scale disturbances have eliminated the seed source for the normal climax tree species, or where microclimatic conditions no longer favor regeneration of the climax species. For example, low-elevation stands of lodgepole pine may assume subclimax status on sites where high forest-floor temperatures and intermittent drought in summer are too extreme for Douglas-fir seedlings to gain a foothold. Similar changes in the microclimate in subalpine lodgepole stands can also make it impossible for Engelmann spruce and subalpine fir to reestablish themselves as climax species.

Mature lodgepole forests, those with trees 100 years old or more, are more open and are characterized by an uneven-aged structure and a better-developed understory. Mixed-species forests occur wherever Douglas-fir, subalpine fir, and Englemann spruce have been able to establish or reestablish themselves. As is true for younger lodgepole forests, shrubs dominate the understory. The most abundant shrub species in montane lodgepole forests are common juniper, wild rose, and kinnikinnik. At higher elevations, these shrub species are largely replaced by buffaloberry, blueberry, red elderberry, and bush honeysuckle. Herbaceous species associated with other montane and subalpine forests may be present in small numbers and include such species as heartleaf arnica, pussytoes, fireweed, wintergreen, spotted coralroot orchid, and pinedrops. The yellow-green, jointed shoots of dwarf mistletoe, a parasitic seed plant that establishes its root system within the bark and outer conducting tissues of the lodgepole, are especially common in open forests.

From left to right: common juniper, kinnikinnik.

Plant Adaptation: Designs for Survival

Serotiny

Lodgepole pine is a fire-adapted species, producing its seed crop in cones that do not open at maturity but remain sealed and tightly attached to the branches for many years, until fire or some other agent breaks the resinous bond that prevents the cone from opening. The closed-cone habit, called serotiny, is typical of a small number of North American pine species. During its lifetime, a lodgepole can accumulate hundreds of hard, prickly cones along its branches. In the event of a fire, the thin film of resin bonding the cone scales together melts and the scales spread open to release a multitude of tiny winged seeds. The seeds are readily dispersed by the wind, germinating in large numbers on the fire-readied seedbed. Serotiny enhances the reproductive success of the lodgepole by retaining the seeds in a protected but viable state until a fire or other similar disturbance reduces competition from other species and provides optimal conditions for germination and growth. Lodgepole seedlings are superbly adapted to the intense sunlight, heat, cold, drought, and lack of humus of the fire-scorched seedbed. The price for this fire-initiated fecundity, however, is the almost impenetrable "dog-hair" stand of saplings that characterizes the young lodgepole forest. In one Colorado study, sample plots in a twenty-two-year-old stand established after fire contained roughly 44,000 trees per acre.

Serotiny is genetically controlled and highly variable in Rocky Mountain populations of lodgepole pine. Individual trees may have either entirely serotinous or nonserotinous cones, or both. In the absence of fire, closed cones open eventually as a result of the mechanical breakdown of the vascular connection between the cone and the parent tree or the deterioration of cone resin with age or with desiccating winds. Studies suggest that Rocky Mountain lodgepoles may even develop a mixed cone serotiny habit with increasing tree age, a distinct evolutionary advantage in that the tree can redirect energy away from the maintenance of old, perhaps nonviable seed to functions more critical to the tree's survival.

Saprophytes and Parasites

The low surface-light levels and impoverished soils typical of many lodgepole pine forests favor plant species that are opportunistic in their strategies for survival. Two groups of plants, saprophytes and parasites, fit this requirement precisely. Saprophytes, such as the coralroot orchids and several species of fungi, contain no chlorophyll and are unable to make their own food through photosynthesis, deriving nutrients from dead organic matter in the forest soil. The mycelium from which the fungal fruiting bodies (the mushrooms) arise may persist underground for years, fruiting when environmental conditions are conducive to growth, remaining dormant when not. When optimal temperature and moisture conditions prevail, a munificence of mushrooms—chanterelles, morels, pine mushrooms, and scaly urchins—can be found on the forest floor. One interesting species, the wood-inhabiting honey mushroom (*Armillaria ostoyae*), can either grow in dead wood as a saprophyte or become parasitic and spread throughout the roots and trunks of living lodgepoles.

Plants such as dwarf mistletoe and pinedrops are true parasites, obtaining all their nutritional resources from a living host plant, usually to the host's detriment. Pinedrops contains no chlorophyll and is parasitic on the roots of conifers. Dwarf mistletoe, on the other hand, contains some chlorophyll and is able to carry on partial photosynthesis, relying on its lodgepole host for water and minerals. In contrast to pinedrops, which is believed to have little impact on its host, the spread of dwarf mistletoe throughout the crown of a lodgepole pine can seriously impact the tree's normal growth rate (both in height and diameter), reduce seed production, and may ultimately kill the tree if the amount of photosynthetically effective needle tissue drops below that needed to sustain the tree. Interestingly, the success of dwarf mistletoe development depends directly on the vigor of the host trees; the more vigorous the host, the more vigorous the mistletoe infestation that will result. In fact, sites with optimal lodgepole growth have a higher proportion of mistletoe-infested trees than do poorer sites.

Parasitic plants found in lodgepole pine forests, from left to right: dwarf mistletoe, pinedrops.

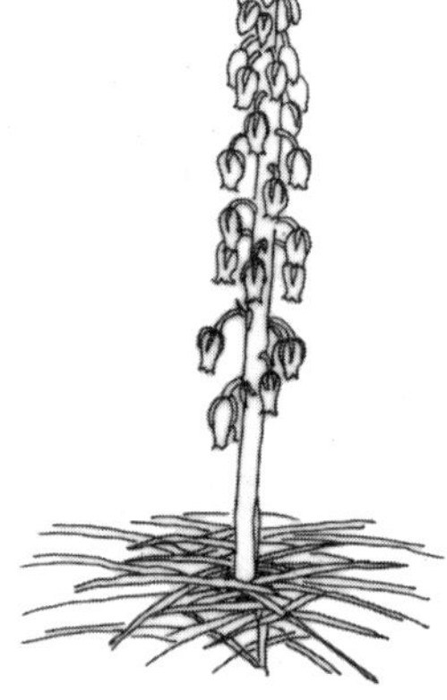

Descriptions of Common Plants

Trees

Rocky Mountain Lodgepole Pine, *Pinus contorta* ssp. *latifolia*. This tall, slender-trunked pine is the common pine of the upper montane and subalpine zones of the northern and central Southern Rockies. Lodgepole pine is identified by the persistent cones that dot its branches and by its greenish yellow, somewhat twisted needles, each about two inches in length and arranged two needles to a bundle. This slow-growing species can live for several hundred years. Male cones are small and cylindrical and grow in clusters at the branch tips. Female cones take up to two years to develop; immature cones are small, prickly globes. At maturity, female cones are woody and yellowish brown in color (weathering to gray), and each cone scale is armed with a short, curved spine. Seeds are long, reddish brown, and winged; good seed crops are produced every one to three years. The very first railroads to penetrate the Rockies did so on ties made from lodgepole pine, most of which were cut in the Medicine Bow Mountains of Wyoming and processed at Tie Siding.

Common Juniper, *Juniperus communis* ssp. *alpina*. This low-growing shrub has a circumpolar distribution and ranges south through the Southern Rockies to New Mexico. It is typically found in dry forests and on open slopes from the foothills to the alpine zone. The sharp, needlelike leaves, frost-blue female cones, cedary fragrance, and prostrate or spreading growth form make common juniper easy to identify. Male and female cones appear on separate plants, although occasionally both sexes can be found on the same plant. Male cones are extremely small and are borne at the tips of branches, disintegrating after pollen release. Female cones resemble berries because of the fusion of the fleshy cone scales. Following fertilization, juniper "berries" require two to three years to reach maturity, changing from pale green to dark blue in color with increasing age. The female cones are an important food source for small mammals and birds and have a long history of medicinal and culinary use.

Shrubs

Kinnikinnik, *Arctostaphylos uva-ursi*. This creeping, prostrate shrub is circumpolar in its distribution and found in open coniferous woods from the foothills to the subalpine zone. Its glossy evergreen leaves, urn-shaped flowers, and deep red berries readily identify kinnikinnik, or bearberry. The oblanceolate leaves have thick cuticles that protect the plant from drought and desiccating winds. In bloom, the delicately scalloped pink flowers hang from trailing branches, largely hidden by the leaves. Shiny green berries, about a quarter of an inch in diameter and ripening to a cherry red at maturity, may persist on the branches for several seasons.

Wild Rose, *Rosa woodsii.* This upright shrub is found throughout the Southern Rockies but is especially common in dry, open woodlands from the foothills to the subalpine zone. Wild rose is distinguished from other shrubs by its thorny floral stems, compound and serrate leaves, and pink, fragrant, five-petaled flowers. Scarlet, fleshy fruits, called hips, develop in late summer; the hips, which remain on the plant after the leaves have fallen, are an important food for various birds and mammals.

Parasitic and Saprophytic Plants

Pinedrops, *Pterospora andromedea.* This unusual plant is a member of the pinesap family (Monotropaceae) and occurs in pine forests from the foothills to the montane zone. Pinedrops is identified by its rich, rusty-rose flowering stalk and its down-hanging, bell-shaped flowers. Clusters of the fleshy, flowering stalks first appear in early summer; stalks average two feet in height, are hairy, and feel somewhat sticky to the touch when fresh, becoming woody as they dry. Pinedrops lack chlorophyll and are parasitic on the roots of conifers, exisiting for most of their life cycle as a mass of brittle, fleshy roots beneath the ground surface and forming an intimate relationship with mycorrhizal fungi. Seed capsules persist on the stalks after maturity, opening along suture zones to release their minute winged seeds; each seed has a large, lacy, and transparent wing that enhances dispersal.

Dwarf Mistletoe, *Arceuthobium americanum.* The distribution of this parasitic seed plant coincides with the distribution of lodgepole pine in North America. The clusters of mustard yellow jointed shoots that sprout directly from the branches and trunk of the host tree identify dwarf mistletoe. These leafless shoots are anchored to the branch of a lodgepole pine by modified roots, called haustoria, that are able to tap into the tree's nutrient and water supply; a severe dwarf mistletoe infestation will weaken and even kill the host tree. Mistletoe plants are either male or female; flowering occurs in spring. Female flowers are wind- or insect-pollinated, and the berrylike fruits, each with a single seed, develop by midsummer. At maturity, typically from late August to early September, the fruit breaks from its base, contracts violently, and shoots the seed several feet into the air; the seed may be expelled at speeds of up to sixty miles per hour and travel distances of up to thirty feet. Each seed is surrounded by a sticky substance that helps it adhere to the surface on which it lands. Seeds that land on or are washed onto a tree branch by the rains will germinate the following spring, establishing their root systems over the next two years; a growth period of three to five years may elapse before the new shoots appear.

Spotted Coralroot Orchid, *Corallorhiza maculata.* This common orchid is found in dry ponderosa pine and lodgepole pine forests from the foothills to the subalpine zone. The orchid's common name refers to the coral-like appearance of its brittle, highly branched root mass. Spotted coral-roots are saprophytes and must obtain their nutrition from dead organic matter in the forest soil; the intertwining of their peculiar root mass with soil-borne fungi and the roots of other plants suggests that this species may be partially parasitic as well. The asparaguslike reddish brown flowering stalks appear in early spring and average about ten inches in height. The small but spectacular flowers appear along a leafless raceme, each flower consisting of a frilly white, purple-spotted lip framed by a fan of reddish brown petals and sepals. Blooming time varies with altitude, extending from late May at lower elevations to mid-July at higher elevations. After flowering, the pendant seed capsules enlarge dramatically, splitting at maturity along longitudinal suture zones to release thousands of dustlike seeds.

Wildflowers

One-sided Wintergreen, *Orthilia secunda.* This attractive member of the wintergreen family (Pyrolaceae) is associated with cool, coniferous forests from the montane to the subalpine. With its rounded evergreen leaves and its erect, one-sided raceme of pale green flowers, this species is easily distinguished from other members of its family, such as **pipsissewa** (*Chimaphila umbellata*) or **green-flowered wintergreen** (*Pyrola chlorantha*). The leaves, though mostly basal, may extend up the lower third of the flowering stem. The flowers consist of five rounded green petals and hang on short pedicels.

Mountain Pussytoes, *Antennaria parvifolia.* This familiar wildflower, a member of the sunflower or composite family, is found in open coniferous forests and forest clearings from the foothills to the subalpine zone. Pussytoes is identified by its stoloniferous (arising from runners), rosettelike growth form, grayish green leaves, and flowers that superficially resemble a kitten's paw. The leaves of this species are wedge-shaped, thick, and covered with fine hairs. Each two- to three-inch flowering stalk arises from a rosette of leaves, the flower head consisting of a tight cluster of white disk flowers.

Fireweed, *Chamerion angustifolium.* This tall, showy member of the evening primrose family (Onagraceae) is often found along roadsides and in areas where fires or other disturbances have occurred. In successional lodgepole stands, fireweed is common only in the early stages of reforestation, disappearing as shading intensifies. Fireweed is distinguished by its spirelike racemes of large, rose-purple flowers and by its slender, lanceolate leaves, which turn red in the fall. The flowers have four petals, eight stamens, a four-lobed stigma, and an inferior ovary (situated below the petals) that elongates as it ripens. At maturity, elongate seed capsules split open to release a multitude of tufted seeds that are easily dispersed by the wind.

Common Plants of the Lodgepole Pine Forest

Trees

Aspen, quaking, *Populus tremuloides*
Fir, subalpine, *Abies lasiocarpa*
Pine, limber, *Pinus flexilis*
    Rocky Mountain lodgepole, *P. contorta* ssp. *latifolia*
    ponderosa, *P. ponderosa*
Spruce, Engelmann, *Picea engelmannii*

Shrubs

Blueberry, *Vaccinium myrtillus*
    broom, *V. scoparium*
Buffaloberry, *Shepherdia canadensis*
Elderberry, red, *Sambucus microbotrys*
Juniper, common, *Juniperus communis* ssp. *alpina*
Kinnikinnik, *Arctostaphylos uva-ursi*
Mountainlover, *Paxistima myrsinites*
Rose, wild, *Rosa woodsii*
Sticky-laurel, *Ceanothus velutinus*

Twinberry (or Bush Honeysuckle), *Distegia* (formerly *Lonicera*) *involucrata*
Waxflower, *Jamesia americana*
Willow, scouler, *Salix scouleriana*

Wildflowers

Arnica, heartleaf, *Arnica cordifolia*
Fireweed, *Chamerion angustifolium*
Locoweed, drop-pod, *Oxytropis deflexa*
Pipsissewa, *Chimaphila umbellata*
Pussytoes, mountain, *Antennaria parvifolia*
Wintergreen, green-flowered, *Pyrola chlorantha*
  one-sided, *Orthilia secunda*

Parasites and Saprophytes

Mistletoe, dwarf, *Arceuthobium americanum*
Orchid, fairy slipper, *Calypso bulbosa*
  spotted coral-root, *Corallorhiza maculata*
Pinedrops, *Pterospora andromedea*

Fungi

Amanita, *Amanita muscaria*
Chanterelle, *Cantharellus cibarius*
Geopyxis (or Fire Cup), *Geopyxis carbonaria*
Morel, black, *Morchella angusticeps*
Mushroom, honey, *Armillaria ostoyae*
  pine (or white Matsutake), *Tricholoma magnivelare*
Puffball, *Calbovista subsculpta*
Russula, *Russula decolorans*
  white-capped, *R. brevipes*
Sticky-cap, yellow, *Tricholoma flavovirens*
Tricholoma, orange, *Tricholoma zelleri*

Environment and Adaptation: Animals of the Lodgepole Pine Forest

Lodgepole pine forests may appear quiet and somewhat empty at first glance. Look more closely, however, and you'll begin to see that these forests offer a critical source of seeds and insects for a fascinating group of conifer forest specialists. The dense growth of trees and the shady character of most successional lodgepole forests result in a depauperate understory, providing little cover or food. Red squirrels, or chickarees, take advantage of the beneficent supply of seed-bearing cones, stockpiling them in caches on the forest floor. Red-backed voles excavate tunnels in the piles of cone scales discarded by the squirrels, feasting on leftover lodgepole seeds and on fungi growing in the moist litter. Though the density of breeding birds is low, the brown creeper and several species of woodpeckers, nuthatches, and chickadees are attracted to these forests by the abundance of insects, each species focusing its foraging activities on different parts of the trees or at different vertical levels. These animals, in turn, attract predators such as the pine marten and the sharp-shinned hawk.

The Chickaree: A Conifer Seed Specialist

John Muir described this small tree squirrel as "a fiery, sputtering little bolt of life." Known by several common names—chickaree, red squirrel, pine squirrel—this ubiquitous conifer seed specialist is easy to spot as it leaps from branch to branch with birdlike agility or delivers one of its scolding, chattering soliloquies. Red squirrels prefer relatively dense stands of lodgepole pine or spruce-fir forests that provide ample supplies of cones and suitably moist, cone-caching sites. Evidence of cone harvesting includes middenlike piles of shucked cone-scales and freshly cut branch tips. Chickarees harvest tightly closed cones, clipping them from the branches in summer and fall and storing them in shallow basins excavated in their middens or at the base of a fallen tree or stump. There is nothing sotto voce about the chickaree when it suspects its foraging territory is being invaded. Not surprisingly, the intensity of territorial behavior within the chickaree's home range varies seasonally and is greatest during the cone-caching period. Though other foods (fungi, fruit, etc.) may be consumed or stored when available, cached cones provide the critical food supply during winter and early spring.

Chickaree midden.

Winter poses a challenge to all animals that remain active throughout the year. During an average winter, the energy needs of a single chickaree are estimated to be about 15,000 kilocalories, which translates into roughly 20,000 to 25,000 seed-bearing lodgepole pinecones to make it through the winter. How do lodgepole pine seeds compare nutritionally to those of Engelmann spruce or Douglas-fir? We know that chickarees relish the seeds of all three species. In the Southern Rockies, studies have shown that Engelmann spruce seeds yield about 15 calories per seed and average about 180 seeds per cone. A Douglas-fir seed, on the other hand, is a nutritional powerhouse at 57 calories per seed but only produces about 45 seeds per cone. The total energy yield per cone for either species is about the same, approximately 2,500 calories; the chickaree would need about 5,000 Engelmann spruce or Douglas-fir cones to get through the winter. Lodgepole pine seeds provide only about a fourth as much caloric energy per cone as those of Douglas-fir or Engelmann spruce. Chickarees living in lodgepole pine forests, however, have a distinct advantage when it comes to harvesting their winter food supply: the lodgepole's serontinous cones can be easily cached in tidy piles on top of the ground or left on the branch for later retrieval. Burial in moist soil, as the squirrel must do for spruce and Douglas-fir cones, would cause the lodgepole cones to open prematurely and the seeds to spoil. With their diet of serotinous cones, the squirrels don't have to harvest all the cones they'll need over the course of the winter but can leave a substantial portion in "long-term storage" on the branches without worrying about losing their bounty to other seed-eating species.

To reach the nutritious seeds enclosed within the resin-sealed lodgepole cone, the chickaree must chew through a succession of extremely woody, spine-tipped cone scales, armament intended to frustrate any seedeater. Studies in the Southern Rockies have shown that chickarees maximize their foraging efficiency in lodgepole forests by discriminative seed predation, selecting trees that have the most easily harvestable cones as well as those that consistently produce a high number of seeds per cone. Coevolution of chickarees and serotinous races of Rocky Mountain lodgepole pine, the overall effect of discriminative seed predation by squirrels, has resulted in the lodgepole's increased reproductive effort toward tissues that protect the seed from predators rather than toward greater seed production. In fact, the seeds in a serotinous cone account for only 1 percent of the cone's total weight.

Coevolution, however, works both ways. In the Southern Rockies, chickarees associated with serotinous races of lodgepole pine have evolved a larger body and heavier jaw musculature than a closely related species, the Douglas squirrel, which is found in the Pacific Northwest and feeds on the more readily obtainable seeds of nonserotinous lodgepoles. A bony ridge atop the skull of the chickaree, nonexistent in most populations of Douglas squirrels, provides additional anchorage for the muscles that work the jaws. For the chickaree and the lodgepole pine, the balance has shifted in the direction of sustainability: the chickaree is able to satisfy its appetite for lodgepole seeds without decimating the entire lodgepole seed crop.

Of Wood-borers and Gleaners

Mountain pine beetles, the most rapacious members of the genus *Dendroctonus*, are boring, tunneling, egg laying, hatching, and maturing in lethal numbers throughout the West's lodgepole pine forests. In recent years, broad swaths of mature beetle-killed lodgepoles have been turning a telltale rusty red, a sure sign that the trees have succumbed to the depredations of tens of millions of beetles no bigger than a grain of rice. Though the mountain pine beetle has coevolved over millions of years with lodgepole and other pine species, recent beetle outbreaks have been especially devastating and widespread. Few forests seem immune to attack. Lodgepole pine forests in California, Oregon, Washington, Idaho, Colorado, Wyoming, Montana, Alberta, and British Columbia are all under siege.

The magnitude of the current pine beetle onslaught is difficult to grasp. In 2003, forest biologists in British Columbia reported that pine beetles destroyed 10 million acres of lodgepole pine—an area roughly the size of Switzerland—in a single year. Closer to home, on the White River National Forest, in north-central Colorado, 90 percent of the lodgepoles across 2.2 million acres are expected to succumb to the beetle's attack. In fact, tens of millions of lodgepole pine are expected to die throughout the Southern Rockies as a result of the current infestation, the scale of the devastation exceeding any outbreak in at least 350 years. Forest biologists suggest that previous outbreaks ended when the beetles exhausted their food supply in a given area or when adverse climatic conditions persisted long enough to impact beetle populations. In this case, with the beetle expanding its elevational range and attacking smaller-diameter and younger lodgepoles than ever before, the prospects for lodgepole pine forests over the next several years seems grim indeed.

Researchers believe that the ecological machinery that sets the stage for a beetle infestation of normal amplitude has gone into overdrive in response to prolonged drought and warmer temperatures throughout western North America. Fire suppression and logging have also played a critical role, creating forests that are uniform in age (100- to 120-year-old trees) and densely stocked with trees. There seems little doubt that temperature has a profound influence on the life history of the mountain pine beetle. Pine beetles are most successful when warmer-than-average annual temperatures permit them to complete their entire life cycle, egg⇒larvae⇒ pre-adult pupae⇒adult, in one year rather than two. A one-year cycle allows the beetles to effectively synchronize their emergence and flight from their lodgepole host. As a consequence, the beetle's ability to mount a massive assault effectively overwhelms the tree's natural defenses and results in a massive die-off of pines. Colder temperatures, on the other hand, force the beetles into a two-year life cycle; under this regime, the larval beetles must endure a second winter during the most vulnerable stage in their development. A two-year life cycle, especially if cold temperatures persist over several years, substantially reduces the likelihood of a synchronized emergence and a mass attack by the beetles. Throughout the range of lodgepole pine, temperatures have been on the rise, with only minor perturbations, since the 1980s, not sharply, but enough to let the pine beetles thrive.

Many of the bird species associated with lodgepole forests are specialists at extracting bark- and wood-boring insects. Nuthatches and brown creepers are equipped with strong feet for clinging to bark and slender pointed bills for picking insects out of bark crevices. Hairy and downy woodpeckers, with their strong grasping feet, picklike bills, long tongues, and stiff-pointed tail feathers that serve to brace the body against the hammering motion of the head, are superbly adapted for digging out wood-boring insects and larvae. The unusually long reach of the woodpecker's barb- tipped tongue is made possible by extensible hyoid bones, which divide into two slender bony and muscular horns that curve back around the base of the skull then up and over the forehead to attach in or near the nostrils. This remarkable adaptation by which the tongue is protruded, supported, and withdrawn enables the woodpecker to probe deep into the feeding and nursery galleries created by wood-boring insects such as the mountain pine beetle.

Life Histories of Selected Animals

Mammals

Chickaree (or Red or Pine Squirrel), *Tamiasciurus hudsonicus.* This tree squirrel is identified by its small size, chattering call, tuftless ears, white eye ring, dark grayish brown back and sides (sometimes tinged with red), and grayish white underparts. In the Southern Rockies, chickarees are most common in lodgepole pine and spruce-fir forests. Diurnal and highly territorial, the chickaree defends not only its nesting area, but also its entire home range. The territorial call is a strident, rolling *cherr* and may be accompanied by vigorous tail-flicking, foot-stamping, and dramatic chases. The chickaree's principal food is conifer seeds, which it obtains by cutting and caching cones from late summer through fall. Other foods, including fungi, berries, buds, flowers, inner bark (cambium), invertebrates, and the sugar-enriched cambial tissues of mistletoe-infested branches, are eaten when available. A ball-shaped nest of grasses and conifer needles constructed on a branch or in a tree cavity is used throughout the year. Chickarees are solitary except during breeding, when females are receptive to males for a single day during estrus. One or more males may court the female, but only the dominant male succeeds in mating, his approach to the female preceded by a melodious series of "appeasement" vocalizations. The altricial young are usually born in April after a gestation period of approximately forty days. Nursed until early summer, the young undergo a period of agility and foraging training before dispersing from the mother's territory in late summer.

Southern Red-backed Vole, *Clethrionomys gapperi*. This beautiful, forest-dwelling vole is distinguished from the deer mouse by its small eyes and ears, its short tail, and the broad patch of reddish hairs that highlights its buffy gray back. In the Southern Rockies, this boreal species occurs mostly in lodgepole pine and spruce-fir forests at higher elevations. Southern red-backed voles are solitary and active throughout the year, retreating into tunnel systems beneath the snowpack in winter. The principal foods include conifer seeds, fungi, berries, bark, and some invertebrates. In contrast to all other voles except the heather vole, southern red-backed voles have rooted rather than evergrowing molars and are thus poorly adapted to the abrasive diet of grasses favored by most voles. In the Colorado Front Range, red-backed voles are reported to have begun breeding activities beneath the snow in late March. Following a gestation period of about eighteen days, the female gives birth to a litter of two to eight altricial young in a small, globe-shaped nest constructed of grasses and other plants. Female voles reach sexual maturity by about two months of age and may produce several litters per season. Red-backed voles seldom exceed twenty months in age.

Birds

Sharp-shinned Hawk, *Accipiter striatus.* This small accipiter is distinguished from the larger **Cooper's hawk** (*A. cooperii*) by its pigeonlike size, square tail, rounded wings, slate blue upperparts, reddish streaking on breast and belly, and white undertail coverts. There is no sexual dimorphism; immature birds are brownish above, whitish and streaked with brown below. Sharp-shinned hawks are associated with coniferous forests and mixed woodlands throughout the Southern Rockies, returning to most nesting areas by early spring; some individuals may be present throughout the year, often staking out bird feeders in mountain residential areas that attract large numbers of small birds. This hawk's style of hunting relies mostly on concealment and ambush, but they are well known for their aerial twists and abrupt changes in direction when pursuing small avian prey. The sharp-shinned hawk typically nests relatively high in an evergreen, constructing a platformlike nest of twigs and branches or renovating the abandoned nest of another raptor. Both sexes incubate the eggs, but the male does most of the hunting during the nesting season. Fledging occurs in as little as twenty-three days.

Downy Woodpecker, *Picoides pubescens.* This bluebird-sized woodpecker is distinguished from the similar hairy woodpecker (*P. villosus*) by its smaller size, small bill, and the dark bars on the outer tail feathers. Though less conspicuous than the hairy, the downy is a common resident of coniferous forests and mountain riparian woodlands throughout the Southern Rockies. These woodpeckers forage by clinging to the trunks and branches of trees, digging out subsurface insects and larvae, or flaking off the bark to get at insect cocoons or eggs. During the summer, the downy may also forage for surface prey on the foliage and branches. The sexes remain apart during the winter and may defend winter feeding territories as well as the site of their roosting hole. Courtship behavior begins in late winter and is initiated by the onset of drumming by both sexes on trees, utility poles, or other resonating surfaces. The territorial call is a slightly softer *pik-pik* than that of the hairy. Once the pair bond is established or renewed, the pair will seek a nest site and both sexes will work at excavating the nest hole. Following egg laying, both sexes incubate the eggs by day, with the male assuming total responsibility at night. Young downy woodpeckers are fed by both parents and are ready to fly within twenty-one to twenty-four days. Fledglings initially follow the parents but disperse as they become more successful at finding food on their own.

White-breasted Nuthatch, *Sitta carolinensis*. This robust, sparrow-sized nuthatch is distinguished from the diminutive **red-breasted nuthatch** (*S. canadensis*) by its larger size and all-white face and breast; the red-breasted nuthatch has a rusty-colored breast and dark eye stripe. White-breasted nuthatches are common residents of the coniferous forests of the Southern Rockies. Most birds are observed foraging for bark insects upside down and sideways on trunks and branches, but ground foraging may also occur. The call of this species, a nasal *yank-yank-yank-yank*, is lower pitched than that of the red-breasted. The white-breasted nuthatch is largely insectivorous except in winter, when it eats seeds and is a common visitor to bird feeders. Winter-foraging flocks, or guilds, often include other nuthatch species, chickadees, brown creepers, and downy woodpeckers. Pairs may remain close to each other during the winter but will normally roost alone. Nesting occurs in early spring, in a natural tree cavity or an abandoned woodpecker or sapsucker hole. Both sexes incubate the eggs, which require about twelve days to hatch. Young nuthatches are able to fly within about two weeks of hatching.

From left to right: red-breasted nuthatch, white-breasted nuthatch.

Brown Creeper, *Certhia americana.* This sparrow-sized bird with its camouflage coloring of streaky brown is a fairly common and permanent resident of the dense coniferous forests of the Southern Rockies. Brown creepers can be difficult to spot and are most often located by their call, a high, lisping *screep*, and then observed spiralling upward along a tree trunk as they forage for bark insects. These birds, equipped with pointed, down-curved beaks, large feet, and stiff tails that serve as braces during foraging, are superbly adapted to their insectivorous niche. Outside the breeding season, brown creepers are solitary but may sometimes be seen foraging in mixed-species flocks. There is some evidence that brown creepers perform altitudinal migrations during cold weather, and communal roosting has been reported. Brown creepers typically nest behind loosened pieces of bark where a branch has fallen away or in abandoned tree cavities, often within fifteen feet of the ground, the female constructing a hammock-shaped nest of plant fibers. Incubation takes only two weeks, and the young fledge within two weeks of hatching.

Common Animals of the Lodgepole Pine Forest

Mammals

Bat, hoary, *Lasiurus cinereus*
Bear, black, *Ursus americanus*
Bobcat, *Lynx rufus*
Chipmunk, least, *Tamias minimus*
    Uinta, *T. umbrinus*
Cottontail, mountain (or Nutall's), *Sylvilagus nuttallii*
Coyote, *Canis latrans*
Deer, mule, *Odocoileus hemionus*
Elk (or Wapiti), *Cervus elaphus*
Ermine (or Short-tailed Weasel), *Mustela erminea*
Hare, snowshoe, *Lepus americanus*
Marten, American, *Martes americana*
Moose, *Alces alces*
Mouse, deer, *Peromyscus maniculatus*
Porcupine, common, *Erethizon dorsatum*

Shrew, masked, *Sorex cinereus*
Squirrel, chickaree (or Red or Pine Squirrel), *Tamiasciurus hudsonicus*
Vole, southern red-backed, *Clethrionomys gapperi*
Weasel, long-tailed, *Mustela frenata*

Birds

Chickadee, mountain, *Parus gambeli*
Creeper, brown, *Certhia americana*
Crossbill, red, *Loxia curvirostra*
Finch, Cassin's, *Carpodacus cassinii*
Goshawk, northern, *Accipiter gentilis*
Grosbeak, evening, *Coccothraustes vespertina*
Grouse, blue, *Dendragapus obscurus*
Hawk, Cooper's, *Accipiter cooperii*
sharp-shinned, *A. striatus*
Jay, gray, *Perisoreus canadensis*
Steller's, *Cyanocitta stelleri*
Junco, dark-eyed, *Junco hyemalis*
Kinglet, ruby-crowned, *Regulus calendula*
Nutcracker, Clark's, *Nucifraga columbiana*
Nuthatch, red-breasted, *Sitta canadensis*
white-breasted, *S. carolinensis*
Owl, great horned, *Bubo virginianus*
northern pygmy, *Glaucidium gnoma*
northern saw-whet, *Aegolius acadicus*
Raven, common, *Corvus corax*
Sapsucker, Williamson's, *Sphyrapicus thyroideus*
Siskin, pine, *Carduelis pinus*
Thrush, hermit, *Catharus guttatus*
Warbler, yellow-rumped, *Dendroica coronata*
Woodpecker, downy, *Picoides pubescens*
Hairy, *P. villosus*

CHAPTER TWENTY-FOUR

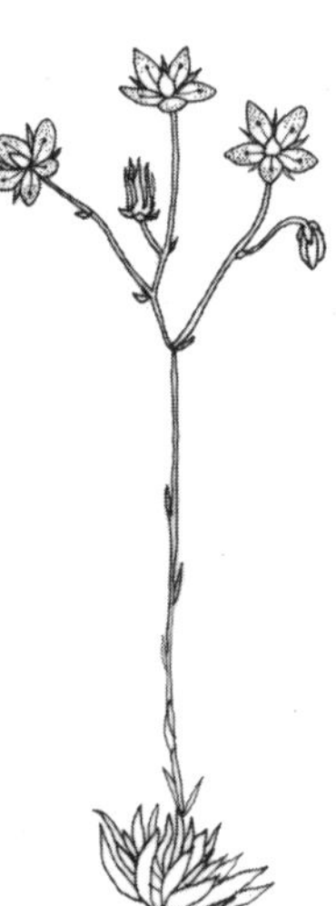

The Wind Forest: Bristlecone Pine and Limber Pine

Venerable in their isolation, the gnarled silhouettes of bristlecone and limber pine grace the mountain skyline. Clinging tenaciously to rocky knobs and ridgetops, these pines endure extremes of every sort: strong winds, cold temperatures, drought, and nutrient-poor soils. The sound of the wind whistling through their branches has a distinctly keening sound. Twisted and flayed to the white sinews of their sapwood by the winds, survivors may have only thin ribbons of living tissue encircling their buttressed trunks. Standing like sentinels above the mountain valleys, their silvered trunks glowing rose at sunset, the magnificent snags continue to transfigure the mountain landscape long after their death.

Ecological Distribution

In the Southern Rockies, open woodlands of limber and bristlecone pine dominate dry, rocky ridges and exposed, south-facing slopes. Limber pine occurs in the Rocky Mountains from Canada to northern New Mexico. In the Southern Rockies, it is found on windswept sites from the foothills to timberline, but it is most common above 9,000 feet. Bristlecone pine is represented by two geographically and taxonomically distinct species. Rocky Mountain bristlecone pine (*Pinus aristata*), the species found in the Southern Rockies, occurs only in Colorado, New Mexico, and the San Francisco Peaks area of Arizona; Great Basin bristlecone (*P. longaeva*), the species that includes the oldest living trees known, is restricted to California,

Nevada, and Utah. A distance of 160 miles separates the Rocky Mountain species from the nearest Great Basin bristlecone populations. In the Rocky Mountains, the northern limits of Rocky Mountain bristlecone pine approximate the fortieth parallel.

In the Southern Rockies, limber and bristlecone pines may each form pure stands on certain sites or may be found in various combinations with other tree species depending on latitude, elevation, and substrate. Bristlecone and limber pines often occur together where their ranges overlap in the central and southern ranges of the Southern Rockies. At the southern end of the Sangre de Cristo Range, limber pine dominates dry slopes between 7,500 and 10,000 feet and takes the place of lodgepole pine as the successional species on open slopes. Above 10,000 feet, limber pine is occasionally replaced on the driest sites by bristlecone pine, although this species is decidedly rare here. Bristlecone pine increases in importance as you move north along the Sangre de Cristos and is especially common on steep, rocky terrain at elevations up to 11,800 feet. A nearly pure stand covering about 300 acres is preserved just east of Costilla, New Mexico, as part of the Clayton Pass–Bristlecone Pine Research Natural Area in Carson National Forest..

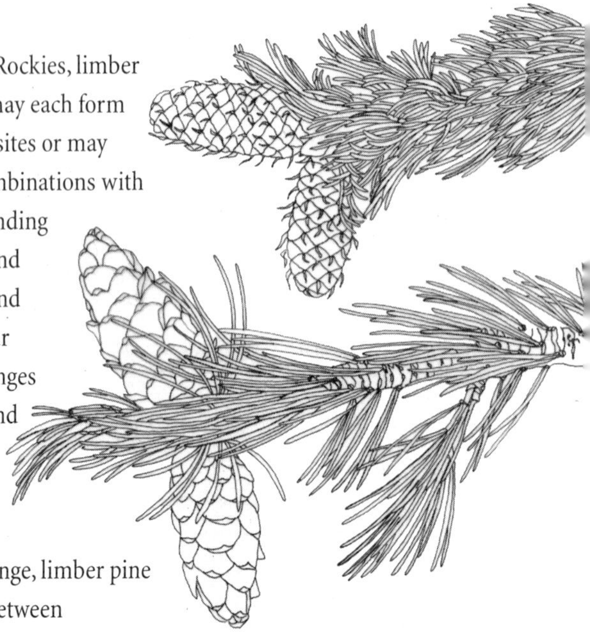

Bristlecone pine (top), limber pine (bottom).

Significant stands of bristlecone have been reported in approximately fifty-four locations in the central and southern ranges of Colorado. In the Spanish Peaks, bristlecone and limber pine form an unusual low-elevation association with woodlands of ponderosa pine and Gambel's oak. At higher elevations, bristlecone pine dominates large portions of the dry subalpine forests typical of this region. North and west of the Spanish Peaks, bristlecone pine becomes increasingly uncommon. In the San Juans, bristlecone pine stands occur only on south-facing slopes north of Creede. In the Sawatch Range, mixed stands of bristlecone and limber pine are prominent along Colorado 82 between Twin Lakes and Independence Pass. A timberline stand of bristlecones believed to include the highest-dwelling erect trees in the Southern Rockies occurs at 12,300 feet on a southwest-facing slope of the Sawatch Range near the historic town of St. Elmo, Colorado. North of this area, pure stands of bristlecone are relatively common in South Park and in the Mosquito Range; in the Pike–San Isabel National Forest, high on the flanks of Mount Bross (14,172 feet), an especially scenic stand of bristlecones is preserved as part of the Windy Ridge–Bristlecone Pine Scenic Area. At the northern limit of the species' range on the Western Slope, stands of bristlecone pine can be seen in upper Gore Canyon (northern Gore Range) and on the rim of Deep Creek Canyon (White River Plateau).

At the southern end of the Colorado Front Range, in the comparatively dry Pikes Peak area, bristlecone is most common on south-facing slopes in the montane and subalpine zones, with limber pine dominating north-facing slopes and filling the role of a successional species in the absence of lodgepole pine. On Mount Evans, bristlecone and limber pine share dominance on high-elevation sites, with bristlecone pine occupying open, south-facing slopes with fine-textured soils and limber pine more prevalent on rocky ridges. A beautiful, easily accessible twelve-acre stand of bristlecone pines, encompassed within the Mount Goliath Natural Area, is located about three miles up the Mount Evans road from Echo Lake. Mixed stands of bristlecone and limber pine are also prominent along I-70 near the town of Silver Plume, Colorado.

Windy Ridge Bristlecone Pine Scenic Area.

Bristlecone pine reaches its northern limits along the Colorado Front Range just west of Nederland, near the historic mining town of Caribou. North and west of this area, limber pine takes the place of bristlecone on dry, windswept sites from timberline down to middle elevations. Some scattered populations of limber pine, such as those at Pawnee Buttes, in northeastern Colorado, occur as low as 5,000 feet. In the Medicine Bow Mountains of Wyoming, limber pine is an important species in lower- and middle-elevation forests, especially because of the rarity of ponderosa pine, but its distribution rarely reaches timberline. In fact, communities of limber pine and aspen often adjoin the sagebrush-grassland transition zone along the mountain valleys of the Medicine Bow Mountains and the Snowy Range.

Physical Environment

Bristlecone and limber pine woodlands occupy areas characterized by strong winds, low temperatures, high solar radiation, a short frost-free season, periodic drought, high surface runoff, and coarse, mostly acidic soils. Average annual precipitation for most sites supporting thriving stands rarely exceeds thirty-five inches; most sites experience greater effective precipitation in summer than in winter. During the winter months, these ecosystems are largely snow-free as a result of wind scour. Tree growth for both Rocky Mountain bristlecone and limber pine appears to be affected by the previous year's climate. El Niño–La Niña events bring heavy snowfalls during El Niños and drought during La Niñas. High monsoonal precipitation in July, August, and September typically results in good early summer growth the following year. The warm fall temperatures associated with La Niña events, on the other hand, appear to reduce growth the following summer because the foliar buds (new needle bundles) fail to harden off sufficiently due to the warm temperatures and are more susceptible to autumn frost-kill.

Community Characteristics

Bristlecone and limber pine woodlands are shaped by the harsh conditions of their environment. In contrast to most other forest types, bristlecone and limber pine woodlands are of limited size, ranging from a few trees to stands encompassing a few hundred acres. They can occur as pure stands, as mixtures of the two species, or as minor constituents in other forest types. Climax stands are typical of the windiest, most xeric environments; in the absence of lodgepole pine, bristlecone and limber pine assume a successional role in areas where fire or logging have removed the preexisting tree cover.

Viewed from a distance, these woodlands are easily distinguished from other forest types. In general, the trees tend to be widely spaced, broad-crowned, and comparatively short, rarely exceeding thirty feet in height. On gentle slopes, these woodlands have an open, grovelike appearance and easy to move through. A high percentage of bare, rocky ground and a sparse understory of shrubs and herbaceous plants are typical of most communities. The most picturesque of these stands usually includes several old trees, many ranging in age between 1,000 and 2,000 years. A dozen bristlecones in the South Park area, for example, exceed 1,600 years of age. These gnarled patriarchs, their trunks ice- and sandblasted to a polished platinum, often support only a few living branches. Timberline populations may be erect or somewhat prostrate, often with spectacularly twisted trunks.

The understory vegetation of bristlecone and limber pine woodlands is highly variable, depending on geographic location, stand elevation, topography, substrate type, and the influence of adjacent vegetation communities. Species diversity tends to be relatively low in most woodlands, except on the most sheltered sites or in successional stands. Shrubs such as common juniper, shrubby cinquefoil, kinnikinnik, and sticky-laurel occur in many stands. Herbaceous species typical of midelevation woodlands include alumroot, stonecrop, false arabis, wallflower, Fendler's sandwort, and alpine penstemon. Species present in high-elevation woodlands include Whipple's penstemon and spotted saxifrage. Favorable sites near timberline may support a mixture of alpine species such as whitlow-wort, alpine clover, alpine thistle, purple fringe, and alpine sandwort.

Plant Adaptation: Designs for Survival

Forever buffeted by fierce winds and clinging tenaciously to rocky ridges, bristlecone and limber pine have evolved strategies that enable them to cope with environmental conditions considered too severe for other tree species. The branches of the limber pine are smooth-barked and flexible, allowing them to bend easily in the wind without breaking. Once established, a limber pine seedling sends down a large taproot, which enables the young tree to anchor itself securely to rocky ridges and bluffs. The ability to retain functional needles for many years, in contrast to the short-lived needles of most conifers, is a characteristic of pines that inhabit high, dry places. The needles of Rocky Mountain bristlecone pine remain functional for ten to fifteen years, requiring the tree to produce only a limited number of new needles each year and ensuring a stable photosynthetic capacity to sustain the tree during times of environmental stress.

Rocky Mountain bristlecones and limber pines are the longest-lived trees in the Southern Rockies. The oldest limber pines occur mostly in central Colorado and include several specimens averaging between 1,000 and a maximum of 1,661 years of age. Rocky Mountain bristlecones claim the greatest antiquity, with several trees dated by tree ring counts at just under 2,500 years in age. In fact, the oldest of these bristlecones had 2,435 countable rings when it was cored in 1992; this tenacious, thirty-foot-tall survivor graces a grove in Park County and has a trunk diameter of four feet. Great Basin bristlecones often exceed 3,000 years in age, and the world's oldest living tree, a bristlecone known as Methuselah growing in the Schulman Memorial Grove in California's White Mountains, has been dated at more than 4,600 years.

We tend to think that any tree living longer than the norm must be growing under optimal conditions, with abundant moisture, moderate temperatures, nutrient-rich soils, and protection from severe weather. Not so for these pine species. The oldest and largest trees typically occupy the harshest, most exposed sites, where soil moisture is scarce and growth is exceedingly slow. Slow-growing trees tend to have extremely narrow growth rings, and therefore denser wood, than fast-growing species. The insect, fungal, and bacterial invasions that plague most trees have little impact on pines growing in severe situations, because the dense, highly resinous wood produced under such harsh circumstances is especially disease resistant. Bristlecones and limber pines growing under more moderate conditions fail to reach great age because the increased moisture available to these trees encourages the production of less dense, less resinous wood, which is more susceptible to disease and decay.

Hardship is a fact of life for both species. For example, young bristlecones (150 years old or less) have bark-encircled trunks, intact cambium, no crown dieback, and as many as eighty or more living limbs. The maximum age at which the trunks of the bristlecones still retain their bark ranges between 400 and 600 years. For longer-lived bristlecones, the passage of time is marked by the gradual loss of bark and cambium to cambial dieback (or cambial retreat), porcupines, and fire; the death of portions of the pine's root system due to parasitic fungi or desiccation; and the periodic attrition of needled limbs as a result of wind damage, drought, and lightning. What living tissues remain—perhaps only a few needled branches and a strip of living bark and cambium—must strike a balance between the size of the living crown and the amount of bark and active xylem needed to sustain it. The oldest bristlecones, those in the 2,000- to 2,500-year-old age class, have trunks with dramatically exposed, erosion-sculpted wood; extensive crown dieback; a prominent dead, erosion-sculpted pith (core) spike; a single strip of living bark (covering only 5 to 10 percent of the trunk); and usually only one living branch. The bristlecone is remarkable in that its dead wood remains sound throughout the life of the tree. In fact, many bristlecones remain upright or intact for hundreds of years after death.

Descriptions of Common Plants

Trees

Rocky Mountain Bristlecone Pine, *Pinus aristata*. Rocky Mountain bristlecone is identified by its five-needled fascicles, the white dots of resin on individual needles, and its bristle-tipped cone scales. The needles are usually strongly curved, less than two inches long, and closely crowded together around all sides of the branches, giving the branch a bottlebrush appearance. The male cones are small, dark orangish, and clustered near the tips of the branchlets. Female cones occur singly or in pairs, near the ends of the branchlets. Bristlecone pines are wind-pollinated. At maturity, the female cones are extremely woody, with purplish brown scales, and are difficult to handle because each scale bears a slender, bristlelike prickle. The seeds are brown and oval shaped, and each has a terminal wing about three times longer than the body of the seed. The minimum age known for seed production in bristlecones is ten years. On favorable sites, mature bristlecones may reach a height of forty feet and will sometimes exceed thirty inches in diameter. Two bristlecones in northern New Mexico hold the record for height and diameter; they are seventy-two feet tall and eleven and a half feet in diameter, and seventy-six feet tall and eleven feet in diameter, respectively.

Limber Pine, *Pinus flexilis.* Limber pine is distinguished from bristlecone, which it superficially resembles, by its longer and less curved needles, the absence of white resin dots on its needles, and the absence of bristles on its cone scales. Limber pine shares with bristlecone pine the arrangement of needles in bundles of five and the distinctly tufted appearance produced by the density of needles encircling the branch. The trunk and branches are smooth-barked and silvery gray when young; the trunk becoming scaly and deeply furrowed with age. The branches are extremely flexible, a characteristic that gives limber pine both its common and scientific names. Male cones are small and reddish; young female cones are round and reddish purple. Mature female cones are woody and elongate and have thick, bristleless cone scales. Each square-tipped cone scale bears two large, winged seeds. A year of heavy seed production normally alternates with several years of light production. The large seeds are especially attractive to Clark's nutcrackers, red crossbills, and other seed predators.

Wildflowers

Yellow Stonecrop, *Amerosedum lanceolatum* (formerly *Sedum lanceolatum*). This attractive, succulent-appearing plant is common on dry, gravelly, or rocky ground from the plains to the alpine

Stonecrop with detail of flower.

tundra. It is identified by its fleshy, simple leaves crowded on short shoots and its star-shaped yellow flowers. The leaves have a waxy covering that prevents water loss, enhancing the plant's survival rate in extremely dry environments. When sufficient water is present, this succulent species flourishes; it remains dormant and somewhat shrunken in size during times of moisture stress.

Common Alumroot, *Heuchera parvifolia.* This member of the saxifrage family (Saxifragaceae) is typical of rock crevices and cliffsides from the montane to the alpine tundra. Alumroot is identified by its roundish lobed leaves arranged in a loose rosette at the base of the plant and by the leafless flowering stalks bearing compact clusters of diminutive green flowers.

Spotted Saxifrage, *Ciliaria austromontana* (formerly *Saxifraga bronchialis*). This lovely wildflower, another member of the Saxifragaceae, is found in dry forested canyons and rocky cliffs from the foothills to the subalpine zone. Spotted saxifrage is easily identified by its matlike growth form, diminutive, awl-shaped leaves, and slender flower stalk bearing several small white flowers. A hand lens reveals the beauty of the flowers, each petal speckled with yellow, orange, and red. The leaves of the spotted saxifrage are evergreen, and mats of this species may form conspicuously green, mosslike cushions on rock ledges during the winter.

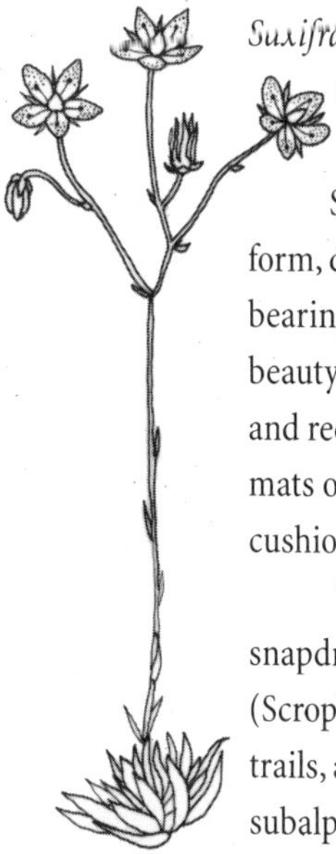

Spotted saxifrage.

Whipple's Penstemon, *Penstemon whippleanus.* This tall snapdragonlike wildflower is a member of the figwort family (Scrophulariaceae) and is common on rocky slopes, along trails, and in open forests from the upper montane through the subalpine zone. Whipple's penstemon is easily distinguished from other high-elevation penstemons by its inch-long, dark purple or wine red flowers and by its robust size. Both dark- and white-flowered forms are often found in the same population.

Purple Fringe, *Phacelia sericea.* This showy species is a member of the waterleaf family (Hydrophyllaceae) and is found on gravelly, open slopes, around boulders, and in disturbed soils of the subalpine zone. Purple fringe is identified by its silky, fernlike leaves and the dense, spiky cluster of purple flowers from which the stamens and pistils protrude conspicuously.

Common Plants of the Bristlecone Pine and Limber Pine Forests

Trees

Douglas-fir, *Pseudotsuga menziesii*
Pine, limber, *Pinus flexilis*
  ponderosa, *P. ponderosa*
  Rocky Mountain bristlecone, *P. aristata*
  Rocky Mountain lodgepole, *P. contorta* ssp. *latifolia*

Shrubs

Blueberry, broom, *Vaccinium scoparium*
Buffaloberry, *Shepherdia canadensis*
Cinquefoil, shrubby, *Pentaphylloides floribunda*
Juniper, common, *Juniperus communis* ssp. *alpina*
Kinnikinnik, *Arctostaphylos uva-ursi*
Raspberry, wild, *Rubus idaeus* ssp. *melanolasius*
Rose, wild, *Rosa woodsii*
Sticky-laurel, *Ceanothus velutinus*

Herbaceous Plants

Alumroot, common, *Heuchera parvifolia*
Arabis, false (or Rockcress), *Boechera drummondii*
Buckwheat, alpine, *Eriogonum jamesii* var. *xanthum*
Candytuft, mountain, *Noccaea* (formerly *Thlaspi*) *montana*
Clover, alpine, *Trifolium attenuatum*
Draba (or Whitlow-wort), *Draba* spp.
Locoweed, Rocky Mountain, *Oxytropis sericea*
Muhly, mountain, *Muhlenbergia montana*
Muttongrass, *Poa fendleriana*
Penstemon, alpine, *Penstemon glaber*
  Whipple's, *P. whippleanus*
Purple Fringe, *Phacelia sericea*
Pussytoes, mountain, *Antennaria parvifolia*
Sandwort, alpine, *Lidia obtusiloba*

Fendler's, *Eremogone fendleri*
Saxifrage, spotted, *Ciliaria austromontana*
Stonecrop, yellow, *Amerosedum* (formerly *Sedum*) *lanceolatum*
Thistle, alpine, *Cirsium scopulorum*
Wallflower, *Erysimiun capitatum*

Environment and Adaptation: Animals of the Bristlecone Pine and Limber Pine Forests

The harsh conditions and limited resources typical of most bristlecone and limber pine woodlands do not support a diverse fauna. Most animals found here are visitors from adjacent communities, attracted by the seasonal crop of pine seeds, the pine's succulent inner bark, or the availability of nest sites in tree cavities or rocky crevices. For much of the year, however, these woodlands stand alone, with only the wind and the occasional porcupine or Clark's nutcracker for company.

The Solitary Diner

Though seemingly clumsy and slow moving on the ground, porcupines are agile tree climbers, using their long, curved claws for gripping and their stout, spine-armored tail for balance and stability. Like the woodpecker, the porcupine uses its tail for support when climbing; the underside of the tail is covered with stiff, downward-pointing bristles set in thick connective tissue, which prevents backsliding. Strong thigh muscles and large foot pads that conform to the substrate at hand make the porcupine look as effortless as a rock climber scaling a favorite pitch. Porcupines are active throughout the year in bristlecone and limber pine woodlands except during the most severe winter weather. Evidence of porcupine activity—patches where bark has been removed and accumulations of inch-long fecal pellets beneath a favorite feeding tree—may be conspicuous in certain areas of heavy use.

Getting up the tree, however, is just half the battle. The porcupine must be able to digest and metabolize the cambium, or inner bark, of these trees, its main source of sustenance and one to which it is uniquely adapted. To combat herbivores, coniferous trees have evolved a battery of defensive strategies that include indigestible, unpalatable, or poisonous substances in their needles and woody tissues and that are designed to reduce the tree's attractiveness to the consumer. Seemingly immune to these defenses, the porcupine attacks the bark of a preferred feeding tree with its rootless incisors, first shaving off the dead outer layer of bark and then concentrating its efforts on the cambium, which it processes into a fine puree with its cheek teeth. To gain the maximum benefit from its diet of woody tissues, at least 75 percent of the porcupine's body cavity is taken up by organs devoted to digestion: stomach, caecum, and intestines. Functionally, the caecum resembles the rumen of an elk or deer, housing the symbiotic microflora necessary to convert otherwise indigestable carbohydrates into metabolizable fatty acids, compounds critical in meeting the porcupine's energy requirements.

Despite the efficiency of the porcupine's digestive processes, the low concentration of nitrogen (a building block of proteins) and the excess of indigestable roughage in its fall and winter diet fail to meet the animal's metabolic requirements, causing it to lose a substantial portion of its body weight over the course of the winter. To minimize the effects of this nutritional shortfall, the porcupine limits the breadth of its diet as well as its movements during the winter, concentrating on foraging areas where its preferred trees, typically those with bark most easily digested by a given animal's intestinal microflora, are abundant. In fact, the porcupine's winter foraging area may be less than 15 percent of that used in summer. With the arrival of spring, porcupines turn their attention to deciduous trees and shrubs, taking advantage of the high protein content of the new buds, catkins, and young leaves. Porcupines generally return to a conifer-based diet by midsummer, the time when the leaves and cambial tissues of deciduous trees begin accumulating tannins and other distasteful compounds that alter proteins and inhibit the intestinal microflora that aids porcupine digestion.

Smart Weapons

Quills are the porcupine's best-known defense against predators when traveling between one foraging area and another. The porcupine's "quiver" of quills numbers in the tens of thousands, and they bristle from every inch of its body, with the exception of its face, belly, and the undersides of its limbs and tail. Each quill ranges between one-half and four inches long and is equipped with a one-way barb designed for burrowing into the predator's flesh. There is more to a porcupine's sense of security, however, than merely possessing an arsenal of quills at the ready. First, the potential predator needs to realize that the porcupine is armed and will use its weaponry if attacked. Porcupines broadcast a distinct, pungent warning odor when their quills are erected defensively. The scent is generated by a special patch known as a rosette, which is equipped with modified quills (called osmetrichia) that serve to increase transmission of the warning odor. Furthermore, the quills contain a fluorescent material that brightens the quills at night, when predators are most likely to be out hunting: an early warning system analogous to the motion-sensor perimeter lighting used to scare off a potential intruder.

How does this amazing system work so that the porcupine is never on the receiving end of its own weaponry? We know that the porcupine doesn't "launch" its quills against a potential enemy, but instead requires body contact with the adversary, leaving behind the barbed quills to finish the job. The base of a porcupine's quill sits beneath the skin, surrounded by a spool-like structure made up of dense connective tissue. This "guard spool" lies just below the hilt of the quill and prevents it from being driven into the porcupine instead of the intended victim. When the porcupine is provoked, it erects its quills and the guard spools realign to allow just enough spring-back upon impact to sever the root of the quill from the anchoring tissue beneath the porcupine's skin. At this point, the quill is released from its "anchor" and lodged in the enemy, allowing the porcupine to scuttle to safety or climb a tree.

Seed Caching

Most coniferous trees rely on the wind to disperse their small, winged seeds. Several mountain pines, however, such as the piñon and the limber pine, depend largely on seed-caching birds for dispersal. Limber pine has evolved characteristics similar to those of piñon, making its cones attractive to foraging Clark's nutcrackers and other seed-eating birds. The seed-bearing cones are conspicuously positioned on the branches, and when the cones mature in late summer, the large, high-energy seeds are displayed temptingly on the newly opened cone scales. Superficially, these traits would seem maladaptive for the tree, since no seedling can grow from a consumed seed. The advantages to the pine in this coevolved system, however, derive from the failure of the birds to recover all the seeds they have cached. Viable seeds that fail to be retrieved have a better chance of germinating and becoming successfully established than those scattered randomly through wind dispersal.

The Clark's nutcracker has evolved both anatomical and behavioral adaptations that make it a proficient harvester of pine seeds. The most striking feature of the nutcracker is its long, sturdy, sharply pointed bill, which it uses as a chisel to pry open green cones or as forceps to extract seeds once the cones have opened. As each seed is extracted, it is subjected to "bill-clicking": the nutcracker rattles the seed in its bill and, assessing its weight or the sound that it makes, determines whether the seed is edible. Inedible seeds are discarded with a toss of the bill, and edible ones, if not eaten at once, are reposited in an expandable pouch located beneath the tongue. This gular pouch, unique to this species, can hold as many as 180 limber pine seeds; its use does not interfere with flock-orienting vocalizations and permits foraging over wide areas. When the pouch is full, the bird flies off to a favored communal caching area, which may be shared with as many as a dozen other nutcrackers. Most caching sites are located on windswept ridges or south-facing slopes that remain largely snow-free throughout the winter. After selecting a site, the nutcracker uses its bill to excavate a small hole in the soil and deposits one to several seeds in it, carefully covering the cache with soil and often marking it with a twig or pebble.

Clark's nutcracker.

In a good cone year, an active nutcracker can store thousands of pine seeds during a fall collecting period, burying many times more seeds than it can possibly consume. Clark's nutcrackers exhibit an extraordinary ability to relocate individual caches. Experiments have shown that seed recovery is dependent not on the nutcracker's sense of smell, but on its ability to recognize the arrangement of objects around or marking a cache. During the winter months, cached seeds not only make up the bulk of the diet, but also provide the extra energy required for winter breeding. Particularly surprising, however, is the fact that pine seeds make up almost the entire diet of the nutcracker's nestlings. The nestlings of most other birds are fed insects because most seeds fail to provide sufficient proteins and fat to ensure normal growth. Limber and piñon pine seeds, however, are unusually high in lipids and proteins, and young nutcrackers appear to thrive on them.

Life Histories of Selected Animals

Mammals

Porcupine, common, *Erethizon dorsatum.* This distinctive rodent is identified by its large size, thickset appearance, the armament of quills cloaking its back, sides, limbs, and tail, and its waddling gait. Porcupines are relatively common in mountain forests throughout the Southern Rockies but are most abundant in open pine woodlands. Their diet changes seasonally, ranging from the inner bark of trees to succulent herbaceous plants. Though timid and rarely known to be aggressive, the porcupine defends itself by turning its back on its attacker, its quills clattering together like so many spears; the animal cannot hurl its quills, but they are so loosely attached that the merest brush against them will result in a painful souvenir for the potential predator or the unwary dog. Solitary but nonterritorial, porcupines may resort to communal denning in cold weather. Breeding, a complicated affair given the armament, occurs in late autumn or early winter. Den sites are chosen in rocky crevices and hollow logs and under abandoned outbuildings. A single precocial young (rarely twins) is born in April or May after a gestation period of about seven months. Maximum longevity is about ten to fifteen years; a radio-collared, free-ranging porcupine was reported to have lived in one area for twenty-one years.

Birds

Clark's Nutcracker, *Nucifraga columbiana.* This pigeon-sized bird is a member of the jay family (Corvidae) and is identified by its gray body, black wings, black (central) tail feathers, long black bill, and, in flight, white wing patches, rump, and outer tail feathers. Clark's nutcrackers inhabit mountain pine forests (especially limber pine and piñon pine woodlands) throughout the Southern Rockies, especially near timberline. This noisy bird, with its nasal croaking call, is gregarious and often forages for pine seeds in large flocks. Clark's nutcrackers breed in February and March, building nests in conifers on wind-sheltered slopes near their seed-caching areas. After fledging, the young follow the parents to the caching site, where the parents continue to feed them until July.

Common Raven, *Corvus corax.* This large, all-black bird is distinguished from the American crow by its larger size, more massive bill, and long, wedge-shaped tail. A member of the Corvidae, this conspicuous, highly intelligent species is widely distributed in the Southern Rockies and can be found from the semidesert shrublands to the alpine tundra. Ravens are omnivorous, functioning both as predator and scavenger opportunistically. They will take live animals when available and plunder the nests of other birds, but they also concentrate on the smorgasbord of carrion supplied by our high-speed highways. Ravens are gregarious except during the nesting season, and large congregations are often reported at winter roosts. Large numbers of ravens may be seen flying and soaring together, carrying out aerial maneuvers and high-spirited play that resembles the mock dogfights of fighter jets. Courtship displays are spectacular, replete with pursuit flights, aerial acrobatics, and close-contact, mutual soaring. Pairs mate for life and remain together throughout the year. The nest site is generally situated on a cliffside, atop a utility pole, or, occasionally, in the top of an abandoned outbuilding. Altricial at birth, ravens are slow in developing and do not fledge until about six weeks of age.

Red Crossbill, *Loxia curvirostra.* This sparrow-sized bird is identified by the reddish body of the male or the yellowish olive body of the female, the dark wings, and the bill with crossed tips. The red crossbill is an irregular and uncommon wanderer in the mountain forests. Pine seeds are its dietary staple, but spruce seeds and the buds and catkins of deciduous trees are also utilized when available. The irregular pattern of this bird's occurrence in any given area is largely a result of seed crop availability from year to year. The crossbill's beak is uniquely adapted to prying open the scales on conifer cones, allowing the seeds to be easily removed by the tongue. When drinking or collecting highway salt, the bird's bill must be held sideways so that the material can be lapped up with the tongue. Red crossbills grasp the branches with their bills, parrot-style, when climbing through the branches of a tree while foraging. The call is somewhat chattering, a series of *jip* notes, often a signal of foraging flocks in the vicinity. Red crossbills nest at any time of the year; the frequency of winter nesting suggests that the nestlings need not be fed solely on insects. The nest is built well out on the branch of a conifer.

Common Animals of the Bristlecone Pine and Limber Pine Forests

Mammals

Bobcat, *Lynx rufus*

Chipmunk, least, *Tamias minimus*
Cottontail, mountain (or Nuttall's), *Sylvilagus nuttallii*
Coyote, *Canis latrans*
Ermine (or Short-tailed Weasel), *Mustela erminea*
Hare, snowshoe, *Lepus americanus*
Marmot, yellow-bellied, *Marmota flaviventris*
Mouse, deer, *Peromyscus maniculatus*
Porcupine, common, *Erethizon dorsatum*
Shrew, masked, *Sorex cinereus*
Squirrel, chickaree (or Red or Pine Squirrel), *Tamiasciurus hudsonicus*
    golden-mantled ground, *Spermophilus lateralis*
Weasel, long-tailed, *Mustela frenata*
Woodrat, bushy-tailed, *Neotoma cinerea*

Birds

Crossbill, red, *Loxia curvirostra*
Finch, Cassin's, *Carpodacus cassinii*
Grosbeak, pine, *Pinicola enucleator*
Jay, gray, *Perisoreus canadensis*
    Steller's, *Cyanocitta stelleri*
Junco, dark-eyed, *Junco hyemalis*
Nutcracker, Clark's, *Nucifraga columbiana*
Nuthatch, white-breasted, *Sitta carolinensis*
Raven, common, *Corvus corax*
Siskin, pine, *Carduelis pinus*
Warbler, yellow-rumped, *Dendroica coronata*
Woodpecker, hairy, *Picoides villosus*

The Snow Forest: Engelmann Spruce and Subalpine Fir

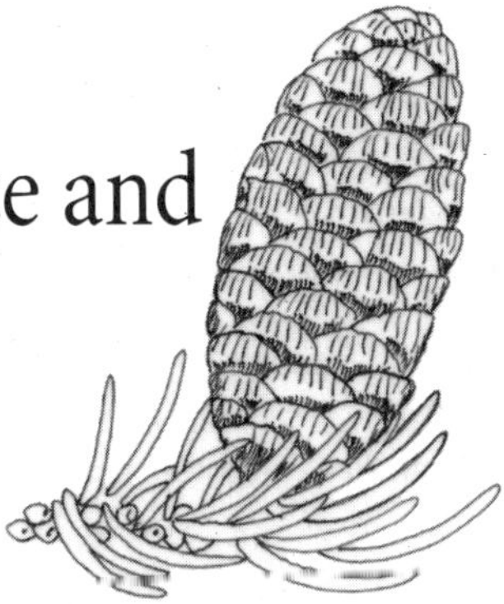

Subalpine fir.

Closing ranks against the open, sun-drenched woodlands typical of lower elevations, forests of Engelmann spruce and subalpine fir share an essential unity with those of the boreal regions of northern Canada. There is always enough of the mysterious in these dark, spired forests to draw one into their midst: enough of the sweet-smoky fragrance of spruce needles, the distant fluting call of a hermit thrush, the soft clucking of a female blue grouse to her chicks, or the fleeting shadow of a marten. Within the cool embrace of the forest, shafts of sunlight pattern the forest floor, spotlighting clumps of curled lousewort amidst a lime green carpet of blueberry and wintergreen.

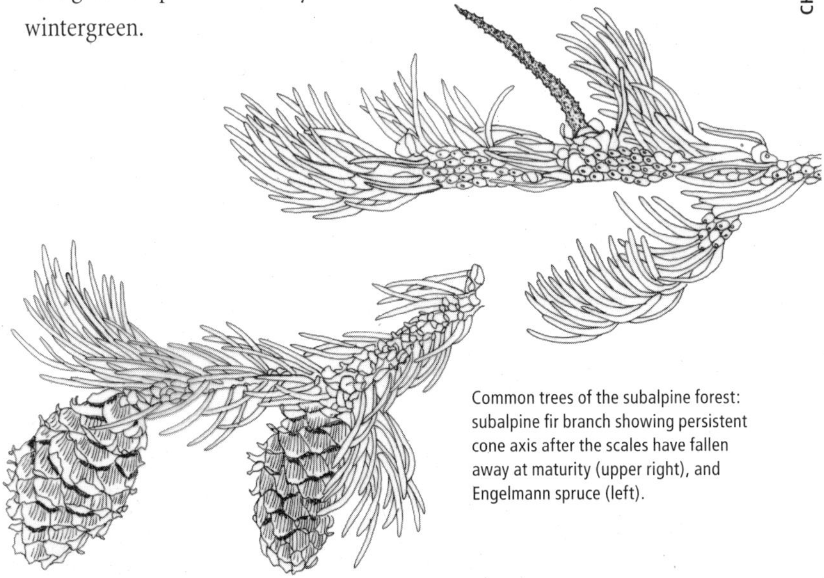

Common trees of the subalpine forest: subalpine fir branch showing persistent cone axis after the scales have fallen away at maturity (upper right), and Engelmann spruce (left).

Ecological Distribution

In the Southern Rockies, Engelmann spruce and subalpine fir dominate the subalpine zone and form extensive, largely homogeneous forests between 9,000 feet and timberline. To understand the distributional patterns that characterize these forests, we must define several terms used in delimiting the upper forest margin. The term *upper timberline,* hereafter referred to simply as timberline, corresponds to the upper elevational limit of fully erect trees. Above timberline, within a narrow and discontinuous transition zone known as the forest-tundra ecotone, trees become increasingly stunted and are finally reduced to prostrate forms in response to the harsh environmental conditions. North American ecologists often use the German word *krummholz* (meaning "crooked wood") to describe these stands of wind-deformed trees, because of their apparent similarity to those in the European Alps. In many timberline areas of the Southern Rockies, trees tend to grow in clusters, forming discrete stands known as tree islands. The term *treelimit* (or *tree line*) defines the elevational boundary marking the cessation of all tree growth, erect or stunted, and the beginning of alpine tundra, the "land above the trees." Because the subalpine forest and the forest-tundra ecotone are part of an ecological continuum, both ecosystem types will be described in this chapter.

Regional Patterns

Within the subalpine forest zone, tree species dominance shifts in response to elevation and latitude. The most majestic spruce-fir forests are found in the western and central ranges, where a generous winter snowpack and high summer precipitation provide ample moisture for optimal growth. In this region, the subalpine forest extends from about 9,500 feet to 11,000 feet and includes a mixture of Engelmann spruce, subalpine fir, stands of aspen, and lush subalpine meadows. On sheltered slopes and in high basins, groves of tall Engelmann spruce are common at timberline. Within the forest-tundra ecotone, both spruce and fir form krummholz islands to about 12,000 feet, but the degree of krummholz development is much less than that found in the windier eastern ranges of the Southern Rockies.

In the central portion of the Southern Rockies, groups of erect

Engelmann spruce and fewer numbers of subalpine fir, as well as islands of krummholz vegetation, reach 12,000 feet on sheltered slopes of the Sawatch Range. In the mountains near Crested Butte, spruce-fir forest begins at about 10,500 feet and extends to nearly 11,500 feet, with an Engelmann spruce–dominated krummholz zone to nearly 12,500 feet on south-facing slopes. In the Park and Sierra Madre ranges, the spruce-fir zone begins at about 10,000 feet, with linear, wind-shaped stands called ribbon forests common along the upper forest margin to nearly 11,000 feet.

At the southern end of the Sangre de Cristo Range, corkbark fir, a variant of subalpine fir identified by its soft, corky bark, shares dominance with Engelmann spruce in the lower subalpine forest. At higher elevations, spruce dominates the forest to treelimit. Treelimit varies from 11,000 feet on northeastern exposures to more than 12,000 feet on southwestern slopes. There is little krummholz development in this area because of the more moderate climate. As one moves north along the Sangre de Cristos, corkbark fir is again restricted to the lower portions of the subalpine forest, and Engelmann spruce dominates the upper forest to treelimit; woodlands of bristlecone pine take the place of spruce-fir forests on the driest subalpine sites. Krummholz communities are rarely encountered here or in the Spanish Peaks to the east. At the northern end of the Sangre de Cristos, corkbark fir continues to be largely absent from the upper subalpine forest, but krummholz becomes increasingly common at timberline.

Farther to the north, in the Colorado Front Range, Engelmann spruce and subalpine fir are codominants throughout most of the subalpine forest zone between 9,500 and 11,000 feet, giving way to limber pine on rocky, windswept slopes. There is usually a dense forest of lodgepole pine at the lower limit of spruce-fir, a result of logging and historic fires since the time of settlement. Engelmann spruce is the dominant species at timberline, which occurs at around 11,000 feet. Extensive krummholz communities occupy the forest-tundra ecotone. Treelimit occurs at around 11,400 feet.

In southern Wyoming, the lower limit of spruce-fir forests also merges with forests dominated by lodgepole pine. Above this zone, dense stands of Engelmann spruce and subalpine fir gradually give way to ribbon forest at about 10,500 feet; well-developed krummholz islands dominated by subalpine fir are common between 11,000 and 11,500 feet. This same pattern is characteristic of the subalpine forest zone in northwestern Colorado.

Physical Environment

Engelmann spruce–subalpine fir forests occupy the highest tree-inhabited environments in the Southern Rockies. The climate is characterized by long, cold winters, short, cool summers, and high annual precipitation. Mean annual temperature is below 40°F, and frost is possible during any month of the year; winter temperatures are relatively moderate when compared to those in the lower basins or valley bottoms, with few record lows exceeding −15°F. Precipitation (measured as water equivalent), mostly as snowfall, is usually greater than twenty-eight inches and is often as much as forty inches annually. Snow depths, even with only minimal drifting, are often greater than five feet and may be augmented periodically by snow blown down from the alpine tundra. In many areas, the deep snowpack, shaded by the trees, persists well into early summer. Winds can be strong, especially near timberline, and are predominantly from the west; windthrow of both living and dead trees is a common phenomenon in these forests.

Forest-Tundra Ecotone

The forest-tundra ecotone is characterized by extreme cold and harsh winds, which severely limit tree growth and reproduction. Throughout most of the ecotone, the average temperature of the warmest month of the year (typically July) is 50°F. In the Southern Rockies, a conspicuous decrease in the elevation of timberline and treelimit occurs with increasing latitude. On average, the growing season is only about fifty days long, and snow is possible at any time of the year. Winter winds, often exceeding eighty miles per hour, sweep the snow from exposed tundra ridges and redeposit it in troughs and depressions in the forest-tundra ecotone. Tree islands and ribbon forests act like snow fences, interrupting the free passage of wind-transported snow and encouraging the development of massive drifts to the lee of these communities.

Timberline Is on the Rise

Throughout western North America, the character of the forest-tundra ecotone is changing as trees expand their elevational range upward. In the Southern Rockies, subalpine forest tree species are currently invading what were once subalpine and lower alpine meadow sites, gradually filling in some of these formerly open habitats with trees. The invasion is discontinuous and not apparent on all sites, however, because conifer seed crops are episodic. While in some areas the expansion of trees into what were once herbaceous habitats may be triggered by postfire succession, recent scientific evidence supports the idea that global climatic change is playing a very significant role. A warmer climate means that the frost-free period lasts longer, soils dry out sooner, and trees can successfully colonize high-elevation areas that had excluded them previously. It is important to remember that elevation ranges provided for spruce-fir forest, timberline, the forest-tundra ecotone, and treelimit are approximate and that change is a constant in any ecosystem.

Community Characteristics

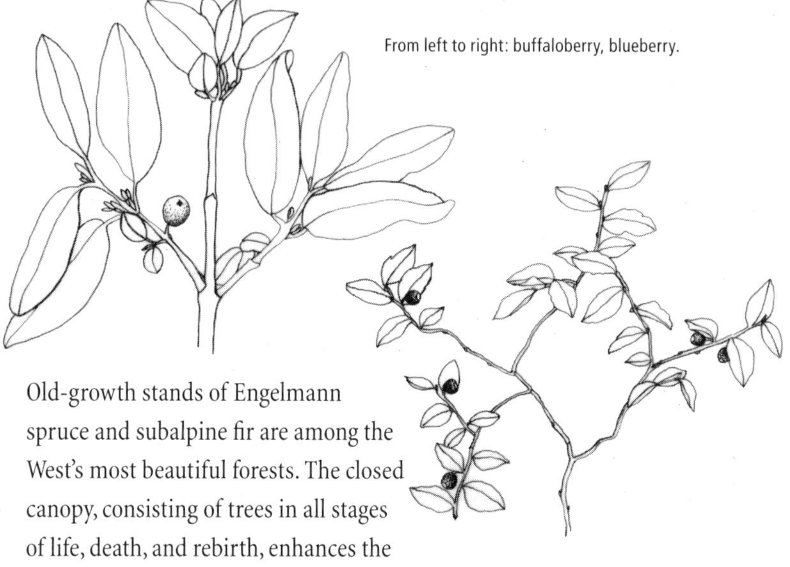

From left to right: buffaloberry, blueberry.

Old-growth stands of Engelmann spruce and subalpine fir are among the West's most beautiful forests. The closed canopy, consisting of trees in all stages of life, death, and rebirth, enhances the feeling of a forest primeval. Within these stands, individual spruce trees may exceed three feet in diameter, 120 feet in height, and average about 450 years in age. In the Southern Rockies, the oldest living Engelmann spruce documented thus far is a majestic 911-year-old patriarch in central Colorado. As the oldest trees die, young ones put on growth spurts to fill the vacated spaces. Silvered snags pocked with nesting cavities stand as venerable reminders of forests past. A crisscross maze of fallen trees, their rotting trunks patterned with moss and lichens, impedes passage. Low-growing blueberries and other shade-loving plants form a dense tangle in some areas, while other parts of the forest floor may have only a scattering of plants. Here and there, a rushing mountain stream or a lush, flower-filled meadow provides a visual counterpoint to the forest's deep-shadowed countenance.

Spruce-fir forests are the domain of a distinctive group of shade- and moisture-loving plants. Many species are the same as or similar to those associated with northern boreal forests. Though the understory is often denser than in other coniferous forests of the Southern Rockies, species diversity is generally low. Broom huckleberry and blueberry, with lesser amounts of red elderberry, high-bush cranberry, Colorado currant, buffaloberry, and mountainlover, where present, dominate the shrub understory. With few exceptions, subalpine forest wildflowers tend to be pale in color; they include such species as pipsissewa, wood nymph, broadleaf arnica, curled lousewort, Gray's lousewort, and twinflower. Several orchids, including the rattlesnake plantain, twayblade, and brownie lady's slipper, are found in especially moist, dense forests. The species composition of forest openings and riparian areas within the subalpine zone is strikingly more diverse than that of the forest itself, including colorful wildflowers such as Parry's primrose, false hellebore, monkshood, chiming bells, aspen sunflower, and trumpet gilia. During wet summers, an array of fascinating and often colorful fungi including coral mushrooms, *Russula*, orange jellies, bird's nests, purple fairy fingers, slime caps, shaggy manes, earth fingers, milky caps, and many others can be found on rotting wood or emerging from the moist litter of the forest floor.

Disturbance and Successional Patterns

The self-perpetuating nature of spruce-fir forests is ensured by the fact that no other tree species can reproduce in the deep shade associated with these stands. In many parts of the Southern Rockies, spruce-fir forests have remained largely undisturbed because of the rarity of severe fires in such moist environments and because their inaccessibility has proven an impediment to extensive logging or other types of exploitation. Unfortunately, mining activities in the late 1800s and early 1900s were responsible for much cutting and burning. In recent years, damaging infestations of the Engelmann spruce beetle and western spruce budworm have spread through these forests.

Common wildflowers of the subalpine forest, clockwise from upper left: twinflower, wood nymph, Parry's primrose, curled lousewort.

When disturbance of climax spruce-fir forests does occur, lodgepole pine or aspen is quick to invade areas below 10,000 feet. These shade-intolerant species eventually produce sufficient shade to limit their own reproduction while creating a suitable microclimate for the establishment of spruce and fir seedlings. Depending on local conditions, the process of conversion may take fifty to one hundred years. On the driest sites, in areas where spruce and fir are unable to regenerate, lodgepole pine or limber pine may form the new climax community. Above 10,000 feet, Engelmann spruce dominates forests disturbed by fires, avalanches, or human activities, largely because its seedlings have a higher survival rate than those of fir and are more sun-tolerant during initial establishment. Reforestation in these high-elevation forests is generally slow, however, because of the harsh environmental conditions.

Community Patterns: The Forest-Tundra Ecotone

Viewed from a distance, the upper limit of the spruce-fir forest may appear as an abrupt boundary, or, as is more often the case, the forest may fragment along its upper margins to form isolated, wind-shaped tree islands and glades. The dominant tree species within the forest-tundra ecotone is Engelmann spruce, but subalpine fir may be common in some communities. Severely stunted aspen are present in rare situations at timberline, and limber pine or bristlecone pine may be found on the driest and most windswept sites. The character of the forest-tundra ecotone is shaped by a rigorous and unforgiving climate. Stunted and wind-battered trees, their crowns often reduced to a one-sided, or "flagged," tuft of foliage on the leeward side of the stem, become increasingly dwarfed toward treelimit. At treelimit, the hardiest survivors are forced to hug the ground, assuming cushionlike and even prostrate growth forms on the most exposed sites.

Forest-tundra ecotone communities are characterized by a rich flora consisting of species associated with both subalpine and alpine ecosystems. Shrubs such as Colorado currant, shrubby cinquefoil, bog birch, willow, and several species of blueberry may form a dense growth in certain krummholz communities. Herbaceous plants such as Jacobs ladder and curled lousewort, both shade-loving species, are found within the shelter of the krummholz islands and ribbon forests. Vegetation between the krummholz communities may consist of a well-developed turf formed by grasses, sedges, soil lichens, mosses, and forbs such as alpine avens, globeflower, and American bistort. In the most exposed, gravelly areas, alpine cushion plants such as moss campion and alpine sandwort are common.

Common wildflowers of the forest-tundra ecotone, from left to right: globeflower, Jacobs ladder.

Plant Adaptation: Designs for Survival

Fungi and the Forest

In spruce-fir forest ecosystems, fungi play two major roles that are absolutely critical to the health and survival of the forest. One group, the saprophytic (wood-eating) mushrooms, functions as decomposers, recycling woody materials throughout the dynamic forest system. The emergent fungal fruiting bodies, the mushrooms we see amidst the litter on the forest floor or sprouting from a tree stump, are supported by miles of microscopic filaments called hyphae that permeate the hidden world of the rotting log or spread out through the soil. If you were to twist thousands of these hyphae together, the end result would be a strand no thicker than a human hair. The hyphae secrete enzymes that break down complex carbohydrates into nutritive sugars, which are then transferred to the mushroom. A second group, the subterranean mycorrhiza, form sheaths around tree roots, assisting in the absorption of water and minerals essential to the tree's growth. In return, the tree feeds the fungi with sugars synthesized in its leaves or needles. All conifers, and even some deciduous species, cannot survive without mycorrhizal fungi.

Purple-colored fairy fingers (*Clavaria purpurea*) often cluster by the dozens in the duff on the forest floor in late summer.

Fungi are the dominant microscopic life-forms in meadow and forest soils, the weight of their total living protoplasm in any given area far exceeding that of all other groups combined. What we didn't know until recently, however, is that many wood-eating fungi have the ability to shift between two very different lifestyles, one as a benign, saprophytic herbivore and the other as a predacious carnivore dining on other microscopic life-forms. The sorts of organisms attacked and consumed by these Jekyll-and-Hyde fungi include nematodes, rotifers, amoebas, copepods, and bacteria. The tactics employed by predatory fungi are amazingly diverse: some produce helicoid-shaped spores that screw into the esophagus during digestion, others behave like microscopic tapeworms and fasten to the gut wall of their victim, some produce spores that function like grappling hooks and harpoons to capture prey, while still another group produces antibiotics that kill bacteria on contact. The most interesting of the Jekyll-and-Hyde fungi in the spruce-fir forests include the shaggy mane, small puffball, orange *Mycena*, and bird's nest; look for them on your next forest hike.

Conifers and the Winter Environment

Spruce and fir exhibit morphological and physiological adaptations that enable them to withstand the stresses of the high-altitude winter environment. In contrast to the broader-crowned conifers typical of lower-elevation forests, the narrow-spired growth form and down-swept branches of spruce and fir minimize snow loading and wind resistance. The spired shape, the result of hormonal suppression of lateral branch growth, becomes especially pronounced along the upper margin of the forest, where many timberline trees resemble upside-down carrots.

Persistent snow loads on the lowest branches of the trees may reduce their resiliency over time, allowing the branches to remain in contact with the moist litter of the forest floor. It is not unusual for branches that remain in contact with soil to produce adventitious roots through a process known as layering. Once layering has commenced, the proximal portion of the branch ceases to grow and the rooted branch stem develops its own vertical, central axis. If the layered branch becomes separated from the parent tree, its root system allows it to persist as an independent tree; multiple layered branches sometimes resemble a ring of saplings growing around the parent tree.

Photosynthesis and Growth

Physiological mechanisms are critical to the survival of trees in cold environments. Annual tree growth depends on the maintenance of a favorable balance between the energy gained as a result of photosynthesis and energy expended through respiration. For substantial rates of photosynthesis to occur, minimal leaf (or needle) temperatures must generally be above 46°F . Studies have shown that Engelmann spruce and subalpine fir are adapted to carry out peak rates of photosynthesis at optimal temperatures lower than are typical for other coniferous species, allowing them to substantially extend their photosynthetic season. In fact, in timberline populations of spruce and fir, the reactivation of photosynthetic processes occurs surprisingly early in the spring, often as much as two months prior to the emergence of new growth.

The photosynthetic apparatus of cold-climate conifers shuts down during midwinter, triggering a corresponding decline in respiratory activity. In milder winter climates, coniferous species are able to carry on positive net photosynthesis whenever temperatures are above freezing. In the subalpine forest, however, winter is essentially a time of physiological drought for trees because water reserves in the soil are frozen and unavailable to the roots. Consequently, winter photosynthetic dormancy provides an adaptive advantage in reducing water loss at a time when potential replenishment is greatly limited and when winter transpiration (evaporative water loss) demands must be met by the expenditure of water reserves stored in the trunk and branches.

Winter Dessication and Freezing Damage

Orange-brown patches of dead needles are often prominent on the upper portions of krummholz trees in spring and are the result of winter desiccation and frost damage. Whereas a photosynthetic season of sufficient duration is essential for the production of new plant tissue, it is equally important that new shoots have time to mature or "harden off" during their first summer season, maximizing their cold tolerance before the onset of winter conditions. Photosynthesis provides the underlying basis for the completion of this growth process. During maturation, individual plant cells develop lignified cell walls, giving the new foliage greater mechanical strength. Needle succulence, the "soft" appearance typical of new growth, declines markedly as the water content of the tissues is reduced, allowing space for ice crystals to form between cells without causing damage; this adaptation is critical because it reduces the susceptibility of new shoots to frost damage. During the final phase of growth, a waxy covering known as a cuticle envelops the needle and substantially reduces evaporative water loss. Needle attrition can occur wherever ice-particle abrasion removes the protective cuticle from the foliage or where an inadequate growing season has failed to allow sufficient time for cuticle development and internal frost-proofing of new growth.

Reproduction

In contrast to pines, which require from two to three growing seasons for cone formation, pollination, and seed maturation, Engelmann spruce and subalpine fir have their reproductive stages compressed into less than four months. The male, pollen-producing conelets burst from their buds in late spring. The succulent, female conelets emerge shortly thereafter, their luminous purplish red scales flared slightly to expose the ovules to wind-borne pollen grains. Following pollination, the cones close their scales and begin a gradual transformation in size and texture, the enclosed seeds ripening during the brief summer growing season. The cones of both species reach maturity in autumn, the scales opening to release the winged seeds to the winds.

Engelmann spruce and subalpine fir require shade, relatively cool temperatures, and a moist seedbed to ensure successful germination and establishment. Seed-based regeneration depends on a favorable sequence of events that includes a good seed crop, adequate wind or animal-aided dispersal to suitable germination sites, and amenable weather conditions during the initial seasons of seedling establishment. Though these conditions are admirably met within the cool, shady, humid environment of the subalpine forest, cone production and seed-based regeneration are considerably less common in the harsh climate of the forest-tundra ecotone. Seedlings that do become established above timberline generally do so in a sheltered microsite, such as in the lee of a rock or within the protection of existing krummholz trees or shrubs. Once established, the seedling must withstand intense sunlight, summer frosts, prolonged periods of drought, frost heaving, snow molds, and browsing damage by small mammals. Successful seedlings often exhibit some sort of beneficial mycorrhizal-rootlet relationship that maximizes the seedling's ability to draw water and nutrients from the soil.

Spiral Grain

Silvery snags, the grain of the wood spiraling upward around the tree, are an elegant presence in old-growth spruce-fir forests. Stripped of bark, these trees reveal the inner geometry of how their cambium (the wood-producing layer) developed over time. As a tree grows, the grain of the wood changes angle because of unequal cell division in the cambium, spiraling to the left when young and then shifting to a right-handed spiral in the outer rings when the tree is larger and older. Biologists believe that the constant angle of the spiral implies genetic control. Adding to the mystery of why a tree's cambium would spiral at all rather than simply grow straight is the fact that trees growing in the Northern Hemisphere spiral mostly to the right, while those in the Southern Hemisphere spiral mostly to the left. Northern Hemisphere tree species grown in the Southern Hemisphere retain their genetically encoded tendency to spiral to the right.

The fire scar on this old-growth Engelmann spruce reveals the cambial spiraling within.

Two hypotheses have been proposed to explain cambial spiraling, one geographic and the other involving an environmentally driven mechanical advantage. It seems most likely, however, that some combination of these two mechanisms provides the most satisfactory answer. In the Northern Hemisphere, more sunlight comes from southerly directions, causing branches on the south side of a tree to grow somewhat longer and leafier. With the prevailing winds coming mostly from the west, the asymmetry of the branches produces a torque or twisting force on the tree trunk, which sets the stage for the spiraling growth pattern we see. The second hypothesis applies to trees growing in windy, mountainous environments, where cambial spiraling clearly adds mechanical strength to the trunk and helps reduce wood fiber breakage from the torsional force of the winds buffeting the tree's crown, an important survival advantage.

Forest Parasites

Witches' Brooms

Anyone who has spent much time in spruce-fir forests has noticed the occasional broomlike masses of stunted and closely packed, sickly looking branches near the top of an Engelmann spruce or a subalpine fir. This bushy proliferation of twigs, which often emits a fetid odor in summer, is called a witches' broom and is the tree's response to an infection caused by a parasitic fungus known as broom rust. Witches' brooms come in all sizes and shapes. Dwarf mistletoes (*Arceuthobium microcarpum*) may also produce witches' brooms, but these proliferations of abnormal branches tend to be smaller and less dramatic than those caused by broom rusts. Like most fungi, rusts reproduce by spores but, in contrast to the familiar mushroom-producing fungi, exhibit a distinctly different life cycle. Broom rusts are among the most complex of all the rusts, producing either four or five spore types and requiring an alternating infection between two nonrelated hosts to complete their life cycle.

The spruce broom rust (*Chrysomyxa arctostaphyli*), which infects Engelmann spruce and Colorado blue spruce, occurs only where kinnikinnick (*Arctostaphylos uva-ursi*), its alternate host, is found in close association. In the case of subalpine fir, the culprit is the fir broom rust (*Melampsorella caryophyllacearum*), and its alternative host is a small wildflower known as chickweed (*Stellaria* spp.); when inhabiting the fir, the fungus produces spores that infect the chickweed, and when inhabiting the chickweed, it produces spores that infect the fir. A witches' broom is an integral part of its tree host, altering branch structure, causing the virtual elimination of cone production by the infected branch, reducing host vigor, and, in severe cases, initiating the destabilization of the forest in which the host is growing.

Snow Molds

Another unusual parasite, a snow fungus (*Herpotrichia* spp.), is responsible for the black, feltlike weft that often envelops the lower branches of conifers newly emerged from the snow. This remarkable fungus thrives in the icy slush of the melting snowpack at temperatures at or below 32°F, its fungal hyphae penetrating and subsequently destroying the needles of its host.

Though extensive infections of *Herpotrichia* can kill small spruce and fir saplings, most infections of mature trees are localized and apparently do little harm to the host. *Herpotrichia* can be especially damaging when it infects the lee side of krummholz islands, where its proliferation is enhanced by the persistence of wind-drifted snow.

Spruce Galls

The strange conelike growth known as a spruce gall, sometimes found on the tips of Engelmann spruce and Colorado blue spruce branches, is caused by an infestation of aphidlike, waxy-tailed insects called adelgids, or woolly aphids. The spruce gall resembles a small greenish purple pineapple in the early stages of development and is easy to identify by its two- to four-inch-long size and its brown, pineconelike appearance at maturity. Adelgids require two hosts, Douglas-fir and spruce, to complete their entire life cycle. Alternating between these two plants, the adelgid's life cycle may take a year or more to complete.

The cycle begins on Douglas-fir in early spring with the laying of eggs on the tree's needles and the production of several generations of adelgids; no galls are produced on Douglas-fir. The feeding activities of the tiny, cottonlike adelgids begin to twist and discolor the needles by late May. By late summer, the adult adelgids that have developed wings fly from their Douglas-fir home to a spruce and deposit eggs that will hatch into immature females that overwinter on the spruce twigs. The wingless adelgids that remained on the Douglas-fir will lay another generation of overwintering eggs amidst the tree's needles. The nymphs overwintering on spruce, on the other hand, mature into adults in spring and lay several hundred eggs near the spruce's new needle buds. These eggs hatch just about the time the needle buds unfurl, and the young nymphs migrate en masse to the new spring growth to feed at the base of the growing needles. Saliva introduced into the plant as a result of the adelgid's feeding activities causes changes in plant development that produce the distinctively shaped spruce gall, which provides a safe, food-rich environment for the developing nymphs. By midsummer, the gall drys out and the chambers open. Winged adult adelgids emerge, flying mostly to the nearest Douglas-fir and begining the entire life cycle anew.

Strategies for Survival above Timberline

Tree Islands

Each tree species responds differently to the harsh environment of the forest-tundra ecotone. Since photosynthetic performance decreases with increasing elevation, most spruce and fir trees above timberline fail to produce cones or, if they do, produce cones with nonviable seeds. Instead, these trees must rely on their ability to reproduce by asexual means, through layering. Though not all rooted branches will develop erect stems, each layered stem has the potential to form a new tree with the same genetic makeup as its parent. In many cases, these layered branches form circular groups of trees or, where winds are especially strong and one-directional, are often elongated in the downwind direction. Limber pine and bristlecone pine are more tolerant of winter desiccation and wind, often developing into erect trees on sites where spruce and fir persist only as prostrate forms. Growth is remarkably slow; a spruce or fir with a trunk diameter of just a few inches may be several hundred years old. These trees, majestic spires in the subalpine forest, are dramatically stunted and grow more or less asymmetrically above timberline, assuming a variety of growth forms and distributional patterns that mirror habitat conditions.

Tree islands capitalize on the strategy of safety in numbers, the clustering of trees providing increased wind protection, mutual mechanical support, ameliorated temperature extremes, higher humidity, and a "black body" (heat-absorbing) effect resulting in earlier snowmelt. In fact, tree thickets can be so dense that they are all but impossible to walk through, except during the winter when they are packed so full of wind-drifted snow that you can walk or ski right over them. Most tree islands consist of one or two tree species and several shrubs. They may be large or small in areal extent, their shapes reflecting the severity and character of the local winds. The persistent, largely one-directional winds that blast these dense thickets, pruning away bark, branches, and foliage from the windward sides and giving the crowns of the tallest trees a distinctly one-sided appearance, govern the orientation of tree islands. Where the winter snowpack affords a protective, sheltered environment, krummholz trees develop a fanlike "skirt" of branches. Cushionlike or prostrate forms are typical of the most severe environments, their wind-pruned surfaces resembling the work of an overzealous bonsai gardener. On gentle slopes, the combination of strong westerly winds and site-specific snow distribution patterns often results in the development of ribbon forests. These distinctive formations consist of multiple parallel bands of stunted trees, some bands measuring more than 300 feet in length and each elongated parallel to the prevailing wind.

Tree island showing leeward flagging of upright Engelmann spruce and the fanlike "skirt" of branches around the base.

Slow downwind "migration" of tree islands occurs where attrition on the windward side is outpaced by growth and layering (asexual) regeneration on the leeward side. Migrating tree islands can be identified by the trail of dead stems and branches left behind as the islands "move" downwind across the forest-tundra ecotone. Research in the Colorado Front Range suggests that some tree islands are moving eastward from their origination point at the rate of several centimeters each year. The dead stems and branches that remain on the windward sides of the trees provide protection for the viable portions, and their removal for campfires or as curiosities can seriously impact the survival of a tree island.

Descriptions of Common Plants

Trees

Engelmann Spruce, *Picea engelmannii.* Engelmann spruce ranges from British Columbia south to New Mexico and Arizona. This conifer is identified by the thin, scaly bark, dark green, sharp-pointed, four-sided needles, and the fine, soft hairs that envelop its twigs; the needles of the closely related **blue spruce** (*Picea pungens*) are sharper and less flexible and typically have a steely blue color. Immature female cones are purplish red; mature cones are brown and papery and hang downward from the branches, sometimes for a year or more after seed dissemination has occurred. Engelmann spruce is relatively long-lived, with many individuals exceeding 450 years of age; in the Southern Rockies, the oldest known spruce is at least 600 years old.

Subalpine fir, *Abies lasiocarpa.* Subalpine fir has the broadest distribution of all North American firs and occurs from the Yukon to southern Arizona and southwestern New Mexico. This tree can be identified at a distance by its narrow, pencil-point crown and by the upright, purple-black cones that decorate the topmost branches. The needles are stalkless, flat, and comparatively blunt, with whitish lines both above and below. On younger trees, the thin, gray bark is patterned with horizontal ridges and conspicuously dotted with resin blisters. On older trees, the bark is broken into narrowly fissured and irregular grayish brown scales. The female cones are borne on the upper side of the topmost branches and remain upright throughout their two-month-long development period. As they reach maturity in early autumn, the cones turn from dark purple to brown and start to fall apart scale by scale, releasing their winged seeds and leaving behind a black, spiky cone core, or "matchstick."

Shrubs

Blueberry (or Huckleberry), *Vaccinium* spp. These diminutive, bright green shrubs are represented by several species in the Southern Rockies, all identified by their small size, alternate arrangement of branches and leaves, narrowly ovate leaves, pinkish urn-shaped flowers, and small red or purple fruits. The most easily identified species is broom blueberry

(*V. scoparium*), with its tiny green leaves, dense branching, and red fruit; the myrtle blueberry (*V. myrtillus*) has larger leaves, a more open and less densely branched habit, and purplish blue fruit. Blueberry flowers are unusual in that the pollen-producing portion, or anther, of each stamen is drawn out into two narrow tubules with a pore at each end. The viscous pollen is extruded through these tubules as the anthers mature, very much like toothpaste out of a tube, and adheres readily to visiting insect pollinators. The fruits are small, tart, and delicious; good fruit years are sporadic and weather dependent.

Buffaloberry, *Shepherdia canadensis*. Buffaloberry is a member of the oleaster family (Elaeagnaceae) and is found from Canada and Alaska south along the Rocky Mountains to central New Mexico. This shrub is readily identified by its opposite leaves and branches, elliptical green leaves, rust-colored scales on the undersides of the leaves and terminal buds, and orange-red berries. The male and female flowers bloom on separate plants, the diminutive and petal-less flowers appearing in early spring, before the leaves emerge. Native people in the northern portions of buffaloberry's range made a froth of the ripe berries that is, to my taste, bitter and inedible in all respects. Bears, foxes, and a few other omnivores relish the berries when available.

Red Elderberry, *Sambucus microbotrys*. This lovely shrub, a member of the honeysuckle family (Caprifoliaceae), is distributed from British Columbia south throughout much of the United States. A common species in moist forests, red elderberry is identified by its compound leaves, pyramidal clusters of cream-colored flowers, and terminal bunches of red berries. Each dark green, pinnately compound leaf consists of a main axis with five to nine finely toothed leaflets; two leaves arise at each node, or attachment point, along the stem. The berries are favored by birds and small mammals but are considered moderately toxic to humans.

Wildflowers

Wood Nymph, *Moneses uniflora*. This diminutive and beautiful member of the wintergreen family (Pyrolaceae) occurs widely in the boreal forests of the Northern Hemisphere and is found in moist subalpine forests throughout the Rocky Mountains. Though frequently overlooked because of its small size, the solitary, nodding, and starlike flower, the basal and oval-shaped leaves, and the distinctive lily-of-the-valley fragrance of its flowers readily identifies the wood nymph.

Curled Lousewort, *Pedicularis racemosa.* Curled lousewort is common in upper montane and subalpine forests from Canada south to New Mexico and California. This species is readily identified by its white sickle-shaped flowers, finely toothed, lanceolate leaves, and multistemmed growth habit. The flowers are distinctive because the upper two petals of the corolla join to resemble the beak of a parrot and the lower three petals are fused to form a slightly twisted lower lip. The leaves and stems often exhibit a pronounced reddish coloration, which intensifies with the coming of autumn and adds color to the forest floor.

Parry's Primrose, *Primula parryi.* Though not a species of dense forests, Parry's primrose is found along streambanks within the subalpine forest and in the forest-tundra ecotone. This showy wildflower, a large-flowered member of the primrose family (Primulaceae), is found from southern Montana and Idaho south through the Rocky Mountains to northern New Mexico and Arizona. Parry's primrose, also known as alpine primrose, is a robust plant with spatulate leaves that arise from a basal rosette and stout stalks that terminate in a clustered raceme of yellow-centered, rose pink flowers. Each individual flower consists of a five-lobed, funnel-shaped corolla that opens out to expose its bright yellow center.

Parry's primrose.

Jacobs Ladder, *Polemonium pulcherrimum* ssp. *delicatum.* This member of the phlox family (Polemoniaceae) is identified by its delicate blue, bell-shaped flowers and the skunklike odor of its compound leaves. Jacobs ladder derives its name from the ladderlike arrangement of small leaflets that make up each compound leaf.

Globeflower, *Trollius albiflorus*. Globeflower is common in moist forest openings in the subalpine forest, where it often grows in association with marsh-marigold and Parry's primrose. It is readily identified by its long-petioled, palmate leaves and its buttercuplike cream or pale yellow flowers. The flowers are unusual in that there are small, nectar-bearing petals between the multiple golden stamens and the sepals.

Heart-leaved Twayblade, *Listera cordata*. This tiny orchid is common in boreal forest habitats from the subarctic of North America south through the Pacific Northwest and the Rocky Mountains to northern New Mexico. Heart-leaved twayblade is readily identified by its small size (less than eight inches tall), its two heart-shaped leaves arising opposite each other at the midpoint of the flowering stalk, and the few-flowered inflorescence. Each flower is small and greenish or slightly reddish in color with a lower lip split into two narrow prongs. Following fertilization of the flowers, the seeds ripen quickly; it is common to find twayblades with both fresh-looking blooms and empty seed capsules from the previous season.

Brownie Lady's Slipper, *Cypripedium fasciculatum*. Brownie lady's slipper is found in subalpine forests in the Rocky Mountains and the Pacific Northwest. Its robust growth form, multiple ovate leaves, and characteristic inflorescence with several nodding purple-brown flowers identify this orchid. Each flower has a bulbous, pouchlike lip and is topped by three slender purplish green petals.

Common Plants of the Spruce-Fir Forest and the Forest-Tundra Ecotone

Trees

Aspen, quaking, *Populus tremuloides*
Fir, corkbark, *Abies arizonica*
  subalpine, *A. lasiocarpa*
  white, *A. concolor*
Pine, Rocky Mountain bristlecone, *Pinus aristata*

limber, *P. flexilis*

Rocky Mountain lodgepole, *P. contorta* ssp. *latifolia*

Spruce, Colorado blue, *Picea pungens*

Engelmann, *P. engelmannii*

Shrubs

Birch, bog, *Betula glandulosa*

Blueberry, broom, *Vaccinium scoparium*

dwarf, *V. cespitosum*

myrtle, *V. myrtillus*

Buffaloberry, *Shepherdia canadensis*

Cinquefoil, shrubby, *Pentaphylloides floribunda*

Cranberry, bush, *Viburnum edule*

Currant, Colorado, *Ribes coloradense* and *R. wolfii*

Elderberry, red, *Sambucus microbotrys*

Juniper, common, *Juniperus communis* ssp. *alpina*

Kinnikinnick, *Arctostaphylos uva-ursi*

Mountainlover, *Paxistima myrsinites*

Pipsissewa, *Chimaphila umbellata* ssp. *occidentalis*

Willow, *Salix* spp.

Wildflowers

Arnica, broad-leaf, *Arnica latifolia*

Avens, alpine, *Acomastylis* (formerly *Geum*) *rossii*

Bishop's Cap, *Mitella pentandra*

Bistort, American, *Bistorta bistortoides*

Chickweed, *Stellaria umbellata*

Chiming bells, *Mertensia ciliata*

Coneflower, black, *Rudbeckia occidentalis* var. *montana*

Daisy, subalpine, *Erigeron peregrinus*

Gilia, scarlet, *Ipomopsis aggregata*

Globeflower, *Trollius albiflorus*

Hellebore, false (or Cornhusk Lily), *Veratrum tenuipetalum*

Jacobs Ladder, *Polemonium pulcherrimum* ssp. *delicatum*

Lady's Slipper, brownie, *Cypripedium fasciculatum*

Orchid, green bog, *Coeloglossum viride*

  northern green bog, *Limnorchis*(formerly *Habenaria*) *hyperborea*

  white bog, *L.* (formerly *Habenaria*) *dilatata*

  lady's tresses, *Spiranthes romanzoffiana*

  rattlesnake-plantain, *Goodyera repens*

Twayblade, heart-leaved, *Listera cordata*

Larkspur, *Delphinium barbeyi*

Lousewort, curled, *Pedicularis racemosa*

  grays, *P. grayi*

Marsh-marigold, *Psychrophila* (formerly *Caltha*) *leptosepala*

Monkshood, *Aconitum columbianum*

Paintbrush, rose, *Castilleja rhexifolia*

Primrose, Parry's, *Primula parryi*

Sunflower, aspen, *Helianthella quinquenervis*

Twinflower, *Linnaea borealis*

Wintergreen, lesser, *Pyrola minor*

  one-sided, *Orthilia secunda*

  swamp (or Pink Wintergreen), *Pyrola rotundifolia* ssp. *asarifolia*

Wood Nymph, *Moneses uniflora*

Fungi

Bird's Nest, common, *Crucibulum laeve*

Boletus, *Boletus edulis*

Coral Mushroom, orange, *Ramaria largentii*

  pixy, *Clavicorona pyxidata*

Earth Tongue, *Neolecta vitellina*

Earth Tongue, clustered, *Cudonia circinans*

Eyelash Cup, *Scutellinia scutellata*

False Morel, hooded, *Gyromitra infula*

Gomphidius, slimy-capped, *Gomphidus glutinosus*

Jellies, orange, *Guepiniopsis alpinus*

Lacterius, orange, *Lacterius olympianus*

Purple Fairy Fingers, *Claveria purpurea*

Russula, emetic, *Russula emetica*

  shrimp, *R. xerampelina*

Environment and Adaptation: Animals of the Spruce-Fir Forests

Animals living in spruce-fir forests year-round must cope with extreme cold, deep snows (which impede travel and foraging), and a short growing season (which limits both the abundance and diversity of food resources). Not surprisingly, the number of species in these high-elevation forests is considerably fewer than that found in forest-edge habitats or in lower-elevation forests. Spruce-fir forests provide critical habitat for boreal species such as the northern three-toed woodpecker, gray jay, pine grosbeak, red crossbill, mountain chickadee, red-breasted nuthatch, chickaree, red-backed vole, marten, and snowshoe hare. Each of these species has adapted to these forests in ways that biologists are continuing to explore.

The arrival of spring and the beginning of the breeding season mark an increase in both species diversity and abundance. The advertisement songs of hermit thrushes, Townsend's solitaires, mountain chickadees, and ruby-crowned kinglets can be heard above the nasal chatterings of nuthatches and the drumming of woodpeckers. In the tree islands that fringe the forest's upper limits, white-crowned sparrows chirp warnings from the tops of flagged trees. Elk and mule deer follow the retreating line of the snowpack, taking advantage of the lush herbage to be found in forest openings. In the heart of the forest, swift-flying predators such as the northern goshawk and the sharp-shinned hawk dart through the maze of branches in pursuit of their prey. Red foxes move silently along game trails, watchful for the unwary showshoe hare or vole. A marten races along a spruce branch, its unwelcome presence announced by the strident chattering of a chickaree. Unfortunately, the large predators that once roamed these dense forests, the grizzly bear, Canada lynx, and the wolverine, have been extirpated in the Southern Rockies. A recent reintroduction program for the lynx is currently underway but has shown only limited success to date.

Plant-Animal Interactions

After a severe winter or when high populations of snowshoe hares or voles are present, it is common to see shrubs and saplings that have been overbrowsed or debarked. Browsing pressure poses a serious problem to woody plants that are already at a disadvantage as a result of the short growing season. Many such plants combat heavy winter browsing through a process called compensatory growth: vigorous sprouting at the stump or the stimulation of resting buds on surviving branches to produce new shoots with an abundance of larger, chlorophyll-rich leaves.

Another antiherbivore strategy is clearly defensive and involves the production of chemical compounds that make the plant's tissues less palatable and even toxic to herbivores. Some plants concentrate the production of these defensive compounds during the early, or juvenile, stages of growth or when heavy browsing initates the regrowth of juvenile shoots. Other plants that grow slowly have a limited capacity for compensatory growth and thus maintain their defensive chemical arsenal throughout all life stages.

When resin- or phenol-rich plant tissues are consumed in sufficient quantities, they can seriously interfere with the digestive and metabolic processes necessary for survival. Herbivores tend to be very selective in their browsing habits, often choosing less-chemically-defended genotypes of a preferred browse species. Snowshoe hares appear to be especially sensitive to the resin content of their preferred browse, selecting more-mature twigs and leaves rather than the more resin-enriched juvenile growth stages. Feeding experiments with captive hares have shown that they will lose weight rapidly and die if fed a monospecific diet of resinous, juvenile-growth-stage twigs. On the other hand, blue grouse and white-tailed ptarmigan often subsist for several months on a monospecific diet of resin- or phenol-rich leaves and buds. How, then, are some animals able to cope physiologically with plant chemical defenses while others must avoid these substances? Blue grouse are apparently able to adapt to a moderately toxic diet, largely through the ability to concentrate and detoxify resins in the caecum and to excrete these substances in the form of caecal droppings. Behavioral observations, however, indicate that such an adaptation requires greater expenditure of energy than does the simple avoidance of heavily defended tissues.

Adaptations to Cold and Deep Snow

Animals that overwinter in the spruce-fir forest adapt to seasonal environmental change through a combination of behavioral, morphological, and physiological mechanisms. The chapter on snow in the first half of this book includes a discussion of several of these adaptations. The unusually broad and flexible hind feet of the snowshoe hare, the dense mat of winter fur that envelops the feet of the marten, and the stiff tufts of feathers that surround the toes of the white-tailed ptarmigan provide floatation and dramatically improve the ability of these animals to move about on the snow.

Mechanisms for maintaining normal body temperature are of critical importance to the overwintering success of both mammals and birds. The temperature at which it becomes necessary for an animal to increase its metabolic rate in order to balance heat loss to the environment is called the lower critical temperature, or LCT. The LCT varies from one species to another and tends to adjust seasonally in most species, generally through changes in insulation thickness. Some animals, such as the chickaree, undergo surprisingly little seasonal LCT adjustment and must rely instead on good nest insulation and high food consumption. The red fox and the porcupine, on the other hand, achieve a substantial drop in their winter LCTs as a result of increased underfur insulation. Gray jays, too, rely on the insulative benefits of their loose, thick feathering, which they can fluff to trap a protective layer of air around the body.

At high elevations, weasels survive at what appears to be the limit of their metabolic capacity. Their unique hunting niche depends on the ability to search through narrow runways and rock piles to find hidden prey unavailable to other predators. Though remarkable for its prowess in tight-squeeze situations, the weasel, with its long, thin body, exposes a relatively large surface area to the air. Weasels are almost constantly expending energy on heat production. Even their resting metabolism is nearly twice that of other mammals of similar mass. Without sufficient food to fuel their metabolic needs, weasels die of starvation after only one or two days. To minimize energy consumption during the winter months, weasels restrict their hunting activities to just a few hours out of each day. Since hunting requires three to five times more energy than resting, time spent in a snug nest prolongs the amount of time the weasel can survive without eating.

In preparation for winter, many animals accumulate reserves of brown fat, a kind of fatty tissue that provides the fuel for metabolic heat production. Birds lack brown fat and, when not generating heat through the muscle activity of flight, must rely on shivering thermogenesis to maintain normal body temperature. Most cold-climate species exhibit an increased capacity for shivering thermogenesis in winter resulting from a seasonal increase in the lipid known as triglyceride and a reduction in the rate of carbohydrate depletion. Chickadees carry this adaptive process one step further, undergoing a torporlike lowering of body temperature triggered by decreasing ambient temperatures. By reducing its body temperature during periods of inactivity, the chickadee effectively minimizes the temperature gradient between body and air, substantially reducing the amount of energy needed to maintain a stable body temperature.

Long-tailed weasel.

There can be little doubt that a persistent snow cover is the primary selective pressure that led to the evolution of seasonal color change in species such as the snowshoe hare and the long-tailed weasel. The debate over the adaptive benefits of white coloration, however, is represented by two opposing points of view. One suggests that the advantages of cryptic coloration for both predator and prey stimulate the seasonal color change. The other relates the issue to energetics and the fact that white coloration serves to minimize heat exchange with the environment. Unfortunately, the arguments in favor of either point of view are inconclusive. In both cases, changes in temperature and photoperiod appear to play a role in initiating color change to coincide with annual changes in snow cover.

Life Histories of Selected Animals

Mammals

Snowshoe Hare, *Lepus americanus*. This lovely hare is about midway in size between a cottontail and a jackrabbit and is distinguished by its unusually broad hind feet, comparatively short ears, and, in winter, white pelage and black-tipped ears; the transitional pelage typical of early spring and late fall is distinctly dappled, changing to a rusty grayish brown during the summer. Snowshoe hares are boreal forest mammals and are associated with densely forested habitat from the Arctic Circle southward along the principal mountain ranges to Tennessee, New Mexico, and central California. Snowshoe hares are herbivorous, nocturnal, and relatively solitary, resting by day in shallow depressions excavated beneath dense shrubbery or under fallen trees. Breeding occurs from March through August, and females generally produce two litters of precocial young a year; juvenile hares are extremely vulnerable to predators such as chickarees, weasels, and martens. Young hares reach adult size between three and five months of age but are unable to breed until the following season.

Snowshoe hare.

Marten, *Martes americana.* The marten is distinguished by its catlike size (one to three pounds), yellowish underside, rich brown upperparts, rounded ears, and bushy, cylindrical tail. This boreal forest specialist is found in lodgepole pine, spruce-fir, and alpine habitats in the Southern Rockies. Martens are mostly nocturnal and solitary, spending daylight hours and severe weather periods resting in tree holes or abandoned squirrel nests; their home range may be as much as four square miles. Active year-round, these arboreal carnivores are adept at hunting in trees for red squirrels, birds, and bird's eggs or on the ground for juvenile snowshoe hares, voles, and other small mammals. During winter, martens take advantage of fallen logs and branches in deep snow as portals to the undersnow runways of mice and voles. Martens are curious and may seem unafraid of humans, often approaching quite closely and emitting a "chuckling" vocalization. Female martens begin breeding at about two years of age and will breed once a year, producing a litter of between one and five kits a year. Mating occurs in summer, but like most mustelids, implantation is delayed for six to eight months. Altricial at birth, young martens develop rapidly and leave the nest at two months of age. Longevity in this species may exceed fifteen years.

Long-tailed Weasel, *Mustela frenata.* This slender-bodied mustelid is easily distinguished from the marten by its size (twelve inches from nose to tip of tail), bounding gait, and fur that is chestnut brown above and golden buff below; winter pelage is white except for the black-tipped tail. The **short-tailed weasel** (*Mustela erminea*) is about half the size of the long-tailed weasel but quite similar overall. In the Southern Rockies, the long-tailed weasel is common in a variety of habitats but is especially prevalent in rocky areas and along streams. Weasels prey mostly on small mammals and ground-nesting birds. The entrance to a weasel burrow is often marked with accumulations of scat. Weasels have scent glands that make them unpalatable to most predators. Long-tailed weasels mate in summer, with ovulation induced by copulation. Implantation of the embryo, however, is delayed until the following spring. A litter of altricial young is born in an underground nest chamber in April. Young weasels develop rapidly, and females are able to begin breeding their first summer.

Birds

Blue Grouse, *Dendragapus obscurus*. This chicken-sized bird is distinguished from other grouse by the sooty gray tail with lighter gray band and mottled gray-brown plumage; males have a yellowish orange comb over each eye. In the Southern Rockies, blue grouse occur in a wide variety of conifer, mixed conifer-aspen, and shrubland habitats, retreating to dense forests of lodgepole pine and spruce-fir during fall and winter. During the courtship period in spring, which peaks from mid-April to late May, males engage in conspicuous displays that include exposing and inflating their yellow, feather-ringed neck crests, strutting, tail fanning, drumming, audible wing-fluttering, and erection of the neck ruff feathers. Wing-fluttering can be heard up to a quarter of a mile away; drumming consists of rhythmic hooting that resembles someone playing on tom-toms. Males are promiscuous, directing their courtship toward any female that comes close. Following mating, females construct a well-concealed nest on the ground; females incubate the eggs and rear the young alone. Following fledging, young grouse remain with the mother until early autumn. Blue grouse are solitary during the winter but may occasionally form small unisexual groups.

Northern Saw-whet Owl, *Aegolius acadicus*. This strikingly colored owl is identified by its robinlike size, yellow eyes, prominent reddish streaking on the breast, white-spotted wings, lack of ear tufts, and reddish facial disk. Northern saw-whet owls are found from northeastern Alaska across Canada and southward to northern Mexico; in the Southern Rockies, the species is most common in dense coniferous forests and riparian woodlands. Saw-whet owls are nocturnal hunters of small mammals; birds and insects may be taken when available. Saw-whet owls are cavity nesters and may begin defending breeding territory as early as February. The species roosts during the day, selecting a site close to its nesting cavity during the breeding season or in dense evergreens during the winter. Vocalizations consist primarily of a repetitious series of whoops said to resemble the sound of a saw blade being sharpened; vocalizations intensify in April and May, ending in June. Nests with young are reported in mid-May, with fledging by late May in most areas. In some cases, females may leave the nest permanently after the nestlings are fully feathered, the male tending the first brood while she seeks a second mate and nests again; this mating system is called sequential polyandry.

Three-toed Woodpecker, *Picoides tridactylus.* The three-toed woodpecker is distinguished from other woodpeckers by its black-and-white, heavily barred sides and variously barred back and, in the male, by the yellow head patch. Though closely tied to the boreal forests of North America and Eurasia, this species is extending its range south into high-elevation spruce-dominated habitat along the Rocky Mountains. Three-toed woodpeckers are insectivorous, concentrating on wood-boring beetles and bark insects; as insect infestations increase, so do the numbers of three-toed woodpeckers. Signs of feasting on bark beetles—a conspicuous mulch of bark plates and wood chips on the ground surrounding a productive feeding tree—are the best evidence of the local occurrence of this uncommon woodpecker. Males attract females by drumming and then performing a head-swaying display. Nests are excavated in snags or other suitable trees and are lined with wood chips. Both the male and female incubate the eggs and rear the young; the male roosts nightly in the nest throughout incubation. Following fledging, families remain together for the summer.

Gray Jay, *Perisoreus canadensis.* Gray jays are identified by their allover gray coloring and darker gray backs and wings. Variously known as the whiskey-jack or camp-robber, the gray jay is notoriously tame and bold and will often take food—with or without permission—out of the hand in the Southern Rockies. This boreal forest specialist is a year-round resident of high-elevation coniferous forests. Vocalizations are highly variable and may include a whistled *wheeoo* and a lower-pitched *chuck*. Gray jays are insectivorous, gleaning insects from the bark and foliage of conifers. This species is often observed caching food, in the form of a saliva-permeated bolus, which sustains the jay during the winter months and provides food for the young, which are born in early spring. During courtship, the male gray jay employs whisper-singing and ritualized feeding of the female. A bulky but well-woven nest is typically constructed on a horizontal branch; insulative materials cached the previous season enable nest building while snow still covers the ground. The pair cooperates in the rearing of the young.

Red-breasted Nuthatch, *Sitta canadensis*. This sparrow-sized bird is distinguished from other nuthatches by its rust-colored underparts, blackish cap, facial stripes, and slate-blue upperparts; females and juveniles have paler underparts. In the Southern Rockies, this species is most common in high-altitude spruce-fir forests but may be found in both mixed-coniferous forests and deciduous woodlands. The nuthatch's call is a nasal *anck-anck-anck* resembling the sound of a toy horn. Red-breasted nuthatches are insectivorous during much of the year and resemble small woodpeckers in the way that they search the bark for food; this species concentrates its foraging activities in the top one-third of a tree and commonly descends a tree headfirst, depending on its feet rather than its tail for support. The winter diet consists largely of conifer seeds, with irruptive migrations occurring when the cone crop is poor. Courtship behavior by the male involves a mixture of wing-drooping and swaying displays punctuated by singing; mated pairs remain together through the winter. The red-breasted nuthatch excavates its own nest cavity, surrounding the entrance with a sticky mass of pitch that is maintained throughout the nesting period.

Ruby-crowned Kinglet, *Regulus calendula*. The grayish olive upperparts, dusky breast, two white wing bars, and silvery eye ring identify this diminutive bird; the male's red crown patch is seldom visible except during the breeding season. In the Southern Rockies, this boreal forest specialist is a common summer resident of spruce-fir and other types of dense coniferous forests, moving south to lowland sites in winter. Kinglets are insectivorous, gleaning insects mostly from the foliage but occasionally catching them on the wing. These tiny birds are extremely active while foraging, jumping and turning repeatedly as they move about the outer foliage of trees and shrubs. The territorial and courtship song is melodious and ends on a series of descending *tew* notes. The nest consists of a feather-lined cup woven of grasses and moss, suspended from a horizontal branch by spiderwebs. The female incubates the eggs, but both parents feed the brood.

Hermit Thrush, *Catharus guttatus.* The speckled breast, olive-brown upperparts, reddish tail, white eye ring, and the nervous twitching of the wings identify this sparrow-sized bird, renowned for its beautiful flutelike song. In the Southern Rockies, this boreal forest specialist is a common summer resident of high-elevation spruce-fir and mixed-coniferous forests. Hermit thrushes are shy and somewhat inconspicuous, except for their beautiful song resonating throughout the forest at dawn and dusk. Their foraging style consists of short, scuffling hops across the forest floor; thrushes supplement their insect diet with berries and other fruit as they become available. Hermit thrushes nest on the ground or, occasionally, a short distance off the ground; the nest is a grass- and fiber-woven cup, often with a middle layer of mud. The female incubates the eggs, but both sexes rear the young.

Common birds of the subalpine forest: hermit thrush (left), ruby-crowned kinglet (right).

Common birds of the forest-tundra ecotone: gray jay (left), white-crowned sparrow (right).

Pine Grosbeak, *Pinicola enucleator*. This robin-sized bird is identified by its plump appearance, dark tail, two white wing bars, and stubby, strongly down-curved beak; males of the species have an allover wash of rosy red, whereas females and immature males have olive-yellow heads. In the Southern Rockies, this boreal forest specialist is associated year-round with high-elevation spruce-fir and mixed-coniferous forests. Pine grosbeaks forage on conifer and other seeds, ranging widely during times of food shortage. When moving from one foraging area to another, their whistling calls and deeply undulating, roller-coasterlike flight styles are reliable field marks. During the breeding season, grosbeaks develop a pair of pouches below the tongue for transporting food to the young. Nesting pairs remain relatively solitary until their broods have fledged, but then form gregarious, loose flocks as they forage through the forest in late summer.

White-crowned Sparrow, *Zonotrichia leucophrys*. This large sparrow is identified by its black-and-white-striped crown (juveniles have buff-and-brown head stripes) and its strongly streaked back and wings. In the Southern Rockies, white-crowned sparrows may be present in a variety of grassland and brushy habitats during migration but are most common in the forest-tundra ecotone during the breeding season. This sparrow is opportunistic, feeding on insects, seeds, flower buds, and moss capsules as available; most feeding occurs on the ground. The song consists of one or more whistled notes followed by a distinctive twittering twill; the alarm call is a loud *pink* or *tseep*. Nesting occurs on the ground or low in a shrub, in a site chosen by the female. The male feeds the female while she incubates the eggs, but the female normally feeds the young during the first few days after hatching; males may assume the majority of the care and feeding of the young while the female begins a second nest.

Common Animals of the Spruce-Fir Forest and Forest-Tundra Ecotone

Mammals

Bear, black, *Ursus americanus*
Bobcat, *Lynx rufus*
Chipmunk, least, *Tamias minimus*
Cottontail, mountain (or Nuttall's), *Sylvilagus nuttallii*
Deer, mule, *Odocoileus hemionus*
Elk (or Wapiti), *Cervus elaphus*
Ermine (or Short-tailed Weasel), *Mustela erminea*
Fox, red, *Vulpes vulpes*
Hare, snowshoe, *Lepus americanus*
Lynx, *Lynx lynx*
Marten, *Martes americana*
Mouse, deer, *Peromyscus maniculatus*
Pocket Gopher, northern, *Thomomys talpoides*
Porcupine, common, *Erethizon dorsatum*
Shrew, montane, *Sorex monticolus*
Squirrel, chickaree (or Red or Pine Squirrel), *Tamiasciurus hudsonicus*
    golden-mantled ground, *Spermophilus lateralis*
Vole, montane, *Microtus montanus*
    southern red-backed, *Clethrionomys gapperi*
Weasel, long-tailed, *Mustela frenata*

Birds

Chickadee, mountain, *Parus gambeli*
Creeper, brown, *Certhia americana*
Crossbill, red, *Loxia curvirostra*
Finch, Cassin's, *Carpodacus cassinii*
Flycatcher, olive-sided, *Contopus borealis*
Goshawk, northern, *Accipiter gentilis*
Grosbeak, pine, *Pinicola enucleator*
Grouse, blue, *Dendragapus obscurus*
Hawk, sharp-shinned, *Accipiter striatus*
Jay, gray, *Perisoreus canadensis*
Steller's, *Cyanocitta stelleri*
Junco, dark-eyed, *Junco hyemalis*
Kinglet, golden-crowned, *Regulus satrapa*
ruby-crowned, *R. calendula*
Nutcracker, Clark's, *Nucifraga columbiana*
Nuthatch, red-breasted, *Sitta canadensis*
white-breasted, *S. carolinensis*
Owl, boreal, *Aegolius funereus*
northern pygmy, *Glaucidium gnoma*
northern saw-whet, *A. acadicus*
Ptarmigan, white-tailed, *Lagopus leucurus*
Solitaire, Townsend's, *Myadestes townsendi*
Sparrow, white-crowned, *Zonotrichia leucophrys*
Thrush, hermit, *Catharus guttatus*
Warbler, Wilson's, *Wilsonia pusilla*
Woodpecker, hairy, *Picoides villosus*
three-toed, *P. tridactylus*

Islands in the Sky: Alpine Tundra

American bistort flourishes on Toll Ridge, Indian Peaks Wilderness Area.

Alpine tundra provides a surprising counterpoint to the rugged, ice-etched massifs of the Southern Rockies. With the coming of summer, alpine meadows are opulent with the colors of wildflowers: yellow, forget-me-not blue, magenta, periwinkle, and rose. Snowbanks still linger along lee slopes, their melting edges fringed by chrome-yellow snow buttercups. Hidden among the willows at the edge of a meltwater pool, a white-tailed ptarmigan clucks softly to her wandering chicks. A short distance upslope, a marmot basks in sunshine, its toast-brown body pressed so closely to the sun-warmed boulder it appears boneless in repose. Nearby, a nasal *eek-eek, eek-eek* reveals the presence of a pika in the labyrinthine corridors of the talus, its carefully harvested pile of bistort and mountain avens air-drying beneath an overhanging rock. High above, cloud shadows dance across the tundra uplands and a strong gust of wind sends a flock of rosy finches scudding downvalley. Tonight, as alpine glow fades from the highest peaks, the male ptarmigan's hauntingly beautiful flight song—*ku-ku-KIIII-KIIERR*—will greet the stars.

In less than two months, summer's green ease will give way to the frost-burnished colors of autumn: copper, russet, and Byzantine gold. The days will shorten quickly, temperatures will drop, and the pulse of life will change; some animals will leave, others must endure whatever comes their way. Winter's arrival transforms the tundra, enveloping everything that it touches in a burka of sparkling white, wind-sculpted anew with each passing storm. For both plants and animals, life here is lived on the edge; those that survive do so at their own peril.

Ecological Distribution

The word *tundra* is Russian and means "land of no trees," by definition a marshy expanse of grassland with areas of permanently frozen ground. It was first used to describe Arctic regions and the distinctive, cold-adapted vegetation associated with lands north of the Arctic Circle. Because of the physiognomic similarities between Arctic plant communities and those found above treelimit on mountains south of the Arctic Circle, plant ecologists refer to these more southerly high-elevation counterparts as alpine tundra.

Alpine tundra ecosystems are found on high mountains throughout the Southern Rockies, extending from treelimit at between 11,200 and 12,000 feet to mountain summits exceeding 14,000 feet. The lower limit of the alpine zone corresponds approximately to the 50°F isotherm for the warmest summer month and is variable from one area to another depending on local environmental and microclimatic factors. There is a general decrease in the elevation of treelimit from south to north along the Southern Rockies. In the absence of a clearly defined forest-tundra ecotone, the lower limit of alpine tundra coincides with timberline and may include isolated patches of subalpine vegetation.

Physical Environment

The alpine zone is defined by extremes: high solar radiation, cold temperatures, and strong winds. Due to the heterogeneity of most alpine areas, great environmental contrasts often occur within short distances and within short time spans. In contrast to temperate environments, where the effects of climatic factors on physical, chemical, and biological processes are somewhat muted and difficult to isolate, the role of climate in shaping the alpine environment is readily apparent. Despite similarities with the Arctic in terms of mean annual temperatures and snow cover duration, several features clearly differentiate midlatitude alpine climates from those of the Arctic. Midlatitude alpine areas experience both diurnal and seasonal differences in solar radiation, whereas the Arctic receives virtually no solar radiation during the six-month span of the Arctic winter; the twenty-four-hour photoperiod of the Arctic summer results in a milder growing season climate overall. Because of their high elevations, however, alpine areas receive intense solar radiation on clear days throughout the growing season, which tends to equalize the total annual radiation input each area receives.

Alpine Temperatures

Cool summer temperatures are the main reason that trees do not grow in Arctic and alpine tundra environments. In the Southern Rockies, the length of the alpine growing (frost-free) season averages about fifty days; daytime temperatures during the summer seldom rise above the high sixties. The alpine temperature regime is subject to highly localized variations resulting from slope and microtopographic differences. For example, while the air temperature a few feet above the ground may make you shiver, the temperature at or near the ground surface, in the zone where plants grow, will be considerably warmer. Alpine plants themselves may play an important role in modifying the air temperatures of their microenvironments. The temperature inside a lilac-colored flower, for example, may exceed that of the surrounding air by several degrees and is considerably higher than that found within a more reflective white flower.

Precipitation

In contrast to most alpine areas, the low annual precipitation associated with Arctic regions rivals that of many deserts. Annual precipitation in the alpine tundra is highly variable but averages around forty inches, most falling as snow during the winter months. During the summer, late-lying and permanent snowfields are common in many alpine areas and are especially prominent where strong winds cause substantial redistribution of winter snow. In sites adjacent to persistent snowbanks, meltwater may be present in abundance throughout much of the growing season; plants growing under such conditions must be adapted to cold, saturated soils and to the rill and gully erosion typical of such sites. Ridges and areas blown free of snow, on the other hand, often experience drought conditions winter and summer.

Wind

Wind is the true architect of the alpine environment. Wind velocity varies significantly from one area to another as well as on a seasonal basis. In the Southern Rockies, average wind speeds of twenty-five to thirty miles per hour are common during the winter, with gusts exceeding 100 miles per hour typical of the period from October to February; gusts greater than 200 miles per hour have been reported along ridges and on some mountain summits. Summer wind velocity is considerably less, averaging between eighteen and twenty miles per hour. Both small- and large-scale topographic features influence the pattern of wind flow. Ridges and other upland sites are typically subjected to the strongest winds and provide the most severe environments for alpine plants in terms of temperature, drought stress, frost action, and wind abrasion.

The effects of wind can be seen in the growth form and plant adaptations of alpine vegetation. Wind effectively reduces air and leaf temperatures, increases transpiration rates, and influences the physiognomy of alpine plants as a result of mechanical abrasion caused by wind-transported snow, ice, and soil particles. The pattern of snow accumulation and snowmelt that results from the redistribution of snow by wind is of critical importance in the establishment of alpine vegetation patterns.

Geology Matters

The spectacular peaks, cliffs, steep slopes, boulder fields, and patterned ground set the alpine stage. Alpine landscapes in the Southern Rockies are highly varied, reflecting differences in rock type, geologic structure, and erosional patterns. Geomorphic processes are intensified by the severe climate and steep terrain. The character of a given alpine site is closely linked to its geologic history, which may include glaciation, frost action, the formation of patterned ground, mass-wasting (downslope movements), or other geomorphic processes. Readers interested in a more detailed discussion of alpine landscape development should refer to Chapter 7.

Tracking Environmental Change

The long-term impacts of warmer growing season temperatures and human-caused increases in atmospheric carbon dioxide and in nitrogen particulate deposition make the alpine tundra a potential bellwether for environmental change. Since its founding in 1921, the University of Colorado's Mountain Research Station, located at the base of Niwot Ridge in the Colorado Front Range, has provided logistical and scientific support for multidisciplinary alpine research. Niwot Ridge was designated as the principal alpine site for the Long-Term Ecological Research program nearly thirty years ago and continues to document and track the ways in which perturbations in global climate, atmospheric chemistry, and increased transmission of solar UVB radiation through the stratosphere are impacting the alpine ecosystems of the Southern Rockies. In the Colorado Front Range, for example, the remaining glaciers and perennial snow and ice patches are in dramatic retreat. In many areas of the Southern Rockies, trees are becoming established at ever-higher elevations, well above current timberline. Though efforts to understand the complex abiotic-biotic interactions that define alpine ecosystems are ongoing and evolving in scope, preliminary results suggest that the primary response of alpine plants and animals to human-caused environmental changes will be a shift in species composition and in total abundance. Most vertebrate researchers fear that the cascading effects of these changes will have the greatest impact on the alpine habitat specialists, such as the pika and the white-tailed ptarmigan.

Community Characteristics

Alpine Plant Communities

Alpine plants are small, hardy, enduring, and infinitely beautiful—perfectly adapted to short, cold growing seasons and dessicating winds. In the Rocky Mountains, tundra plant communities consist almost solely of perennial plant species: gramineous plants (grasses, sedges, and rushes), herbaceous species, ferns, low-growing shrubs, lichens, and mosses. Annual species, plants that sprout, flower, and produce seed in a single growing season, are common in lower elevation ecosystems but are extremely rare in the alpine. Of the roughly 313 vascular plant species (plants with specialized water- and nutrient-conducting tissues) that make up the alpine flora of the Southern Rockies, more than 40 percent are restricted to alpine habitats. Not surprisingly, sixty-seven of our alpine species also occur in the circumpolar Arctic and reach their southernmost limits of distribution in the Southern Rockies. Only a small number of genera and species are endemic to the alpine of the Southern Rockies or to the Rocky Mountains as a whole. Interestingly, several alpine taxa occur in the Southern Rockies and are also common in the high, arid mountains of central Asia (the Altai-Pamir area).

Old-man-of-the-mountain, facing east.

Visitors to the alpine tundra are often astonished by the diversity of plant communities found within relatively short distances. Alpine ecologists describe tundra vegetation as a mosaic of plant communities arranged into types or continua along environmental gradients that reflect the topography, amount and duration of winter snow cover, temperature, wind exposure, and availability of moisture during the growing season. Superimposed on these environmental gradients are differences in soil chemistry, substrate stability, and disturbance impacts resulting from the activities of pocket gophers and other herbivores. In alpine areas, even a few inches of difference in microtopography, such as might be caused by the presence of a rock or small shrub, can modify wind flow patterns, snow drifting, and other attributes of the microhabitat.

Microhabitat, in combination with the tolerance ranges of individual plant species, plays a critical role in the structure, composition, and distribution of alpine plant communities. To a large degree, the patterns that result can be correlated with available moisture. The harshest environments for tundra plants are found on rocky ridges and other windswept winter-snow-free sites. Only the hardiest and most drought-resistant species, such as lichens, mosses, and a few cushion plants, are encountered on such sites. At the opposite end of the moisture spectrum, in areas where snow accumulates to substantial depths during winter and persists late into the growing season, the snow-free period may be too brief to allow for the completion of plant reproductive cycles. The most favorable sites for plants are those where the snow cover provides winter protection but melts early enough to permit a long period of summer growth.

In the Southern Rockies, alpine plant communities can be grouped into six general types: (1) alpine grasslands, (2) alpine meadows, (3) fellfields, (4) snowbeds, (5) alpine wetlands, and (6) alpine talus, scree slopes, and rock crevices. Because of the heterogeneity of the alpine environment, most communities are small, and several distinctly different types may be present in close proximity.

Alpine Grasslands

Alpine grasslands, or dry meadows, are distinctive in appearance andare characterized by dense carpets of turflike, or tussock-forming, perennial grasses, sedges, and an array of herbs and fruticose lichens. These communities are best developed on level to gently rolling sites that are largely snow free during the winter and have deep, well-drained, relatively fine-textured soils; suitable sites also include boulder-strewn, frost-patterned uplands, as well as the stabilized surfaces of rock glaciers and gently sloping moraines. Once established, these durable communities stabilize slopes and reduce erosion, promoting continued soil development and enhancing water absorption. Soil moisture is highly variable from one site to another and reflects winter snow accumulation patterns. Sites range from extremely xeric areas where strong winds create snow-free conditions throughout much of the winter to areas where a shallow winter snow cover delivers sufficient soil moisture to ensure a comparatively lush growth of grasses, sedges, and forbs.

The species associations that characterize specific habitat types form a continuum between xeric-adapted associations and associations that thrive under more mesic conditions. Three types of dry, turflike grasslands occur in the alpine zone of the Southern Rockies: (1) elk sedge, or kobresia, turf (dominated by *Kobresia myosuroides*), (2) false elk sedge turf (dominated by *Carex elynoides*), and (3) rock sedge turf (dominated by *Carex rupestris*). Some alpine ecologists suggest that kobresia turfs represent the climatic climax ecosystem of high tundra regions of the Southern Rockies.

Kobresia turfs are most common on ridgetops, summits, and passes that are relatively snow-free in winter and not excessively windy. Similar kobresia-dominated turf communities can also be found on exposed tundra slopes in the Alps, the Urals, Iceland, Greenland, and the eastern coast of Siberia. Studies of kobresia stands in Rocky Mountain National Park have shown that the restriction of kobresia to sites that are largely snow-free most of the winter results from the fact that kobresia requires approximately six to seven months to complete vegetative and floral development and is therefore intolerant of prolonged snow cover. Compact tussocks of kobresia dominate a typical stand, with a scattering of herbaceous species such as alpine harebell, moss gentian, alpine meadowrue, alpine forget-me-not, alpine primrose, and western yellow paintbrush. As these turfs age, kobresia, with its dense root system, tends to dominate herbaceous species, which are less able to compete for water. In many alpine areas, kobresia turfs are a favorite grazing area for elk and bighorn sheep.

False elk sedge turfs tolerate a shallow snow cover and have a higher proportion of exposed soil and rock. These turfs are less cushiony underfoot than those of kobresia, although the two species are similar in appearance. Differences between the two are especially conspicuous in the fall, when the straw color of false elk sedge contrasts sharply with the burnished copper swards of kobresia. During early summer, herbs such as alpine parsley, old-man-of-the-mountain, greenleaf chiming bells, and alpine clover provide a colorful display. Rock sedge turfs, in contrast to the more common communities dominated by kobresia or false elk sedge, form small, somewhat open stands in areas with less-well-developed soils. Forbs are less prominent in this community type and include such species as alpine potentilla and draba.

Alpine Meadows

Alpine meadows, in contrast to the compact economy of sedge-dominated turfs, are luxuriant in their profusion of forbs and grasses, providing a summerlong tapestry of wildflower color. Not surprisingly, alpine meadows include more species of wildflowers, grasses, and mosses than are found

Common plants of alpine meadows, from left to right: alpine avens, sky pilot, American bistort.

in any other tundra community in the Southern Rockies. Because of their affinity for moist environments, alpine meadows are found on gentle lee slopes and in shallow basins where they are protected from the harsh winter climate by a blanket of early-melting snow; on some sites the snow cover may persist into late June or early July. Soils tend to be less rocky than those of the alpine grasslands and are relatively deep, rich in organic material, and well drained. Alpine meadows include a variety of vegetation associations whose distribution can be correlated with soil moisture and snow cover duration.

Meadows dominated by alpine avens and other colorful wildflowers are typical of the most wind-sheltered and moist sites. These meadows are among the most strikingly beautiful tundra communities because of the great diversity of associated tundra plants, including sky pilot, American bistort, alpine wallflower, western yellow paintbrush, mountain harebell, alp lily, narcissus anemone, and alpine chiming bells. During some years, spectacular displays of American bistort or the endemic old-man-of-the-mountain lend an unparalled monochromatic splendor. Summer's end is heralded by the elegant, trumpet-shaped flowers of Arctic and blue-bottle gentians and by a firestorm of autumn color that transforms the foliage of alpine avens to burgundy red and splashes the tundra with gold and ochre.

Old-man-of-the-mountain.

Though less visually dramatic than the wildflower-rich communities, subalpine and alpine meadows dominated by tufted hairgrass occur in both the Northern and Southern hemispheres and are common throughout the Southern Rockies. Hairgrass meadows are typical of sites that are covered with snow too long to be tolerated by kobresia but lack sufficient moisture to support wetland sedges such as Rocky Mountain sedge. In early summer, blueleaf potentilla, alpine avens, alpine ragwort, alpine chickweed, and Parry's clover bloom brightly among the hairgrass tussocks.

Animal-Disturbed Communities

Grazers, both large and small, are attracted to alpine grasslands and meadows. Mounds of loose soil and the sinuous castings, or "gopher eskers," left behind by the winter burrowing activities of northern pocket gophers may be conspicuous in areas with deeper soils. During years when heather, long-tailed, and montane vole populations are high, large patches of vegetation may be severely grazed and meadow areas riddled with small holes and tunnel systems. Animal-disturbed sites, especially those in which pocket gophers or other burrowers have exposed substantial amounts of bare soil, are typically invaded by a distinctive group of species that includes sky pilot, alpine chiming bells, and alpine avens, with lesser amounts of American bistort, yarrow, black-headed sage, and old-man-of-the-mountain. In areas of shallow snow accumulation, Arctic sage, Parry's clover, or tufted hairgrass may dominate sites that have experienced repeated digging and grazing by pocket gophers. The occurrence of fellfield species such as moss campion and whiproot clover in overgrazed grassland or meadow sites can often be explained by the ability of these species to take advantage of disturbance.

Fellfields

Fell is the Gaelic word for rock, and the term *fellfield* refers to the distinctive plant communities associated with rocky, windswept ridgetops and exposed, windward slopes. Rocks and patches of gravel are conspicuous, and the soils tend to be coarse textured, with little organic matter and limited profile development; the most severe sites are characterized by periodic deflation of the soil as a result of wind scour. Fellfield communities are characterized by a diversity of plant species whose cushion and matlike growth forms enable them to survive the harsh fellfield environment, which is remarkably similar to a desert in terms of the severity of its environment. Fellfield plants are subject to severe desiccation both winter and summer as a result of wind exposure, the impoverished and permeable nature of coarse soils, and the lack of a winter snow cover.

From a distance, fellfields may appear somewhat barren when compared with other tundra communities. In late spring and early summer, however, they resemble a colorful Persian carpet. More than half of the vegetation is made up of cushion-forming plants such as alpine phlox and moss campion. The cushion growth form, which has evolved independently in diverse plant families, consists of a tightly interwoven cluster of branches and shoots connected to a long central taproot. Rosette-forming species such as big-rooted spring beauty and mat-forming species such as dwarf clover and mountain dryad are especially common in certain communities. Based on differences in environmental factors and species composition, three major fellfield types are recognized in the Southern Rockies: (1) fellfields dominated by cushion plants, (2) fellfields dominated by mat-forming species, and (3) fellfield microterraces dominated by mountain dryad.

Phlox (left), moss campion (right).

Cushion Plant Communities

Fellfields dominated by cushion plants are found throughout higher alpine areas of the Southern Rockies. These communities are most common on nonglaciated and relatively stable surfaces that are blown free of snow during the winter. Because of the environmental extremes typical of such sites, they generally have a higher proportion of bare rock and gravel than vegetation cover; cushion plants constitute more than 70 percent of the vegetation cover on such sites. The most common cushion-forming species include moss campion, alpine nailwort, alpine phlox, alpine sandwort, and alpine forget-me-not. Dwarf clover and a sprinkling of drought-adapted erect species such as the little alpine sunflower and spike woodrush may also be found in some communities. Soil lichens and mosses are especially prominent, in sharp contrast to the situation in other fellfield habitats.

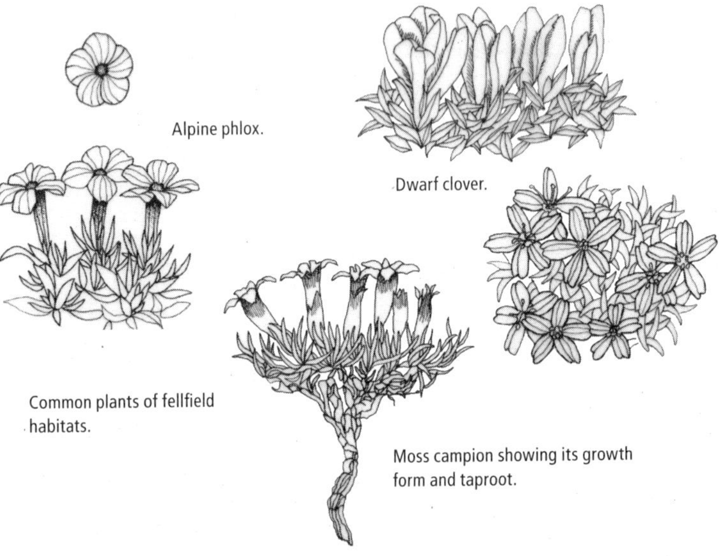

Alpine phlox.

Dwarf clover.

Common plants of fellfield habitats.

Moss campion showing its growth form and taproot.

Cushion and mat-forming species play critical roles in colonizing and stabilizing newly exposed rock and gravel habitats. With their tiny, highly modified leaves, long taproots, and compact growth forms, these plants are able to outcompete erect species in invading barren, exposed sites. Though cushion plants may be found in other alpine communities, they tend to be less vigorous and are subject to invasion and competition from erect species. In certain situations, cushion plants form the stable vegetation type for a given site, whereas in others, these communities represent a stage of succession in the establishment of a grassland or dry meadow. On sites undergoing succession, cushions of moss campion and alpine sandwort provide a suitable substrate for the establishment of seedlings of kobresia, alpine avens, western yellow paintbrush, alp lily, and many other species.

Mat-forming Plant Communities

Fellfield communities dominated by mat-forming species are typical of lower alpine sites where the conditions are less severe than those associated with cushion-plant communities and where a shallow snow cover may be present periodically during the winter months. Communities dominated by extensive mats of alpine clover tend to be most common on level to gently sloping sites with a more favorable moisture regime than is associated with most fellfield communities. In late June and early July, a rose-colored carpet of alpine clover gives way to the scattered flowers of alpine wallflower, goldflower, alpine chiming bells, and alpine reedgrass. In some years, old-man-of-the-mountain may produce a spectacular display. Soil lichens and mosses are considerably less important in these communities than in those dominated by cushion plants.

Mountain Dryad Communities

Fellfield communities dominated by mountain dryad are associated with extremely windy sites that are blown free of snow throughout much of the winter. Most communities are found on unstable slopes, with a preference for north-facing slopes, and on soils that tend to be finer textured and moister than is typical of other fellfield habitats. A large proportion of bare ground and a patchy vegetation cover characterize most communities. With the coming of summer, the dryad's large white flowers provide a showy display,

Mountain dryad in fruit, with detail of mountain dryad flower.

repeated once again when the mature fruits unfurl their plumes in late summer. Occurring in association with mountain dryad are species such as mat saxifrage, Arctic bluegrass, draba, and goldbloom saxifrage. Soil lichens and mosses may be especially prominent in this community.

Mountain dryad is an important pioneer species and soil builder in dry tundra sites because of its wind tolerance, long stout roots, and matlike profusion of branches. In some cases, this diminutive evergreen plant forms stepped terraces in which the plants occupy the "riser" of each terrace while the "tread" remains largely free of vegetation cover. These terracettes generally parallel the contour of the slope and form as a result of the combined influences of surficial frost creep, wind, and the restraining influence of the roots of the mountain dryad.

Snowbed Communities

During the long alpine winter, snow accumulates along the walls of cirques and other leeward slopes, in shallow basins, and to the lee of boulders or other obstacles to the wind. In some areas, snowbanks linger well into summer, whereas others persist from one year to the next. Snowbed communities are typical of sites where snowbanks persist well into the alpine summer. Environmental conditions in snowbed communities contrast sharply with those of other alpine habitats. Plants covered by winter snow experience warmer and more constant air and soil temperatures, higher humidity, and greater protection from wind desiccation and abrasion. A late-lying snow cover may also prevent plants from breaking dormancy prematurely and provides a consistent supply of soil moisture once growth begins. On the other hand, a persistent snow cover foreshortens the growing season, in some cases to such an extent that certain species may be unable to complete reproduction within the narrow window of exposure. Once the snow has melted, saturated soils on slopes are subject to solifluction, while those on level surfaces may experience active frost heaving and needle-ice development. Summer soil temperatures in snowbed sites are also lower than those in nonsaturated areas because of the evaporation of meltwater.

The character and species composition of a given snowbed community corresponds to the duration of the snow cover, which determines the length of the growing season and the amount of moisture present in the soil. Snowbed communities often exhibit concentric bands or zones that mark the progressive stages in the seasonal melt-back of a late-lying snowbank. These zoned communities may be conspicuous, with an outer ring of snow buttercups in full bloom while an inner ring of buttercups may just be greening as they emerge from beneath the snow.

In more complex situations, plant species associations may reflect differences in meltwater drainage and localized variations in snow-cover duration. Several distinctive snowbed communities are recognized: (1) microorganism-dominated snowbed communities, (2) sedge-dominated snowbed communities, (3) rush-dominated snowbed communities, and (4) Sibbaldia- and Lepraria-dominated snowbed communities.

Microrganism-dominated Snowbed Communities

Permanent and late-lying snowbanks contain a diversity of cold-adapted microorganisms, including bacteria, algae, fungi, and protozoa. These highly specialized organisms form a distinctive microecosystem, complete with producers, consumers, and decomposers. The most conspicuous of these organisms are the snow algae, of which several species occur in the snowbanks of the Southern Rockies. Streaks and patches of red or pinkish snow are especially prominent when you slide, or glissade, down a snowfield that contains the resting cells of the single-celled alga *Chlamydomonas nivalis*, a species of green algae found in the water that surrounds snow crystals; when disturbed by a hiker or a glissader, pink snow smells like overripe watermelon. First appearing in late May or early June, the reddish coloration of *Chlamydomonas* is due to the presence of carotenoid pigments (especially xanthin) intensified by the aggregations of large resting spores, which become concentrated in depressions on the snow surface as a result of flowing meltwater. These pigments protect chlorophyll from the intense sunlight and harmful ultraviolet radiation typical of high elevations.

Snow algae persist as spores in the old snow of permanent snowbanks, but they may also appear in snowbanks that melt completely. Though *Chlamydomonas* algal cells are present throughout the year in certain snowbanks, germination is dependent on the presence of meltwater in the snow. Though the optimal temperature for growth is around 32°F, the species is unable to grow when temperatures exceed 50°F. When the temperature drops below freezing, photosynthesis ceases, as do the algae's vegetative

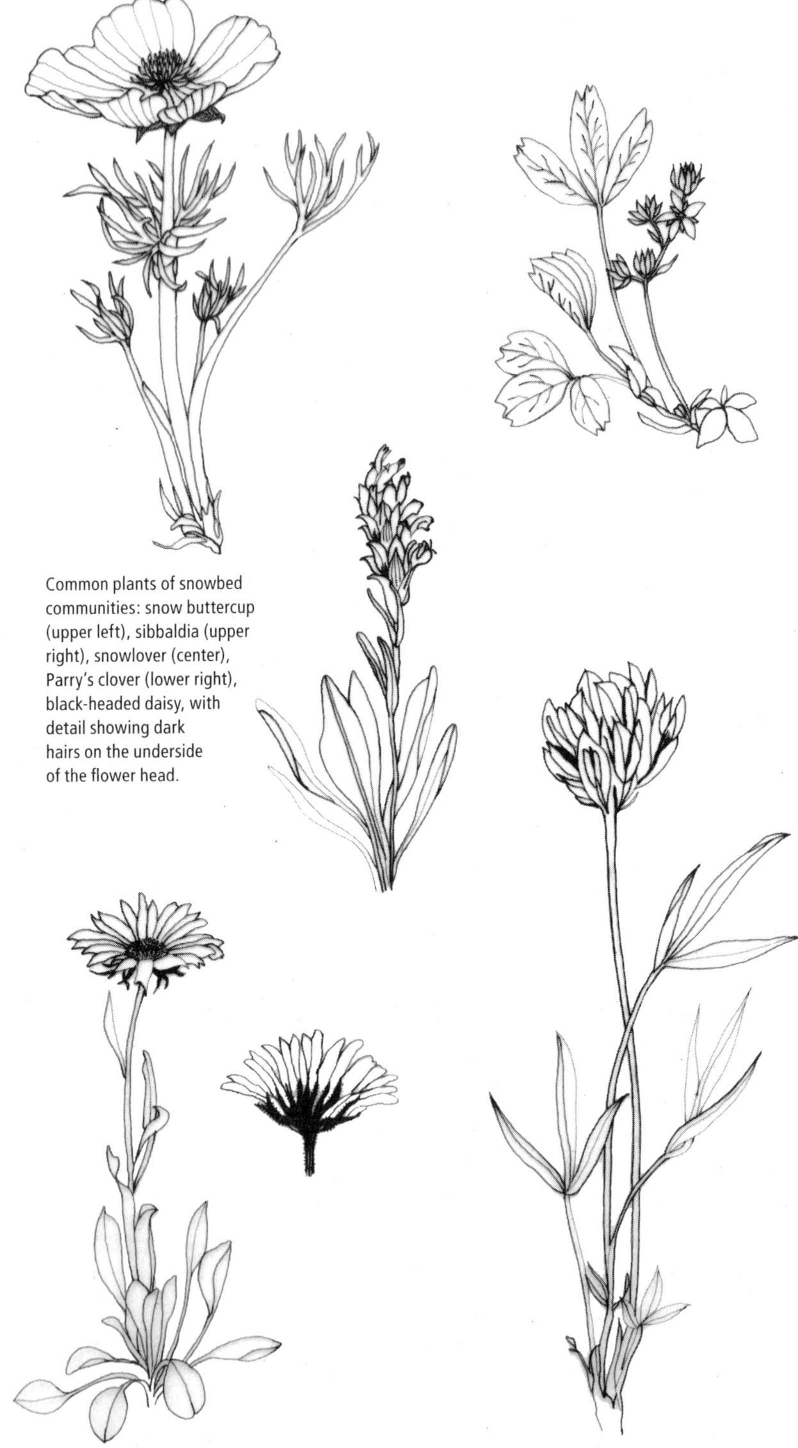

Common plants of snowbed communities: snow buttercup (upper left), sibbaldia (upper right), snowlover (center), Parry's clover (lower right), black-headed daisy, with detail showing dark hairs on the underside of the flower head.

stages; there is no effect, however, on resting spores. When temperatures warm and sufficient water is present, the free-swimming algal cells are able to reproduce and form spores within a few days. Several studies suggest that these motile algal cells concentrate radionuclides in the snowpack. Despite its enticing aroma, do not eat watermelon snow; though the algae isn't toxic, consumption generally ends in intestinal distress.

Sedge-dominated Snowbed Communities

Snowbed communities dominated by Crandall's sedge and black sedge occupy shallow depressions and other sites that remain snow covered for as long as eleven months of the year. These extremely late-melting sites are characterized by wet to fully saturated soils, variable proportions of bare soil and rock, and intensive but relatively shallow frost activity. The degree of vegetation cover reflects the duration of the snow cover. The dull green, droopy tussocks that typify this species readily identify communities dominated by Crandall's sedge. Other snow-tolerant species, such as Drummond's rush, Baffin fescue, black-headed daisy, and alpine pussytoes, may also be common. Few species complete flowering in this community, because of the short growing season and the effects of cold meltwater; several snowbed species reproduce by vegetative means.

Rush-dominated Snowbed Communities

Snowbed communities dominated by Drummond's rush are common in late-lying snow areas and are typical of shallow nivation depressions and other sites with a slightly longer snow-free period than those dominated by Crandall's sedge. In some cases, communities dominated by Drummond's rush may develop around the perimeter of Crandall's sedge stands. Soils in rush-dominated snowbed sites are normally fast-drying. The dark green color and wiry appearance of Drummond's rush give this community a distinctive appearance. When in bloom, the diminutive rose-colored flowers of the rush demand a closer look with a 10x hand lens; the florets are an exquisite surprise with their feathery pink stigmas, yellow stamens, and brown ovaries. Several other flowering species are also common in this community, including saffron ragwort, black-headed daisy, snow buttercup, and alpine willowherb.

Sibbaldia- and *Lepraria*-dominated Snowbed Communities

Snowbed communities dominated by *Sibbaldia* and the grayish white soil lichens *Lepraria arctica* and *Stereocaulon* spp. occupy sites that are snow-free for at least seven to twelve weeks, well drained, and have relatively fine-textured soils. Though this community may appear quite barren from a distance, closer examination reveals a fairly high herb and lichen cover. In many areas, *Lepraria* tends to form polygonal units a few inches in diameter, each unit separated by narrow dessiccation cracks. The flowering species snow buttercup, alpine avens, and Parry's clover are often common. Sites with slightly less-persistent snow cover may support Arctic willow, alpine Timothy, tufted hairgrass, and snowlover.

Alpine Wetland Communities

Nourished by melting snowbanks, wetlands of every size and configuration dot the alpine tundra of the Southern Rockies. Alpine wetlands, with their saturated soils, cold temperatures, and active frost processes, are strikingly similar to wetlands found in Arctic regions. In fact, Arctic wetland species such as koenigia (an extremely tiny annual), Arctic saxifrage, and golden saxifrage reach their southernmost limits of distribution in the Southern Rockies. Wetland habitats are highly variable, ranging from exposed, gravelly

Common plants of alpine wetlands, left to right: Rocky Mountain sedge, rose (or queen's) crown, with detail of individual floret, and elephantella.

surfaces inundated by shallow meltwater rivulets for most of the growing season to communities characterized by shallow standing water and a luxuriant growth of water-loving plants. Most communities are situated on relatively flat surfaces below late-lying snowbanks, in the catchment areas of alpine basins, and adjacent to ponds, lakes, and streams.

Bare Gravel Surfaces

Wetland communities developed on saturated gravels are common along streams and in frost-active areas supplied with meltwater from snowbanks or other sources. Gravel habitats with shallow, continuously flowing water should be examined closely for the reddish, seedlinglike leaves of koenigia. This inconspicuous plant, one of the few annual species to be found in the alpine tundra, takes root in the cold meltwater washed gravels, in mats of the moss *Calliergon sarmentosum*, or in small bits of sedge peat. Showy species such as rose crown, as well as several small rushes (*Juncus castaneus, J. biglumis*, and *J. triglumis*) and Nelson's sedge, are often present in gravelly habitats.

Sedge-dominated Wetlands

Wetland sites characterized by shallow standing water are found downslope from persistent snowbanks, adjacent to ponds and lakes, and on solifluction terraces. These communities often remain saturated throughout the growing season and are dominated by a luxuriant growth of deep green, stiff-leaved tussocks of Rocky Mountain sedge. In lower alpine sites, especially those in somewhat wind-sheltered areas, Nelson's willow may share its wetland

Marsh-marigold.

habitat with marsh-marigold, globeflower, elephantella, rose crown, star gentian, and little gentian. At higher elevations, alpine lousewort, alpine willowherb, and alpine bistort are the most common flowering species in wetland sites. Despite the dense vegetation cover, pocket gopher activity is limited because of the high water table. Voles are common in sedge-dominated wetlands, their nests and runways concentrated in the better-drained and most hummocky sites.

Talus, Scree, and Rock Crevice Communities

Rocky habitats are found along the bases of cliffs, around the fronts of rock glaciers and moraines, in blockfields, and on slopes mantled with loose rock rubble. During the winter, snow accumulates between the rocks, ensuring a dependable supply of moisture throughout the growing season. The spaces between the rocks provide a remarkably sheltered environment for plants, affording protection from both wind and cold. Plants associated with rocky habitats tend to be present in small numbers and are restricted to sites with ample soil and moisture. Many species are rugged pioneers, with either long, shallow root systems or with massive taproots that enable them to make the best possible use of their limited space and substrate.

Slope orientation, the degree of protection provided by the rock, and the stability of the substrate largely determine the species composition of a particular habitat. Species typical of lower elevations, such as death camas, prickly currant, and Colorado columbine, grow in lush profusion in the warmest, most stable, and wind-sheltered sites. Gently sloping talus and scree are dominated by species such as alpine thistle, talus ragwort, and alpine sorrel. Soil-filled rock crevices support big-rooted spring beauty, alumroot, spotted saxifrage, alpine rock-jasmine, and goldbloom saxifrage. Species that are less tolerant of full sun and strong winds, such as alpine kittentails, dwarf columbine, nodding saxifrage, and adoxa, are found beneath overhanging ledges and boulders.

Plant Adaptation: Designs for Survival

Alpine plants exhibit a variety of adaptations that enable them to survive and even flourish in the harsh alpine climate. Morphological adaptations play a critical role in modifying the complex energy environment to which these plants are subjected. To the first-time visitor, the most striking characteristics of alpine plants are their low growth forms and small sizes. By sacrificing height and leaf size, alpine plants take advantage of the more moderate microclimate near the ground surface, exposing as little plant tissue as possible to cold temperatures and desiccating winds. Additionally, alpine plants may have as much as 90 percent of their biomass below ground, investing their energies in an extensive root or rhizome system that provides them with vital life support during times of water or nutrient stress. Species growing in the most drought-prone habitats often exhibit a rosettelike growth form, minute leaves, or fleshy, succulent leaves that permit substantial water storage.

Lichen Pioneers

Lichens are especially conspicuous in alpine environments, surviving well on bare rock surfaces, on tundra soils and adjacent to snowbeds, and amidst the ground-hugging plants of the alpine grasslands and meadows. These hardy pioneers are extremely well suited to colonizing inhospitable habitats because their basic biology bundles together two organisms, each with radically different attributes, into a more efficient, functional life-form. In essence, the fungal component of the lichen provides a latticelike structure, a means of attachment to a rock or other substrate, and moisture retention while the algae or cyanobacteria contribute to photosynthetic gain, which allows the lichen to grow and proliferate. Patches of crustose (crust-forming) lichens pattern rock outcrops and bouldery deposits throughout the mountains in a colorful mosaic of greens, browns, oranges, yellows, and black. Crustose lichens are extremely slowgrowing, requiring anywhere from less than a year to several decades (a function of light and temperature) to expand a mere 1⁄16 of an inch. Lichens found growing on moraines and other rocky substrates near glaciers may be thousands of years old, and they have been used by geologists to measure the ebb and flow of glacier ice over time.

The stems, leaves, and flower buds of alpine plants are especially vulnerable. In the most severe environments, delicate tissues such as those of the mountain dryad are covered with a thick, waxy cuticle. The leaves of other species are coated with hairs of various types that provide insulation from the cold, reduce water loss due to transpiration, and moderate damage to leaf tissues caused by high levels of ultraviolet radiation. Conspicuous examples are the silky weft of hairs that cloaks the leaves and stem of old-man-of-the-mountain and the dark purple, heat-absorbing hairs that distinguish the black-headed daisy. Studies of alpine plants show that thick hairs reflect some visible light that, when too intense, actually slows photosynthesis. Dark hairs, such as those that envelop the buds and flowers of the black-headed daisy, are especially effective in trapping visible wavelengths of solar energy and thus accelerating flowering and seed development.

Solar-Tracking Flowers

Round and parabolic-shaped flowers dominate cold-climate environments. In contrast to the diversity of floral color and shape typical of midsummer, white and yellow saucer-shaped flowers are most common in alpine meadows and other moist sites soon after snowmelt. These flowers, because of their shape and highly reflective petals, function as solar collectors by focusing heat and light on the plant's reproductive organs. The snow buttercup's petals, for example, are coated with an oily substance and have starchy granules in their cells, both adaptations that increase reflectivity. By maximizing the limited heat budget of the alpine summer, these adaptively shaped flowers accelerate the development of pollen and seeds and may also provide a beneficial microclimate—a floral "solar furnace"—for their pollinators. Some species, such as old-man-of-the-mountain, maximize their solar advantage by simply facing eastward and providing a wind-sheltered basking surface for pollinating insects.

Floral heliotropism, the ability of some plants to orient their flowers to face the sun, confers a survival advantage for several Arctic and alpine species, including snow buttercup, marsh-marigold, alpine poppy, and mountain dryad. The most common pattern of floral movement for heliotropic species is to keep the axis of the parabolic (bowl-like) petal surfaces nearly perpendicular to incoming solar radiation. In fact, the temperature within a saucer-shaped heliotropic flower may be as much as 14°F warmer than the surrounding air. Researchers studying the snow buttercup, which tracks the sun throughout the day, discovered that this species' tracking response is triggered by special sensors in the stem just below each flower that exhibit spectral sensitivity to blue light as opposed to other wavelengths; these sensors signal a shift in the plant growth hormone auxin away from the sunlit side of the plant. In the case of the snow buttercup, heliotropism ultimately results in increased pollen production and a higher rate of pollen grain receipt and germination; when combined, these advantages account for a nearly 45 percent increase in overall reproductive success when compared to nonheliotropic species.

Snow buttercup.

The Perennial Advantage

Alpine plants must metabolize, grow, and reproduce at consistently cold growing-season air temperatures. Most alpine vascular plants are herbaceous perennials, a few species are biennial, and only 1 to 2 percent of our alpine flora consists of annuals. Annual species, such as the diminutive little koenigia, are at a distinct disadvantage because they need to complete the entire life cycle from germination to seed production within the short span of the alpine summer. Perennial species, on the other hand, can complete their life cycles more rapidly because they do not need to invest valuable time in germination or in the initial stages of growth.

Most tundra perennials, in contrast to lower-elevation species, enter winter with preformed shoots and flower buds that enable them to initiate growth as soon as environmental conditions become favorable. These preformed buds develop in late summer or early fall and overwinter within a protective shroud of dead leaves and other tissue. Once dormancy is broken in the spring, elongation and flowering proceed rapidly, relying on the availability of carbohydrates stored in the root system during the previous growing season. Flowering success, then, depends largely upon environmental conditions at the time preformed buds developed, rather than on the growth conditions of the current season.

Photosynthesis and Growth

The ability to initiate photosynthesis at low temperatures and to draw on stored carbohydrates for rapid initial growth in the spring are essential for species that must cope with the short, cold alpine growing season. Many alpine vascular plants are able to carry on photosynthesis at daytime temperatures as low as 32° F, substantially lower than temperatures reported for plants growing in more moderate climates. The great majority of alpine plants are "summer-green," having leaves that survive for a single summer as well as preformed vegetative buds. The overwintering strategy of summer-green perennials requires massive storage of carbohydrates in roots or rhizomes, which provides the critical food reserves to fuel spring growth. In fact, spring growth is often so rapid that respiration greatly exceeds photosynthetic production and food is consumed at a faster rate than it can be made. As shoot growth slows and flowering is completed, the respiration rate declines and the necessary replenishment of carbohydrate reserves in the roots begins.

Winter photosynthetic activity is reported for alpine species with evergreen leaves, such as the mountain dryad, and for a unique group of species classified as having "winter-green" leaves, such as kobresia, tufted hairgrass, and alpine forget-me-not. Winter-green plants have leaves that develop during one summer and survive into the next, contrasting with evergreen species, which last several seasons. The winter-green growth strategy maximizes photosynthetic activity over a longer time span than is possible for summer-green species and concentrates the winter storage of carbohydrates (mostly sugars) in the immature leaves, an advantage that minimizes the time needed for translocation and provides an even quicker jump-start for the resumption of growth in the spring.

Anthocyanins and Alpine Plants

Alpine plants owe their spectacular colors to green-reflecting chlorophylls and the pigments carotene (yellow and orange-reds) and anthocyanin (reds and blues). Colored pigments are present in all green leaves and are visible to varying degrees depending on the proportion of pigment to chlorophyll present in the leaf tissue at any given time or season. Oil-soluble carotenoids absorb energy from the blue and green wavelengths of the incoming light spectrum, which they pass on to chlorophyll. Anthocyanin, a water-soluble pigment synthesized from sugars stored in the roots, helps to block ultraviolet radiation at high elevations and serves to protect plant tissues from radiation damage. Most obvious to us, of course, is the range of colors it produces in plants, from reds when the cell sap is acidic to blues when sap is alkaline; anthocyanin is responsible for the red skin of apples and all blue flowers. Cold temperatures tend to reduce the chlorophyll content in plant tissues, which encourages the accumulation of anthocyanin in the leaves and young stems of alpine plants. Anthocyanin serves to enhance a plant's cold tolerance, acting as a "sink" for excess sugars produced during the cool, bright weather of spring and fall. The bright reddish colors typical of the foliage of many alpine plants just after snowmelt and again at the end of the growing season is due to higher-than-normal levels anthocyanin; this phenomenon is especially pronounced in snow buttercups and other species growing in environments with late-lying snow.

Reproduction in Alpine Environments

The ultimate measure of a species' fitness in any environment is its ability to reproduce successfully. Many alpine plants reproduce sexually, producing flowers and viable seeds during summers when there is adequate sunshine and warmth. Because of the shortness and severity of the alpine summer, however, the seeds of most species mature too late in the season to meet the right combination of temperature and sufficient moisture over time for germination to occur during the same growing season. In fact, in some species, the ripening process may not reach completion until the year following flowering. During some years, weather conditions may not favor flowering, seed production, or germination.

The availability of moisture and suitably warm temperatures set the stage for successful germination in the alpine environment. In most cases, germination takes place in early summer, shortly after snowmelt. Seedlings must have sufficient time to develop root systems and store enough carbohydrates to allow survival through the long, cold winter. Late summer germination in species of drier habitats appears to be inhibited by lack of soil moisture, low temperatures, and insufficient time for seedling development. Species typical of wet meadows and other sites that retain soil moisture throughout the growing season normally produce seeds with built-in dormancy mechanisms that protect against premature germination. Seedling growth is very slow in most species; a plant needs several years to grow large enough and store enough carbohydrates to produce flowers.

Many alpine species reproduce by means of runners, stolons, rhizomes, and bulblets. Such methods circumvent the environmental constraints that often interfere with fertilization and seed production and allow rapid colonization of newly exposed ground. Whiplash saxifrage, like the strawberry, sends out threadlike runners across the surface of the ground. At the end of each runner is a tiny plant that draws nourishment from the parent until it has developed its own set of roots, at which time the runner withers away. One of the most interesting reproductive strategies is that of alpine bistort (*Bistorta vivipara*), which produces bulblets along its flowering stalk. The Latin epithet *vivipara* refers to the plant's ability to bear "young" without going through the seed and seedling process. The viviparous bistort produces both flowers and bulblets; the delicate white flowers are at the top of the flowering stalk and the bulblets toward the bottom. The bistort's flowers have never been known to produce viable seed in our region. The bulblets, on the other hand, drop from the parent plant and are able to establish themselves during the same growing season in which they were "sown," often sprouting green shoots while still attached to the flowering stalk.

Descriptions of Common Plants

Wildflowers

Moss Campion, *Silene acaulis* ssp. *acaulescens.* Races of this cushion-forming species are found in the Arctic and in nearly every alpine tundra area in the Northern Hemisphere. Its bright pink, five-petaled flowers, narrow green leaves, cushionlike growth form, and long taproot identify moss campion. This species generally grows in fellfields and dry meadows and is one of the first colonizers of barren gravel areas. On average, cushions growing under optimal conditions may be anywhere from 75 to 100 years of age; the oldest known moss campion is a 350-year-old cushion with a diameter of nearly two feet.

Black-headed Daisy, *Erigeron melanocephalus.* This species is recognized by its small size, basal rosette of spoon-shaped leaves, white ray flowers, and the dark purple hairs that cover the underside of its flower head and upper stem. A similar species, the **one-flowered daisy** (*E. simplex*), lacks these dark hairs and is found in less moist habitats. Black-headed daisy is found in areas with late-lying snow.

Old-Man-of-the-Mountain, *Rydbergia grandiflora.* This large, conspicuous sunflower derives its common name from the silky hair that covers its stems, foliage, and flowering heads. Old-man-of-the-mountain is distinguished by its east-facing, bright yellow ray and disk flowers and by its feathery leaves. This species stores food in its root system for several years before producing flowers, the entire plant dying once the seed matures.

Rose Crown, *Clementsia* (or *Sedum*) *rhodantha.* This showy alpine wildflower, also known as queen's crown, is identified by its ball-shaped cluster of rose-colored flowers and by the prominent midrib that marks the underside of each succulent, lanceolate leaf. Rose crown is endemic to the Southern Rockies and is found in alpine wetlands and other moist habitats.

Parry's Clover, *Trifolium parryi.* Of the three species of clover endemic to the alpine zone of the Rocky Mountains, Parry's clover, with its strongly scented, ball-shaped cluster of flowers, is the most "cloverlike." Other distinguishing characteristics include the uniformly purple or rose-purple flowers, the papery bracts that subtend the individual flowers, and the trifoliate (leaves consisting of three leaflets) leaves; the superficially similar alpine or whiproot clover (*T. dasyphyllum*) has bicolored flowers and smaller, narrower leaves.

Dwarf Clover, *Trifolium nanum*. The short-stalked, one- to three-flowered inflorescenses, matlike growth form, and tiny leaves distinguish dwarf clover from other clover species. This species is slow growing and typical of exposed habitats such as fellfields.

Alpine Phlox, *Phlox pulvinata*. Alpine phlox is distinguished by its five-petaled, fragrant blue flowers and its compact, matlike growth form. Blooming in late June and early July, this species transforms barren-seeming fellfields with splashes of palest blue. *P. condensata* is the common alpine phlox of the southern half of the Southern Rockies.

Sky Pilot, *Polemonium viscosum*. This showy species is identified by its terminal cluster of blue, funnel-shaped flowers and by its distinctly whorled leaflets. A paler blue race of sky pilot, *P. grayanum*, is common from Mount Evans southwestward through the Southern Rockies. Though white mutants of sky pilot are common, they should not be confused with the sticky-leaved, cream-colored flowers of *P. brandegei*, which occurs in unstable alpine screes and similar rocky habitats.

American Bistort, *Bistorta bistortoides*. Easily identified by its tall, flowering stalk, whitish to pinkish compact and cylindrical flower heads, and lanceolate leaves; in some years, American bistort is a conspicuous midsummer-blooming species from the upper montane to the alpine meadows. Though the flowers of bistort lack petals, the five sepals (actually called tepals) appear petal-like; at the base of each flower is a tiny brown sheath called a stipule. Unlike the more diminutive **alpine bistort** (*B. vivipara*), American bistort reproduces by seeds rather than by bulblets.

Alpine Sorrel, *Oxyria digyna*. The cluster of basal kidney-shaped leaves and begonialike flowers identify alpine sorrel, a species typical of alpine rockslides and other rocky habitats. The prefix *oxy* means "sour" in Greek, and the leaves of this species are distinctly sour-sweet and a good source of vitamin C.

Big-rooted Spring Beauty, *Claytonia megarhiza*. This spectacular species is distinguished by its rosette growth form, broadly spatulate leaves, and encircling ring of white-pink flowers. Big-rooted spring beauty is typical of rocky terrain at high elevations. **Pygmy bitterroot** (*Oreobroma pygmaea*, formerly *Lewisia pygmaea*), a diminutive and magenta-flowered relative, is found in the gravelly soils of shallow snowbed sites.

White Marsh-Marigold, *Psychrophila* (formerly *Caltha*) *leptosepala*. Marsh-marigold is identified by its white tepals (petals and sepals that are indistinguishable), broadly heart-shaped basal leaves, and preference for subalpine and alpine snowbed and wetland habitats. Once flowering is completed, the fruits (called follicles) become swollen and conspicuous.

Snow Buttercup, *Ranunculus adoneus*. This showy species, with its ruffled, glossy yellow tepals (petals and sepals are indistinguishable) and finely dissected leaves, is commonly found around melting snowbanks. Snow buttercups are often encountered poking their brilliant yellow flower buds through the melting snow and have been reported to bloom beneath several feet of snow. This species is endemic to the Rocky Mountains.

Alpine Avens, *Acomastylis* (formerly *Geum*) *rossii*. Alpine avens is one of the most common alpine wildflowers, easily recognized by its yellow roselike flowers and fernlike leaves. There is probably no greater habitat generalist in the alpine tundra. Alpine avens is found in a variety of upland habitats characterized by light winter snow covers and well-drained soils. With the coming of fall, the buildup of anthocyanins in the leaves turns these plants a rich burgundy rust.

Mountain Dryad, *Dryas octopetala* ssp. *hookeriana*. Mountain dryad is identified by its white eight-petaled, roselike flowers, finely toothed, evergreen leaves, and elegantly plumed seed heads. Locally abundant on gravelly, windswept slopes, this species often forms large single-species stands.

Sibbaldia, *Sibbaldia procumbens*. This diminutive member of the rose family is distinguished by its prominent green sepals, tiny yellow petals, and three-part, triple-notched leaves. Sibbaldia is always associated with areas of late-lying snow.

Whiplash Saxifrage, *Hirculus platysepalus* ssp. *crandallii* (formerly *Saxifraga flagellaris*). Whiplash saxifrage is easily identified by its upright, five-petaled yellow flowers, stoloniferous (runner-producing) growth habit, and glandular-pubescent leaves. This small but beautiful saxifrage is a pioneering species, most often encountered in barren, gravelly sites and rocky crevices.

Snowlover, *Chionophila jamesii*. This lovely little member of the figwort family is distinguished by its one-sided raceme of creamy-white, flattened, snapdragonlike flowers. The genus name is Greek and refers to snowlover's preference for snow accumulation sites. The Latin epithet honors Edwin James, naturalist on the 1820 Long Expedition, who was first to collect the snowlover.

Elephantella, *Pedicularis groenlandica*. Elephantella, with its fernlike leaves and distinctive magenta flowers, each resembling the head of an elephant, is one of our easiest alpines to identify. This species has a broad elevational range but is most common in moist meadows and wetlands in the subalpine and lower alpine zones.

Grasses, Sedges, and Rushes

Kobresia, *Kobresia myosuroides*. This member of the sedge family is one of the dominant climax species on dry, peaty tundra. Kobresia has short, slender, and curving leaves, a simple, bisexual spikelet, and can be distinguished from the superficially similar false elk sedge (*Carex elynoides*) by the open sheath that encloses the ovary in the carpellate floret. This species forms a dense, rhizomatous turf that turns a rich bronze-yellow in autumn.

Rush, Drummond, *Juncus drummondii*. This delicately beautiful rush grows in a spraylike "tuft," each plant consisting of a group of round, jointless stems up to twelve inches tall. The leaves are reduced to sheaths at the base of each stem, and each stem is topped by a cluster of one to three florets, each with a lavender-hued, lilylike flower.

Rocky Mountain Sedge, *Carex scopulorum*. Rising from a weblike network of rhizomes, the stems of Rocky Mountain sedge form a dense turf in subalpine and alpine wetlands. This is a robust sedge whose flowering stems well exceed the erect leaves. Each stem is topped by an erect, terminal staminate (male) inflorescence and subtended by a cluster of carpellate (female) inflorescences.

Common Plants of the Alpine Tundra

Shrubs

Birch, bog, *Betula glandulosa*
Cinquefoil, shrubby, *Pentaphylloides floribunda*

Willow, arctic, *Salix arctica* ssp. *petraea*
planeleaf, *S. planifolia*
snow, *S. reticulata* ssp. *nivalis*

Grasses, Sedges, and Rushes

Bentgrass, alpine, *Agrostis variabilis*
Bluegrass, alpine, *Poa alpina*
arctic, *P. arctica* ssp. *grayana*
Letterman's, *P. lettermanii*
snowbed, *P. abbreviata* ssp. *pattersonii*
Fescue, alpine, *Festuca brachyphylla*
Baffin, *F. baffinensis*
Hall's, *F. hallii*
Hairgrass, tufted, *Deschampsia cespitosa*
Kobresia (or Elk Sedge), *Kobresia myosuroides*
Rush, Drummond's, *Juncus drummondii*
chestnut, *J. castaneus*
three-glumed, *J. triglumis*
two-glumed, *J. biglumis*
Sedge, black, *Carex nigricans*
Crandall's, *C. crandallii* (formerly *C. pyrenaica*)
ebony, *C. ebenea*
false elk, *C. elynoides*
fish-scale, *C. chalciolepis*
Hepburn's, *C. nardina* ssp. *hepburnii*
Nelson's, *C. nelsonii*
rock, *C. rupestris*
Rocky Mountain, *C. scopulorum*
Timothy, alpine, *Phleum commutatum*
Trisetum, spike, *Trisetum spicatum*
Wheatgrass, Scribner's, *Elymus scribneri*
slender, *E. trachycaulus*
Woodrush, Spike, *Luzula spicata*

Wildflowers

Adoxa (or Moschatel), *Adoxa moschatellina*
Alp Lily, *Lloydia serotina*
Alumroot, common (or Alpine Alumroot), *Heuchera parvifolia*
Anemone, narcissus (or Alpine Anemone), *Anemonastrum narcissiflorum*
Angelica, Gray's, *Angelica grayi*
Avens, alpine, *Acomastylis* (formerly *Geum*) *rossii*
Bistort, alpine, *Bistorta vivipara*
    American, *B. bistortoides*
Bitterroot, pygmy, *Oreobroma* (formerly *Lewisia*) *pygmaea*
Braya, dwarf, *Braya humilis*
Buttercup, snow, *Ranunculus adoneus*
Butterweed, Frémont's, *Senecio fremontii* var. *blitoides*
Camas, subalpine death, *Anticlea* (formerly *Zigadenus*) *elegans*
Campion, alpine, *Gastrolychnis drummondii*
    moss, *Silene acaulis*
Candytuft, mountain, *Noccaea* (formerly *Thlaspi*) *montana*
Chickweed, alpine mouse-ear, *Cerastium beeringianum* ssp. *earlei*
    field, *C. arvense*
Chiming bells, greenleaf, *Mertensia lanceolata*
Clover, Alpine or Whiproot, *Trifolium dasyphyllum*
    Brandegee's, *T. brandegei*
    dwarf, *T. nanum*
    Parry's, *T. parryi*
Columbine, Colorado blue, *Aquilegia coerulea*
    dwarf, *A. saximontana*
Daisy, black-headed, *Erigeron melanocephalus*
    one-headed, *E. simplex*
    pinnate-leaved, *E. pinnatisectus*
    subalpine, *E. peregrinus*
Draba, Gray's peak, *Draba grayana*
    thick, *D. crassa*
    white, *D. cana*
Dryad, mountain, *Dryas octopetala* ssp. *hookeriana*

Elephantella, *Pedicularis groenlandica*
Fern, alpine lady, *Athyrium distentifolium* var. *americanum*
Christmas, *Polystichum lonchitis*
Fireweed, alpine, *Chamerion latifolium*
Forget-me-not, alpine, *Eritrichum aretioides*
Gentian, Arctic, *Gentianodes algida*
bottle, *Pneumonanthe parryi*
moss (or Siberian Gentian), *Chondrophylla prostrata*
rose, *Gentianella amarelle* var. *acuta*
star, *Swertia perennis*
Gilia, snowball, *Ipomopsis spicata* ssp. *capitata*
Goldflower, *Tetraneuris brevifolia*
Harebell, alpine, *Campanula uniflora*
common (or Mountain Harebell), *C. rotundifolia*
King's Crown, *Tolmachevia integrifolia*
Kittentails, alpine, *Besseya alpina*
Koenigia, *Koenigia islandica*
Lousewort, alpine, *Pedicularis scopulorum*
Marsh-marigold, *Psychrophila* (formerly *Caltha*) *leptosepala*
Meadowrue, alpine, *Thalictrum alpinum*
Nailwort, Rocky Mountain (or Alpine Nailwort), *Paronychia pulvinata*
Old-man-of-the-mountain, *Rydbergia grandiflora*
Onion, alpine, *Allium geyeri*
Paintbrush, rose, *Castilleja rhexifolia* and *C. haydenii*
Paintbrush, western yellow, *Castilleja occidentalis* and *Castilleja puberula*
Parsley, alpine, *Oreoxis alpina*
Penstemon, Harbour's, *Penstemon harbourii*
Phlox, alpine, *Phlox pulvinata*
Poppy, alpine, *Papaver radicatum* ssp. *kluanensis*
Primrose, alpine (or Rock-jasmine), *Androsace chamaejasme*
fairy (or Alpine Primrose), *Primula angustifolia*
Parry's, *P. parryi*
rock, *A.septentrionalis*
Purple Fringe, *Phacelia sericea*
Ragwort, alpine, *Ligularia holmii*

Rose Crown (or Queen's Crown), *Clementsia* (or *Sedum*) *rhodantha*
Sage, arctic, *Artemisia arctica* ssp. *saxicola*
  black-headed (or Alpine Sage), *A. scopulorum*
Sandwort, alpine, *Lidia* (formerly *Minuartia*) *obtusiloba*
  Fendler's, *Eremogone fendleri*
Saussurea, Weber's, *Saussurea weberi*
Saxifrage, goldbloom, *Hirculus serpyllifolius* ssp. *chrysanthus*
  nodding, *Saxifraga cernua*
  snowball, *Micranthes rhomboidea*
  spotted, *Ciliaria austromontana*
  whiplash, *H. platysepalus* ssp. *crandallii*
Senecio, dandelion, *Ligularia taraxacoides*
  purple-leaved, *L. soldanella*
Sibbaldia, *Sibbaldia procumbens*
Sky Pilot, *Polemonium viscosum*
  honey, *P. brandegei*
Snowlover, *Chionophila jamesii*
Sorrel, alpine, *Oxyria digyna*
Spring Beauty, big-rooted, *Claytonia megarhiza*
Thistle, alpine, *Cirsium scopulorum*
Violet, twin-flower, *Viola biflora*
Wallflower, western, *Erysimum capitatum*
Willowherb, alpine, *Epilobium anagallidifolium*

Lichens

Antler (or Worm) Lichen, *Thamnolia vermicularis* (white)
Lichen, finger, *Dactylina arctica* (creamy yellow to brownish)
  golden, *Acarospora chlorophana* (bright yellow to greenish yellow)
  Iceland, *Cetraria islandica* (brown)
  jewel, *Xanthoria elegans* (orange)
  map, *Rhizocarpon geographicum* (bright green and black)
  snow, *Cetraria nivalis* (yellow)
  white soil, *Lepraria* spp., *Stereocaulon* spp.
Parmelia, *Parmelia alpicola* (brownish black; crustose)
Rock Tripe, *Umbilicaria* spp.

Environment and Adaptation: Animals of the Alpine Tundra

Pika.

The beauty and beneficence of the alpine summer belie the ferocity and harsh realities that arrive with the winter winds. Animals that live and prosper in the alpine environment do so at the limits of their genetic tolerance. Very few animal species are year-round residents of the alpine tundra. Of the nineteen resident mammalian species, the majority—shrews, pikas, voles, pocket gophers, yellow-bellied marmots, and weasels—are small-bodied and can utilize the more moderate microenvironment at or beneath the ground surface. In most years, the rigors of the winter environment force large mammals such as bighorn sheep and elk to move to lower elevations in search of more-sheltered areas for grazing. Of the half dozen or so birds that breed in the alpine, only the white-tailed ptarmigan remains year-round. No avian or mammalian species is restricted to the alpine zone, although several species are as common here as they are at lower elevations.

The majority of animal species encountered in the alpine zone are present only during the breeding season; others visit on an occasional basis or during migration. Several birds nest in the alpine tundra but winter at lower elevations: brown-capped rosy finches, horned larks, water pipits, rock wrens, spotted sandpipers, ravens, prairie falcons, and black swifts. Elk graze in the tundra during the summer and early autumn, lured by the lush growth of grasses and herbs. Coyotes and red foxes wander up from the mountain valleys, attracted by secluded alpine meadows with an abundance of small mammals and ground-nesting birds. Golden eagles and red-tailed and ferruginous hawks may be seen soaring above timberline as they hunt. Mountain bluebirds, gulls, and kestrels are often conspicuous in late summer and early autumn, when Mormon crickets, grasshoppers, and other insects abound in tundra meadows.

Survival Strategies

Survival in the alpine requires the capacity to withstand climatic extremes and to aquire adequate food. This means that the amount of heat produced by metabolism of food or fat reserves must offset that which is lost to the environment. Reproductive success, of course, provides the final measure of a species' ability to adapt to the exigencies of the alpine environment. Escaping environmental extremes is largely a function of behavior and the degree to which an animal is able to move about within its environment to avoid energetically stressful conditions. Birds are the most mobile, of course, with some species migrating large distances to benign overwintering areas while others simply move back and forth, either diurnally or seasonally, between the alpine tundra and protective cover or roosting sites in the subalpine or montane zones. Small mammals are generally able to survive the winter by hibernating, using sheltered microhabitats, storing food, or using adaptive hunting strategies that expose them as little as possible to climatic extremes.

The Hibernators

The overwintering success of most alpine animals depends on the ability to avoid subfreezing temperatures and excessive heat loss to the environment. For mammals and birds, maintaining a high, constant body temperature is achieved by increasing metabolic heat production severalfold. When food is scarce or unavailable, the higher rate of food intake necessary to fuel metabolic processes is most threatening to small mammals, whose metabolic rates are already at comparatively high levels. Hibernation enables these species to conserve energy by allowing their body temperatures to drop to within a few degrees of freezing, greatly reducing the metabolic rate, heart rate, respiration, and other energetically costly functions.

A mammalian hibernator spends the winter in a state of dormancy in an underground burrow or other subterranean shelter where the temperature rarely drops below freezing. Among alpine mammals, hibernation is best-developed in the marmots and the ground squirrels. The annual cycles of these herbivorous animals follow a predictable sequence of events: spring emergence from hibernation, mating, gestation, lactation, emergence of young, prehibernatory fattening, autumnal immergence, and hibernation until the following spring. Spring emergence is cued to environmental factors associated with the onset of vegetative growth, such as increasing air and soil temperatures and a reduction in the snow cover. In the latter stages of hibernation, the increasing frequency of alternating bouts of torpor (dormancy) and arousal enables the animal to monitor and respond to ambient conditions and to emerge at the most opportune time. Arousal from hibernation is energetically costly, however, because the animal must metabolize a considerable amount of its brown fat reserves in order to rewarm its organs and muscle tissues. Premature depletion of these reserves is a common cause of death in hibernating mammals.

Yellow-bellied Marmots: Hibernation and the Group Advantage Two resources are of critical importance to the overwintering and reproductive success of yellow-bellied marmots: suitable burrow sites and lush herbage for food. Yellow-bellied marmots are active above ground for about four months in summer and fall and hibernate during the remainder of the year. Highly social and territorial, marmots form colonies that consist of a single adult male, a harem of several adult females, several yearlings, and multiple litters of young. Burrows are used as nurseries, resting sites during the day and night, protection from inclement weather, refuges from predators, and communal hibernacula. Marmots spend up to 80 percent of their lives in their burrows, moving between a preferred hibernaculum and an assortment of summer residence burrows.

Within the marmot social system, competition for the best food and burrows is counteracted by the advantages of group living. The colony provides a measure of social protection, increased alertness to predators, and assurance of a suitable hibernaculum, advantages that ultimately ensure colony members a better chance of survival. By sharing home burrows with the colony's juveniles and yearlings, adults enhance their parental investment by providing a safe alternative to premature dispersal. The eventual dispersal of

the yearlings after a period of two years reduces competition within the colony and maintains optimal colony size. Larger colonies are at a distinct disadvantage because of the greater foraging territory required, the longer distances that must be traveled to obtain food, and the increased risk of predation during foraging trips.

Yellow-bellied marmots appear to have an almost enviably simple life. As the mammalogist David Armstrong suggested, their daily routine resembles that of tourists on well-earned vacations at the beach: "Marmots are gourmands and heliophiles—they eat and they sunbathe." The diet of yellow-bellied marmots consists largely of succulent vegetation. Consumption of other food resources, insects and animal matter, occurs when their preferred food plants are in short supply or of poor quality. Foraging begins shortly after emergence from hibernation, with individuals fanning out short distances from the home burrow. Most breeding occurs within two weeks of emergence, ensuring that the female and her young have enough time to accumulate sufficient fat to survive hibernation. Foraging intensifies during the months of July and August, the lush vegetation being converted metabolically into brown fat reserves for the long-haul winter period. To attain their optimal prehibernation weight, juvenile marmots typically remain active later in the season than adults. The failure of females to produce litters in consecutive years in alpine habitats suggests that the postweaning growth period may not be sufficient to allow postpartum females to accumulate the necessary energy reserves both to survive hibernation and to achieve reproductive success the following spring.

Using Microhabitats

Small mammals that do not hibernate or are unable to migrate long distances generally escape climatological extremes by burrowing or taking advantage of sheltered microenvironments under rocks, snow, and vegetation. These animals are of two types: species that continue foraging throughout the winter, making use of whatever protective cover is available, and those that store food for winter consumption. The first group includes both herbivorous and carnivorous species, such as the northern pocket gopher, shrews, weasels, and most voles. The second group includes the pika, least chipmunk, and deer mouse.

The Burrower's Strategy

Northern pocket gophers are common in the alpine tundra of the Southern Rockies. These solitary mammals spend most of their lives below ground, leaving behind enormous networks of foraging tunnels and burrow mounds; the largest burrow system known may exceed 300 feet in length, representing nearly three tons of soil. In fact, these prodigious earth movers are thought to be one of the dominant geomorphic agents in alpine areas where their populations are high. It is uncertain whether the pocket gopher's restriction to areas with winter snow cover reflects a need for protective cover to permit winter foraging beneath the snow or whether the snow is necessary as a buffer against cold temperatures. Evidence of wintertime activity is conspicuous and frequently involves extensive burrowing through the snow to get to new sources of food; such tunnels are then used to dump excavated soil, producing complex patterns of earth tubes, called "gopher eskers," which are exposed on the surface when melt out occurs.

A Network of Runways

Voles, like pocket gophers, prefer habitats with winter snow cover. In contrast to pocket gophers, however, voles forage primarily along the ground surface, their carefully clipped runways often crisscrossing areas with lush sedge or other herbaceous cover. When montane and long-tailed vole populations are high, surface runways, ball nests, piles of rice-shaped feces, ropelike cords of clipped vegetation, and heavily grazed areas are especially conspicuous when the snow melts in the spring. One alpine species, the heather vole, does not construct a runway system except in the immediate vicinity of its nest, and caches food near the nest throughout the year. Most voles, however, do not begin caching food until a protective blanket of snow covers the ground, either to avoid predators or to protect their food stores from being robbed by other small mammals. One study in the Colorado Front Range describes the amazing results of a single, three-week caching effort by montane voles. The voles began harvesting pygmy bitterroot tubers beneath snow that fell during a September storm, creating an extensive series of runways and root-foraging trenches. When the snow melted three weeks later, four separate caches were revealed, yielding a total of 887 pygmy bitterroot tubers, an aggregate energy store of 395 kilocalories! In practical terms, the results of three weeks or less of industrious root-gathering by the voles yielded sufficient reserves to support a single winter-acclimated vole for about twenty-two days without additional foraging. While the voles are busy caching their winter food stores in autumn, they are also building up small but energy-rich brown fat reserves in critical parts of the body. These brown fat reserves will generate heat by fueling the vole's metabolic furnace, allowing the vole to cope with cold temperatures during the long, dark winter beneath the snow.

Pikas: Life in the Talus

The pika is the quintessential alpine mammal, superbly adapted to life in high places. This small member of the *Lagomorpha* inhabits talus slopes and blockfields, which provide refuge from predators, shelter from the sun and from midday heat (pikas are very heat sensitive), and protection from the harsh conditions typical of an alpine winter. The pika's strident, high-pitched territorial calls and nasal squawks are delivered from a lookout rock or sometimes from within the talus, the sound perfectly pitched to carry well in open country. In contrast to other members of the hare and rabbit family, the pika lacks a visible tail and its ears and feet are extremely small, which helps to reduce heat loss through the extremities. The gray-brown color of pikas' fur perfectly matches their rocky habitat, making them hard to spot unless you see them moving about or hear their vocalizations. Additionally, the feet have furred soles, providing a nonskid surface for negotiating rocky surfaces.

Like other lagomorphs, pikas produce two types of feces. The more common type is a dry, fibrous pellet consisting of indigestible waste. The second type is amorphous, soft, and somewhat tarry in appearance and high in protein and other nutrients. The pika reingests the soft feces for an additional round of processing in the digestive system, maximizing the nutritional and caloric contents of its herbaceous diet. Pika urine is highly concentrated and viscous, which allows the excretion of waste products with a minimum consumption of water, an advantage in an environment where free water is often unavailable. Chalk-colored deposits of urine, often encircled by orange patches of the nitrogen-loving lichen *Xanthoria elegans*, are often conspicuous on rocks within the pika's home territory.

To survive, pikas require good foraging habitat (alpine meadows) in close proximity to large patches of suitably blocky talus in which to den. Consequently, pikas are extremely territorial and mostly solitary except during the breeding season. Three main seasonal patterns of activity characterize the typical pika year: breeding from April through June, territorial maintenance and haying from July through October or November, and winter foraging and utilization of stored hay piles. Breeding occurs in late spring as temperatures increase and the alpine snowpack begins to melt. Male-female territorial overlap is prevalent at this season, but the level of aggression between individuals is fairly low. A litter of up to five altricial young is born within about thirty days of mating and coincides with the melting of the snow cover and the appearance of new vegetation. Pikas are the fastest growing of all lagomorph species and may reach adult size within three months of birth. A second, postpartum mating occurs shortly after the birth of the first litter, after which time territorial boundaries are redrawn and vigorously defended by both sexes; although females may initiate two litters per season, a second litter is weaned only if the first litter is lost to predation or as a result of the poor physiological condition of the mother. Reabsorbtion of an entire litter may occur in response to extremely adverse weather conditions.

Vocalizations during the breeding season are varied and consist of "tooth-chattering" (during aggressive encounters), a trill-like call normally delivered by courting males, single-note alarm calls, and long-call exchanges between males and females and between individuals of the same sex. There are distinctive dialect differences in the calls of pikas that result from the islandlike nature of their far-flung geographic distribution.

The best time to observe pikas is during the busy haying season, when they are utterly focused on foraging activities. Vegetation is clipped with the teeth and carried in mouthfuls to a sheltered location among the rocks. Each haypile amounts to a bushel or so of plant material, and the complex of haypiles associated with one individual may consist of as many as thirty different species of plants; on Niwot Ridge, in the Colorado Front Range, the

Pika.

haypiles of one population of pikas averaged twenty-eight kilograms of fresh vegetation per pika, an amount the researcher estimated would require at least 14,000 individual foraging trips over the course of the eight- to ten-week summer harvest periods. Recent research suggests that pikas are able to assess the nutritional value of the available plant foods and harvest accordingly. Though pikas generally avoid harvesting plants that contain high levels of toxic chemicals, they will sometimes cache moderately toxic species in their haypiles because these plants tend to resist decomposition the longest and can be consumed once the toxins decay.

Territorial activity is extremely vigorous during the haying period, with both male and female pikas defending solitary territories in the vicinity of their haypiles. Territorial behavior includes sharp single-note calls, often delivered from the top of conspicuous rocks; scent marking, accomplished by the rubbing of their cheek glands on rocks within the territory; energetic chases; and occasional skirmishes.

With the onset of winter, pikas greatly restrict their movements and foraging activities. Pikas do not rely on their hay piles as their exclusive winter food source; rather, the hay pile serves as insurance against an unusually harsh winter. During good weather, winter foraging continues via tunnels built beneath the snow. As the snowpack deepens over the course of the winter or in times of bad weather, pikas reduce their physical activity and rely on their hay piles for food. Vocalizations are often heard during winter, typically in response to a territorial intrusion or the presence of a predator.

Fossil evidence suggests that pika lineages have persisted in North America for at least 50,000 years and that the modern distribution and virtual isolation of pikas on "mountaintop islands" is the result of climatic changes over the last 10,000 years. The American pika has proven to be extremely vulnerable to the challenges posed by global warming and could well become the first North American mammal to disappear as a direct consequence of human-caused climatic change. With a high average body temperature of 104.2°F and a relatively low lethal body temperature of 109.6°F, the pika is physiologically and behaviorally restricted to cool alpine microclimates. Over the past century, the Western Interior has warmed by at least 1°F; computer models suggest the region will warm by an additional 4.5 to 14.4°F during the next 100 years. For the pika, when behavioral thermoregulation fails, there is nowhere to go but farther up the mountain. In the Great Basin, Sierra Nevada pikas have disappeared from at least eight of the twenty-five mountainous localities where they were once common, and the trend there appears to be accelerating. Similar population declines are occurring in Washington, Oregon, Nevada, Idaho, Montana, Utah, Wyoming, Colorado, and New Mexico. In October of 2007, the Center for Biodiversity petitioned the Secretary of the Interior to list the pika as threatened or endangered under the United States Endangered Species Act. With climate change regarded as the primary driving force behind the current population crisis and the continuing trend towards ever-warmer, drier conditions, future prospects for the pika seem grim indeed.

Mountain Monarchs

Rugged terrain with abundant escape cover in the form of cliffs, ledges, and talus slopes provide optimal habitat for the two mountain monarchs of the Southern Rockies: the bighorn sheep (also called mountain sheep) and the mountain goat. The mountain goat, a nonnative species associated with glaciated subalpine and alpine tundra in the northern and coastal ranges of western North America, was first introduced into Colorado in 1948 by the Colorado Division of Wildlife, with the questionable intent of providing a huntable population. Subsequent introductions in 1950, 1961, 1964, 1968, 1970, and 1971 have allowed mountain goats to become well established in portions of the San Juan Mountains, Gore Range, Collegiate Range, and on Mount Evans. The mountain goat's reliance on free water or snow and on the presence of mineral licks within their home ranges restricts the species to suitable habitat at timberline or above year-round.

Most bighorn sheep, although well adapted to withstand alpine conditions, migrate seasonally to lower elevations where protected winter range remains available to them. In areas where migration routes have been interrupted by human developments, bighorn sheep generally remain in the alpine throughout the year. Indiscriminate hunting, competition with domestic livestock, and introduced sheep diseases decimated bighorn populations throughout the region prior to the 1950s. Today, as a result of both natural recovery and reintroduction efforts, populations are on the increase again in many areas. In Rocky Mountain National Park, the current population is estimated to be several hundred animals. Biologists are continuing to assess the impact and potential problems associated with the introduction and spread of mountain goats into areas historically occupied by bighorn.

Precipitous terrain offers considerable protection from all but the most determined predators. Sheep and goats are remarkably surefooted and adept at moving about their precarious habitats. Bighorn sheep have hooves modified for gripping rocky substrates: the posterior portion of each toe is formed into a round, rubbery pad, and the toes are independently movable and somewhat pincerlike. The mountain goat's hoof, unlike that of other ungulates, has a slightly convex and pliable pad that extends beyond the outer cornified shell. This adaptation permits even greater traction and dexterity. In addition to having remarkable mobility, bighorn rely on keen binocular vision and a well-developed sense of smell to detect danger. If several sheep are together, individuals generally face in different directions so that all approaches are under surveillance.

Bighorn sheep are among the most specialized of all grazers; their ability to survive on a diet of dry, abrasive grasses and herbs of comparatively poor quality gives them a competitive advantage over elk or other grazers. To counteract tooth wear, bighorn sheep, like most grazers, have evolved very long, broad molar teeth that continue to emerge throughout the sheep's life. Like other ruminants, bighorns harbor microorganisms in a specialized chamber of the digestive tract, the rumen, which break down plant cellulose and convert it to volatile fatty acids (acetic, proprionic, and butyric acid) and transform plant protein into amino acids. In contrast to humans, who primarily use glucose to power their metabolic processes, ruminants fuel their metabolic machinery with volatile fatty acids. Bighorn sheep have relatively large rumens compared to other ruminants of equal size, suggesting that the diet on which sheep survive requires a longer processing time than is necessary for soft browse or more succulent forages.

Gregariousness and ritualized social behavior enhance survival of mountain sheep and goats in extreme environments. The basic unit of mountain sheep society is the band; several bands constitute a herd. Bighorn segregate by sex into male (ram) bands and female-and-juvenile bands. Rams follow the largest-horned male during major movements, whereas females tend to follow the lead of an older lamb-leading ewe. Typically, rams have areas where they concentrate in spring and again before the rut begins in November, and where dominance fights occur. The coexistence of rams is governed by a dominance hierarchy; rams apparently judge the dominance rank of other rams by their horn sizes. Mountain sheep society does not differentiate conduct between individuals based on sex, but only between larger (dominant) and smaller (subordinate) animals. The organization and predictability of sheep society appears designed to maximize familiarity with the habitat, minimize energy wasted, discourage the dispersion of juveniles, and promote adherence to traditional home ranges from one generation to the next.

Birds of the Alpine Tundra

For most of the year, the alpine tundra is a beautiful but harsh environment. Most birds accept the gift of mobility, winging their way beyond the howling chinooks and frigid cold of an alpine winter. Spring and summer in the alpine tundra, however, offer a truce that lasts for a few sweet weeks. Though bird species diversity is comparatively low in alpine regions, the handful of species that breed in the tundra, the white-tailed ptarmigan, water pipits, horned larks, rosy finches, white-crowned sparrows, rock wrens, and the rare black swift, partition the limited resources to ensure success.

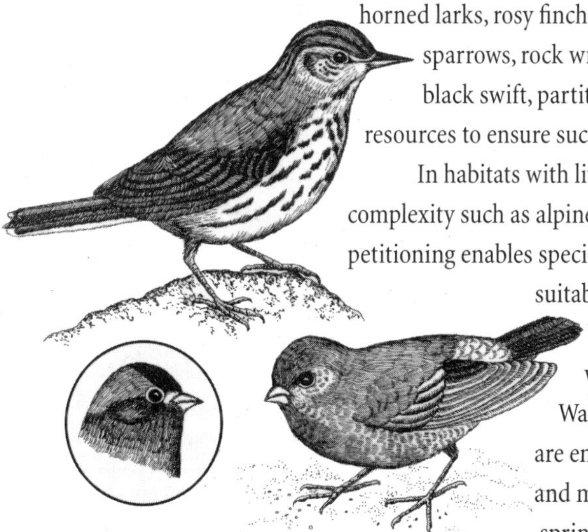

In habitats with little structural complexity such as alpine tundra, resource petitioning enables species to appropriate suitable niche space and to avoid competition with other species. Water pipits, for example, are entirely insectivorous, and much of their food in spring and early summer consists of cold-numbed or dead insects gleaned

Common birds of the alpine tundra, from top to bottom: water pipit, brown-capped rosy finch, inset of gray-crowned rosy finch.

from the surfaces of snowbanks or plucked from moist ground. Pipits nest on the ground, tucking their cup-shaped nests under the overhanging edges of rocks or beneath the protective cover of grass tussocks; the eggs are chocolate brown, providing both camouflage and additional heat gain. Horned larks, also ground nesters, forage on snowbanks for insects but gather seeds and other plant foods for at least a quarter of their diet. White-tailed ptarmigan nest in shallow depressions in a snow-free area protected from the wind; the rudimentary nest is softened with some grasses and a few feathers, and one side of the nest is left open for escape. The ptarmigan's diet varies seasonally, with nitrogen-rich snow buttercup leaves favored in early spring and willow catkins, bistort bulblets, snowball saxifrage, alpine avens flowers, and the blooms of chickweed filling out the menu in summer. With the coming of fall and winter, the ptarmigan's diet shifts from flowers to seeds, willow buds, and willow twigs. To cope with the increased consumption of more cellulose-rich plant tissues, the ptarmigan must rely on bacteria-aided digestion in the cecum. Ptarmigan chicks start out their lives on a diet of insects, gradually adding flowers and leaves to the mix; the chick's diet shift corresponds to the delayed development of the cecum and long intestine.

Rosy finches are essentially seedeaters, though they feed their nestlings a diet of insects and are often observed foraging opportunistically along the edges of receding snowbanks. But rosy finches, in contrast to ground-nesting white-tailed ptarmigan, water pipits, and horned larks, are obligate cliff nesters, placing their nests in rock crevices and under overhangs that provide shelter from the weather. White-crowned sparrows build their nests in tree islands or in boggy willow areas near timberline; when you hear the exquisite trilling song of the male white-crowned sparrow defending its territory, it usually means there's a nest nearby.

Several alpine birds practice behavioral temperature regulation. On days that are windy and cold, if the sun is out, horned larks are often observed basking in the sunshine on the lee sides of rocks or taller clumps of vegetation. On cold nights, horned larks may dig shallow roosting holes in the ground with their bills and sleep with their backs approximately level with the ground surface. The use of roosting holes exposes only a minimal amount of the horned lark's body surface and reduces radiative and convective heat losses. In much the same way, the white-tailed ptarmigan makes use of the insulative value of snow by seeking out soft patches in which to tunnel and roost at night and during periods of inclement weather. During the long alpine winter, ptarmigan spend anywhere from a few hours to a few days in these snow burrows, benefitting by a reduction in heat loss of up to 45 percent.

The courtship and territorial displays of alpine birds resemble those of species associated with grasslands or other open habitats. Male water pipits engage in elaborate song flights, which consist of a steep vertical ascent accompanied by a simple, somewhat liquid song and followed by a descent to the ground, during which the bird raises and spreads its tail, dangles its legs, flutters its wings, and quickens the tempo of its song. The male horned lark begins its song flight by suddenly rising with rapid wingbeats, climbing in irregular circles (rising vertically if flying into a strong wind) to a height of several hundred feet. Singing repeatedly, the male continues to flap and soar in circles before folding its wings and plunging to the ground, only to pull out at the last moment and sail across the ground before alighting on a clump of vegetation.

Solar-powered Insects

Most insects become sluggish and are unable to fly at low temperatures. Flies, with their remarkably low energy requirements and their tolerance of cool temperatures, assume considerable importance as pollinators in alpine environments. Several other flying insects, including bumblebees and some butterflies, are able to warm up their flight muscles by muscular thermogenesis, a physiological process in which heat is produced internally in a manner analogous to shivering in warm-blooded animals. Bumblebees require a thoracic temperature of nearly 85°F before they are able to fly. To maintain this temperature, the bumblebee must find food at a rate at least equal to the rate at which fuel is consumed in foraging. The bee's ability to move about as a result of muscular thermogenesis when temperatures are low and most other nectar-feeding insects are inactive confers a competitive advantage and helps to ensure an adequate food supply.

Butterflies gain the heat they need for metabolic processes and locomotor activity largely from the sun or from their surroundings. Research has shown that butterflies require thoracic temperatures of at least 80°F to initiate flight. Scale color and pubescence, as exemplified by the dark gray scaling of the Rocky Mountain parnassian or the ebony, plushly furred wings of the Magdalena alpine, are important morphological adaptations that increase the solar efficiency of the wings. By changing the orientation of the wings, either through basking to maximize heat gain or by closing the wings dorsally to reduce overheating, butterflies are able to maintain a range of optimal body temperatures similar to those of warm-blooded animals. To further maximize their solar gain, butterflies seek out wind-sheltered microhabitats, such as the flower head of old-man-of-the-mountain, for basking.

Magdalena alpine.

Basking positions vary from species to species, and a given subfamily of butterflies often exhibits a characteristic basking style. A great many species simply press the thorax and abdomen closely to a warm rock or other surface. Members of the subfamily Coliadinae (sulfurs) tilt sideways to present the ventral surface of the hind wings perpendicular to the angle of the sun. Several genera of Satyridae (satyrs, wood nymphs, browns, alpines, and arctics), the Lycaenidae (blues, coppers, and hairstreaks), and the Pierinae (whites and orange tips) are body baskers, angling the wings narrowly to maximize solar gain to the body. Most Papilionidae (swallowtails and parnassians) and Nymphalidae (angle-wings, checkerspots, tortoiseshells, admirals, and painted ladies) are open-wing baskers, undoubtedly the most efficient position for rapidly elevating body temperature.

Insects on Ice

Confronted by the rigors of winter, insects enter a state of hibernation or arrested development known as diapause. During diapause, there is no growth or metamorphosis, and the metabolic rate is substantially reduced. In alpine environments, some insects overwinter as eggs, some as larvae, some as pupae, and a few as adults. In most cases, hibernating or diapausal insects seek a sheltered hibernaculum, either by shallow burrowing in soil or vegetation or by crawling under rocks or into crevices, where they are buffered from fluctuating air temperatures. Insects that normally complete their life cycles in one season at lower elevations may take two or more seasons at higher elevations. Most butterflies, moths, spiders, and beetles follow this developmental pattern. High-elevation flies and mosquitoes, on the other hand, complete developmental stages in a single season and can reproduce several times in spite of the brevity of the alpine summer.

Alpine insects generally achieve winter hardiness in one of two ways. Some insects, such as beetles, survive the cold by lowering the freezing point of their tissues through the synthesis of compounds such as glycerol or even ethylene glycol, the ingredient in common automobile antifreeze. Other insects actually induce freezing in parts of their bodies. The key to surviving self-induced freezing is to prevent dehydration and ice formation inside cells while allowing other body cavities (the gut, blood, and spaces between the cells) to gradually fill with ice. These insects, such as the familiar "woolly bear" caterpillar (the overwintering larval stage of the tiger moth), have the ability to synthesize glycerol and other compounds that reduce the proportion of bodily water locked up in ice.

Life Histories of Selected Animals

Mammals

Pika, *Ochotona princeps.* This small, quick-moving mammal is approximately the size of a juvenile cottontail and has brownish gray fur, rounded ears, and no visible tail. Pikas are restricted to the alpine and subalpine zone and are found almost exclusively in talus or other rock rubble near meadows that provide adequate forage. Vocalizations include a variety of high-pitched, single- and multiple-note calls, and nasal squawks. These diurnal herbivores are active year-round, gathering vegetation during the summer months and storing it in small hay piles for use during the winter. Territories are maintained through scent marking, vocalizations, chases, and a variety of aggressive behaviors. One litter of altricial young is born in late June or early July.

Yellow-bellied Marmot, *Marmota flaviventris.* The yellow-bellied marmot, the largest of the ground-dwelling squirrels, is identified by its rusty brown upperparts, grizzled whitish fur about the mouth and chin, and yellowish brown belly. Marmots are encountered in rocky outcrops with adjacent meadows for foraging and are common from the upper foothills to the alpine tundra. These diurnal herbivores are active during the late spring and summer and hibernate during the remainder of the year. Highly social, they form small colonies consisting of a single adult male, a harem of adult females, yearlings, and young. Vocalizations include high-pitched whistles, squeals, and tooth-chattering. Breeding occurs in spring, shortly after emergence from hibernation, and each female gives birth to a single litter of altricial young.

Ermine (or Short-tailed Weasel), *Mustela erminea.* The short-tailed weasel, or ermine, is identified by its small size (adults average eight inches in total length), slender body, and black-tipped tail. In summer, the weasel's upperparts are a rich brown and the belly and chin are pale buff; winter pelage is pure white, except for the black-tipped tail. Like most mustelids, the short-tailed weasel is carnivorous, feeding on small mammals, birds, and insects. Active mostly at dawn and dusk, short-tailed weasels are solitary and maintain winter and summer hunting territories. Mating occurs in late spring, shortly after the female gives birth, but gestation is prolonged for about ten months by delayed implantation.

Bighorn Sheep (or Mountain Sheep), *Ovis canadensis.* Bighorn sheep, or mountain sheep, are medium-sized, stocky ungulates with a whitish rump patch and horns. Horns are not shed as antlers are, and the most massive, fully curled horns are characteristic of the oldest rams. The horns of the female are spikelike; the horns of juvenile males resemble those of the female, becoming broader based and more curled with increasing age. Bighorns prefer remote, rocky terrain with quick access to escape cover and meadows for grazing. Bighorn sheep are diurnal and active throughout the year, alternating bouts of intense grazing with periods of rest and rumination. Lambing occurs in late May and early June; single lambs are typical, but twin lambs are also reported in some populations.

Birds

White-tailed Ptarmigan, *Lagopus leucurus.* The white-tailed ptarmigan is largely restricted to alpine tundra and is identified by its grouselike appearance, white tail, and by the male's reddish eye combs. Winter plumage is white except for the dark bill and red eye comb; summer plumage is mottled brown and black on top and white below. Vocalizations are varied and include soft, henlike clucking and a high-pitched *ku-kriee-kriee* most often heard at dawn or dusk. White-tailed ptarmigan are herbivorous, relying heavily on the buds and woody twigs of alpine willows during the winter. The summer diet consists of a diversity of green leaves and flowers; seeds and the bulblets of alpine bistort may also be important. Male territorial establishment consists of "flight screams," "ground challenging," and intimidating postures. Males are typically monogamous, and pair bonds are maintained throughout the breeding season. Climatic events control the timing of breeding and nesting. The female ptarmigan builds a simple scrape nest on the ground, and the male assists the female by acting as sentry at the nest. Juveniles remain with the mother through autumn.

Ptarmigan; nest with eggs.

Horned Lark, *Eremophila alpestris.* The bold black mustache, black ear tufts, and white outer tail feathers (bordering an otherwise black tail) distinguish the horned lark. This species is most often encountered in open country and occurs from the shortgrass prairie to the alpine tundra. Horned larks forage for seeds and insects while walking or running over the ground. Males establish and defend breeding territories; the male performs territorial song flights, courtship feeding, and other displays. The female selects a nest site on the ground and excavates a hole for the cup-shaped nest of grass with her bill, often "paving" the nest site on one side with small stones.

Water Pipit, *Anthus spinoletta.* Water pipits are sparrow-sized birds with brownish gray upperparts and pinkish buff, moderately streaked underparts. Pipits prefer low-elevation grasslands and meadows during migration but are largely restricted to alpine tundra during the nesting season. This species is often observed foraging along the ground or on snowbanks for insects and seeds; the pumping motions of its tail as it moves or perches provide a good field mark to watch for. Territorial males engage in elaborate song flights and ground-perched singing. Pipits nest on the ground, constructing cup-shaped nests of grasses tucked beneath rocks or plant tussocks; pipit eggs are a soft, chocolate brown.

Rosy-finch, *Leucosticte australis, L. tephrocotis,* and *L. atrata.* Rosy-finches hybridize in areas of overlap and, in the Southern Rockies, include three subspecies distinguished by head pattern and body color. The **brown-capped rosy-finch** (*L. australis*) is identified by its brown cap and brighter rose underparts, wings, and rump; this subspecies occurs in the Southern Rockies year-round. The **gray-crowned rosy-finch** (*L. tephrocotis*), a winter resident in our region, is distinguished by its silver-gray crown and blackish forehead; this subspecies nests largely north and west of the Southern Rockies and is a common breeding bird on the Alaskan tundra. The rare **black rosy-finch** (*L. atrata*) has distinctly darker plumage and breeds in the Great Basin and northwestern Rockies. Winter flocks in the Southern Rockies may number several hundred birds and include more than one subspecies. On their breeding grounds, brown-capped rosy-finches forage for seeds and occasional insects on the ground and on snowbanks; rosy-finches have gular pouches beneath their tongues for transporting food to the nest site. During the breeding season, aggressive encounters between territorial males are frequent and vigorous. Territorial behavior is unusual in that the area defended by the male changes with the movement of the female. This close defense of the female, with the male shadowing her wherever she goes, arises out of the strong preponderance of males in both breeding and wintering populations. Rosy-finches nest in crevices and holes in cliffs; the female builds the nest and incubates the eggs but is assisted by the male in caring for the nestlings.

Common Animals of the Alpine Tundra

Mammals

Badger, American, *Taxidea taxus*
Bobcat, *Lynx rufus*
Chipmunk, least, *Tamias minimus*

Coyote, *Canis latrans*
Deer, mule, *Odocoileus hemionus*
Elk (or Wapiti), *Cervus elaphus*
Ermine (or Short-tailed Weasel), *Mustela erminea*
Goat, mountain, *Oreamnos americanus*
Jackrabbit, white-tailed, *Lepus townsendii*
Marmot, yellow-bellied, *Marmota flaviventris*
Marten, *Martes americana*
Mouse, deer, *Peromyscus maniculatus*
Pika, *Ochotona princeps*
Pocket Gopher, northern, *Thomomys talpoides*
Sheep, bighorn (or Mountain Sheep), *Ovis canadensis*
Shrew, dwarf, *Sorex nanus*
  masked, *S. cinereus*
Squirrel, golden-mantled ground, *Spermophilus lateralis*
Vole, heather, *Phenacomys intermedius*
  long-tailed, *Microtus longicaudus*
  montane, *M. montanus*
Weasel, long-tailed, *Mustela frenata*
Woodrat, bushy-tailed, *Neotoma cinerea*

Birds

Bluebird, mountain, *Sialia currucoides*
Dipper, American, *Cinclus mexicanus*
Eagle, golden, *Aquila chrysaetos*
Falcon, prairie, *Falco mexicanus*
Gull, Franklin's, *Larus pipixcan*
Hawk, red-tailed, *Buteo jamaicensis*
Hummingbird, broad-tailed, *Selasphorus platycercus*
  rufous, *S. rufus*
Kestrel, American (formerly Sparrow Hawk), *Falco sparverius*
Lark, horned, *Eremophila alpestris*
Pipit, water, *Anthus spinoletta*
Ptarmigan, white-tailed, *Lagopus leucurus*
Raven, common, *Corvus corax*

Robin, American, *Turdus migratorius*
Rosy-Finch, *Leucosticte australis, L. tephrocotis,* and *L. atrata*
Sandpiper, spotted, *Actitis macularia*
Sparrow, white-crowned, *Zonotrichia leucophrys*
Swift, black, *Cypseloides niger*
Wren, rock, *Salpinctes obsoletus*

Butterflies

Alpine, Colorado, *Erebia callias*
    common, *E. epipsodea*
    Magdalena, *E. magdalena*
    Theano, *E. theano*
Arctic, Melissa, *Oeneis melissa*
    polixenes, *O. polixenes*
Blue, arctic, *Agriades aquilo*
    high mountain, *A. franklinii*
    Shasta, *Icaricia shasta*
Checkerspot, rockslide, *Charadrius damoetas*
Copper, lustrous, *Chalceria cupreus*
Fritillary, bog, *Proclossiana eunomia*
    Mormon, *Speyeria mormonia*
    mountain, *Boloria napaea*
    Uncompahgre, *Boloria improba acrocnema*
Parnassian, Rocky Mountain, *Parnassius smintheus*
Skipper, alpine checkered, *Pyrgus centaureae*
Sulphur, Mead's, *Colias meadii*
Tortoiseshell, Milbert's, *Aglais milberti*
White, western, *Pontia occidentalis*

Selected References

Regional Books

Evans, Howard Ensign, and Mary Alice Evans. *Cache La Poudre: The Natural History of a Rocky Mountain River*. Niwot, CO: University Press of Colorado, 1991.

Houk, Rose. *Black Canyon of the Gunnison*. Tucson, AZ: Southwest Parks and Monuments Association, 1991.

Julyan, Bob, and Tom Till. *New Mexico's Wilderness Areas: The Complete Guide*. Denver: Westcliffe Publishers, 1999.

Norton, Boyd, and Barbara Norton. *Backroads of Colorado: Your Guide to Colorado's 50 Most Scenic Tours*. Stillwater, MN: Voyageur Press, 1995.

Rennicke, Jeff. *The Rivers of Colorado*. Colorado Geographic Series, no. 1. Billings and Helena, MT: Falcon Publishing, 1985.

———. *Colorado Mountain Ranges*. Colorado Geographic Series, no 2. Billings and Helena, MT: Falcon Publishing, 1986.

Rozinski, Bob, Wendy Shattil, and Audrey DeLella Benedict. *Valley of the Dunes: Great Sand Dunes National Park and Preserve*. Golden, CO: Fulcrum Publishing, 2005.

Sellers, Judith B., and Williard Clay. *Colorado Wild: Preserving the Spirit and Beauty of Our Land*. Stillwater, MN: Voyageur Press, 2002.

Trimble, Stephen. *Great Sand Dunes: The Shape of the Wind*. Globe, AZ: Southwest Parks and Monuments Association, 2001.

Thybony, Scott, Robert G. Rosenberg, and Elizabeth Mullett Rosenberg. *The Medicine Bows: Wyoming's Mountain Country*. Caldwell, ID: Caxton Press, 2000.

History and Archaeology

Benedict, James B. Center for Mountain Archeology Research Reports; Numbers 1–9. Ward, CO: Center for Mountain Archeology, 1978–2007.

———. "Tundra Game Drives: An Arctic-Alpine Comparison." *Arctic, Antarctic, and Alpine Research* 37, no. 4 (2005): 425–34.

Cassells, E. Steve. *The Archaeology of Colorado*, rev. ed. Boulder, CO: Johnson Books, 1997.

Eberhart, Perry. *Guide to the Colorado Ghost Towns and Mining Camps*. Chicago: Swallow Press, 1969.

Evans, Howard Ensign. *The Natural History of the Long Expedition: 1819–1820.* New York: Oxford University Press, 1997.

Lavender, David. *Colorado River Country.* New York: E. P. Dutton, Inc., 1982.

———. *The Rockies.* Lincoln: University of Nebraska Press, 1968.

Noble, David Grant, ed. *Bandelier National Monument: Geology, History, and Prehistory.* Santa Fe, NM: School of American Research, 1980.

Simmons, Virginia McConnell. *The San Luis Valley: Land of the Six-Armed Cross.* Boulder: University Press of Colorado, 1999.

Sprague, Marshall. *The Great Gates: The Story of Rocky Mountain Passes.* Lincoln: University of Nebraska Press, 1964.

Viola, Herman J. *Exploring the West.* Washington, DC: Smithsonian Books, 1987.

General Touring, Hiking Guides, and Maps

Colorado Trail Foundation. *The Colorado Trail: The Trailside Databook.* Colorado Trail Foundation, 2002.

Cushman, Ruth Carol, and Glenn Cushman. *Boulder Hiking Trails.* Boulder, CO: Pruett Publishing, 1995.

Dannen, Kent, and Donna Dannen. *Rocky Mountain National Park Hiking Trails (Including Indian Peaks)*, 9th ed. Guilford, CT: Globe Pequot Press/Falcon Publishing, 2002.

Gaug, Maryann. *Hiking Colorado: A Guide to Colorado's Greatest Hiking Adventures.* Guilford, CT: Globe Pequot Press/Falcon Publishing, 2003.

Jacobs, Randy, ed., with Robert M. Ormes. *Guide to the Colorado Mountains, 10th Edition.* Golden, CO: The Colorado Mountain Club Press, 2000.

Martin, Craig. *100 Hikes in New Mexico*, 2nd ed. Seattle: Mountaineers Books, 2002.

National Scenic Byways Online (New Mexico, Colorado, and Wyoming). Byway directory, www.byways.org/browse/states, 2006.

Pixler, Paul. *Hiking Trails of Southwestern Colorado.* Boulder, CO: Pruett Publishing, 1981.

Roach, Gerry. *Colorado's Fourteeners: From Hikes to Climbs*, 2nd ed. Golden, CO: Fulcrum Publishing, 1999.

Smith, Marc. *Hiking Wyoming's Medicine Bow National Forest.* Casper, WY: Open Space Publications, 2003.

Warren, Scott S. *100 Classic Hikes in Colorado,2nd Edition.* Seattle: Mountaineers Books, 2001.

Winger, Charlie. *The Essential Guide to Great Sand Dunes National Park and Preserve.* Golden, CO: Colorado Mountain Club Press, 2003.

Geology

Benedict, James B. "Downslope Soil Movement in a Colorado Alpine Region Rates, Processes, and Climatic Significance." *Arctic and Alpine Research* 2, no. 3 (1970).

Beus, Stanley S., ed. *Centennial Field Guide Vol. 2, Rocky Mountain Section of the Geological Society of America*. Boulder, CO: Geological Society of America, 1987.

Bjornerud, Marcia. *Reading the Rocks: The Autobiography of the Earth*. Cambridge, MA: Westview Press, 2005.

Blackstone, D. L. *Traveler's Guide to the Geology of Wyoming*. Laramie: Wyoming Geological Survey, 1971.

Bridge, Raymond. *The Geology of Boulder County*. Boulder, CO: Lone Eagle Publications, 2004.

Chronic, Halka, and Felicie Williams. *Roadside Geology of Colorado*, 2nd ed. Missoula, MT: Mountain Press, 2002.

Crumpler, L. S., and J. C. Aubele. *Volcanoes of New Mexico: An Abbreviated Guide for Non-Specialists: Volcanology in New Mexico*. Bulletin 18. Albuquerque: New Mexico Museum of Natural History and Science, 2001.

Goff, F., B. Kues, M. Rogers, L. McFadden, and J. Gardner, eds. *The Jemez Mountains Region*. Guidebook 47. Socorro: New Mexico Geological Society, 1996.

Hansen, Wallace R. *The Black Canyon of the Gunnison: In Depth*. Tucson, AZ: Southwest Parks and Monuments Association, 1987.

Hopkins, Ralph Lee, and Lindy Birkel Hopkins. *Hiking Colorado's Geology*. Seattle: The Mountaineers, 2000.

Lockley, M. G., B. J. Fillmore, and L. Marquardt. *Dinosaur Lake: The Story of the Purgatoire Valley Dinosaur Tracksite*. Special Publication 40. Denver: Colorado Geological Survey, 1997.

Mathews, Vincent. *Messages in Stone: Colorado's Colorful Geology*. Denver: Department of Natural Resources, 2003.

Mathez, Edmond A., and James D. Webster. *The Earth Machine: The Science of a Dynamic Planet*. New York: Columbia University Press, 2004.

McPhee, John. *Rising from the Plains*. New York: Farrar Straus Giroux, 1986.

Mears, Brainerd, Jr., et al. *A Geologic Tour of Wyoming from Laramie to Lander, Jackson, and Rock Springs*. Circular no. 27. Laramie: Geological Survey of Wyoming, Public Information, 1986.

Tweto, Ogden, comp. *Geologic Map of Colorado*. Denver: United States Geological Survey, 1979.

Voynick, Stephen M. *Colorado Gold: From the Pike's Peak Rush to the Present*. Missoula, MT: Mountain Press, 1992.

———. *Colorado Rockhounding: A Guide to Minerals, Gemstones, and Fossils*. Missoula, MT: Mountain Press, 1994.

Climate

Ives, J. D., and R. G. Barry, eds. *Arctic and Alpine Environments*. London: Methuen, 1974.

Keen, Richard A. *Skywatch: The Complete Western Weather Guide, Revised Edition*. Golden, CO: Fulcrum Publishing, 2004.

Price, Larry W. *Mountains and Man: A Study of Process and Environment*. Berkeley: University of California Press, 1981.

Schaefer, Victor J., and John A. Day. *A Field Guide to the Atmosphere*. The Peterson Field Guide Series, No. 26. Boston: Houghton Mifflin, 1981.

Snow and Winter Environments

Armstrong, Betsy, and Knox Williams. *The Avalanche Book*. Golden, CO: Fulcrum Publishing, 1986.

Halfpenny, James C., and Roy Douglas Ozanne. *Winter: An Ecological Handbook*. Boulder, CO: Johnson Books, 1989.

LaChapelle, Edward B. *Field Guide to Snow Crystals*. Seattle: University of Washington Press, 1969.

Marchand, Peter J. *Life in the Cold: An Introduction to Winter Ecology, 3rd Edition*. Hanover, NH: University Press of New England, 1996.

General Natural History and Ecology

Arno, Stephen F., and Ramona P. Hammerly. *Timberline: Mountain and Arctic Forest Frontiers*. Seattle: Mountaineers Books, 1984.

Bowman, William D., and Timothy R. Seastedt, eds. *Structure and Function of an Alpine Ecosystem: Niwot Ridge, Colorado*. New York: Oxford University Press, 2001.

Cushman, Ruth Carol, and Stephen R. Jones. *The Shortgrass Prairie*. Boulder, CO: Pruett Publishing, 1988.

Cushman, Ruth Carol, Stephen R. Jones, and Jim Knopf. *Boulder County Nature Almanac*. Boulder, CO: Pruett Publishing, 1993.

Floyd, M. Lisa., ed. *Ancient Piñon-Juniper Woodlands: A Natural History of Mesa Verde Country*. Boulder, CO: University Press of Colorado, 2003.

Gellhorn, Joyce. *Song of the Alpine: The Rocky Mountain Tundra through the Seasons*. Boulder, CO: Johnson Books, 2002.

Halfpenny, James C., ed. *Ecological Studies in the Colorado Alpine: A festschrift for John Marr.* Occasional Paper 37, Institute of Arctic and Alpine Research. Boulder: University of Colorado.

Holtmeier, Friederich-Karl. *Mountain Timberlines: Ecology, Patchiness, and Dynamics*. Kluwer Academic Publishers, Dordrecht, The Netherlands, 2003.

Jones, Stephen R., and Ruth Carol Cushman. *The North American Prairie*. The Petersen Field Guide Series. New York: Houghton Mifflin, 2004.

Lanner, Ronald M. *The Piñon Pine: A Natural and Cultural History*. Reno: University of Nevada Press, 1981.

———. *Made for Each Other: A Symbiosis of Birds and Pines*. New York: Oxford University Press, 1996.

Marchand, Peter J. *Autumn: A Season of Change*. Hanover, NH: University of New England Press, 2000.

Marr, John W. *Ecosystems of the East Slope of the Colorado Front Range*. University of Colorado Studies, Series in Biology No. 8. Boulder: University of Colorado, 1967.

Murphy, Alexandra. *Graced by Pines: The Ponderosa Pine in the American West.* Missoula, MT: Mountain Press, 1994.

Mutel, Cornelia Fleisher, and John C. Emerick. *From Grassland to Glacier: The Natural History of Colorado and the Surrounding Region*, 2nd ed. Boulder, CO: Johnson Books, 1992.

Shepperd, Wayne D., Dan Binkley, Dale L. Bartos, Thomas J. Stohlgren, and Lane G. Askew, compilers. *Sustaining Aspen in Western Landscapes: Symposium Proceedings; June 13–15, 2000; Grand Junction, CO.* Proceedings RMRS-P-18. Fort Collins, CO: U.S. Department of Agriculture, Forest Service, Rocky Mountain Research Station.

Suzuki, David, and Wayne Grady. *Tree: A Life Story*. Vancouver, BC: Greystone Books, 2004.

Windell, J. T., B. E. Williard, D. J. Cooper, S. Q. Foster, C. F. Knud-Hansen, L. P. Rink, and G. N. Kiladis. *An ecological characterization* of *Rocky Mountain montane and subalpine wetlands.* U. S. Fish and Wildlife Service Biological Report 86(11), 1986.

Zwinger, Ann H., and Beatrice E. Willard. *Land Above the Trees: A Guide to American Alpine Tundra*. New York: Harper & Row, 1972.

Plant Field Guides

Beidleman, Linda H., Richard G. Beidleman, and Beatrice E. Willard. *Plants of Rocky Mountain National Park*. Helena, MT: Falcon Publishing, 2000.

Corbridge, James N., and William A. Weber. *A Rocky Mountain Lichen Primer*. Niwot, CO: University Press of Colorado, 1998.

Ells, James. *Rocky Mountain Flora*. Golden, CO: The Colorado Mountain Club Press, 2006.

Evenson, Vera Stucky. *Mushrooms of Colorado and the Southern Rockies*. Englewood, CO: Westcliffe Publishers, 1997.

Freeman, Craig C., and Eileen K. Schofield. *Roadside Wildflowers of the Southern Great Plains*. Lawrence: University Press of Kansas, 1991.

Guennel, G. K. *Guide to Colorado Wildflowers: Plains & Mountains*, vol. 1. Englewood, CO: Westcliffe Publishing, 1995.

———. *Guide to Colorado Wildflowers: Mountains*, vol. 2. Englewood, CO: Westcliffe Publishing, 2004.

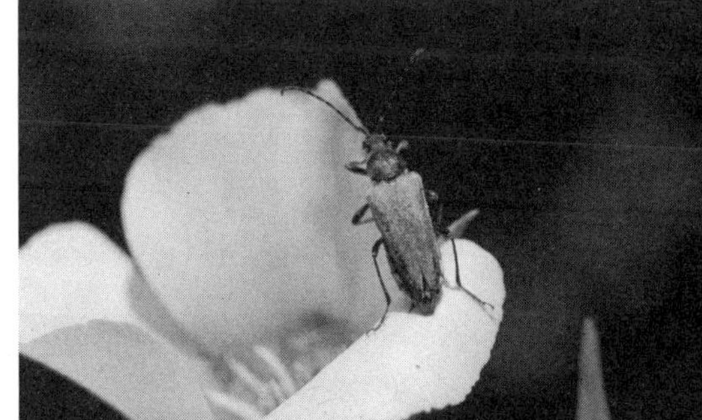

Harrington, H. D. *Edible Native Plants of the Rocky Mountains*. Albuquerque: University of New Mexico Press, 1967.

Martin, William C., and Charles H. Hutchins. *Spring Wildflowers of New Mexico*. Albuquerque: University of New Mexico Press, 1984.

———. *Summer Wildflowers of New Mexico*. Albuquerque: University of New Mexico Press, 1986.

Robertson, Leigh. *Southern Rocky Mountain Wildflowers*. Guilford, CT: Globe Pequot Press/Falcon Publishing, 1999.

Russo, Ron. *Field Guide to Plant Galls of California and Other Western States*. Berkeley: University of California Press, 2006.

Weber, William A., and Ronald C. Wittman. *Colorado Flora: Eastern Slope*. Niwot, CO: University Press of Colorado, 2001.

———. *Colorado Flora: Western Slope*. Niwot, CO: Colorado Associated University Press, 2001.

Wingate, Janet L., and Lorraine Yeatts. *Alpine Flower Finder: The Key to Rocky Mountain Wildflowers Found Above Treeline*. Boulder, CO: Johnson Books, 2003.

Mammals

Adams, Rick A. *Bats of the Rocky Mountains: Natural History, Ecology, and Conservation*. Boulder: The University Press of Colorado, 2003.

Armstrong, David. *Rocky Mountain Mammals*. Niwot, CO: Colorado Associated University Press, 1987.

Boyce, Mark S., and Larry D. Hayden-Wing, eds. *North American Elk: Ecology, Behavior and Management*. Laramie: The University of Wyoming Press, 1979.

Connor, Douglas A. "Life in a Rock Pile." *Natural History* (June 1983): 51–57.

Dearing, D. "The manipulation of plant toxins by a food-hoarding herbivore, the North American pika, Ochotona princeps." *Ecology* 78:774–781.

Elbroch, Mark. *Mammal Tracks & Sign: A Guide to North American Species*. Mechanicsburg, PA: Stackpole Books, 2003.

Findley, James S., et al. *Mammals of New Mexico*. Albuquerque: University of New Mexico Press, 1975.

Fitzgerald, James P., Carron A. Meaney, and David M. Armstrong. *Mammals of Colorado*. Niwot, CO: University Press of Colorado and Denver Museum of Natural History, 1994.

Ogara, Bart W., and Jim D. Yoakum. *Pronghorn Ecology and Management* (A Wildlife Management Institute Book). Boulder, CO: University Press of Colorado, 2004.

Valdez, Raul, and Paul R. Krausman, eds. *Mountain Sheep of North America*. Tucson: University of Arizona Press, 1999.

Wallmo, O. C., ed. *Mule and Black-tailed Deer of North America*. Lincoln: University of Nebraska Press, 1981.

Birds

Elbroch, Mark, and Eleanor Marks. *Bird Tracks & Sign: A Guide to North American Species*. Mechanicsburg, PA: Stackpole Books, 2001.

Gellhorn, Joyce. *White-tailed Ptarmigan: Ghosts of the Alpine Tundra*. Boulder, CO: Johnson Books, 2007.

Harrison, Hal H. *A Field Guide to Western Bird's Nests*. The Peterson Field Guide Series, No. 25. Boston: Houghton Mifflin, 1979.

Kingery, Hugh E., ed. *Colorado Breeding Bird Atlas*. Denver: Colorado Bird Atlas Partnership, 1998.

Sibley, David Allen. *The Sibley Field Guide to Birds: Western North America*. New York: Chanticleer Press, Inc., 2003.

Wheeler, Brian K., and William S. Clark. *A Photographic Guide to North American Raptors*. Princeton, NJ: Princeton University Press, 2003.

Amphibians and Reptiles

Hammerson, Geoffrey. *Amphibians and Reptiles in Colorado*. Niwot, CO: University Press of Colorado and Colorado Division of Wildlife, 1999.

Fish

Woodling, John D. *Game Fish of Colorado.* Pub Code DOW-M-1-25-84. Denver: Colorado Division of Wildlife, 1980.

———. *Colorado's Little Fish: A Guide to the Minnows and Other Lesser-Known Fishes in the State of Colorado*. Denver: Colorado Division of Wildlife, 1985.

Invertebrates

Angel, Leslie. *Butterflies of Rocky Mountain National Park*. Boulder, CO: Johnson Books, 2005.

Cranshaw, Whitney, and Boris Kondratieff. *Guide to Colorado Insects*. Engelwood, CO: Westcliffe Publishers, 2006.

Glassberg, Jeffrey. *Butterflies through Binoculars: A Field Guide to the Butterflies of Western North America*. New York: Oxford University Press, 2001.

Opler, Paul A., and Amy Bartlett Wright. *Peterson Field Guides: A Field Guide to Western Butterflies*. New York: Houghton Mifflin, 1999.

Pyle, Robert Michael. *The Audubon Society Field Guide to North American Butterflies*. New York: Alfred A Knopf, 1981.

Ward, J. V., and B. C. Kondratieff. *An Illustrated Guide to the Mountain Stream Insects*. Niwot, CO: University Press of Colorado, 1992.

Weissmann, Michael J., Linda P. Clement, and Boris Kondratieff. *Insects and Other Arthropods of Great Sand Dunes National Monument*. Tucson, AZ: Southwest Parks and Monuments Association, 1993.

Index

NOTE: Page numbers in *italics* refer to illustrations. Page numbers in **boldface** refer to major discussions or species descriptions. Scientific names are indexed only if no English name is available. Index entries for all plant or animal species are listed under the appropriate category heading: AMPHIBIANS, BIRDS, FUNGI, INSECTS, MAMMALS, TREES, WILDFLOWERS, etc.

A

Acclimatization, to altitude, 152; to seasonal changes, 185

Acid rain, lichens and, 356

Adaptive radiation, 81, 93

Adiabatic heating, 164

Agriculture, 25, 30, 43, 45–47, 51

Air, density, 151–152; pollution, 159; pressure and winds, 152–153

Air mass source areas, 150–151, 154, 166

Albuquerque Low, 168

Alder, mountain, 411, 416

Algae, snow, 589, 591

Allelopathy, 236–237, 487

Alluvial-fan deposits, 90, 114

Alpine Loop, National Backcountry Scenic Byway, 29

Alpine tundra, animal adaptations, **609–628**; climate, **576–578**; common plants, **601–608**; definitions, **574–575**; plant adaptations, **594–600**; plant communities, **579–594**

Altithermal, 141–142

Altitude, air density and, 151–152; blue sky, 157, 170; mountain sickness, 152; plant adaptations to, 157; temperature and, 151; vegetation zonation, 196

Amazonite, 78, 114

AMPHIBIANS, at high altitude, 424; decline of mountain toads and frogs, 425
- canyon treefrog, 318
- Great Basin spadefoot toad, 318
- Great Plains toad, 225, 229
- mountain (or boreal) toad, 437
- New Mexico spadefoot toad, 229
- northern leopard frog, 432–433, 437
- plains spadefoot toad, 225, 229
- tiger salamander, 229, 432, 437
- western chorus frog, 396, 433, 437
- Woodhouse's toad, 229, 437

Amphibolite, 74

Ancestral Arctic Ocean, 96–97

Ancestral Rockies, 56, *70*, 79, 87–88, 90–91, 96

Andesite, 77, 118, 121

Animas Glacier, 136; River, 29, 90; Valley, 132

Anorthosite, 58, 77

Antero, Mount, 35

Anticline, *100*, 105, 112

Ants, ant-plant mutualism, 374; *Formica* spp., 374; harvester ant (*Pogonomyrmex* spp.), 253; honey ant, 318; velvet ant, 272

Aquatic ecosystems, aquatic animals, 455–460; description, 439; lentic ecosystems (still water), 445–455; lotic ecosystems (flowing water), 439–445

Aquatic invertebrates (insects and true bugs), general, 440, 486–487; water boatmen, *449*, 456–457; water strider, *449*

Aquatic invertebrates (non-insect), copepods, 459; discussion of, 455–457; fairy shrimp, 457; fingernail clam, 459; hot spring snail, 460; horsehair worms *460*; pea clam, 459 opossum shrimp, 460

Arapaho Glacier, *128*

Arapaho Indians, 13, 44

Archaeology, archaeological sites, 25–26, 50, 101, 140–141; prehistoric game-drive hunting, 141, 142

Archean eon, 57–58, 71–72

Archosauria, 93, 95

Arizona monsoon, 170

Arkansas Canyon, 86, 89;

River, 9, 17, 20, 112, 126; Valley, 35, 123, 137

Arkosic rocks, 90–91

Arroyo Peñasco Formation, 86

Artesian wells, 51, 126

Aspen forests, autumn color, 472–473; clones and clonal growth, 470–472; common animals, 482–494; common plants, 473–481; community characteristics, 464–468; description, 461–464; plant adaptations, 468–472

Asteroid impact, 55, Chicxulub impact, 108

Atmospheric circulation, 152–154

Avalanches, 172, 181–184; causes, 178, 181–185; Colorado Avalanche Information Center, 182, 185; safety, 184–185; types, 183–184

B

Baca Ranch, 23, 51

Bacteria, 173, 186, 233, 265–266

Bajada, 90, 114

Bandelier Natl. Monument, 25–26, 61

Bandelier tuff, 125

Basalt, 60, 118–119, 122–124

Basement rocks, 71–72, 78

Basin and Range, 99

Bates Hole, 122

Batholiths, 54, 58, **61–62**, 76, 113, 118

Battlement Mesa, **30–31**, 125

Bayou Salado, 47–48

Bear River, 39

Beaver, **426**, 434; beaver sign, *420*

Beetle, mountain pine, **510–512**

BEETLES
- carrion, 272
- darkling, 253
- ips, 318, 347
- mountain pine, **510–512**
- sawyer, pine, 347
- ten-lined June, *253*

Belden Formation, 89

Benthic zone, 453

Bermuda High, 170

Berthoud Pass, 18, 46, 113–114, 169, 182

Beulah Limestone, 86

Big Thompson Canyon, 74, 137; River, 47

Biodiversity, 195–196

Birch, river, **411–412**, 416; bog, 379, **413**, 417, 560, 604

Birds of prey, identification of, *250*

BIRDS
- blackbird, Brewer's, 228, 395; red-winged, 395, 431
- bluebird, mountain, 271, 317, 346, 393–394, 395, 493, 627; western, 317, 346, 395
- bunting, lark, 224, 228
- bunting, lazuli, 286–287, 317
- bushtit, 289, 314, 315, 317
- chat, yellow-breasted, 435
- chickadee(s), black-capped, 289, 360–361, 362; mountain, 289, 317, 346, 360, 362, 493, 517, 573
- coot, American, 435
- cowbird, brown-headed, 395
- crane, sandhill, 435
- creeper, brown, 346, 362, 516, 517, 573
- crossbill, red, 346, 362, 435, 517, 534–536, 573
- crow, American, 228
- cuckoo, yellow-billed, 435
- curlew, long-billed, 228
- dipper, American (ouzel), *423*, 430, 435, 627; quote from John Muir, 422
- duck, mallard, 435
- eagle, bald, 435; golden, 228, 252, 268, 271, 317, 395, 627
- falcon, American kestrel, 228, 395, 627; prairie, 228, 395, 627
- finch, black rosy, 626; brown-capped rosy, *619*, 626, 628; Cassin's, 346, 361, 362, 517, 536, 573, 626, 628; gray-crowned rosy, *619*, 626, 628
- flicker, northern, 289, 317, 346, 362, 435, 493
- flycatcher, ash-throated, 317; Cordilleran, 435, 493; dusky, 289, 493; gray, 289; Hammond's, 493; olive-sided, 573; Pacific-slope, 346; willow, 435
- gnatcatcher, blue-gray, 289, 315, 317
- goldfinch, American, 228, 395
- grosbeak, black-headed, 346, 362; evening, 344–345, 346, 362, 517; pine, 536, 571, 573
- grouse, blue, 362, 493,

517, 567, 573; sage, 268–269, 271; mating display of sage grouse, *266*; sharp-tailed, 395; greater prairie-chicken, 228; white-tailed ptarmigan, 573, 624–625, 627
gull, Franklin's, 627
hawk, Cooper's, 362, 435, 493, 514, 517; ferruginous, 228, 248–249, 252, 271; northern goshawk, 362, 489, 493, 517, 573; northern harrier, 228, 392, 395, 435; red-tailed, 228, 252, 271, 289, 317, 346, 392, 395, 493, 627; rough-legged, 228, 252, 271, 395; sharp-shinned, 346, 363, 493, 514, 517, 573; Swainson's, 223, 228, 253
heron, black-crowned night, 428, 435; great blue, 428, 435
hummingbird, black-chinned, 271, 289, 317, 435; broad-tailed, 271, 289, 346, 387, 393, 395, 435, 493, 627; rufous 393, 395, 493, 627
ibis, white-faced, 435
jay, gray, 517, 536, 568–569, 571, 573; piñon, 306–308, 313–314, 317; Steller's, 306, 317, 343–344, 346, 363, 493, 517, 536, 573; western scrub, 285–286, 289, 317
junco, dark-eyed, 346, 358, 361, 363, 395, 493, 517, 536, 573
killdeer, 228, 435
kingbird, eastern, 228; western, 228, 395, 435
kingfisher, belted, 430, 435
kinglet, golden-crowned, 363, 573; ruby-crowned, 363, 517, 569–570, 573
lark, horned, 224, 228, 253, 271, 395, 625, 627
longspur, chestnut-collared, 201; Lapland, 228; McCown's, 228
magpie, black-billed, 228, 346, 395, 435, 493
meadowlark, western, 224, 228, 395
merganser, common, 428, 436
mourning dove, 228, 317, 346
nighthawk, 228, 346, 396
nutcracker, Clark's, 306, 308, 317, 346, 363, 517, 534, 536, 573
nuthatch, pygmy, 344, 346, 363; red-breasted, 346, 363, 515, 569; white-breasted, 317, 346, 363, 493, 515, 517, 536, 573
oriole, Bullock's, 431, 436
osprey, 436
owl, boreal, 573; burrowing, 222–223, 228; flammulated, 342–343, 346, 493; great-horned, 346, 359–360, 363, 396, 436, 493, 517; northern pygmy, 347, 493, 517, 573; northern saw-whet, 347, 363, 436, 493, 517, 567–568, 573
western screech, 436, 493
peewee, western wood, 347, 436, 494
phalarope, Wilson's, 436
phoebe, Say's, 228, 253, 317, 436
pipit, water, 396, *619*, 625–626, 627
plover, mountain, 223–224, 228; snowy, 436
ptarmigan, white-tailed, 186, *188*, 620, 624–625, 627
raven, 253, 271, 317, 347, 363, 396, 517, 534, 536, 627
robin, American, 309, 347, 396, 436, 493, 628
sandpiper, spotted, 429, 436, 628
sapsucker, red-naped, 489, *490*, 493; Williamson's, 343, 347, 489–490, 493, 517
shrike, loggerhead, 228, 249, 253, 272, 396
siskin, pine, 345, 347, 363, 517, 536
snipe, common, 396, *423*, 429–430, 436
solitaire, Townsend's, 309–310, 317, 347, 363, 573
sparrow, Brewer's, 229, 249, 253, 272, 289, 396; chipping, 317, 347, 396; fox, 432, 436; grasshopper, 229; lark, 229, 253, 272, 396; Lincoln's, 396, 431–432, 436; sage, 272; savannah, 394, 396; song, 432, 436, 493; vesper, 224–225, 229, 253, 272, 396; white-crowned, 396, 436, 571–572, 573, 628
swallow, bank, 436; barn, 229; cliff, 436; northern rough-winged, 436; tree, 347, 436, 490, 493; violet-green, 347, 396, 436, 490, 493

swift, black, 436, 628; white-throated, 317, 436
tanager, western, 344, 347, 363
teal, green-winged, 428–429, 436
thrasher, sage, 269, 272
thrush, hermit, 363, 517, 570, 573; Swainson's, 363, 436
titmouse, juniper, 289, 314, 318
towhee, canyon, 253, 289, 318; green-tailed, 269, 272, 289; spotted, 287, 289
turkey, wild, 289
warbler, black-throated gray, 289, 318; Grace's, 347; MacGillivray's, 289, 436; orange-crowned, 290, 318; Virginia's, 286, 290, 318; Wilson's, 430–431, 436, 573; yellow, 436; yellow-rumped, 347, 363, 436, 491–492, 493, 517, 536
waxwing, Bohemian, 309; cedar, 309, 436
woodpecker, downy, 347, 360, 363, 436, 514–515, 517; hairy, 347, *358*, 360, 363, 494, 514, 517, 536, 573; Lewis's, 436; northern three-toed, 568, 573
wren, canyon, 286, 318, 437; house, 286, 290, 318, 347, 491, 494; marsh, 437; rock, 286, 290, 318, 628
vireo, plumbeous (formerly solitary), 347, 491, 493; warbling, 436, 491, 493
vulture, turkey, 229, 253
yellowthroat, 431, 437

Black Canyon of the Gunnison, 71, 88, 137; Natl. Park, 31–32, 62, 74, *75*, 81

Black Forest area, geology of, 115; ponderosa pine in, 115

Blanca Peak, 20, 50, 90

Blue Mesa Reservoir, *120*

Blue River, 36–38, 123

Boulder Creek Granite, 76

Boundary Peak, 124

Box Canyon, *78*, 85

Bross, Mount, 36

Brazos Mountains, 26

Buffalo Pass, 42, 167

Buffalo Peaks, 21, 35–36, 47

Bunchgrasses, 205, 208, 241

BUTTERFLIES

admiral, Weidemeyer's, 437, 494
alpine, Colorado, 628; common, 437, 628; Magdalena, 628; Theano, 628
arctic, chryxus, 347, 396; Melissa, 628; polixenes, 628
blue, arctic, 628; arrowhead, 290; greenish, 437; high mountain, 628; Shasta, 628
checkerspot, anicia, 396; arachne, 396; rockslide, 628
copper, blue, 272, 396; lustrous, 628; ruddy, 396; tailed, 290
crescentspot, northern, 396; pearly, 396; silvery, 494
elfin, western pine, 347
fritillary, Aphrodite, 290; Atlantis, 396; bog, 628; Mormon, 628; mountain, 628; northwestern, 437; Uncompahgre, 628
hairstreak, Colorado, 290, *290*; juniper, 318
mourning cloak, 437
orangetip, 437; southern Rocky Mountain, 347
parnassian, Phoebus, 396; Rocky Mountain, 396, 628
ringlet, ochre, 396
satyr, Ridings', 229
skipper, alpine checkered, 628, plains gray, 229; simius, 229
skipperling, garita, 396
sooty-wing, saltbush, 253
sulphur, Queen Alexandra's, 396; Mead's, 628
swallowtail, anise, 494; pale, 437; two-tailed, 290; western tiger, 494
tortoiseshell, Milbert's, 628
white, sagebrush, 272; spring, 437; western, 628
wood nymph, Great Basin, 253, 318; large, 290

C

Cache la Poudre, Canyon, 135; River, 46, 137, 444

CACTI

brittle, 304
candelabra (cholla), 214, 294, 304
claret cup, 295, **301**, 304
hedgehog, **301**, 304
hen-and-chickens, 214
mountain ball, **330–331**, 333
nipple, 214
prickly-pear, yellow, 214,

246, 304; spiny, 214, 246, 304

Caldera, 54, 78, 118–119, 124

Cambrian period, 57, 80–82

Cameron Pass, 14

Camp Hale, 34

Capulin Volcano Natl. Monument, 23, 125

Carr, willow, 399

Castle Peak, 32, 120

Castle Rock Conglomerate, 115

Caterpiller(s), western tent (*Malacosoma* spp.), **486**, 494

Cattle ranching, 45–46, 48

Cave of the Winds, 78, 82–83

Cenozoic era, 54–55

Center pivots, 51, 204

Central City Mining District, 113

Central Colorado Trough, 56, 88–89, 107

Chaffee Group, 84

Chalk Cliffs, 34

Challenger Peak, 20

Chama River, 22, 28

Cheyenne, 13

Cheyenne Belt, 58, 72, 74, 77

Chimayosos Peak, 74, 85

Chinese Wall, volcanic rocks of, 38

Chinle Formation, **94**, 95, 97

Chugwater Formation, 94–95

Cimarron Range, 21, 125

Circumboreal species, 196

Cirques, 36, 42, 47, 131, 135, 140–142, 147, 179

Clayton Pass–Bristlecone Pine Research Natural Area, 520

Climate, definitions, 148–149; effects of altitude, 151–152; effects of latitude and continentality, 149; glacial-interglacial transition, 140; over geologic time, 54–56; Pleistocene-Holocene fluctuations, 128, 133, 141

Climax vegetation, concepts, 191–192, 196, 197

Cloud types, crest cloud, 160, 163, *164*; lens-shaped, 162; mountain wave clouds, *148*, 162–163; rotor cloud, 163; thunderhead, *170*

Coal, 55, 64, 104

Collegiate Range, 34, 121

Colorado–Big Thompson Project, 46

Colorado Front Range, **14–18**; Ancestral Rockies, 88; Arapaho Glacier, *128*; cirques, 131; climate research, 156; dating glaciation, 135, 137; Eocene alluvial deposition, 114; faulting, 112; Front Range Highland, 106; Frontrangia, 56, 88–91; glaciers, 129, 132, 145; granites, 76–77; Holocene ice advances in, 140; prehistoric game drives, 142; Laramide orogeny, 106; mineralization, 113; Niwot Ridge, *180*; post-Laramide erosion surface, 117; Precambrian outcrops, 74; rock glaciers, 147; Silurian rocks, 84; weather, *163–164*, 165, 170

Colorado Lineament, 73–74

Colorado Mineral Belt, 55, 105, 112, **113–114**, 117, 121

Colorado Natl. Monument, 29, 88, 95, 97–98

Colorado Piedmont, 112

Colorado Plateau, 29, 97, 104–105, 125, 141

Colorado River, 112, 126; age of, 126–127; ancestral, 29; Cretaceous outcrops along, 104; diversion of, 10; Glenwood Canyon, 38; Gore Canyon, 37, 46; Grand Valley of, 30; headwaters of, 9, 16, 41, 46–47; life in, 444–445; National Scenic Byway, 46

Colorado Sag, 80, 82

Colorado Salt Works, 48

Columnar jointing, 60, *120*, 122

Comanche Natl. Grassland, 201

Comanches, 19

Como Bluff, 98

Continental Divide, and climate, **10**; crest clouds, 160, 163; description and map, **7–9**, *8*, 17, 136; Eisenhower Memorial Tunnel, 182; Francisco Coronado and, 20; at Independence Pass, 35; mountain wave cloud, *148*; spring storms, 169; Trail Ridge Road, 15

Continentality, 149–150

Convection, 151, 160–161

Coriolis force, 153

Cornices, 180, *181*

Craton, 58, 67, *70*, 71–72, 84, 87

Crawford State Park, 32

Creede Mining District, 113

Crestone Conglomerate, 90

Crestone Needle, 20, 90; Peak, 20

Cretaceous period, 55, 99–109

Cricket, Mormon, 272

Cripple Creek Mining District, 113

Cryptogamic crust, 370

Cuchara Pass, 19, 121

Cuesta, 101

Culebra Peak, 21

Cumulus clouds, 161

Curecanti Rec. Area, 32

Cutler Formation, 56, 90–91

Cyclonic storms, 153–154, 160–161, 167, 169

D

Dakota Group, 55, 101

Dakota Hogback, 97, 101, 104, 107

Dams and diversions, Colorado River diversion projects, 46–47; impact on wetlands, 398

Dating, geologic, **129–130**, 135, 137, 139–140

Dawson Arkose, 114–115

Deep Creek Canyon, 38, 84, 86

Denver Basin, 88, 107, 116

Denver Formation, 114

Devonian period, 57, 84–85

Diamond-bearing rock, 71, 84. *See also* kimberlite

Diatreme, 84. *See also* kimberlite

Dikes, 19, **61–62**, *75*, 76–77, 81, 113, 121

Dillon Pinnacles, *120*

Dinosaurs, 56, 95, 98; extinction of, 55; trackways of, 98; *Allosaurus*, 98; *Apatosaurus*, 98; *Brontosaurus*, 98; *Camarasaurus*, 98; *Camptosaurus*, 98; *Ceratosaurus*, 98; *Dimetrodon*, 92; *Diplodocus*, 98; *Stegosaurus*, 98

Dinosaur Natl. Monument, 39, 91, *92*, 98, 127, *294*

Dolores Formation, 94–95

Dolores River, 28, 95

Dune, deposits, 97; dunefields, 54–56, 91, **138–139**

Dust devils, 152, 203, 233

Dyer Dolomite, 84

E

Eagle River, 34

Earth's core, 66, 71; crust, 66, 80; mantle, 66, 71, 80; structure, 66

Ecological concepts, 191–194; amplitude, 191–193, balance, 194; competition, 192, 194, 335, 483–484

Ecoregion, definition, 7, 190–191; conservation, 191

Ecosystem, definition and concepts, 190–192, 196

Ecotone, definition, 190; forest-tundra, 541, 545

Elbert Formation, 85

El Diente, 27

Elkhead Range, 42–43

Elk Mountains, **32–34**; cirques of, 131; rock glaciers, 147; volcanism in, 54, 117, 125

Elk River, 39, 41, 43

Ellingwood Point, 20

El Niño, 155–156, 522

Endangered species, 196

Endemic species of Southern Rockies, 195

Engineer Mountain, 29, 90, 136; Pass, *27*

Entrada Sandstone, 55, **94**, 97

Environmental change, accelerating warming phase, 143; balancing human needs, 51; high-altitude, 425; human wrought, 2–3, 398; impacts of drought, 398; increasing salinity of groundwater, 408; South Park water issues, 49; super-interglacial period, 143; volcanism and climate, 122. *See also* global warming

Eocene epoch, 55

Eolus Granite, 76

Erosion, glacial, **130–133**; post-Laramide, 117, 125; Tertiary erosion surface, 117

Evans, Mount, 17

Evolution, 81, 92, 100–101, 110, 195

Extinctions, 54, 55, 92, 107, 109, **139**, 195–196

F

Faults, 21, 73–74, 88, 105, 112, 117, 123, *127*

Fellfields, 584–588

Fen, 49, 399

FERNS AND FERN ALLIES
fern, alpine lady, 607
fern, Christmas, 607
horsetail (scouring rush), *Equisetum* spp., 418
quillwort, 455

Fire-adapted plants, 258, 276, 319, 326–327, 352, 495; serotiny, **500–501**

FISH, impacts of nonnative fish, 3; native species in Colorado River, *443*
Astraspis (jawless fossil fish), 83
chub, boneytail (native), 458; humpback (native), 458; roundtail (native), 458; Rio Grande (native), 459
dace, longnose (nonnative), 459; speckled (native), 459
minnow, fathead (nonnative), 459; northern pike (formerly Colorado squawfish, native), 3, 445
sculpin, mottled (native), 459
stickleback, brook (nonnative), 458
sucker, flannelmouth (native), 459; razorback (native), 459; white (nonnative), 459
trout, species accounts, **457–458**; brook (nonnative), **458**, 459; brown (nonnative), **458**, 459; cutthroat (nonnative), **458**, 459; greenback cutthroat (native); **458**, 459; rainbow (nonnative), **458**, 459

Fish Canyon Tuff, 61

Flagstaff Mountain, fossil soil on, 78

Flatirons, 90, *100*

Flat Top Mountain, 38

Flattop Mountain, *141*

Flat Tops, **38–39**, 60, 125, 167; Scenic Byway, 39

Florissant Fossil Beds Natl. Mon., **121**

Foothills vegetation zones, 196, **197**

Fossil flora, Creede, 122; Florissant, 122

Fossils, invertebrate, 81–83, 85, 92, 102; mammal, 122; plant, 95, 97, 116; Therapsid reptiles, 92; vertebrate, 95, 102, 116.
See also dinosaurs

Fountain Formation, 56, 90–91

Four Corners area, 85, 101

"Fourteeners," **7**, 17, 20, 27, 29, 32, 34, 36, 90, 123

Fox Hills Sandstone, 104

Frémont, John Charles, 41, 199, 385

Frémont Limestone, 57, 83

Frost creep, 145–146, 588

FUNGI, general, 353, 469–470, 501, 546, *547*
amanita, 470, 481, 507
bird's nest, 561
boletus, 470, 481, 561
bracket, violet-pored, 481
chanterelle, 507
conk, aspen, 481
coral mushroom, orange, 561; pixie, 561
earth tongue, 561
eyelash cup, 561
fairy fingers, purple, *547*, 561
firecup, 507
gomphidus, slimy-capped, 561
heartrot, white, 482
honey mushroom, 501, 507
jelly, orange, 561
lacterius, orange, 561; white, 470, 481
morel, black, 507; false hooded, 561
pine (or white Matsutake) mushroom, 507
puffball, 507
russula, 470, 481, 507, 561
snow mold fungus, **552–553**
sticky-cap, yellow, 507
tricholoma, orange, 507

G

Gall, piñon spindle, 318; sagebrush sponge, 272; sagebrush stem, 272; spruce, *406*, 412, 553; woolly stem, 253

Gambel's oak woodland, *273*; and fire, 276

Gangplank, 11, 125–126

Garden of the Gods, 90

Generalist species, 193

Geologic history of the Southern Rockies, 54–58, 69–147; map, *111*

Ghost Ranch, 95, 97

Glaciation, Bull Lake, 54, **134–135**; Holocene, **140–143**; Pinedale, 54, 134, **135–137**; pre–Bull Lake, 54, **134**; record of, 129, *130*, 131–133

Glen Eyrie Formation, 89

Glenwood Canyon, 38, 78, 81, 84–86, 89

Global warming, 3, 142, 156, 463, 541–542; bison remains in melting glacier, 142

Glorieta Pass, 20

Gneiss, *76*

Gold, 18, 36, 42, 47, 48, 113–114; placer gold, 36, 42, 48, 114

Gore Range, 36, **37**, 39, 88, 106–107, 123, 125

Grand Canyon, 71, 74, 85

Grand Ditch, 46

Grand Hogback, 38, 104, 107

Grand Mesa, **30–31**, 60, 125, 129, 135; Scenic and Historic Byway, 30

Grand Valley, 29–30, 241

Granite, *76*; grus, 78

GRASSES
- arrowgrass, 379, 418
- barley, foxtail, 213, *368*, 379
- bentgrass, alpine, 605
- blow-out grass, *193*
- bluegrass (*Poa* spp.), 479; alpine, 605; arctic, 605; Letterman's, 605; snowbed, 605
- bluestem, big, *210*, 213; little, 213; sand, 213
- buffalograss, *204*, **211**, 214
- cheatgrass, 214, 246, 256, 263, 303, *368*, 379
- cordgrass (*Spartina*), 214
- dropseed, pine, 332
- feathergrass, New Mexican, 303
- fescue alpine, 605; Arizona, 263, 332, 379; Baffin, 605; Hall's, 605; Idaho, 263, 379; mountain, 332; spike, 332 Thurber's, 280, **375**, 379, 479
- galletagrass, *210*, **211**, 214, 246, 263, 304
- grama, blue, 204, **211**, 214, 246, 256, 263, 280, 295, 303, 332, 379; hairy, 214, 246; sideoats, *210*, **211**, 214, 263, 280, 304
- hairgrass, tufted, **375**, 379, 418, 605
- Indiangrass, 214
- Junegrass, 214, 256, 263, 304, 332, *368*, **375**, 379, 479
- mannagrass, 418, 454
- muhly, alkali, 214, 245–246; mountain, 280, 332, *368*, **375**, 379, 528; ring, 214, 244–246, *245*
- muttongrass (*Poa*), 263, 304, 528
- needle-and-thread, *210*, **211–212**, 214, 256, 263, 379; green, 214, 379
- oatgrass, Parry's, 332, **375**, 379; poverty, 332; timber, **375**, 379
- oniongrass, purple, 480
- redtop, 379
- reedgrass, Canadian, 379, 418
- ricegrass, Indian, *193*, 244, 246, 263, 295, 304, 379
- ryegrass, desert, 246
- sacaton, alkali, 214, 246
- saltgrass, 214, 246, 380
- sandreed, 214
- squirreltail, 214, 263, 380
- switchgrass, 214
- three-awn, 214, 380
- timothy, alpine (native), 605; timothy (nonnative), 380
- trisetum, spike, 380, 605
- wheatgrass, alpine, 605; crested, 380; Scribner's, 605; slender, 380; western, *210*, **212**, 214, 263, 380
- wild rye, blue, 480; giant, 263

Grassland ecosystems, alpine tundra grasslands and meadows, **580–584**; mountain grasslands and meadows, **364–396**; shortgrass prairie, **199–229**

Grays Peak, 17

Great Diamond Hoax, 11–12

"Great Divide," 7. *See also* Continental Divide

Great Plains Grassland Biome, 200

Great Sand Dunes, 49, 139; Natl. Park, 20, *21*, 50, 52, 138

Greenhorn Limestone, 101

Greenhorn Mountain, 18–19

Green River, 444; Basin, 104

Green River Formation, 115; fossil-rich, 116

Groaning Cave, 38, 86

Groundwater resources, 126

Growing season, 159

Gunnison River, 29–32, 61; Basin, 241; Valley, 159

H

Habitat, defined, 194

Halophytes (salt-loving plants), 234–235

Harding Sandstone, 57, 83

Hardscrabble Limestone, 86

Hermosa Group, 90

Hibernation, 185, **610–611**; of yellow-bellied marmot, **611–612**

High Creek Fen, 49

High Plains, 125, 139, 168–169, 203

Highway of Legends, 19

Hispanic settlers, 51

Hogback escarpment, 53, *100*, 101

Holocene epoch, 54, 128

Home Moraine, 135

Hoodoos, *120*

Hoosier Pass, 35–36

Horseshoe Park, 132, 137

Hot springs, 14, 23–24, 34–35, 42, 46, 112

Huerfano, Butte, 62; Park, 90

Hypsithermal, 141. *See also* Altithermal

I

Ice Age, 54, 128, 139

Ignacio Formation, 81

Igneous rocks, **59–61**, 76, **113**, 114

Independence, Mountain, 44–45; Pass, 33, 35, 131

Indian Peaks, 16, 140

Indicator species, 193

INSECTS, infestations of, 324, **339–341**, 352, **359**, 545, **510–512**; maximizing heat gain, 621–622
- caddisfly, 440, *441*
- cicada, Putnam's, 290, 318
- dragonfly, 459
- leafminer, aspen blotch, 494
- mayfly, 272, *441*, 440–442, 455, 460
- stonefly, *441*, 460
- tarantula, 253
- walkingstick, Colorado, 272
- water scavenger, 459

Invasive (or alien) plant species, 194, 256, 257, *368*, 408

Iridium layer, 107–108, *109*

Iron Dike, 77

J

Jelm Formation, 95

Jemez Mountains, general, **22–25**, 124–125; Jemez and Guadalupe rivers, 23; Jemez State Mon., 23, *24*; Natl. Scenic Byway, 23–24; volcanic field, 54, 124

Jet stream, 152–154, 166–167

Jurassic period, 55–56, 96–98

K

Karst, 86, 113

Kelsey Lake Diamond Mine, 12

Kennaday Peak, 115

Kenosha Pass, 18, 36, 47

Kerogen, 115

Kimberlite, 12, 57, 71, 84

Kit Carson Peak, 20

Kremmling Bluffs, *103*; ammonites (*Placenticeras meeki*) in, 102

krummholz, defined, 538

K-T boundary, 55, **107–108**, *109*

L

Laccoliths, **61–62**

Land grants, Mexican, 51–52

Lands End Road, 30

La Niña, 155–156, 522

Lapse rate, 151, 158

Laramide Orogeny, 55, 99, **104–105**, *106*, 110, 112–113; uplifts, 54

Laramie, Basin, 115, 145; Mountains, **10–12**, 72, 77, 115, 122, 206; River, 112, 135

Laramie Formation, 104

Las Vegas Range, 22

Latin names, 198

Lava Cliffs, 61

Leadville Limestone, 57, 64–65, 84–86

Leadville Mining District, 114; lead ore, 113

Life zones, 189–190

LICHENS
- antler (or worm), 608
- finger (*Dactylina arctica*), 608
- golden (*Acarospora chlorophana*), 608
- Iceland (*Cetraria islandica*), 608; in alpine tundra, 595–596
- jewel (*Xanthoria elegans*), 608, 617
- map (*Rhizocarpon geographicum*), 130, 608
- old man's beard (*Usnea* spp.), 130, 132, 134, 136, 352, 356, 357
- parmelia (*Parmelia alpicola*), 608

rock tripe (*Umbilicaria* spp.), 608
snow (*Cetraria nivalis*), 608
soil (*Lepraria* spp.), 591–592, 608
soil crust (*Stereocaulon* spp.), 608

Limnetic zone, 451–452

Lionshead, the, 89

Lipalian Interval, 58, 77–78

Little Ice Age, 54, 142

Little Bear Peak, 20

Little Snake River, 39, 43

Littoral zone, 450–451

LIZARDS
collared, 253, **315–316**, 318
lesser earless, **226**, 229
plateau striped, 229, 253, 272, **287–288**, 290, 318, 347
racerunner, six-lined, 229
sagebrush, 253, **270**, 272, 290, 318
short-horned, 251, 253, 290, 396
side-blotched, **316**, 318
skink, many-lined, 229, 253; variable, 290, 347
tree, 318
western whiptail, 318

Lizard Head Pass, 27, 97

Lodgepole pine forests, *495*, **498–499**; mountain pine beetles and the forest, **510–512**; role of saprophytes and parasites, 501–502; serotiny, **500–501**

Long Canyon Trail, 108

Longs Peak, 17, 131; Diamond, 15, 77

Loveland Pass, 18, 113, 182

Lykins Formation, 94

Lyons Sandstone, 56, 91

M

Madera Formation, 89

Madison Limestone, 86

MAMMALS, burrowers, 383–384; grazers, 385–386
badger, American, 227, 252, **268**, 270, 288, 394, 626
bat, big brown, 227, **389**, 394; hoary, 516; little brown, 227, 345, 362, 395, **425–426**, 434; long-eared, 345; long-legged myotis, 317, 362, 435, 492; small-footed myotis, 289; pallid, 316; silver-haired, 394, **487–488**, 492; Townsend's big-eared, 288
bear, black, 288, 434, **488–489**, 492, 516, 572; "bear register" tree, *485*, 486
beaver, 426, 484–485
bighorn (mountain sheep), 395, 617–619, **624**, 627
bison, *209*
bobcat, 288, 516, *535*, 572, 626
chipmunk, cliff, 288; Colorado, **283**, 288, 316, 342, 345, 362; Hopi, 288, 316; least, 252, 270, **283**, 288, 316, *334*, **342**, 345, 362, 394, 434, 492, 516, 536, 572, 626; Uinta, 516
coyote, 227, 252, 270, 288, 316, 345, 362, **390–391**, 394, 434, 492, 516, 536, 627
deer, mule, 252, *270*, **285**, 288, 316, 345, 362, 394, 434, 492, 516, 572, 627
elk (or wapiti), 288, 345, 362, **391**, 394, *434*, 485, 492, 516, 572, 627
fox, gray, 252, 288, **312**, 316; red, 394, **427–428**, 434, 572; swift, 227
goat, mountain, 617–618, 627
gopher, northern pocket, 252, 271, 346, *384*, **390**, 395, 572, 613, 627; plains pocket, 227; valley pocket, 252, 395; "gopher eskers," 584
hare, snowshoe, 362, 492, 516, 536, **565–566**, 572; black-tailed jackrabbit, **220**, 227, 247–248, 252, 271, 288, 316; white-tailed jackrabbit, **220**, 227, 247, 252, 271, 394, 627
lion, mountain (cougar or puma), 288, **312–313**, 316, 345, 362
lynx, 572
marmot, yellow-bellied, 288, 345, 394, 536, **623–624**, 627
marten, pine, 516, **566**, 572, 627
mink, **426**, 434
mouse, brush, 289, **311**, 316; deer, 227, 252, 271, 289, 316, 345, 362, 394, 434, 492, 516, 536, 572, 627; Great Basin pocket, 289; northern grasshopper, 227, 252, 271, 394; northern rock, 289, **311**, 317; piñon, **311**, 317; plains harvest, 227; plains pocket, 227; silky

pocket, 227, 252, 394; western harvest, 394; western jumping, 395, 434, **488**, 492
moose, 492, 516
muskrat, **426**, 434
pika, *609*, 614–617, **623**, 627
porcupine, 289, 317, 346, 492, 516, **529–531**, **533**, 536, 572
prairie dog, black-tailed, **221–222**, 227; Gunnison's, **267–268**, 271; white-tailed, 252, **267**, 271
pronghorn, **222**, 227, 252, 271, 395
rabbit, desert cottontail, 227, 247, 252, 270, 288, 316; mountain (or Nuttall's), 270, 288, 316, 345, 362, **389**, 394, 434, 492, 516, 536, 572
raccoon, **427**, 435, *437*
rat, Ord's kangaroo, 227, 248, 252, 271, 394; water conservation and, 238
ringtail, 289, **312**, 317
shrew, dwarf, 346, 627; least, 227; masked, 227, 362, **388–389**, 395, 492, 517, 536, 627; Merriam's, 227; montane, 362, 395, 435, 492, 572; water, **425**, 435
skunk, striped, 228, 252, **427**, 435; western spotted, **284–285**, 289, 317
squirrel, Abert's (or tassel-eared), 337–339, **341**, *346*, 346; chickaree (red or pine), 362, 492, **512–513**, 517, 536, 572; rock, **283–284**, 289, 317; pine squirrel midden, *509*
squirrel, ground, golden-mantled, *334*, **341–342**, 346, 362, 395, 492, 536, 572, 627; thirteen-lined, **221**, 228; white-tailed antelope, 289; Wyoming, 271, *384*, **389–390**, 395
vole, heather, 627; long-tailed, 395, 435, 492, 627; montane, 346, 384–385, **390**, 395, 435, 492, 572, 627; prairie, 228; southern red-backed, 362, **513**, 517, 572; sagebrush, **267**, 271, 395, 613–614
weasel, long-tailed, 228, 271, 289, 317, 346, 362, 395, 435, 492, 517, 536, **566–567**, 572, 627; short-tailed (or ermine), 345, 492, 516, 536, **567**, 572, **624**, 627
woodrat, bushy-tailed (or packrat), 271, 289, **311–312**, 317, 346, 362, 536, 627; Mexican, **284**, 289, 317, 346

Mancos Shale, 55, 103–104, 241; and saltbrush badlands, *240*

Manitou Limestone, 82

Map(s), Continental Divide and major rivers, *8*; physiographic provinces, *4*; Southern Rocky Mountains, *6*; geology, *111*

Maroon Bells, 32, 90

Maroon Formation, 56, 90–91

Marr, John, **196**; and vegetation classification, 196–198

Mass-wasting, 145–147

Mat-forming plants, 209, 240, 243, 245, 587

Medano Creek, 138–139; Pass, 20, 138

Medicine Bows, *13*, 14, 72–73, 80, 106, 115; Holocene ice advances, 140

Medicine Peak Quartzite, 73, 115

Mesa Verde Formation (or Group), 55, 104

Mesozoic era, 55–56

Metamorphic rocks, **65**, *76*

Microclimates, 185, 190, 200, 499, 576

Middle Park, 43, **45–47**, 106, 116, 122, 187; aquifer, 48; cold, 159

Mineralization, 55, 113–114

Minturn Formation, 89

Miocene epoch, 54

Mississippian period, 57, 85–86

Mistletoe, parasitic, 333, 357, **504–505**, 507, 552

Mitten Park Fault, *127*

Moenkopi Formation, 94

Molas Formation, 86

Molybdenum, 114

Monarch Pass, 35, 85

Monocline, *100*

Montane vegetation zones, 196, **197**

Moraines, glacial, 133, 135, 137, 140

Moraine Park, 132–134, 137

Morrison Formation, 56, 97–98

Mosquito (*Drosophila* spp.), 460

Mosquito Pass, 36–37; Range, **35–37**, 47, 81–82, 88, 123, 131

Moss, water (*Calliergon sarmentosum*), 455, 593; "peat moss" (*Sphagnum* spp.), 407

Mountain building, 56, **66–68**, 88, 96, 112–113, 117; age of the Rockies, 53

Mountain parks (basins), definition, 43–44; North Park, **44–45**; Middle Park, **45–47**; South Park, **47–49**; San Luis Valley, **49–52**

Mountain ranges, Colorado Front Range, **14–18**; Elkhead Range, **42–43**; Elk Mountains, **32–34**; Gore Range, **37**; Grand Mesa (and Battlement Mesa), **30–31**; Jemez Mountains, **22–25**; Mosquito Range, **35–36**; Nacimiento Mountains, **26**, 86, 88; Pajarito Plateau, 25–26; Park Range and the Sierra Madre, 41–42; Rabbit Ears Range, **39–41**; Sangre de Cristo Range, **20–22**; San Juan Mountains, **26–29**; Sawatch Range, **34–35**; Spanish Peaks, **19–20**; Tenmile Range, **36**; Uncompahgre Plateau, **29**; West Elk Mountains, **31–32**; Wet Mountains, **18–19**; White River Plateau and the Flat Tops, **38–39**

Mountain Research Station (Univ. of Colo.), 17, 578

Mount Goliath Natural Area, 521

Mount Princeton batholith, 121

Muddy Pass, 41

Mudflows, 145–147

Muir, John, 319, 350, 422

Mushrooms. *See* Fungi

Mycorrhizal symbiosis, 325; aspen and, **469**, Douglas-fir and, **352–353**; mycelium, 501; spruce-fir forests and, **546–547**

N

Nature Conservancy, The, 49, 51

Navajo, 23, 50

Navajo Sandstone, 55, 97

Needle Mountains, 26, 76, 107

Needle Rock, 62

Neoglacial, 142

Never Summer Mountains, 117, 122, 136

Niche, definition, 194

Niobrara Formation, 102

Niwot Ridge, 17, *145*, *180*

North Gate Canyon, 44

North Park, 43, **44**, *45*, 104, 106, 122; cold, 159; dune fields, 138

North Platte River, 41, 44

O

Oil and natural gas, 101, 116

Oil shale, 115; development of, 116

Old-growth forest, 335

Oligocene epoch, 54

Oligocene volcanoes, 117–118, 122

Ordovician period, 57, 82–83

Ore-deposit types, 113–114

Orogeny, 68, 71; Cordilleran, 96, 105; Laramide, 55, 99, **104–105**, *106*, 110, 112–113; Nevadan, 99; Sevier, 99–100, 105. *See also* mountain building

Orographic precipitation, 160–161

Ouray Limestone, 85

Outwash, 137; glacial, 132

Overgrazing, 49, 201, 203–206, 256

Oxalic acid, 237

P

Pacific Decadal Oscillation, 155–156

Painted Wall, 62, 74, *75*

Pajarito Plateau, **25**, 26, 61, 124

Paleocene epoch, 55

Paleo-Indian hunters, 50, 54, 139, 141

Paleozoic era, 57; features of, *70*

Palmer Divide, 168

Pangaea, 56, 79, 87, 91–93, 95–96, 203

Paonia State Park, 32

Paradox Basin, 85, 88

Parasites, 501; dwarf mistletoe, *502*, 504–505, 552; fir broom rust, 552; pinedrops, *502*, 504; root, 232, 262; snow mold fungus, 552; spruce broom rust, 552

Park Range, **41–42**, 167; Ancestral Rockies, 88; dating glaciation, 137;

glacial effects, 137; Holocene ice advances, 140; Laramide orogeny, 106; volcanism, 117, 125; weather, 170

Parting Sandstone, 84

Pathfinder Uplift, 88

Patterned ground, 143, **144–145**, 146

Pawnee Buttes, 122; Pawnee Natl. Grassland, 201

Peaks of Southern Rockies, *6;* Columbia, 34; Democrat, 36; Elbert, 34; Evans, 17, 76; Harvard, 34; Lincoln, 36; Massive, 34; Mount of the Holy Cross, 34; Oxford, 34; Princeton, 34; Richthofen, 122; Shavano, 35; Sneffels, 136; Sopris, 31–32, 62, 147; Tabeguache, 35; Werner, 42; White, 114; Wilson, 27; Yale, 34

Pecos Baldy Peak, 74, 85

Pecos River, cliff-forming metamorphic rocks, 74

Pennsylvanian period, 56, 87–90; map, *87*

Periglacial landscapes, 143–147

Permian period, 56, 91

Phantom Canyon, 83

Photosynthesis, in alpine plants, 598

Physiographic provinces, *4*

Piceance Basin, 88, 104, 107, 115–116

Picketwire Dinosaur Tracksite, *98*

Pierre Shale, 55, 102, *103*

Pikes Peak, 17; Batholith, 61, 77–78, 114; Granite, 58, 77, 112

Piñon-juniper woodlands, chemical defenses, **296**; drought adaptations, **295**; ecological distribution, **291–295**; seed caching and seed dispersal, **305–310**

Pioneer species, 191–192

Plains Indians, 13, 199

Plant-herbivore defenses, 236, 296, 373, 487, 562–563

Plate tectonics, **66–68**, 80, 87, 93, 95–96, 105; collision-suturing of continental plates, 56, 87–88; plates, map of, *67*

Pleistocene epoch, 54, 128

Pleistocene glaciers, Cache la Poudre Glacier, *136*; Colorado River Glacier, 136; Uncompahgre Glacier, 136

Pliocene epoch, 54

Plutons, 55, **61–62**; stocks, **61–62**, 76, 113–114

Polar easterlies, 153

Ponderosa pine forests, animal adaptations, 334–339; ecological distribution, 320–321; fire ecology, 326–327; mountain pine beetle, 339–341; mycorrhizal adaptations, 325

Porphyry, 60, 114

Precambrian era, **58**, **69–78**; map of features, *70*; ore deposition, 113; provinces, **71**

Precipitation, by seasons, 166–171; convectional, 161–162; cyclonic, 161; East Slope–West Slope differences, 10; glaciations and, 133; orographic effects, 160–161; rain shadow, 50; schematic diagram of chinook, *163*, 164–165.

Prehistoric hunters, 130; and game-drive systems, *141*, 142; use of quartzite, 101

Profundal zone, 452–453

Proterozoic eon, 57–58, 71, **72–74**

Puebloans, 25, 50; ruins of Giusewa, 23, *24*

Purgatory Peak, 21

Pyroclastic rocks, 119, 124–125; defined, 60

Q

Quandary Peak, 36

Quaternary period, 54

R

Rabbit Ears Range, **39**, **41**, 122

Rain shadow, 50, 126, 161

Rampart Range, 78, 115, 117

Ranges of the Southern Rockies, 5; description, **10–43**; map of, *6*

Raton Basin, 89, 104, 107

Rawah Peaks, 13–14

Redbeds, 94

Red Mountain Pass, 29, 136, 182

Red Rocks Park, 90, 97

Redwall Limestone, 85

Reintroduction of species, 196, 617

Rhyolite, 60, 118

Rime crystals, *172*, 173

Rio Grande features, Basin, 241; Gorge, 124; Rift, 22,

54, 112, 118–119, 123–125; River, 9, 22, 28, 112, 138, 444; Valley, 123, 159

Riparian forests, 398

Rise of the Rockies, 104

Rivers, map of, *8*

Roaring Fork River, 443; Valley, 132

Roches moutonnées, 131

Rock glaciers, 147

Rockwood Quarry, 85–86

Rocky Mountain front, 54, 74, 117

Rocky Mtn. Natl. Park, **15–16**, 61, 74, *181*, *185*; and Colorado River, 9; glaciation, 131, 135, *136*, 137, 142, 145–146; Iron Dike, 77; prehistoric hunting blind, *141*; volcanism in, 122; and water diversion, 46

Rollins Pass, 18, 46

Rossby waves, 153–154, 162

Royal Gorge, 35, 74, 137

Rumination, physiology and importance, 217, 385–386, 618

RUSHES (*Juncus* spp.)
- baltic, 246, 379
- bulrush (tule), 418, 454, 455
- chestnut, 593, 605
- Drummond's, **604**, 605
- subalpine, 380, 418
- three-glumed, 593, 605
- two-glumed, 593, 605
- woodrush (*Luzula*), 418; spike woodrush, 605

S

Salt, plant adaptations to, **234–235**, as plant cell antifreeze, 235

Salt springs of South Park, 47–48

San Antonio Peak, 60, 124

San Cristobal Lake, 119, 146

San Francisco Peaks, 189

San Jose Formation, 116

San Juan Basin, 101, 104, 107, 116

San Juans, **26–29**; Cambrian rocks, 80–81; domal uplift, 112; evidence for Precambrian erosion, 76; fossil soil exposures, 86; glaciation of, 129, 131–132, 134, 136–137; pyroclastic rocks, 61; redbeds, 95; rock streams, 147; volcanism, 54, 114, 117, 124; weather, 168, 170

San Juan Tuff, 119

San Juan volcanic field, 119, *120*, 121

San Luis People's Ditch, 51

San Luis Valley, 43, **49–52**, 89, 123–124, 126, 241; aquifer, 48, 50–51; basalt, 119; cold, 159; dunes, 138; faulting, 113; mat saltbrush badlands, 240; Pennsylvanian uplift, 88

Sand Wash Basin, 88

Sangre de Cristo Formation, 56, 90–91

Sangre de Cristos, *1*, **20–22**, *52*, 123; Ancestral Rockies, 88; Cambrian dikes, 81; cirques, 131; cliff-forming metamorphic rocks, 74; faulting, 113; glacial effects, 137; lack of post-Laramide erosion surface, 117; Laramide orogeny, 106; Mississippian rocks, 86; Pennsylvanian rocks, 89; redbeds, 95; rock glaciers, 147

Saprophytes, **501**; spotted coralroot orchid, **505**

Sastrugi, *180*

Sawatch Range, **34**, 123; Ancestral Rockies, 88; Cambrian rocks, 81–82; glacial effects, 131, 135; granites, 76–77; rock glaciers, 147; volcanism, 54, 117, 121, 125

Sawatch Sandstone, 64, 81

Sawatch–San Luis highland, 106

Sawtooth Peak, 9, 145, *164*, *170*

Sea level, changes during geologic history, 55, 102

SEDGES (*Carex* spp.)
- *C. oreocharis*, 380
- *C. pachystachya*, 380
- *C. pennsylvanica* ssp. *hellophila*, 333
- *C. stenophylla* ssp. *eleocharis*, 380
- *C. utriculata*, 407
- *C. vallicola*, 263
- *C. xerantica*, 333
- Black (*C. nigricans*), 605
- Cottongrass (cottonsedge), 418
- Crandall's (*C. crandallii*), 605
- Ebony (*C. ebenea*), 605
- Elk (*Kobresia myosuroides*), **581–582**, **604**, 605

Elk, false (*C. elynoides*), 581–582, **604**, 605
Fish-scale (*C. chalciolepis*), 605
Geyer (*C. geyeri*), 280, 357, 480
Hepburn's (*C. nardina* ssp. *hepburnii*), 605
Nelson's (*C. nelsonii*), 605
Rock (*C. rupestris*), 581, 605
Rocky Mountain (*C. scopulorum*), 592, **604**, 605
Spikerush, 246, 418, 455
Water (*C. aquatilis*), 407

Sedimentary rocks, 62–64; environmental evidence in, 63–64; evaporites, 89–90

Seed caching, **306–308**; Clark's nutcracker, 531, *532*, 533

Seismicity, 123

Seral species, 192, 498

Serotiny, **500–501**

Sevier, Orogeny, 99–100, 105; Thrust Belt, *106*

Shadow Mountain Reservoir, 16

Sherman Granite, 58, 77, 115

Shirley Basin, 115, 241

Shrublands, mountain shrublands and Gambel's oak woodlands, **273–290**; sagebrush shrublands, **254–272**; semidesert, sagebrush, and mountain shrublands, discussion and summary of all shrubland ecosystems, **230–239**; semidesert shrublands, **240–253**

SHRUBS
bitterbrush, **260**, 262, 279, 303, 332
blueberry (*Vaccinium*), 479, **556–557**; broom huckleberry, 506, 528, **557**, 560; dwarf, 560; myrtle, 506, **557**, 560
buckbrush (New Jersey tea), 279, 332
buffaloberry (or soapberry), 506, 528, **557**, 560; silver, 279
chokecherry, 262, **278–279**, 332, 357, 417, 479
cinquefoil, shrubby (potentilla), 332, 417, **474**, 479, 528, 560, 604
cliffrose, Mexican, 279, 303
cranberry, highbush, 560
currant, Colorado, 560; golden, 279, 417; gooseberry, 417, 479; prickly, 379; wax, **328**, *329*, 332
dogwood, red-osier, 417, 479, **473**
elderberry, red, 417, 506, **557**, 560
grape, Oregon (holly grape), 332
greasewood, 241–242, 243, 244–245, 262, 417
hackberry, netleaf, **411**, 417
hawthorne, 417; river, 279
hopsage, spiny, 262
juniper, common, **299**, 332, 357, 479, 503, 506, 528, 560
maple, Rocky Mountain, 357, **413**, 417, 479
mock orange, littleleaf, **300**, 303
mountainlover, **354**, 357, 479, 506, 560
mountain-mahogany, **277**, 279, 303, 332; curl-leaf, 279, 303; little-leaf, 279, 303
mountain (or ocean) spray, 279, **300**, 303
ninebark, 357, **474**, 479
oak, wavy-leaved, 279
plum, wild, 213, 279, 417
rabbitbrush, 213, 245, **259**, 262, 279, 303, 379; flax-leaved, 303; small, 245; sticky-leaved, 245, 262, 303, 379
raspberry, boulder (Rocky Mountain thimbleberry), **328**, 332, 357
raspberry, wild, 357, 479, 528
rose, wild, 262, 279, 357, 479, 504, 506, 528
sagebrush, big (Great Basin), 213, 245, 255, 258, **259**, 262, 280, 303, 332, 379, 479; black, 258, 262; dwarf, 258, 262; hoary, 258, 262; mountain, 255, 258, **259**, 262, 280; Wyoming, 262
saltbush, general, 241, *242*, 262, 303; four-winged, 213, **243**, 245; Gardner's, 245; mat, **243–244**, 245; shadscale, **243**, 245; silverscale, 213; spiny hopsage, 245
snakeweed, broom, 213, 245, 262, 280
snowberry, roundleaf, 263, 278, 280, 479; western, 213
squaw-apple, *280*
sticky-laurel, **474**, 479, 506, 528
sumac, 213, **278–280**,

303; smooth, 280
thimbleberry, 357, 479
winterfat, 213, 244, 246

Shrub-steppe, **231**, 241

Sierra Grande Uplift, 88

Sierra Madre, **41–42**, 72–73, 170

Sills, **61–62**, 113

Silurian period, 57, 83–84

Silver ore, 36, 48, 113–114

Silver Plume Granite, 58, 77

Skyline Drive, 101

Sky Line Trail, 22

Slab avalanches, 183–184

Slope, orientation of, 157–158; winds, 165

Slumgullion Earthflow, 119, 146

SNAKES
bullsnake, 229, 253, 272, 290, 318, 437
coachwhip, 229
garter snake, plains, 229; western terrestrial, 396, **433–434**, 437, 494
hognose, western, **226–227**, 229
milk snake, 347
racer, 229
rattlesnake, western, 229, 251–253, 272, 290, 318
smooth green, **288**, 290, 437, 494

Snow, amounts of, 160, 166; crystal formation, 173–175; density of, 179; depth hoar, *177*, 187; equi-temperature metamorphism, 176; firn, 176; graupel, 173–174; impacts on plants and animals, 185–188; as insulation, 186; International Snow Classification, *174*; melt-freeze metamorphism, 176, 178; metamorphism of, 175–178, 188; névé, 176; powder snow, 176; sintering, 176–177, 184; snowflakes, 174; temperature-gradient metamorphism, 176–178, 184; thermodynamic instability of new snow, 176; wind redistribution of, 179

Snowpack, animal adaptations to, 187–188; isothermal, 175, 178; metamorphism of, 175–178, 188; mountain snowpack, 173; release fractures in, 183; snowbed plants, 588–592; structure, 175; subnivean environment, 185–187, weakening, 177; windblown dust in, 175

Snowy Pass Supergroup, 73

Snowy Range, *13*, 137

Soil characteristics, alkaline, 234, 242, 294; calcareous, 293; fossil, 78, 86; fungi in, 547; moraine, 135; nutrient poor, 499; organic, 399; oxygen levels, 408; red, 86; saline, 234, 242; sandy, 256

Solar radiation, 156–158

Solar-tracking flowers (heliotropism), 596; snow buttercup, *597*

Solifluction, 145–146

South Park, 35–36, 43, **47–49**, 88–89, 106, 121

South Platte River, 47, 126; ancestral, 115; Valley, 159

South Table Mountain, 107

Southern Rockies, Continental Divide, 7–10; geographic location, 5–7; high peaks in, 7

Southwest monsoon, 170

Spanish Peaks, **19–20**, 121

Species of special concern, 196

Stone stripes, *145*

Stromatolites, *73*, 82, 86

Subalpine spruce-fir forest, adaptations to snow, **563–565**; conifers and the winter environment, **548–551**; discussion and description, **537–573**; Engelmann spruce and subalpine fir forests, forest-tundra ecotone, **545–546**; fungi, role of, **546–548**; plant-animal interactions, **562–563**

Subalpine vegetation zones, 196, **198**

Subduction, 67–68, 96, 105

Submergence of North America, 57

Subnivean living, 186–187

Succession, 191–192, 196, 371, 453–454, 465–467, 543, 545; and communities, 197, 407

Sundance Sea, 55, 96–97

Suture zones, 95

Sweet Home Mine, 114

Syncline, *100*, 105

T

Tallgrass prairie, species, 208

Talus, 147

Taos Mountains, 21

Taos Valley, 44

Taylor, Pass, 32–33

Tectonics, 55; defined, 66

Temperature, 158–159

Tenmile Range, **35–37**, 123

Tennessee Pass, 85, 89

10th Mountain Division, 34

Tepee Buttes, 102

Tepee rings, 44

Tererro Formation, 86

Terpenes, 296, **309–310**

Tertiary period, geologic chart, 54–55; geologic events of, 110–127; large animals of, 116–117

Thermals, 161, 203, 233

Thermogenesis, 186

Thirty-Nine Mile volcanic field, 121

Thunderheads, 162, *170*; thunderstorms, 170, 201, *202*

Thunder Mountain, 16, 30

Tiger Wall, Yampa River, *40*

Timberline, defined, 538; rising, 541

Todilto Limestone, **94**, 97

Toledo Caldera, 124

Torreys Peak, 17

Trail Ridge Road, 15, *16*, 74, 122, 145–146, *185*

Transcontinental Arch, 57, *70*, 80, 82, 86, 96

Trappers Peak, 125; volcanic rocks of, 38

Tree islands, 554, *555*

Treelimit (or tree line), 190; defined, 538

TREES
- alder, mountain, *405*, 411
- aspen, quaking, 416, 462, **473**, 479, 506, 559
- ash, mountain, 357, 416
- birch, river, *405*, 411–412
- box-elder, **411**, 416
- cottonwood, Frémont, **410**, 416; lanceleaf (hybrid), 416; narrowleaf, *405*, **410–411**, 416; plains, 213, *401*, **410**, 416; Rio Grande, **410**, 416
- Douglas-fir, 332, 349, **353**, **354**, 416, 528; Native American story about, 348–349; scientific naming of, **350**
- fir, Arizona, 559; subalpine, **412**, 479, 506, *537*, **556**, 559; white, 353, *406*, **412**, 416, 559
- hackberry, netleaf, 411
- juniper (cedar), alligator, 292; oneseed, **299**, 303; Rocky Mountain, **299**, 303, 332, 353; Utah, **299**, 303
- locust, New Mexican, 279, 417
- oak, Gambel's, 236, **276–277**, 303, 332, 479
- pine, Great Basin limber, 518; limber, 332, 353, 506, *520*, **526**, 528, 560; lodgepole, 353, 479, *495*, 496, *497*, 502–503, 506, 528, 560; Mexican white, 417; piñon, 296, **298–299**, 303; ponderosa, 279, 321, **327–328**, 332, 353, 506, 528; Rocky Mountain bristlecone, 518, *520*, **525–526**, 528, 559
- poplar, balsam, 417
- spruce, Engelmann, 417, 479, 506, *537*, **556**, 560; blue, *406*, **412**, 417, 556, 560
- willow, arctic, 605; Bebb, 417; blue, 413, 417; bluestem, 417; Geyer, 417; mountain, 413, 417; peach-leaved, 403, 411, 417; planeleaf, 413, 417, 605; plain's sandbar, 412, 417; Scouler, 507; sandbar, 412, 417; snow, 605; subalpine, 417; wolf, 417

Triassic period, 56, 93–96

Triassic redbeds, 94

Trinidad Lake St. Park, 108

Trout Creek Canyon, 83; Pass, 35, 48, 85, 89

Truchas Peaks, 21–22, 74, 85

Tuff, 61, *118*, 119, 122, 125

Turbulence, clear-air, 162

Turquoise, formation of, 124

Turtle, Box, **226**, 229

U

Unaweep Canyon, 29, 81, 95, 97

Uncompahgre Plateau, 29, 88; River, 136

Uncompahgria, 56, 88, 90–91, 96

Unconformity, 78

Uplift, Miocene–Pliocene, 123

Upslope conditions, 160–161

U.S. Air Force Academy, 114

U.S. Endangered Species Act, and mountain toads, 425; and picas, 617

U.S. Fish and Wildlife Service, 196

U-shaped valleys, 128

Utes, 19, 28, 39, 43–44, 47–48, 50, 138

V

Valles Caldera, 22–23, 25, 124

Vedauwoo Rocks, 10, 77

Vegetation zones, 196, **198**

Vertebrates, and adaptive radiation, 93; colonizing the land, 84; early, 83

VINES
- grape, wild, 418
- virgin's bower, 418

Volcanism, 60, **117–122**, 124

W

Wagon Wheel Gap, 60, 119, *120*

Wall Mountain Tuff, 61

Water, conservation, 234; diversion, 46–47, 51; rights, 49, 51

Wave cyclones, 154

Weather, defined, 149; mountain effects on, 160–166; seasonal, 166–171

Weathering and erosion, solution weathering, 86

Weber Formation, 56, 91–92

West Elk Breccia, 31, 61, 120

West Elks, 28, **31–32**, 61, 112; Scenic Byway, 32; volcanism in, 117, 119–120

Western Interior Basin, 55, 96–97, 100; Seaway, 55, *99*, 102, *106*, 107

Wetlands, animal descriptions and lists, **425–437**; community characteristics of lowland and foothill wetlands, **401–402**; ecological distribution, **398–399**; montane wetlands, **402–404**; nesting in, **422–423**; physical environment, **400**; plant adaptations, **408–410**; plant descriptions and lists, **410–419**; subalpine wetlands, **404–407**; successional wetlands, **407**; wetland animals, **419–425**

Wet Mountains, **18–19**, 86, 88, 89, 106, 121, 170

Wheeler Geologic Area, 28, 61, *118*, 119

Wheeler Survey, 22

White River, 39

White River Formation, 122

White River Plateau, **38–39**, 91, 112; Cambrian rocks, 81; caves, 86; Cretaceous rocks, 104; Laramide orogeny, 106; Pleistocene glaciation, 129; Silurian rocks, 84; volcanism, 125

Wild and Scenic Rivers System, 28

Wilderness Areas, Big Blue, 27; Eagles Nest, 37; Flat Tops, 38–39; Holy Cross, 34; Indian Peaks, 9, 17, *128*, *130*, 131–132, 141, *145*; La Garita, 27; Lizard Head, 27; Lost Creek, 15; Maroon Bells–Snowmass, 32; Mount Sneffels, 27; Mount Zirkel, 41; Pecos, 22; Rawah Peaks, 14; South San Juan, 27; Weminuche, 27; West Elk, 31; Wheeler Peak, 21

WILDFLOWERS
- alumroot, common, **527**, 528, 606
- anemone, narcissus, 606; windflower, 481
- angelica, giant, 418; Gray's, 606
- arnica, broad-leaf, 560; heartleaf, **356**, 357, *475*, **477**, 480, 507
- aster, common purple, 263, 333, 357; golden, 263, 280, 295, **301**, 304; tansy, 304; white prairie, 214
- avens, alpine (mountain), *582*, 603
- balsamroot, 256, **261**, 263, 280, 480
- bedstraw, 380, 480
- beeplant, yellow, 304
- begonia, sand, 214
- bergamot, wild (beebalm), 380
- bindweed, field, 214
- bistort, alpine (viviparous), 600, **602**, 606; American, 380, 560, *574*, *582*, **602**, 606; water (smartweed), 455
- bittercress (brook-cress), **414**, 418
- bitterroot, pygmy, *263*, **602–603**, 606; sagebrush, 263, 380
- black-eyed Susan, 380, **478**, 480
- bladderpod, 295; double, 304
- bladderwort, great 454; small, 454
- blanketflower, 281, 333, 380
- blazingstar, plains, 214
- blue-eyed grass, 380
- blue-eyed Mary, 357

braya, dwarf, 606
broomrape, tufted, 214, *232*, **262**, 263
buckwheat, alpine, 528; buckwheat, 263; desert, 246, 256, 263, 304; James's, 333; subalpine, 281, 380; sulphur flower 263, 281, **331**, 333, 382
burreed, 454
buttercup, 380, 418; birdfoot, 454; floating, 454; heart-leaved, 454; small-flowered crowfoot, 454; snow, *590*, *597*, **603**, 606; spearwort, 455; water crowfoot, 454
camas, death, 380, 606;
campion, alpine, 606; moss, *585–586*, **601**, 606
candytuft, mountain, 333, 528, 606
cattail, 454
chickweed, 333, 552, 560, 606; alpine mouse-ear, 606
chicory, 214
cicely, sweet, 480
chiming bells (bluebells), **414**, 418, 480, 560; greenleaf (alpine), 606; southwestern, 480
cinquefoil, mountain, 480; soft, 380
clover, alpine, 528; Brandegee's, 606; dwarf, *586*, **602**, 606; Parry's, *590*, **601–602**, 606; prairie, 215; red, 380; whiproot, **602**, 606
columbine, Colorado, 17, 380, *476*, **477**, 480, 606; dwarf, 606; western red, **477**, 480
coneflower, black, 380, **477–478**, 480, 560; prairie, 214
coltsfoot, sweet, 454
cow parsnip, **414**, *415*, 418, 480
creeper, Virginia, 418
dandelion, 381, 480
draba, 528, 606
dryad, mountain (or alpine), *587*, **603**, 606
duckweed (*Lemna* spp.), 454
elephantella, *418*, 592, 604
evening primrose, prairie, **212**, 215; white, 205; white stemless, 215; yellow stemless, 215
fireweed, 480, **506**, 507; alpine, 607
fleabane, or daisy (*Erigeron* spp.), black-headed, *590*, **601**, 606; desert, 246, 295, 304; Eaton's, 263; little, 263; one-flowered, 601; one-headed, **601**, 606; pinnate-leaved, 606; prairie, 215; showy, 381, *475*, **477**, 480; subalpine, **376–377**, 381, 560, 606; trailing, 333
forget-me-not, alpine, 607
four-o'clock, Colorado, 295, **301**, 304
gaura, scarlet, 215, 281
gayfeather, 215
gentian, arctic, 607; blue bottle, 381, 607; fragrant, 381; fringed, 381; green (monument plant); 381; moss (Siberian), 607; prairie, 381; rose, 607; star, 418, 607
geranium, common wild (rose-colored), 478; sticky, 478; white, 478
gilia, ballhead, 304; prickly, 304; scarlet, 263, 281, **302**, **378**, 381, 560; snowball, 607; trumpet, *380*
globeflower, 418, *546*, **559**, 560
golden banner, **377**, 381, 480
goldflower, 607
groundsel, arrowleaf, **416**, 419; butterweed, 606; Fendler's, 333, 381; New Mexican, 333
gumweed, 215, 295, 333, 381
harebell, common, 381, *475*, **476**, 480, 607; common, alpine, 607; Parry's, 381, 480
hawkweed, white-flowered, 357
hollyhock, mountain, 418
hyacinth, wild, 246
Jacob's ladder, *546*, **558–559**, 560
king's crown, 607
koenigia (*Koenigia islandica*), 607
larkspur, Nuttall's (mountain), 256, 260, **261–262**, 263, 333, 480; prairie, 215; subalpine, **414**, 418, 561
lily, alp, 606; avalanche (glacier), *198*, 381, 480, 560; corn (false hellebore), **378**, 381, 480, 560; desert mariposa, 246, *246*; mariposa, 263, 281, 381, 474, *475*, 480; sand, 212; wood, 480
locoweed, Colorado, 215, **377–378**, *381*; drop-pod, 507; Rocky